1989-1990

TO

ANTIQUES DEALERS

1989-1990

GREEN
SLOAN'S
GUIDE ™

TO
ANTIQUES DEALERS

Antiques Dealers
Appraisers Auctioneers
Antiquarian Booksellers
Conservators Consultants
Period Restoration Specialists
Reproduction Repairs

NEW ENGLAND

Susan P. Sloan
Editor

THE ANTIQUE PRESS
Boston

ISBN 0-929233-01-8
ISSN 0898-090X
L. of C. 88-83822

Attention: Historical societies, museums, antiques study groups:
This directory is available at quantity discounts on bulk purchases for education, business or sales promotions use. For information, please contact our Group Sales Department, The Antique Press, 105 Charles Street - #140, Boston, MA 02114 (617)723-3001

Printed and bound in the United States of America

DEDICATION

In memory of Kenneth E. Alm

TABLE OF CONTENTS

1

INTRODUCTION

Introduction, 2
How to Use This Guide, 4
Explanation of a Sample Entry, 6
Thoughts on Buying Antiques, 7
Abbreviations and Terms Explained, 8
Key to the Use of QuickCodes™, 10
Key to Association Acronyms, 12

15

FINE ARTS COLLECTIONS AND COURSES OF INTEREST TO
ANTIQUES COLLECTORS

*Historic Deerfield, Deerfield; Museum of Fine Arts, Boston; The Society for the
Preservation of New England Antiquities, Boston; Peabody Museum, Salem;
Sotheby's, New York; Colonial Williamsburg, Williamsburg;
Winterthur, Winterthur*

27

BRIEF PROFILES OF THE IMPORTANT PERIODICALS COVERING
THE ANTIQUES TRADE IN NEW ENGLAND

31

MAPS

Connecticut, 33
Maine, 34-35
Massachusetts, 36-37
Cape Cod, 38
New Hampshire, 41
Rhode Island, 39
Vermont, 40

43
LISTINGS OF ANTIQUES DEALERS, ANTIQUARIAN BOOKSELLERS, AUCTION HOUSES, APPRAISERS, AND PERIOD RESTORATION SPECIALISTS

Connecticut, 43
Maine, 115
Massachusetts, 161
New Hampshire, 283
Rhode Island, 329
Vermont, 347

379
INDEXES

An Alphabetical Index of Business Names, 381
QuickCode™ Index: Alphabetical List of QuickCodes™, 406
Index to Multiple Dealer and Group Shops, 453

464
LISTING

466
ORDER FORM

ACKNOWLEDGMENTS

A number of people have been especially helpful in the conception and compilation of this directory. Emyl Jenkins first suggested the idea in "Maine Antique Digest" in February 1987.

Arlene Russell worked along side me for the last eight months, serenely patient throughout the entire compilation process. She has ensured that consistency and accuracy were maintained - and always in good cheer. Terry Pittaro was a very effective advertising manager, an often frustrating job.

Hartnett House put in tremendous effort to create small, legible and attractive maps. Ingrid Monke wrote the article on Fine Arts Study Courses with sparkle and enthusiasm. Gail Gardner of Boston drew the basket of mixed fruit and flowers.

One of the interesting things about this publication was the way it was put together. Extensive use was made of the sophisticated software packages available for producing a camera-ready manuscript. The original data was delivered to Ideas InPrint, a design, layout and typesetting firm in Salem, Massachusetts. The text was formatted into the complex book design incorporated herein - with no conventional paste-up. The text was then published using Ventura Publisher 2.0 with the Professional Extension. Thus, the entire book was produced on personal computers using DeskTop Publishing Hardware and Software.

Paul Parisi and Gretchen Wright of Ideas InPrint were patient and cooperative in preparing many of the ads and guiding the manuscript through the desktop publishing process. Dennis Cohen programmed the PC loaded with Enable from The Software Group to perform all the functions necessary to efficiently compile this directory.

And finally, loving thanks to Arthur, who first mastered the computer, and then kept it and me functioning when I thought eternal frustration was just a way of life. Without him I would have quit long ago.

▼

Introduction

INTRODUCTION

SLOAN'S GREEN GUIDE TO ANTIQUES DEALERS is the quintessential guide for antiques buyers, dealers, collectors, travelers, interior decorators, consultants and ordinary folk planning an antiques tour through New England or a Saturday afternoon "antiquing". It eliminates the guesswork in antiquing by answering the questions who, where and when with respect to buying, selling and repairing antiques. Whether one has been purchasing antiques in New England for twenty years or is contemplating the first trip, one will find more useful information between the covers of "Sloan's Green Guide" than any other single publication.

The New England antiques trade is composed of a large cast of participants in the six states of Connecticut, Maine, Massachusetts, New Hampshire, Rhode Island and Vermont. Included are dealers - retail, private and wholesale; auction houses of all sizes and focus; appraisers; a huge antiquarian book trade; conservators; consultants; repair and restoration specialists and those engaged in the reproduction and replication of antiques. Most of them are here - alphabetized, organized, categorized and indexed - in a fashion enabling the reader to access them easily.

In the design of this publication, we have incorporated features that respond to the needs of those being listed and those utilizing the listings. Dealers and other antiques-related businesses are given generous space to describe and list the inventory and/or services they offer. This information follows the obligatory name, address and telephone number at the beginning of each listing. Business hours, with indications as to seasonal variations, travel directions from easily identified reference points, parking availability and charge cards accepted, if any, are shown to aid the reader in travelling, shopping and buying efficiently. The listees are categorized by QuickCodes™, i.e. numbers assigned to eighty-seven categories of antiques and antiques-related services. The placement of these QuickCodes™ at the beginning of each entry enables the reader to rapidly identify dealers in an area of interest, i.e. Americana or Objets d'Art, without reading through the entire listing. Finally, these QuickCodes™ are the basis for the eighty-seven indices at the end of the book, listing the businesses according to inventory and services provided.

As a service to our readers, we have taken a slight departure from our title to list some services that are not strictly antiques, but of an ancillary nature. Thus we have included the needlework shop on Nantucket which produces beautiful reproductions of old-fashioned hooked rugs, the fellow in Maine who repairs columns and the firm in Massachusetts who sells the only authentic milk paint available in New England. These businesses provide a service to individuals recreating a "period" environment and thus we feel will be of interest to some of our readers. We would wish to include more of these listings in future editions.

There are many skilled craftsmen in New England whose services are eagerly sought for the reproduction or replication of fine period antiques - from the replication of Goddard Townsend furniture to fine Chippendale style hardware. The quality of their products and their reputations are excellent and they are appropriately listed in this book.

We have made every attempt to be thorough. This includes thousands of dollars invested in mailings and telephone calls, and hundreds of hours on the phone and editing and proofreading copy. If a listing falls short of its potential, it is not for the lack of effort. Readers are encouraged to share information with us, whenever they feel that ours falls short of the mark. Additions, deletions, and amplifications of current listings are all welcomed and forms are provided at the end of the book to transmit information.

How to Use This Guide

THIS GUIDE IS composed of five sections. After the introductory material, the first section is devoted to a survey of antiques study courses and important educational opportunities at selected museums, historic restorations and collections. The institutions we have listed are a representative selection of the opportunities available. This section may be used as a starting point from which to obtain more information.

In the second section, pertinent periodicals serving the New England antiques community are profiled. These tabloids and magazines provide the antiques enthusiast with comprehensive information including calendars, previews, and reviews of auctions, antiques shows and exhibits taking place in New England. "Sandwiched" in amongst the reviews you may find thought provoking articles about trends in the trade and blow-by-blow descriptions of the latest antiques dispute being adjudicated, either in the court of public opinion or the courts, per se. It all makes for fascinating reading and the periodicals listed are highly recommended. A profile of each publication is given along with subscription information and phone numbers.

The third section contains the maps of the six New England states. These maps have been specifically designed in that they indicate only the towns listed in this guide and the numbered roads connecting them. The maps have no scale and it would be unwise to use them to calculate the time it will take to travel between two points. Their purpose is to permit one to easily identify the location of cities mentioned.

The fourth and largest section is comprised of the listings of dealers by state. Antiques dealers constitute the majority of these listings but businesses which provide antiques-related services are also included. Among these are appraisers, auction houses, antiquarian booksellers, restoration and repair services, consultation, conservation, cabinetmaking, replication and reproduction services. The entries are organized alphabetically 1) by state, 2) by city, and 3) by business name. Dictionary-style headers inform the reader of the geographical location of the businesses on a given page.

Dealer entries include the business name, address, phone number, and three numbers called QuickCodes™. QuickCodes™ indicate categories of antiques or antiques-related services which the business either sells or provides. A description, often in the dealer's own words, as to the inventory, information as to size, hours, days closed, charge cards accepted, services available, year established, associations, travel directions, and parking are also included.

Clarification of some of the terms used in the listings is relevant here. "Size" refers to size of the retail space. Medium indicates 501 to 2000 square feet; Large indicates 2001 to 9999 square feet and Huge indicates over 10,000 square feet of retail space. If there is no indication as to "Size", either the retail space is under 500 square feet or the information was not available. "Assoc" refers to association memberships which the business maintains. Acronyms are shown and these are explained elsewhere in the Guide. "GR12" in the QuickCodes™ means a group shop with twelve dealers. "MDS20" means a multiple dealer shop with twenty dealers.

If you seek antique porcelain dealers in Boston, first refer to the "KEY TO THE USE OF QuickCodes™" to determine the QuickCode™ number for dealers in pottery and porcelain. In this case, it is "63". Run your eye down the Boston listings for "63" to quickly identify dealers in antique porcelain. For a more comprehensive identification of porcelain dealers in New England refer to the "Businesses Indexed by Inventory or Services" in the indices at the back of the book.

Finally, dealers are indexed alphabetically and cross-indexed by inventory. The first index is an alphabetical listing of all business names. Eighty-seven indices list dealers according to the categories of merchandise stocked or services offered. If you are interested in Americana, refer to the Americana index for dealers in New England that specialize in this field. The entire listing of index categories is contained in the "KEY TO THE USE OF QuickCodes™".

"Sloan's Green Guide" is designed to facilitate quick reference whether you are a collector, a traveler or an estate executor looking to value and dispose of an estate. We hope that you will find it useful and easy to use. We are interested in hearing your comments.

EXPLANATION OF A SAMPLE ENTRY

WEINER'S ANTIQUE SHOP
22 Beacon St, 02108
(617)227-2894   **29 36 63**

One of Boston's most interesting shops featuring a large selection with variety & quality. Continuous family ownership for 93 years. **Pr:** $25-15000. **Est:** 1896 **Serv:** Appraisal, brochure, purchase estates. **Hours:** Mon-Fri 9-4 Sat 11-4. **Size:** Medium. **Cc:** MC/V. **Assoc:** AAA NAWCC. Paul Weiner **Park:** Local Garage. **Loc:** Directly across the street from the Gold Dome of the State House on Beacon Hill.

QuickCodes™ showing categories of antiques to be found or services available here: in this case, Decorative Accessories, Furniture, and Pottery & Porcelain

Price range of inventory

Services available

Retail square feet

Associations of which the dealer or business is a member

Parking availability

Year established

Business hours indicating seasonal changes if any

Charge cards accepted

Travel directions from an easily identified reference point

THOUGHTS ON BUYING ANTIQUES

THE PURPOSE OF this book is to provide a comprehensive directory for antiques buyers, antiques dealers, consumers of antiques-related services and travelers in New England who seek to quickly and easily identify vendors of products and services which meet an individual need. The directory attempts to present as much factual information as possible about each business. It leaves the evaluation of a particular dealer or vendor to the potential customer. The reader should not infer from the inclusion of a listing any endorsement on the part of the editor.

The best purchase in any field is an informed purchase. In buying antiques, the knowledge one brings to the selection and purchase of a particular piece will determine the pleasure and satisfaction derived from owning it. Nothing can surpass knowledge obtained from years of experience and scholarship. This information can be obtained by reading widely articles published in one's field of interest. Subscribe to the magazines and periodicals which cover the antiques trade and collecting - a few of which are mentioned in our section on periodicals. Go to museums and galleries and develop an eye for what the experts consider the finest examples. Determine the valid criteria for evaluating the age and quality of a given piece. Talk to experts. Avail yourself of the many lectures, seminars and workshops that are held each year in New England and elsewhere on the evaluation, purchase, and care of fine antiques. Go to antiques shows and examine the pieces that interest you until you can distinguish between the merely acceptable and the truly superb.

Antiques dealers generally love their inventory and they will respond to an interested, well-informed client. A good dealer cultivates a customer, because although the individual may not purchase today, there is always the possibility that tomorrow he or she may become an avid client, intent on assembling a truly fine collection in a particular field.

ABBREVIATIONS AND TERMS EXPLAINED

Assoc: ASSOCIATIONS A listing of association acronyms indicating the dealer's memberships

By appt only BY APPOINTMENT ONLY Dealer who does not maintain shop hours. To view the inventory, call ahead for an appointment and an address. One may anticipate this dealer works with the serious collector.

C   CENTURY

Cc: CHARGE CARDS accepted

Est: ESTABLISHED Indicates the year in which the dealer entered the antiques trade.

GR20   GROUP SHOP Indicates a collection of antiques and /or collectibles dealers under one roof, in this example: 20 dealers

Int   INTERSECTION

Jct   JUNCTION

L or R   LEFT or RIGHT

Loc: LOCATION Travel directions to the business address from the nearest easily identified reference point

MDS15   MULTIPLE DEALER SHOP Indicates a collection of antiques dealers under one roof, in this example: 15 dealers

MI   MILES

min   MINUTES

N, S, E or W NORTH, SOUTH, EAST or WEST

Park: PARKING availability

Pr: PRICE RANGE Indicates the range of prices in individual
            pieces in a dealer's inventory

SS   STOP SIGN

Serv: SERVICES available from this dealer, often at an extra charge.
            These may include consultation, appraisals, repairs, restorations
            and shipping, among others.

Shows: Antiques Show Participation. EL indicates the Ellis Memorial
            Antiques Show in Boston. WAS indicates the New York City
            Winter Antiques Show.

Size: Retail square footage. Medium indicates under 2000 square feet.
            Large indicates under 10,000 square feet and Huge indicates
            over 10,000 square feet.

Sum   SUMMER

Win   WINTER

KEY TO THE USE OF
"QuickCodes™"

TO FACILITATE RAPID reference in "Sloan's Green Guide" a coding system is used for identifying eighty-seven selected categories of antiques and antiques-related services. Numbers, referred to as QuickCodes™, have been assigned to these categories. Businesses have been queried as to their inventory and services and then assigned a maximum of three QuickCodes™.

These QuickCodes™ appear on the third line of each entry in bold face type, supplementing the text description. Thus, if one is in Essex, Massachusetts with thirty minutes to spare, one can quickly scan the QuickCodes™ to determine which dealers sell the category of antiques of particular interest. So informed, the reader is able to travel directly to the dealer of choice, bypassing the "pottery and porcelain" dealer when looking for "barometers".

The eighty-seven categories of antiques and antiques-related services and the QuickCodes™ assigned to them appear on the facing page.

1	Americana	45	Garden Statuary
2	Andirons/Fenders	46	Interior Decoration
3	Antiquities	47	Jewelry
4	Appraisal	48	Lace/Linen
5	Architectural Antiques	49	Lead Soldiers
6	Arms/Military	50	Lighting
7	Art Deco/Art Nouveau	51	Maps
8	Auction	52	Miniatures
9	Autographs/Manuscripts	53	Mirrors
10	Barometers	54	Models
11	Baseball Cards	55	Music/Musical Instruments
12	Bookbinding/Restoration	56	Nautical/Marine Items
13	Books/Antiquarian	57	Needlework/Samplers
14	Books	58	Objets d'Art
15	Bottles	59	Oil Paintings
16	Brass/Copper/Metalwork	60	Oriental Art
17	Bronzes	61	Paperweights
18	Buttons/Badges	62	Photographs
19	Cabinet Makers	63	Porcelain/Pottery
20	Cameras/Daguerreotypes	64	Post Cards
21	Carpets/Rugs	65	Primitives
22	Chair Caning	66	Prints/Drawings
23	Clocks/Watches	67	Quilts/Patchwork
24	Coins/Medals	68	Repairs
25	Conservation	69	Replication
26	Consultation/Research	70	Reproduction
27	Country Antiques	71	Restoration
28	Crocks/Stoneware	72	Scientific/Medical Instruments
29	Decorative Accessories	73	Sculpture
30	Decoys	74	Services to Period Homes
31	Display Stands/Glass	75	Shipping/Packing/Storage
32	Dolls/Toys	76	Shop Signs
33	Ephemera	77	Silver
34	Folk Art	78	Sporting Art/Equipment
35	French Antiques	79	Stamps
36	Furniture	80	Textiles
37	Furniture/American	81	Tools
38	Furniture/Continental	82	Tribal Art
39	Furniture/English	83	Victorian Antiques
40	Furniture/Oak	84	Vintage Cars/Carriages
41	Furniture/Painted	85	Vintage Clothing/Costumes
42	Furniture/Pine	86	Wicker
43	Furniture/Reproduction	87	Weather Vanes
44	Glass		

KEY TO ASSOCIATION ACRONYMS

AAA	Appraisers Association of America
AADA	Associated Antique Dealers of America Inc
AADLA	Art & Antique Dealers League of America Inc
ABAA	Antiquarian Booksellers Association of America
ADA	Antique Dealers' Association of America
AIC	American Institute for Conservation of Historic & Artistic Works
ANS	American Numismatic Society
AR	The Appraisers' Registry
ARLIS/NA	Art Libraries Society of North America
ASA	American Society of Appraisers
AWI	American Watchmakers Institute
AWG	Association of Women Gemologists
BADA	British Antique Dealers Association
BCoADA	Berkshire County Antiques Dealers Association
BHI	British Horological Institute
CADA	Connecticut Association of Dealers in Antiques Inc
CAI	Certified Auctioneers Institute
CCADA	Cape Cod Antique Dealers Association Inc
GIA	Gemological Institute of America
GSAAA	Granite State Antique Dealers & Appraisers Association
IIC	International Institute for Conservation of Historic & Artistic Works
ILAB	International League of Antiquarian Booksellers
ISA	International Society of Appraisers
ISFAA	International Society of Fine Arts Appraisers

JBT	Jewelers Board of Trade
MAA	Maine Auctioneers Association
MABA	Maine Antiquarian Booksellers Association
MADA	Maine Antiques Dealers Association Inc
MJSA	Manufacturing Jewelers & Silversmiths of America
MRIAB	Massachusetts & Rhode Island Antiquarian Booksellers
MSAA	Massachusetts State Auctioneers Association
NAA	National Auctioneers Association
NAADAA	National Antique & Art Dealers Association of America Inc
NADA	National Association of Dealers in Antiques Inc
NAWCC	National Association of Watch & Clock Collectors
NEAA	New England Appraisers Association
NEBA	New England Booksellers Association
NECA	New England Conservation Association
NHABA	New Hampshire Antiquarian Booksellers Association
NHADA	New Hampshire Antiques Dealers Association Inc
NSAA	North Shore Antiques Dealers Association
NTHP	National Trust for Historic Preservation
ORRA	Oriental Rug Retailers of America
PSMA	Professional Show Managers Association
PVADA	Pioneer Valley Antiques Dealers Association
SSADA	South Shore Antiques Dealers' Association
SADA	Suburban Antique Dealers Association
SNEADA	Southeastern New England Antique Dealers Association Inc
SPNEA	Society for the Preservation of New England Antiquities
VAA	Vermont Auctioneers Association
VABA	Vermont Antiquarian Booksellers Association
VADA	Vermont Antiques Dealers' Association Inc

NOTES

Fine Arts
Collections
And
Study Courses

FINE ARTS COLLECTIONS AND COURSES OF INTEREST FOR THE COLLECTOR

TOURING EARLY AMERICAN homes and outstanding collections of decorative arts can, of course, do much to enhance your knowledge of antiques, and with some of the greatest collections in New England, or nearby, valuable and worthwhile opportunities to do just that abound. In addition, a number of institutions conduct courses and seminars, lectures and gallery talks, on their collections. While some programs are full-time, in-depth courses geared to professionals, others are aimed at collectors and connoisseurs. The following list is by no means exhaustive, but simply highlights some of the finest opportunities available to those interested in expanding their knowledge of antiques. Because course topics, fees, and dates vary from year to year, it is best to contact the organizations at the address listed for up-to-date information. Fees given here simply serve as a general guideline. Members often qualify for reduced rates and special programs, and membership fees tend to be quite reasonable.

HISTORIC DEERFIELD
Box 321
Deerfield, MA 01342
(413) 774-5581
*Fees: Most lectures and colloquies are free; short workshops and forums are low cost
($10-$60); three or four day forums - $350-$400.*

STRETCHED OUT ALONG the main street of Old Deerfield Village in the
Connecticut Valley is a remarkable collection of fifty-two houses, built over a
period spanning the early eighteenth to twentieth centuries. The institution of
Historic Deerfield, incorporated in 1951, owns and operates twelve of the
houses, which represent the changing styles of Connecticut River domestic
architecture. Shown only by guided tours, the buildings are open every day of
the year. Tour themes revolve around the collections and the way in which
they are exhibited in the houses.

Famous for its exceptional collection of early American furniture, Deerfield
exhibits one of the major collections (more than 10,000 objects) of Americana
and related decorative arts of the seventeenth, eighteenth and early nineteenth
centuries. Holdings include the George Alfred Cluett Collection of American
furniture and the Lucius D. Potter Collection of furniture, and brassware
along with many impressive examples of early American textiles (especially
needlework), silver, pewter, glass, brass candlesticks, and paintings.

Historic Deerfield operates an extensive series of educational programs
throughout the year - lectures, films, and many colloquia and workshops
geared to collectors and connoisseurs. Topics cover just about every interest:
historic interiors, design and construction of American furniture, American
presentation silver, schoolgirl needlework, identifying base metal artifacts,
today's market for Americana, and so on. Trips to other museums and historic
sites are sponsored as well. Members of Friends of Historic Deerfield often
receive reduced rates as well as the chance to register early for special classes
and programs.

Three- and four-day forums that focus on a special topic are occasionally offered. A recent forum on ceramics included workshops, tours, and lectures on Chinese export porcelain and English ceramics as well as American-made wares, and for another, three prominent scholar-curators discussed master-works of furniture, silver, ceramics, and brass in the Historic Deerfield collections.

College students interested in pursuing a career in the museum or historic preservation field may apply for the nine-week Summer Fellowship Program in early American History and Material Culture, a well-respected program that is now more than thirty years old. By examining the history, life, arts, and material culture of the town, the students develop the skills needed to conduct architectural and historical research on early America.

MUSEUM OF FINE ARTS
465 Huntington Ave
Boston, MA 02115
(617) 267-9300, ext. 363
Fees: Lectures and courses, $7.50-$120.

THE HISTORIC CITY of Boston is the home of one of the country's oldest museums, and masterworks from the extensive collections of the Museum of Fine Arts provide valuable records of major historic events as well as examples of the finest works produced in early America.

Holdings include such beautiful American silver objects as Paul Revere's celebrated Liberty Bowl and a commemorative tankard by Benjamin Burt from the M. and M. Karolik Collection; exquisitely crafted chests, rockers, settees, and other furniture originally owned by local families who made fortunes on the China trade during the clipper ship era; as well as outstanding paintings by the renowned John Singleton Copley, Fitz Hugh Lane, and Gilbert Stuart.

Gallery talks and illustrated lectures complement the permanent collections and special exhibitions. With such impressive resources, a fairly extensive program of events is offered from month to month. Listings appear in the calendar, which is sent to members; membership benefits include free admission to the museum and reduced rates for the generally low-cost lectures and talks. Prominent historians, curators, and other specialists speak on Oriental influences in British and American furniture, Boston and Philadelphia furniture, American folk painting, or eighteenth century silver, to name just a few of the subjects covered in the past. Art tours, such as a visit to Salem's historic sites or a bus ride through Boston's old neighborhoods, are offered as well.

SOCIETY FOR THE PRESERVATION OF NEW ENGLAND ANTIQUITIES

Harrison Gray Otis House
141 Cambridge St
Boston, MA 02114
(617) 227-3956

Fees: Modest — $3 to $40 — for most events; slight reductions offered to members

PRESERVING NEW ENGLAND'S heritage is the aim of the Society for the Preservation of New England Antiquities (SPNEA), which has holdings of more than one hundred buildings, including twenty-three house museums and eleven study properties. Founded in 1919 by William Sumner Appleton (one of the first to develop techniques for documenting and preserving historic buildings), SPNEA has the largest and best documented collection of New England decorative arts (more than 30,000 objects), placing special emphasis on wallpaper, textiles, architectural elements, ceramics, glass, pewter, furniture and toys.

Today SPNEA is the largest regional preservation organization in the country, with a renowned Conservation Center (located at the Lyman Estate in Waltham, Massachusetts) and extensive archives and publications related to the field. The Conservation Center conducts research into methods of preserving buildings and restoring architectural details as well as historic furnishings and offers its services as consultant to organizations and individuals around the country. Conservators and curators have written widely on their research; to obtain a list of SPNEA publications, write to the address listed above.

Three centuries of New England life can be studied by visiting SPNEA's museum properties, which are located throughout New England. Like the Harrison Gray Otis House in Boston, some houses are restored in the style of a particular period; others, described as "collector's houses" (for instance, the Winslow Crocker House in Yarmouth Port, Massachusetts) contain outstanding decorative arts collections. Houses that have remained in one family for several generations are also open for tours. The SPNEA brochure, "House Guide", summarizes the contents of the house museums, giving open hours and location as well. Study properties, for the most part unfurnished, serve as examples of distinctive architectural styles and are also open for visits if arrangements are made in advance (call 617/227-3956).

PEABODY MUSEUM OF SALEM
East India Square
Liberty and Essex Sts.
Salem, MA 01970
(508)745-9500 (recorded message)
(508)745-1876

Fees: Admission $4, Memberships start at $25. Gallery talks are free, films are free or $1 above admission. Fees, if any, for lectures, special events and courses run $6 - $50

LOCATED ON EAST India Square at the heart of the historic district is the Peabody Museum of Salem. Recently merged with the China Trade Museum of Milton and boasting a newly opened Asian Export Art Wing, the Peabody is the repository of one of the most beautiful collections of Chinese export porcelain in the country. It includes hundreds of pieces of China trade wares made for the American market. The quality is breathtaking.

In addition there are paintings, gold, silver, furniture and textiles relating to this fascinating period in maritime history thoughtfully displayed throughout rooms in the Asian Export Wing. Each year the Museum offers over 100 programs including concerts, films and classes. Gallery talks include tours of the new Asian Export Wing, Asian Export Art, Furniture & Paintings. Past courses have included Chinese Export Art, Chinese Folk Crafts and Japanese Calligraphy.

SOTHEBY'S WORKS OF ART PROGRAM
1334 York Ave.
New York, NY 10021
(212) 606-7822

Fees: For Works of Art Program, tuition is $12,875 (does not cover meals, housing, and supplemental fees); short-term courses, $25-$300.

SOTHEBY'S, THE WORLD-famous auction house founded in 1744, counts among its staff some of the most knowledgeable experts in the art world. A visit to any Sotheby's Americana auction is a fine way to study antiques and to obtain Sotheby's estimate of their value. Sotheby's educational program, one of the most outstanding, was originally developed at Sotheby's in London as an apprenticeship program for the company's art experts. The Works of Art Program was opened to the general public in 1974, and in 1985 Sotheby's began a Works of Art Program in New York, focusing on American Arts.

The American Arts Course is a full-time nine-month program of intensive professional study designed primarily for those interested in pursuing careers related to the American art field, though collectors who want to expand their knowledge of this field have participated as well. The hands-on course emphasizes connoisseurship, practical experience, and the workings of the art market. If space permits, interested individuals may be allowed to take selected lecture programs from the American Arts Course on an audit basis.

Lectures, study sessions, field trips, and attendance at art auctions train students to identify period styles from 1650 to the present in the decorative arts - furniture, silver, ceramics, glass, and textiles - and the fine arts - paintings, sculpture, prints, drawings, and photographs.

Enrollment is limited to twenty-three; candidates must demonstrate their qualifications for the program by one of the following: a BA degree in Art History or a related field, substantial experience in the art field, or demonstrated talent in a field such as cabinet making, interior design, etc. Writing ability and an interview are also required.

The Works of Art Program also offers short-term courses and symposia (from evening lectures to four-day seminars) for individuals who would like to expand their knowledge of a specific field, including fine arts conservation and antique jewelry, among others. (Specific details on current offerings are available by calling 212/606-7822).

COLONIAL WILLIAMSBURG FOUNDATION
PO Box C
Williamsburg, VA 23187
(804) 229-1000

Fees: Modest — $1.50 — for lectures, Antiques Forum, $220, exclusive of room and board, Learning Week in Archaeology, $650 for a two-week session, $400 for one-week.

COLONIAL WILLIAMSBURG, THE one-time capital of Virginia now restored to its eighteenth-century appearance, is a splendid example of a working town in colonial America. Period furnishings fill the houses, both original and reconstructed, and craftsmen in costume demonstrate their trades. The houses illustrate vividly the different social classes and occupational groups of colonial society.

The DeWitt Wallace Decorative Arts Gallery displays antique objects from the seventeenth through the nineteenth centuries-more than 8,000 examples of the finest craftsmanship in early American furniture, porcelain and pottery, silver, pewter, brass and textiles.

Williamsburg sponsors its widely acclaimed Antiques Forum at the end of January/early February. The six-day forum has been held every year since 1948, and includes audio-visual presentations, formal lectures, study tours, and workshops conducted by experts and scholars from across the country. Past topics include the quality in antiques of the eighteenth century and the development of style during the Queen Anne period (1688-1745). Registration for this popular course is limited; first-come, first-served.

Colonial Williamsburg offers a number of other educational opportunities as well. In 1988, a learning weekend surveyed the contributions and influences of Black artists and early craftsmen in America. A lecture series focused on Virginia's architecture, folk art, colonial music and furniture. The Department of Archaeological Research sponsors Learning Weeks in Archaeology, during which participants work on excavations at several Historic Area properties. Six two-week sessions (twelve openings per session) are held during the summer.

WINTERTHUR
Route 52
Winterthur, DE 19735
(302) 656-8591, extension 313, for Guild information
(302) 654-1548, to reserve tours
Fees: Seminar on American Home, $285; conferences and workshops, $25-$95; tours, $8-$12.50.

NESTLED IN DELAWARE'S Brandywine Valley stands the greatest museum of American furniture and decorative arts: Winterthur, the former home of Henry Francis du Pont, houses - under one roof - a vast collection of American antiques and affords the public the incredible opportunity - unequaled elsewhere - to see the changing styles in American furniture and decorative arts over a two hundred year period. Surrounded by spectacular gardens, the grand house contains nearly two hundred rooms and displays of outstanding examples of domestic architecture, furniture, textiles, pewter, silver, ceramics, paintings, and prints dating from about 1640 to 1840. Each room - parlor, bedroom, dining room, and so on - is decorated with period settings, with careful attention to every detail. Du Pont purchased the rooms from houses that were being destroyed or renovated, then had them installed in Winterthur, and furnished them with antiques he collected. In 1951 the building was opened to the public as a museum, and people have been coming in droves ever since to see this magnificent collection.

The museum provides numerous opportunities to learn about American antiques, and among its offerings are special tours of the rooms, as well as lectures and seminars on subjects related to the collections. Its membership organization, the Winterthur Guild, has been sponsoring tours, seminars, lectures and special events for members since 1976, and membership information can be obtained by calling the number listed above. In addition, Winterthur operates three graduate training programs, a research library, and clinics on identifying and caring for historic and artistic objects. Also open to the public are three historic homes in Odessa, Delaware, which have been restored and furnished with period antiques.

In 1986 the Guild began offering an annual four-day seminar (held in March) on "The American Home". Focusing on a specific period in American design, these seminars explore such topics as the Chippendale style period from 1760 to 1790 through lectures and small workshops on connoisseurship and conservation. Participants have a wide variety of workshop and tour topics to choose from - furniture, finishes, textile conservation, and silver connoisseurship, for example. Registration is limited to 100 persons; the group splits up into small sections for the workshops.

From time to time, the museum offers short one- and two-day conferences on special subjects: One successful program covered the material culture of Philadelphia, while another focused on Belter furniture and the Rococo Revival interior. "Influence of the Past: Perspectives on Interior Design Today", a national conference on traditional design and its effect on today's interiors and designers, held in the fall of 1988, attracted professionals in the field as well as interested laymen, who discussed such topics as recreating period rooms, historical accuracy in period rooms, and the compatibility of historical design and a contemporary life-style.

The museum regularly operates special one- and two-hour reserved tours of its collections on various topics. "American Interiors" traces the changes in American taste from 1700 to 1840. "A Diverse Nation" examines the ethnic and regional diversity exemplified in the room settings of Shakers, the English, Dutch New Yorkers, and Germans of Pennsylvania. American silver, Federal furniture, Chinese export porcelain, and Oriental rugs are covered in "A Fare of Specialty Wares", while "American Craftsmanship" focuses on the design history of American decorative arts and the development of furniture construction.

And finally, museum curators provide assistance in identifying and dating American art objects from 1640 to 1840; advance reservations must be made for this free service. Offering advice on the condition and care of paintings, artworks on paper, and decorative art objects are graduate students and faculty members of the Winterthur Art Conservation Program.

Periodicals

PERIODICALS

The following list surveys some of the more important and fascinating periodicals covering the New England antiques scene:

MAINE ANTIQUE DIGEST

A monthly tabloid in six or more sections covering the marketplace for Americana - country and formal furniture, fine and folk art, and accessories. Originally started as a magazine covering only Maine, it has over 25,000 subscribers in all 50 states and foreign countries.

"Maine Antique Digest" covers the market for art and antiques as news. It goes well beyond the press releases that fill most trade papers. Along with a calendar of auctions and shows advertised within, it carries auction results and fascinating inside information about the antiques business. If you only subscribe to one periodical this would be high on the list of choices. Editor Samuel C Pennington

$29 One Year $50 Two Years Maine Antique Digest, Box 645 Waldoboro ME 04572 (207)832-7534

The Magazine ANTIQUES

This beautiful monthly magazine covers the Eastern Seaboard and attracts advertisers from across the country. Covering the decorative and fine arts, it seeks to stimulate appreciation and improve the connoisseurship of its readers. Illustrated primarily in four-color, articles cover historic houses, both public and private, ceramics, glass, silver, furniture, textiles, folk art, painting, sculpture, gardens and architecture. Regular features include Current and Coming, Queries, Books about antiques, Editorials, What's where when. Since 1922, "the" antiques publication in the United States. Editor and Publisher Wendell Garrett

$38 One Year The Magazine Antiques Old Mill Road POB 1975 Marion OH 43305 1-800/237-2160

ANTIQUES & THE ARTS WEEKLY

"Antiques & The Arts Weekly" or "The Bee" as it is more familiarly known was first published in October, 1969. In a weekly tabloid format of between 160 and 220 pages, the paper is filled with articles, and advertising from auctioneers, antiques dealers, show managers and private parties either seeking to sell or buy antiques. The paper reviews auctions, antique shows, and museum exhibits and informs its readers of shop openings, museum events and upcoming sales and shows. It runs a weekly index of shows and auctions advertised within. Another excellent source of information. Mailed Second Class every Tuesday. Editor R. Scudder Smith

$32 One Year $56 Two Years Antiques & The Arts Weekly 5 Church Hill Rd, Newtown CT 06470 (203)426-8036

NEW ENGLAND ANTIQUES JOURNAL

A monthly tabloid publication, first published in 1983, containing educational feature articles about antiques, auction reviews and previews, show reviews, book reviews, a calendar of events, news about shows, shops, exhibits, etc. It includes some interesting in-depth articles on particular areas of collecting. Editor Bryan Mc Mullin

$14.95 One Year $25 Two Years New England Antiques Journal 4 Church St Ware MA 01082 (413)967-3505

THE REVIEW Cape Cod's Arts & Antiques Magazine

A beautiful bi-monthly magazine covering the Cape. In its third year of publication, its articles cover a wide variety of arts and antiques subjects as they relate to Cape Cod, Martha's Vineyard and Nantucket. Especially important is "What New With What's Old" an extensive section devoted to antiques-related news notes and items from shops, cooperatives, individual dealers and collectors. Includes Antiques Shop Review, Gallery Review, Book Review, Cape Cod Portfolio, and Ad Index. Editor Alison Lapetina

$15 One Year (six issues) The Review Box 34 Centerville MA 02632 (508)775-7001

THE REGISTER

A weekly Cape Cod newspaper with a monthly magazine supplement devoted to Cape Cod Antiques & Arts. This attractive little newspaper carries advertising from many Cape antiques dealers that you may not find elsewhere. During the weeks Cape Cod Antiques & Arts supplement is not published, a column by the same name appears.

$24.95 Off Cape One Year The Register Box 400 Yarmouth Port MA 02675 (508)362-2111

Maps

LOCATOR MAPS

Specially-designed locator maps, identifying those towns listed in this guide, follow. The maps inform the reader of the relative concentration of antiques-related businesses in a given town and indicate the numbered road thereto. As with any other map, the printed size of the town name reflects its size as measured by the number of inhabitants - only here the inhabitants are antiques dealers and antiques-related services - as opposed to the entire population.

The categories are three:

Town Name	Number of antiques-related businesses
small type	one - five
medium type	six - fourteen
large type	over fifteen

Thus in Connecticut, the map identifies Woodbury with thirty-eight listings in large type and Hartford with only three listings in small type. Due to lead-time required to produce maps, the readers will discover instances where rule does not apply since additions and deletions to the database have been made up until the last minute.

Road maps should be used in conjunction with these locator maps to determine distances and estimate travel times.

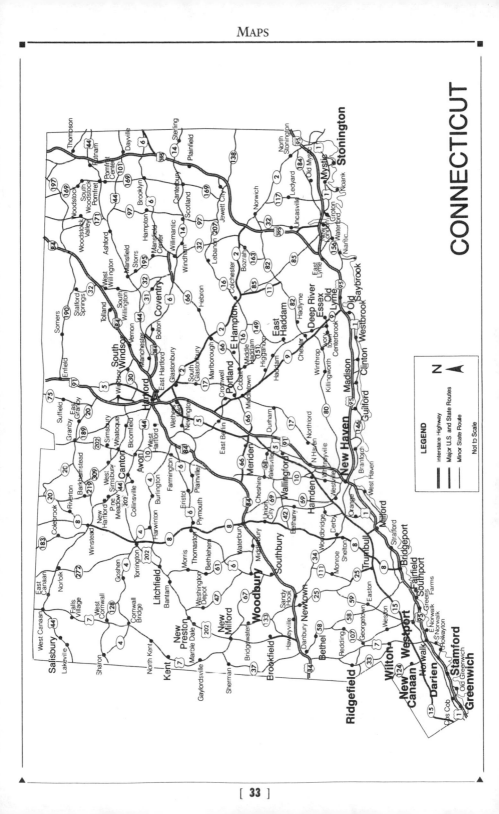

CONNECTICUT

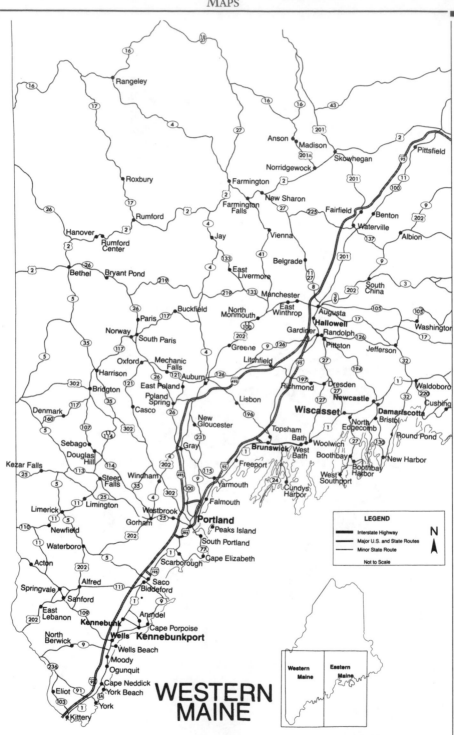

WESTERN
MAINE

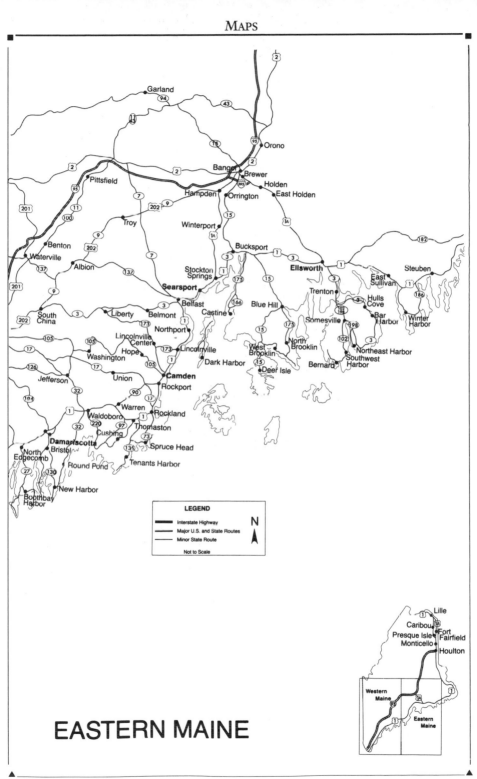

EASTERN MAINE

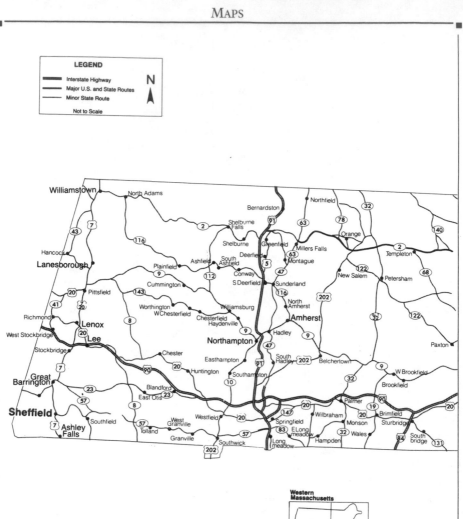

WESTERN
MASSACHUSETTS

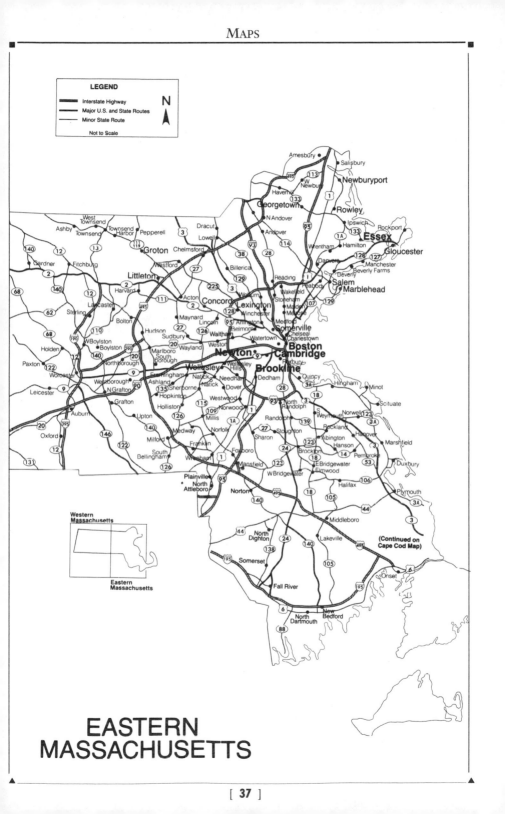

EASTERN MASSACHUSETTS

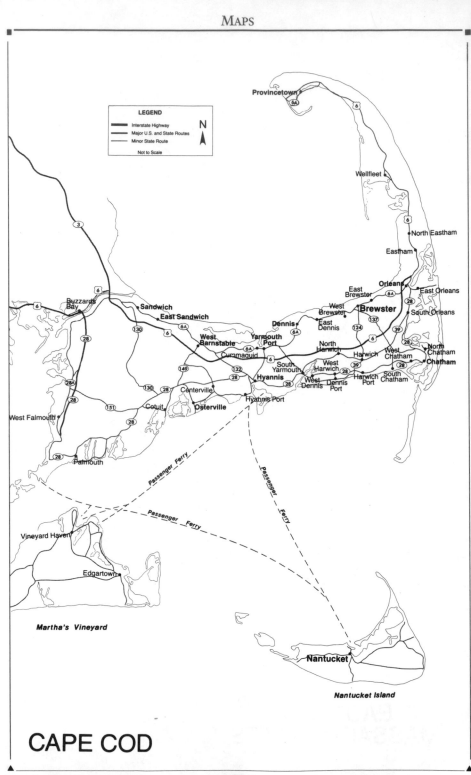

CAPE COD

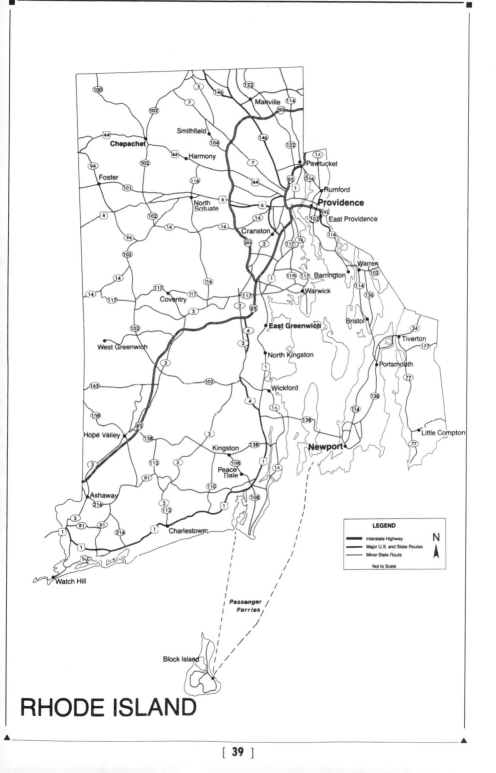

RHODE ISLAND

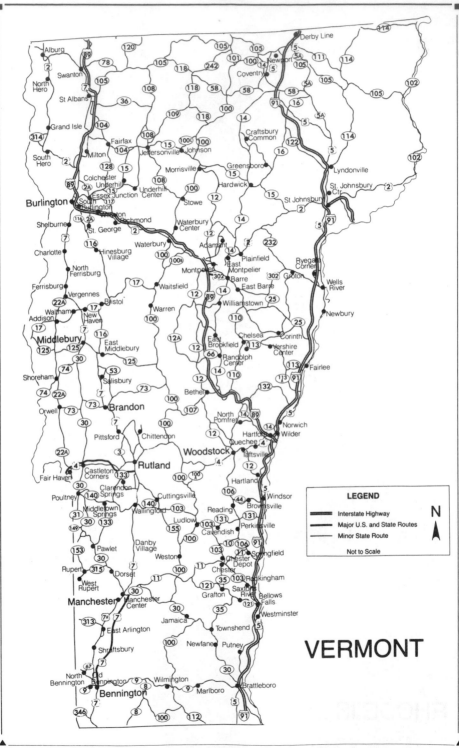

VERMONT

NEW HAMPSHIRE

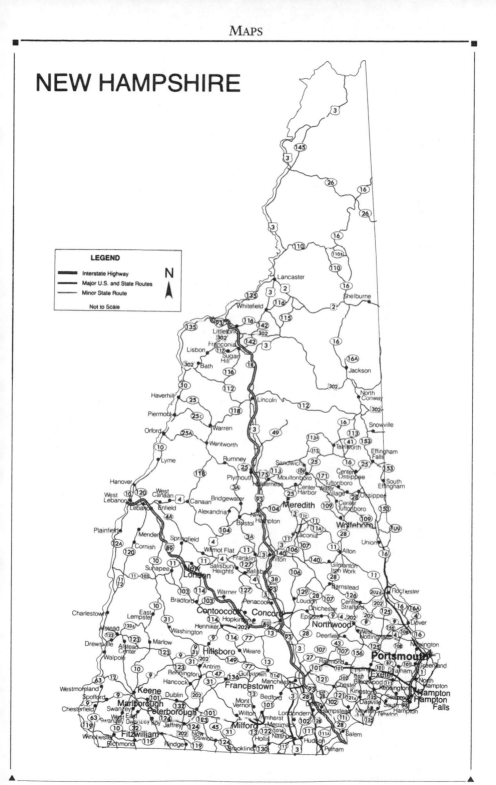

Connecticut

Ashford

CLASSICS IN WOOD
PO Box 211, 06278
(203)429-6020   43
Reproduction tables, chairs & accessories of the Colonial period. *Serv:* Reproduction, brochure $2.00. *Hours:* BY APPT. *Loc:* Call for Directions.

JERALD PAUL JORDON GALLERY
PO Box 71, 06278
(203)429-7954   5 74
An extensive resource of period building & architectural materials through the Federal period. *Serv:* Installation, purchase period architectural pieces. *Hours:* BY APPT. *Loc:* Call for Directions.

MERRYTHOUGHT
Rte 44, 06278
(203)429-8827   1 43 65
18th & 19th C country antiques, furniture & accessories, mostly American, complemented by handcrafted articles from contemporary American artisans - weather vanes, lighting, antique tin items, reproduction Windsor chairs & Colonial tables. *Pr:* $25–5000. *Serv:* Brochure $2, catalog of handcrafted items $2, purchase antiques. *Hours:* By chance/appt. *Size:* Medium. *CC:* MC/V. Jeri Dunphy *Park:* On site. *Loc:* Rte 44 approx 1 MI E of Rte 89, next to Scout Camp entrance, look for Sign of the Swan.

Avon

AUTHENTIC REPRODUCTION LIGHTING
Box 218, 06001
(203)677-4600   50 70
Authentic reproductions of 18th C tin lighting, realistically priced for use in early homes, electrified or for use with candles - handmade in the Colonial manner. *Serv:* Made-to-order, catalog $2.75. *Hours:* BY APPT.

EAGLES NEST
Old Avon Village, 06001
(203)678-0790   11 24 79
Baseball cards, coins & stamps. *Hours:* Tue-Thu 12-4 Fri 12-5 Sun 12-6. *Park:* Nearby.

IMPERIAL DECORATING & UPHOLSTERY
41 Sandscreen Rd, 06001
(203)673-4734   22 68 71
Reupholstery of antique pieces, furniture repair & restoration, chair caning, rush seat weaving & Shaker tape weaving. *Hours:* Mon-Fri 9-5 by chance/appt. *Park:* In front. *Loc:* 1 MI from Int of Rtes 44 & 10, Rte 202 in Avon Ctr.

NATURAL SELECTION BOOKS
PO Box 1375, 06001
(203)651-0557   13
Antiquarian books on natural history. *Serv:* Search service. *Hours:* BY APPT. *Assoc:* CAB. Keith Neitman

GARLAND AND FRANCES PASS
87 Paper Chase Trail, 06001   16
Antique metalware: pewter, brass, copper, iron & tin. *Pr:* $25–5000. *Hours:* By appt.

RUTH TROIANI FINE ANTIQUES
1 Mulberry Lane, 06001
(203)673-6191   **39 57 59**

17th & 18th C needlework, American & English paintings of animals & children, 17th & 18th C treen, early metalware, early English oak & walnut furniture. *Est:* 1963. *Serv:* Everything guaranteed as represented. *Hours:* BY APPT ONLY. *Shows:* ELLIS.

Bantam

KENT & YVONNE GILYARD ANTIQUES
Rte 202W, 06750
(203)567-4204   **37 63 80**

18th & 19th C American country furniture, textiles, china & paintings. *Est:* 1978. *Serv:* Antique restoration. *Hours:* Daily 10-5 sometimes CLOSED WED, call suggested. *Park:* On site. *Loc:* 4 MI W of Litchfield Ctr.

GOOSEBORO BROOK ANTIQUES
Old Turnpike Rd, 06750
(203)567-5245   **28 36 67**

Furniture, baskets, quilts, stoneware & collectibles. *Est:* 1972. *Hours:* All Year. *Loc:* 2 MI W of Bantam Ctr.

WESTON THORN ANTIQUES
Rte 202, 06750
(203)567-4661   **39 59 63**

An attractive collection of English, Continental & American furniture, old reproductions, paintings, silver, porcelain & rugs, housed in 2-story building & barn in scenic Litchfield County. *Pr:* $1–10000. *Est:* 1982. *Serv:* Appraisal, purchase estates. *Hours:* Fri,Sun 11-5

Sat 11-5:30, else by chance/appt. *Size:* Large. *Assoc:* AAA. *Park:* On site. *Loc:* Rte 202, 4 MI SW of Litchfield CT.

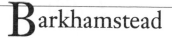
Barkhamstead

BETTY MESSENGER
125 Gavitt Rd, 06035
(203)379-2171   **13 33**

Magazines - over 800 titles, also books & ephemera. *Hours:* BY APPT most mornings/evenings. *Assoc:* CAB.

Bethany

THE ANTIQUARIUM
166 Humiston Dr, 06525
(203)393-2723   **13 33**

20,000 volumes of antiquarian books & ephemera. *Serv:* Catalogs, appraisal, search service. *Hours:* BY APPT ONLY. *Assoc:* CAB. Lee Ash

WHITLOCK FARM, BOOKSELLERS
20 Sperry Rd, 06525
(203)393-1240   **13 51 66**

Antiquarian books: Americana, farming, gardening & horticulture, natural history, prints & maps. *Serv:* Appraisal, search service, catalog. *Hours:* Tue-Sun 9-5. *Assoc:* ABAA CAB. Gilbert Whitlock

ROBERT B WILLIAMS
57 Lacey Rd, 06525
(203)393-1488   **13 59 66**

Specializing in antiquarian & out-of-print dog books, dog paintings, drawings & etchings, a select group of dog figurines. *Pr:* $15–5000. *Est:* 1980.

Serv: Appraisal, catalog, purchase estates, search service. *Hours:* BY APPT ONLY. *CC:* MC/V.

Bethel

DIERINGERS ARTS & ANTIQUES
186 Greenwood Ave, 06801
(203)748-5034   **30 34 65**
Fine selection of white ironstone, decoys, quilts, handwovens, prints, folk art, country furniture, kitchen smalls & primitive art. *Hours:* Tue-Sat 10-5:30. Win: Thu-Sat 10-5. *Loc:* At the Opera House.

J THOMAS MELVIN
20 P T Barnum Sq, 06801
(203)744-5244   **36 59 60**
Furniture, paintings, Oriental porcelains & period brass. *Hours:* BY APPT. *Assoc:* CADA.

PICKWICK HOUSE ANTIQUES
153 Greenwood Ave, 06801
(203)743-6170   **21 23 44**
Eight rooms with china, glass, rugs & tall case clocks. *Est:* 1968. *Serv:* Appraisal, estate sales. *Hours:* Daily 10-6 CLOSED WED,SUN. *CC:* AX/MC/V. *Assoc:* CADA NEAA. Elizabeth Nightingale *Park:* Nearby. *Loc:* Between Wilton & Danbury.

Bethlehem

WOODY MOSCH CABINETMAKERS
23 Wood Creek Rd, 06751
(203)266-7619   **19 74**
18th C & Shaker antique reproduction furniture, 18th C architectural woodworking & custom cabinetry. *Est:* 1976. *Hours:* BY APPT. *Park:* On site. *Loc:* Call for directions.

THE NEW ENGLAND SHOP
151 N Main St, 06751
(203)266-7826   **32**
Used furniture, antiques & stuffed dolls. *Est:* 1972. *Hours:* Wed-Sun 10-6. Rena Meyer *Park:* In front. *Loc:* I-84 to Rte 6 to Rte 61.

Bloomfield

ARS ANTIQUA BOOKS
50 Silo Way, 06002
(203)242-3466   **13**
Antiquarian books specializing in American music & musicology, ethnonomusicology, hymnology, early music, music history & reference, also medieval & Renaissance literature, art & architecture. *Pr:* $5–1000. *Est:* 1983. *Serv:* Catalog (free), search service. *Hours:* BY APPT ONLY. *Assoc:* CAB. Llyn Kaimowitz

Bolton

AUTUMN POND ANTIQUES
29 Westridge Dr, 06043
(203)643-9709   **1 37 59**
Specializing in 18th & early 19th C American furniture & accessories. *Serv:* Purchase estates. *Hours:* By chance/appt suggested. *CC:* MC/V. *Assoc:* CADA. Norma Chick *Park:* On site. *Loc:* 84E to 384E Exit 4: toward Bolton.

HAILSTON HOUSE INC
59 West St Rte 85, 06043
(203)646-2877   **27 36 63**

Two authentic New England barns brimming full of traditional furniture, decorative accessories, eclectic lighting, one-of-a-kind nautical furniture, situated in a charming country setting accented with garden ornaments. *Pr:* $10–10000. *Est:* 1976. *Serv:* Consultation. *Hours:* May-Dec Mon,Fri 11-5 Sat,Sun 10:30-6,Jan-Apr Sat,Sun 10:30-5. *CC:* MC/V. *Assoc:* MADA. Frances Hailston *Park:* On site. *Loc:* Rte 84, Rte 384 Bolton Exit: Rte 85S, 1.5 MI.

QUAKER LADY ANTIQUES
222 West St Rte 85, 06040
(203)643-7738   **27 37 65**

An historical 1735 farmhouse specializing in early American furniture accented with accessories & collectibles. *Est:* 1982. *Serv:* Purchase estates. *Hours:* Sat,Sun 10-6 BY APPT. *CC:* MC/V. Andrea Sauer *Loc:* 20 min E of Hartford off I-384, call for detailed directions.

Bozrah

CHARLES GALLERY
432 Fitchville Rd, 06334
(203)889-4901   **59 78**

American 19th & 20th C paintings, specializing in hunting, fishing & wildlife. *Hours:* BY APPT ONLY. Charles A Connell, Jr

Branford

BRANFORD RARE BOOK & ART GALLERY
779 E Main St, 06405
(203)488-5882   **9 13 66**

Americana, manuscript items, prints maps, postal history & fine art. *Serv:* Catalog, appraisal. *Hours:* Tue-Sat 11-5 Sun 12-5. *Assoc:* CAB. John R Elliott

BARBARA CHAMBERS RESTORATIONS
779 E Main St, 06405
(203)488-9568   **68 71**

Repair & restoration of antique & contemporary fine porcelain, pottery & china, chipped crystal, glass, dolls' heads & lamps. *Serv:* Repairs, restoration. *Hours:* Year round Mon-Sat BY APPT. *Park:* On site. *Loc:* From New Haven I-95 Exit 56: L onto Leetes Island Rd, at 3rd light Rte 1 turn R, approx 1 MI.

YESTERDAY'S THREADS
564 Main St, 06405
(203)481-6452   **47 80 85**

Men's, women's, & children's clothing & accessories from 1840s thru 1940s, Victorian whites, Edwardian wedding dresses, tuxedos, day dresses, evening wear, parasols, vintage textiles, samplers & yardages, Victorian & modern jewelry. *Est:* 1977. *Serv:* Repairs, restoration. *Hours:* Sep-Jun Mon,Wed,Fri 12:30-5 Sat 10-4, Jul-Aug by chance/appt. *Park:* In front. *Loc:* I-95 Exit 55 (Cedar St): toward Branford, 1.5 MI to end, turn R onto Main St, approx 3 blocks.

Bridgeport

GRAYNOOK ANTIQUES & INTERIORS
72 Park Ave, 06604
(203)334-3621   36
Furniture & decorative accessories.
Est: 1976. *Serv:* Interior design.
Hours: BY APPT. *Loc:* Call for directions.

MARC THE 1ST ANTIQUES
3142 Fairfield Ave, 06605
(203)576-9221   **29 37 77**
American furniture, silver & decorative accessories. *Est:* 1983. *Hours:* Tue-Sat 11-5 or BY APPT. *Assoc:* CADA.
Park: On site. *Loc:* I-95 Exit 25 (Fairfield Ave): approx 7 min.

Bridgewater

THE DOLL ROOM
Rte 133 & Stuart Rd, 06752
(203)354-8442   32
Antique & collectibles dolls & doll-related items. *Hours:* BY APPT.

Bristol

RICHARD BLASCHKE
670 Lake Ave, 06010
(203)584-2566   **31 74**
Curved china cabinet glass. *Est:* 1960.
Serv: Cut glass by appt, brochure.
Hours: Mon-Fri 10-4:30 Sat 12-5
CLOSED TUE. *CC:* MC/V. *Park:*
On site. *Loc:* I-84 Exit 31.

DICK'S ANTIQUES
670 Lake Ave, 06010
(203)584-2566   **40 83**
Oak, walnut & Victorian furniture & accessories. *Est:* 1960. *Serv:* Brochure.
Hours: Mon-Fri 10-4:30 Sat 12-5
CLOSED TUE. *CC:* MC/V. *Park:*
On site. *Loc:* I-84 Exit 31.

Brookfield

BERT & PHYLLIS BOYSON
23 Cove Rd, 06804
(203)775-0176   13
Antiquarian books: children's, illustrated, science, technology & general nonfiction. *Hours:* BY APPT. *Assoc:* CAB.

EUROPEAN COUNTRY ANTIQUES
833 Federal Rd Rte 7, 06804
(203)775-2872   27
18th & 19th C English, Irish & French country furniture, china & paintings.
Hours: Year round Wed-Sun 12-5. *CC:*
MC/V. *Park:* Nearby. *Loc:* I-84 Exit 7:
3 min.

MC CAFFREY BOOTH ANTIQUES
436 Federal Rd, 06804
(203)775-1629   **36 43**
Antique & reproduction formal furniture. *Serv:* Refinishing, French polishing, restoration. *Hours:* Tue-Sat 11-5:30. *CC:* MC/V. Thomas E Mc Caffrey *Park:* On site. *Loc:* I-84 to Rte 7, L onto Federal, on Rte 202.

Brookfield Center

ANTIQUE CLOCK SHOP
128 Whisconier Rd Rte 25, 06805
(203)775-4753   23 68 71
Antique, shelf & tall clocks. *Est:* 1975.
Serv: Repair, restoration. *Hours:* Daily
10-5. Pierre T Tunison *Park:* On site.
Loc: 3 MI N of I-84, on Rte 25.

Brooklyn

HEIRLOOM ANTIQUES
10 Winding Rd, 06234
(203)774-7017   36 50
Fine antiques & early lamps. *Serv:*
Fabric lampshades, lamp parts, lamp
repairs, appraisal. *Hours:* Daily 12-5
CLOSED WED. *Assoc:* NEAA. Cath-
arine H Williams *Loc:* Rte 169 Brooklyn Ctr S of the traffic light at Int Rte
6, behind Mortlake Fire Company.

Burlington

HADSELL'S ANTIQUES
191 Geo Washington Tnpk, 06013
(203)673-2344   44
Two floors of depression glass & quality glass & related items of the era. *Pr:*
$25–500. *Est:* 1982. *Serv:* Appraisal,
purchase estates, repairs. *Hours:* Fri-
Sun 1-5 by chance/appt. *Size:* Medium. Luther A Hadsell *Park:* On site.
Loc: From Unionville Ctr, S on Rte
177, R at 2nd light after bridge (Burlington Rd), at next SS, R on Geo
Washington Tnpk, 1 MI.

Canterbury

CACKLEBERRY FARMS
ANTIQUES
16 Lisbon Rd, 06331
(203)546-6335   27
A small country shop featuring country
collectibles. *Pr:* $1–3000. *Serv:* Cater-
ing to the trade. *Hours:* By
chance/appt. *Size:* Medium. *CC:*
MC/V. *Park:* On site. *Loc:* Rte 395
Exit 89: Rte 14 to Canterbury, 1st L
past firehouse, 600 yds from corner on
L.

STONE OF SCONE ANTIQUES
19 Water St, 06331
(203)546-9917   1 6 13
Located in the rural setting of
Connecticut's quiet corner, featuring a
large selection of rare & out-of-print
books - New England history a specialty - antique firearms & rare caliber
reloading tools, antique jewelry & general line of smalls. *Pr:* $10–3000. *Est:*
1976. *Serv:* Appraisal. *Hours:* Mon-Fri
12-8 Sat 10-8 Sun 10-5:30. *CC:* MC/V.
Assoc: CAB NEAA. Jan Stratton *Park:*
On site. *Loc:* I-395N Exit 83A: L on
Rte 169, 8 MI, L at Rte 14, 3 MI, L
onto Water St, 500 ft on R.

Canton

1784 HOUSE ANTIQUES
Canton-on-the-Green Rte 44, 06019
(203)693-2622   37 44 63
Quality furniture, paintings, glass, por-
celain, Meissen, Sevres & Limoges.
Hours: Mon-Sun 10-5. Mrs. Myrtle
Colley *Park:* In front. *Loc:* Rte 44:
white house on the Village Green.

ANTIQUES AT CANTON VILLAGE
Canton Village Rte 44, 06019
(203)693-2715 {MDS20}
Featuring 18th & 19th C furniture & accessories of the highest quality. *Pr:* $50–5000. *Est:* 1988. *Hours:* Wed-Mon 10-5 Sun 12-5. *CC:* MC/V. *Loc:* From Hartford, I-84W Farmington Exit: follow signs to Farmington Ctr, Rte 10 to Avon, L on Rte 44 to Canton.

BALCONY ANTIQUES
81 Albany Turnpike, 06019
(203)693-2996 {GR17}
Oldest group shop in Connecticut displaying furniture, decorative accessories & paintings. *Hours:* Mon-Sat 10-4:30. *Park:* On site. *Loc:* In the Finishing Touch Building.

BOOK STORE
Rte 44, 06019
(203)693-6029 13
General stock of antiquarian books: modern firsts & academic. *Hours:* Wed-Fri 10-6 Sat 10-5 Sun 12-5. *Assoc:* CAB. Stephen Powell

CANTON BARN AUCTIONS
79 Old Canton Rd, 06019
(203)693-0601 8
Auction every Saturday night January-mid December at 7:30, preview 5-7:30. Merchandise from homes, estates. No reserve, no buyers premium. *Hours:* BY APPT. Richard E Wacht *Park:* On site. *Loc:* Off Rte 44, turn onto Old Canton Rd at Citgo station.

THE HOUSE OF CLOCKS
Rte 44 148 Albany Turnpike, 06019
(203)693-2066 23
Antique & European tall clocks & regulator wooden works clocks. *Est:* 1976. *Serv:* Appraisal, repairs, restoration.

Hours: Tue-Thu 10-1 Wed,Fri,Sat 10-4 BY APPT. *Assoc:* NAWCC. *Park:* On site. *Loc:* Near Int of Rtes 44 & 177.

Cheshire

J MUENNICH ASSOCIATES, INC
1185 S Main St, 06410
(203)272-5944 4
Jewelry appraisal & portable gemological services - diamonds & gemstones/antique & period jewelry. *Hours:* Tue-Sat 9-2 (office hours). *Assoc:* AWA GIA ISA. Jill M Muennich

Chester

ONE-OF-A-KIND INC
21 Main St, 06412
(203)526-9736 36 47
Quality antique furniture, jewelry, rugs, porcelain, pottery & primitives. *Pr:* $25–5000. *Est:* 1975. *Serv:* Appraisal, purchase estates. *Hours:* Wed-Sat 10-5 Sun 12-5. *Size:* Medium. *Assoc:* NEAA. Thomas Perry *Park:* In front. *Loc:* From Hartford: 91S to Rte 9S, Exit 6 (L), 1 MI to Chester Ctr.

PERIOD LIGHTING FIXTURES
1 Main St, 06412 50 74
Entirely handmade reproductions of 17th & 18th C chandeliers, lanterns & sconces in copper, pewter, distressed tin & wood. *Serv:* Catalog (refundable)$3.

SAGE AUCTION GALLERIES
Rte 154, 06412
(203)526-3036   **4 8**

Auctioning antiques & fine home furnishings from Essex & Clinton homes.
Serv: Appraisal. Paul Sage

Clinton

HEY-DAY ANTIQUES
PO Box 133, 06413
(203)669-8800   **21**

Oriental rugs. *Est:* 1973. *Serv:* Repair, cleaning, appraisal, purchase estates. *Hours:* BY APPT. *Loc:* Call for directions.

MEURS RENEHAN
101 E Main St, 06413
(203)669-7055   **23 34 65**

European clocks principally early German & Dutch, Japanese clocks, folk art & primitives. *Serv:* Appraisal, restoration, conservation, repair. *Hours:* BY APPT ONLY. *Assoc:* NAWCC.

STEPHEN H SMITH, CABINETMAKER
25 Liberty St, 06413
(203)669-9172   **19**

Handmade, reproduction furniture, including fine chests, desks & tables. *Serv:* Cabinet makers. *Hours:* By appt.

VAN CARTER HALE FINE ART
36 W Main St, 06413
(203)669-4313   **4 26 59**

Fine American paintings, watercolors & prints with an emphasis on Connecticut & New England artists. Art appraisal to the trade with a computer bank of over 10,000 American & Canadian artists with auction records. *Pr:*

$300–20000. *Serv:* Specialty is identifying artists from a partial signature. *Hours:* BY APPT. *CC:* MC/V. *Assoc:* NEAA. *Park:* On site. *Loc:* I-95 Exit 63: S on 81 for .5 MI, R on Boston Post Rd (US1), 6th bldg on L.

Colchester

BARBARA WOOD BROWN
179 S Main St, 06415
(203)537-2286   **57 67**

Country furniture & accessories with quality quilts & coverlets a specialty. *Hours:* BY APPT.

LES TROIS PROVINCES
526 Westchester Rd Rte 149, 06415
(203)267-6057   **35 36 63**

One of the country's largest collections of 18th & 19th C country French antique furniture & accessories, tables, armoires & buffets, displayed in period rooms in the historic Champion House. *Est:* 1970. *Hours:* Wed-Sat 10-5 Sun 12-5. John Adams *Park:* In front. *Loc:* From Hartford: Rte 2 Exit 16: S to Rte 149, from Middletown: Rte 66E to Rte 16, R onto Rte 149 8 MI N of Goodspeed Opera.

NATHAN LIVERANT & SON
48 S Main St, 06415
(203)537-2409   **37 59**

Fine American antiques & paintings for the discriminating collector displayed in an 1831 meeting house. *Est:* 1920. *Serv:* Will buy an single piece or an entire collection. *Hours:* Mon-Sat 10-5. *Loc:* Located between Hartford & New London.

NADEAU'S AUCTION GALLERY
489 Old Hartford Rd, 06415
(203)537-3888   **8**
Antique and estate auctions. No
buyer's premium. *Serv:* Purchase estates, consignments, appraisals, truck-
ing available. *CC:* MC/V. Edwin
Nadeau *Park:* Ample. *Loc:* From
Hartford: Rte 84 to Rte 2 toward New
London. Exit 17 L at SS. First L then
first R, first bldg on L..

Colebrook

COLEBROOK BOOK BARN
Rte 183, 06021
(203)379-3185   **13**
Antiquarian books: Americana, American & English literature, rare books,
salesmen's samples & publisher's
leather bindings. *Serv:* Appraisal, catalogs. *Hours:* Sat,Sun 10-5 appt advised.
Assoc: ABAA CAB. Robert Seymour

RINHART GALLERIES
Upper Grey, 06021
(203)379-9773   **4 13**
Antiquarian books: American history,
presidents, photography & graphic
arts. *Serv:* Catalogs. *Hours:* BY APPT
ONLY. *Assoc:* NEAA. George R Rinhart

Collinsville

COUNTRY LANE BOOKS
PO Box 47, 06022
(203)693-2245   **13**
Antiquarian books: children's books,
Civil War, literature, voyages & West-
ern Americana. *Hours:* BY APPT
ONLY. *Assoc:* ABAA. Edward T
Myers

**LAWRENCE GOLDER, RARE
BOOKS**
PO Box 144, 06022
(203)693-8110   **13**
Antiquarian books: rare or scarce
Americana, early voyages & travels, the
West, Colonial, Indians, wars, Canadi-
ana & the Arctic. *Serv:* Catalog, ap-
praisal. *Hours:* BY APPT ONLY.
Assoc: CAB.

Cornwall Bridge

THE BRASS BUGLE
Rte 45, 06754
(203)672-6535   **1 65 80**
In an 18th C barn: furniture, primitives, collectibles, fabrics, quilts, glass,
china, lamps & tools. *Est:* 1962. *Hours:*
May-Nov 11 daily 8-5. *CC:* MC/V.
Louise M Graham *Park:* On site. *Loc:*
1 MI off Rte 7 on Rte 45.

Cos Cob

THE BOOK BLOCK
8 Loughlin Ave, 06807
(203)629-2990   **9 12 13**
Press books & fine printing, literature,
rare books, fine bindings, autograph
letters & manuscripts. *Serv:* Restoration, bookbinding. *Hours:* BY APPT
ONLY. *Assoc:* ABAA CAB. David
Block

PIERCE-ARCHER ANTIQUES
391 Valley & Palmer Hill Rd, 06807
(203)869-1130   **39**
Fine English antiques, importers of
17th-19th C English furniture & decorative accessories. *Est:* 1967. *Serv:*
Master picture framer. *Hours:* Mon-

Fri 9:30-5:30 Sat 9:30-4:30. *CC:* AX/MC/V. Eugenia Pierce Archer *Park:* On site. *Loc:* At the Int.

Coventry

ALLINSON GALLERY INC
46 Fieldstone Ln, 06238
(203)742-8990   **4 59 66**

Oils, watercolors, etchings, lithographs, woodcuts & Japanese woodblock prints. *Est:* 1977. *Serv:* Appraisal. *Hours:* BY APPT. *Assoc:* AAA. Jane Allinson PhD *Park:* Nearby. *Loc:* I-84 Coventry Exit: 8 MI.

ANTIQUE DE-LIGHTS
1205 Main St, 06238
(203)742-6104   **30 36 50**

Lamps, decoys, vintage radios & furniture. *Hours:* Thu-Sun 10-5. *Loc:* Between Village Restaurant & firehouse.

COVENTRY ANTIQUE CENTER
Rte 31, 06238
(203)742-1647   **{GR}**

Toys, dolls, linens, jewelry & vintage clothing. *Serv:* Doll repair. *Hours:* Wed-Sun 10-5. Mary Woodman

COVENTRY BOOK SHOP
1159 Main St Rte 31, 06238
(203)742-9875   **13**

A general stock of antiquarian books. *Serv:* Appraisal, search service. *Hours:* Tue-Sat 12-5. *Assoc:* CAB. John R Gambino

HANDS OF TIME
209 Woodbridge Rd, 06238
(203)742-9844   **34 65 80**

Antiques, collectibles & folk art featuring fabrics, upholstery, pillows & primitives. Lynda M Pellegren *Loc:* In the Capt Cyrus Jones House.

MEMORY LANE ANTIQUE CENTER
2224 Boston Turnpike Rte 44, 06238
(203)742-0346   **{GR23}**

Silver, china, glass, furniture, primitives, jewelry & quilts. *Est:* 1985. *Serv:* Appraisal, consultation, purchase estates. *Hours:* Year round Wed-Sun 10-5. *CC:* MC/V. Gail Dickenson *Park:* On site. *Loc:* I-84 Exit 67: 2 MI S to corner of Rtes 31 & 44.

OLD COUNTRY STORE ANTIQUES
1141 Main St, 06238
(203)742-9698   **36**

Seven rooms of furniture & decorative accessories. *Est:* 1973. *Hours:* Wed-Sun 10-5 & by chance. *Park:* In front. *Loc:* On Rte 31.

KATHLEEN SULLIVAN-CHILDREN'S BKS
861 Main St, 06238
(203)742-7073   **13**

19th & 20th C children's & illustrated books. *Serv:* Appraisal, search service. *Hours:* BY APPT. *Assoc:* CAB.

VILLAGE ANTIQUES
1340 Main St Rte 31, 06238
(203)742-5701   **{GR12}**

In a reproduction of an 1890s village - a potpourri of antiques & collectibles, on 2 floors of an old barn. *Pr:* $1-5000. *Est:* 1973. *Serv:* Appraisal, auction, purchase estates, kiln-fired shade matching. *Hours:* Wed-Sat 9-5 Sun 10-4. *Size:* Large. *CC:* MC/V. *Park:* On site. *Loc:* Corner of Rtes 31 & 275.

WILDFLOWER
1199 Main St Rte 31, 06238
(203)742-7482   **27 32 34**

Small, historic shop filled with country antiques, antique toys, unique collectibles, fine contemporary folk art & a large selection of artist teddy bears. *Pr:* $40–3000. *Serv:* Purchase estates. *Hours:* Wed-Sun 10-5, best to call ahead. *Size:* Medium. Sylvia R Jucker *Park:* On site. *Loc:* I-84/Rte 31S, directly to Main St in Coventry.

Cromwell

CUSTOM HOUSE
6 Kirby Rd, 06416
(203)828-6885   **29 50**

A specialty shop for custom lamp shades: hand sewn, pierced, botanical, fabric & paper lamination - displayed on antique Chinese porcelain & early oil & kerosene lamps with a selection of antique accessories. *Pr:* $25–1000. *Est:* 1968. *Serv:* Consultation, interior design, custom mounting & wiring. *Hours:* Sep 15-July 15 Mon-Fri 10-4 Sat 9:30-12:30. *Size:* Medium. Eunice Buxton *Park:* On site. *Loc:* I-91 Exit 21: 1st R, 2nd L.

HORTON BRASSES
Nooks Hill Road, 06416
(203)635-4400   **16 70**

Manufacturers of brass hardware for antique furniture. Superior reproductions of Queen Anne, Chippendale, Hepplewhite, Sheraton, Victorian & early 1900s drawer pulls, knobs, hinges, finials, escutcheons, iron & architectural hardware. *Est:* 1930. *Hours:* Aug 24-Jul Mon-Fri 9:00-3:45. *CC:* MC/V. *Loc:* I-91 Exit 21: call for directions.

Danbury

CARNIVAL HOUSE ANTIQUES
17 Padanaram Rd Rte 37, 06811
(203)792-6746   **33 44 63**

Three large rooms full of period furniture, carnival & depression-era glass, china, jewelry, pottery & Coca Cola collectibles. *Pr:* $4–1500. *Hours:* Apr-Dec Wed-Sun 11-5 CLOSED JAN-MAR. *Size:* Medium. *CC:* MC/V. Mary Lou Zdanowski *Park:* In front. *Loc:* I-84W Exit 6: E Exit 5 onto Rte 37N, approx .5 MI past McDonald's on R.

ORPHEUS BOOKS
4 Abbott Ave, 06810
(203)792-4990   **13 55**

Books on music. *Serv:* Catalog. *Hours:* BY APPT ONLY. *Assoc:* CAB. Irving Goldstein

TIME AFTER TIME
9 Main St, 06811
(203)743-2801   **78**

Billiard supplies, custom & antique tables from the mid-1800s, run by a professional billiard player. *Est:* 1958. *Serv:* Billiard room interior design, appraisal, repair, restoration. *Hours:* Mon-Sat, CLOSED WED in JUL/AUG. *Size:* Medium. Ed O'Connell *Park:* On site. *Loc:* I-84 Exit 5: 3 min.

Darien

1860 HOUSE OF ANTIQUES
682 Post Rd, 06820
(203)655-8896   **{GR4}**

Four rooms & a large barn of country & formal American, English & French furniture, brass, prints, Quimper, mirrors, majolica, copper, lamps, Staffordshire, toys, flow blue, quilts, fireplace furnishings & childhood folk art. *Pr:* $25–2500. *Est:* 1977. *Hours:* Mon-Sat 11-5. *Assoc:* CADA. Lonny Fitz-Gerald *Park:* On site. *Loc:* Between 119 & 12 off I-95.

ANTIQUES UNLIMITED
1090 Post Rd, 06820
(203)655-5133   **34 37 63**

18th & 19th C American furniture with appropriate accessories, formal & country, fine art & folk art, the expected & the unexpected. *Hours:* Mon-Sat 10-5 Sun by chance/appt. *Size:* Large. *CC:* MC/V. Sally Case *Park:* Nearby lot. *Loc:* I-95 Exit 11: (L from New Haven, R from NYC), 300 ft on R.

GILANN SUMMER BOOK SHOP
4 West Ave, 06820
(203)655-4532   **11 13 33**

Children's books, first editions, baseball cards & ephemera. *Pr:* $5–and up. *Serv:* Appraisal, catalog, search service, mail order Jul/Aug. *Hours:* Sum: Wed-Sun 11-5, 301 West St open year round. *CC:* MC/V. *Assoc:* NEAA. *Park:* On site. *Loc:* Across from Darien Railroad Station.

EMY JANE JONES ANTIQUES
770 Boston Post Rd, 06820
(203)655-7576   **40 42 47**

Seven rooms of furniture in oak, pine, walnut & mahogany, beautiful antique jewelry & accessories. *Serv:* Appraisal, consultation, repair. *Hours:* Mon-Sat 10:30-4:30 Sun 1-5. *CC:* AX/MC/V. *Park:* In front. *Loc:* In the heart of Darien.

LA CALECHE
1089 Post Rd, 06820
(203)655-3993   **35 46**

An elegant shop displaying the finest 17th, 18th & 19th C French antiques with original French paintings, antique mirrors, Quimper, decorative & fine arts personally selected by the French owner. *Pr:* $1500–15000. *Est:* 1987. *Serv:* Consultation, interior design. *Hours:* Mon-Sat 10-5:30 Sun 11-5. *Size:* Medium. *CC:* MC/V. Jany Caroli *Park:* In front. *Loc:* I-95 Exit 11E: on Post Rd .2 MI.

H P MC LANE ANTIQUES INC
1076 Post Rd, 06820
(203)655-2280   **16 63 77**

American & English furniture, silver, paintings, brass, boxes, prints, Oriental & European porcelain & lamps. *Hours:* Tue-Sat 10-5. *Park:* In front. *Loc:* I-95 Exit 11E.

PURPLE DOOR ANTIQUES
1975 Post Rd, 06820
(203)655-4742   **{GR4}**

18th & 19th C furniture, quilts, glass, porcelain, redware, stoneware, folk art, toys & more. *Hours:* Daily 10-5 Sun 11-4. *CC:* MC/V. Mary Stasik *Park:* On site. *Loc:* I-95 Exit 10: S on Noroton Ave to Post Rd, L & on L.

CATHERINE SYLVIA REISS
23 Tokeneke, 06820
(203)655-8070   **66**

Antique prints, national historic town views, American, illustrated. *Est:* 1977. *Serv:* Fine matting, framing. *Hours:* Mon-Sat 10:30-5:30. *CC:* MC/V. *Loc:* I-95 Exit 12.

ROSE D'OR
973 & 980 Boston Post Rd, 06820
(203)655-4668   **36 44 60**

Consignment of antiques, furniture, lamps, china, glass, Oriental art, paintings & bronzes. *Hours:* Mon-Sat 10-5 Sun 12-5. *Size:* Large. *Park:* On site. *Loc:* I-95 Exit 11N or 11S: near Darien RR.

DORRIE SCHREINER GALLERY ANTIQUE
111 Old Kings Hwy S, 06820
(203)655-4677   **1 60 73**

Orientalia, Americana, fine arts, American & European paintings & sculpture. *Est:* 1972. *Serv:* Appraisal. *Hours:* BY APPT.

SEVERED TIES
995 Post Road, 06820
(203)656-2131

Antiques & quality consignments: furniture, decorative accessories, art, silver & estate jewelry. *Est:* 1988. *Serv:* Consignments. *Hours:* Mon-Sat 10-5. *Park:* Nearby.

WIND-BORNE FRAME & RESTORATION
559 Post Rd, 06820
(203)655-9735   **25 59 71**

Fine art gallery featuring 19th & early 20th C paintings & prints. Professional fine art conservation services performed by qualified experts. All media & art objects accepted. Antique frame restoration, fine custom framing. *Serv:* Conservation, frame repair, gold leafing, reproduction, restoration,framing. *Hours:* Tue-Sat 10-5. *Size:* Medium. *CC:* MC/V. R Blaikie Hines *Park:* On site. *Loc:* I-95 Exit 13: L off ramp onto Post Rd/Rte 1, 1 MI from Exit on R.

WINDSOR ANTIQUES LTD
1064 Post Rd, 06820
(203)655-2330   **37 63 78**

Large stock 18th & 19th C English & American furniture, Chinese export porcelains, samplers, folk art, sporting art, paintings & fireplace equipment. *Est:* 1975. *Hours:* Mon-Sat 10:30-5, CLOSED AUG. David Kemp *Park:* On site. *Loc:* I-95 Exit 13 or 11.

Deep River

W B GOTTLEIB - BOOKS
385 Winthrop Rd, 06417
(203)526-9462   **13**

Antiquarian books: modern first editions, poetry, travel, juveniles & theatre. *Hours:* Daily 12:30-5:30. *Assoc:* CAB. William B Gottleib *Loc:* On Rte 80.

RIVERWIND ANTIQUE SHOP
68 Main St, 06417
(203)526-3047   **42 65**

Primitives, pine & unique treasures. *Hours:* Tue-Sat 10:30-5 Sun 12-5. Peggy Maraschiello *Loc:* Corner of Main & Spring sts.

Derby

BOOKS BY THE FALLS
253 Roosevelt Dr Rte 34, 06418
(203)734-6112   **13 14**

Four rooms of antique & out-of-print books in an old red brick building by the waterfall. *Est:* 1983. *Serv:* Appraisal. *Hours:* Year round daily 10-5. *Size:* Large. *Assoc:* CAB. Ronald A Knox *Loc:* Rte 8 Exit 15: L thru town, 1 MI to old red brick factory by waterfall.

Durham

HODGE PODGE LODGE
114 Main St, 06422
(203)349-8697   **29 36**

Furniture & decorative accessories.
Hours: By chance/appt. *Assoc:* CADA.
George Gorton

East Haddam

CENTERPIECE ANTIQUES
Rte 149, 06423   **6 36**

Furniture, military smalls & the unusual. *Hours:* Wed-Mon 11-5.

CONNECTICUT RIVER BOOKSHOP
Goodspeed Plaza, 06423
(203)873-8881   **13**

General out-of-print & rare books,
specializing in nautical, hunting &
fishing, New England, art & architecture, children's & Americana subjects.
Pr: $10-500. *Est:* 1987. *Serv:* Nautical
catalog, appraisal. *Hours:* Thu-Sat
10:30-5 Sun 12-5. *Size:* Medium.
Assoc: CAB. Frank Crohn *Park:* On
site. *Loc:* I-95 Exit 69: Rte 9N to Exit
7 (E Haddam), located right in town.

MAGIC HORN LTD
95 Ray Hill Rd, 06423
(203)873-1346   **13 33**

Children's & illustrated, big little
books, limited ephemera & general
stock of antiquarian books. *Serv:* Limited search service. *Hours:* Sat,Sun 11-
6 by chance/appt. *Assoc:* CAB. Fred
Miller

OLD BANK HOUSE GALLERY
90 Main St, 06423
(203)873-8224   **60 66 78**

In a handsome 1820 bank overlooking
the CT river, an extensive selection of
antique & original prints, beautiful
French matting & marbleized papers.
Interesting collection of books & an-
tiques provide pleasant browsing. *Pr:*
$25-8000. *Est:* 1979. *Serv:* Custom
framing, conservation, interior design.
Hours: Everyday BY APPT. Winifred
Rapp *Park:* On site. *Loc:* CT Rte 9
Exit 7: follow signs to Goodspeed
Opera House, located 1 MI N of
Goodspeed on Rte 149.

East Hampton

BELLTOWN TRADING POST
Rte 66, 06424
(203)267-0280   **36**

Period furniture & collectibles. *Serv:*
Auctions, estate sales. *Hours:* Thu-Sun
10-5 or BY APPT.

BIBLIOLATREE
Country Store Rte 66, 06424
(203)267-8222   **13**

35,000 volumes of antiquarian books.
Hours: Sat,Sun 1-on, weekdays by
luck. *Assoc:* CAB. Paul O Clark

GRAND ILLUSIONS
26 Barton St, 06424
(203)267-8682

A small collection of kaleidoscopes:
high quality brass, wood & leather
models from the 1800s by Bush &
Brewster. *Serv:* Repairs by referral,
mail order list available. *Hours:* By
appt only.

OLD BANK ANTIQUES
66 Main St, 06424
(203)267-0790 {GR50}

Furniture from every period attractively arranged & accented with glassware, Orientals, clocks, mirrors & a large selection of jewelry. *Pr:* $5–2500. *Est:* 1984. *Hours:* Wed-Sun 10-5 Thu 10-9. *Size:* Large. *CC:* AX/DC/MC/V. *Park:* Nearby lot. *Loc:* From Hartford: I-84 Exit 55: Rte 2, Exit 13, R onto Rte 66, L at 2nd light.

OPERA HOUSE ANTIQUES
95 Main St, 06424
(203)267-0014 **36 59 83**

Country & formal furniture, Victoriana, glassware, accessories, paintings, prints & collectibles. *Est:* 1986. *Serv:* Appraisal, auction, purchase estates. *Hours:* Wed-Sun 10-5. *Size:* Medium. *Park:* On site. *Loc:* From Hartford: Rte 2 Exit 13: R onto Rte 66, L at 2nd light.

East Lyme

STEPHEN & CAROL HUBER INC
82 Plants Dam Rd, 06333
(203)739-0772 **34 41 57**

Needlework specialists covering English & American 17th-19th C. Samplers, silk embroideries, tent stitch pictures, bedcovers, domestic handwoven fabrics always in stock. American painted furniture 17th-19th C & appropriate accessories. *Pr:* $25–200000. *Serv:* Appraisal, conservation, consultation, interior design. *Hours:* Appt suggested. *Size:* Large. *Loc:* Please call for directions & appointment.

East Norwalk

THE CLOCKERY
14 Van Zant St, 06855
(203)838-1789 **23 68 71**

Antique clock specialists with 100 clocks on display in the showroom. *Pr:* $100–8000. *Est:* 1973. *Serv:* Repair, restoration. *Hours:* Tue-Sat 10-4:30. *CC:* MC/V. *Assoc:* AWI BHI NAWCC. Floyd Taylor *Park:* On site. *Loc:* I-95 Exit 16: to Rte 136, .5 MI S.

Easton

RED SLEIGH
1093 Black Rock Tnpk, 06612
(203)268-2783 **34 42 65**

Affordable country pine, primitives, folk art & interesting smalls. *Pr:* $10–1500. *Serv:* Consultation, purchase estates, repairs, restoration. *Hours:* Nov-May Mon-Sat 11-4:30. *Size:* Large. *Assoc:* CADA. William Pirozzoli *Park:* On site. *Loc:* Merritt Pkwy Exit 5: N 7.5 MI toward Redding.

Enfield

ENFIELD MALL INTERNATIONAL
Hazard Ave, 06082

Flea market every Sunday. *Loc:* I-95, Exit 47, inside Mall.

Essex

A MATHEWS ANDERSON ANTIQUES
2 Captains Walk, 06426
(203)767-1214　　　　**21 27 44**

An antique barn with 3 floors of country furniture, Oriental rugs, flint glass & collectibles. Herb garden, herbs & dried arrangements. *Est:* 1986. *Serv:* Brochure. *Hours:* Apr-Dec Wed-Sun, Jan-Mar BY APPT. *Size:* Medium. *Park:* On site. *Loc:* I-95S Exit 68 (Essex/Hartford): Rte 9, Exit 3, R .5 MI on Rte 156, on corner of Rte 156 & Captains Walk.

FRANCIS BEALEY AMERICAN ARTS
3 S Main St, 06426
(203)767-0220　　　　**1 37 59**

Fine period American furniture of the 18th & early 19th C, American Impressionist paintings - fireplace furnishings a specialty. *Pr:* $1000–100000. *Serv:* Consultation. *Hours:* Sep 15-Jun Mon-Sat 11-4, else Mon-Fri 11-4. *Size:* Medium. *Park:* Nearby lot. *Loc:* 4 MI N of I-95, from the W: Exit 65 (Rte 153), from the E: Exit 69 (Rte 9).

BONSAL-DOUGLAS ANTIQUES
59 Main St, 06426
(203)345-3441　　　　**38 56 59**

Superb marine paintings, fine 16th-early 17th C European furniture shown in a 17th C showroom in historic Essex. Sherry served daily at 4:00 pm. *Pr:* $500–25000. *Serv:* Consultation, interior design, select estate purchases, exhibit at shows. *Hours:* Sum: Wed-Sun 12-5, Win: Tue-Sat 11-5. Isabelle D Seggerman *Park:* On site.

Loc: I-95 Exit 69: Rte 9, Exit 3 (Essex) which is Rte 154, follow signs & rd directly into Main St Essex.

ESSEX ANTIQUES CENTER
8 Main St, 06426
(203)767-1291　　　　{GR22}

Quality American furniture, Staffordshire, glass, pottery & porcelain, quilts, jewelry, primitives & folk art in an historic 1800's Colonial in the center of the village. *Hours:* Daily 11-5. *CC:* MC/V. *Park:* On site. *Loc:* In the ctr of Main St in a white colonial.

ESSEX AUCTION & APPRAISAL
PO Box 27, 06426
(203)767-1204　　　　**4 8**

Liquidators of estate & household contents, commercial & residential, single pieces or entire contents, direct purchases or consignment. *Serv:* Appraisal, accept mail/phone bids, mailing list. *Hours:* BY APPT. *Assoc:* ASA ISA. *Loc:* Call for directions.

ESSEX COLONY ANTIQUES
Rte 153 & Ingham Hill Rd, 06426
(203)767-2721　　　　{GR10}

Country, Federal & Victorian fine arts in a large red 1792 Colonial. *Est:* 1986. *Serv:* Purchase estates. *Hours:* Daily 10:30-5:00. *CC:* AX/MC/V. Frank Coulom *Park:* On site. *Loc:* I-95 Exit 65N: 3 MI.

THE ESSEX FORGE
Old Dennison Rd, 06426
(203)767-1808　　　　**2 50 70**

Reproduction chandeliers, indoor lighting, sconces, fireplace equipment, lanterns & standing lamps. *Est:* 1969. *Hours:* Mon-Sat 10-5. *CC:* MC/V. Wallace Lawder *Park:* On site. *Loc:* 1st door on L on North Main St.

HASTINGS HOUSE
Box 606, 06426
(203)767-8217   **45 60 80**
Textiles, objets d'art, European & Oriental antiques, Japanese scrolls & screens, unusual 19th C garden furniture & statuary. *Est:* 1968. *Serv:* Purchase estates. *Hours:* BY APPT ONLY. *Assoc:* AADLA. *Shows:* WAS. Philip H McNemer *Loc:* Call for Appt.

TURTLE CREEK ANTIQUES
60 S Main St, 06426
(203)767-1204   **37**
American furniture & decorative accessories. *Serv:* Auction. *Hours:* Wed-Sun 11-5. *CC:* MC/V. *Assoc:* ISA. Penny Parker *Park:* Nearby. *Loc:* I-95 Rte 9 Exit 3: to traffic signal, follow sign to Essex Ctr, at 1st SS turn R onto S Main St.

VALLEY FARM ANTIQUES
134 Saybrook Rd, 06426
(203)767-8555   **6 16 63**
Furniture, guns, pewter, jewelry, china & glass. *Est:* 1960. *Serv:* Appraisal, consultation, purchase estates. *Hours:* Tue-Sat 10-4. *Assoc:* NEAA. Ellsworth E Stevison *Park:* Nearby. *Loc:* 2 min off I-95.

WHITE FARMS ANTIQUES
2 Essex Sq, 06426
(203)767-1876   **37**
Specializing in 18th & 19th C American country furniture & accessories. *Est:* 1985. *Hours:* Tue-Sat 10-5. Dan Stix *Park:* Nearby. *Loc:* In the center of town.

Essex (Centerbrook)

BRUSH FACTORY ANTIQUES
33 Deep River Rd Rte 154, 06409   **{GR}**
Housed in a newly-renovated historic factory building, furniture & decorative accessories. *Hours:* Tue-Sun 11-5. *Loc:* I-91 to Rte 9S Exit 4: R off ramp .5 MI on L. From I-95, Rte 9N, Exit 4, R, .75 MI on L.

CHARLES & PATRICIA THILL ANTIQUE
The Factory Bldg-Middlesex Tnpk, 06409
(203)767-1696
American & European antiques. *Serv:* Appraisal.

Fairfield

PATRICIA BARGER
66 Wilson St, 06432
(203)372-2536
18th & 19th C antiques & accessories. *Hours:* BY APPT ONLY.

JAMES BOK ANTIQUES
1954 Post Rd, 06430
(203)255-6500   **16 29 36**
Period furniture, early brass & accessories. *Hours:* By chance/appt. *Assoc:* NHADA. *Loc:* On US Rte 1.

CONNECTICUT BOOK AUCTION
251 Carroll Rd, 06430
(203)259-1997   **8 13 51**
Book auctions - including ephemera, maps & photographs - held 3 times yearly. *Est:* 1976. *Serv:* Appraisal, ac-

cept mail/phone bids, catalog, purchase estates. *Hours:* BY APPT
ONLY. Y J Skutel

ENSINGER ANTIQUES LTD
3921 Park Ave, 06432
(203)374-1586   **36 63**
Specializing in Chinese export porcelain & period furniture. *Hours:* BY
APPT ONLY. Gail Ensinger

G G G ANTIQUES
Box 63, 06430
(203)254-3630   **4 47**
Fine antique & estate jewelry. *Serv:*
Appraisal, purchase estates. *Hours:* BY
APPT & shows. *CC:* AX/MC/V. *Assoc:*
ASA GIA ISA. Ellen Grober

PATTY GAGARIN ANTIQUES
Banks North Rd, 06430
(203)259-7332   **21 29 41**
Fine American painted furniture,
weather vanes, rugs & accessories.
Hours: BY APPT.

LEMANOIR COUNTRY
FRENCH ANTIQUES
10 Sanford St, 06430
(203)255-1506   **35 36 63**
Fine quality 18th & 19th C French
provincial furniture & accessories &
old Quimper faience. *Pr:* $35–15000.
Hours: Tue,Thu-Sat 10:30-5 BY
APPT, CLOSED JAN,JUL,AUG.
Size: Medium. *Park:* In front. *Loc:* I-
95 Exit 21: L onto Post Road, to 3rd
Light, white building on L of Int.

A. LUCAS, BOOKS
89 Round Hill Rd, 06430
(203)259-2572   **13**
19th & 20th C first editions. *Serv:* Appraisal, search service. *Hours:* Please
phone first. *Assoc:* CAB. Alexander
Lucas

MUSEUM GALLERY BOOK
SHOP
360 Mine Hill Rd, 06430
(203)259-7114   **13 14**
Books on the fine arts. *Hours:* BY
APPT. *Assoc:* CAB. Henry B Caldwell

WINSOR ANTIQUES
43 Ruane St, 06430
(203)255-0056   **35 39**
Specializing in English & French
country furniture & English Windsor
chairs, furnishings from the 17th to
late 19th C & a large selection of decorative accessories. *Pr:* $25–20000.
Est: 1983. *Hours:* Year round Tue-Sat
10-5. *Size:* Large. *CC:* MC/V. *Assoc:*
CADA. Paul Winsor *Park:* On site.
Loc: I-95 Exit 21 (Mill Plain Rd): S to
Jct Rte 1, L on Post Rd to 1st light, R
on Ruane St, 1st bldg on L.

F alls Village

R & D EMERSON,
BOOKSELLERS
103 Main St, 06031
(203)824-0442   **13**
In an old church: antiquarian & rare
books. *Hours:* Daily 12-5 CLOSED
JAN,FEB. *Size:* Large. *CC:* MC/V.
Assoc: ABAA CAB. Robert C Emerson
Park: In front.

F armington

LILLIAN BLANKLEY COGAN
ANTIQUARY
22 High St, 06032
(203)677-9259   **37**
Specialist in 17th & 18th C original
New England furniture & the appro-

priate accessories - nothing post-revolutionary. *Est:* 1928. *Hours:* BY APPT ONLY. *Assoc:* AADLA. *Shows:* WAS. *Loc:* Situated at "Hearts & Crowns".

5:30 Sun 12-5:30, CLOSED WED. Pat Shiple *Park:* On site. *Loc:* Between Rtes 107 & 102.

Gaylordsville

BITTERSWEET SHOP
Rtes 7 & 55, 06755
(203)354-1727   {GR14}
Formal & country furniture, paintings, quilts & decorative accessories. *Est:* 1978. *Hours:* Apr-Dec daily 10-5, CLOSED WED Sun 12-5. *CC:* MC/V. Mark Estabrooks *Park:* On site. *Loc:* 40 min N of Danbury on Rte 7.

MICHAEL HALL ANTIQUES
Kent Rd Rte 7, 06755
(203)355-4750   50 60 80
American & European furniture, pottery, porcelain, glassware, textiles, linens, lighting fixtures, chandeliers & Oriental works-of-art. *Hours:* By chance/appt. *Park:* On site. *Loc:* From Gaylordsville Iron Bridge, on Rte 7 less than .25 MI on Housatonic River side, travelling N.

Georgetown-Wilton

WHITE DOVE ANTIQUES
951 Danbury Rd Rte 7, 06829
(203)544-8100   {GR}
Shaker, tiger maple, primitives, hooked rugs, game boards, decoys & 19th C pine & cherry. *Est:* 1980. *Serv:* Interior design. *Hours:* Mon-Sat 11-

Glastonbury

MAURER & SHEPHERD, JOYNERS
122 Naubuc Ave, 06033
(203)633-2383   70 74
Reproduction of authentic 17th & 18th C Colonial joinery - windows, door frames & columns. *Est:* 1976. *Serv:* Consultation, reproduction. *Hours:* Mon-Fri 8:30-5:30. Hap Shepherd *Loc:* 5 min outside of Hartford, off Rte 2.

MARY S SWIFT ANTIQUES
1401 Main St, 06033
(203)633-2112   30 34 36
A small friendly shop next to an 18th C house, with country furniture, hooked rugs, quilts, decoys & unusual accessories. *Pr:* $25–2000. *Est:* 1972. *Hours:* Mon-Sat BY APPT. *Size:* Medium. *Park:* On site. *Loc:* Main St is Rte 17 in Glastonbury.

ROY & BETSY THOMPSON ANTIQUES
20 Chestnut Hill Terr, 06033
(203)659-3695   1 36
Specializing in 17th & 18th C New England furniture & decorative accessories & 19th C American paintings. *Est:* 1968. *Serv:* Appraisal, consultation. *Hours:* BY APPT. *Assoc:* ADA NEAA. *Park:* On site. *Loc:* From Hartford: Rte 2E Exit 7: follow S Glastonbury signs approx 3 MI on L.

Goshen

ANGLER'S & SHOOTER'S BOOKSHELF
Goshen, 06756
(203)491-2500   **13 78**
Antiquarian books: angling, hunting, shooting, Derrydale press & sporting art. *Hours:* BY APPT ONLY. *Assoc:* ABAA. Col Henry A Siegel

GOSHEN ANTIQUE CENTER
North St Rte 63N, 06756
(203)491-2320   **{MDS28}**
Distinctive dealers in an 1830s Colonial house listed in the National Register of Historic Places filled with beautiful antiques from America, Europe & Asia, artistically displayed. *Serv:* Appraisal. *Hours:* Daily 10:30-5:30 CLOSED TUE. *CC:* AX/MC/V. Maya Schaper *Park:* On site. *Loc:* 6 MI N of Litchfield.

TRADE WINDS, THE 1749 HOUSE
Rte 63S, 06756
(203)491-2141   **60 63**
Chinese ceramics - mostly porcelains & decorative accessories. *Est:* 1986. *Hours:* By chance/appt. *Loc:* 6 MI from Litchfield.

Granby

GRANBY ANTIQUES EMPORIUM
381 Salmon Brook, 06035
(203)653-2355   **{GR}**
Folk art, furniture, china, glass, jewelry, linens, pictures & tools. *Hours:* Daily 12-5 Sat,Sun 10-5 CLOSED WED. *CC:* MC/V. *Loc:* On Rte 10N.

WILLIAM & LOIS M PINKNEY
240 N Granby Rd, 06035
(203)653-7710   **13 66**
Antiquarian books: Western Americana, New England, New York, limited editions club, first editions, children's books, cookbooks, natural history, hunting & fishing, sheet music, prints, literary biography & criticism. *Serv:* Appraisal, search service. *Hours:* Mon-Fri 9-5, call ahead on weekends. *Assoc:* ABAA CAB.

Greenwich

AMERICAN TRADITION GALLERY
335 Greenwich Ave 2nd fl, 06830
(203)869-8897   **59**
Specializing in American painters 1830-1930, especially Connecticut artists. *Serv:* Appraisal. *Hours:* Sum: Tue-Fri 11-4 or BY APPT.

ANTAN ANTIQUES LTD
12 W Putnam Ave, 06830
(203)661-4769   **29 35 59**
French & English 18th & 19th C decorative accessories & furniture. *Est:* 1978. *Hours:* Mon-Sat 10:30-5. *CC:* AX/MC/V. *Assoc:* NEAA. Monique Olmer *Park:* On street. *Loc:* Corner of Greenwich Ave.

ANTIQUES & INTERIORS AT THE MILL
334 Pemberwick Rd, 06830
(203)531-8118   **29 36**
A beautiful collection of 18th & 19th C antique furniture & accessories in the railroad building of a restored mill. *Pr:* $20–6000. *Est:* 1985. *Serv:* Appraisal, consultation, interior design. *Hours:* Jan 2-Dec 25 Tue-Sat 10:30-5 & BY

APPT. *Size:* Medium. *CC:* MC/V. Doris W Ross *Park:* On site. *Loc:* Merritt Pkwy King St Exit: (from S:R, from N:L) on King, at 2nd light, L on Glenville, 1st R after Fire Station.

BANKSVILLE ANTIQUES
1064 North St, 06830
(203)869-9673   **5 21 36**

Fine 18th & 19th C country & formal furniture & accessories, architectural pieces, majolica & quilts. *Serv:* Consultation, search service, refinishing. *Hours:* Tue-Sat 9-5. *CC:* AX/MC/V. Elizabeth Watson *Park:* On site. *Loc:* Merritt Pkwy Exit 31: North St 4 min.

BETTERIDGE JEWELERS INC
117 Greenwich Ave, 06830
(203)869-0124   **4 47**

From pre-Columbian to Tiffany: Carefully chosen antique & estate jewelry for the serious collector. *Serv:* Appraisal. *Hours:* Tue-Sat 9-5. *Assoc:* AAA. Albert E Betteridge III

CHELSEA ANTIQUES OF GREENWICH
14 W Putnam Ave, 06830
(203)629-2224   **4 24 63**

Four showrooms of English & American furniture, Persian rugs, sterling silver, English & Continental porcelain, crystal, bronze, Oriental porcelain, art & print section 18th & 19th C works, jewelry, gold & silver coins. *Pr:* $15–15000. *Est:* 1949. *Serv:* Appraisal. *Hours:* Year round Mon-Sat 10:30-5. *Size:* Medium. *Assoc:* NEAA. *Park:* Nearby lot. *Loc:* On Boston Post Road in central Greenwich opposite "Greenwich Chateau" the highest building in town.

CONSIGN IT
115 Mason St, 06830
(203)869-9836   **36 47 77**

Wonderful antique consignment shop, with large turn-over, quality merchandise from Greenwich's finest homes. *Pr:* $100–10000. *Est:* 1980. *Serv:* Appraisal, purchase estates. *Hours:* Mon-Sat 10-5. *Size:* Large. *Assoc:* NEAA. Randi Conway *Park:* On site. *Loc:* I-95 Exit 3: .5 MI to Mason St, parallel to Greenwich Avenue.

ELAINE DILLOF
60 William St, 06830
(203)629-2294   **35 37 39**

French, English & American furniture. *Hours:* Mon-Sat 11-5. *Park:* Nearby.

GEORGIAN ANTIQUES
382 Greenwich Ave, 06830
(203)625-0004   **39 59 63**

Fine English furniture, porcelain & paintings. *Serv:* Appraisal. *Hours:* Mon-Sat 10-5. Carol Thomasy *Park:* In front. *Loc:* Downtown Greenwich.

RENE GROSJEAN ANTIQUES
51 Greenwich Ave, 06830
(203)869-7114   **23 47**

Antique & estate jewelry & watches. *Est:* 1943. *Serv:* Restoration, repair. *Hours:* Tue-Sat 9:30-5. *Park:* In front. *Loc:* 1 block from Post Rd.

GUILD ANTIQUES
384 Greenwich Ave, 06830
(203)869-0828   **29 37 39**

English & American furniture, Chinese export porcelain & decorative accessories. *Hours:* Mon-Sat 10-5. *CC:* MC/V. George Rich *Park:* In front. *Loc:* 2 MI from Exit 3, NY Thruway.

HALLOWELL & CO
340 W Putnam Ave, 06830
(203)869-2190   **6 72 78**

Fine vintage sporting & collector firearms. *Pr:* $500–50000. *Serv:* Appraisal, catalog, purchase estates. *Hours:* Mon-Sat 10-6. *Size:* Medium. *CC:* AX/MC/V. Morris L Hallowell *Park:* In front. *Loc:* West Putnam Ave is US Rte 1.

HENRI-BURTON FRENCH ANTIQUES
79 E Putnam Ave, 06830
(203)661-8529   **35**

Located in an historic building - quality 18th & 19th C French furniture & accessories from country to formal, armoires, commodes, tables, chairs, Quimper, faience, lamps & decorative objects. *Est:* 1987. *Hours:* Mon-Sat 9:30-5:30. *Size:* Medium. *CC:* MC/V. *Park:* On site. *Loc:* I-95 Exit 4: (from NYC: L, from New Haven: R), .2 MI to lights, L onto Putnam, 1 MI on R.

THE HOUSE THAT JACK BUILT
115 Mason St, 06830
(203)661-0029   **32 34 67**

Large selection of antique birdhouses & cages. Folk art, quilts, pottery, early American toys & whirligigs. *Loc:* Village Square.

LIBERTY WAY ANTIQUES
One Liberty Way, 06830
(203)661-6417   **29 36 44**

Furniture, art, decorative accessories & early American pattern glass. *Est:* 1987. *Serv:* Appraisal. *Hours:* Mon-Sat 10-5:30. *CC:* AX/MC/V. Joy Shannon *Park:* On site. *Loc:* I-95 Exit 3: follow Arch St N, cross Greenwich Ave, L to Mason St, L on Elm St, 2nd parking lot drive.

STEFANO MAGNI ANTIQUES/FINE ART
95 E Putnam Ave, 06830
(203)622-7550   **38 58 59**

Large gallery of expertly selected fine European antiques & fine art from the 16th C Renaissance-19th C. Beautiful Italian ceramics, European porcelain, exotic African & Asian decorative objects. *Pr:* $100–50000. *Est:* 1987. *Serv:* Appraisal, brochure, consultation, restoration. *Hours:* Tue-Sat 9:30-5:30 Sun 12-5. *Size:* Large. *CC:* AX. *Park:* On site. *Loc:* Greenwich Central business district, 2 blocks from Greenwich Ave, across from 1st Nat'l Supermarket in Fine Arts Building.

PROVINCES DE FRANCE
22 W Putnam Ave, 06830
(203)629-9798   **35 59**

Fine French 18th & 19th C antiques - a large selection of provincial & country furniture, faience & accessories, fine paintings, watercolors & prints. *Hours:* Mon-Sat 10-5:30 Sun 12-5, Jun til Sep 15 CLOSED SUN. *Size:* Medium. *CC:* AX/MC/V. Jenny Kechejian *Park:* In front. *Loc:* I-95 Exit 3: .5 block from Greenwich Ave, on Rte 1.

DAVID A SCHORSCH
1037 North St, 06830
(203)869-8797   **1 87**

Fine American antiques & weather vanes. *Serv:* Consultants & brokers. *Hours:* BY APPT ONLY.

SCHUTZ & COMPANY
Dewart Rd, 06830
(203)629-3387   **4**

Appraisal of 19th & 20th C American & European painting & sculpture. *Hours:* BY APPT ONLY. *Assoc:* AAA. Herbert Schutz

SOPHIA'S GREAT DAMES
1 Liberty Way, 06830
(203)869-5990   **47 80 85**

Quality antique clothing & period accessories from the 1880s-1950s, nostalgia & collectibles, specializing in costume jewelry. *Est:* 1981. *Serv:* Consultation, repairs, restoration. *Hours:* Mon-Sat 10-5:30. *Size:* Medium. *CC:* AX/MC/V. Sophia O'Connor *Park:* On site. *Loc:* 1 MI off I-95.

Guilford

A SUMMER PLACE
21 Boston St, 06437
(203)453-5153   **86**

Antique wicker. *Serv:* Buy wicker. Mary Jean Mc Laughlin *Loc:* On the Green.

ARNE E AHLBERG
1090 Boston Post Rd, 06437
(203)453-9022   **36**

Antique furniture & decorative accessories. *Serv:* Appraisal. *Hours:* BY APPT.

CORNUCOPIA ANTIQUE CONSIGNMENTS
1058 Boston Post Rd, 06437
(203)453-8677   **1 47 80**

Two floors of furniture, china, glass, silver, paintings, jewelry & textiles. *Est:* 1985. *Serv:* Interior design. *Hours:* Jun-Dec Tue-Sat 10-5 Sun 11-3, Jan-May CLOSED SUN. *Size:* Medium. *CC:* MC/V. *Park:* On site. *Loc:* I-95 Exit 58: Rte 77, turn toward Guilford, at traffic light turn R, 3rd bldg on L, red carriage.

LAMB HOUSE FINE BOOKS
21 Boston St, 06437
(203)453-8803   **13**

Select out-of-print titles of 20th C literature, New England history, Americana, art & architecture, antiques, travel & gardening. *Hours:* Tue-Sat 11-6 Sun 12-5. Lory McCaskey *Loc:* On-the-Green.

Haddam

WILD GOOSE CHASE
831A Rte 154, 06438
(203)345-3459   **36**

Antiques & furniture. *Hours:* Thu-Sun 10-5. John Iverson

Hamden

AMERICAN WORLDS BOOKS
PO Box 6305 Whitneyville Sta, 06517
(203)776-3558   **13**

Antiquarian books: American literature, scholarly studies of American authors, American cultural history & business history. *Serv:* Catalogs, appraisal, search service. *Hours:* BY APPT ONLY. *Assoc:* CAB. Nolan E Smith

ANTIQUE BOOKS
3651 Whitney Ave Rte 10, 06518
(203)281-6606   **13**

Antiquarian books in 3 buildings emphasizing early Americana in all fields except poetry & fiction. *Pr:* $10–300. *Serv:* Catalog, appraisal. *Hours:* By chance/appt suggested. *Size:* Large. *Assoc:* CAB. Willis O Underwood *Park:* On site. *Loc:* Rte 91 Exit 10: Rte 10 (Whitney Ave), R after the 4th light.

BOOKCELL BOOKS
90 Robinwood Rd, 06517
(203)248-0010   **13**

Antiquarian books: the sciences, technology, children's & illustrated. *Serv:* Catalogs, appraisal, search service. *Hours:* BY APPT ONLY. *Assoc:* CAB. Dorothy Kuslan

GALLERY 4
2985 Whitney Ave, 06518
(203)281-6043   **44 48 77**

Antiques, silver, cut glass, Limoges, linens, books, trade cards, china, pattern glass, quilts, fine art, Eskimo, American Indian, Oriental art. *Est:* 1976. *Hours:* Mon-Sat 10-6. *CC:* MC/V. *Loc:* I-95 Exit 10: 200 yds N.

MCBLAIN BOOKS
2348 Whitney Ave, 06518
(203)281-0400   **13**

A general line of antiquarian books including those on Africa, Asia, the Pacific, Black America, Latin America & the Middle East. *Serv:* Catalogs. *Hours:* BY APPT ONLY. *Assoc:* ABAA CAB. Philip A McBlain *Park:* On site. *Loc:* 2 blocks off Wilbur Cross Parkway.

Hartford

BACON ANTIQUES
95 Maple Ave, 06114
(203)524-0040   **36 44 63**

Furniture, decorative accessories, glass & china. *Est:* 1947. *Serv:* Appraisal, purchase estates. *Hours:* Mon-Sat 9-5. *CC:* MC/V. *Park:* On street. *Loc:* 100 yds from Main St.

THE JUMPING FROG
161 S Whitney St, 06105
(203)523-1622   **13**

Antiquarian books: modern first editions, military history, biography, literary criticism, autographed books, illustrated, science fiction, mysteries, drama, music, sports, Norman Rockwell covers & advertisements. *Est:* 1983. *Serv:* Appraisal, catalog ($1), purchase estates. *Hours:* Wed-Sat 10-6 Sun 1-6, else by chance/appt. *Size:* Medium. *Assoc:* CAB. Bill McBride *Park:* In front. *Loc:* I-84 Exit 46: R at 2nd Light, .5 block on L.

THE UNIQUE ANTIQUE
The Hartford Civic Center, 06103
(203)522-9094   **47**

One of the largest selections of antique & estate jewelry in the East including Victorian, mourning, art nouveau, deco, vintage, costume & precious gemstones. *Pr:* $25–2000. *Serv:* Purchase estates. *Hours:* Mon-Fri 10-9 Sat 10-6 Sun 12-5, Sum: Sun by chance. *Size:* Medium. *CC:* AX/MC/V. Joanne Douglas

Harwinton

JOHN M DAVIS INC
PO Box 262, 06791
(203)485-9182   **37 39 60**

English & American furniture, accessories & Chinese export porcelain. *Est:* 1973. *Serv:* Appraisal, conservation, purchase estates, interior design. *Hours:* BY APPT ONLY. *Loc:* 10 min E of Litchfield.

RYAN'S ANTIQUES
8 Burlington Rd Rte 4, 06791
(203)485-9600 **27 81**

Tools, kitchen items, large variety of antiques & collectibles & country furniture. *Hours:* Sum: daily by chance/appt. *Loc:* Rte 8 Exit 42: E 3 MI on Rte 4.

H ebron

DAVID & DALE BLAND ANTIQUES
124 Slocum Rd, 06248
(203)228-3514 **36**

Specializing in 18th C furniture. *Assoc:* NEAA.

H igganum

BRYCE GEORGE MUIR
Nelson Pl, 06441
(203)345-4741

Furniture, prints & decorative accessories. *Hours:* BY APPT.

I voryton

COMSTOCK HSE ANTIQUE RESTORATION
28 Comstock Ave, 06442
(203)767-2211 **25 68 71**

Conservation of fine antique furniture. *Serv:* Conservation, repairs, restoration. *Hours:* BY APPT ONLY. *Assoc:* NEAA. Timothy D Robin *Park:* On site.

J ewett City

JEWETT CITY EMPORIUM
144 N Main St Rte 12, 06351
(203)376-9808 **{GR20}**

Antiques, collectibles, estate jewelry, diamonds, coins, furniture, linens & old lace. *Est:* 1983. *Serv:* Appraisal. *Hours:* Wed-Sun 10-5. *Size:* Large. *CC:* MC/V. Deanna Denis *Loc:* I-395 Exit 84: 1.5 MI on Rte 12.

LEONE'S AUCTION GALLERY
Wedgewood Dr, 06351
(203)642-6248 **8**

Estates sales, antiques & collectibles auctions. *Assoc:* NAA.

JOHN WALTON INC
Box 307, 06351
(203)376-0862 **1 37**

Specializing in American antiques of the 17th-early 19th C, the largest stock of original examples in New England. *Serv:* Written guarantee, buy back policy, purchasing. *Hours:* Mon-Sat BY APPT ONLY. *Loc:* Offer limousine Service from the airport or railroad station.

K ent

THE FORRER'S
N Main St Rte 7, 06757
(203)927-3612 **27 32 81**

Early American country & formal furniture, accessories, toys, banks, tools, porcelain, china, folk art & Staffordshire early china. *Est:* 1966. *Serv:* Appraisal, purchase estates. *Hours:* Wed-Mon 9-5 by chance/appt.

Size: Medium. *CC:* AX/MC/V. Edward E Forrer *Park:* On site. *Loc:* Rte 7, 35 MI N of Danbury.

GOLDEN THISTLE ANTIQUES
Rte 7, 06757
(203)927-3790   **37 38 63**
American & European furniture, porcelain & glass. *Est:* 1967. *Hours:* Fri-Mon 11-5, else BY APPT. *Park:* Nearby. *Loc:* Ctr of town.

HARRY HOLMES ANTIQUES
Rte 7, 06757
(203)927-3420   **23 36**
18th & 19th C furniture & clocks. *Est:* 1968. *Serv:* Purchase estates. *Hours:* Daily 9-5 CLOSED WED. *CC:* MC/V. *Park:* On site. *Loc:* 5 MI N of Village of Kent.

HOLMES RESTORATIONS
Kent Falls, 06757
(203)672-0125   **71**
American & European formal & country antiques, restorations of modern furniture, copper, brass, iron, chair seats woven, non-commercial stains used & milk paints made in shop. Michael Holmes

KENT ANTIQUES CENTER
Kent Station Sq Main St, 06757
(203)927-3313   **{GR7}**
Quality country antiques, accessories & collectibles from the 18th-20th C located in a restored 150 year-old farmhouse. *Hours:* Daily 11-5 CLOSED THU. *CC:* MC/V. *Loc:* On Rte 7 behind the RR station, N of the monument.

ELIZABETH S MANKIN ANTIQUES
Rte 341 E, 06757
(203)927-3288   **37 59 63**
American formal & country period furniture, paintings, accessories & English ceramics. *Est:* 1953. *Hours:* Mon-Sat 11-5. *Assoc:* NHADA. *Park:* On site. *Loc:* 1.9 MI from the traffic light in Kent.

OLDE STATION ANTIQUES
Main St Rte 7, 06757
(203)927-4493   **29 36**
American, French & English fine antiques & reproductions. *Serv:* Interior design, restoration. *Hours:* Daily 10-5 CLOSED MON. *CC:* MC/V. Gene Stillwagon *Park:* On site. *Loc:* N of the ctr of town.

PAULINE'S PLACE
Main St Rte 7, 06757
(203)927-4475   **47**
Antique & estate jewelry, 14k, 18K, 21K gold-Georgian to contemporary. *Est:* 1978. *Serv:* Repairs. *Hours:* Jan-May daily 11-5 CLOSED WED,THU. *CC:* AX/MC/V. *Park:* In front. *Loc:* Approx .25 MI N of monument on Main St.

Killingworth

THE BERGERON'S ANTIQUES
294 Rte 81, 06417
(203)663-2122   **38 40 42**
Furniture : including, English oak pub tables & Continental armoires. *Pr:* $25-5000. *Est:* 1972. *Serv:* Purchase estates, repairs, restoration. *Hours:* By Chance/Appt. *Size:* Large. *CC:* MC/V. *Assoc:* CADA. Rebecca Bergeron *Park:* On Site.

LEWIS W SCRANTON ANTIQUES
224 Roast Meat Hill, 06417
(203)663-1060   **16 28 41**

Specializing in early American painted furniture in as-found condition, New England slipware, redware, stoneware & other related early accessories. *Est:* 1968. *Serv:* Purchase estates. *Hours:* By chance/appt suggested. *Assoc:* ADA. *Park:* On site. *Loc:* I-95 Exit 63: Rte 81N, 5 MI, R at circle onto Rte 80, .8 MI, R at 1st crossroad, 3rd house on R.

Lakeville

AMERICANA
Main St, 06039
(203)435-2494   **34 36 67**

Antique quilts, furniture, folk art & accessories. *Hours:* Year round Mon-Thu 10-5 Fri,Sat,Sun 11-5. Suzanne Feldman

BAD CORNER ANTIQUES & DECORATION
Rtes 41 & 44, 06039
(203)435-9369   **33 36 65**

Primitives, American advertising & furniture. *Est:* 1965. *Hours:* May-Oct daily 11-5. Gail A Vaill *Park:* On site. *Loc:* Adjacent to Iron Masters Motel.

LISA C INC
Main St, 06039
(203)435-0721   **85**

Fine vintage clothing including Victorian whites & wedding gowns from 1900s-1950s. *Hours:* Daily 10-5 or by appt. *Loc:* In the center of town.

Lebanon

THE ETCETERA SHOPPE
Rte 87 On The Green, 06249
(203)642-6847   **48 85**

Antique baby dresses, vintage clothing, linen & lace. *Est:* 1981. *Serv:* Repair & restoration of antique gowns, period & floral designs. *Hours:* By chance/appt. Nancylee S Gaucher *Park:* On site. *Loc:* I-395, Rte 32N out of Norwich, to Rte 87.

Lisbon-Jewett City

MR & MRS JEROME BLUM
Ross Hill Rd, 06351
(203)376-0300   **16 37 50**

Brass chandeliers, lighting, wall sconces, American country furniture & 17th & 18th C brass. *Hours:* BY APPT ONLY. *Shows:* ELLIS. *Loc:* I-395 Exit 84 (Jewett City).

Litchfield

COUNTRY HOUSE CONSIGNMENTS
West St Rte 202, 06759
(203)567-8826   **16 36 63**

Antiques, brass, china, furniture, glass, lamps, linen, paintings, prints, pewter, rugs & silver. *Est:* 1980. *Hours:* Mon-Sun 10-4. *CC:* MC/V. *Park:* On site. *Loc:* .1 MI W of the Green, in a red building.

D W LINSLEY INC
Rte 202W, 06759
(203)567-4245   **39 40 42**

Exceptional English country pine &

period oak furniture displayed on 3 floors. *Est:* 1973. *Hours:* Wed-Sun 11-5. *CC:* AX. *Park:* On site. *Loc:* 2 MI from Litchfield adjacent to the White Memorial.

LITCHFIELD AUCTION GALLERY
Harris Plains, 06759
(203)567-3126   **8**
Sunday auctions held twice monthly featuring Americana, fine art & folk art. 10% buyers premium. *Serv:* Appraisal, accept mail/phone bids, brochure, catalog, consultation. *Hours:* Tue-Fri 9:30-5, CLOSED non-auction weekends. *Size:* Large. *CC:* MC/V. *Park:* On site. *Loc:* From N: Rte 7 to Rte 63 to 202W, From NYC: Rte 684 to 84 in Danbury, Brookfield Exit (Rtes 7 & 202) follow Rte 202.

THOMAS MC BRIDE ANTIQUES
West St, 06759
(203)567-5476   **44 59 77**
Furniture, decorations, silver, American & European paintings, Victorian, early American & French glass. *Est:* 1966. *Hours:* Mon-Fri 9:30-5 weekends BY APPT, CLOSED Dec 15-Apr. *Park:* On site. *Loc:* Red barn next to Town Hall.

JOHN STEELE BOOK SHOP
South St near the Green, 06759
(203)567-0748   **13 64**
Antiquarian & second-hand books, Connecticut history, post cards. *Hours:* Tue-Sat 11-5:30 Sun 1-5 & BY APPT. *Assoc:* CAB. William Keifer *Loc:* Next to the Litchfield Historical Society.

HARRY W STROUSE
306 Maple St, 06759
(203)567-0656   **58 77**
Two rooms of 18th & 19th C antiques & decorations in a 1749 house. Specializing in silver & objets d'art, furniture, glass, china, rugs, tools, paintings, prints, fabric, pewter, crocks, andirons, books, brass, copper & wrought iron. *Pr:* $25–5000. *Est:* 1971. *Serv:* Appraisal, auction, consultation, interior design, purchase estates. *Hours:* By chance/appt. *Size:* Medium. *Park:* On site. *Loc:* 1.5 MI N from Rte 202, just past Our Lady of Grace Church.

PETER H TILLOU - FINE ARTS
Prospect St, 06759
(203)567-5706   **34 59 73**
European & American paintings of 17th-19th C, 18th C American furniture, sculpture & American folk art. *Est:* 1955. *Hours:* BY APPT ONLY. *Shows:* WAS. *Loc:* Call for Appt.

THOMAS D & CONSTANCE R WILLIAMS
Brush Hill Rd, 06759
(203)567-8794   **16 63**
18th & 19th C pewter & Chinese export porcelain. *Serv:* Appraisal. *Hours:* BY APPT.

WOOD*WORKS
The Cove Rte 202, 06759
(203)567-9767   **68 71**
American & European antiques restoration, fine woodworking, French polishing, faux finishes, marbleizing & grain painting. *Est:* 1975. *Hours:* BY APPT. Barry Strom *Park:* On site. *Loc:* Call for directions.

Madison

ANTIQUES AT MADISON
837 Boston Post Rd, 06443
(203)245-7856   35 37 39
American, English & French furniture
& antique decorative objects. *Pr:*
$100–3000. *Est:* 1986. *Hours:* Apr-Jan
15 Wed-Sat 11-5 Sun 1-5, Jan 16-Mar
Sat 11-5 Sun 1-5. *Size:* Medium. *CC:*
AX/MC/V. Joan Fernandez *Park:* On
site. *Loc:* I-95 Exit 61: to downtown
Madison.

KIRT & ELIZABETH CRUMP
387 Boston Post Rd Rte 1, 06443
(203)245-7573   23 37
18th & 19th C clocks including tall
case clocks, pillar & scroll & other
shelf clocks & mantle clocks, period
timepieces & American furniture. *Est:*
1976. *Serv:* Appraisal, consultation,
repair & restoration of clocks only.
Hours: By chance/appt. *Assoc:* ADA
BHI NAWCC. *Park:* On site. *Loc:* I-
95 Exit 61: approx 1 MI.

P HASTINGS FALK SOUND VIEW PRESS
206 Boston Post Rd, 06443
(203)245-2246   26 59 66
Specialist in 19th & early 20th C
American art, paintings by women &
vintage photographs. Publisher of
25,000 entry biographical dictionary
"Who Was Who in American Art",
dictionary of signatures & monograms
of American artists. *Serv:* Brochure,
catalog, consultation, purchase estates.
Hours: BY APPT ONLY. *CC:* MC/V.
Peter H Falk *Loc:* Call for Appt &
directions.

NOSEY GOOSE
33 Wall St, 06443
(203)245-3132   27 41 86
Painted & country furniture, accesso-
ries & antique wicker. *Est:* 1980.
Hours: Mon-Sat 10-5. *CC:* MC/V.
Betty-Lou Morawski *Park:* On site.
Loc: I-95 Exit 61S: Rte 1, L at light, 1st
L off Rte 1.

ON CONSIGNMENT OF MADISON
77 Wall St, 06443
(203)245-7012
Consignment furniture, china, porce-
lain, Oriental rugs & silver. *Est:* 1985.
Serv: Consignment shop. *Hours:* Tue-
Sat 10-5. *Park:* On site. *Loc:* From
Boston Post Rd: US Rte 1, L onto Wall
St, between library & post office on
Wall St.

ORDNANCE CHEST
PO Box 905, 06443
(203)245-2387   6 24 78
Antique firearms, books, medals,
edged weapons - mostly pre-WW II,
pre-1898 weapons & military collectibles. *Pr:* $10–1500. *Est:* 1976. *Serv:*
Appraisal, catalog (3 issues/$5), pur-
chase estates, search service. *Hours:*
BY APPT ONLY. *CC:* MC/V. *Loc:*
Call for directions.

RIVER CROFT
220 River Rd, 06443
(203)245-4708   16 68 71
Repair, restoration, polishing of brass,
copper, iron, perform fabrication,
welding, brazing, soldering of metals
& electrified lamps. *Serv:* Repairs, restoration. *Hours:* Mon-Fri 9-5 Sat 9-12.
Bob Cole *Park:* On site. *Loc:* I-95 Exit
62S: Rte 1, L onto Rte 1, 1st L onto
Mill Rd, .75 MI, sign hangs from tree
at end of driveway on R.

SHAFER AUCTION GALLERY
82 Bradley St, 06443
(203)245-4173 **4 8**

Auctions approximately twice monthly, always on Sunday evening at 7:00pm, with a 2 hr preview beforehand. Quality home furnishings & antiques. Left bids. *Est:* 1969. *Serv:* Appraisal, consignment. *Hours:* By chance. *Assoc:* CAA NAA. *Park:* On site. *Loc:* I-95 Exit 61: S on Rte 79, 1st L, 3rd building on R.

Manchester
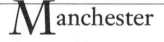

BOOKS & BIRDS
519 E Middle Tnpk, 06040
(203)649-3449 **13**

Antiquarian books: including birds, nature, Connecticut, hunting & fishing, military & history, gardening & cooking & children's books. *Serv:* Appraisal, search service. *Hours:* Tue-Sat 11-4:30 Thu til 8, call for Sun & Mon hours. *Assoc:* CAB. Gil Salk *Loc:* 1 MI E of Main St.

CONNECTICUT CANE & REED CO
134 Pine St, 06040
(203)646-6586 **22**

Complete stock of all chair seating & wicker repair supplies. Largest selection on the East Coast. *Serv:* Antique restoration & basketry supplies, same day shipments. *Hours:* Mon-Fri 9-5 Sat 10-4. *Size:* Large. *CC:* AX/MC/V. Joanne Parkinson *Park:* On site. *Loc:* Off Rtes 44 & 6.

Mansfield Center

SHIELA B AMDUR - BOOKS
PO Box 151, 06250
(203)423-3176 **13**

Antiquarian books relating to medicine, psychiatry & New England. *Hours:* BY APPT. *Assoc:* CAB.

JACK COLLINS WOODWORKING
RR1 Box 243, 06250
(203)455-0086 **70 71**

Restoration lumber - authentic new materials for restoration. Seasoned wide Eastern white pine, red oak, white oak, Pennsylvania cherry, hard maple, genuine mahogany, slow growth Northern hard pine & clear pine. *Serv:* Custom milling, brochure $1.00 restoration lumber. *Hours:* BY APPT.

Marble Dale

LIMEROCK FARMS ANTIQUES
Rte 202, 06777
(203)355-1208 **27**

Country American furniture, tables & cupboards in cherry & pine. *Est:* 1977. *Hours:* Sat,Sun 11-5 & holidays. Leiliah J Diekman *Park:* On site. *Loc:* 4 MI from New Milford toward Litchfield.

EARL J SLACK ANTIQUES
Rte 202, 06777
(203)868-7092 **37 39 59**

English & American furniture, paintings, English & Oriental porcelains thoughtfully displayed in a 19th C house. *Est:* 1975. *Hours:* Sat,Sun 11-5. *Loc:* Between New Milford & Litchfield by a red brick church.

Marlborough

THE CONNECTICUT GALLERY
4 Austin Dr, 06447
(203)295-9544   **59**

Art of all periods, specializing in Connecticut Impressionism. *Hours:* Tue-Sat 10-5 Thu 10-8 Sun 1-5. Helen K Fusscas

Meriden

DUNN'S MYSTERIES OF CHOICE
251 Baldwin Ave, 06450
(203)235-0480   **13**

Antiquarian books: detective fiction, true crime, Ayn Rand, H.L. Mencken, libertarianism, atheism & anarchism. *Serv:* Catalog. *Hours:* BY APPT ONLY. *Assoc:* CAB. William Dunn

FAIR WEATHER ANTIQUES
763 Hanover Rd, 06450
(203)237-4636   **33 36 64**

Decorative antiques, furniture, post cards, ephemera & collectibles. *Hours:* Mon,Thu-Sat 11-4, Oct-Apr Sun 1-4. *Assoc:* CADA.

ORUM SILVER CO
51 South Vine St, 06450
(203)237-3037   **68 71**

Repairing, restoring & replating of antiques & old silver, gold, nickel, brass & copper plating, cleaning, buffing & polishing of all types of metal, repairing & refinishing of pewter. *Serv:* Brochure. *Hours:* Mon-Fri 8-4:30 or by chance/appt. Joe Pistilli *Park:* In front. *Loc:* I-91N or S to Meriden, off Rte 691 W near Meriden Sq.

Middle Haddam

MIDDLE HADDAM ANTIQUES
Rte 151, 06456
(203)267-9221

Antiques & collectibles. *Hours:* Mon-Fri 1-5 Sat,Sun 10-5. Janet Freidenberg

THE VILLAGE ATTIC
Middle Haddam Rd, 06456
(203)267-8903

A discriminating choice of eclectic items for the collector. *Hours:* Thu-Sat 10-4. Elsie Johnson

Middlebury

MICHAEL C DOOLING
72 North St, 06762
(203)758-8130   **13**

Antiquarian books: Americana, architecture, art, bindings & travel. *Serv:* Appraisal, catalog. *Hours:* Evenings & weekends BY APPT. *Assoc:* CAB.

Middletown

COUNTRY ANTIQUES AT MIDDLETOWN
808 Washington St, 06457
(203)344-8536   **36 40 83**

Five-room historical house & barn filled with Victorian, formal, country & primitive furnishings, china & collectibles, specializing in Victorian oak, walnut & quality mahogany furniture. *Pr:* $10–2000. *Serv:* Appraisal, auction, consultation, interior design, purchase estates, repair. *Hours:* May 15-Aug Wed-Sat 10-5 Sun 11-5 or by chance/appt. *Size:* Medium. *CC:*

MC/V. Jean Deschesnes *Park:* On site. *Loc:* From Hartford: I-91S, Rte 66 Washington St Exit: 2 MI on R. From New Haven: I-91N, Rte 66 Middletown Exit: 5 MI on L.

MARGARET & PAUL WELD
PO Box 416, 06457
(203)635-3361   **1 2 5**

18th & 19th C American antiques, including country furniture, hearth equipment, iron, early tools, architectural items & decorative accessories. *Est:* 1957. *Hours:* BY APPT ONLY. *Assoc:* NHADA.

M ilford

ANTIQUES OF TOMORROW
93-95 Gulf St, 06460
(203)878-4561   **40 59 60**

Antiques, furniture, dolls, toys, paintings & Orientals. *Pr:* $25–1000. *Est:* 1974. *Serv:* Appraisal, consultation, custom woodwork, purchase estates, repairs. *Hours:* Daily 10-3:30. *Size:* Medium. *CC:* MC/V. Mary Paternoster *Park:* On site. *Loc:* 4 min from either Merritt or Wilbur Pkwys.

KAYES CONSIGNMENTS
2001 Bridgeport Ave, 06460
(203)874-5578   **36 47**

Furniture, jewelry, china & collectibles. *Est:* 1982. *Hours:* Tue-Sat 10-4, call advised. Kay Pazda *Park:* On site. *Loc:* I-95 Exit 35: turn R at end of ramp, L at 1st light.

JENNY LEES ANTIQUES
4 Daniel St, 06460
(203)878-5068   **32 36**

18th C furniture, dolls & accessories. *Serv:* Auction. *Hours:* Mon-Sat 10-2 or by chance. Ginny Kabe

MILFORD ANTIQUE CENTER
51 River St, 06460
(203)874-8111   **{GR4}**

Antiques & collectibles, furniture, nautical & primitives. *Est:* 1985. *Hours:* Daily 10:30-5. *Park:* Nearby. *Loc:* 1 block from Town Hall across from 7-11.

MILFORD EMPORIUM
16 Daniel St, 06460
(203)878-3677   **40 43**

Refinished turn-of-the-century oak & walnut furniture & reproductions. *Est:* 1976. *Hours:* Mon-Fri 3-6 Sat 10-4 Sun 9-3. Peter Goodfellow *Park:* On site. *Loc:* 1 block from post office.

MILFORD GREEN ANTIQUES GALLERY
19-21 River St, 06460
(203)874-4304   **{GR}**

Antiques, collectibles & decorative accessories art deco, Victorian glass, matting & framing, ephemera & magazines. *Hours:* Tue-Sat 10:30-5:30 Sun,Mon by chance. Dave Williams *Loc:* Downtown.

R & J GLASSWARE
88 Boston Post Rd, 06460
(203)877-3280   **44 79**

Depression glass & stamps, china, linens & a general line. *Est:* 1981. *Hours:* Tue-Sun 10-4. Robert Carr *Park:* On site. *Loc:* I-95 Exit 36.

STOCK TRANSFER
119 Broad St, 06460
(203)874-1333   **36 47 59**
Large consignment shop specializing
in fine home furnishings, collectibles,
jewelry & paintings. *Est:* 1982. *Hours:*
Tue-Sat 10-4. *Size:* Large. *Park:* On
site.

TREASURES & TRIFLES
580 Naugatuck Ave, 06460
(203)878-7045   **36 47**
Furniture, advertisements & jewelry.
Hours: Daily 12-5. Billy Byrnes

WISHING WELL ANTIQUES
753 Boston Post Rd, 06460
(203)874-5538
A general line of antiques. *Est:* 1987.
Hours: Tue-Fri 4-8 Sat,Sun 10-5.
Sandy Chechoski *Park:* On site. *Loc:*
I-95 Exit 39: 1 MI S.

Monroe

BARBARA'S BARN ANTIQUES
418 Main St Rte 25, 06468
(203)268-9805   **27 33 47**
Variety of antiques & collectibles, specializing in country furniture, costume
jewelry & children's books, sheet
music, fiesta, blue willow, Maxfield
Parrish & Wallace Nutting prints.
Hours: Tue-Fri 11:30-4:30 Sat,Sun
11:30-5. *Size:* Medium. Barbara A Gil-
more *Park:* On site.

Morris

MARTINGALE FARM ANTIQUES
Rte 61, 06763
(203)567-5178   **27**
Two-story barn with country furniture

& accessories. *Est:* 1984. *Hours:* Thu-
Sun 9-5. *Assoc:* CADA. *Park:* On site.
Loc: 10 MI N of Woodbury, next to the
Morris Historical Society.

T'OTHER HOUSE ANTIQUES
Litchfield Rd, 06763
(203)567-9283   **44 63**
China, pattern glass & general line.
Est: 1948. *Hours:* By chance/appt.
Park: On site. *Loc:* Near White
Flower Farms.

Mystic

5 CHURCH STREET ANTIQUES
5 Church St, 06355
(203)536-0610   **29**
Antique consignment shop. *Hours:*
May-Dec Fri-Tue 10:30-5, Jan-Apr
Sat,Sun 10:30-5. *Size:* Medium. *CC:*
MC/V. *Park:* In front. *Loc:* Rte 27 at
Mystic Seaport, S towards downtown,
R on Holmes St, L onto Church St, 1st
L into large parking lot.

MYSTIC FINE ARTS
Factory Square Courtyard, 06355
(203)572-8141
Fine arts auction house specializing in
American & European paintings, watercolors, prints & sculpture in six sales
a year. *Serv:* Appraisal, consignments
accepted, restoration. *Hours:* By appt.
Albert E Goring

**MYSTIC RIVER ANTIQUES
MARKET**
14 Holmes St, 06355
(203)572-9775   **{GR35}**
Fine antiques, collectibles, memorabilia, paintings, books, furniture &
pottery. *Est:* 1985. *Hours:* Daily 10-5.
CC: MC/V. Linda R Schuster *Park:*
On site. *Loc:* I-95 Exit 89.

ORIENTAL RUGS LTD
12 Water St, 06355
(203)572-9233   21
Large selection of antique Oriental carpets & selection of new carpets. *Est:* 1980. *Serv:* Appraisal, consultation. *Hours:* Mon-Sat 10-5 or BY APPT. *CC:* MC/V. *Assoc:* NHADA. Karen DiSaia *Park:* Nearby. *Loc:* Historic Factory Square.

TRADE WINDS GALLERY
20 W Main St, 06355
(203)536-0119   51 66
Specializing in antique maps & prints from around the world & a general line of art. *Pr:* $25-1500. *Est:* 1974. *Hours:* Jun-Sep Mon-Sat 10-6 Sun 11-5, else CLOSED SUN. *Size:* Medium. *CC:* AX/MC/V. Thomas K Aalund *Park:* In front. *Loc:* Just W of the drawbridge in downtown Mystic.

New Canaan

ACAMPORA ART GALLERY
134 Elm St, 06840
(203)966-6090   59
Specializing in 19th-early 20th C American paintings with focus on Hudson River School & American Impressionists. *Pr:* $2500-75000. *Est:* 1970. *Hours:* Tue-Sat 10-4. *Park:* In front. *Loc:* From Merritt Pkwy going N Exit 37: L to middle of town to SS, L turn .5 block on L - Elm St.

ENGLISH HERITAGE ANTIQUES, INC
13 South Ave, 06840
(203)966-2979   39 59 63
Fine English 18th & 19th C formal furniture, paintings, porcelain & accessories displayed on three spacious

gallery levels. Everything guaranteed to be as represented. Located in the heart of the beautiful village of New Canaan. *Est:* 1978. *Serv:* Brochure, purchase estates. *Hours:* Mon-Sat 10-5. *Size:* Large. *CC:* AX/MC/V. *Assoc:* AADLA NEAA. Cecily R Collins *Park:* Nearby lot. *Loc:* Merritt Pkwy Exit 37: N 2 MI, opposite Mobil, 1 hr from NYC.

HASTINGS ART, LTD
138 Main St, 06840
(203)966-9863   59
Fine 19th & 20th C American paintings, specializing in Hudson River School and American Impressionism. *Serv:* Appraisal, conservation, restoration, framing. *Hours:* Tue-Sat 10:30-4:30. *CC:* MC/V. *Park:* In front. *Loc:* From NYC: Exit 37, L at bottom of ramp, to New Canaan, 1st shop on Main St.

LISSARD HOUSE
62 Main St, 06840
(203)972-3473   42 66 78
Irish pine furniture, antiques & reproductions, sporting painting & prints. *Est:* 1987. *Serv:* Irish tea room on premises. *Hours:* Tue-Sat 9:30-5. *CC:* AX/MC/V.

MANOR ANTIQUES
90 Main St, 06840
(203)966-2658   39 58 59
Direct importers of personally selected fine quality English & French furniture & objets d'art. *Est:* 1983. *Serv:* Appraisal, interior design. *Hours:* Mon-Sat 10-5 Sun 12-4 & BY APPT. *Size:* Medium. *CC:* AX/DC/MC/V. *Assoc:* NEAA. Florence M Byrne *Park:* Nearby lot. *Loc:* Merritt Pkwy Exit 38N: Rte 106, L turn, R on Main St.

THE MORRIS HOUSE
Box 1524, 06840
(203)966-9778 **37**
Fine American furniture & decorative accessories from the early American scene pre-1840. *Pr:* $50–50000. *Est:* 1944. *Serv:* Consultation. *Hours:* BY APPT ONLY. Joan Morris *Park:* On site.

NEW CANAAN ANTIQUES
120 Main St, 06840
(203)972-1938 **{MDS5}**
Fine quality period American, English & French furniture, 19th C paintings, 18th & 19th C porcelains & other fine accessories beautifully displayed in 7 rooms in one of New Canaan's earliest buildings. *Est:* 1984. *Serv:* Brochure. *Hours:* Mon-Sat 10-5. *Size:* Large. *Park:* Nearby lot. *Loc:* Merritt Pkwy Exit 37 or 38: to Ctr of New Canaan, corner of Main & Elm Sts.

SALLEA ANTIQUES
110 Main St, 06840
(203)972-1050 **29 35**
Distinctive English & French boxes: tea caddies, lap desks, toiletry boxes, decanter boxes, medical & apothecary boxes, gun boxes, sewing boxes, game boxes, snuff & tobacco boxes, glove boxes, jewelry boxes, humidors: wood, tortoise shell, ivory & brass. *Hours:* Mon-Sat 10-5 Sun 12-4, call ahead. *CC:* MC/V. *Shows:* ELLIS. Sally B Kaltman *Park:* Nearby. *Loc:* On Main St in New Canaan.

JOYCE SCARBOROUGH ANTIQUES
3 South Ave, 06840
(203)972-3644 **39 42**
English country furniture - especially pine - plus accessories & kitchenware. *Pr:* $5–4000. *Est:* 1974. *Hours:* Mon-

Sat 10-5 Sun BY APPT. *CC:* AX/MC/V. *Park:* Nearby lot. *Loc:* Ctr of town across from municipal parking lot.

SEVERED TIES, INC
111 Cherry St, 06840
(203)972-0788 **29 36**
Furniture, decorative accessories, art, silver & estate jewelry. *Serv:* Consignments. *Hours:* Mon-Sat 10-5 Sun 1-5. *Assoc:* CADA NEAA. William Dale *Park:* Adjacent. *Loc:* Off Merritt Pkwy.

THE SILK PURSE
118 Main St, 06840
(203)972-0898
Consignment shop for fine home furnishings. *Hours:* Mon-Sat 10-5 Sun 12-5. *CC:* MC/V. *Park:* Nearby.

THE STUDIO
86 Main St, 06840
(203)966-1332 **50**
Custom lamps & lampshades & miscellaneous English antiques. *Hours:* Mon-Sat 10-5:30. *CC:* MC/V. *Assoc:* CADA. *Park:* Nearby.

New Hartford

GALLERY FORTY FOUR
Rte 44, 06057
(203)236-1146 **59**
Specializing in 19th & early 20th C American paintings. *Est:* 1966. *Serv:* Framing, restoration, appraisal. *Hours:* Tue-Sat 10-5. *Park:* On site. *Loc:* 7 min from Rte 8 & Rte 44 in Winsted CT.

VILLA'S AUCTION GALLERY
Rte 7N, 06057
(203)379-7151   **8**

Antique & estate auctions. Estate liquidation. Richard Villa *Park:* On site. *Loc:* From Hartford: Follow Rte 44 W to Canaan Ctr, take Rte 7N.

New Haven

EDWIN C AHLBERG
441 Middletown Ave, 06513
(203)624-9076   **37 71**

Formal & semi-formal antiques & New England furniture. *Serv:* Repairs, refinishing, appraisals. *Hours:* Mon-Fri 8-5 Sat 8-12 Sun 1-5. *Shows:* ELLIS. *Loc:* On Rte 17, .5 MI N of Exit 8 on I-91.

ANN MARIE'S VINTAGE BOUTIQUE
1569 Chapel St, 06511
(203)787-1734   **47 85**

Vintage clothing, beaded & mesh antique bags, embroidered shawls & deco jewelry.

ANTIQUE CORNER
859 Whalley Ave, 06515
(203)387-4550   **{GR9}**

Three floors of antiques including furniture, wicker, oil paintings, antique & estate jewelry, art pottery, quilts & silver. *Est:* 1981. *Serv:* Purchase estates. *Hours:* Mon-Sat 10:30-5 Sun 12-4. *Size:* Medium. *CC:* MC/V. Rhona Harris *Park:* On site. *Loc:* Merritt Pkwy Exit 59.

THE ANTIQUES MARKET
881 Whalley Ave, 06515
(203)389-5440   **39 63**

Extensive stock of old Wedgwood, Irish Belleek & period English furniture. *Est:* 1968. *Hours:* Daily 10:30-5. *CC:* AX/MC/V. *Assoc:* CADA. Miriam Levine *Park:* On site. *Loc:* Merritt Pkwy Exit 59.

ARK ANTIQUES
Box 3133, 06515
(203)387-3754   **16 77**

Fine American craftsman silver, jewelry & metalwork of the early 20th C, with special focus on the arts & crafts movement. *Pr:* $50–35000. *Serv:* Catalog $15 annually. *Hours:* Sep 15-Jun BY APPT & shows. Rosalie Berberian *Loc:* Call for Appt & directions.

BRYN MAWR BOOK SHOP
56 1/2 Whitney Ave, 06510
(203)562-4217   **13**

Antiquarian books: art, biography, children's, fiction, religion & philosophy. *Hours:* Win: Wed-Fri 12-3 Sat 10-1, Sum: Wed-Thu 12-3 BY APPT. *Assoc:* CAB. Meigs, Carter & Darling

CITY POINT ANTIQUES
19 Howard Ave, 06509
(203)776-2202   **66 80**

Early textiles, prints, decorative accessories, Yale memorabilia & Dutch tiles. *Est:* 1980. *Hours:* Sat-Sun 10-5 or BY APPT. *Loc:* Opposite Chart House.

THOMAS COLVILLE FINE ART
58 Trumbull St, 06511
(203)787-2816   **59 66**

Specializing in antiques from the 19th & early 20th C, French & Dutch paintings, watercolors & drawings. *Est:* 1972. *Serv:* Appraisal, consultation, purchase estates, repair. *Hours:* BY APPT. *Loc:* At the Int of 95 & 91, Exit 3.

FROM HERE TO ANTIQUITY
900 Whalley Ave, 06515
(203)389-6722   **44 59 63**

Specializing in American art & American art pottery. *Pr:* $10–20000. *Serv:* Appraisal, consultation, interior design, purchase estates, repairs. *Hours:* Wed-Sat, else by chance/appt. *Size:* Medium. *CC:* MC/V. D B Smernoff *Park:* On site. *Loc:* Merritt Pkwy Exit 59.

GIAMPIETRO ANTIQUES
153 1/2 Bradley St, 06511
(203)787-3851   **34 59**

American folk art & decorative art for the serious collector. *Est:* 1977. *Hours:* BY APPT ONLY. *Assoc:* ADA. Kathryn Giampietro *Loc:* Call for directions.

SALLY GOODMAN ANTIQUES
901 Whalley Ave, 06515
(203)387-5072   **47 77**

Antique & estate jewelry, furniture, decorative accessories & silver. *Est:* 1976. *Serv:* Appraisal, consultation, purchase estates. *Hours:* Daily 10-5, Sum: CLOSED SUN. *Size:* Medium. *CC:* MC/V. *Assoc:* ASA. Steven Goodman, GIA *Park:* On site. *Loc:* Merritt Pkwy Exit 59: 1 MI.

HAROLD'S LTD INC
871-873 Whalley Ave, 06515
(203)389-2988

Fine European & American antiques - Irish pine to American four poster beds, china, jewelry, silver, Oriental rugs, lighting fixtures & Orientalia. *Est:* 1968. *Serv:* Appraisal, purchase estates, restoration. *Hours:* Mon-Sat 10-5 Sun 12-4. *CC:* AX/MC/V. *Assoc:* CADA NEAA. *Park:* On site. *Loc:* Merritt Pkwy Exit 59: R onto Whalley Rd, 1.5 MI.

HER MAJESTY'S ANTIQUES
317 Bassett St, 06511
(203)787-0096   **63 83**

Located in Gowie-Normand house - New Haven's only Victorian museum. All substyles of Victorian furniture. Diverse & colorful selection of advertising tins & many patterns of Roseville pottery. *Serv:* Consultation, interior design. *Hours:* BY APPT. *Size:* Medium. *CC:* MC/V. Seth C Hawkins *Park:* On site. *Loc:* Rte 15 Exit 60 (Dixwell Ave): S 1.5 MI to Bassett St, R for 1 block.

PETER G HILL & ASSOCIATES
PO Box 1892, 06508
(203)624-5101   **5**

Architectural antiques.

JASMINE
One Elm St, 06510
(203)785-1430   **29 36**

Fine 18th & 19th C American, English & Chinese furnishings & accessories. A source for reproduction fabrics, tapestries & bed linens. *Est:* 1983. *Serv:* Interior design. *Hours:* Mon-Sat 10-6, Sep-Dec 24 extended evening hrs. *Size:* Medium. *CC:* AX/DC/MC/V. *Assoc:* NTHP. David Gillman *Park:* On site. *Loc:* Rte 91 Trumbull St Exit: L onto Orange St, L onto Elm St, 1 block on the L across from WTNH 8.

MILTON H KASOWITZ
895 Whalley Ave, 06515
(203)389-2514

General line of furniture & decorative accessories including brass, copper, jewelry, glass, lamps, gold & silver. *Est:* 1953. *Serv:* Appraisal, purchase estates. *Hours:* Mon-Sat 10-4:30. *CC:* DC/MC/V. *Park:* In back.

WILLIAM REESE COMPANY
409 Temple St, 06511
(203)789-8081   **13**

Antiquarian books: Western & general Americana, English literature, some early printed & color plate books. *Serv:* Catalog, appraisal. *Hours:* Mon-Fri 9-6 BY APPT. *Assoc:* ABAA CAB. Terry Halladay

SHANNON FINE ARTS INC
PO Box 3570, 06525
(203)393-2033   **59**

High quality American paintings. *Est:* 1976. *Hours:* BY APPT. Gene Shannon *Loc:* Call for directions.

R W SMITH-BOOKSELLER
51 Trumbull St, 06510
(203)776-5564   **13**

Art reference - especially American Colonial to the present, photography, architecture & 20th C design & American decorative arts - 20,000 titles in stock. *Pr:* $10–3500. *Est:* 1975. *Serv:* Catalog($3.50), purchase estates, search service a specialty. *Hours:* By chance/appt. *Assoc:* ABAA ARLIS/NA ILAB NEBA. Raymond W Smith *Park:* In front. *Loc:* I-91 Exit 3: thru light at end of Exit, 1 block on R in John Slade Ely House.

C A STONEHILL INC
282 York St, 06511
(203)865-5141   **9 13**

English literature & history, incunabula & manuscripts. *Serv:* Appraisal. *Assoc:* ABAA. Robert J Barry Jr

VILLAGE FRANCAIS
555 Long Wharf Dr, 06411
(203)562-4883   **35**

Country French antiques & fabrics from Provence. *Loc:* Long Wharf Maritime Center.

WEST GATE ANTIQUES
896 Whalley Ave, 06515
(203)387-2078   **23 36 58**

Fine selection of antique, objets d'art & furniture. *Est:* 1972. *Serv:* Appraisal, consultation. *Hours:* Mon-Sat 11-5. *CC:* MC/V. Christopher S Velush *Park:* On site. *Loc:* Merritt Pkwy Exit 59: R off ramp 1 MI.

WESTVILLE ANTIQUE CENTER
871 Whalley Ave, 06515
(203)387-1866   **{GR10}**

American, European & Oriental furniture, accessories, silver, jewelry, prints, paintings, maps, china, lamps & wallcoverings. *Serv:* Appraisal, interior design, consultation. *Hours:* Mon-Sat 10-5 Sun 12-4. George E Jordan *Park:* In front. *Loc:* Merritt Pkwy Exit 59.

WHITLOCK'S INC
17 Broadway, 06511
(203)562-9841   **13**

Attractive antiquarian & rare books in all fields. *Est:* 1900. *Serv:* Appraisal, purchase estates, search services. *Hours:* Mon-Sat 9:30-5:30. *Size:* Medium. *CC:* MC/V. *Assoc:* CAB. Reverdy Whitlock *Park:* Nearby lot. *Loc:* Located in downtown New Haven.

New Milford

BRUCE W ANDERSON ANTIQUES
264 Kent Rd W, 06776
(203)355-9073   **23 40 59**

Antique & custom furniture including Victorian, Empire, oak, clocks &

paintings. *Est:* 1980. *Assoc:* NAA
NEAA. *Park:* On site. *Loc:* From Rte
84 to Rte 7N which is Kent Rd.

AUCTION BARN
Rte 109, 06776
(203)355-3866   **8**
Antique & estate auctions from local
homes. No buyer's premium. *Serv:*
Purchase estates, accept consignments.
Ted Gall *Loc:* Midway between New
Milford & Washington on Rte 109.

BIT OF COUNTRY
Rte 202, 06776
(203)354-6142   **27 40**
Antique oak furniture, solid brass beds
& white iron beds. *Est:* 1981. *Hours:*
Daily 10-5:30 Sun 1-5. *CC:* MC/V.
Park: On site. *Loc:* I-84 Exit at Rte 7.

**CRICKET HILL
CONSIGNMENT**
49 Bank St, 06776
(203)354-8872   **43 44 63**
Formal & country antiques & reproduction furniture, porcelain, glass &
accessories. *Est:* 1982. *Hours:* Daily
11-5 CLOSED TUE. *CC:* MC/V.
Park: On site. *Loc:* 1 block off the
Village Green.

LEON-VANDERBILT
22A Bennitt St, 06776
(203)354-5662   **36 71**
Specializing in antique furniture. *Serv:*
Furniture restoration, purchase furniture in any condition. *Hours:* Mon-Sat
9-5.

**PHOENIX ANTIQUE
RESTORATION**
Five Old Town Park Rd No 39, 06776
(203)354-6646   **19 71**
18th C cabinet work, fine French polishing, painted finishes, veneer & carving. Paul Gannon

TIMELESS BOOKS
8 Caldwell Dr, 06776
(203)355-4839   **13**
A general stock of antiquarian books:
juvenile series & children's illustrated.
Hours: BY APPT. *Assoc:* CAB. Dorothy A Gereg

TRI-COUNTY LIQUIDATORS
Rte 109, 06776
(203)355-3866   **8**
Auction every Friday night at 7pm. Ted
Gall

New Preston

BLACK SWAN ANTIQUES
Rte 45 Main St, 06777
(203)868-2788   **39**
17th & 18th C English country furniture, unique examples of Elizabethan,
William & Mary & Queen Anne
pieces. *Est:* 1985. *Serv:* Purchase antiques. *Hours:* Thu-Mon 10-5 Sun 12-
5, CLOSED TUE & WED. Hubert
van Asch van Wyck *Loc:* Rte 202 on
Rte 45.

BRITANNIA BOOKSHOP
Church St, 06777
(203)868-0368   **13 58 66**
Antiquarian bookshop specializing in
old British & Irish books, old prints,
paintings & curios. Situated in an historic 18th C village in a restored cider
mill overlooking a dramatic waterfall

& mill pond. *Hours:* May-Sep Thu-Sun 11-5 & BY APPT, Nov-Apr Fri-Sun 11-5. *Size:* Medium. *CC:* AX/MC/V. *Assoc:* CAB. Barbara C Tippin *Park:* On site. *Loc:* Rte 84E, Exit 7 to Rte 7, N to New Milford, 202E to Rte 45 New Preston Ctr.

THE R COGSWELL COLLECTION
5 Main St, 06777
(203)868-9108   **37 67**

Country & formal antique furniture & accessories & a large collection of quilts. *Est:* 1987. *Hours:* Thu-Mon 11-5 or BY APPT. *CC:* AX/MC/V. Victor Terek *Park:* On site. *Loc:* I-84 New Milford Exit: Rte 202 into New Preston to Main St.

TIMOTHY MAWSON BOOKS & PRINTS
Main St, 06777
(203)868-0732   **13 66**

Gardening & horticulture, cookery & gastronomy, decorative arts & botanical prints. *Serv:* Catalog, appraisal, search service. *Hours:* Thu-Sun 11-5:30 or BY APPT. *Assoc:* ABAA CAB. *Park:* Nearby.

JONATHAN PETERS
5 Main St, 06777
(203)868-9017   **29 48**

Unique collection of fine & imported linens & home accessories including furniture, wicker, baskets, handmade bandboxes, frames, English botanicals, flower holders & Limoges boxes. *Hours:* Mon-Sat 11-5 Sun 12-5. *CC:* AX/MC/V. Betsey Nestler *Park:* Nearby. *Loc:* In the center of New Preston.

STRAWBERRY HILL ANTIQUES
Rte 202, 06777
(203)868-9133   **39 63 66**

English formal & country furniture, Chinese export porcelain, framed engravings & prints. *Hours:* Mon,Thu-Sat 10:30-5:30 Sun 12:30-5.

TREBIZOND RARE BOOKS
Main St, 06777
(203)868-2621   **13**

Antiquarian books: English, Continental & American literature, voyages & travels, Americana & 18th C British books. *Hours:* By chance/appt. *Assoc:* ABAA CAB. Williston Benedict

TRUMPETER
5 Main St, 06777
(203)868-9090   **9 66 83**

19th & 20th C prints - historical & architectural - Victorian smalls & framed autographs. *Est:* 1978. *Serv:* Framing. *Hours:* Wed-Sun 11-5. *CC:* AX/MC/V. *Park:* On site. *Loc:* Just past Jct of Rtes 202 & 45.

Newington

CONNECTICUT ANTIQUE WICKER
1052 Main St Rear, 06111
(203)666-3729   **86**

A large selection of antique wicker. *Est:* 1980. *Serv:* Restoration, purchase estates, consultation, appraisal. *Hours:* BY APPT, please call for hours. Henry Spieske *Park:* On site. *Loc:* Call for directions.

DOLL FACTORY
2551 Berlin Turnpike Rte 5-15, 06111
(203)666-6162   **85**

Vintage clothing from the 1920s to

present. *Serv:* Rental. *Hours:* Tue-Sat 1:30-6:30. *Size:* Medium. *CC:* MC/V. Louise S Chinelli *Park:* On site. *Loc:* From Hartford, Rte 91S, Rte 15-5 which is Berlin Tnpk to Newington CT.

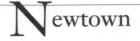
Newtown

BANCROFT BOOK MEWS
86 Sugar Ln, 06470
(203)426-6338　　　　　　13
Antiquarian books: music, theatre & dance. *Serv:* Search service. *Hours:* BY APPT. *Assoc:* CAB. Eleanor Bancroft

CODFISH ANTIQUES
Box 361, 06470
(203)426-6055　　　**29 37 63**
Pottery, small American furniture & accessories. *Hours:* BY APPT. Elizabeth W Long

JANE COTTINGHAM ANTIQUES
187 S Main St, 06470
(203)426-4000　　　　　　**66**
Watercolor & oil paintings, old photographs, botanical prints & early advertising. *Hours:* Tue-Sat 10-5 Sun 12-5. *Loc:* Corner Pecks Lane & Rte 25.

MARIE LOUISE KANE
13 Fox Run Lane S, 06470
(203)426-5974　　　　　　**4**
Fine arts appraisals. *Hours:* BY APPT.

THE PAGES OF YESTERYEAR
Old Hawleyville Rd, 06470
(203)426-0864　　　　　　13
Nonfiction antiquarian books. *Serv:* Appraisal. *Hours:* BY APPT. *Assoc:* CAB. John Renjilian

POVERTY HOLLOW ANTIQUES
Poverty Hollow Rd, 06470
(203)426-2388　　　**44 50 63**
Furniture, lamps, china & glass. *Hours:* Thu-Sun or by chance. Marge Bennett *Loc:* Short distance from I-84.

Noank

STONE LEDGE ART GALLERIES
59 High St, 06340
(203)536-7813　　　　　　**59**
Specializing in 19th C fine art. *Serv:* Framing, restoration, art appraisal. *Hours:* Tue-Sat 9-5.

Norfolk

NOBODY EATS PARSLEY
114 Litchfield Rd Rte 272 S, 06058
(203)542-5479　　　　　　**33 64**
Post cards & ephemera. *Est:* 1982. *Serv:* Appraisal. *Hours:* Weekdays by chance. *Park:* On site. *Loc:* Rte 44 to Norfolk, Rte 272S, 10 houses up on the R.

North Kent

GOODE HILL ANTIQUES
Rte 7, 06757
(203)927-3872　　　**28 32 36**
Country & formal furniture, stoneware, flow blue & old pull toys. *Hours:* By chance/appt. *Park:* On site. *Loc:* 3 MI N of Kent in a white Colonial.

MAVIS
Rte 7, 06757
(203)927-4334 **32 44 47**

Country stencilled furniture & accessories, glass, china, linens, baskets, jewelry & dolls. *Est:* 1973. *Hours:* Mon-Sat 11-6 Sun 12:30-6. Mavis L Scholl *Park:* On site. *Loc:* 3 MI N of Monument.

Norwalk

BARTER SHOP
140 Main St Rte 7 & 123, 06851
(203)846-1242 **15 33 55**

Three buildings of antiques, collectibles, old books, magazines, old records, post cards, bottles, ephemera, Victorian, oak, art deco furniture, tools, pictures, prints, paintings & frames, musical instruments, photographia & militaria. *Pr:* $1–15000. *Hours:* Year round Mon-Sun 10-7:30. *Size:* Huge. *CC:* MC/V. Richard A Bucciarelli *Park:* On site. *Loc:* CT Thruway Exit 15 (Rte 7): .25 MI S on Rte 123 (7) OR Merritt Pkwy, Exit 39 (Main Ave), 1 MI S on L.

EAGLES LAIR ANTIQUES
565 Westport Ave, 06851
(203)846-1159 **37 59**

Specializing in American & Continental furniture, fine art, paintings & decorative accessories. *Est:* 1970. *Serv:* Consultation, repair. *Hours:* Daily 10-6, CLOSED WED,SUN. *CC:* AX/MC/V. Alexis Mihura *Park:* On site. *Loc:* Merritt Pkwy Exit 41: S 1 MI to Westport, Rte 1, L 1 MI.

KEVIN B MCCLELLAN
12 France St, 06850
(203)846-9814 **4 8**

Estate appraisals/liquidation & tag sales. *Serv:* Appraisal for insurance, estate tax or family division.

MELINDA VENTRE
26 Keeler Ave, 06854
(203)866-1833 **67 80**

Coverlets & early textiles. *Hours:* BY APPT.

WINGS OF A DOVE
CONSIGNMENT
217 Westport Ave, 06850
(203)847-6284 **21 36 66**

Furniture, Oriental rugs, paintings & prints. *Hours:* Mon-Sat 10-5. *Park:* In front.

Norwich

1840 HOUSE
47 8th St, 06360
(203)887-2808   **27**
Country furniture & accessories. *Est:*
1964. *Hours:* By chance/appt. *Assoc:*
CADA. Olive J Buddington

NORWICHTOWN ANTIQUE CENTER
12 New London Turnpike, 06360
(203)887-1870   **{GR14}**
Pine, oak collectibles, glassware & estate jewelry. *Hours:* Tue-Sat 10:30-5.

WALTS ANTIQUES
193 Taftville-Occum Rd Rte 97, 06360
(203)822-8791   **23 24 44**
Americana, cut glass, satin, Steuben, Tiffany & clocks. *Pr:* $25–5000. *Hours:* BY APPT ONLY. Walter Jorczak *Park:* On site. *Loc:* I-395 R at Exit 83: 1st house on R.

Old Greenwich

NEW ENGLAND SHOP
250 Sound Beach Ave, 06870
(203)637-0326   **21 44 63**
China, glassware, rugs & furniture. *Hours:* Mon-Sat 9-5. Barbara Regan *Park:* Accessible.

Old Lyme

BRIGER FAIRHOLME JONES
23 Lyme St, 06371
(203)434-2467   **29 36**
Antique furniture & decorative accessories for the discriminating collector.

Est: 1987. *Hours:* Tue-Sat 10-5 or BY APPT. Paul Briger *Park:* In front. *Loc:* I-95 Exit 70.

THE COOLEY GALLERY
25 Lyme St, 06371
(203)434-8807   **59 71**
Specializing in fine American paintings, late 19th & early 20th C painting, drawings & watercolors. *Est:* 1984. *Serv:* Appraisal, period framing, restoration. *Hours:* Tue-Sat 10-5, else BY APPT. Jeffrey W Cooley *Park:* In front. *Loc:* I-95 Exit 70.

THE ELEPHANT TRUNK
24 Lyme St, 06371
(203)434-9630   **29**
Quality consignments, antiques, paintings, decorative accessories, rugs, silver & upholstered furniture. *Hours:* Tue-Sat 10-5 or BY APPT. *Park:* In front. *Loc:* I-95 Exit 70: S on Rte 156.

GARY R PARTELOW REPRODUCTIONS
34 Lyme St, 06371
(203)434-2065   **43 70**
Reproduction of classic American designs - some 17th & all 18th C - Windsor, Queen Anne, Chippendale & ladderback chairs, candlestick tables, mahogany lowboys & highboys. *Est:* 1983. *Serv:* All furniture is custom. *Hours:* Mon-Sat 8:30-5. *Park:* In front. *Loc:* I-95 Exit 70.

WHITLEY GALLERY
60 Lyme St, 06371
(203)434-9628   **59 60 63**
18th & 19 C American & European furniture, specializing in Impressionists of the Old Lyme Colony, Oriental art, pottery, porcelain, crystal & deco-

rative accessories. *Hours:* Wed-Sat 11-5 BY APPT. Joseph Whitley *Park:* In front. *Loc:* I-95 Exit 70.

Old Mystic

OLD MYSTIC FLEA MARKET
Rte 27 at I-95, 06372
(203)536-2223

Antiques & collectibles. *Est:* 1983. *Serv:* Free parking, free admission. *Hours:* Sun 10-5. Sonny Hendel *Loc:* 1 MI N of Mystic Seaport.

Old Saybrook

ESSEX-SAYBROOK ANTIQUES VILLAGE
985 Middlesex Turnpike, 06475
(203)388-0689   {GR85}

Furniture, primitives, glass, china, brass clocks, linens, jewelry, paintings, silver, pottery, decoys & toys. *Est:* 1983. *Serv:* Truck & UPS shipping. *Hours:* Year round daily 11-5. *CC:* AX/MC/V. *Park:* On site. *Loc:* Rte 95 Exit 69: Rte 9, Exit 2, L at end of ramp, .5 MI to Village.

THE HOUSE OF PRETTY THINGS
49 Sherwood Terr, 06475
(203)388-5920   **32 44 63**

Glass, porcelain figurines & dolls. *Est:* 1975. *Hours:* Mon-Sat 10-5. *CC:* MC/V. *Assoc:* CADA NEAA. Frank Burton *Park:* On site. *Loc:* Rte 9 to Old Saybrook.

LITTLE HOUSE OF GLASS
1560 Boston Post Rd, 06475
(203)399-5127   **44 63**

Furniture, china & glass. *Est:* 1956. *Hours:* Fri-Wed 10-5. *Park:* In front. *Loc:* I-95 Exit 66: approx 2 MI.

PRESENCE OF THE PAST
488 Main St, 06475
(203)388-9021   **63**

Haviland & Noritake china. *Est:* 1977. *Serv:* China matching. *Hours:* BY APPT ONLY. Jan Fenger *Loc:* Call for directions.

SWEET PEA ANTIQUES
851 Middlesex Turnpike, 06475
(203)388-0289   **44 47 63**

China, glass, estate jewelry, furniture & decorative accessories. *Est:* 1983. *Hours:* Tue-Sat 11-5. *CC:* MC/V. *Park:* On site. *Loc:* 5 min from I-95, to Rte 154N, on the L.

TOUCH OF CLASS
1800 Boston Post Rd, 06475
(203)399-6694   **86**

Antique & reproduction wicker. *Est:* 1977. *Serv:* Repair, restoration. *Hours:* Seasonal Spring-Fall daily 10-6. *CC:* MC/V. *Park:* On site. *Loc:* I-95 Exit 66: on Rte 1.

Old Wethersfield

WILLARD RESTORATIONS INC
141 Main St, 06109
(203)529-1401   **71 74**

Authentic restoration of historic structures. *Hours:* BY APPT.

Pawcatuck

WOODS ANTIQUES
38 W Broad St Rte 1, 06378
(203)599-8090   **40 83 86**
Oak & Victorian furniture, wicker, fine
china, glass & estate jewelry. *Hours:*
Mon-Fri 10-4 Sat,Sun 10-2.

Pine Meadow

1847 HOUSE ANTIQUES
Church St off Rte 44, 06061
(203)379-0575   **27 63**
Country antiques & accessories in a
rustic shop: coverlets, cupboards, baskets, pottery & country furniture. *Est:*
1978. *Serv:* Purchase estates. *Hours:*
Thu-Tue 12-5. Barbara C Krohner
Park: On site.

PINE MEADOW ANTIQUES
Rte 44, 06061
(203)379-9333   **36**
Vast assortment of 19th & 20th C furniture & collectibles, American & English country & Victorian antiques.
Est: 1973. *Serv:* Auctioneers, estate appraisal. *Hours:* Daily 10-5. *CC:* MC/V.
Assoc: NAA. Rae Cameron *Park:* On
site. *Loc:* Between Canton & Winsted.

Plainville

ROBERT T BARANOWSKY
337 New Britain Ave, 06062
(203)747-3833
A general line of antiques. *Hours:*
Daily 11-4:30. *Loc:* I-84 Exit 34.

THE BOOK EXCHANGE
327 New Britain Ave, 06062
(203)747-0770   **13**
A general stock of antiquarian books:
literature, science fiction, philosophy,
religion, comics, mysteries, bestsellers,
occult, counterculture & used records.
Hours: Mon,Wed,Sat 10-6 Thu,Fri
10-8 Sun 10-5. *Assoc:* CAB. Paula Rose

GOLDEN SALES & AUCTIONS
161 Woodford Ave, 06062
(203)676-9178   **8**
Auction house featuring antiques &
collectibles. *Serv:* Accept consignments. Ron Maynard *Loc:* I-84 Exit 34:
Crooked St Exit to Woodford Ave.

WINTER ASSOCIATES INC
21 Cooke St, 06062
(203)793-0288   **1 8 66**
Appraisals for estate & insurance of
antiques & household furnishings,
purchase or take on consignment sin-
gles items or entire estates, conduct
auctions selling antiques & fine furnishings. *Serv:* Catalogs($3-$5), consultation. *Hours:* Mon-Fri 9-5. *CC:*
MC/V. *Assoc:* NEAA. Linda Stamm
Park: On site. *Loc:* Direct train from
NYC to nearby Berlin, Robertson Airport in Plainville OR I-84 Exit 34: Rte
372W, R after 3rd light.

Pomfret

BO & CO
PO Box 162, 06258
(203)928-3939   **13**
Antiquarian books: technology & social history (English & American

1837-1900). **Serv:** Catalogs. **Hours:** BY APPT ONLY. **Assoc:** CAB. Elizabeth B Wood

POMFRET ANTIQUE WORLD
Rte 101, 06259
(203)928-5006   **{GR90}**
Furniture, pottery, porcelain & country paintings. **Est:** 1984. **Hours:** Daily 10-5 CLOSED WED. **CC:** MC/V. **Park:** On site. **Loc:** W from Int of Rtes 169 & 101.

 Pomfret Center

COUNTRY COTTAGE
ANTIQUES
Rte 101, 06259
(203)774-0063   **{GR40}**
Furniture, paintings, country, glass, porcelain, pottery, jewelry & quilts. **Hours:** Thu-Sat 10-5. **Loc:** 2.5 MI from Pomfret Antique World.

MEADOW ROCK FARM
ANTIQUES
Rte 169, 06259
(203)928-7896   **1 41 42**
In the barn on the old golf course, a collection of early American country pieces & accessories. **Est:** 1970. **Hours:** Apr-Jan 10 Mon-Sat 9:30-5 Sun 12-5, Jan 11-Mar by chance. **Size:** Medium. Georganna Dickson **Park:** On site. **Loc:** Just S of Sturbridge & N of Mystic on Rte 169.

POMFRET BOOK SHOP
Rtes 44 & 169, 06259
(203)928-2862   **13 51 64**
New England books & town maps, atlases & post cards. **Serv:** Catalog, appraisal, search service. **Hours:** BY APPT. **Assoc:** CAB. Roger Black

PRISCILLA H ZIESMER
RFD 2 Box 87, 06459
(203)774-4429   **29 37 59**
American furniture, paintings & accessories. **Hours:** Shows & by appt. **Assoc:** ADA.

 Portland

CRANE'S ANTIQUES, ETC
Rte 66, 06480
(203)342-3270   **44 63**
Glassware, china & used furniture. **Hours:** Wed-Sat 11-5 Sun 11:30-5. **Park:** In front. **Loc:** .5 MI E of Rte 17.

 Putnam

GRAMS & PENNYWEIGHTS
39 Front St, 06260
(203)928-6624   **{GR30}**
18th & 19th C country & formal furniture, silver, art glass, Oriental rugs, objets d'art, lamps, jewelry, quilts, dolls, paintings, pottery, toys, bronzes & primitives. **Est:** 1987. **Hours:** Mon-Fri 10-6 Sat,Sun 10-5 CLOSED WED. **Park:** On site. **Loc:** I-395 Exit 97: Rte 44 to Front St downtown Putnam.

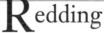 Redding

MELLIN'S ANTIQUES
PO Box 115, 06875
(203)938-9538   **37 63 66**
Specializing in Canton Chinese export porcelain maintaining a large selection of forms supplemented with high quality 17th & 18th C brass, unusual decoratives boxes, 19th C bird & flower prints in custom frames all in a pleasing

room setting. *Pr:* $25–10000. *Est:* 1977. *Serv:* Appraisal, brochure, consultation, interior design. *Hours:* By chance/appt. *Size:* Medium. *Assoc:* ADA. Rich Mellin *Park:* On site. *Loc:* Off Rte 7 Fairfield County, call for directions.

SERGEANT
Great Pasture Rd, 06875
(203)938-9366   **5 37**
18th & 19th C American furniture, architectural elements, French & English furniture. *Serv:* House restoration service. *Hours:* BY APPT ONLY. *Assoc:* AAA. Gary Sergeant *Park:* In front. *Loc:* 1 MI S of Redding ctr.

Ridgefield

ATTIC TREASURES
58 Ethan Allen Hwy Rte 7, 06877
(203)544-8159
Furniture, decorative accessories & depression glass. *Est:* 1980. *Hours:* Afternoons best. *Park:* On site. *Loc:* N of 95 & Merritt Pkwy, 10 MI on Rte 7.

RUTH COATES ANTIQUES
605 Ethan Allen Hwy, 06877
(203)438-9014   **60**
Continental & Oriental antiques & accessories. *Hours:* Daily 11-5 Wed BY APPT, CLOSED TUE. *CC:* MC/V. *Park:* On site. *Loc:* On Rte 7 between Rtes 35 & 102.

COUNTRY VILLAGE ANTIQUES
346 Ethan Allan Hwy Rte 7, 06877
(203)438-1100   **{GR10}**
Ten shops featuring country furniture, antique fishing tackle, tools, primitives, linens, glass, china & quilts.

Hours: Mon-Sat 10:30-5:30 Sun 12-5. Bonnie Olbrich *Park:* On site. *Loc:* Between Rtes 102 & 35.

THE CHARLES DALY COLLECTION
PO Box 2697, 06877
(203)438-7341   **13**
Antiquarian bookseller carrying books on angling, firearms, hunting exploration & natural history. *Assoc:* ABAA. Howard B Walzer

GIORDANO GRAZZINI
Ridgefield, 06877
(203)431-8726   **71**
Florentine antiques & restoration. *Serv:* Hand carving/turning, French polish, inlay & veneer work. *Hours:* Call for appt & directions.

GREENWILLOW ANTIQUES
Copps Hill Common 109 Danbury Rd, 06877
(203)431-6212   **36 44 63**
Formal & country furniture, fine china & glass. *Hours:* Mon-Sat 11-5. *CC:* MC/V. Lynn Brinker *Park:* On site.

GERALD GRUNSELL & ASSOCIATES
450 Main St, 06877
(203)438-4332   **4 23 71**
Dealers in fine European 18th & 19th C clocks. *Est:* 1953. *Serv:* Restorations undertaken, appraisals. *Hours:* Tue-Sat 9-5. *Assoc:* FBHI NAWCC. *Park:* Nearby. *Loc:* 20 min N of I-95.

HUNTER'S CONSIGNMENT
426 Main St, 06877
(203)438-9065   **47 63 77**
Quality antiques & furnishings, antique jewelry, china, crystal & silver. *Est:* 1986. *Hours:* Mon-Sat 10-5 Sun 11-3. *CC:* MC/V. *Park:* On site.

ISLAND HOUSE ANTIQUES
346 Ethan Allen Hwy, 06877
(203)431-6326 **42**
Irish pine furniture & 18th C antiques.
Hours: Mon-Sat 10-5:30 Sun 12-5.
CC: AX/MC/V. *Park:* Ample. *Loc:* On
Rte 7.

THE METAL MENDER
7 Silver Spring Park Rd, 06877
(203)438-3695 **71**
Restoration to pewter, copper, brass &
steel. *Hours:* Tue-Sat 9-5. Bill
Vishnosky *Park:* On site.

THE RED PETTICOAT
113 West Ln, 06877
(203)431-9451 **1 43**
Located in the 1740 Benjamin Rockwell house, seven rooms of 18th &
19th C antiques, fine reproductions,
lamps, collectibles, accessories, folk
art, old wicker & ephemera all in a
beautiful country setting. *Pr:* $5-
10000. *Serv:* Purchase estates. *Hours:*
Tue-Sat 10-5:30 Sun 12-5:30. *Size:*
Large. *CC:* MC/V. *Park:* On site. *Loc:*
Rte 35S, Main St Ridgefield, 4 MI S of
fountain.

RIDGEFIELD ANTIQUE SHOPS
197 Ethan Allen Hwy, 06877
(203)431-3702 **{GR5}**
Furniture, dolls, toys, smalls & vintage
clothes. *Hours:* Daily 11-5. *Park:*
Ample. *Loc:* On Rte 7.

THE SILK PURSE
470 Main St, 06877
(203)972-0898 **36 63 77**
Two large shops full of furniture, silver,
china, glassware & pictures from the
finest homes in Fairfield county. *Pr:*
$25 2500. *Hours:* Mon-Sat 10-5 Sun
12-5. *Size:* Medium. *CC:* MC/V. *Park:*
In front.

UNDER THE DOGWOOD TREE
13 Catoonah St, 06877
(203)438-9860 **47**
Victorian, contemporary & estate jewelry. *Est:* 1986. *Serv:* Appraisal, consultation, repairs, restoration. *Hours:*
Wed-Sat 10:30-5. *CC:* MC/V. Marty
Brayer *Loc:* Across from the post office.

Riverside

ESTATE TREASURES
1162 E Putnam Ave, 06878
(203)637-4200 **44 47 77**
Consignment shop of antiques, furniture, china, sterling, glassware & estate
jewelry. *Est:* 1978. *Hours:* Mon-Sat
10-5:30 Sun 12-5. Lillian London
Park: In front. *Loc:* I-95 Exit 5: L .5
block.

Riverton

ANTIQUES AND HERBS OF
RIVERTON
Rte 20, 06065
(203)379-3673 **48 77**
Victorian silver plate, new linens &
baskets. *Hours:* Tue-Sat 11-4:30. *Loc:*
Off Rte 44.

Rowayton

WILLIAMS PORT ANTIQUES
143 Rowayton Ave, 06853
(203)866-7748 **36 56**
Formal & country furniture, silver,
brass, baskets, quilts, lamps, nauticals
& unusual accessories. *Serv:* Appraisal.
Hours: Mon-Sat 10-5 Sun by

chance/appt. *CC:* MC/V. *Assoc:* CADA
NEAA VADA. Andy Williams *Park:*
In front. *Loc:* I-95 Exit 11 or 12: to Rte
136, 1.5 MI to Rowayton Ctr.

Salisbury

BUCKLEY & BUCKLEY ANTIQUES
Main St Rte 44, 06068
(203)435-9919   37 50 57
Specialize in William & Mary, country
Queen Anne & other high forms of
American country furniture (1680-
1860) & period accessories. *Est:* 1976.
Serv: Appraisal, consultation, interior
design, purchase estates. *Hours:* Wed-
Mon 11-5 Sun 1-5 appt suggested.
Size: Medium. Gloria Buckley *Park:*
On site. *Loc:* Rte 44, .25 MI W of
Town Hall.

RUSSELL CARRELL
Rte 44, 06068
(203)435-9301   41 63
18th & early 19th C painted furniture
& pottery. *Est:* 1946. *Serv:* Antique
show promotion. *Hours:* BY APPT
ONLY. *Loc:* Call for directions.

COLLECTORS
Rte 44 Fairacres Farm, 06068
(203)824-5662   37 39 63
Fine English, American & French 18th
C furniture, porcelain & pottery. *Est:*
1963. *Hours:* By appt only. Andelm
Ortiz *Park:* On site. *Loc:* On Rte 44.

MICHAEL COX ANTIQUES
Main St, 06068
(203)435-0062   39
English & French furniture. *Hours:*
Wed-Fri 10-5 Sat,Sun 11-4. *Loc:* On
Rte 44.

LION'S HEAD BOOKS
Academy St, 06068
(203)435-9328   13
Antiquarian & new books on gardening, landscape,design. *Hours:* By appt
& mail order. Mike McCabe

SALISBURY ANTIQUES CENTER
Library St off of Rte 44, 06068
(203)435-0424   {GR10}
Formal (English & American), country
& primitive furniture, paintings, quilts
& jewelry. *Est:* 1981. *Hours:* Mon-Sat
10-5 Sun 11-4. *CC:* MC/V. *Park:* In
front. *Loc:* Off Rte 44 in downtown
Salisbury.

THREE RAVENS ANTIQUES
Main St Rte 44, 06068
(203)435-9602   1 30 67
Unusual American antiques & accessories, American paintings & graphics,
woodcarvings, early furniture, unusual
pottery, weather vanes, quilts & coverlets. *Hours:* Year round daily 10-5 by
chance/appt. *Assoc:* BCoADA. Florie
Corbin *Park:* Nearby. *Loc:* At Int of
Rtes 41 & 44 in Salisbury near the
White Hart Inn.

Sandy Hook

CHISWICK BOOK SHOP INC
98 Walnut Tree Hill Rd, 06482
(203)426-3220   13
Rare books, press books & fine printing, printing & printing history, typog-
raphy & type specimens, papermaking
& marbleing & calligraphy. *Serv:* Catalog. *Hours:* BY APPT ONLY. *Assoc:*
ABAA. Herman Cohen

cotland

**OLD ENGLISH ANTIQUES &
TEA ROOM**
Rtes 97 & 14, 06264
(203)456-8651   **39 47 48**

English antiques including furniture,
linen & jewelry. *Serv:* An English tea
room. *Hours:* Thu-Mon 11-5 or BY
APPT. Brenda Mlyniec

haron

RANDALL AND KOBLENZ
RR 1 Box 115F, 06069
(203)364-5710   **34 47 65**

Antiques & estate jewelry, country furniture, folk art & primitives. Lynn
Randall

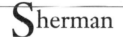herman

PAST TIME BOOKS
Rte 39N, 06784
(203)354-2515   **13**

A general stock of antiquarian books:
illustrated, children's classics, New England authors, self-help & how-to
books & medieval studies. *Serv:* Appraisal, search service. *Hours:* By
chance/appt. *Assoc:* CAB. Steve
Lorusso

**SCARLET LETTER BOOKS &
PRINTS**
Box 117, 06784
(203)354-4181   **13 66**

Antiquarian books: children's, illustrated, 19th C wood engravings &

original illustrator art. *Hours:* BY
APPT ONLY. *Assoc:* ABAA. Kathleen
A Lazare

imsbury

C RUSSELL NOYES
9 Hopmeadow St, 06070
(203)658-5319   **16 37**

Furniture of 18th & early 19th C, cop-
per, woodenware, tin & accessories.
Est: 1955. *Hours:* Daily 9-5 CLOSED
JAN-MAR 15. *Park:* On site. *Loc:* On
Rte 10 between Avon & Simsbury.

omers

OLD HICKORY ANTIQUES
Hickory Hill, 06071
(203)749-2113   **36 44 63**

High style country furniture of the
18th & 19th C - some in paint - early
blown glass & cut sponge pottery.
Hours: BY APPT. *CC:* MC/V. *Assoc:*
VADA. Tom Corcoran

South Glastonbury

RIBA AUCTIONS
Main St, 06073
(203)633-3076   **4 8**

Three auctions of autographs, photographs, prints, posters & historical
ephemera. 10% buyer's premium. *Est:*
1984. *Serv:* Appraisal, catalog, consultation, consignments. *Hours:* BY
APPT. Brian Riba *Park:* On site. *Loc:*
S of Hartford.

South Norwalk

BEAUFURN INC
16 S Main St, 06854
(203)838-3221   **43**
Country French antique reproduction furniture imported from France. *Serv:* Catalog $10. *Hours:* Mon-Fri 9-5 BY APPT ONLY. *Size:* Medium. *Park:* Municipal parking lot. *Loc:* From NYC: I-95 N Exit 14: R to 3rd traffic light, R onto S Main St, L onto Haviland St for parking area.

FAIENCE
120 Washington St, 06854
(203)853-4444   **36 46**
Antique furniture & interior design. *Hours:* Mon-Thu 10-6 Fri,Sat 10-10 Sun 1-5. *CC:* AX/MC/V. Sue Westphal *Park:* On site. *Loc:* In Historic District of South Norwalk.

MECHANICAL MUSIC CENTER INC
89B N Main St, 06854
(203)852-1780   **55**
Various automatic music instruments, victrolas, music boxes, player pianos & self-playing organs. *Est:* 1975. *Serv:* Reproducing pianos & piano rolls, restoration, repair. *Hours:* Tue-Sat 9:30-4:30. *CC:* MC/V. Fran Mayer *Park:* On site. *Loc:* Adjacent to Maritime Ctr.

OLD WELL ANTIQUES
135 Washington St, 06854
(203)838-1842   **27 32 41**
American country painted furniture, period furniture & accessories, vintage toys & holiday goods. *Pr:* $1–5000. *Est:* 1985. *Serv:* Appraisal, auction. *Hours:* Tue-Sat 11-5. Patrick J Padula *Park:* Nearby lot. *Loc:* I-95 Exit 15.

WASHINGTON STREET BOOK STORE
119 Washington St, 06854
(203)866-9204   **13**
General stock of antiquarian books in all subjects. *Hours:* Tue-Sun 10-6, extended hrs before Christmas & in summer. *Assoc:* CAB. Christopher Grahame-Smith

South Willington

KINGSMILL BOOK SHOP
Rte 32, 06265
(203)429-6694   **13**
Recent fiction, literary criticism, theology & philosophy. *Hours:* Fri 1-5 Sat 11-4, CLOSED JAN,FEB. *Assoc:* CAB. Bill Peters

SOUTH WILLINGTON ANTIQUES
Rte 32, 06279
(203)429-5595   **5 29 36**
Fourteen rooms & barn with furniture & decorative accessories - everything from the early country furniture to pieces of the 50s & period costumes. Resource for decorators, dealers & theatre groups. *Pr:* $1–5000. *Est:* 1958. *Serv:* Appraisal, restoration, delivery. *Hours:* Wed-Sun 10-4 or BY APPT. *Size:* Large. *CC:* MC/V. Donna Burns *Park:* On site. *Loc:* I-84 Exit 70: S approx 4 MI on the L.

South Windsor

COUNTRY BARN
1135 Sullivan Ave, 06074
(203)644-2826   **27 34 65**
Large 150-year-old barn featuring antique country furniture, primitives,

kitchen collectibles & folk art. *Pr:* $50–25000. *Est:* 1982. *Serv:* Purchase estates. *Hours:* Mar 15-Dec Daily, Jan,Mar BY APPT. *Size:* Large. Jo Patelli *Park:* On site. *Loc:* I-84N S Windsor Exit: L on Buckland to Sullivan Ave.

EARLY NEW ENGLAND ROOMS
37 Mc Guire Rd, 06074
(203)282-0236   **19 70 74**

The millwork facility for Sunderland Homes, reproducing period house features: raised paneling, cupboards, doors, entries, windows & kitchen cabinetry. *Serv:* Catalog ($10), reproduction woodwork. Edward Sunderland

HORACE PORTER ANTIQUES
728 Deming St, 06074
(203)644-0071   **37**

18th & 19th C American furniture. *Hours:* Sat 9-5 & BY APPT. David Bland *Loc:* I-84 Exit 63: .5 MI N on Rte 30.

SUNDERLAND PERIOD HOMES INC
37 Mc Guire Rd, 06074
(203)528-0890   **74**

Authentic 18th C & reproduction period homes. Complete architectural drawings of framing included with all structures. *Serv:* Complete contracting, millwork & restoration consulting services. Edward Sunderland

TIME PAST ANTIQUES
673 Main St, 06074
(203)289-2119   **23**

American, English & Continental clocks & fine antiques. *Est:* 1981. *Serv:* Appraisal, consultation, restoration & repairs (guaranteed). *Hours:* Mon-Fri 9-5. *CC:* MC/V. *Assoc:* NAWCC.

Park: On site. *Loc:* Just across the Bissell Bridge on Rte 91. 6 MI from downtown Hartford.

JOHN A WOODS, APPRAISERS
347 S Main St, 06074
(203)289-3927   **4 14 26**

A medical book dealer offering appraisals of books, documents & manuscripts. *Est:* 1976. *Serv:* Catalog, consultation, purchase estates, library development. *Assoc:* AAA ASA.

South Woodstock

SCRANTON'S SHOPS
Rtes 169-171, 06281
(203)928-3738   **{GR90}**

Seven rooms of antiques & handcrafted items in an early New England blacksmith's shop. *Est:* 1982. *Hours:* Mon-Fri 11-5 Sat,Sun 10-6. *Size:* Large. *CC:* DC/MC/V. *Park:* On site. *Loc:* I-395 Exit 97: toward Putnam, R on 171 for 5 MI, on the L across from fairgrounds.

Southbury

CHISWICK BOOK SHOP, INC.
Professional Bldg Village St, 06488
(203)264-7599   **13**

Illustrated, press, rare & press books, book arts & Officina Bodoni. *Hours:* BY APPT ONLY. *Assoc:* ABAA. Herman Cohen

THE HONEY POT
88 Main St S, 06488
(203)264-9966   **47**

Antique jewelry including: rings, bracelets, brooches, pins, pendants, necklaces, earrings, chains, watch chains, fobs, diamonds & stickpins. *Serv:* Repair, bead & pearl restringing. *Hours:* Tue-Fri 10-5 Sat 10-4. *CC:* MC/V. *Loc:* I-84, Exit 15.

GARY LUNDIN
Box 341, 06488
(203)264-5803   43
Antique reproduction tables, cupboards, chests & custom furniture.

SOUTHBURY ANTIQUES CTR
750 Main St, S, 06488
(203)262-6313   **{GR15}**
Quality shop of country & formal furniture & decorative accessories. *Est:* 1988. *Hours:* Tue-Sun 10-5. *CC:* MC/V. Kenlynne Pritchard *Park:* On site. *Loc:* I-84 Exit 14: R onto S Main St.

I M WIESE, ANTIQUARIAN
Roxbury Sta Rte 67, 06488
(203)354-8911   5
American antiques & antique building materials. *Hours:* BY APPT.

Southport

CHELSEA ANTIQUES
293 Pequot Ave, 06490
(203)255-8935   **{GR3}**
Furniture, china, glass & jewelry. *Serv:* Consignments. *Hours:* Tue-Sat 10:30-5. *Loc:* I-95 Exit 19.

PAT GUTHMAN ANTIQUES
281 Pequot Rd, 06490
(203)259-5743   16
Antiques & accessories for the kitchen & keeping room from America, England & the Continent. *Serv:* Demon-

strations, lectures, guest exhibitors. *Hours:* Tue-Sat 10-5 & BY APPT. *Shows:* ELLIS. *Loc:* I-95 Exit 19.

GWS GALLERIES
2600 Post Rd, 06490
(203)255-4613   59
American & English formal furniture & decorative accessories & oil paintings. *Hours:* Mon-Sat 9:30-5:30. Graham Stiles

HANSEN & CO
244 Old Post Rd, 06490
(203)259-5424   4 6
Appraisals of antique firearms & military accoutrements. *Serv:* Consultation, purchase estates. *Hours:* Mon-Fri 10-7 Sat 10-5. *CC:* MC/V. *Assoc:* AAA. Kenneth M Levin

JOSKO & SONS AUCTIONS
Box 817, 06490
(203)255-1441   8
Periodic auctions of antiques & collectibles from area homes. *Serv:* Auctioneer. Bill Josko

OLD SOUTHPORT BOOKS
65 Station St, 06490
(203)255-2277   13
Antiquarian books: children's, sporting, Americana & military. *Serv:* Appraisal, search service. *Hours:* BY APPT. *Assoc:* CAB. Molly Vogel

POMEROY ANDERSON
PO Box 787, 06490
(203)255-3095   4 26
Independent fine arts appraiser, specializing in paintings & sculpture. Art consultant, lecturer, author & researcher. *Serv:* Appraisal, auction, consultation, purchase estates. *Hours:* BY APPT. *Assoc:* ASA. Margaret P Anderson ASA

J B RICHARDSON GALLERY
362 Pequot Ave, 06490
(203)259-1903   **21 34 37**

American country & formal furniture, folk art & Oriental rugs. *Hours:* Thu-Sat 11-5 or BY APPT. *Assoc:* ADA.

THE STOCK MARKET
3519 Post Rd, 06490
(203)259-1189   **37 38 39**

English, Continental & American formal & country furniture, silver, paintings & decorative accessories. *Hours:* Mon-Sat 10:30-5.

TEN EYCK-EMERICH ANTIQUES
351 Pequot Ave, 06490
(203)259-2559   **37 63**

18th & 19th C English & American furniture & porcelain. *Hours:* Tue-Sat 11-5.

LAURENCE WITTEN RARE BOOKS
Box 490, 06490
(203)255-3474   **9 13**

Medieval & Renaissance manuscripts, early printed & illustrated books, illumination & incunabula. *Hours:* BY APPT ONLY. *Assoc:* ABAA.

Stamford

FENDELMAN & SCHWARTZ
555 Old Long Ridge Rd, 06903
(914)725-0292   **4**

Fine arts, antiques & household contents appraisal firm for probate, fine arts insurance, gift & IRS evaluations. Sale of art or antiques collections can be handled privately, at public sale or auction. *Serv:* Appraisal. *Hours:* BY APPT. *Assoc:* AAA ASA ISA. Helaine Fendelman

AVIS & ROCKWELL GARDINER
60 Mill Rd, 06903
(203)322-1129   **13 59 66**

American antique prints & paintings. *Hours:* BY APPT ONLY. *Assoc:* AADLA ABAA. *Park:* Nearby.

STEVE NEWMAN FINE ARTS
201 Summer St, 06905
(203)323-7799   **73**

19th & 20th C American & European sculpture. *Hours:* Wed-Fri 11-5 Sat 12-5.

RAPHAEL'S ANTIQUE RESTORATION
655 Atlantic St, 06902
(203)348-3079   **71**

Antique furniture restoration, veneer replacement, carving & French polishing. *Est:* 1947. *Serv:* References available. *Hours:* Mon-Fri 8-5 Sat 8-2:30. *Park:* On site. *Loc:* I-95S Exit 7 (Atlantic St): 2 blocks turn L, under thruway & railroad bridges, 1 block on R.

SHIPPAN POINT GALLERY
66 Fairview Ave, 06902
(203)324-7643   **37 39 59**

A brick Colonial displaying 19th & 20th C American & British paintings & some 18th & early 19th C furniture in three rooms. *Pr:* $1500–10000. *Serv:* Appraisal, consultation. *Hours:* Sat,Sun 10-6 BY APPT. Thomas Pikul *Park:* On site. *Loc:* I-95 Exit 8 (Elm St): traveling W from New England, I-95 Exit 8 (Atlantic St): traveling E from New York.

UNITED HOUSE WRECKING
535 Hope St, 06906
(203)348-5371   **5 16 74**

A fabulous collection of antique interior & exterior doors & architectural treasures including stained glass, furniture, statuary, brass & copper, Victorian gingerbread, plumbing fixtures, nautical & subway items, prints, ironwork & weather vanes. *Serv:* Shipping & delivery. *Hours:* Mon-Sat 9:30-5:30 Thu til 8. *CC:* AX/MC/V. *Park:* On site. *Loc:* I-95 Exit 9S: R onto Cortland (Rte 106), L on Glenbrook into Church St, R on Hope, R beyond Glenbrook Shopping Ctr.

ALEXANDRA WISE ANTIQUES
105 Broad St, 06901
(203)964-9295   **47 77**

Antique jewelry & silver - Victorian through modern - fancy silver serving pieces, selection of unique costume jewelry from the '30s, '40s & '50s. *Est:* 1978. *Serv:* Repairs. *Hours:* Mon-Fri 12-5. *CC:* MC/V. *Park:* Nearby lot. *Loc:* I-95 Atlantic St Exit (7 going N, 8 going S): R onto Broad St, Landmark Building on R, next to Town Ctr.

Sterling

ROBERT H GLASS AUCTIONEERS
Rte 14, 06377
(203)564-7318   **8**

Antiques & estate auctions. 10% buyer's premium. *Assoc:* CAI. Gwendolyn Glass

Stonington

CHRISTOPHER & KATHLEEN COLE
Rte 1, 06378
(203)599-2188   **16 37 65**

Specializing in American country antiques, including early iron for the hearth, treenware, architectural elements, accessories & furniture. *Pr:* $20–1000. *Est:* 1979. *Hours:* All year by chance/appt. *Size:* Medium. *CC:* MC/V. *Park:* On site. *Loc:* I-95 Exit 91: S off ramp to N Main St, .3 MI, L on N Main St to Rte 1E, 3 MI.

DOWNSTAIRS AT HARBOR VIEW
60 Water St, 06378
(203)535-4191   **29 47**

Antiques, accessories & vintage jewelry. *Hours:* Wed-Sun 1-4 evenings BY APPT.

NEIL B EUSTACE
156 Water St, 06378
(203)535-2249   **29 37**

American formal furniture, decorative arts & accessories of the 18th & early 19th C. *Hours:* By chance/appt.

RAYMOND IZBICKI
145 Water St, 06378
(203)535-1737   **47 77**

Select jewelry, silver & art. *Hours:* Wed-Sun 10-4.

ANN LEHMANN ANTIQUES
158 Water St, 06378
(203)535-4306   **1 34 57**

American primitive & folk art. *Est:* 1987. *Hours:* Tue-Sat 11-4 Mon,Sun by chance/appt.

MARY MAHLER ANTIQUES
117 Water St, 06378
(203)535-2741   **29 36**
18th & 19th C furniture & accessories.
Hours: Mon-Sat 11-5.

RONALD NOE ANTIQUES
135 Water St, 06378
(203)535-2624   **29 36**
Specializing in mahogany dining furniture & formal accessories. *Hours:*
Mon-Sat 10-5 Sun 12-4.

OPUS I
120 Water St, 06378
(203)535-2655   **21 36 63**
18th & 19th C furniture, Rose Medallion, Canton, brass, paintings, Windsor chairs & Oriental rugs. *Hours:* By
chance/appt. Carolyn Gunn

ORKNEY & YOST ANTIQUES
148 Water St, 06378
(203)535-4402   **21 29 37**
18th & 19th C American furniture,
Oriental rugs, paintings & appropriate
accessories of antique & international
appeal. *Pr:* $20–25000. *Est:* 1972.
Serv: Auction, purchase estates.
Hours: Mon-Sat 9-5 most Suns. *Size:*
Large. *CC:* AX/MC/V. Carolyn Orkney *Park:* On site. *Loc:* I-95 Exit 91:
follow signs to Stonington Borough, 3
min off I-95, on Water St.

QUESTER GALLERY
On The Green, 06378
(203)535-3860   **54 56 78**
Extensive collection of 19th & 20th C
paintings, sculptures & prints, specializing in maritime, sporting, wildlife &
American Impressionist subjects. Sea-focused collection includes fine ship &
yacht models, furniture & antique
scrimshaw. *Pr:* $500–250000. *Est:*
1860. *Serv:* Appraisal, brochure, catalog $12.50, conservation, consultation.
Hours: Apr-Sep 7 Mon-Sat 11-6 Sun
1:30-5. *Size:* Medium. *Assoc:* ISA
NEAA. James P Marenakos *Park:* In
front. *Loc:* From N: I-95 Exit 91: L for
.3 MI, L on N Main thru light, L @ SS,
R @ next SS, over RR overpass, L on
High, 1 block.

QUIMPER FAIENCE
141 Water St, 06378
(203)535-1712   **63**
A unique shop dealing exclusively
Quimper pottery. *Est:* 1690. *Serv:* Catalog ($2).

MARGUERITE RIORDAN
8 Pearl St, 06378
(203)535-2511   **1 57 59**
American furniture, fine paintings and
works of art for the serious collector.
Hours: Appt suggested. *Shows:* WAS.

VICTORIA STATION
109 Water St, 06378
(203)535-3258   **36 59 63**
19th C furniture, paintings, glass &
china. *Hours:* Weekends 10-5 or BY
APPT.

WATER STREET ANTIQUES
114 Water St, 06378
(203)535-1124   **38 39 59**
English & Continental furniture,
paintings & accessories. *Hours:* Daily
10-5.

Stony Creek

STONY CREEK VILLAGE STORE
118 Thimble Island Rd, 06405
(203)488-3060   **44 63**
Antiques, furniture, pottery, porcelain

& glass. *Est:* 1960. *Serv:* Purchase estates, manage estate sales, auctioneer. *Hours:* Mon-Sun 9-5. Alice Green *Park:* In front. *Loc:* I-95 Exit 56S: 3 MI.

Storrs

RAINBOW BOOKS
146 Moulton Rd, 06268
(203)429-5343   **13**

Children's books & a general stock of antiquarian books. *Serv:* Search service. *Hours:* BY APPT. *Assoc:* CAB. Caroline C Lucal

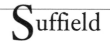

Stratford

AMERICA'S PAST
82 Boston Ave, 06497
(203)378-7037   **59**

19th & 20th C American paintings. *Hours:* By appt. Ivan Seresin

Suffield

NIKKI & TOM DEUPREE
480 N Main St, 06078
(203)668-7262   **7 34 41**

Small, top quality inventory constantly changing, with emphasis on design & condition. *Pr:* $100–30000. *Serv:* Appraisal. *Hours:* Appt suggested. *Assoc:* ADA. *Loc:* 5 MI N of Bradley International Airport.

Thompson

RUSSIAN BEAR ANTIQUES
Box 33 RR 2, 06277
(203)928-4276   **29 37**

Fine American 18th & 19th C furniture & accessories. *Serv:* Appraisal, purchase estates. *Hours:* Sat,Sun 1-5 or by chance/appt. Camille Strong *Loc:* 15 MI S of Worcester MA, 1.5 MI from Int of 395 & 44.

Tolland

HUNT COUNTRY ANTIQUES
68 Hartford Turnpike, 06084
(203)871-9063   **36 39 42**

Direct importer of 18th & 19th C English, Irish & European pine country furniture & accessories, featuring armoires, tables, dressers & unusual pieces. *Pr:* $50–3000. *Serv:* Interior design. *Hours:* Mon, Wed-Sat 11-5 Sun 12-5. *Size:* Medium. *CC:* MC/V. Corinne Palmer *Park:* In front. *Loc:* From Hartford, Rte 84E, Exit 67 (L), Rte 30 (R), approx 1.25 MI on L in Colonial Sq.

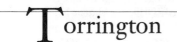

Torrington

COUNTRY AUCTION SERVICE
PO Box 1532, 06790
(203)542-5212   **8**

Purchase & sale of antique furniture, furnishings & collectibles - single items & complete estates - consignment arrangements available. Inquiries handled with discretion. No buyer's premium. *Serv:* Estate appraisal & liquidation, consultation, purchase estates. *Hours:* BY APPT. *Assoc:* NAA. I Joseph Stannard

NORMAN'S ANTIQUES
37 Volkmann Ln, 06790
(203)489-7440   **36 40 43**

Furniture from 1800s to turn-of-the-century, candlestands to tables, chairs, bookcases, wardrobes, country pine, oak, maple, walnut & mahogany. *Pr:* $25–1500. *Est:* 1982. *Serv:* Custom woodwork, purchase estates, repairs, reproduction, stripping. *Hours:* Mon-Sat 9-5 CLOSED WED,SUN. *Size:* Large. *CC:* MC/V. Norman Mailhot *Park:* Nearby lot. *Loc:* Rte 8 Exit 44: Rte 202 toward Torrington, L onto Volkmann, 1st bldg on L, white brick.

NUTMEG BOOKS
354 New Litchfield St Rte 202, 06790
(203)482-9696   **13 33**

Used, rare & out-of-print books, paper & ephemera. *Serv:* Catalog, appraisal, search service. *Hours:* Daily 12-5, or by chance/appt. *CC:* MC/V. *Assoc:* CAB. Deborah Goring *Park:* On site. *Loc:* .5 MI from downtown W toward Litchfield.

Trumbull

APPRAISAL ASSOCIATES
93 Canterbury Ln, 06611
(203)268-6403   **4**

Appraise antique autos, mansions for insurance & acquisition. *Est:* 1973. *Serv:* Appraisal, consultation. *Hours:* Daily 9-5. *Assoc:* ASA. Ralph G Okrepkie

GWENDOLYN DONAHUE
Old Barn Rd, 06611
(203)268-3988   **27**

Country antiques. *Hours:* BY APPT.

ZIMMERS HEIRLOOM CLOCKS
124 Strobel Rd, 06611
(203)261-2278   **23 71**

Wide variety of clocks, including Banjo, Welch & Waltham. *Serv:* Clock restoration. *Hours:* Call ahead.

Wallingford

ANTIQUE CENTER OF WALLINGFORD
28 South Orchard St, 06492
(203)269-7130   **{GR3}**

A renovated barn filled with oak & other furniture, country items, pottery, pressed glass, tinware, post cards, book & collector's items. A browser's paradise. *Pr:* $1–1000. *Est:* 1966. *Hours:* Daily 1-5. *Size:* Medium. *Park:* On site. *Loc:* 1 block E of Rte 5, across from the cemetery.

IMAGES, HEIRLOOM LINENS/LACE
145 Quinnipiac St, 06492
(203)265-7065   **46 48 80**

Specializing in American & European estate linens/lace & other early textiles - linen sheet sets, shams, banquet cloths, especially hard-to-find large tablecloths, rounds, squares, runners, doilies, pillowcases, quilts, coverlets & Marseille spreads. *Pr:* $2–1200. *Est:* 1988. *Serv:* Appraisal. *Hours:* Mon-Fri 10-3 Sat 11-3 or by chance/appt. *CC:* MC/V. Debra S Bonito *Park:* On site. *Loc:* I-91 Exit 14: 6 MI. Merritt Pkwy Exit 64: 2 min.

MAISON AUCTION COMPANY INC
128 East St, 06492
(203)269-8007   **4 8**
Antique & estate auctions. No buyer's premium. *Serv:* Appraisal, auctioneer. Bill Ulbrich *Loc:* I-91 Exit 12: R at exit onto Rte 5N to 2nd signal light. L over RR bridge onto John St. R at end on to East St.

LEE MOHN ANTIQUES AND ART
30 N Colony St, 06492
(203)269-3313   **58 63 64**
A general line of antiques. *Est:* 1988. *Hours:* Wed-Sun 11-5. *Size:* Medium. *Park:* Nearby lot. *Loc:* I-91 Exit 13: 2 MI N on Rte 5 OR Wilbur Cross Pkwy Exit 66: 2 MI S.

WALLINGFORD ANTIQUES COLLECTIVE
36 N Main St 2nd Fl, 06492
(203)265-9037   **{GR15}**
Quality group shop with clocks, furniture, silver, quilts, glass, china, inkwells, lighting fixtures, post cards, vertu, decorative accessories, books, microscopes & ephemera. *Pr:* $5–5000. *Hours:* Thu-Sun 10-4. *Assoc:* NAWCC. *Park:* In front. *Loc:* I-91 Exit 14 OR Merritt Pkwy Exit 64: located in Simpson Court at corner of Center St.

Washington Depot

STEPHEN CALCAGNI
Titus Rd, 06794
(203)868-7667   **37 39 60**
Fine art & antiques specializing in din-

ing tables, chairs, sideboards, mirrors, china & Chinese export porcelain. *Est:* 1978. *Serv:* Appraisal, purchase estates, repairs, conservation. *Hours:* Mon-Sat 12-5. *Park:* On site. *Loc:* I-84 Exit 15: Rte 6 to Rte 47 to Washington.

HICKORY STICK BOOKSHOP
Rte 47, 06794
(203)868-0525   **13**
Antiquarian books: Connecticut, New England, Alexander Calder, Gladys Taber & Eric Sloane. *Serv:* Search service. *Hours:* Mon-Sat 9-6 Sun 11-5. *Assoc:* CAB. Thomas P Whitney

THE TULIP TREE COLLECTION
Washington Mews Rte 47, 06794
(203)868-2802   **21 41 42**
A carefully selected collection of antique & reproduction painted, pine furniture & reproduction upholstered furniture, complemented by rag & kilim rugs, lamps & accessories. *Pr:* $10–3000. *Serv:* Appraisal, interior design, reproduction, architectural design. *Hours:* Year round Tue-Sun. *Size:* Large. *CC:* AX/MC/V. Robert B Winston *Park:* Nearby lot. *Loc:* From S: I-84 Rte 6 N: L Rte 47 to Washington Depot From N: Rte 202 to Rte 47 to Washington Depot.

West Cornwall

DEBORAH BENSON BOOKSELLER
River Rd, 06796
(203)672-6614   **13**
Antiquarian books: early medical, diabetes, modern firsts, foredge, books about books, Alice in Wonderland &

inscribed books. *Serv:* Appraisal, search service. *Hours:* By chance/appt. *Assoc:* CAB. Deborah Covington

BARBARA FARNSWORTH
Rte 128, 06796
(203)672-6571   13

Antiquarian books: horticulture, art, literature, prints & decorated trade bindings. *Serv:* Appraisal, search service. *Hours:* By chance/appt. *Assoc:* ABAA CAB.

INDIAN LANE FARM
187 Johnson Rd, 06796
(203)672-0255   34 37 59

Specializing in 18th & 19th C American & English furniture, decorative arts, folk art & fine art. *Est:* 1988. *Serv:* Appraisal. *Hours:* Wed-Sat 11-5 Sun 1-5. *CC:* AX/MC/V. John A Wright *Park:* On site. *Loc:* Johnson Rd is 1 MI N off Rte 43 from the Jct of Rtes 4, 128 & 43 at Mohawk Mtn in West Cornwall.

West Hartford

SAMUEL S T CHEN
104 Shepard Rd, 06110
(203)561-0765   4

Appraisal of Oriental art - including painting & calligraphy, jade & hardstones, pottery & porcelain, bronze & cloisonne & snuff bottles. *Est:* 1977. *Serv:* Appraisal. *Hours:* BY APPT ONLY. *Assoc:* AAA.

ROBIN FERN GALLERY
165 Robin Rd, 06119
(203)233-2781   59

Specializing in 19th & 20th C American & European art. *Pr:* $200–7000.

Hours: BY APPT ONLY. Elizabeth B Beksha *Park:* In front. *Loc:* I-84 Exit 43.

ALICE KUGELMAN
19 Sunset Terr, 06107
(203)521-6482   4

Independent appraiser specializing in 18th & 19th C furniture & silver, estate liquidation & museum consultant. *Est:* 1970. *Hours:* BY APPT. *Assoc:* AAA ASA.

PARK PLACE ANTIQUES
322 Park Rd, 06119
(203)233-6380   (GR2)

Specializing in antique & collectible jewelry, brass, metalwork & hard cover books. *Est:* 1975. *Hours:* Year round daily 11-6 CLOSED SUN. *Size:* Medium. *CC:* AX/MC/V. Fran O'Connell *Park:* On site. *Loc:* Rte 84W Exit 43: 1 block on R.

W HARTFORD BK SHOP AT PARK PLACE
322 Park Rd, 06119
(203)233-6380   13

A general stock of used, out-of-print & rare books. *Serv:* Appraisal, search service. *Hours:* Mon-Sat 11-5:30 Thu 11-9 Sun by chance. *Assoc:* CAB. Michael Polasko

West Haven

ARTISTIC VENTURES GALLERY
608 Second Ave, 06516
(203)934-0191   59

"Art between the wars", American paintings - 1920s-1940s, dealer to dealer. *Pr:* $1000–10000. *Serv:* Purchase estates. *Hours:* BY APPT ONLY. Lydia Bornick *Park:* Nearby lot. *Loc:* Call for directions.

JOSEPH LOUIS NACCA
52 Fern St, 06516
(203)933-4668   **36**
18th & 19th C furniture, specializing in the Empire period. *Hours:* Mon-Fri 8-4:30. *Park:* In front. *Loc:* I-95 Exit 43: make a R U-turn, go up Highland St, 2nd L.

West Redding

LINCOLN & JEAN SANDER INC
235 Redding Rd Rte 107, 06896
(203)938-9873   **37**
18th C New England furniture & related accessories. *Serv:* Appraisal, consultation. *Hours:* BY APPT. *Assoc:* ADA. *Park:* In front. *Loc:* 12 MI from Rte 84, 2 MI from Rte 7, 10 MI from Merritt Pkwy.

West Simsbury

NANCY DAVIS
202 Farms Village Rd, 06092
(203)651-8638   **27**
American country antiques. *Hours:* BY APPT.

West Willington

RONALD & PENNY DIONNE
Glass Factory Schoolhouse Rd, 06279
(203)487-0741   **29 37**
American furniture & decorative ac-

cessories with emphasis on the 18th C. *Hours:* BY APPT. *Assoc:* NHADA. *Loc:* I-84 Exit 69: 1 MI E.

RANDALL NELSON
40 Fisher Hill Rd, 06279
(203)429-3830   **70 71 74**
Architectural restoration & reproduction, interior & exterior work, restoration in terra cotta & stone - residential & commercial. *Est:* 1980. *Hours:* BY APPT.

Westbrook

THE CAPTAIN STANNARD HOUSE
138 S Main St, 06498
(203)399-7565   **{GR3}**
Federal, Victorian & country furniture. *Est:* 1987. *Hours:* Daily 11-5. *Size:* Medium. *CC:* AX/MC/V. Elaine Grandmaison *Park:* On site. *Loc:* I-95 Exit 65: R .25 MI into town ctr, L at 2nd light, at end of st.

HANES RUSKIN
Box 820, 06498
(203)399-5229   **2 16 63**
18th & early 19th C American furniture & period accessories including paintings, fireplace equipment, Delft, Chinese export porcelain, English ceramics, needlework & 17th & 18th New England metalware. *Serv:* Appraisal. *Assoc:* ISA. Joyce Hanes

Weston

MILLICENT RUDD BEST
190 Goodhill Rd, 06883
(203)227-3966   **36 63 77**
Furniture & decorative arts, porcelain,

ceramics & silver. *Serv:* Appraisal. *Hours:* BY APPT ONLY. *Assoc:* AAA.

SANDI OLIVER FINE ART
11 Tubbs Springs Dr, 06883
(203)226-4469   **58**
Fine art. *Serv:* Appraisal. *Hours:* BY APPT ONLY. *Assoc:* NEAA. *Park:* Ample. *Loc:* Off Rte 53.

Westport

CONNECTICUT FINE ARTS, INC
2 Gorham Ave, 06880
(203)227-8016   **4 59 66**
Art appraisals of 19th & 20th C American & European drawings, paintings, prints & sculpture. Buying & selling 19th & 20th C works of art. *Est:* 1968. *Serv:* Appraisal, consultation. *Hours:* BY APPT ONLY. *Assoc:* AAA. Burt Chernow

CONSIGNMART
877 Post Rd E, 06880
(203)226-0841
Jewelry, paintings, furniture & silver. *Hours:* Mon-Sat 10-5:30. *Park:* Ample. *Loc:* I-95 Exit 18.

COUNTRY SWEDISH ANTIQUES
35 Post Rd W, 06880
(203)222-8212   **27**
Direct import of Swedish antiques & reproductions. *Pr:* $100–5000. *Est:* 1985. *Hours:* Tue-Sat 10-5. *Size:* Medium. *CC:* MC/V. Dick De Jounge *Park:* On site. *Loc:* I-95 Exit 17: to Int of Rte 1, or Merritt Pkwy, Exit 41 to Int of Rte 1.

THE FAMILY ALBUM
283 Post Rd E, 06880
(203)227-4888   **34 47 67**
Antique jewelry, quilts, vintage prints & folk art. *Hours:* Mon-Sat 9:30-5. *CC:* MC/V. *Park:* Playhouse Square. *Loc:* Next to Westport County Playhouse, Exit 40 or 41 off Merritt Pkwy.

FRIEDMAN GALLERY
135 W Post Rd E, 06880
(203)226-5533   **7 47 50**
Specialize in 20th C decorative arts with an emphasis on art deco, furniture, jewelry, lighting, radios & juke boxes. *Pr:* $50–10000. *Est:* 1980. *Hours:* Tue-Sat 10:30-5:30. *Size:* Medium. *CC:* AX/MC/V. Michael Friedman *Park:* Nearby lot. *Loc:* Downtown Westport across from the post office.

GUTHMAN AMERICANA
Box 392, 06881
(203)259-9763   **13**
Antiquarian books on American Revolution, French & Indian War & Colonial warfare. *Hours:* BY APPT ONLY. *Assoc:* ABAA. *Shows:* WAS. William H Guthman *Loc:* Call for directions.

L'OBJET D'ART LTD
Riverside Commons 57 Wilton Rd, 06880
(203)454-1830   **38 39 60**
Offering an important selection of eclectic 18th & 19th C formal & elegant provincial European furniture & accessories as well as fine Oriental antiques. *Pr:* $1000–45000. *Est:* 1982. *Serv:* Appraisal, consultation & special projects, purchase estates, restorations. *Hours:* Apr-Oct Tue-Fri 11-5 Sat 11-6, Nov-Mar Tue-Sat 10:30-6. *Size:* Medium. Michael G Delhaise *Park:* On site. *Loc:* Merritt Pkwy Exit 41: Rte 33

S, 1500 ft past 1st traffic light on R side OR I-95, Exit 17 Rte 33 N, 600 ft past Jct on L.

DORVAN L MANUS
179 Compo Rd, 06880
(203)227-8602　　　　　　**37 39**

18th & 19th C tables, English & American furniture & decorative accessories. *Serv:* Restoration of gilt mirrors. *Hours:* BY APPT.

PARC MONCEAU
18 Riverside Ave Rte 33, 06880
(203)227-8887　　　　　　**27 35**

18th & 19th C country French furniture & accessories including armoires, buffets, tables, chairs, bureaus & many interesting accessories. *Est:* 1985. *Serv:* Restoration. *Hours:* Tue-Sat 10-5. *Size:* Large. Joanna Farber *Park:* Nearby lot. *Loc:* I-95 Exit 17: N on Rte 33 to 18 Riverside Ave OR Merritt Pkwy, Exit 41, S on Rte 33 to 18 Riverside Ave.

PRINCE OF WALES
1032 Post Rd E, 06880
(203)454-2335　　　　　　**39 42**

Specialists in fine quality 18th & 19th C English pine furniture & accessories. *Hours:* Tue-Sat 10-5 Sun 1-5 BY APPT. *Size:* Large. *CC:* MC/V. *Park:* Accessible.

SAM SLOAT COINS, INC
136 Main St, 06880
(203)226-4279　　　　　　**24 79**

Coins, stamps & precious metals. *Est:* 1961. *Serv:* Appraise estates of coins. *Hours:* Mon-Fri 9-4 Sat 9-12. *Park:* On site. *Loc:* I-95 Exit 17 OR Merritt Pkwy Exit 42.

THINGS
142 Main St, 06880
(203)227-3666　　　　　　**36 77 78**

Interesting mix of furniture, silver, wood carvings, Orientalia, hunt prints & country Japanese. *Pr:* $5–9000. *Serv:* Interior design. *Hours:* Mon-Sat 10:00-5:30 Sun by chance, Nov 24-Dec 24 Sun 12-5. *Size:* Medium. *CC:* AX. Barbara Kelley *Park:* Nearby lot. *Loc:* I-95 Exit 17: N to Post Rd, R 2 blocks, L onto Main St, 2nd block on R OR Merritt Pkwy Exit 41.

TODBURN
243 Post Rd W, 06880
(203)226-3859　　　　　　**27 32 86**

Wicker furniture, dolls, accessories & country furniture. *Serv:* Restoration of wicker furniture. *Hours:* Mon-Sat 10-5. *Park:* On site. *Loc:* I-95 Exit 17.

TURKEY HILL BOOKS
46 Turkey Hill Rd S, 06880
(203)255-0041　　　　　　**13**

Antiquarian books: firsts, fiction, children's signed, limited editions & fine bindings. *Serv:* Appraisal, search service. *Hours:* BY APPT. *Assoc:* CAB. Jack Grogins

Wethersfield

CLEARING HOUSE AUCTION GALLERIES
207 Church St, 06109
(203)529-3344　　　　　　**4 8**

Family-owned & operated full-time auction gallery, 2 sales per week. One major catalog auction per month, usually on Friday. Auctions every Wednesday at 7pm, with a 1-hour preview. *Est:* 1947. *Serv:* Appraisal. *Hours:* Office: daily 8-5, Gallery: BY APPT. *CC:*

MC/V. Thomas G Le Clair *Park:* On site for 300 cars. *Loc:* I-91 Exit 26 (Marsh St): S of Hartford.

Willimantic

ANTIQUES & THINGS
River Plaza, 06226
(203)456-4544   **47 48 85**
Vintage clothing, linens, jewelry, furniture, kitchenware & stained glass. *Hours:* Wed-Fri 9-4:30 Sat,Sun 9-1. Cheryl Hines

ERNEST ELDRIDGE AUCTIONEER
201 Church St, 06226
(203)423-0525   **8**
Complete auction service with bi-weekly auctions. *Serv:* Appraisal, accept phone bids, consultation, no buyer premium. *Assoc:* CAA. *Park:* In front. *Loc:* 30 MI E. of Hartford.

Wilton

ARCHIVES HISTORICAL AUTOGRAPHS
119 Chestnut Hill Rd, 06897
(203)226-3920   **9 13**
Autograph letters, documents, manuscripts & signed books. *Assoc:* ABAA. Warren P Weitman

AMABEL BARROWS ANTIQUES
372 Ridgefield Rd, 06897
(203)762-9054   **4**
Management of estate sales, specializing in antiques. Complete household furnishings (minimum value $15,000) sold in situ. *Pr:* $1–30000. *Est:* 1965. *Serv:* Appraisal. *Hours:* ESTATE SALES ONLY. *Assoc:* CADA NEAA.

CASTLE ANTIQUE IMPORTERS
681 Danbury Rd, 06897
(203)544-8863   **42**
Large selection of pine & mahogany furniture. *Serv:* Free delivery within a reasonable distance. *Hours:* Sat-Sun 9-9 weekdays 9-6 BY APPT. *Size:* Large. *Park:* On site. *Loc:* On Rte 7.

THE PINE CHEST, INC.
30 Deepwood Rd, 06897
(203)762-0521   **27 37 74**
American country furniture & accessories - specializing in mid 18th-late 19th C items.. *Est:* 1985. *Serv:* Custom woodwork, repairs. *Hours:* BY APPT. *Assoc:* CADA. Michael West *Park:* On site. *Loc:* Call for directions.

THOMAS SCHWENKE, INC
Jct Rtes 7, 33 & 106, 06897
(203)834-2929   **37**
A renovated 1791 house featuring a large stock of Federal furnishings. *Hours:* By appt. *Loc:* In the Elijah Betts House.

GEORGE SUBKOFF ANTIQUES, INC.
643 Danbury Rd Rte 7, 06897
(203)834-0703   **37 39 59**
A large shop stocked with fine period American, English & Continental furniture of the 18th & early 19th C, good paintings & decorations. *Hours:* Tue-Sat 10-5:30 Sun 12-5. *Size:* Large. *Assoc:* AADLA. *Park:* On site. *Loc:* On Rte 7.

VALLIN GALLERIES
516 Danbury Rd, 06897
(203)762-7441   **45 60**
Chinese & Asian art & antiques, fine porcelains, pottery, paintings, textiles & Oriental garden ornaments from neolithic through 19th C. *Est:* 1940.

Serv: Purchase estates or single items. *Hours:* Wed-Sat 10:30-5 Sun 1-5, else BY APPT. *Assoc:* AADLA ASA CINOA. Peter Rosenberg

MARIA & PETER WARREN ANTIQUES
1030 Ridgefield Rd, 06897
(203)762-7353   **35 37 39**
Period American, English & French furniture, antiques & decorative arts. *Hours:* BY APPT ONLY.

WAYSIDE EXCHANGE
300 Danbury Rd, 06897
(203)762-3183   **21 29 36**
Furniture, rugs & decorative accessories. *Est:* 1961. *Hours:* Mon-Sat 10:30-4:30 Sun 12-5. *Park:* On site. *Loc:* Rte 7.

Windham

THE TIN LANTERN
273 Back Road, 06280
(203)423-5676   **50 70**
Reproductions of traditionally handmade early American chandeliers, sconces, lanterns & reflector ovens. *Hours:* Mon-Fri 9-5 Wed 1-5 Sat 9-2. A J Styger

Windsor

CEDRIC L ROBINSON-BOOKSELLER
597 Palisado Ave, 06095
(203)688-2582   **13**
Antiquarian books: Americana, architecture Civil War & Confederacy, American literature, voyages, travels &

exploration. *Serv:* Catalog, appraisal. *Hours:* Mon-Sat 9-5 BY APPT. *Assoc:* ABAA CAB.

Winsted

VERDE ANTIQUES & BOOKS
64 Main St, 06098
(203)379-3135   **13 33**
Antiquarian books: first editions, children's illustrated & ephemera. *Serv:* Appraisal. *Hours:* Thu-Sat afternoons by chance/appt. *Assoc:* CAB. Ginny Dethy

Winthrop

JAS E ELLIOTT ANTIQUES
453 Winthrop Rd, 06417
(203)526-9455   **4 39 63**
Specializing in British pottery & porcelain of 18th & 19th C, Federal, Empire & Regency furniture, early ABC plates & mugs & other fine quality decorative accessories. *Pr:* $50–10000. *Est:* 1959. *Serv:* Appraisal, consultation, purchase estates. *Hours:* May-Dec Thu-Sat 12-5, else BY APPT. *Size:* Medium. *Assoc:* AADLA CINOA NEAA. *Shows:* ELLIS. *Park:* On site. *Loc:* I-95 Exit 64: Rte 80, Jct of 145.

Woodbridge

WOODBRIDGE BOOK STORE
Meeting House Ln The Center, 06525
(203)387-3815   **13**
A general stock of antiquarian books. *Hours:* TUE ONLY 10-4. *Assoc:* CAB. Betty Bell

Woodbury

ANTIQUE FURNITURE RESTORATION
187 Washington Rd, 06798
(203)266-4295   **71**

French polishing, restoration of old finishes, veneers & inlays, complete & proper structural restoration. *Serv:* Will purchase antique furniture in any condition. *Hours:* Mon-Sat 9-5. Mark Bieluczyk

ANTIQUES ON THE GREEN
14 Green Circle, 06798
(203)263-2558   **16 65 67**

Located in a 1700s newly-restored Colonial, American primitive furniture & accessories, quilts, baskets & pewter. *Pr:* $25–5000. *Est:* 1987. *Hours:* Wed-Sun 12-5 by chance/appt. *Size:* Medium. Roger Bjornberg *Park:* On site. *Loc:* Int of Rtes 6 & 47, behind North Green at Canfield Corner.

THE BAY TREE ANTIQUES
745 Main St, N, 06798
(203)263-5611   **29 39 66**

Ten showrooms of fine imported 18th & 19th C English formal & country furniture as well as accessories in a pre-Revolutionary home & barn. *Pr:* $25–10000. *Est:* 1985. *Hours:* Mar-Dec Wed-Sat 10-5 Sun 11-5 & BY APPT. *Size:* Large. *CC:* MC/V. James R Buczynski *Park:* On site. *Loc:* Rte 84 Exit 15 (Rte 6): N thru Southbury & Woodbury, 2 MI N of Woodbury town ctr.

BOOKS ABOUT ANTIQUES
139 Main St, N, 06798
(203)263-0241   **14**

Specializing in books relating to antiques, decorative arts, folk art, fine arts, interior design, architecture & crafts. *Est:* 1988. *Serv:* Special orders, search service. *Hours:* Mon-Sat 10-5:30 Sun 12-4. *Size:* Medium. *CC:* MC/V. Greg Johnson *Park:* In front. *Loc:* I-84 Exit 15: E on Rte 6, 5.7 MI on L.

BRITISH COUNTRY ANTIQUES
50 Main St, N, 06798
(203)263-5100   **35 39 42**

Eleven spacious house & barn showrooms featuring exceptional quality authentic 18th & 19th C English & French country furniture in pine, fruitwoods, elm & oak, paint-decorated armoires, many unusual accessories, known for beautifully-finished antiques. *Est:* 1977. *Serv:* Brochure, custom woodwork, interior design. *Hours:* Year round Tue-Sun 10-5. *Size:* Large. *CC:* MC/V. Ed Adolph *Park:* On site. *Loc:* I-84 Exit 15: Rte 6 E for 5 MI, on R, 1 hr 45 min from NYC.

CARRIAGE HOUSE ANTIQUES
403 Main St, S, 06798
(203)266-4021   **1 37**

A choice selection of American furniture from 1780-1840 tastefully displayed in a 19th C carriage house. *Serv:* All pieces guaranteed. *Hours:* By chance/appt. *Size:* Medium. *CC:* MC/V. Nancy Huebner *Park:* On site. *Loc:* Across from the cannon & Civil War Monument on Main St.

CLAPP AND TUTTLE
Main St, S, 06798
(203)263-2207   **21 37 66**

Furniture, paintings, Persian rugs, prints & fine art. *Est:* 1955. *Serv:* Museum-quality custom framing, restoration. *Hours:* Tue-Sat 9:30-5, Sep-May open Sun. *CC:* AX/MC/V. *Park:* In front. *Loc:* On Rte 6 in Middle Quarter Plaza.

HAROLD E COLE ANTIQUES
661 Washington Rd, 06798
(203)263-3332   **1 37 71**
17th, 18th & 19th C New England furniture & accessories for advanced dealers & collectors. *Est:* 1960. *Serv:* Appraisal, consultation, purchase estates, restoration. *Hours:* By chance/appt. *Park:* On site. *Loc:* 3 MI from Int of Rtes 47 & 6.

COUNTRY LOFT ANTIQUES
88 Main St, N, 06798
(203)266-4501   **21 35**
A beautifully refurbished rustic 125

year-old barn specializing in country French & English antiques, Oriental & kilim rugs. *Est:* 1985. *Serv:* Interior design. *Hours:* Wed-Sat 10-5 Sun 12-5. Carole Winer *Park:* On site. *Loc:* .2 MI N of Jct 47 on Rte 6.

CROSSWAYS ANTIQUES
4 Main St, S, 06798
(203)263-4100   **16 39 53**
English Georgian furniture & accessories of the period including porcelains, trays, mirrors, brass & prints. *Est:* 1964. *Hours:* Mon-Sat 10:30-5 Sun 1-5. *Size:* Medium. James E Boudreau *Park:* In front. *Loc:* At the corner of Rtes 6 & 47.

DARIA OF WOODBURY
82 Main St, N, 06798
(203)263-2431   **34 37 65**

Early American furniture, folk art, early kitchen items & primitives. *Est:* 1968. *Serv:* Appraisal, consultation, purchase estates, restoration. *Hours:* Daily 10-5. H Daria Mattox *Park:* On site.

DAVIS ANTIQUES
289 Main St, S, 06798
(203)263-5700   **23 47**

Clocks & estate jewelry. Roger S Davis

DAVID DUNTON/ANTIQUES
Rte 132 Off Rte 47, 06798
(203)263-5355   **1 37 59**

Antiques of the highest quality from the American Federal period with appropriate accessories. *Est:* 1974. *Serv:* Conservation. *Hours:* Sat,Sun 12-5 appt suggested. *Size:* Large. *Park:* In front. *Loc:* I-84 Exit 15: Rte 6 to Rte 47, L on 47 to Rte 132 R onto 132, 2nd house on L 10 Min from I-84.

CRAIG FARROW CABINETMAKER
451 Main St, S, 06798
(203)263-0495   **68 70 71**

Specializing in early New England 17th & 18th C furniture copies. *Est:* 1979. *Serv:* Repairs, restoration, reproduction. *Hours:* Tue-Sat 9-5. *CC:* MC/V. *Park:* On site.

GILDAY'S ANTIQUES
1917 Main St, N, 06798
(203)274-1555   **37 50**

Fine 19th C furniture, lamps, paintings & Oriental rugs. *Est:* 1985. *Serv:* Purchase estates. *Hours:* Wed-Sun 10-5:30 or BY APPT. *CC:* MC/V. *Assoc:* CADA. Ed Gilday Healy *Park:* On site. *Loc:* Near the Watertown Line, Exit 15 on I-84, E on Rte 6, 10 MI.

GRASS ROOTS ANTIQUES
12 Main St, N, 06798
(203)263-3983   **29 44 77**

18th & 19th C country & formal antiques on 2 floors in a renovated silk mill - including glass, china, pictures, silver, jewelry & decorative accessories. *Est:* 1972. *Serv:* Purchase estates. *Hours:* Tue-Sat 11-5 Sun 1-4. *CC:* MC/V. Ethel Greenblatt *Park:* In front. *Loc:* I-84 Exit 15.

KENNETH HAMMITT ANTIQUES
346 Main St, S, 06798
(203)263-5676   **2 37 53**

Authentic 18th & 19th C American furniture & accessories - mostly formal - including highboys, lowboys, chests, tables, chairs, candlestands, mirrors, silver, paintings, rugs, samplers & fireplace tools. *Est:* 1954. *Serv:* Fully guaranteed. *Hours:* Mon-Sat 10-5:30. *Size:* Large. *Park:* On site. *Loc:* I-84 Exit 15: approx 6 MI.

FRANK C JENSEN ANTIQUES
142 Middle Rd Turnpike, 06798
(203)263-0908   **37**

17th, 18th & 19th C American furniture & accessories. *Est:* 1953. *Serv:* Reproductions, restorations. *Hours:* By chance/appt, please call ahead. *Park:* On site. *Loc:* I-84 Exit 15: R at 3rd light, off Rte 6, .5 MI on R.

MILL HOUSE ANTIQUES
Main St, N, 06798
(203)263-3446   **29 35 39**

Huge selection of English & French antique furniture & decorative accessories in 17 showrooms. *Est:* 1962.

Hours: Daily 9-5 CLOSED TUE.
Size: Large. *Park:* On site. *Loc:* I-84
Exit 15: 7.5 MI N.

**GERALD MURPHY ANTIQUES
LTD**
60 Main St, S, 06798
(203)266-4211   39 63
18th & 19th C English & country furniture, desks, clocks, watercolors, porcelains, pottery, brass, pewter & linens
for the discriminating buyer, all in a
Greek revival house located in the
Woodbury historic district. *Est:* 1984.
Serv: Purchase estates. *Hours:* Wed-
Mon 11-5. *Size:* Medium. *CC:* MC/V.
Patricia Murphy-Sadlier *Park:* On
site. *Loc:* I-84 Exit 15: 5 MI E on Rte
6.

PETER A NELSON
881 Main St, S, 06798
(203)263-5881   29 37
American antique furniture & quality
decorative arts to 1840. Buying di-
rected toward interests of the serious
collector. *Serv:* All pieces sold with a
guarantee. *Hours:* Mon-Sat 10-5.
Assoc: AAA ADA.

NEW ENGLAND FIREBACKS
161 Main St, S, 06798
(203)263-4328   2 70 74
Reproduction American 18th C firebacks, handcasted in Connecticut. *Est:*
1986. *Serv:* Mail order, brochure.
Hours: At Woodbury Blacksmiths &
by appt. Patricia Eustou *Park:* On site.

NININGER & COMPANY LTD
4 Main St, S, 06798
(203)266-4661   19 70 71
Occasional tables of distinction with a
fine selection for sale in the gallery,
designers & crafter of special order

furniture, restorers & conservators of
fine antiques. *Pr:* $600–6000. *Est:*
1979. *Serv:* Brochure, conservation,
custom woodwork, repairs, replication, reproduction. *Hours:* Wed-Mon
10:30-5 Sun 1-5. *Size:* Medium. *CC:*
MC/V. *Park:* In front. *Loc:* At the Int
of Rtes 6 & 47.

ART & PEGGY PAPPAS
ANTIQUES
PO Box 335, 06798
(203)266-0374   1 5 43
17th, 18th & 19th C American antiques & reproductions, 18th, 19th &
20th C architectural elements for restoration & decoration, including hardware, flooring, beams, mantles,
windows, doors & cutstones. *Serv:*
Consultation, custom woodwork, purchase estates, replication, reproduction. *Hours:* BY APPT ONLY.

PINE WOODS ANTIQUES
681 Main St, N, 06798
(203)266-0700   41 42
Featuring painted & polished pine furniture & accessories from Scandinavia.
Hours: Thu-Sun 10-5 or BY APPT.
Loc: 1.8 MI from Rte 47.

THE POLISHED SNEAKER
137 Main St, S, 06798
(203)266-4847
Consignment antiques & used furniture. *Est:* 1986. *Hours:* Tue-Fri 11-4
Sat,Sun 11-5. *CC:* MC/V. *Park:* In
front.

EMILIE J RAHHAL
319 Main St, S, 06798
(203)263-4646   21
Oriental & Navajo rugs. *Hours:* By
Chance/Appt.

RAMASE
266 Washington Rd Rte 47, 06798
(203)263-3332   **5 74**
General old building materials including hewn beams, wide flooring, paneled room ends, wall boards, doors, moldings, mantels, old window glass, old brick, early American hardware, cupboards & weathered barn siding. *Est:* 1960. *Hours:* Fri-Sat 8-4 BY APPT. Harold Cole *Park:* On site. *Loc:* 1.5 MI from Int of Rtes 46 & 7.

MONIQUE SHAY ANTIQUES
920 Main St, S, 06798
(203)263-3186   **36 41**
Three large barns of 19th C Canadian antiques including painted armoires, cupboards, tables & chairs. *Pr:* $100–10000. *Hours:* Daily 10-5. *Size:* Huge. *Park:* On site. *Loc:* I-84 Exit 15: to Rte 6N, 3 MI on L.

SOUTHFORD ANTIQUES
813 Main St, S, 06798
(203)263-5028   **37 47 83**
Early American, Victorian & country furniture & accessories & vintage jewelry. *Est:* 1979. *Serv:* Appraisal, conservation, purchase estates, repairs. *Hours:* Mon-Fri 11-4:30 Sat,Sun 12-5 CLOSED TUE. Jean Reeve *Park:* On site. *Loc:* I-84 Exit 15: to Rte 6N, 6 MI.

STERLING AUCTIONS LTD
289 Main St, S, 06798
(203)263-5700   **8**
Auctions featuring furniture, clocks, paintings, jewelry, china, silver, rugs, guns & toys. *Serv:* Purchase single items or estates, accept consignments.

EVE STONE & SON ANTIQUES
319 Main St, S, 06798
(203)266-4802   **16 37 83**
Fine, rare & unusual distinctive formal & country American furniture, 17th & 18th C English & Dutch copper & brass. *Serv:* Appraisal, consultation. *Hours:* Wed-Mon 10-6. *CC:* AX/MC/V. Susan Stone-Downs *Park:* On site. *Loc:* I-84 Exit 15: to Rte 6N, in ctr of town.

ROBERT S WALIN ANTIQUES
547 Flanders Rd, 06798
(203)263-4416   **34 37**
18th & 19th C American furniture, accessories & folk art. *Est:* 1966. *Serv:* Purchase estates. *Hours:* By chance/appt suggested. *Park:* On site. *Loc:* I-84 to Rte 6, 3 MI N of the town of Woodbury.

MADELINE WEST ANTIQUES
Main St, S (At War Memorial), 06798
(203)263-4604   **29 60**
Decorative accessories for the intermediate & advanced collector, Oriental paintings, prints, fine porcelain & Staffordshire plates. *Est:* 1960. *Hours:* Daily 10-5.

WEST COUNTRY ANTIQUES
334 Washington Rd Rte 47, 06798
(203)263-5741   **27 42**
Specialize in 18th & 19th C English, Irish & European polished pine & country furniture & decorative items. *Est:* 1982. *Hours:* Wed-Sun 10-5. *CC:* MC/V. *Park:* On site. *Loc:* I-84 Exit 15: 1.5 MI N of Main St on Rte 47.

WOODBURY BLACKSMITH & FORGE CO
161 Main St, S, 06798
(203)263-5737   **2 71 74**
Early American wrought iron hardware, custom fireplace tools, accessories, brackets, hangers & hooks, latches, hinges, door knockers & foot

scrapers. *Serv:* Custom order, catalog ($2). *Hours:* Mon-Fri 8-5 Sat BY APPT. *CC:* MC/V. *Park:* On site.

WOODBURY HOUSE
494 Main St, S, 06798
(203)263-3407   **1 4 23**

Americana, books & clocks. *Est:* 1968. *Serv:* Appraisal. *Hours:* Thu-Sat 12-5. *CC:* MC/V. *Assoc:* ISA CAB CADA. Bernie McManus *Park:* On site.

WOODBURY PEWTERERS
Rte 6, 06798
(203)263-2668   **16 70**

Reproduction of early American pewter - including pieces from the Henry Ford Museum, the Mystic Seaport collection & a personal collection. Some factory seconds at a discount. *Serv:* Repairs of their own pieces. *Hours:* Mon-Sat 9-5, Christmas-Apr Mon-Fri. Ray Titcomb *Park:* On site. *Loc:* I-84 Exit 15.

Woodstock

ARMAN ABSENTEE AUCTION
PO Box 174, 06281
(203)928-0873   **8**

Antiques reference books & books on collecting auctioned periodically. *Serv:* Catalogs. David Arman

Woodstock Valley

NORMAN C HECKLER & CO
Bradford Corner Rd, 06282
(203)974-1634   **8**

Full-service public auction company specializing in auction sales of bottles, flasks, fruit jars & glass objects. *Serv:* Accept mail bids.

Yalesville

VICTOR A DENETTE
BOOKS/EPHEMERA
31 Chapel St, 06492
(203)269-9818   **13**

A general stock of antiquarian books. *Serv:* Appraisal, search service. *Hours:* Tue-Sat 9-5. *Assoc:* CAB.

UNIQUE ANTIQUES & COLLECTIBLES
409 Main St, 06492
(203)265-7255   **23 55 83**

Interesting shop in turn of century post office with a diverse line of antiques & collectibles & a bargain barn. *Pr:* $1–2500. *Est:* 1984. *Serv:* Appraisal, purchase estates, repair, restoration. *Hours:* Tue-Fri 10-5 Sat 11-5 Sun by chance/appt. *Size:* Medium. Rick Termini *Park:* On site. *Loc:* Rte 68 to Britannia Spoon Restaurant to Main St, 200 yds up. I-91 Exit 15: to Rte 68 W to Main St, Yalesville.

Maine

Albion

COCK HILL FARM
Bessey Ridge Rd, 04910
(207)437-2345   **32 34 65**
Folk art, toys, primitives, comic books, comic toys & memorabilia. *Hours:* BY APPT. *Assoc:* MADA. Barbara J Thornsjo

Alfred

ALFRED TRADING COMPANY
Village Sq, 04002
(207)324-8355   **27 40 42**
Country antiques, tools, oak & pine furniture, quilts, linens & tins. *Hours:* Open all year. Fred Price

PATRICIAN DESIGNS
1 Court St, 04002
(207)324-3555   **27 40**
Refinished oak furniture, country & Victorian accessories. *Est:* 1978. *Hours:* Sum: daily 10-5, Win: by chance/appt. *CC:* MC/V. Patricia Marley *Loc:* Rtes 202, 4 & 111.

SHIRETOWN ANTIQUE CENTER
Rte 202, 04002
(207)324-3755   **{GR50}**
Country furniture, primitives, oak & collectibles. *Est:* 1983. *Hours:* Jun-Sep Mon-Sat 10-5 Oct-May CLOSED TUE. *Size:* Medium. *CC:* MC/V. Joan Sylvester *Park:* In front. *Loc:* 1 MI N of Alfred Village Sq.

Anson

PHILL A MC INTYRE & DAUGHTERS
PO Box 231, 04911
(207)696-5809   **8**
Antique & estate auctions usually held at the Morrill auction facility in Gray Maine. 10% buyer's premium. *Serv:* Auctioneer.

Arundel

ARUNDEL ANTIQUES
US Rte 1,
(207)985-7965   **{GR200}**
A large group shop featuring a wide selection of antiques. *Hours:* Daily 10-5 CLOSED TUE,WED. Joanne S Desjardins *Loc:* Between Biddeford & Kennebunk.

Auburn

MORIN'S ANTIQUES
195 Turner St, 04210
(207)782-7511   **40**
Specializing in refinished oak for home & office. *Hours:* Mon-Fri 9-5. Diane Landry, Mgr

ORPHAN ANNIE'S
96 Court St, 04210
(207)782-0638   **7 77 85**
Art glass by Tiffany, Durand, Steuben, Lalique, Daum, Leverre Francais, decorative lighting from art nouveau & art deco periods, perfumes, jewelry, vintage clothing, pottery, silver, Orientalia & collectibles. *Pr:* $5–5000. *Est:* 1977. *Serv:* Purchase estates.

Hours: Mon-Sat 10-5 Sun 12-5. *CC:* AX/MC/V. Daniel Poulin *Park:* On site. *Loc:* ME Tnpk Exit 12: 2.5 MI to Auburn, R at 3rd light, 4 blocks, on R, across from County Court House.

Augusta

PINE TREE STABLES
ANTIQUES
1095 Riverside Dr, 04330
(207)622-4857   **23 44 50**

Art glass, baskets, primitives, watches, clocks, cut glass, flow blue, majolica, lamps, lanterns, prints, brides baskets & rose bowls. *Hours:* Tue-Sun 9-5. *Assoc:* MADA. Harold Bulger *Loc:* On Rte 201.

READING TREASURES
BOOKSHOP
W River Rd, 04330
(207)622-2047   **13**

A general collection of antiquarian books with an emphasis on early children's literature, Maine books & New England writers. *Serv:* Search service. *Hours:* Year round Tue-Fri afternoons Sat mornings or BY APPT. *Assoc:* MABA. Gertrude Harrington

WHITE BARN ANTIQUES
Riverside Dr, 04330
(207)622-6096   **32 44 63**

Glass, china, toys, still banks & furniture. *Hours:* Apr-Dec Mon-Sat 10:30-3 Sun by chance. *Assoc:* MADA. Eleanor N Merrill *Loc:* Rte 201N, 6 MI N of Memorial Bridge.

Bangor

T J BURKE ORIENTAL RUGS
48 Columbia St, 04401
(207)942-8872   **21**

Antique/semi-antique Oriental rugs, carpets, kilims, tapestries & tribal trappings. *Pr:* $100–35000. *Est:* 1978. *Serv:* Appraisal, conservation, purchase estates, repairs, restoration. *Hours:* Mon-Fri 10-5:30 Sat 10-2 Sun BY APPT, call ahead. *Size:* Medium. *Park:* In front. *Loc:* I-95 Hammond St Exit: take 1 R, on R past YMCA & Court House, from Main St 2nd L (Cross St) to Int Columbia St.

GAMAGE ANTIQUES
60 Main St, 04401
(207)945-6226   **36 50 59**

Formal & country furniture, lamps, paintings, rugs, china, glass & jewelry. *Hours:* Mon-Sat. *Assoc:* MADA. Hedda Gamage

LIPPINCOTT BOOKS
624 Hammond St, 04401
(207)942-4398   **13 33**

Four centuries of old & rare books, wide variety of subjects - especially Maine, ephemera, periodicals & some uncommon books. *Pr:* $1–1000. *Est:* 1975. *Serv:* Appraisal, purchase estates. *Hours:* Tue-Sat 10-5:30. *Assoc:* MABA. Bill Lippincott *Park:* In front. *Loc:* I-95 Exit 46: bear R, .5 MI on R.

Bar Harbor

ROSE W OLSTEAD
200 Main St, 04609
(207)288-5494   **1 37**

A select grouping of American period

furniture & decorative accessories displayed in room like settings - including nautical items, lighting devices & metal ware. *Est:* 1946. *Hours:* Mon-Sat 10-5:30.

STEVE POWELL
The Hideaway, 04609
(207)288-4665   13
Large stock of antiquarian mystery books & related items. *Pr:* $5–1500. *Est:* 1983. *Serv:* Catalog. *Hours:* BY APPT. *CC:* MC/V. *Assoc:* MABA. *Park:* On site.

Bath

RECENT PAST
17 Western Ave, 04530
(207)443-4407   48 83
Victorian & country specializing in textiles & linens. *Hours:* By chance/appt. *Assoc:* MADA. Pauline J Thibodeau

TRIFLES
21 Elm St, 04530
(207)442-8474   29
Decorative accessories - antique smalls of the 19th C, emphasis on classically oriented pieces. *Est:* 1986. *Serv:* English tea room serving lunch & afternoon tea. *Hours:* Mon-Fri 11-4 rainy Sats. Helen Robinson *Park:* In front. *Loc:* 2 blocks from Rte 1 in downtown Bath.

Belfast

ANDREWS & ANDREWS
Rte 1, 04915
(207)338-1386   8
Auctioneers offering antiques from area estates. *Serv:* Appraisal. Daniel W Andrews

APEX ANTIQUES
98 High St, 04915
(207)338-1194   5 36
A Victorian carriage house featuring American & European formal & country furniture, architectural details & accessories. *Hours:* Sum: daily 9-6, Win: by chance/appt. *Assoc:* MADA. G Davanzo

BOOKLOVER'S ATTIC
Rte 1, 04915
(207)338-2450   13
Antiquarian books: American first editions, music, maritime, aviation, Americana, science fiction, hunting, fishing, exploration, recordings (lp's): jazz, Broadway shows, sound tracks, classical & vocal. *Hours:* May-Oct 11-6 daily CLOSED TUE. *Assoc:* MABA. Peter Plumb *Park:* Nearby. *Loc:* Rte 1 N just over bridge.

CHECKERED PAST ANTIQUES CENTER
117 High St, 04915
(207)338-5571   {GR17}
Furniture, country, primitives & small amount of glass. *Est:* 1987. *Hours:* Sum: Mon-Sat 10-5 Sun by chance/appt, Win: Tue-Sat 10-5. *Park:* Nearby. *Loc:* Downtown.

AVIS HOWELLS ANTIQUES
21 Pearl St, 04915
(207)338-3302   **37**

In a white Victorian home, specializing in things Shaker or Canton & American furniture pre 1850. *Hours:* By chance/appt. *Assoc:* MADA. *Loc:* At corner Court & Pearl Sts.

Belgrade

BORSSEN ANTIQUES
Rte 135, 04917
(207)495-2013   **40**

A large selection of oak furniture. *Est:* 1967. *Serv:* Restoration, refinishing. *Hours:* All year Daily. *Loc:* 1.5 MI S of Town Hall.

Belmont

BARBARA PATTERSON'S ANTIQUES
Rte 3, 04915
(207)342-5766   **63 67**

Cupboards, quilts & rugs, American art pottery, amusing & decorative objects & functional early furniture. *Hours:* Daily CLOSED THU, summer evenings. *Assoc:* MADA. *Loc:* 8 MI W of Belfast in an old red Cape.

Bernard

1895 SHOP
1 Steamboat Wharf Rd, 04612
(207)244-7039   **23 44 64**

Glass, china, collectibles, post cards, lamps & clocks. *Hours:* Seasonal. Louise Kelley *Loc:* Off Rte 102.

ANTIQUE WICKER
Just Off Rte 102, 04612
(207)244-3983   **86**

Two hundred pieces of antique wicker in stock at all times. *Est:* 1976. *Serv:* Will ship anywhere. *Hours:* Sum: daily 10-5, Win: anytime by chance/appt. Edward Higgins *Park:* On site. *Loc:* 4 MI beyond Southwest Harbor.

NANCY NEALE TYPECRAFT
Steamboat Wharf Rd, 04612
(207)244-5192   **12 16**

Specialists in antique woodtype & pieces relating to printing, type trays, type sticks, metal fonts & complete fonts. Unique museum-like shop displaying type made from 1880s to 1940s. Cuts used for illustrations & newspapers, Hebrew type & German type. *Serv:* Catalog, mail order, collages representing family history made to order. *Hours:* Jun-Aug by chance/appt.

THE OLD RED STORE
2 Steamboat Wharf Rd, 04612
(207)244-3349   **44 63**

Mainly china, glass & small furniture. *Est:* 1974. *Hours:* Jun 15-Sep 15 Mon-Fri 10-1 2-5, else by chance/appt. Paul Hinton *Park:* Nearby.

ONCE UPON A TIME
Rte 102, 04612
(207)244-3745   **7 40 47**

Extensive collection of silver, gold, costume jewelry, art deco - Victorian to 1950s - including art nouveau, Edwardian, quilts, linens, china & oak furniture displayed in a small barn. *Pr:* $5–300. *Est:* 1971. *Hours:* Jun-Sep 9-6 by chance/appt. *CC:* MC/V. Doris Simon *Park:* In front. *Loc:* 3 MI past Southwest Harbor, .5 MI short of Bernard.

Biddeford

BIDDEFORD ANTIQUE CENTER
Rte 1, 04005
(207)284-6433 **{GR40+}**
Furniture, paintings, primitives, linens, fine glass, china & collectibles. *Est:* 1987. *Hours:* Daily 9:30-4:30 Nov-Mar CLOSED TUE,WED. *CC:* MC/V. Dolly Curran *Park:* On site. *Loc:* I-95 Exit 4: N on Rte 111 to Rte 1, S about 1.5 MI.

ELI THE COBBLER ANTIQUES
30 Morin St, 04005
(207)282-1028 **44 47**
Oriental & art glass & jewelry. *Est:* 1972. *Hours:* Year round Mon-Fri 9-3. *Loc:* Just around the corner from the Biddeford Antique Center.

Blue Hill

EMERSON'S ANTIQUES
Main St, 04614
(207)374-5140 **29**
Antiques & decorative accessories - mostly New England & pre-1845. *Est:* 1963. *Hours:* Mon-Fri 10-5 Sat 11-3. *CC:* MC/V. Brad Emerson *Park:* On street.

LIROS GALLERY
Main St, 04614
(207)374-5370 **51 59 66**
Fine paintings, old prints, maps & Russian icons. *Est:* 1966. *Serv:* Restoration. *Hours:* Year round Mon-Fri 9-5 Sat BY APPT. *CC:* AX/MC/V. *Park:* On street. *Loc:* Next to Jonathans Restaurant in Blue Hill.

Boothbay

BLUE UNICORN
Rte 27, 04537
(207)633-6499 **44**
Furniture, flint, Heisey, toy glass & china. *Hours:* Seasonally daily 10-5 Sun 12-5. *Assoc:* MADA. Glenn Buell

Boothbay Harbor

BAY STREET ANTIQUES
2 Bay St, 04538
(207)633-3186 **3 44 63**
Art glass (Tiffany, Nash, Daum, Galle, Lalique) early 20th C American art pottery (Newcomb, Ohr, Rookwood, Grueby), American Indian baskets & pottery, art nouveau, arts & crafts, art deco, Chinese items, Japanese prints, folk art & ephemera. *Pr:* $5–7500. *Est:* 1980. *Hours:* Jun 15-Sep Mon-Sat 10-5. *Assoc:* MADA. Tom R Cavanaugh *Park:* On site. *Loc:* Follow Atlantic Ave to Bay Street, turn L (E side of Boothbay Harbor).

COLLECTOR SHOP
Lakeside Dr & Middle Rd, 04538
(207)633-2215 **23 36 44**
Furniture, glass, china, clocks, lamps, tin & post cards. *Est:* 1982. *Hours:* Most days 10-5. Ed Swett *Park:* On site. *Loc:* 5th business on L after Boothbay post office.

GLEASON FINE ART AT MCKOWN ST
16 McKown St, 04538
(207)633-2336 **59 66**
19th & 20th C American paintings, with emphasis on artists who have ties to the Boothbay Harbor region, in-

cluding Monhegan Island. *Pr:* $5–10000. *Est:* 1987. *Serv:* Appraisal, consultation, purchase estates. *Hours:* May-mid Oct Tue-Sat, else by chance/appt. *CC:* AX/MC. Dennis Gleason *Loc:* Rte 27 to Boothbay Harbor, in white house at McKown Sq.

JOSEPHINE HURD ANTIQUES
92 Commercial St, 04538
(207)633-4732   **44**

Early glass & large selection of Portland glass patterns. *Hours:* Jul-Sep daily 10-4. *Assoc:* MADA. *Loc:* White house with goblets in the window.

Brewer

FRAN & DEAN'S ANTIQUES
21 Silk St, 04112
(207)989-5740   **65 81**

Tools & primitives. *Hours:* BY APPT ONLY. *Assoc:* MADA. Frances Pennypacker

MCLEOD MILITARY ANTIQUES
1087 N Main St, 04412
(207)989-1429   **6 20**

Maine's only shop devoted to military antiques, all wars & all nations - Nazi, Japanese, G.I., Viet Cong, Union or Confederate. *Pr:* $1–1000. *Serv:* Appraisal, catalog, consultation, purchase estates. *Hours:* Daily 12-5. *CC:* MC/V. Ralph McLeod *Park:* In front. *Loc:* Rte 9 in Brewer is N Main Street, 3 MI E of ctr of town.

SCOTT'S BOOKS
121 Parker St, 04412
(207)989-2459   **13**

12,000-15,000 volumes, hard covers,

nonfiction & many subjects. *Hours:* By chance/appt. *Assoc:* MABA. Scott Servisky

Bridgton

BRIDGTON BOOK HOUSE
Depot St, 04009
(207)647-2546   **13**

General collection in various categories. *Hours:* Jul-Labor Day Mon,Tue,Thu,Fri 10-4:30 Sat 10-1. *Assoc:* MABA. Elizabeth Medbury *Loc:* Off Rte 302.

M SPENCER
RFD 2 Box 123, 04009
(207)647-8144   **59 66**

Large selection of fine paintings & prints. *Hours:* BY APPT ONLY.

WALES & HAMBLEN ANTIQUE CENTER
134 Main St, 04009
(207)647-8344   **{GR30}**

Victorian, oak & country furniture & decorative accessories. *Serv:* Restoration, refinishing. *Hours:* Daily 10-5.

Brooklin

GEORGE & PATRICIA FOWLER, BOOKS
Reach Rd, 04616
(207)359-2070   **13**

Antiquarian books: Western Americana, children's literature, storytelling modern literature, letters, memoirs & biography. *Serv:* Search service, catalog. *Hours:* MAIL ORDER ONLY. *Assoc:* MABA.

Brunswick

CROSS HILL BOOKS
9 Noble St, 04011
(207)729-8531   13
Specializing in nautical books. Catalogs issued concerning sea, ships, sailing, maritime & naval history & yachting. *Pr:* $5–500. *Est:* 1977. *Serv:* Appraisal, free catalog, search services. *Hours:* BY APPT. *Assoc:* MABA. William W Hill *Park:* In front. *Loc:* US Rte 1, Pleasant St to Main St, R onto Main St S for .5 MI, R on Noble 2nd house on L.

ROBERT E DYSINGER - BOOKS
5 Stanwood St, 04011
(207)729-1229   13
19th C Americana & American literary first editions. *Serv:* Search service. *Hours:* By chance/appt. *Assoc:* MABA.

GORDON'S BOOKSHOP
14 Center St, 04011
(207)725-2500   13
Antiquarian books: travel, natural science, art, WW I, WW II, maritime & marine. *Hours:* Mon-Sat 10-5. *Assoc:* MABA. Marilyn A Gordon

MARILYN NULMAN, BOOK REPAIR
9 Noble St, 04011
(207)729-6449   12 68
Book repair & book binding, acid-free slipcases. *Hours:* BY APPT ONLY. *Assoc:* MABA.

OLD BOOKS
136 Maine St, 04011
(207)725-4524   13
Large selection with emphasis on liter-

ature. *Hours:* Mon-Sat 10-5 CLOSED THU,SUN. *Assoc:* MABA. Clare C Howell

CHARLES VINCENT - BOOKS
1 Maple St, 04011
(207)729-7854   13
Rare antiquarian books & collectibles in all subjects. *Hours:* By chance/appt. *Assoc:* MABA.

WALFIELD THISTLE
381 Bath Rd, 04011
(207)443-3986   13
8,000 used, out-of-print & scarce books. *Hours:* Mon-Sat 10-5. *Assoc:* MABA. Jean Thistle

Bryant Pond

MOLL OCKETT
Rte 26, 04219
(207)665-2397   13 33 44
Specialize in out-of-print books, advertising, ephemera, small collectibles & pattern glass. *Pr:* $1–300. *Est:* 1968. *Serv:* Appraisal, purchase estates. *Hours:* Apr-Oct Thu-Mon 10-5. *Size:* Large. *Assoc:* MABA. Basil Seguin *Park:* On site. *Loc:* On Rte 26, between Bethel & Norway.

Buckfield

PATRICIA LEDLIE-BOOKSELLER ABAA
Bean Rd, 04220
(207)336-2969   13
One of New England's largest selections of natural history books: books on birds, invertebrates, mammals & reptiles. *Hours:* By chance/appt. *Assoc:* ABAA MABA.

Camden

ABCDEF BOOKSTORE
23 Bay St, 04843
(207)236-3903 13
Americana, European history, literature, music & art. *Hours:* May-Oct 10:30-5 CLOSED JAN-MAR. *Assoc:* ABAA MABA. Lilian Berliawsky

LEVETT'S ANTIQUES
24C Bayview St, 04843
(207)236-8356 **29 36**
18th & 19th C furniture & accessories. *Est:* 1976. *Hours:* Mon-Sat 10-5. Georgia G Levett *Park:* On site. *Loc:* .5 block off Rte 1 in ctr of town.

THE RICHARDS ANTIQUES
93 Elm St US 1, 04843
(207)236-2152 **36 50**
Furniture & accessories for the discriminating collector, lamps a specialty. Large inventory of Woodstock & other fine lamp shades. *Pr:* $1-5000. *Est:* 1948. *Serv:* Purchase estates, repairs, restoration. *Hours:* Jun-Oct daily 10-5 CLOSED WED,SUN, else BY APPT ONLY. *Assoc:* MADA. Chad Richards *Park:* In front. *Loc:* Rte 1, on L entering Camden from S.

SCHUELER ANTIQUES
10 High St Rte 1, 04843
(207)236-2770 1 36 59
Located in a renovated carriage house, where a range of American furniture, decorative accessories, complimentary art & decoys attractively displayed. *Est:* 1947. *Hours:* Jun-Oct 15 Tue-Sat 10-5 Sun 1-5. *Size:* Medium. *Assoc:* MADA. Gay Schueler *Park:* On site. *Loc:* Thru Camden heading N, R at top of town (where Rte 1 heads toward Belfast), 4th house on L.

STONE SOUP BOOKS
35 Main St, 04843
(207)785-2782 **13 14 33**
Out-of-print books - 10,000 titles - specializing in Maine, maritime & poetry. *Est:* 1982. *Hours:* Jun 15-Sep 15 daily 10:30-5, else Fri,Wed 12-5 Sat 10:30-5. *Assoc:* MABA. Paul Joy *Park:* In front. *Loc:* Ctr of downtown Camden, on waterfront side of Main St.

Cape Elizabeth

HANSON'S CARRIAGE HOUSE
3 Two Lights Rd, 04107
(207)767-3608 1 27 80
Country furnishings, textiles, spinning & weaving tools, Shaker & Indian items. *Hours:* Jun-Oct daily 10-5 BY APPT. *Assoc:* MADA. Jean Hanson

LOMBARD ANTIQUARIAN MAP/PRINTS
Box 281, 04107
(207)799-1889 **13 51 66**
Rare 16th-19th C maps, charts of all world regions, specializing in New England, Maine, Winslow Homer wood engravings, early botanical, bird & animal engravings. *Serv:* Catalog, sale by phone & mail, search service. *Hours:* BY APPT ONLY. *Assoc:* MABA MADA. Reginald T Lombard Jr

Cape Neddick

THE BARN AT CAPE NEDDICK
US Rte 1, 03902
(207)363-7315 {GR12}
Smalls, glass, oak & pine furniture, pottery & general line. *Est:* 1986.

Hours: Daily 10-5. *CC:* MC/V. Gerald McDaniels *Park:* On site. *Loc:* I-95 York Exit: Rte 1, 3 MI N.

CRANBERRY HILL ANTIQUES/LIGHTING
Rte 1, 03902
(207)363-5178   **50 65**
General line of antiques in as found condition, largest lampshade/lamp parts selection north of Boston. *Pr:* $1–4000. *Est:* 1971. *Serv:* Appraisal, repairs, replication, reproduction, restoration. *Hours:* Jun-Sep Wed-Mon 9:30-5, else Wed-Mon 10-4. *Size:* Large. *CC:* MC/V. Tony Anni *Park:* On site. *Loc:* I-95N The Yorks/Ogunquit Exit: R to Rte 1N, L onto Rte 1N, 3.2 MI on L, diagonally across from Cape Neddick Inn.

Cape Porpoise

PADDY'S COVE ANTIQUES
Ward Rd, 04014
(207)967-4842   **27 65**
Country furniture, cupboards, accessories & primitives. *Est:* 1976. *Hours:* May-Nov daily 10-5, Win: BY APPT. *Assoc:* MADA. Priscilla Flannery *Park:* On site. *Loc:* 2 MI from Kennebunkport off Rte 9.

Caribou

AUNTIE BEA'S ANTIQUES
Madawaska Rd, 04736
(207)498-8721   **44**
Depression, carnival, pattern, cut glass, tin primitives, baskets, small furniture, dolls & doll furniture,. *Hours:* Sum:

Daily 9-9, else weekends & evenings. Roger Thompson *Loc:* Off I-89 on the Madawaska Rd.

THE BARN DOOR
724 N Main St, 04736
(207)492-0432   **23 67 81**
Cupboards, primitives, clocks, oil lamps, quilts, tools, tin, woodenware, furniture, advertising items, brass bells & wooden sculptures. *Est:* 1968. *Hours:* Sum: Tue-Sat 9-5, Win: Fri-Sat 9-5. Valeska Lombard *Park:* Nearby. *Loc:* Just N of the airport.

CHARLOTTE'S DOLLS & COLLECTIBLES
Madawaska Rd, 04736
(207)498-8937   **32**
Dolls: old, new & antique. *Hours:* Year round daily 9-9 by chance. Charlotte St Peter *Loc:* Just off I-89 on the Madawaska Rd.

JUDY'S ANTIQUES
Sweden St Plaza, 04736
(207)498-2006   **27 44 63**
Glass, china, collectibles, baskets, country items, kitchenware, Roseville pottery, furniture & woodenware. *Est:* 1985. *Hours:* All year Mon-Sat 9:30-5. *CC:* MC/V. Judy Solman *Park:* Nearby. *Loc:* 1 block from post office.

Castine

BARBARA FALK - BOOKSELLER
Rte 166A, 04421
(207)326-4036   **13 33**
Antiquarian books: literature, children's, women writer's & ephemeral material. *Hours:* Year round by chance/appt call ahead. *Assoc:* MABA.

Cundys Harbor

BOOK PEDLARS
Holbrook St, 04011
(207)729-0087   **13**

Out-of-print Maine books, children's illustrated books & Americana. *Hours:* By chance/appt. *Assoc:* MABA. Wally O'Brien

Cushing

NEVILLE ANTIQUES
Pleasant Point Rd, 04563
(207)354-8055   **10 56**

Barometers, nautical antiques, porcelains, children's furniture & decorative accessories. *Hours:* BY APPT ONLY. *Assoc:* MADA. *Loc:* 9 MI from Thomaston off Rte 1.

Damariscotta

ROGER & BEE BENNETT
Bristol Rd, 04543
(207)563-5013   **44 50 81**

Quality early American pattern glass (1830-1890), including Portland & Sandwich glass, lamps & some early tools. *Hours:* Late May to mid Oct. *Assoc:* MADA. *Loc:* Call for directions.

BROOKMEAD FARM
Bus Rte 1, 04543
(207)563-5410   **36 44 47**

Furniture, glass, china & jewelry. *Hours:* Daily 9-4. Eric Jensen

COOPER'S RED BARN
Bus Rte 1, 04543
(207)563-3714   **13 44 81**

Two story barn filled with books, furniture, glass, antique tools & old picture frames. *Est:* 1945. *Hours:* Daily 9-5. *Size:* Large. *Park:* On site. *Loc:* .75 MI heading E out of Damariscotta.

ELLIOTT HEALY PHOTOGRAPHICA
Egypt Rd, 04543
(207)563-5841   **13 51 62**

Photography books & images, fine arts, books on antiques, illustrated & children's books, prints & maps. *Hours:* BY APPT ONLY. *Assoc:* MABA.

THE MAPLES
Bristol Rd, 04543
(207)563-8565   **27 30 83**

Country & Victorian antiques, crafts, folk art & decoys. *Est:* 1985. *Hours:* May-Oct daily 10-5, else BY APPT. *Park:* On site. *Loc:* 2 MI from downtown on Rte 130 heading S.

PINE CHESTS & THINGS
Bristol Rd, 04543
(207)563-3267   **27 30 65**

Country furniture, primitives, looms, spinning wheels & duck decoys. *Est:* 1962. *Hours:* By chance/appt. *Assoc:* MADA. Richard Else

PATRICIA ANNE REED ANTIQUES
Bristol Rd HC 61, 04543
(207)563-5633   **5 34 59**

Gallery full of Americana, early furniture, paintings, porcelain, toys, fabrics, folk art, architectural pieces & decorative objects. *Serv:* Appraisal, consultation, interior design, purchase estates. *Hours:* May 15-Oct Mon-Sat 9-6 Sun by chance/appt. *Size:* Medium. *Park:* On site. *Loc:* .5 MI from Baptist Church, toward Pemaquid Point.

PETER/JEAN RICHARDS FINE ANTIQUE
The Bristol Rd Route 130, 04543
(207)563-1964   **37 39 77**
Fine 18th & early 19th C American & English furniture & accessories, including silver, brass, tea caddies, paintings & rugs. *Serv:* Appraisal, consultation, purchase estates. *Hours:* May 15-Sep Mon-Sat 10-6, else BY APPT. *CC:* AX/MC/V. *Assoc:* MADA NHADA. *Park:* On site. *Loc:* Rte 1, Business Rte 1 into Damariscotta, S on Rtes 129-130, toward Pemaquid & Bristol, .7 MI to shop in red barn on L.

Deer Isle

BELCHER'S ANTIQUES
Reach Rd, 04627
(207)348-9938   **1 34**
Three large rooms & attached barn of 19th C farmhouse featuring advertising items, country furniture & unusual accessories. *Pr:* $50–1500. *Serv:* Restoration. *Hours:* Jul-Sep daily 10-5, else by chance/appt. *Size:* Medium. Linda Friedmann *Park:* In front. *Loc:* Rte 15 on Deer Isle, .1 MI from Reach Road Monument, clearly marked with highway signs.

Denmark

BRUCE D COLLINS FINE ART
RR1 Box 113, 04022
(207)452-2197   **8**
Periodic auctions of American & European paintings & graphics. 10%

buyer's premium. Absentee & telephone bidding can be arranged. *Serv:* Auctions, consignments accepted, catalogs. *Loc:* Auctions held at Seaboard Auction Gallery, Rte 236 Eliot ME. Rte 95 N Exit 3B.

C E GUARINO
Berry Rd, 04022
(207)452-2123   **8 51 66**
Absentee auction house holding six auctions a year in historical American ephemera, antique prints, maps, photographs, posters & Indian artifacts. *Est:* 1973. *Serv:* Auction, mailing list, appraisal. *CC:* MC/V. *Park:* On site. *Loc:* Rte 117 1 MI from the Village of Denmark.

Dresden

MATHOM BOOKSHOP & BINDERY
Blinn Hill Rd, 04342
(207)737-8806   **9 12 13**
Antiquarian books: Maine, women's studies, modern first, autographs, scholarly & out-of-print, literature, history & poetry. *Hours:* By chance/appt best to call ahead. *Assoc:* MABA. Lewis Turco

East Lebanon

MICKLESTREET RARE BOOKS/MOD 1STS
RFD 1, 04027
(207)457-1042   **13**
10,000 volumes including medicine, architecture, Americana, literature, theatre & fine printing. *Serv:* Catalogs issued. *Hours:* BY APPT ONLY.

Assoc: MABA. Viola Morris *Loc:* Off Rte 202 corner of New Road and Jim Grant Rd.

East Livermore

ALDEN PRATT, BOOKS
Star Rte, 04228
(207)897-6979   13

Used & out-of-print books, including Maine town & country histories, books of local interest & Civil War. *Hours:* BY APPT. *Assoc:* MABA. *Loc:* Rte 133 to Rte 106N, 1 MI.

East Winthrop

LAKESIDE ANTIQUES
Rte 202, 04364
(207)377-2616   {GR45}

Two floors of pine, oak, walnut, Victorian furniture, cupboards, chests, tables, tools, toys & Victorian accessories. *Hours:* Daily 7-5, Win: CLOSED MON,TUE. Ormond Piper *Loc:* 4 MI W of ME Tnpk on Rte 202.

Eliot

BOOKS & AUTOGRAPHS
287 Goodwin Rd, 03903
(207)439-4739   9 13 62

Signed & limited editions of 20th C writers, autographs, letters, manuscripts, signed photographs with emphasis on the performing arts, including the opera, movies & theatre. *Hours:* Year round BY APPT ONLY. *Assoc:* ABAA MABA. Sherman R Emery

SEABOARD AUCTION GALLERY
Rte 236, 03903
(207)439-4515   8

Antique and Estate auctions. *Assoc:* MAA NHAA NAA. Martin Willis *Loc:* I-95 Exit 3-B: Southbound Exit 2 in Kittery Rte 236 N Approx 3 MI. 5 MI from Portsmouth.

Ellsworth

BIG CHICKEN BARN - BOOKS
Rte 1, 04605
(207)667-7308   13

Collection of 90,000 books, magazines & paperbacks including Maine, nautical, religion, Americana, mysteries, children's, cookbooks & medical. *Hours:* Mar-Christmas, Spring & Fall daily 9-4, Sum: daily 9-5. *Assoc:* MABA. Annegret Cukierski

CALISTA STERLING ANTIQUES
Bayside Rd Rte 230, 04605
(207)667-8991   29 36

Formal & country period furniture & accessories in 2 shops. *Est:* 1934. *Hours:* May-Oct daily 10-5:30, Nov-Apr by chance/appt. *CC:* MC/V. *Assoc:* MADA. *Park:* In front. *Loc:* 4 MI from ctr of Ellsworth, look for signs.

CINDY'S ANTIQUES
Bucksport Rd, 04605
(207)667-4476   40 77 86

Country, Victorian, oak furniture, wicker, smalls, decoys, flint glass & silver. *Hours:* Daily. *Assoc:* MADA. Lawrence Clough *Loc:* Rtes 1 & 3.

DOWNEAST ANTIQUE CENTER
40 Water St, 04605
(207)667-9351   **{GR13}**

Furniture, decorative accessories, jewelry, post cards & toys. *Est:* 1988. *Serv:* Chair caning. *Hours:* Year round Mon-Sat 9-5 Sun 12-5, CLOSED Dec 26-Jan 1. *CC:* MC/V. A L Jenkins *Park:* On site. *Loc:* 1 block from Union River Bridge on Water St.

Eustis

MACDONALD'S MILITARY
Coburn Gore, 04936
(207)297-2751   **13 62**

Civil War books, papers & photographs, other military & wars & Maine fish & game. *Serv:* Catalogs issued every six weeks - send two stamps. *Hours:* BY APPT ONLY. *Assoc:* MABA. Thomas L MacDonald

Fairfield

JULIA & POULIN ANTIQUES
Skowhegan Rd, 04937
(207)453-2114   **40**

Antique oak furniture. *Est:* 1967. *Hours:* Mon-Sat 9-5. *CC:* MC/V. *Park:* In front. *Loc:* I-95 Exit 36: 1 MI.

JOHN D JULIA ANTIQUES
Rtes 23 & 201, 04937
(207)465-3004   **40 42 86**

Oak, pine, mahogany, wicker & walnut furniture & smalls. *Est:* 1972. *Serv:* Hand carved decoys & wooden animals. *Hours:* TO THE TRADE, call suggested. *Loc:* I-95 Exit 36.

JAMES D JULIA AUCTIONEERS
Skowhegan Rd Rte 201, 04937
(207)453-7904   **8 30 59**

Dealing in fine quality furniture, jewelry, paintings. Special catalog auctions include decoys. Also a showroom with items for sale. *Pr:* $10–100000. *Serv:* Appraisal, brochure, catalog (free), purchase estates. *Hours:* Mon-Fri 9-5. *Size:* Medium. *Assoc:* MAA MADA NAA. *Park:* In front. *Loc:* I-95 Exit 36: on Rte 201, 1 MI N of Fairfield Village.

THISTLE'S
16 Main St, 04937
(207)453-9817   **13 36 66**

Furniture, table-top antiques, & antiquarian books & prints. *Pr:* $10–500. *Serv:* Purchase estates. *Hours:* Mon-Sat 10-5 Sun BY APPT. *Size:* Medium. *Assoc:* MABA. David G Thistle *Park:* On site. *Loc:* I-95 Exit 35 (Fairfield): 1.1 MI S on Main St.

Falmouth

HARD CIDER FARM ORIENTAL RUGS
45 Middle Rd Rte 9, 04105
(207)775-1600   **21**

Fine oriental rugs - antique to modern, large collection of Persian & tribal rugs. *Est:* 1975. *Serv:* Appraisal, conservation, consultation, repairs, restoration. *Hours:* Tue-Sat 10-5 appt appreciated. *Size:* Medium. *CC:* AX/MC/V. R W Tirrell *Park:* On site. *Loc:* I-295 Exit 10 (Falmouth): Rte 9W, L onto Middle Rd, 1.8 MI.

Farmington

ANTIQUES FROM POWDER HOUSE HILL
North St, 04938
(207)778-2946　　　**44 63 81**

Quality tools, china, glass & wood. *Hours:* By chance/appt. *Assoc:* MADA. Wendell A Sweatt *Loc:* At Court House take Anson St for .25 MI, R on North St, 1st house.

MAPLE AVENUE ANTIQUES
23 Maple Ave, 04938
(207)778-4850　　　**27 65**

Primitives, accessories & country furniture. *Hours:* By chance/appt. *Assoc:* MADA. Frank P Dingley *Loc:* Opposite Agway Store on Rte 2.

TOM VEILLEUX GALLERY
Rtes 4 & 149, 04938
(207)778-3719　　　**59 66**

American Impressionists & American women artists for the discriminating collector. Provincetown prints. *Est:* 1972. *Serv:* Purchase American paintings, appraisals, consultation, restoration. *Hours:* BY APPT ONLY.

Farmington Falls

FALLS BOOK BARN
Main St, 04940
(207)778-3429　　　**13 33**

Antiquarian books: biography, classics, cooking, criminology, history, juvenile, Maine, nature, poetry, religion, fiction & ephemera. *Hours:* Year round 10-4 by chance Win: unheated. *Assoc:* MABA. Ethel Emerson

Fort Fairfield

JANDRA'S WOODSHED
24 High St, 04742
(207)473-7331

Furniture, china, glass, oil lamps & stoneware. *Hours:* Mon-Sat 9-5 & BY APPT. *Assoc:* ISA. John C Anderson

Freeport

BOOK CELLAR
36 Main St, 04032
(207)865-3157　　　**13**

Nostalgic fiction, juveniles & biography. *Serv:* Search service. *Hours:* Year round mornings, mostly mail order. *Assoc:* MABA. Dean Chamberlin

FREEPORT ANTIQUE MALL
Rte 1, 04032
(207)865-0607　　　**{GR30}**

Primitives, jewelry, glass, china, pottery, stoneware, furniture & toys. *Hours:* Daily year round. *Loc:* I-95N Exit 17: 5 min S of downtown Freeport.

OLD THYME SHOP
207 Main St, 04032
(207)865-3852　　　**27**

Country pieces & accessories. *Hours:* Mon-Fri 10-4. Barbara Perry

Gardiner

BUNKHOUSE BOOKS
Rte 5A, 04345
(207)582-2808　　　**13**

Maine town & county histories, non-fiction & fiction on Maine, sporting books, novels & general books. *Hours:* May-Oct weekday afternoons. *Assoc:* MABA. Isaac Davis

MCKAY'S ANTIQUES
75 Brunswick Ave, 04345
(207)582-1228   **16 63 65**
Metals, pottery, early china, iron, brasses, tin, firkins & primitives. *Est:* 1980. *Hours:* Sum: daily 10-5 CLOSED MON, Win: by chance/appt. *CC:* MC/V. Irene McKay *Park:* Nearby. *Loc:* On Rte 201 beside 7-11.

MORRELL'S ANTIQUES
106 Highland Ave, 04345
(207)582-4797   **44 63 83**
Quality glass (art, cut & pattern), fine china & choice Victorian collectibles. *Hours:* By chance/appt. *Assoc:* MADA. Hazel I Morrell

PORT OF GARDINER ANTIQUES
252-262 water St, 04345
(207)582-2441   **{GR}**
Furniture, glass, china & collectibles. *Hours:* Tue-Sat 9-5. Loretta Brinzow

FRED ROBBINS
210 Brunswick Ave Rte 201, 04345
(207)582-5005   **6 20 49**
Military, political & campaign material, daguerreotypes & lead soldiers. *Est:* 1968. *Serv:* Appraisal. *Hours:* Mon-Sat 10-5. *Assoc:* NPIC PTAD. *Park:* Nearby. *Loc:* 2 MI from I-95.

Garland

FREDERICA DEBEURS - BOOKS
Upper Garland Rd, 04939
(207)924-7474   **13**
Antiquarian book shop: Specializing in art books & books on science & technology. *Pr:* $1–850. *Est:* 1981. *Serv:* Appraisal, free catalog, search service. *Hours:* By chance/appt. *Assoc:* MABA. *Park:* On site. *Loc:* From Dexter, 5 MI E on Rte 94, take dirt road on L (sign), bookstore is just beyond bend to R.

Gorham

COUNTRY SQUIRE ANTIQUES
Mighty St, 04038
(207)839-4855   **21 44 59**
Bohemian, cranberry & satin glass, porcelain, Limoges lamps, paintings, rugs & furniture. *Est:* 1972. *Hours:* Appt preferred. *Assoc:* MADA. Ed Carr *Park:* On site. *Loc:* 11 MI from Exit 8 on ME Tnpk, 4 MI from ctr of Gorham.

LONGVIEW ANTIQUES
Longview Dr, 04038
(207)839-3020   **21 65 67**
Primitives, quilts, paintings, hooked rugs & country furnishings. *Hours:* Mon or by chance/appt. *Assoc:* MADA. Helen A Woodbrey

Gray

THE BARN ON 26 ANTIQUE CENTER
Rte 26 Poland Spring Rd, 04039
(207)657-3470   {GR20}
Oak, pine, primitives, country items, furniture & glass. *Est:* 1977. *Hours:* May-Oct Tue-Fri 10-5, Nov-Apr daily 10-4 CLOSED MON,TUE. *CC:* MC/V. Fran Demers *Loc:* I-95 Exit 11: 3.5 MI.

Hallowell

BERDAN'S ANTIQUES
151 Water St, 04347
(207)622-0151   **27 34 65**
Furniture, coverlets, folk art, primitives, stoneware, quilts, advertising items & country items. *Est:* 1963. *Hours:* Mon-Sat 10-5 CLOSED SUN & HOLIDAYS. *Assoc:* MADA NHADA. Betty M Berdan *Loc:* Downtown.

D & R ANTIQUES
202 Water St, 04347
(207)623-3020   **23 44 50**
Clocks, china, glass & lamps. *Hours:* Daily 9-5. *Assoc:* MADA. Rowland Hastings

GARY F ELWELL ANTIQUES
15 Middle St, 04347
(207)623-4653   **23 34**
Victorian & revival furnishings, folk art, primitives American tall clocks in a fully-restored mansion in the heart of a national historic district. *Est:* 1966. *Serv:* Appraisal, consultation, clock restoration, purchase estates. *Hours:*

Daily 9:30-6. *Assoc:* NAWCC NEAA. *Park:* On site. *Loc:* 2 blocks from Water St & City Hall.

JAMES H. LE FURGY BOOKS & ANT.
163 Water St, 04347
(207)293-2863   **1 41 59**
American painted furniture & accessories pre-1860 in original condition, 19th & 20th C American paintings, American Indian art, new & out-of-print reference books on the fine & decorative arts. *Pr:* $20-2000. *Serv:* Appraisal, purchase estates. *Hours:* Mon,Wed,Fri,Sat 10-5 appt suggested. *Size:* Medium. *Park:* In front. *Loc:* ME Tnpk Augusta Exit: Rte 202, toward Augusta at rotary turn R on State St S to Hallowell(State St turns to Water St).

MAINELY ANTIQUES
200 Water St, 04347   **44 63**
In a shop overlooking the Kennebunk River: Specializing in American pottery, fiesta & Heisey. *Hours:* Daily 10-4 CLOSED SUN. *Assoc:* MADA.

MOTHER GOOSE ANTIQUES
172 Water St, 04347
(207)623-1752   **47**
Fine antique jewelry. *Est:* 1982. *Hours:* Mon-Sat 9-5. *CC:* AX/MC/V. *Loc:* Downtown.

JOSIAH SMITH ANTIQUES
181 Water St 2nd fl, 04347
(207)622-4188   **44 60 63**
Emphasizing early glass & ceramics, Oriental items with Japanese pottery a specialty, art pottery, art from all periods small, decorative furniture & accessories. *Pr:* $25-2500. *Est:* 1980. *Hours:* All year most days 10-7. *Assoc:*

MADA. Bruce Weber *Park:* Nearby lot. *Loc:* On Rte 201 (Main St), entrance to 2nd fl shop is on Academy St.

LEON TEBBETTS BOOK SHOP
164 Water St, 04347
(207)623-4670   13

Antiquarian books: a general collection of 30,000 volumes in all categories, fiction & nonfiction. *Hours:* Jun-Oct Daily 10-5, Nov-May Sat 10-5 Sun BY APPT. *Assoc:* MABA.

Hamden

GARY W WOOLSON, BOOKSELLER
RFD 1 Box 1576, 04444
(207)234-4931   13 51 66

General line of used & antiquarian books, maps, prints & a few paintings. Specializing in Maine, natural history, literature, art/architectural history. *Pr:* $1–500. *Est:* 1967. *Serv:* Appraisal, lists. *Hours:* Mon-Wed 12-4 by chance/appt. *Assoc:* MABA. *Park:* On site. *Loc:* I-95 Exit 43: toward Winterport on Rte 69, Rte 9, 2 MI, sign in front.

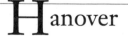
Hanover

LYONS' DEN ANTIQUES
Rte 2, 04237
(207)364-8634   23 30 36

Glass, china, tools, clocks, 18th & 19th C furniture, primitives & decoys. Hours: Daily 9-5. Size: Large. Nancy Lyons Loc: 10 MI W of Rumford.

Harrison

JEFF KOOPUS
Maple Ridge Rd, 04040
(207)583-4860   70

A one-man shop specializing in authentic handcrafted country & formal furniture. All work done on a custom basis by commission. *Serv:* Reproduction furniture.

Holden

DOUGLAS MARSHALL
Copeland Hill Rd, 04412
(207)989-6230   27 34

Maine country furniture & decorative accessories, folk art & primitive hooked rugs. *Hours:* Year round by chance/appt. *Assoc:* MADA.

Hope

THE BLUEBERRY PATCH
Box 975, 04847
(207)763-4055   1 44

Early Americana & collectibles. Fine collection of carriage/wagon wheels, wagons & sleighs. *Est:* 1986. *Serv:* Brochure, purchase estates. *Hours:* BY APPT: Jun 15-Oct 5 Mon-Sat 10-6 Sun 1-6. *Size:* Large. Merle V Zimmer *Park:* On site. *Loc:* From downtown Camden, Rte 105W, approx 7.5 MI.

Hulls Cove

HULLS COVE TOOL BARN
Box 144, 04644
(207)288-5126   **59 81**

Antiques, old tools, old books, paintings & prints. *Hours:* Year round Sat,Sun 9-5, Apr-Oct Weekdays 9-5. *Loc:* Rte 3 towards Bar Harbor,turn onto Breakneck Rd at the Hulls Cove General Store.

Jay

RIVER OAKS BOOKS
RFD 2 Box 5505, 04239
(207)897-3734   **13**

Antiquarian books: a general collection with emphasis on illustrated books, mystery, Americana, juvenile, nature, Maine books. *Serv:* Mail order. *Hours:* Year round by chance/appt. *Assoc:* MABA. Nick Bogdon *Loc:* Just off Rte 140.

Jefferson

BUNKER HILL ANTIQUES
Rte 213, 04348
(207)563-3167   **27 65 67**

Primitives, country furniture & accessories, white ironstone & Mulberry china, toys, prints & paintings, quilts & coverlets. *Hours:* By chance/appt. *Assoc:* MADA. Joanne Vose

Kennebunk

DYNAN FINE ARTS
Rte 1N, 04043
(207)985-7763   **36 59**

Furniture & paintings. *Hours:* By chance/appt. Celeste Dynan

J J KEATING INC
Rte 1N, 04043
(207)985-2097   **8 70**

Full array of antiques as well as antique reproductions. *Est:* 1957. *Serv:* Appraisal, auction, purchase estates, reproduction. *Hours:* May-Oct Tue-Sun, Nov-Apr Thu-Sat. James J Keating *Loc:* I-95 Exit 3: N on US Rte 1.

JUDITH A KEATING, GG
Rte 1N, 04043
(207)985-4181   **4**

Appraisals of antique & estate jewelry, watches, silver & antique ladies' accessories (fans, pocketbooks, sewing). *Hours:* BY APPT. *Assoc:* MADA.

RICHARD W OLIVER AUCTIONEERS
Rte 1 Plaza 1, 04043
(207)985-3600   **8**

Auctioneers of antiques, decoys, Oriental art, glass, china, golf & fishing items, guns. 10% buyer premium, 20% deposit on mail/phone bids. *Serv:* Appraisal, purchase estates, mailing list. *Hours:* Mon-Fri 9-5 Sat 10-4. *Assoc:* NAA NEAA. Betsy Brown *Park:* On site. *Loc:* I-95 Exit 3: E to US Rte 1, then L.

RIVERGATE ANTIQUES MALL
Old Post Rd Rte 1N, 04043
(207)985-6280   **{GR100}**

Full line of antiques & collectibles,

china, glass, furniture, jewelry & pottery. *Est:* 1987. *Hours:* Year round daily 10-5. *Park:* On site. *Loc:* .5 MI N of Kennebunk on Rte 1.

VICTORIAN LIGHT/WATERTOWER PINES
29 York St Rte 1S, 04043
(207)985-6868   **50 71**

Victorian & turn-of-the-century chandeliers, wall sconces, floor & table lamps in a 120 year-old carriage barn. Select from kerosene, gas & early electric lighting which may be in original condition or completely restored. *Pr:* $5–30000. *Serv:* Brochure, consultation, repairs, restoration. *Hours:* Mon-Sat 9:30-5 Sun 12:30-5 appt suggested. *Size:* Medium. *CC:* MC/V. Judy Oppert *Park:* In front. *Loc:* I-95 Exit 3: to Kennebunk, Rte 1S, look for Watertower which is at back of property.

Kennebunkport

ANTIQUES AT NINE
61 Western Ave, 04046
(207)967-0626   **5 37 38**

Featuring formal & country furnishings both American & Continental, architectural elements, books, art, textiles, accessories. Fresh merchandise daily. Summer lodging available in housekeeping cottages near the beach. *Pr:* $10–30000. *Est:* 1980. *Serv:* Appraisal, auction, interior design, purchase estates. *Hours:* Year round daily 10-5. *Size:* Large. *CC:* MC/V. Jim Biondi J Carlson *Park:* On site. *Loc:* On the Kennebunk-Kennebunkport town line, Rte 9, 3.5 MI E of Rte 1, between Wells & Kennebunk Exits 2 & 3 off ME Tnpk.

CATTAILS ANTIQUES
Rte 35 Lower Village, 04046
(207)967-3824   **27 59 66**

Country furniture, baskets, quilts, paintings, prints, wicker furniture, linens, silver, country accessories, some Shaker smalls, folk art & nautical items. *Pr:* $5–2500. *Est:* 1977. *Serv:* Appraisal, consultation, interior design picture framing. *Hours:* May-Oct 15 Mon-Fri 10-5 Sat 9-5 Sun 11-5, else by chance. *CC:* AX/MC/V. *Assoc:* MADA. Cathleen Ellenberger *Park:* On site. *Loc:* I-95 Exit 3 (in ME): S on Rte 35, 4-5 MI, on L.

BARBARA DOHERTY
Pearl St, 04046
(207)967-4673   **30 34 45**

18th & 19th C country furniture, accessories, folk art, quilts, baskets, decoys & garden things. *Hours:* Daily 10-5 or by chance/appt. *Assoc:* MADA. *Loc:* Next door to "The Goose Hangs High".

GIBRAN ANTIQUE GALLERY
Ocean Ave, 04046
(207)967-5556   **47 77 83**

Estate jewelry, old Hummels, Victorian furnishings & silver. *Est:* 1985. *Hours:* Sum: daily 10-9, Oct-Christmas Fri,Sun. *CC:* MC/V. *Park:* Nearby. *Loc:* Across from the old Fire Station.

MARIE PLUMMER GOETT
Spring St, 04046
(207)967-5282   **29 36 50**

Furniture, lighting, accessories from the 17th, 18th, 19th C in an 18th C house overlooking Dock Square. *Hours:* Daily 10-5 or by chance/appt. *Assoc:* MADA.

THE GOOSE HANGS HIGH
Pearl St, 04046
(207)967-5717 **65**

A barn full of antiques including American primitives. *Est:* 1968. *Hours:* Apr-Nov by chance/appt CLOSED SUN. *Assoc:* MADA. Jean Pineo *Loc:* Look for the goose over the barn entrance across from the Captain Jefferd's Inn.

MARITIME MUSEUM SHOP
Ocean Ave, 04046
(207)967-4195 **17 56**

Nautical & general antiques, bronzes, paintings, campaign & camphorwood furniture, scrimshaw & navigational instruments. *Hours:* May 15-Oct 15 daily 10-4 CLOSED SUN. *Assoc:* MADA. *Park:* On site. *Loc:* At Booth Tarkington's former Boathouse.

NAUTICAL ANTIQUES
Box 765, 04046
(207)967-3218 **56 59**

Specialist in marine antiques, scrimshaw, marine paintings, carvings, folk art, campaign furniture & prisoner of war work. *Est:* 1972. *Serv:* Appraisal, catalog $3. *Hours:* BY APPT ONLY. *Size:* Medium. John F Rinaldi *Park:* On site. *Loc:* 1.5 hrs from Boston, .5 hr from Portland.

OLD FORT INN & ANTIQUES
Old Fort Ave, 04046
(207)967-5353 **30 44 65**

Selection of period antiques including English & European country pine, decoys, primitives, china, cut glass & early advertising items. *Pr:* $25–900. *Hours:* Apr 15-Dec 15 daily 9-5, Dec 16-Apr 14 BY APPT ONLY. *CC:* AX/DC/MC/V. *Assoc:* MADA. Sheila Aldrich *Park:* In front. *Loc:* I-95 Exit 3: L on Rte 35, follow signs to Kennebunkport, over drawbridge, R to Ocean Ave, L at Colony Hotel, R, .25 MI.

PORT ANTIQUES
Ocean Ave, 04046
(207)967-5119 **47 77**

Antique & estate jewelry, collectibles, silver, furniture & paintings. *Est:* 1985. *Serv:* Appraisal, purchase estates. *Hours:* Tue-Sun 9-5. *CC:* AX/MC/V. Chris Coughlin *Park:* Nearby. *Loc:* Corner of Arundel Wharf.

RANDS ANTIQUES ON RAND GREEN
Western Ave Rte 9, 04046
(207)967-4887 **29 42**

Refinished English pine furniture & decorative accessories. *Est:* 1944. *Hours:* Mar-Dec daily 10-5. *CC:* MC/V. *Assoc:* MADA. *Park:* Nearby. *Loc:* I-95 Exit 3: to Rte 9.

SAML'S STAIRS ANTIQUES
Main St Rte 9, 04046
(207)967-2880 **36 59 77**

18th & 19th C furniture, paintings, silver, china, doorstops & accessories. *Est:* 1986. *Serv:* Appraisal, consultation, repair. *Hours:* Mon-Sat 10-4 BY APPT ONLY CLOSED WED. Bruce L Johnson *Loc:* Just off Rte 1.

WINDFALL ANTIQUES
Ocean Ave, 04046
(207)967-2089 **60 63 77**

Porcelain, American & European silver, 19th C art, Orientalia & glass. *Hours:* May 15-Oct daily 10-5 CLOSED TUE. *Assoc:* MADA. Anne Kornetsky *Park:* Nearby. *Loc:* Near Colony Hotel.

WINTER HILL FARM
Wildes District Rd, 04046
(207)967-5879   **29 37 38**
Two floors of Continental, English &
American furniture accented with fine
accessories displayed in restored barn.
Pr: $10–3000. *Est:* 1985. *Serv:* Re-
pairs, restoration. *Hours:* May-Oct
daily 10-5, Nov-Apr Wed-Mon 10-5.
Size: Medium. John Dickinson *Park:*
On site. *Loc:* From Kennebunkport,
Rte 9E, to Maine St, bear L at fork, .5
MI on Wildes District Rd, on L at top
of hill.

Kittery

WILLIAM CORE DUFFY
Box 445, 03904
(207)439-6414   **77**
Early American silver for the knowledgeable collector. Exceptional silver
from all periods. *Est:* 1976. *Serv:* Appraisal, purchase estates. *Hours:* BY
APPT ONLY. *Loc:* Call for directions.

THE WINDSOR CHAIR
36 Rogers Rd, 03904
(207)439-2164   **43**
Handcrafted 18th C reproduction
Windsors & fine period furniture. *Est:*
1983. *Hours:* BY APPT. *CC:* MC/V.
Madeleine Godnig *Park:* On site. *Loc:*
I-95 Exit 2 (Kittery): to Rte 236S, at
traffic circle continue .7 MI, bear R at
fork at cemetery, on L.

Lille

THE OLD HOMESTEAD
US Rte 1, 04749
(207)895-3353   **34 42 65**
Country pine furniture, small primi-

tives, children's items, folk art, baskets,
kitchen wares, some oak & Victorian
items. *Hours:* Daily by chance/appt.
Assoc: MADA NEAA. Les Dumond

Limerick

RYAN M COOPER
PO Box 149, 04048
(207)793-8863   **56 62**
19th & 20th C maritime photography,
including sailing vessels, naval vessels,
steamers, whaling vessels, yachting &
harbor views. *Serv:* Illustrated list
available ($2). *Hours:* BY APPT. *Assoc:*
PHSNE. *Loc:* Call for directions.

TOM JOSEPH & DAVID RAMSAY
Rte 5, 04048
(207)793-2539   **1 5 45**
Early American furniture in original
paint, paintings, folk art, garden statuary, architectural items & student
lamps. *Est:* 1976. *Hours:* BY APPT.
Assoc: ADA NHADA PTADA. *Loc:*
On Rte 5, 50 yds from Jct of Rte 160.

Limington

EDWARD & ELAINE CASAZZA
Douglas Rd, 04049
(207)637-2599   **21 59 65**
Furniture, primitives, paintings, rugs
& country. *Hours:* Year round Mon-
Sat 8-4:30. *Loc:* .25 MI from Jct of Rtes
25 & 117.

ROBERT O STUART
Jo Joy Rd, 04049
(207)793-4522   **29 37**
Specializing in fine 18th & 19th C
American furniture & decorative ac-
cessories. *Est:* 1976. *Serv:* Appraisal,

restoration, consultation. *Hours:*
Mon-Sat 9-6 Sun 12-5 call ahead.
Park: On site. *Loc:* Off Rte 117, 28 MI
W of Portland.

Lincolnville

DUCK TRAP ANTIQUES
Rte 1, 04849
(207)789-5575   **44 63**
Large selection of flow blue for the
beginner or advanced collector, china,
glass, pewter & furniture. *Hours:* May-
Nov call for appt. *Assoc:* MADA. Nat-
alie Mac Innis *Loc:* 7 MI N of Camden.

Lincolnville Beach

BETTY'S TRADING POST
Rte 1, 04849
(207)789-5300   **24 32 36**
Furniture, glass, jewelry, dolls & old
coins. *Hours:* Year round. *Assoc:*
MADA. Betty Smith

GOOSE RIVER EXCHANGE
Rte 1, 04849
(207)789-5241   **13 20 33**
Books, post cards, photographica,
posters, advertising & ephemera. One
of the most unique paper Americana
specialists in New England. *Pr:* $2–
2000. *Est:* 1977. *Hours:* Jul-Sep 4 daily
10-6, else by chance/appt. *Size:* Medium. Kenneth N Shure *Park:* In
front. *Loc:* Rte 1 in Lincolnville Beach,
opposite Lobster Pound Rest.

**MAINE ANTIQUE
MERCHANTS LTD**
Rte 1 (Northport), 04849
(207)338-1444   **{GR}**
Antiques of the early American com-

munity. *Hours:* Apr 15-Oct 15 Tue-
Sat, Win: by chance/appt. *Assoc:*
MADA. Ellen Katonah *Loc:* 2.5 MI N
of Lincolnville Beach.

**NORTH HOUSE FINE
ANTIQUES**
Rte 1 Waterside, 04849
(207)789-5252   **29 36 63**
Quality 18th & 19th C decorative arts
with emphasis on English ceramics.
Pr: $50–5000. *Hours:* May 15-Oct 15
Mon-Sat 9-6, Oct 16-May 14 Fri-Sun
10-5. *Size:* Medium. *CC:* MC/V.
Assoc: MADA. Judith Noel *Park:* In
front. *Loc:* Rte 1, 6 MI N of Camden
or 10 MI S of Belfast.

SIGN OF THE OWL
Box 85 RR2, 04849
(207)338-4669   **40 60 63**
General selection including some pine
& oak furniture, china, glass, specialize
in Orientalia - old & reproduction -
porcelain & art. *Pr:* $20–1200. *Est:*
1986. *Serv:* Appraisal, interior design,
bed & breakfast. *Hours:* May-Oct
Wed-Mon 10-6, Nov-Dec Wed-Sun
11-5. *Size:* Medium. *CC:* MC/V. John
E Trowbridge *Park:* On site. *Loc:* US
Rte 1, 9 MI N of Camden.

Lisbon

**OLD LISBON SCHOOLHOUSE
ANTIQUES**
Rte 196, 04252
(207)353-6075   **{GR3}**
Large Victorian schoolhouse filled
with a general line from 1800 to 1950s.
Pr: $10–500. *Est:* 1973. *Serv:* Ap-
praisal, consultation, purchase estates.
Hours: Apr 15-Nov 15 Thu,Sat 11-4
or by chance/appt call ahead. *Size:*

Large. Burtt Warren *Park:* On site. *Loc:* I-95 at Topsham take Rte 196N, or at Auburn, Rte 196S, to Lisbon.

adison

BOOKS BOUGHT AND SOLD
125 Main St, 04950
(207)696-8361   **13**

Antiquarian books: 5000 better used, out-of-print esoteric books, literature, history & records. *Hours:* Daily 8:30-5. *Assoc:* MABA. C Seams

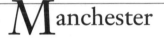anchester

BLUE WILLOW FARM
Worthing Rd, 04351
(207)623-4893

Blue willow, collectibles & country crafts. *Est:* 1984. *Hours:* Jun-Oct Mon-Fri 1-5, else by chance/appt. Vicki Oliver *Park:* On site. *Loc:* 1.5 MI off Rte 17.

CHARLES ROBINSON RARE BOOKS
Pond Rd, 04351
(207)622-1885   **13 51 66**

Rare & fine books in many fields. Illustrated books, maps & fine prints of the 19th & 20th C a specialty. *Pr:* $25–2000. *Est:* 1974. *Serv:* Appraisal, auction. *Hours:* BY APPT ONLY. *Assoc:* MABA. *Loc:* Rte 202, 2.3 MI, on L.

echanic Falls

MCMORROW AUCTION COMPANY
Box 825 RFD #1, 04256
(207)345-9477   **8**

Antiques, commercial, farm & estates. *Serv:* Auction, appraisal. *Assoc:* CAI NEAA. Jody McMorrow

oody

THE GRAY'S ANTIQUES
Rte 1 & Tatnic Rd, 04054
(207)646-8938   **{GR7}**

Furniture, linens, glass & oil paintings. *Est:* 1987. *Hours:* Daily 10-5. *CC:* MC/V. Jean Gray *Park:* On site. *Loc:* Just over the Ogunquit line.

KENNETH & IDA MANKO
Seabreeze Dr, 04054
(207)646-2595   **27 34**

Offering a choice stock of country furniture, paintings & folk art for the advanced collector, dealer & decorator. One of the finest 19th C antique weather vane selection in New England. *Est:* 1973. *Serv:* Appraisal, consultation. *Hours:* Summer & Fall: daily 9-5 or by chance. *Assoc:* NEAA. *Park:* On site. *Loc:* 3 MI from I-95.

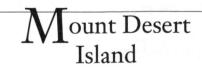ount Desert Island

WIKHEGAN BOOKS
PO Box 370, 04660
(207)276-5079   **13 33**

Antiquarian & used books with em-

phasis on decorative & fine arts, nautical, Down East, Maine authors, eastern
woodlands, Indians, natural history,
women & ephemera. *Serv:* Search service. *Hours:* Phone or mail order call
ahead. *Assoc:* MABA. J Fuerst

New Gloucester

DONALD CHANDLER - BOOKS
Rte 231, 04260
(207)926-4653 13

Antiquarian books: emphasis on
Americana & Maine books. *Hours:*
Year round by chance/appt. *Assoc:*
MABA.

New Harbor

RICHARDSON BOOKS LTD
Box 169, 04554
(207)677-2429 13

Antiquarian books: Jane Austen, Vir-
ginia Woolf, the Bloomsbury Group,
Winston Churchill. *Serv:* Catalogs.
Hours: BY APPT ONLY. *Assoc:*
MABA. Peggy Richardson

New Sharon

ATTIC OWL BOOKS
PO Box 1802, 04955
(207)778-2006 13

Antiquarian books: 2000 rare, out-of-
print & philosophy books including
philosophers' biographies, aesthetics,
ethics, epistemology, logic, metaphysics & philosophies of mind, science,
religion, mathematics & education.
Serv: Search service. *Hours:* Primarily

catalog mail order, can be seen by appt
year round. *Assoc:* MABA. William L
Reid

FREDERICK BAUER
RFD 1 Box 460, 04955
(207)778-9682 8

Auctioneers of antiques from area estates. Absentee bids discouraged. Frederick A Bauer

Newcastle

BARN STAGES BOOKSHOP
Pump St, 04553
(207)563-8335 13

A general, eclectic, balanced collection
of 20,000 used & out-of-print books-
both hardback & paperback-gathered
for readers & browsers & arranged by
category. An annex 2 miles from the
main shop houses 3,000 children's
books. *Pr:* $1–50. *Est:* 1985. *Hours:*
May 15-Sep 15 Mon-Fri 1-5 (ANNEX
ONLY Sun 1-5), else BY APPT. *Assoc:*
MABA. Barbara W Yedlin *Park:* In
front. *Loc:* Main St (Bus Rte 1), .1 MI
from Newcastle.

**DIFFERENT DRUMMER
ANTIQUES**
Glidden St Off Bus Rte 1, 04553
(207)563-1836 50

Lighting devices, as well as a variety of
furniture & accessories. *Est:* 1983.
Serv: Consultation, purchase estates.
Hours: Apr-Oct daily 9-5, Nov-Mar by
chance/appt. *Size:* Medium. *Assoc:*
MADA. J M Warner *Park:* On site.
Loc: 100 ft off Bus Rte 1, signs posted.

FOSTER'S AUCTION GALLERY
Rte 1, 04553
(207)563-8150   **8**

Fine antiques, 15-20 estate sales per year, Aug 1-2 annual summer auction - Americana, fine arts. Accept mail/phone bids, 10% buyers premium. *Est:* 1953. *Serv:* Appraisal, estate liquidation, mailing list. *Hours:* Daily 9-4. *Assoc:* MAA NAA. Robert L Foster Jr *Park:* On site. *Loc:* From Wiscasset, 3 MI N, on L, on Rte 1.

MARY HODES
Mills Rd Rte 215, 04553
(207)563-5151   **16 36 81**

Furniture, Mettlach, pewter, tin, china & tools. *Est:* 1970. *Hours:* Apr-Oct Daily 11-5. *Loc:* 1 MI from Rte 1.

CONSTANCE H HURST
Bus Rte 1 at Newcastle Sq, 04553
(207)563-8222   **29 39**

Imported 17th, 18th, 19th C English period furniture & accessories. *Serv:* Purchase estates. *Hours:* Mon-Sat 10-5, Win: Mon-Sat 10-4. *Park:* Nearby. *Loc:* From Rte 1N, take Bus Rte 1.

KAJA VEILLUX ART & ANTIQUES
Newcastle Sq Bus Rte 1, 04553
(207)563-1002   **23 47 59**

Furniture, paintings, sconces, rugs, clocks, jewelry & decorative items. *Serv:* Appraisal, estate auctions. *Hours:* Daily 9-5, Win: CLOSED SUN. *Assoc:* MADA NEAA.

MILLING AROUND
Academy Hill, 04553
(207)563-1241   **27 80**

Antiques, textiles, bobbins & country furnishings. *Est:* 1979. *Hours:* Sum: afternoons & weekends, else BY APPT.

Assoc: MAA. Dirk Poole *Park:* Nearby. *Loc:* US Rte 1 Newcastle/Damariscotta Exit: 1st L.

NEWCASTLE ANTIQUES
Rte 1, 04553
(207)563-5714   **3 56 59**

Oil paintings, antiquities, early American furniture & accessories & marine antiques. *Est:* 1978. *Hours:* Daily. Ellen Perez *Loc:* 4 MI N of Wiscasset Bridge.

GORDON NICOLL
Mills Rd Rte 215, 04553
(207)563-5808   **21 59 60**

Paintings, Oriental & Indian art & rugs. *Est:* 1972. *Hours:* Tue-Sat 10-5 or BY APPT. *Park:* Nearby.

SAIL LOFT
PO Box 278, 04553
(207)563-5671   **13**

Antiquarian books: illustrated, children's & natural history. *Pr:* $2–450. *Est:* 1933. *Serv:* Appraisal, search service. *Hours:* By chance/appt. *Assoc:* MABA. Harriet Williams *Park:* In front. *Loc:* Behind post office.

TRUEMAN AUCTION CO
RR1 Box 455A, 04553
(207)586-6680   **8**

A prompt, professional auction company with low commission rates. Complete estates or single items handled confidentially. Prompt settlement of accounts. *Serv:* Appraisal, brochure, consultation. *Hours:* Daily 7-7. Lawrence B Trueman

Newfield

JOHN BAUER SONIA SEFTON ANTI
Elm Street, 04056
(207)793-8950   **29 37 82**
American Indian art & American period furniture & accessories. *Pr:* $150–15000. *Serv:* Appraisal, consultation. *Hours:* BY APPT. *Loc:* I-95 Exit 5 (Saco): Rte 5W, 20 MI, Rte 11W, 4 MI, Willow Brook Museum, look for mill pond/house, 4th house on R.

Norridgewock

SNOWBOUND BOOKS
PO Box 458, 04957
(207)634-4398   **13**
Antiquarian books: out-of-print, used & rare books with special emphasis on military, Americana, children's books, Maine, mysteries, sporting & fiction. *Hours:* By phone/mail only. *Assoc:* MABA. Marla Bottesch

North Berwick

YOUNG FINE ARTS GALLERY, INC.
PO Box 313, 03906
(207)676-3104   **59**
Works by - Albert, Bacon, Brown, Grant, Hart, Birney, Lafarge, Richards, Ripley, Smillie, Sonntag, Vedder, West, Woodbury, Wyant, 19th C American & European paintings. *Serv:* Auctions 5 times a year. illustrated listing $15. *Hours:* BY APPT. George Young *Loc:* Auctions at Seaboard Gallery in Elliot, ME.

North Edgecomb

THE DITTY BOX
Rte 1, 04543
(207)882-6618   **1 57 63**
In an 1840 meeting house, featuring a large collection of American furniture & decorations, with emphasis on country items. Also Staffordshire portrait figures, paintings, pewter, Currier & Ives prints. *Pr:* $10–3000. *Est:* 1963. *Serv:* Appraisal, brochure. *Hours:* Jun 25-Oct 15 Mon-Sat 10:30-5 Sun 12-5, else by chance/appt. *Size:* Medium. *Assoc:* MADA. Muriel Lewis *Park:* On site. *Loc:* W side of Rte 1, on North Edgecomb/Newcastle line, 2 MI N of Wiscasset Bridge - 2 MI S of Foster's Auction Gallery.

EDGECOMB BOOK BARN
Cross Point Rd, 04556
(207)882-7278   **13**
30,000 books, out-of-print & rare, illustrated, children's, Marine, Americana & Maine. *Hours:* Sum: daily 11-6, Win: BY APPT. *Assoc:* MABA. Frank McQuaid

M.A.H. ANTIQUES
Eddy Rd, 04556
(207)882-6960   **66**
Prints: botanicals, historical & natural history. *Hours:* Mar-Nov BY APPT ONLY. Sally S Walt *Park:* On site. *Loc:* 1 MI from Rte 1 across the river from Wiscasset.

JACK PARTRIDGE
Rte 1, 04556
(207)882-7745   **1 39 58**
18th C English & American furniture, paintings & objets d'art. *Est:* 1927. *Hours:* May-Oct 15 daily 9:30-6.

Shows: WAS, ELLIS. **Loc:** 3 MI N of
Wiscasset facing Pioneer Motel on R
going N on Rte 1.

North Monmouth

JOYCE B KEELER - BOOKS
Wilson Pond Rd, 04265
(207)933-9088   **13**
Antiquarian books: diverse general
collection, including science fiction &
fantasy, children's books 1870-1970,
nostalgic fiction, regional Americana
& Maine books. **Serv:** Mail order.
Hours: BY APPT ONLY. **Assoc:**
MABA.

Northeast Harbor

PINE BOUGH
Main St, 04662
(207)276-5079   **1 13 50**
Dealing in select 18th, 19th & 20th C
American antiques, accessories in
treen, iron, glass, American lighting a
specialty. Also antiquarian books &
ephemera. **Pr:** $1–10000. **Serv:** Ap-
praisal, consultation, purchase estates.
Hours: Jun-Aug Mon-Sat 10-5, else by
chance/appt. **CC:** AX/MC/V. Joanne
Fuerst **Park:** In front. **Loc:** Within 5
MI of Acadia Nat'l Park, at head of Sea
St, on Main St in heart of Village.

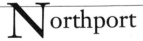

Northport

LORD SEAGRAVE'S
Coastal Rte 1, 04915
(207)338-1424   **9 13 33**
Autographs, manuscripts, antiquarian
books, decoys, ephemera, oak furni-

ture, maps, nautical & marine items,
post cards, prints, glass, Civil War
items & primitives. **Pr:** $10–5000.
Serv: Appraisal, auction, catalog ($1),
purchase estates. **Hours:** Daily 10-5.
Size: Medium. **CC:** MC/V. **Assoc:**
MABA NEAA. Ron Seagrave **Park:**
On site. **Loc:** Rte 1, 10 MI N of Camden.

Norway

DIXON'S ANTIQUES
16 Deering St, 04268
(207)743-6881   **16 37 66**
Early New England furniture, pressed
glass, Wedgwood, prints & paintings,
primitives, copper & ironware. **Hours:**
By chance/appt.

Ogunquit

BEAUPORT INN ANTIQUES
96 Shore Rd, 03907
(207)646-8680   **44 63**
Small furniture, china, glass & decorative accessories. Dan Pender **Park:**
Nearby. **Loc:** Off US Rte 1 on the road
to Perkins Cove.

POTPOURRI ANTIQUES
Rte 1, 03907
(207)646-3529   **47**
Specializing in fine antique jewelry. **Pr:**
$25–5000. **Est:** 1961. **Serv:** Purchase
estates. **Hours:** May-Sep BY APPT
ONLY. **Assoc:** MADA. Thomas N
Zankowich **Park:** On site. **Loc:** Rte 1
.25 MI N of Ogunquit Ctr, large prominent sign.

Orono

THE GREEN DOOR ANTIQUE SHOP
92 Main St, 04473
(207)866-3116   **44 63 77**

European & American antiques, period Irish silver a specialty, china & glass. *Serv:* Appraisal & estate sales. *Hours:* By chance/appt, call ahead. *Assoc:* MADA. Eileen O'Callaghan

Orrington

MERRIMAC'S ANTIQUES
Rte 15, 04474
(207)989-2667   **40 44 83**

One floor of glass, china, baskets. One room of furniture - Victorian, oak & some pine, dealing mainly in art glass. *Pr:* $25–5000. *Serv:* Appraisal. *Hours:* May-Nov Mon-Sat 10-4 by chance/appt. Mary MacDonald

Oxford

OXFORD COMMON ANTIQUE CENTER
Rte 26, 04270
(207)743-7652   **{GR18}**

Folk art, decoys, maritime antiques, Americana, quilts, Victoriana, toys & oak furniture. *Est:* 1986. *Hours:* Daily 10-5, Jan-Mar Thu-Sun 10-5. *CC:* MC/V. *Park:* On site. *Loc:* Between South Paris & Oxford 1 MI S of Norway.

Paris

HAUNTED BOOKSHOP
Paris Hill, 04271
(207)743-6216   **13**

Antiquarian books: general collection of used, out-of-print & rare books. *Serv:* Search service. *Hours:* Year round by chance/appt, extended summer hours. *Assoc:* MABA. Wini Mott

Peaks Island

ISLAND TO ISLAND ANTIQUES
PO Box 82, 04108
(207)766-2261   **34 65**

Folk art & primitives. *Hours:* BY APPT ONLY. Robert T Foley

Pittsfield

KENNISTON'S ANTIQUES
Rte 2, 04967
(207)487-5032   **36 63 77**

Primitives, glass, china, furniture, paintings, jewelry, baskets, silver & books. *Hours:* Apr-Nov or BY APPT. *Assoc:* MADA. Barbara Kenniston

Pittston

PHIPPS OF PITTSTON
Rte 27, 04345
(207)582-3555   **28 42 63**

Refinished pine & other natural wood furniture, ironstone, yellow ware, pottery & items for the decorator. *Hours:* Spring-Fall daily CLOSED SUN. *Assoc:* MADA. Maggi Phipps *Loc:* Between Wiscasset & Gardiner.

KENNETH AND PAULETTE TUTTLE
Rtes 194 & 27, 04345
(207)582-4496 **21 37 84**

18th & early 19th C American country & formal furniture, decorative Oriental rugs & vintage Ford automobiles. *Serv:* Everything guaranteed as represented. *Hours:* By chance. *Assoc:* MADA.

Poland Spring

CIDERPRESS BOOKSTORE
Cleve Tripp Rd RFD 1, 04274
(207)998-4338 **13**

Antiquarian books: a general collection with emphasis on literature, science, history, philosophy, natural history & books by & about women. *Hours:* Mar 15-Dec 15 by chance/appt. *Assoc:* MABA. Virginia Chute *Loc:* From Rte 26 take Range Hill Rd.

Portland

F O BAILEY ANTIQUARIANS
141 Middle St, 04101
(207)774-1479 **4 8**

One of Maine's oldest auction houses dealing in fine furniture, paintings, rugs, glassware, porcelain, gold & silver items. 10% buyer's premium. *Est:* 1819. *Serv:* Appraisal, auctioneers, restoration & refinishing. *Hours:* All year. *Assoc:* MADA. Joy Piscopo *Loc:* I-295 Exit Franklin St: at 5th set of lights turn R onto Middle St, gallery on R at next Int.

BARRIDOFF GALLERIES
26 Free St, 04101
(207)772-5011 **59**

19th & 20th C American paintings. *Est:* 1975. *Serv:* Appraisal, consultation. *Hours:* Mon-Fri 10-5 Sat 12-4. Annette Elowitch *Park:* Nearby. *Loc:* 2 blocks from the Portland Museum.

CARLSON AND TURNER BOOKS
241 Congress St, 04101
(207)773-4200 **9 13 66**

Over 40,000 volumes, good selection of reference books, fine art & decorative prints. *Pr:* $3-3000. *Est:* 1974. *Serv:* Appraisal. *Hours:* Tue-Sat 10-5. *CC:* MC/V. *Assoc:* MABA NEAA. Norma C Carlson *Loc:* I-295 Franklin St Exit: R at 2nd light, 150 yds on L across from Eastern Cemetery.

CUNNINGHAM BOOKS
762A Congress St, 04104
(207)775-2246 **13**

Antiquarian books: an organized general collection of used & out-of-print books. *Hours:* Year round Mon-Sat 11-6. *Assoc:* MABA. Joan Pickard

FLYNN BOOKS
466 Ocean Ave, 04103
(207)772-2685 **13**

Antiquarian books: a general collection, including rare & fine press books, Americana, the West & selected Maine & New England books. *Hours:* BY APPT ONLY. *Assoc:* MABA. Anita Flynn *Park:* On site. *Loc:* I-295 Exit 8 (Washington Ave): L at 3rd light onto Ocean Ave, corner of Victor Rd, red house.

MILK STREET ANTIQUES
8 Milk St, 04101
(207)773-8288 **28 34 67**

Fine 18th & 19th C American country & formal furniture, pottery, china, stoneware, toys, paintings, quilts, textiles, Oriental rugs, folk art & decoys. *Est:* 1976. *Serv:* Wholesale to the trade. *Hours:* Mon-Sat 10-6. *CC:* MC/V. Kimberly Washam *Park:* Nearby. *Loc:* Next to the Regency.

NELSON RARITIES, INC
One Monument Sq, 04101
(207)775-3150 **7 23 47**

Extensive collection of estate jewelry, specializing in art deco, art nouveau & period jewelry, also stones, watches & silver. *Serv:* Catalog. *Hours:* Mon-Fri 9:30-5 weekends by appt. *Assoc:* MADA. Andrew Nelson

F M O'BRIEN-ANTIQUARIAN BOOKS
34 & 36 High St, 04101
(207)774-0931 **9 13 66**

Specializing in Americana & general literature, with an emphasis on Maine books, autographs, paintings & prints. *Est:* 1934. *Serv:* Appraisal, build collections for libraries. *Hours:* BY APPT ONLY. *Assoc:* ABAA MABA. *Park:* On site. *Loc:* I-95 Exit 7 at S Portland: follow Gull signs to waterfront Commercial St to High St up to 5th house on L with long drive.

OCTAVIA'S ANTIQUES
247 Congress St, 04101
(207)772-2668 **50 83**

Victorian era furniture, accessories & lighting. *Est:* 1983. *Hours:* Year round Tue-Sat 10-5:30. *Loc:* 2 min off I-95.

OUT-OF-PRINT SHOP
112 High St, 04101
(207)775-3233 **13**

Antiquarian books: a general collection of nonfiction. *Hours:* Wed-Fri 11-6 Sat 12-5:30. *Assoc:* MABA. Pat Murphy

PAST TENSE ANTIQUES
247 Congress St, 04101
(207)772-3355

Eclectic selection of antiques from all periods specializing in 1950s memorabilia. *Est:* 1988. *Hours:* Year round Mon-Sat 11-5. Calvin S Muse *Park:* On street.

PORT 'N STARBOARD
195 Commercial St, 04101
(207)773-0520 **54 56 66**

Ship & shore merchants located in a restored waterfront warehouse featuring marine paintings, prints, ephemera, photography, maps, charts, books, instruments, scrimshaw, ship models, 1/2 hulls, folk art & decoys. *Pr:* $3–3000. *Est:* 1984. *Serv:* Appraisal, consultation, interior design. *Hours:* Father's Day-Labor Day Mon-Sat 9-9, else Mon-Sat 10-6. *Size:* Medium. *CC:* AX/MC/V. Michael Leslie *Park:* On site. *Loc:* I-295, follow WATERFRONT signs, on corner of Dana & Commercial Sts.

MARY ALICE REILLEY
83 India St, 04101
(207)773-8815 **42 44 65**

A large selection of pine, also primitives, glass, china & country accessories. *Assoc:* MADA.

REMEMBER WHEN
15 Pleasant St, 04101
(207)761-7946 **48 59 80**

A small shop in Portland's latest area of

restoration. Collectibles, decorative accessories, clothing & beautifully prepared & presented vintage textiles, especially linens. Some furniture & art work. *Pr:* $25–500. *Est:* 1987. *Hours:* Apr 20-Oct 20 Tue-Sat 10-6, Oct 21-Apr 19 Tue-Sat 11-5. Emily Materson *Park:* In front. *Loc:* I-295 Exit 7: S to Fore St, turn R, up Pleasant St at Int with Fore (at blinking light).

ALLEN SCOTT/BOOKS
1B Dana St, 04101
(207)774-2190   **13**
Antiquarian books: carefully selected collection of 10,000 quality books for collectors & libraries including first editions, art, architecture, psychology, travel, Americana, maritime, literature, books on books & history. *Hours:* Year round Mon-Sat 11-6 & BY APPT. *Assoc:* MABA. *Loc:* In the Old Port Exchange.

VENTURE ANTIQUES
101 Exchange St, 04101
(207)773-6064   **44 63 67**
19th C furniture, china, glassware, quilts & lamps. *Hours:* Mon-Sat 10-5. *Assoc:* MADA. Isabel Thatcher

VOSE SMITH ANTIQUES
647 Congress St, 04101
(207)773-6436   **16 17 80**
Antique copper, brass, bronze, cloisonne, paisley shawls & a large collection of curtain tie-backs. *Hours:* All year CLOSED SUN. *Assoc:* MADA. Donald W Harford

WILMA'S ANTIQUES & ACCESSORIES
86 Middle St, 04101
(207)772-9852   **27 44 63**
Country & formal furniture, fine glass & china, braided & hooked rugs, paint-

ings & accessories. *Est:* 1979. *Serv:* Purchase estates. *Hours:* Mon-Sat 10-5. *Size:* Medium. *CC:* MC/V. *Assoc:* MADA. Wilma D Taliento *Park:* On site. *Loc:* I-95 Franklin St Exit: thru 5 sets of lights, turn L, 2nd shop on R.

Presque Isle

THE COUNTRY STORE
667 Main St, 04769
(207)764-6192   **32 36 44**
General line of antiques & collectibles. *Serv:* Purchase estates. *Hours:* Mar-Dec Mon-Sat 10-5, Jan-Feb Mon-Sat 12-4. *Size:* Large. *CC:* MC/V. Angie Graves *Park:* On site. *Loc:* Diagonally across from McDonald's.

Rangeley

BLUEBERRY HILL FARM
Saddleback Rd, 04970
(207)864-5647   **44 67**
Antiques, quilts, glass & advertising. *Hours:* Jul-Aug Thu-Sat 10-4. Stephanie Palmer

Richmond

THE LOFT ANTIQUES
9 Gardiner St, 04357
(207)737-2056   **29 48 85**
Early clothing, accessories, fine laces, linens & decorative items. *Hours:* By chance/appt. *Assoc:* MADA. Kay Pierce *Loc:* I-95 Exit 26.

Rockport

**JOAN HARTMAN ELLIS
ANTIQUE PRINT**
19 High St, 04856
(207)236-4524 **66**
18th & 19th C engravings, lithographs
& woodcuts, including botanicals, natural history, American & European
views & caricatures. *Pr:* $25–500. *Est:*
1962. *Hours:* Appt suggested. *Park:* In
front. *Loc:* In Rockport Village on
Amesbury Hill.

KATRIN PHOCAS LTD
19 Main St, 04856
(207)236-8654 **37 39 59**
Two floors of English & American furniture of 17th, 18th & 19th C, accessories & fine art at harborside. *Pr:*
$25–10000. *Est:* 1987. *Hours:* Jun-Sep
Tue-Sat 10-5, JUL,AUG Sun 12-5.
CC: AX/MC/V. *Park:* In front.

WINDY TOP ANTIQUES
59 Pascal Ave, 04856
(207)236-4514 **16 18**
Small, tidy shop specializing in buttons, copper & brass, also china, glass
& some soft goods. *Est:* 1970. *Serv:*
Appraisal. *Hours:* Jun 15-Oct 15 Mon-
Fri 10-4 by chance/appt. Marion H
McGee *Park:* On site. *Loc:* Rte 1N to
Rte 90 at Waldoboro, to dead end,
shop on R, next to general store.

Round Pond

CARRIAGE HOUSE
Rte 32, 04564
(207)529-5555 **13 66**
Antiquarian books: emphasis on non-
fiction, large & varied selection of
Americana, marine & illustrated
books, prints, furniture & primitives.
Est: 1961. *Hours:* Sum: daily 9-5 Win:
by chance/appt. *Assoc:* MABA. Roy
Gillespie *Loc:* 1 MI S of Round Pond
Village.

THE HOLMES
Rte 32, 04564
(207)529-5788 **27 29 59**
Country furniture, books, paintings &
decorative accessories. *Hours:* Jul-Aug
Mon-Fri 9-5 or BY APPT. *Park:* On
site.

ROUND POND ANTIQUES
Rte 32, 04564
(207)529-5568 **27 36 59**
Furniture, country items & paintings.
Hours: Tue-Sat 10-5.

TIME AND AGAIN ANTIQUES
Rte 32S, 04564
(207)677-2715 **36 44 63**
Carrying fine pattern glass, including
Portland & Sandwich; china, including
flow blue, Mulberry & white ironstone; furniture, predominantly 19th
C, some 18th C. *Pr:* $50–3000. *Est:*
1982. *Serv:* Purchase estates. *Hours:*
May-Oct daily 9-4, Nov-Jun by
chance/appt. *Size:* Medium. *CC:*
MC/V. Joan Staples *Park:* On site. *Loc:*
From Damariscotta, Rte 130 to Bristol
(6 MI), L at Town Hall toward Rte 32,
2.5 MI, at Rte 32 turn R, 3 MI on L.

Roxbury

YANKEE GEM CORP
Rte 19, 04275
(207)364-4458 **6 24 32**
Large barn offering glass, china, pewter, primitives, guns, coins, toys, furni-

ture & paintings. *Hours:* May-Nov Daily, Sat & Winters by chance. *Assoc:* MADA. Dean A Mc Crillis *Loc:* 9 MI N off Rte 2.

Park: On site. *Loc:* Rte 1, N of Saco take R off Main onto Beach out to Ferry Rd.

Rumford

CONNIE'S ANTIQUES
190 Lincoln Ave, 04276
(207)364-8886   **48 64 85**
Clothing, linens, post cards, dolls, jewelry, toys, furniture, primitives, glass & china. *Hours:* By chance/appt, call advised. *Assoc:* MADA. Constance P Goudreau *Loc:* .75 MI off Rte 2, big blue house on top of hill.

Rumford Center

GROVE FARM ANTIQUES
Star Rte, 04278
(207)369-0259   **29 66 85**
Glass, paintings, prints, decorative arts & vintage clothing. *Hours:* May-Oct by chance/appt. Burton S de Frees *Loc:* From Rte 2 at Rumford Ctr go N 6 MI, then 1.2 MI on E Andover Rd.

Saco

F P WOODS, BOOKS
48 Ferry Rd, 04072
(207)282-2278   13
Specializing in Americana, literature, Shaker, utopian & communal material. *Pr:* $20–4000. *Est:* 1978. *Serv:* Appraisal, catalog, purchase estates, search service. *Hours:* BY APPT ONLY. *Assoc:* MABA. Frank P Woods

Sanford

BOOK ADDICT
Pine Tree Dr, 04073
(207)324-2243   13
Antiquarian books: a general collection including biography, history, adventure, nature, sports & fiction. *Hours:* May-Oct BY APPT. *Assoc:* MABA. David H Foshey

JOHN LEEKE, PRESERVATION CONSULT
Country Club Rd #2, 04073
(207)324-9597   **5 26 74**
Helping homeowners, tradesmen, contractors, architects & museums understand their historic buildings - involving problem solving, project management, planning, maintenance, programming & training. *Serv:* Conservation, consultation, repair, restoration, replication, reproduction. *Hours:* BY APPT ONLY.

Scarborough

TOP KNOTCH ANTIQUES
14 Willowdale Rd, 04074
(207)883-5303   40
Antiques, collectibles & oak furniture, signs, toys & tools. *Serv:* Consignments accepted. *Hours:* Daily & some evenings. *Loc:* From Rte 1 follow signs.

Searsport

ANTIQUES AT THE HILLMANS
Rte 1, 04974
(207)548-6658   **28 50 67**

Fine china, lamps, dolls, linens, stoneware, quilts, Victorian walnut & oak furniture. *Hours:* Apr-Oct daily. *Assoc:* MADA. Les Hillman *Loc:* 2.75 MI N of town.

BETTER DAY'S ANTIQUES
Rte 1, 04974
(207)548-2467   **40 83 86**

Victorian walnut, oak, mahogany & wicker furniture. *Est:* 1977. *Serv:* Appraisal, purchase estates. *Hours:* Daily 9-5. Melinda Frazee *Loc:* 1.5 MI S of village of Searsport.

THE CAPTAIN'S HOUSE ANTIQUES
E Main St, 04974
(207)548-6344   **21 37 60**

Formal American furniture of the 18th & 19th C. Specializing in Chinese export porcelain. Large selection of Canton, Rose Medallion & Mandarin Oriental carpets. *Hours:* Jun-Aug Mon-Sat 10-5 Sun 1-5. *Size:* Medium. Elizabeth Hoeschle *Park:* On site. *Loc:* 25 MI N of Searsport on US 1, between Camden & Bar Harbor.

GOLD COAST ANTIQUES
Rte 1, 04974
(207)548-2939   **32 50 52**

Antique dolls, doll accessories, doll dressmaking, old ivory, china, signed cut glass, Limoges, paintings, early oil lamps, miniatures & furniture. *Hours:* By chance/appt. *Assoc:* MADA. Vasco Baldacci

PRIMROSE FARM ANTIQUES
Rte 1, 04974
(207)548-6019   **28 80 81**

Country antiques, furniture, textiles, Shaker items, stoneware, baskets, tools, fine glass, china & ironstone. *Est:* 1973. *Hours:* Apr-Oct daily 9-5 CLOSED SUN. *Assoc:* MADA. Liz Dominic *Loc:* 3 MI N of Village.

PUMPKIN PATCH ANTIQUE CENTER
Rte 1, 04974
(207)548-6047   **{GR25}**

Eclectic array of Americana & Maine antiques in a two-story shop. *Hours:* Daily 9-5, Win BY APPT. *Assoc:* MADA. Bob Sommer

RED KETTLE ANTIQUES
Rte 1, 04974
(207)548-2978   **27 32 40**

Victorian walnut & oak furniture, country furniture & accessories & French & German dolls. *Hours:* All year by chance/appt. *Assoc:* MADA. Ginny Middleswart *Loc:* 3 MI N of Village on Rte 1.

Sebago

THE GALLERY SHOP
Off Rte 7, 04024
(207)787-3370   **14 44 63**

Finest in glass & ceramics, 18th to 20th C, excellent selection of related books. *Serv:* Jones Museum of Glass & Ceramics. *Hours:* May-Nov 14 Mon-Sat 9:30-5 Sun 1-5. *Assoc:* MADA NHADA.

Skowhegan

MAIN(E)LY BOOKS
178 Madison Ave, 04976
(207)474-3185 13
Antiquarian books: hunting, fishing, music, entertainment & military history. *Hours:* Year round BY APPT ONLY. *Assoc:* MABA. Robert Chandler

South Casco

VARNEY'S VOLUMES
Quaker Ridge Rd, 04015
(207)655-4605 13
General collection of out-of-print & rare books with specialty in children's & Maine. *Pr:* $5–250. *Est:* 1978. *Serv:* Mail orders anytime. *Hours:* Jul-Aug daily 10-5 CLOSED WED & SUN, else by chance/appt. *Assoc:* MABA. A. Lois Varney *Park:* On site. *Loc:* 25 MI NW of Portland just off Rte 302 between Portland & White Mts, turn R at Thomas Inn & Playhouse.

South China

COUNTRY ANTIQUES
Rte 32 Off Rte 3, 04358
(207)445-2315 1 15 27
Country furniture, specializing in pine - refinished & original paint - country smalls & primitives, kitchen utensils, iron, spongeware, yellow ware, redware, stoneware, & old tools. *Hours:* Daily by chance/appt. Karl Rau *Park:* In front. *Loc:* Rte 3E from Augusta, turn S onto Rte 32, 100 yds to shop.

GRAY MATTER SERVICE
Rte 3, 04358
(207)445-2245 13
Books: rare, used, out-of-print, collectibles, folk art & antiques. *Hours:* Apr-Dec Mon-Thu 10-5 Fri-Sun 1-5, Win: by chance, mail order. *Assoc:* MABA. Mabel Charles

South Portland

J. GLATTER BOOKS
146 Ocean St, 04106
(207)799-7283 13
Antiquarian books: 12,000 books. *Hours:* Year round Wed-Fri 11-5 Sat 12-4. *Assoc:* MABA. Jack Glatter

Southwest Harbor

MARIANNE CLARK FINE ANTIQUES
Main St Rte 102, 04679
(207)244-9247 27 29 37
Authentic 18th & 19th C country & formal furniture & accessories. *Pr:* $25–25000. *Hours:* Jun 15-Oct Mon-Sat 10-5. *Size:* Large. *Assoc:* AADA MADA. *Park:* On site. *Loc:* Rte 3 thru Ellsworth, to Int of Rte 102, to SW Harbor, on Mt Desert Island.

Springvale

HARLAND EASTMAN - BOOKS
66 Main St Rte 109, 04083
(207)324-2797 13 14
Old & rare books, a general collection with emphasis on Maine local history, Maine nonfiction, Maine authors, 19th & 20th C boys' & children's books. *Pr:*

$5–500. *Serv:* Appraisal. *Hours:* By chance/appt. *Size:* Medium. *Assoc:* MABA. *Park:* In front. *Loc:* 1.5 MI N of Int of Rtes 109 & 202, no sign.

GEORGE E MILKEY BOOKS
7 Frost St #2, 04083
(207)324-5510 13

Antiquarian books: out-of-print & rare books including Americana, literature, ships & the sea, natural history & scholarly books. *Hours:* Year round daily 9-9. *Assoc:* MABA.

Spruce Head
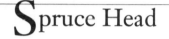

ELFAST'S ANTIQUES
Patten Point Rd, 04859
(207)594-9377 63 67 80

Specialize in a large selection of British china & pottery, including stick sponge, gaudy Welsh, blue & white, soft paste, yellow ware & ironstone, as well as quilts, rugs, textiles, country furniture & related accessories. *Est:* 1972. *Hours:* Jun-Oct daily 10-5, Sep-Jun by chance/appt. *Assoc:* MADA. Bruce Elfast *Loc:* Follow signs from Rte 1 between Thomaston & Rockland.

Steep Falls

WARD'S BOOK BARN
Box 6, 04085
(207)675-3348 13

Antiquarian books: old fiction - much before 1900 - biography, military & rare books. *Hours:* Year round daily 9-8. *Assoc:* MABA. Ellery Ward

Stockton Springs

BRICK HOUSE ANTIQUES
Rte 1 @ Sandy Point, 04981
(207)567-3173 17 37 81

18th & 19th C American & French furniture, primitives, art glass, china, tools, metals, bronzes, lamps & paintings. *Hours:* Jun-Sep or by chance. *Assoc:* MADA. Violet K Paddock

VICTORIAN HOUSE BOOK BARN
E Main St, 04981
(207)567-3351 13

Antiquarian books: old, out-of-print & scarce books. *Serv:* Mail & phone orders, search service. *Hours:* Apr-Dec daily 8-8 Jan-Mar by chance/appt. *Assoc:* MABA. Andrew B MacEwen

Thomaston

ANCHOR FARM ANTIQUES
184-186 Main St, 04861
(207)354-8859 47 63 77

Two large rooms featuring sterling silver, jewelry, china, lamps, tools & furniture. *Est:* 1975. *Serv:* Appraisal, purchase estates. *Hours:* By chance/appt. *Size:* Large. *Assoc:* MADA. Muriel D Knutson *Park:* In front. *Loc:* Rte 1 next to ME State Prison.

WEE BARN ANTIQUES
4 1/2 Georges St, 04861
(207)354-6163 32 36 47

Furniture, accessories, silver, jewelry, art glass, toys & fine china. *Hours:* All year. *Assoc:* MADA. Gwen B Robinson *Loc:* Just off Rte 1.

Topsham

MERRYMEETING ANTIQUES
Pleasant Point Rd, 04086
(207)729-9251   **44 59 63**
Fine art, cut glass, china, pewter &
paintings. *Hours:* All year by
chance/appt. *Assoc:* MADA. Ellie V
Carver

TOPSHAM FAIR MALL
Rte 196, 04086
(207)729-7913   **{GR}**
Victoriana, country, samplers, prints,
china, books, jewelry, glassware & Oriental art. *Hours:* Mon-Thu 9:30-5:30
Fri til 9 Sun 12-5. *Loc:* I-95 Exit 24.

Trenton

**THE ACADIA MEWS ANTIQUE
CENTER**
Rte 3 Bar Harbor Rd, 04605
(207)667-7323   **65 86**
Quality furnishings, antique wicker,
country, folk art & primitives. *Est:*
1953. *Hours:* May-Oct Mon-Sat 11-4.
Loc: 7 MI from Ellsworth on the way
to Bar Harbor.

MAYO ANTIQUES GALLERY
Rte 3, 04605
(207)667-2586   **21 36 86**
Formal, Victorian, country, wicker,
paintings, baskets, rugs & collectibles.
Serv: Auction, appraisal. *Hours:* Year
round Mon-Sat 10-5. *CC:* MC/V.
Nancy Mayo *Park:* In front. *Loc:* Between Ellsworth & Bar Harbor.

Troy

GREEN'S CORNER ANTIQUES
Rte 202, 04987
(207)948-2355   **27 40 83**
A large barn full of oak, mahogany &
pine furniture, thousands of small
items, doorstops, kitchenware, toys,
signs, tools & stoneware. Also stock
farm-related items - cupboards, frames
& lighting. *Pr:* $1-1000. *Est:* 1975.
Serv: Appraisal, consultation, purchase
estates, repairs. *Hours:* Year round
daily, appt suggested. *Size:* Large. Ron
Reed *Park:* On site. *Loc:* From Water-
ville, Rte 139, Rte 202 in Unity, 4 MI
on L N of Unity.

Union

EBENEZER ALDEN HOUSE
Union, 04862
(207)785-2881   **37 59 63**
Fine 18th & 19th C American furni-
ture, paintings, Oriental porcelains,
primitives & country pieces. *Hours:*
All year appt suggested. *Assoc:* MADA.
Hazel Marcus *Loc:* Int of Rtes 235 &
17, next to Firehouse.

Waldoboro

**WILLIAM EVANS,
CABINETMAKER**
W Main St, 04572
(207)832-4175   **19 70 71**
Traditional handmade furniture to
order. Restoration of quality formal
antiques by a European-trained craftsman. *Serv:* Conservation, custom
woodwork, reproduction, restoration.

Hours: By chance/appt. **Park:** On site.
Loc: In The Village on Main St 1st bldg
W of the bridge on the N Side.

OLD LIBRARY BOOKSTORE
Friendship St, 04572
(207)832-6330   **13**
Antiquarian books: 10,000 arranged by
category. **Hours:** Mon-Fri 9:30-4 Sat
9:30-1. **Assoc:** MABA. Martha Melan-
son

Warren

ABLE TO CANE
67 Main St, 04864
(207)273-3747   **22**
Caning, basketry & wicker material.
Serv: Repairs on all types of antique
seats.

Warren Village

VILLAGE ANTIQUE GROUP
SHOP
Union & Main Sts, 04864
(207)273-2860   **{GR9}**
Country, linens, silver, jewelry, glass,
china & collectibles. **Hours:** May-Oct
daily 10-4.

Waterboro

WATERBORO EMPORIUM
Rte 202, 04067
(207)247-4128   **11 42 80**
Pine & oak furniture, baseball cards,
jewelry, ephemera, linens, rugs, textiles, depression & pattern glass.

Hours: Sep-May Fri-Sun 10-4 Jun-
Aug 9-5. Sherry Porter **Loc:** On the
Square.

Wells

1774 HOUSE ANTIQUES
Rte 1, 04090
(207)646-3520   **27 65 67**
Cupboards, country, primitives, quilts,
decorative accessories & small furniture - always interesting & unique
items. **Hours:** Daily. Stan Tufts **Loc:**
Across from Bo-Mar Hall.

THE ARRINGTONS
Rte 1, 04090
(207)646-4124   **13**
Antiquarian books: emphasis on Amer-
icana & military history. **Hours:** Mar-
Nov daily 9-5, Nov-Mar by
chance/appt. **Assoc:** MABA. Eleanor
Arrington

BO-MAR HALL
Rte 1, 04090
(207)646-4116   **{GR85}**
Lots of furniture, antiques & collectibles. **Hours:** Daily 10-5. **Loc:** I-95 Exit
2.

THE BOOK BARN
US Rte 1, 04090
(207)646-4926   **9 11 13**
Large general bookstock, baseball
cards & comicstock. **Serv:** Appraisal,
catalog (no charge), purchase estates.
Hours: Apr-Nov daily 10-5, Dec-Mar
Sat,Sun 10-5. **Size:** Medium. **CC:**
MC/V. **Assoc:** MABA. Ann Polizzi
Park: Nearby lot. **Loc:** I-95 Exit 2: L at
ramp onto Rte 109E, R to Rte 1S, 100
yds on L, next to shopping ctr.

COUNTRY BARN
US Rte 1, 04090
(207)646-5507   **33 40 42**
Refinished oak & pine furniture, ephemera, tinware, china, glass & primitive & country accessories. *Hours:* May-Oct Tue-Sun 10-5. *Assoc:* MADA. Edward T Goebel

COREY DANIELS
Shady Ln Drakes Island, 04090
(207)646-5301   **34 37 45**
Large selection of visually appealing European antiques for house & garden, choice American folk art & furniture. *Est:* 1971. *Serv:* Purchase estates. *Hours:* Daily by chance/appt. *Loc:* From Rte 1, R on Drakes Island Rd, R on Shady Ln.

EAST COAST BOOKS
Depot St Rte 109, 04090
(207)646-3584   **9 13 66**
Collection of used & out-of-print books & remainders, specializing in fine art prints, drawings, watercolors, historical paper & autographs of the 17th thru 20th C. *Pr:* $10–5000. *Est:* 1976. *Serv:* Appraisal, auction (accept mail bids), catalog, purchase estates. *Hours:* Apr-Oct 15 daily 10-6, else BY APPT. *CC:* AX/MC/V. *Assoc:* MABA. Merv Slotnik *Park:* On site. *Loc:* I-95 Exit 2: .5 MI E of Exit.

THE FARM
Mildram Rd, 04090
(207)985-2656   **16 39 53**
Specializing in English antiques with a large stock of English formal & country furniture, mirrors, lighting, silver, pottery & porcelain, metalware & Chinese export porcelain for the discriminating collector. *Pr:* $25–10000. *Hours:* Sum: daily 10-4 CLOSED WED. Win: Weekends. *Size:* Large.

Thomas Hackett *Park:* On site. *Loc:* From US Rte 1, 2.5 MI W on Coles Hill Rd to Mildram Rd, turn L, farm is on the R.

HARDINGS BOOK SHOP
US Rte 1, 04090
(207)646-8785   **13 51 66**
A very large stock of quality old & rare books, maps & prints, Maine & New England town histories meticulously arranged. *Hours:* Apr-Dec daily 9-5, Jan-Mar Fri-Sun 9-5. *Size:* Medium. *Assoc:* ABAA MABA MADA. Douglas N Harding *Park:* On site. *Loc:* I-95 Exit 2: E to Rte 1, turn L, on the L.

R JORGENSEN ANTIQUES
Rte 1, 04090
(207)646-9444   **2 39 59**
Eleven extensive showrooms of fine period antiques - formal & country - American, British Isles, French & Scandinavian furniture & accessories displayed in lovely room settings. *Hours:* Daily 10-5 CLOSED WED. *Assoc:* MADA NHADA. *Park:* On site. *Loc:* I-95 Exit 2: E to Rte 1, N until large sign on the L.

A DAVID PAULHUS BOOKS
Burnt Mill Rd, 04090
(207)646-7022   **13 59 66**
Antiquarian books - emphasis on Americana & fine bindings, paintings & prints. *Hours:* Year round by chance/appt. *Assoc:* MABA.

RIVERBANK ANTIQUES
Rte 1 - Wells Union Antique Ctr, 04090
(207)646-6314   **5 38 45**
Two floors of 18th & 19th C American & English C American, English & Continental furniture & decorations, including garden ornaments & archi-

tectural elements. *Pr:* $5–10000. *Est:* 1976. *Serv:* Purchase estates. *Hours:* May-Nov Mon-Sat 10-5 Sun 12-5, Mar-Apr CLOSED TUE-THU. *Size:* Large. Lynn E Chase *Park:* On site. *Loc:* I-95 Exit 2: Rte 1, .25 MI N, bldg #9 at Wells Antique Ctr.

SNUG HARBOR BOOKS
Rte 1, 04090
(207)646-4124   **9 13 66**
Large stock of scarce & out-of-print books, with emphasis on Americana, Civil War, the West & fine bindings; also prints & autographs. *Hours:* Jun-Labor Day daily 9-6, off season weekends 10-5 or BY APPT. *Assoc:* MADA.

WELLS ANTIQUE MART
Rte 1, 04090
(207)646-8153   **{GR85}**
Furniture, decorative accessories, glass, china, quilts, metalwork, jewelry, lace & linens, quilts. *Hours:* Year round: daily 9-5 CLOSED TUE. *Park:* In front. *Loc:* I-95 Exit 2.

WELLS UNION ANTIQUE CENTER
US Rte 1, 04090
(207)646-6612   **{GR15}**
Nine individually owned shops with 15 dealers carrying a wide range of country, formal, American, English & Continental furniture, paintings & accessories, garden statuary, architectural, glass, china, jewelry & collectibles. *Pr:* $1–10000. *Est:* 1982. *Hours:* May-Nov daily, Dec-Apr CLOSED TUE, WED. call ahead. *Size:* Huge. *CC:* MC/V. *Park:* On site. *Loc:* I-95 Exit 2: L off Exit on Rte 109, to Rte 1, at light take L, .25 MI on R.

West Bath

F BARRIE FREEMAN ANTIQUES
Quaker Point Farm, 04530
(207)442-8452   **29**
Period decorative accessories. *Hours:* BY APPT. *Loc:* Bath is at Int of I-95 & Rte 6.

West Brooklin

LOUISA GOODYEAR ANTIQUES
Old Friends Barn, 04616
(207)359-8949   **27 33 65**
Maine furniture, country implements, primitives, oddities & collectibles. *Pr:* $1–500. *Est:* 1970. *Serv:* Purchase estates. *Hours:* May 15-Oct 15 Mon-Sat 11-5, Oct 16-May 14 by chance/appt. *Assoc:* MADA. *Park:* On site. *Loc:* 5 MI from Dear Isle Bridge, or Sedgewick, L toward Brooklin, 1 MI.

West Southport

CATHERINE HILL ANTIQUES
Cozy Harbor, 04576
(207)633-3683   **32 36 65**
Furniture, primitives, toys, decorative items in the shed. *Hours:* By chance/appt. *Loc:* 1 block off Rte 27 between Boothbay Harbor & Newagen.

Westbrook

PEG GERAGHTY-BOOKS
41 The Hamlet, 04092
(207)854-2520   **13 33**
Antiquarian books: emphasis on

children's books, Americana & paper ephemera. *Hours:* Year round BY APPT ONLY. *Assoc:* MABA.

Windham

CIDER MILL ANTIQUE MALL
Rte 302, 04062
(207)892-5900 {GR}
Furniture, glass, jewelry, china, oak, mahogany, period clothing & primitives. *Hours:* Daily 10-5 Thu til 7. *Loc:* ME Tnpk Exit 8: 9 MI from Portland in the Sebago Lake Region.

Winter Harbor

POND HOUSE ANTIQUES
Main St E, 04693
(207)963-2992 16 28 66
Large shop featuring primitives, country, pewter, copper, brass, stoneware, decoys, quilts, paintings, prints. *Pr:* $25–1000. *Est:* 1985. *Serv:* Purchase estates. *Hours:* May 15-Oct 15 daily 9-5 by chance/appt. *Size:* Medium. Elsie R Fanning *Park:* In front. *Loc:* Rte 1N out of Ellsworth, Rte 186.

Winterport

RICHARD & PATRICIA BEAN
Rte 1A, 04496
(207)223-5381 37 63
18th & 19th C American furniture & Chinese porcelain. *Loc:* 12 MI from Bangor Airport.

Wiscasset

COACH HOUSE ANTIQUES
Pleasant St, 04578
(207)882-7833 36 59 65
Country & formal furniture, primitives, paintings & unusual accessories. *Est:* 1966. *Hours:* All Year, Win: by chance/appt. *Assoc:* MADA. William Glennon

LILAC COTTAGE
Main St On The Green Rte 1, 04578
(207)882-7059 16 37 39
19th C American & English furniture, porcelain, pewter & decorative items. *Hours:* Jun-Sep daily 10-5 CLOSED SUN. *Assoc:* MADA. Shirley Andrews

MARINE ANTIQUES
US Rte 1, 04578
(207)882-7208 54 56 72
Selected marine antiques including ship paintings, scrimshaw, models, instruments & carvings, also campaign furniture. *Pr:* $500–50000. *Serv:* Appraisal, consultation. *Hours:* By chance/appt. *Size:* Large. John T Newton *Park:* In front.

MARSTON HOUSE AMERICAN ANTIQUES
Main St at Middle St, 04578
(207)882-6010 1 32 41
18th & 19th C American country furniture & accessories in original paint, primitives, folk art, birdhouses, baskets, toys, quilts, rugs & linens. *Pr:* $100–10000. *Est:* 1987. *Hours:* Apr-Oct daily 10-5, else by chance/appt. *Size:* Medium. *CC:* AX/MC/V. *Assoc:* NHADA. Paul Mrozinski *Park:* On

site. *Loc:* Rte 1 to Wiscasset, in ctr of town at corner of Main St (Rte 1) & Middle St.

MUSICAL WONDER HOUSE
18 High St, 04578
(207)882-7163   **55**

Antique music boxes, wind-up phonographs, records & player pianos. *Pr:* $950–50000. *Est:* 1963. *Serv:* Appraisal, conservation, consultation, purchase estates, repairs, rest. *Hours:* May 2-Oct daily, else BY APPT ONLY. *CC:* AX/MC/V. Danilo Konvalinka *Park:* In front. *Loc:* Rte 1 to Wiscasset, 50 MI N of Portland, 150 MI N of Boston.

NONESUCH HOUSE
1 Middle St, 04578
(207)882-6768   **{GR9}**

18th & early 19th C formal & country furniture, accessories, paintings, prints, rare books, quality smalls, nautical & folk art. *Est:* 1982. *Hours:* Apr-Nov daily 10-5. *CC:* MC/V. Dan Anspach Terry Lewis *Park:* Nearby. *Loc:* 80 ft from Rte 1.

MARGARET B OFSLAGER
Main St, 04578
(207)882-6082   **21 65 67**

American antiques, country, hooked rugs, paintings, quilts & primitives. *Loc:* At Main & Summer St.

AARON & HANNAH PARKER ANTIQUES
US Rte 1, 04578
(207)882-6160   **32 48 67**

Decorative accessories, quilts, linens, toys, formal furniture, ironstone & ephemera. *Est:* 1983. *Hours:* Year round daily 9-5, Jan-Feb Wed-Sat 9-5.

Size: Large. *CC:* MC/V. *Assoc:* MADA. *Park:* On site. *Loc:* 2.5 MI S of Wiscasset.

PORRINGER & BRUCE MARCUS ANTIQUE
Water St, 04578
(207)882-7951   **37**

Specializing in 17th, 18th & 19th C furniture. *Est:* 1976. *Serv:* Appraisal, consultation. *Hours:* Year round Mon-Sat 10-4:30. Barbara Darling *Park:* Nearby. *Loc:* On the waterfront by the Old Ships.

SHEILA & EDWIN RIDEOUT
12 Summer St, 04578
(207)882-6420   **27 57 63**

American, English 18th & 19th C pottery, samplers, needlework pictures, country & furniture. *Hours:* Sum: Tue-Fri 10:30-6 else by chance/appt. *Assoc:* MADA.

SPRIG OF THYME ANTIQUES
US Rte 1, 04578
(207)882-6150   **34 41 65**

Early Cape Cod house filled with country painted furniture & proper accessories, folk art & other country needs. *Hours:* Apr-Oct daily 10-5, else by chance/appt. Linda P Heard *Park:* On site.

PATRICIA STAUBLE ANTIQUES
Rte 1 & Pleasant St, 04578
(207)882-6341   **{GR4}**

American country & period furniture & accessories, art, folk art, pottery, textiles & hooked rugs. *Pr:* $50–12000. *Est:* 1965. *Serv:* Appraisal, interior design, purchase estates. *Hours:* May-Nov Mon-Sat 10-5, Dec-Apr by chance/appt. *Size:* Large. *CC:* V. *Assoc:* MADA. *Park:* On site. *Loc:* Rte 1 - in town.

TWO AT WISCASSET
Main St, 04578
(207)882-5286   1 34 50
American country furniture with original paint a specialty, paintings, folk art, toys, early lighting & hooked rugs. *Pr:* $25–2500. *Est:* 1974. *Hours:* Apr 15-Nov 15 daily, call ahead if coming a long distance. *Assoc:* MADA. Doris Stauble *Loc:* Rte 1.

WISCASSET BAY GALLERY
Water St, 04578
(207)882-7682   59 66 71
Specializing in fine 19th & early 20th C American & European paintings with a focus on New England artists. The gallery is continually acquiring choice samples of work by both noted & less known artists who came to Maine to paint its rugged coast. *Pr:* $250–5000. *Est:* 1985. *Serv:* Appraisal, brochure, conservation, purchase estates, restoration. *Hours:* May-Oct Thu-Tue 10-5, Nov-Dec 21 Sat 10-4. *Size:* Medium. *CC:* MC/V. Keith S Oehmig *Park:* On site. *Loc:* N on Rte 1, last road on L before bridge, S on Rte 1, 1st road on R after bridge.

Woolwich

ANTIQUES ETC
Rte 1, 04579
(207)443-4550   44 48 63
Victorian glass, china, linens, pictures, furniture, accessories & country smalls. *Hours:* May-Sep daily 10-5. *Assoc:* MADA. Pauline Thibodeau *Loc:* .5 MI N of Bath Bridge on US Rte 1.

Yarmouth

GERALD W BELL AUCTIONEER
139 Main St, 04096
(207)989-3357   8
Auctioning antiques & estate jewelry. 10% buyer's premium. *Serv:* Accept phone bids.

NATHAN D CUSHMAN INC
Box 281, 04096
(207)846-4197   77
Silver specialist - fine antiques. *Hours:* BY APPT.

THE RED SHED
12 Pleasant St, 04096
(207)865-4228   36 48 77
Four rooms of antique furniture & accessories including sterling & Victorian silver, fine china, jewelry, glass, linens & post cards. *Hours:* Mar-Dec 23 daily 10-4 CLOSED SUN. *Assoc:* MADA.

W M SCHWIND, JR ANTIQUES
17 E Main St Rte 88, 04096
(207)846-9458   36 59 66
Shop in 1810 house featuring country & formal furniture, paintings, prints, ceramics, glass, rugs & related accessories. *Est:* 1967. *Hours:* Year round, Sum: Mon-Fri 10-5. *Assoc:* MADA.

SUMNER & STILLMAN
PO Box 225, 04096
(207)846-6070   13
First editions of English literature from 1835-1935: Alcott, Conrad, Cooper, Crane, Dickens, Doyle, Eliot, Emerson, Hardy, Harris, Hawthorne, Irving, James, Kipling, Longfellow, Melville, Meredith, Poe, Stevenson, Stow, Thackeray, Thoreau & Trollope.

Serv: Catalogs. *Hours:* BY APPT ONLY. *Assoc:* ABAA MABA. Richard S Loomis Jr

York

LAWRENCE FORLANO
Chases Pond Rd, 03909
(207)363-7009   21
Antique & old decorative Oriental carpets. *Est:* 1960. *Serv:* Cleaning & repair. *Hours:* Daily 10-5, call ahead advisable. *Park:* On site. *Loc:* I-95 York Exit: .5 MI.

GORGEANA ANTIQUES
Southside Rd, 03909
(207)363-3842   **44 63**
Specializing in fine quality glass, china & collectibles. *Hours:* All year by chance/appt. *Assoc:* MADA. Julia Upham *Loc:* .5 MI E of Rte 1S of York River.

MARITIME AUCTIONS
US Rte 1, 03909
(207)363-4247   **8**
Nautical auctions, firehouse, railroad, scientific instrument auctions, absentee bids, 10% buyers premium, mari-

time art. Auctions held at Seaboard Auction Gallery. *Serv:* Catalogs issued, mailing lists, accept consignment. *Hours:* Summer by chance/appt. Chuck DeLuca

POST ROAD ANTIQUES & BOOKS
Chase's Pond Rd, 03909
(207)363-7922   **13 29**
General line of period antiques & accessories & old & rare books. *Hours:* Tue-Sat 10-5 or BY APPT.

JOHN LARKIN SGRO
337 Rte 1S, 03909
(207)363-2784   **29 36**
Furniture, accessories advertising & smalls.

York Beach

SAMUEL WEISER BOOKS
PO Box 612, 03910
(207)363-7290   **13**
Antiquarian books: Oriental philosophy, metaphysics & the arcane traditions. *Hours:* BY APPT ONLY. *Assoc:* MABA. Glen Houghton

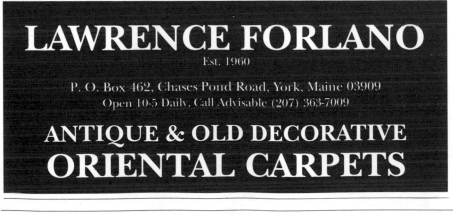

▼

Massachusetts

Abington

ABINGTON AUCTION GALLERY
728 Brockton Ave, 02351
(617)857-2001 **8**
An antiques & quality household merchandise specialized auction gallery for Americana & Victorian items. All auctions conducted Saturday at 6:30 with a 3-hour preview. *Est:* 1985. *Serv:* Appraisal, auction, estates purchased. *Hours:* Office Mon-Fri 10-5. Charles D Glynn *Park:* On site. *Loc:* 15 min from Rte 24 on Rte 123, 20 min from Rte 3.

Acton

ENCORES
174 Great Rd Rte 2A, 01720
(508)263-1515 **27 42**
Two rooms of European country furniture & fine reproduction pieces - featuring an extensive selection of quality pieces including armoires, cupboards, sideboards, tables & chairs, dressers, buffets, desks, coffee tables, painted & one-of-a-kind pieces. *Pr:* $300–3000. *Hours:* Mon-Sat 10-5 Thu til 8 Sun 1-5. *Size:* Large. *CC:* MC/V. Nancy Lenicheck *Park:* In front. *Loc:* I-95 Rte 2 W: 9 MI, at rotary take 2nd Exit, Rte 2A/119, 1.5 MI on L.

SEAGULL ANTIQUES
60 Great Rd, 01720
(508)263-0338 **7 36 77**
An everchanging array of quality antiques from period to deco - furniture, sterling & accessories. *Pr:* $25–5000. *Serv:* Appraisal, purchase estates. *Hours:* Sep-Jun Tue-Sat 10-4:30 Sun

12:30-4:30, Sum: Tue-Sat 10-4:30. *Size:* Medium. *CC:* MC/V. Carole Siegal *Park:* In front. *Loc:* I-495 Exit 31: to Littleton Common, Rte 2A E, 10 min to Great Rd, OR RTe 128, to Rte 2W, to Rte 2A W, 15 mins to Great Rd.

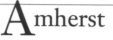Amherst

AMHERST ANTIQUARIAN MAPS
51 Mc Clellan St, 01002
(413)256-8900 **51 66**
Old, rare, original maps, charts & prints from the 16th-19th C. *Pr:* $10–3000. *Serv:* Occasional catalog ($2). *Hours:* Year round by chance appt. *CC:* MC/V. *Assoc:* MRIAB. Jon Rosenthal *Park:* In front. *Loc:* In Amherst Ctr, less than .25 MI from the post office.

BOOK MARKS
1 E Pleasant St, 01002
(413)549-6136 **13**
Antiquarian books: photography, art, architecture, illustrated, literary criticism, literature & music. *Hours:* Mon-Sat 10-5. *Assoc:* MRIAB. Fred Marks *Loc:* Located in the Carriage Shops.

R & R FRENCH ANTIQUES
657 S Pleasant St Rte 116, 01002
(413)253-2269 **2 36**
18th & 19th C furniture, lighting, fireplace tools, ceramics, pewter & textiles. *Hours:* Mon-Sat by chance/appt. *Assoc:* PVADA. Rachael C French

GRIST MILL ANTIQUES
Rte 116 & 26 Mill Ln, 01002
(413)253-5296 **33 36 44**
An eclectic collection of furniture, glass, ephemera, advertising, post

cards, political memorabilia, posters, kitchenware, fountain pens, lighting - mostly from the Victorian era through the 1930s. *Est:* 1978. *Serv:* Consultation, interior design, purchase estates. *Hours:* Feb-Dec Thu-Mon 10-5 Sun 12-5. *Size:* Large. *Assoc:* PVADA. Hill Boss *Park:* On site. *Loc:* Rte 116, 1 MI S of Amherst Commons.

LEIF LAUDAMUS, RARE BOOKS
62 Orchard St, 01002
(413)253-5188 13
Antiquarian books: bibliography, early printing, history of science, incunabula, medicine, Bibles, illustrated, foreign language & rare books. *Serv:* Appraisal, catalog. *Hours:* BY APPT. *Assoc:* MRIAB.

POLISSACK ANTIQUE JEWELRY
233 N Pleasant St, 01002
(413)549-1630 23
Vintage wristwatches. *Hours:* TO THE TRADE. *Loc:* Rte 91N Exit 19: Carriage Shops.

ROSENTHAL PAPER RESTORATION
51 Mc Clellan St, 01002
(413)256-0844 25 71
Conservation & restoration of flat printed paper. *Hours:* BY APPT ONLY. *Assoc:* AIC NECA. Bernice M Rosenthal

VALLEY BOOKS
199 Pleasant St, 01002
(413)256-1508 13 14
Two floors of used, discounted new & old books on all subjects, first editions & out-of-print books. Specializing in literature, the arts, history & sports. *Est:* 1975. *Serv:* Appraisal, catalog, search service. *Hours:* Sep-May Mon-

Fri 10:30-5:30 Sat 10-5 Sun 12-5, else 10-5. *Size:* Medium. *CC:* AX/MC/V. *Assoc:* MRIAB NEBA. Lawrence Pruner *Park:* In front. *Loc:* I-91 Amherst Exit (Rte 9E): 6 MI to lights at Amherst College, turn L, go thru 2 lights & look for store on R.

WOOD-SHED ANTIQUES
156 Montague Rd, 01002
(413)549-1720 16
Iron, tin & wooden items from the kitchen & pantry & white textiles. *Pr:* $25–250. *Serv:* Brochure. *Hours:* Apr-Nov Mon-Wed,Fri 10-6. Bea Q Wood *Park:* On site.

Andover

ANDOVER ANTIQUARIAN BOOKS
68 Park St, 01810
(508)475-1645 13 51 66
In a Victorian business complex, a select stock of unusual new & old books, maps & prints. Book arts & crafts shows held regularly. Coffee & tea available. *Pr:* $1–500. *Est:* 1977. *Serv:* Appraisal, catalog,˙ search service, repairs, restoration. *Hours:* Mon-Sat 10-5. *Size:* Medium. *CC:* MC/V. *Assoc:* ABAA MRIAB. V David Roger *Park:* On sight. *Loc:* Located across from Park St Village, 2 blocks E of Main St & Old Town Hall.

NEW ENGLAND GALLERY INC
350 N Main St, 01810
(508)475-2116 37
18th C American furniture & accessories. *Est:* 1969. *Serv:* Appraisal, purchase estates. *Hours:* Tue-Sat 9-4 appt suggested. Robert A Blekicki *Park:* Nearby. *Loc:* Rte 495 Exit 41A.

Arlington

Ashby

IRREVERENT RELICS
102 & 106 Massachusetts Ave, 02174
(617)646-0370   **1 28 42**
Specializing in a country look for folks with city sophistication & city spaces. 2 shops full of the weird & wonderful from hooked rugs to pastoral paintings. *Pr:* $5–2500. *Serv:* Conservation, consultation, interior design, purchase estates, repairs. *Hours:* Tue,Wed 12-6 Thu 12-8 Fri 12-5 Sat 10-6, call ahead advised. *Size:* Medium. Kristin Duvalle *Park:* On site. *Loc:* 2 blocks N of Int of Rte 16 & Massachusetts Ave, approx 1.5 MI N of Porter Sq, 3 MI N of Harvard Sq.

SCIENTIA BOOKS
432A Massachusetts Ave, 02174
(617)643-5725   **13**
Specializing in antiquarian books on medicine, science & evolution, scholarly books on history of medicine & history of science. *Est:* 1985. *Serv:* Appraisal, catalog, search service. *Hours:* BY APPT ONLY. *Assoc:* MRIAB. Malcolm J Kottler *Loc:* From Rte 128, take Rte 60 (Pleasant St) Exit 80: 1 MI then R at Int of Pleasant & Massachusetts Ave.

SECOND TYME AROUND
1193A Massachusetts Ave, 02174
(617)646-5789   **47 48 77**
Antique & costume jewelry, linens, sterling & furniture. *Hours:* Mon,Tue,Fri,Sat 10-5 Thu 10-8. *CC:* MC/V. *Park:* In front.

COUNTRY BED SHOP
Richardson Rd, 01431
(508)386-7550   **19 43 70**
Country & high style reproduction beds, chairs & tables. Each piece made to order. *Pr:* $1000–8000. *Est:* 1972. *Serv:* Catalog ($4), replication, reproduction, custom work. *Hours:* Mon-Sat 8-5 appt suggested. Alan W Pease *Park:* On site. *Loc:* Call for directions.

Ashley Falls

DON ABARBANEL
East Main St, 01222
(413)229-3330   **16 57 63**
Needlework, brass, metalwork, English pottery, Delft, Chinese export porcelain & formal accessories. *Hours:* Daily 10-5, call ahead in winter. *Assoc:* BCoADA. *Park:* In front. *Loc:* Just off Rte 7A.

ASHLEY FALLS ANTIQUES
Rte 7A, 01222
(413)229-8759   **37 47**
18th & 19th C American furniture & antique jewelry. *Hours:* Daily 9:30-5:30. *Assoc:* BCoADA. Jeanne Cherneff *Park:* Nearby.

CIRCA
Rte 7A, 01222
(413)229-2990   **38 63**
Majolica - English, American & French - Canton, American & Continental furniture. *Hours:* Fri-Mon 10-5. *Assoc:* BCoADA. *Park:* On site.

LEWIS & WILSON
E Main St, 01222
(413)229-3330　　　　**39 59 60**

English, French & Oriental furniture, paintings, china, ginger jars & lighting fixtures. *Hours:* Daily 10-5. *Assoc:* BCoADA. Don Lewis *Park:* On site. *Loc:* Renovated train station, green with yellow trim, just off Rte 7A.

RUSSELL LYONS
Rte 7A, 01222
(413)229-2453　　　　**29 38**

Continental furniture & decorative accessories. *Hours:* Daily by chance/appt. *Park:* In front.

ROBERT THAYER AMERICAN ANTIQUES
E Main St, 01222
(413)229-2965　　　　**1 37**

Specializing in Americana. *Serv:* All items unreservedly guaranteed as represented. *Hours:* By chance/appt. *Park:* On site. *Loc:* Just off Rte 7A.

THE VOLLMERS
Rte 7A Box 325, 01222
(413)229-3463　　　　**6 27 59**

Country furniture, paintings, firearms & accessories. *Hours:* Daily 10-5, TUE by chance. *Assoc:* BCoADA. Diana Vollmer *Park:* On site.

Auburn

KENNETH ANDERSON
PO Box H, 01501
(508)832-3524　　　　**4 13**

A general stock of antiquarian books relating to hunting, fishing, golf, tennis & mountaineering. *Serv:* Appraisal. *Hours:* Mail order only. *Assoc:* ABAA.

AUBURN FLEA MARKET
773 Southbridge St Rte 12, 01501
(508)832-2763

Sunday flea market with 150 indoor & outdoor selling spaces. *Serv:* Space - $10. *Hours:* Sun 9-4. *Loc:* I-90 Exit 10 OR I-290 Exit 7 OR I-395 Exit 7: follow Rte 12S .5 MI.

Barnstable Village

BARNSTABLE VILLAGE ANTIQUES
3267 Main St, 02630
(508)362-8538　　　　**{GR7}**

Fine period furniture, Oriental porcelain, American primitives, tools, scales, country furniture, glass, textiles, china, Staffordshire & clocks. *Est:* 1985. *Hours:* Daily 10-5. Daniel Cobb *Park:* In front. *Loc:* In the village.

CAPE COD SHOPPER
3217 Main St Rte 6A, 02630
(508)775-2895　　　　**{GR2}**

Glass & paper antiques & collectibles: 25,000 post cards, sheet music & ephemera, pressed & depression glass, commemorative glass & pottery, bottles, nostalgia collectibles & jewelry. *Est:* 1983. *Serv:* Appraisal, consultation. mail order. *Hours:* Apr 15-Dec 21 Tue-Sat 10:30-4, Dec 22-Apr 14 BY APPT. *Assoc:* CCADA. Jane Sheckells *Park:* In front. *Loc:* From Rte 6 Exit 6: Rte 132 to Rte 6A, turn R, just past Barnstable County Court House in Barnstable Village Ctr.

Belmont

CROSS & GRIFFIN
468 Trapelo Rd, 02178
(617)484-2837
General line of furniture & decorative accessories. *Est:* 1961. *Hours:* Tue-Sat 10-4. *CC:* MC/V. *Park:* On street. *Loc:* Rte 128, Trapelo Rd Exit: toward Belmont, 4 MI at Waverly Square.

PAYSON HALL BOOKSHOP
80 Trapelo Rd, 02178
(617)484-2020   13
Antiquarian bookseller. *Serv:* Search service. *Hours:* Tue-Fri 10-7 Sat 10-4. *Assoc:* MRIAB. Clare M Murphy

Bernardston

BERNARDSTON BOOKS
503 South St, 01337
(413)648-9864   13 14
Out-of-print books history, biography, anthropology, military, natural history, Black history, fiction classics, theology & religion, philosophy of history, linguistics, sociology, art & music, poetry & literary criticism. *Pr:* $5–500. *Est:* 1986. *Serv:* Conversation, purchase estates. *Hours:* By chance/appt. *Size:* Large. *Assoc:* MRIAB. A L Fullerton *Park:* On site. *Loc:* I-91 Exit 28: Rte 10S OR I-91 Exit 27: Rte 5N.

Beverly

A R M ASSOCIATES
3 Bass St, 01915
(508)532-3506   4 84
Appraisal of antique & special interest cars. *Serv:* Appraisal. *Hours:* BY APPT. *Assoc:* ISA. Anthony R Miller

JEAN S MC KENNA BOOK SHOP
10 Longview Terr, 01915
(508)927-3067   13
Antiquarian books: biography, children's, illustrated, literature, local history & fiction. *Serv:* Appraisal, search service. *Hours:* BY APPT. *Assoc:* MRIAB.

PRICE HOUSE ANTIQUES
137 Cabot St, 01915
(508)927-5595   22 36 86
Featuring quality antique wicker, oak & mahogany furniture & accessories. *Pr:* $25–700. *Est:* 1976. *Serv:* Expert wicker repairing, chair caning, natural rush seating. *Hours:* Tue-Sat 10-4. *CC:* MC/V. Kathy Pignato *Park:* Nearby lot. *Loc:* Rte 128 to Rte 62E, 2 MI take R onto Cabot St, .5 MI on L.

Blandford

ROBERT F LUCAS
Main St, 01008
(413)848-2061   9 13
Antiquarian books: 19th C Americana, Thoreau, transcendentalism, 19th C Hawaiiana, Poe, manuscript Americana & whaling. *Serv:* Appraisal, catalog. *Hours:* BY APPT. *Assoc:* ABAA MRIAB. *Loc:* On Rte 23.

Bolton

ROBERT W SKINNER INC
Rte 117, 01740
(508)779-6241   4 8

New England's auction gallery, with regular auctions of Americana, Victoriana, dolls & toys, arts & crafts, Oriental rugs, paintings & prints, bottles & glass, jewelry & American Indian art. *Serv:* Fine art & antiques appraisal, nine catalog subscriptions available. *Hours:* Mon-Fri 10-5. *Size:* Large. Nancy Skinner *Park:* On site. *Loc:* I-495 exit 27: W on Rte 117 to Bolton.

Boston

ALBERTS-LANGDON, INC.
126 Charles St, 02114
(617)523-5954   60 63

Fine Far Eastern art, ceramics, paintings & furniture. *Serv:* Appraisal. *Hours:* Sep-Jul Mon-Fri 10-4. Russell Alberts *Park:* Nearby. *Loc:* At the corner of Charles & Revere Sts.

FRANCESCA ANDERSON GALLERY
8 Newbury St, 02116
(617)262-1062   59

American paintings by 20th C New England realists. *Est:* 1983. *Serv:* Appraisal. *Hours:* Tue-Sat 10-6 Sun 12-5. *Park:* Local garage. *Loc:* Between Arlington & Berkeley Sts.

ANTIQUARIAN BOOKSELLERS INC
234 Clarendon St, 02116
(617)266-5790   13

Fine books from the 15th C to the present featuring Americana, fine bindings & printing, first editions & printing history. *Serv:* Expert appraisals, catalog. *Hours:* Tue-Sat 10-5. *Assoc:* ABAA. David L O'Neal

ANTIQUE PORCELAINS LTD
33 Fayette St, 02116
(617)426-5779   35 60 63

A fine collection of Chinese export, Staffordshire, Imari, faience & other choice pieces in a restored Federal townhouse in downtown Boston. *Serv:* Consultation, interior design. *Hours:* BY APPT. *Size:* Medium. *CC:* AX/MC/V. *Assoc:* SADA. Anne F Kilguss *Park:* Nearby lot. *Loc:* From

ALBERTS-LANGDON, INC.
ORIENTAL ART
126 CHARLES STREET
BOSTON, MASSACHUSETTS 02114
(617) 523-5954

Arlington St go S to Piedmont St, turn L 1 block, R on Church St, 3 blocks to Fayette St, 4th house on L.

ARABY RUG
667 Boylston St, 02116
(617)267-0012　　　　21
Antique & semi-antique rugs from the Middle East. *Serv:* Expert cleaning & washing, rugs demothed & stored. *Hours:* Mon-Sat 9-6. Arthur Mahfuz *Loc:* Across from the Boston Public Library.

ARKELYAN RUGS
67 Chestnut St, 02108
(617)523-2424　　　　21
Specializing in Portuguese needlepoint rugs. A fine selection of elegant wool hand-made rugs in stock at all

Rare
Masterpieces
Rich In
Imagination

"America's
most exquisite collection
of rare antique rugs, fine
oriental rugs & kilims."

Araby RUG

667 Boylston Street
Boston
(617) 267-0012

times. *Serv:* Shop offers a custom design service. *Hours:* By appt, please call ahead. Sum: See Nantucket MA listing. Cindy Lydon

ARS LIBRI
560 Harrison Ave, 02118
(617)357-5212　　　　13
Dealers in rare & scholarly books on the fine arts, illustrated books from the 15th to the 20th C. Stock of art reference material includes monographs, catalogues, Raisonne periodicals & documents relevant to all periods/fields of art history. *Hours:* Mon-Fri 10-6 Sat 11-5. *Assoc:* ABAA. Elmer Siebel

AUTREFOIS
125 Newbury St, 02116
(617)424-8823　　　　35 38 50
Large selection of country French & Continental furnishings including lighting, decorative accessories, Oriental porcelains & garden planters. *Serv:* Custom lamp mountings. *Hours:* Mon-Sat 10-5. *Size:* Medium. *CC:* AX/DC/MC/V. Maria Rowe *Park:* Nearby Lot.

BEACON HILL FINE ARTS/ANTIQUES
49 River St, 02114
(617)720-1195　　　　39 59 77
Elizabethan, Chippendale and Liberty period furniture accessories selected in England. Georgian miniatures; drawings; manuscripts; books; boxes for: documents, jewelry, cutlery, tea, tobacco & snuff; Napoleonic lap desks; ivory; bronze; treen & silver. *Pr:* $10-5000. *Est:* 1988. *Serv:* Catalog (free), interior design - entry hall & libraries only, consultation. *Hours:* Daily 11-7,

Portuguese Needlepoint Rugs

Elegant, handmade wool rugs from Lisbon. Extremely durable with non-fading colors, these fine rugs are perfect for traditional or contemporary interiors. We keep a wide selection of rugs in stock at all times and also specialize in custom orders. Open by appointment.

Cindy Lydon, Arkelyan Rugs
67 Chestnut Street, Boston, MA 02108 (617) 523-2424
June 15 - Sept. 15   72 Orange Street, Nantucket, MA 02554 (508) 228-4242

B E L G R A V I A

A Unique Source of Antiques
& Decorative Furnishings

At Belgravia, you will find a carefully culled array of 18th & 19th C furniture, period mirrors and wall sconces, Chinese export porcelain, contemporary and fine art, chosen for the discriminating individual or decorator, and always with a ...

A Certain Style

222 Newbury Street; Boston, MA 02116
(617) 267-1915; Monday-Saturday, 10-6

call for evening hours. Jana Coply *Park:* Local garage. *Loc:* 1 block W of Charles St on Beacon Hill.

BEDELLE INC
50 School St, 02108
(617)227-8925 **17 47**
Antique jewelry, bronzes, glass & paintings. *Hours:* Mon-Fri 9:30-4. *Size:* Medium. Charles Richman *Park:* Nearby garage. *Loc:* Down from the Parker House.

BELGRAVIA ANTIQUES INC
222 Newbury St, 02116
(617)267-1915 **29 36 60**
A unique collection of 18th & 19th C English & French furniture interspersed with deco pieces, decorative lamps, mirrors & Oriental porcelain.

Pr: $25–15000. *Hours:* Mon-Sat 10-5:30. *Size:* Medium. *CC:* AX/MC/V. Carolyn Schofield *Park:* Nearby.

BESCO PLUMBING
729 Atlantic Ave, 02111
(617)423-4535 **68 74**
Domestic & imported plumbing antiques. *Serv:* Stripping, polishing, plating, worn parts rebuilt. *Hours:* Mon-Fri 9:30-5:30 Sat 10:30-4.

JAMES BILLINGS
70 Charles St, 02114
(617)367-9533 **29 38 39**
18th & early 19th C English & Continental furniture, paintings, prints & accessories. *Pr:* $250–25000. *Serv:* Complete interior design service. *Hours:* Mon-Sat 10-6. *Size:* Medium.

CC: AX/MC/V. *Assoc:* BADA CINOA. James Billings Lise Davis *Park:* In front. *Loc:* Approach Charles St from Storrow Dr. Located in the Charles St Meeting House.

THOMAS G BOSS-FINE BOOKS
355 Boylston St 2nd Fl, 02116
(617)227-1527 13

Rare & collectible books & bookplates. 19th & 20th C English & American literature, detective fiction, Sherlock Holmes, signed & inscribed books, autographs, press books fine bindings, books about books, 19th C book auction catalogs. *Hours:* BY APPT. *Assoc:* ABAA. Thomas G Boss

BOSTON ANTIQUE COOPERATIVE I&II
119 Charles St, 02114
(617)227-9811 {GR14}

In the heart of Beacon Hill two levels with a diverse selection from 17th C to art deco. *Est:* 1981. *Hours:* Daily 10-6 Sun 12-6. *CC:* MC/V. *Park:* Nearby.

BOSTON BOOK ANNEX
906 Beacon St, 02215
(617)266-1090 9 13

A general stock of antiquarian books: American & English literature, first editions, East Asia, autobiography & Maine. *Serv:* Appraisal, catalog, search service. *Hours:* Mon-Sat 10-10 Sun 12-10. *Assoc:* ABAA MRIAB. Helen Kelly *Park:* Nearby.

THE BOSTON HAMMERSMITH
46 Westland Ave Suite 42, 02115
(617)542-1949 68

Expert repairs of silver, pewter & Sheffield. *Est:* 1973. *Serv:* Repairs, restoration. Kristina Karnalovich

BOSTON ORNAMENT COMPANY
24 Penniman Rd, 02134
(617)787-4118 70 74

Ornamental plaster & concrete. Clayton Austin

BRATTLE BOOK SHOP
9 West St, 02111
(617)542-0210 4 9 13

One of Boston's oldest & largest antiquarian bookstores, 3 floors of used & rare books. *Pr:* $1–25000. *Serv:* Appraisal, purchase estates, 1-800-447-0210. *Hours:* Mon-Sat 9-5:30. *Size:* Large. *CC:* AX/MC/V. *Assoc:* ABAA MRIAB. Kenneth Gloss *Park:* Nearby lot. *Loc:* Between Washington & Tremont in downtown Boston, 1 block from Jordan Marsh, off the Boston Common.

BRODNEY INC
811 Boylston St, 02116
(617)536-0500 29 47 77

Paintings, jewelry, antiques, objets d'art, bronzes & silver. *Serv:* Purchase single items & estates. *Hours:* Mon-Sat 9:30-5 Jul,Aug CLOSED WEEKENDS. *Assoc:* AADLA. Richard G Brodney *Loc:* Opposite Prudential Center.

BROMER BOOKSELLERS INC
607 Boylston St, 02116
(617)247-2818 4 13

Antiquarian books: first editions, early printed, books about books, children's, illustrated & miniature books, fine bindings & printings. *Serv:* Appraisal, catalog, search service. *Hours:* Mon-Fri 9:30-5:30 most Sats 10-4. *Assoc:* ABAA MRIAB. David Bromer *Park:* Nearby. *Loc:* At Copley Sq in Boston's Back Bay.

MAURY A BROMSEN ASSOCIATES, INC
770 Boylston St, 02199
(617)266-7060 **4 9 13**

Antiquarian books: autographs, bibliography, Americana & Latin Americana. *Serv:* Appraisal. *Hours:* BY APPT. *Assoc:* ABAA. *Park:* Nearby.

BROOKS, GILL & CO INC.
132 Canal St, 02114
(617)523-2923 **21**

Oriental rug specialists. *Est:* 1904. *Hours:* Tue-Sat 9-5 Wed til 8:15. *Park:* Nearby lot. *Loc:* Between North Station & Faneuil Hall Marketplace.

BUDDENBROOKS
753 Boylston St, 02116
(617)536-4433 **13**

Antiquarian books: fishing, hunting, nautical, travel, explorations, voyages, first editions, literature, color plates, fine bindings, children's & illustrated. *Est:* 1975. *Serv:* Appraisal, catalogs, search service. *Hours:* Sun-Sat 8-11:30pm. *Size:* Large. *CC:* AX/MC/V. *Assoc:* ABA ABAA MRIAB NEBA. *Park:* Nearby lot. *Loc:* I-91 to Prudential Ctr Exit, Copley Sq to Boylston St, between Exeter & Fairfield.

J R BURROWS & COMPANY
6 Church St, 02116
(617)451-1982 **71 74**

Reproduction & restoration of carpet, wallpaper & textile designs of the 19th C. *Est:* 1984. *Serv:* Consultation, interior design. *Hours:* BY APPT. John R Burrows *Loc:* In Bay Village.

CENTER FOR ANTIQUES CONSERVATION
PO Box 370, 02130
(617)524-2899 **68 71 74**

Restoration of antique furniture, wooden artifacts, paintings. Decorative carving, wood & brass inlay, painted surfaces, structural stabilization, gilding & decorative veneer, upholstery, rushwork & caning & French polish. *Est:* 1974. *Serv:* Appraisals, pickup & delivery, consultation. *Hours:* Call for information. *Assoc:* NEAC. Robert F Lamboy

HOWARD CHADWICK ANTIQUES
40 River St, 02108
(617)227-9261 **2 29 36**

A small shop on Beacon Hill filled with American & English furniture, brasses, pictures, porcelains & lamps. *Est:* 1979. *Serv:* Appraisal, consultation.

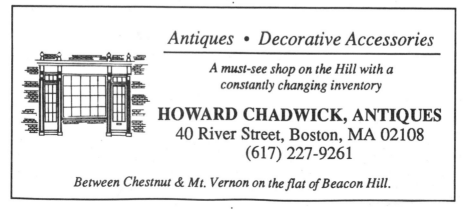

Hours: Oct 15-May 15 Mon-Sat 11-4, else Tue-Thu 11-4. *Loc:* 2 short blocks N of Beacon St on River St, .5 block W of Charles St.

sultation, restoration of frames. *Hours:* Tue-Fri 9-6 Sat,Mon 10-5. *Assoc:* ABAA. *Shows:* ELLIS. D. Roger Howlett III *Park:* Nearby.

CHESTNUT & COMPANY
84 Chestnut St, 02114
(617)227-0990   **29**

A general line of antiques & decorative accessories. *Serv:* Faux painting, interior design, custom lamps. *Hours:* Mon-Sat 10-6. *CC:* AX/MC/V. *Park:* Nearby. *Loc:* At Chestnut & River Sts.

CHOREOGRAPHICA
82 Charles St, 02114
(617)227-4780   **13**

Antiquarian books: antiques, cookery, dance, embroidery, needlework, music, theatre, opera & art. *Hours:* Mon-Sat 9:30-5 Sun 9:30-4. *Assoc:* MRIAB. Ernest Morrell *Park:* Nearby.

CHILDS GALLERY
169 Newbury St, 02116
(617)266-1108   **59 66 73**

Fine American & European paintings, prints, drawings, watercolors & sculptures. *Est:* 1937. *Serv:* Appraisal, con-

COLLECTOR'S SHOP
WEIU 356 Boylston St, 02116
(617)536-5651   **21 47 48**

Consignment antiques: American furniture, decorative accessories, lighting fixtures, silver, oil paintings, Ori-

The Women's Educational and Industrial Union

invites you to visit the

Collector's Shop

**It's filled with antiques and fine collectibles.
Consigned merchandise accepted.**

Mastercard and Visa accepted.

356 Boylston Street • Boston • 536-5651
Near the Public Garden

A non-profit organization whose sales support varied social services.

entalia, pottery & porcelain, crystal, glassware, Native American art, metalwork & fine linens. *Hours:* Mon-Sat 10-6. Dolores V Cleland *Park:* Nearby. *Loc:* .5 block W of the Public Garden on Boylston St.

ISABELLE COLLINS OF LONDON
115 Newbury St, 02116
(617)266-8699   **39 42**
Specialist in antique English country & pine furniture. *Hours:* Tue-Sat 10-5. *Park:* Nearby. *Loc:* Between Clarendon & Dartmouth Sts.

COMENOS FINE ARTS
81 Arlington St, 02116
(617)423-9365   **59 66 73**
American Impressionist paintings concentrating on the Boston School - featuring paintings, watercolors & drawings. *Est:* 1976. *Serv:* Consultation, purchase estates. *Hours:* Mon-Sat 9:30-5:30 Sun 12-5. *Size:* Medium. *CC:* MC/V. *Park:* On site (valet). *Loc:* Opposite Park Plaza Hotel, up the street from Ritz-Carlton & Public Garden.

CRANE COLLECTION
121 Newbury St, 02116
(617)262-4080   **59**
Gallery of American paintings featuring 19th & early 20th C art including Boston School, Hudson River School, American Impressionism & Tonalist works. Changing quarterly exhibitions. Artists include: Bruce Crane, LD Eldred, JJ Enneking & Herman Herzog. *Pr:* $250–100000. *Serv:* Appraisal, conservation, purchase estates. *Hours:* Tue-Sat 10-5 BY APPT. *Size:* Medium. *Park:* Nearby lot. *Loc:* Between Clarendon & Dartmouth Sts, park in lot between Dartmouth & Exeter Sts.

DIVINE DECADENCE
535 Columbus Ave, 02118
(617)266-1477   **7 29 36**
An innovative shop featuring a unique blend of 20th C interior furnishings, specializing in art deco, moderne & mid-century - including designer furniture, sculpture, lighting, vintage rattan, neon clocks, jukeboxes & advertising. *Serv:* Custom neon. *Hours:* Tue-Sat 12-6 Sun 12-5 or BY APPT. *CC:* AX/MC/V. *Loc:* From Copley Pl, Dartmouth St E, L onto Columbus Ave, 8 blocks on L.

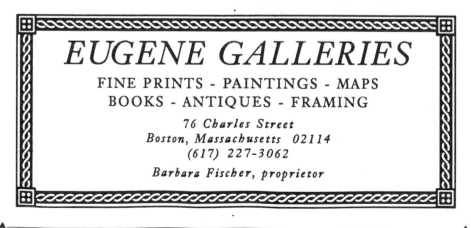

EUGENE GALLERIES
FINE PRINTS - PAINTINGS - MAPS
BOOKS - ANTIQUES - FRAMING
76 Charles Street
Boston, Massachusetts 02114
(617) 227-3062
Barbara Fischer, proprietor

EUGENE GALLERIES
76 Charles St, 02114
(617)227-3062   51 59 66

Fine prints - botanicals, historical & city views, maps, paintings & books. *Est:* 1954. *Serv:* Framing. *Hours:* Mon-Sat 10:30-5:30. *CC:* MC/V. Barbara Fischer *Park:* Nearby garage. *Loc:* Between Mt Vernon & Pinckney Sts.

FINE TIME VINTAGE TIMEPIECES
279 Newbury St, 02116
(617)536-5858   23 47

Timepieces - wristwatches, clocks, jewelry & pocketwatches. *Est:* 1983. *Serv:* Appraisal, repair, restoration, search services. *Hours:* Sum: Tue-Sat 11-6, Win: Tue-Sun 11-6. *Assoc:* NAWCC. William Zeitler *Loc:* Corner of Gloucester & Newbury Sts.

THE FINEST HOUR
274 Newbury St, 02116
(617)266-1920   23 68 71

In an elegant Boston townhouse - wide selection of vintage wristwatches & exotic watchbands in dozens of skins & colors. *Pr:* $150-5000. *Serv:* Repair, restoration, purchase old/unusual watches. *Hours:* Mon-Sat 11-7 Sun 1-6. Thomas Thompson

FIRESTONE AND PARSON
Ritz Carlton Hotel, 02108
(617)266-1858   47 77

Period jewelry from the Victorian era to the present, English & early American silver. *Pr:* $500-100000. *Serv:* Appraisal, brochure, purchase estates. *Hours:* Oct-May Mon-Sat 9:30-5, Jun-Sep Mon-Fri 9:30-5. *Assoc:* NAADAA. Edwin Firestone *Park:* Nearby. *Loc:* Across from the Public Garden.

THE FORTRESS CORPORATION
99 Boston St, 02125
(617)288-3636   75

Modern, new 10 story building which provides Museum-Quality brand storage. Advanced temperature & humidity control systems, vertical carousel storage technology, & 24 hour security. For antiques, fine arts, vintage cars, & other valuable possessions. *Hours:* Mon-Fri 8-6, Sat 9-3. *Park:* On site. *Loc:* Just off the Southeast Expressway on Boston St.

FUSCO & FOUR ASSOCIATES
1 Murdock Terr, 02135
(617)787-2637   7 26

Specialists in art deco & art moderne, with a computer bank of art deco prices, auction records, dealers, & societies nationwide. A full-service marketing & public relations agency for the arts & antiques field. *Est:* 1979. *Serv:* Appraisal, consultation, interior design. *Hours:* BY APPT ONLY. Tony Fusco Robert Four *Loc:* Call for directions.

GOODSPEED'S BOOK SHOP INC
7 Beacon St, 02108
(617)523-5970   13 51 66

Rare books, prints, autographs, genealogies & Americana. *Hours:* Mon-Fri 9-5 Sat 10-3, Jun 15-Labor Day CLOSED SAT. *Assoc:* ABAA. George T Goodspeed *Park:* Nearby lot. *Loc:* 1 block E of the State House.

GRAND TROUSSEAU
88 Charles St, 02114
(617)367-3163   47 85

A small, romantic shop on Beacon Hill, filled with antique clothes & jewelry. Carrying wearable clothing from

IT'S NOT NICE TO KEEP GRANDFATHER IN THE BASEMENT.

Your Grandfather deserves better treatment—the kind we offer at The Fortress® for all your valuable collectables, art, even vintage automobiles. We're a new, one-of-a-kind storage facility that provides impenetrable electronic security, a temperature and humidity-controlled environment, and personal service. Give us a call at 617-288-3636 for more information. The Fortress, 99 Boston Street, Boston, MA 02125.

FORTRESS®
MUSEUM QUALITY STORAGE ®

1890-1940 in all sizes, Victorian & Edwardian gowns & wedding dresses, beaded flapper dresses, embroidered shawls & all manner of accessories. *Pr:* $25–1000. *Est:* 1985. *Serv:* Consultation on re-creating a total period look. *Hours:* Daily 12-5 or BY APPT. *CC:* AX/MC/V. Candace Savage *Park:* Local garage.

GEORGE I GRAVERT ANTIQUES
122 Charles St, 02108
(617)227-1593   **29 38**

Decorative European furniture & accessories. *Est:* 1958. *Hours:* Mon-Fri 10-5 or by appt. *Park:* Nearby. *Loc:* At the corner of Charles & Revere Sts.

GROGAN & COMPANY
890 Commonwealth Ave, 02215
(617)566-4100   **4 8**

Boston's only full service auction & appraisal company. *Est:* 1987. *Serv:* Appraisal, accept mail/phone bids, catalog, consultation, purchase estates. *Hours:* Mon-Fri 9-5:30 Sat,Sun BY APPT. Michael B Grogan *Park:* On site.

H GROSSMAN
51 Charles St, 02114
(617)523-1879   **1 37 63**

American furniture, china & glass. *Est:* 1923. *Hours:* Mon-Sat 9-5. Hyman Grossman *Park:* Nearby. *Loc:* On Beacon Hill.

GUIDO
118 Newbury St, 02116
(617)267-0569   **59 71**

19th & 20th C American & Boston School paintings & gold leaf frames. *Est:* 1967. *Serv:* Restoration, gold leaf frames, appraisal. *Hours:* Tue-Sat 9:30-5:30. *Loc:* Clarendon & Dartmouth Sts.

HALEY & STEELE INC
91 Newbury St, 02116
(617)536-6339   **1 56 66**

Print dealers & custom picture framers, specializing in 18th, 19th & 20th C published prints, English sporting art, American topographical & historical views, botanicals, natural history & marine. *Pr:* $25–3500. *Est:* 1899. *Serv:* Appraisal, catalog, conservation, consultation, interior design, repairs. *Hours:* Sep-Jul Mon-Fri 10-6 Sat 10-5 Aug Mon-Fri 9-5 Sat 10-5. *Size:* Medium. *CC:* AX/MC/V. Abigail Driscoll *Park:* Nearby lot. *Loc:* Between Berkeley & Clarendon Sts in the Back Bay.

HARPER & FAYE INC
60 Federal St, 02110
(617)423-9190   **4 47**

Fine antique & estate jewelry in gold & platinum. *Pr:* $450–25000. *Est:* 1985. *Serv:* Appraisal, consultation. *Hours:* Mon-Sat 9:30-5:30 CLOSED AUG. *CC:* AX/MC/V. *Assoc:* GIA. *Park:* Local garage. *Loc:* MBTA Red Line to Downtown Crossing. R 1 block down Washington St, R down Franklin St, L opposite the Shawmut Bank.

HERITAGE ART
112 Mount Vernon St, 02108
(617)523-2793   **1 26 59**

Oil, watercolor & pastel artwork of rediscovered 19th & early 20th C painters in the Boston area, period Tonalist, Luminist, & Impressionist paintings of Boston & greater metropolitan subjects. *Pr:* $300–3000. *Est:* 1986. *Serv:* Appraisal, consultation, purchase estates. *Hours:* Nov-Apr 15 Mon-Fri 10-6 Sat,Sun 12-5, May 16-Oct BY APPT.

Assoc: AADLA. Fred Gorman *Park:* Local garage. *Loc:* In Boston, from Cambridge St to Int of Charles/Mt Vernon Sts, proceed up Beacon Hill 1 block.

HIGHGATE GALLERIES
81 Commercial St, 02109
(617)720-4112　　　　**36 44 46**
Formal French & English furniture, displayed in room settings & small vignettes, along with some Victorian & deco accessories. *Pr:* $100–10000. *Serv:* Interior design. *Hours:* Daily 9-5. *Size:* Medium. *CC:* MC/V. Irving S Camielle *Park:* In front. *Loc:* Mercantile Wharf Building, directly opposite Waterfront Park.

HOMER'S JEWELRY & ANTIQUES
44 Winter St, 02108
(617)482-1973　　　　**47 77**
Antique & estate jewelry, silver. *Est:* 1882. *Hours:* Mon-Sat 9:30-5. Dan Cohen *Park:* Local garage.

PRISCILLA JUVELIS INC
150 Huntington Ave, 02215
(617)424-1895　　　　**9 13 66**
Antiquarian books: artist books, art bindings, fine bindings & printing, first editions, illustrated books, literature, manuscripts & drawings. *Serv:* Appraisal, catalog. *Hours:* BY APPT ONLY. *Assoc:* ABAA MRIAB.

KAY BEE FURNITURE COMPANY
1122 Boylston St, 02215
(617)266-4487　　　　**17 21 23**
Used furniture, Oriental rugs, clocks, bronzes, paintings, china, glass & prints. *Hours:* Mon-Fri 9-5:30 Sat 9-5. Leonard Kadish *Loc:* Between the Fenway & Massachusetts Ave.

KNOLLWOOD ANTIQUES
517 Columbus Ave, 02118
(617)536-8866　　　　**7 29 83**
Located in the historic South End at Greenwich Park, a two-level shop containing furniture, decorations, lighting, American art pottery, arts & crafts furniture, carpets, mirrors, paintings & 18th & 19th C engravings. *Est:* 1988. *Serv:* Consultation, interior design. *Hours:* Jan-late Nov Mon-Sat 9-6 Wed til 9, else Mon-Sun 9-9. *Size:* Medium. *CC:* MC/V. Richard A Lavigne *Park:* On Site. *Loc:* From Prudential Ctr take W Newton St to corner of Columbus, take R, go 2 blocks to corner of Greenwich Park & Columbus Ave.

LYNNE KORTENHAUS
6 Faneuil Hall N, 02109
(617)973-6406　　　　**4**
Appraisal of American & European paintings & drawings; Impressionist & modern sculpture. *Serv:* Appraisal. *Hours:* By appt. *Assoc:* AAA.

RALPH KRISTIANSEN BOOKSELLER
Box 524 Kenmore Sta, 02215
(617)424-1527　　　　**13**
Antiquarian books: detective fiction, science fiction, fantasy & literature. First editions, fine & rare, out of print. *Serv:* Catalog, purchase estates. *Hours:* Mail order only. *Assoc:* ABAA MRIAB.

LACE BROKER
252 Newbury St, 02116
(617)267-5954　　　　**48 80**
A charming selection of fine old laces, linens & fabrics for the decorator or the collector & remnants for the person who sews. *Pr:* $2–1500. *Est:* 1979. *Serv:* Appraisal, purchase estates, repairs, restoration. *Hours:* May-Dec

daily 10-6 Sun 12-5. *CC:* MC/V. Linda Zukas *Park:* Nearby lot. *Loc:* 1 block from the Prudential Bldg.

DAVID LAWRENCE GALLERY
303B Newbury St, 02115
(617)236-4898 37 50

An eclectic mix of 18th & 19th C Continental, English & American furniture, lighting, mirrors & decorative accessories. All items guaranteed as represented. *Est:* 1975. *Serv:* Appraisal, purchase estates, custom upholstery, repairs, restoration. *Hours:* Oct-May Tue-Sat 12-5, May-Oct Tue-Sat 12-7 & BY APPT. *Size:* Medium. *CC:* AX/DC/MC/V. Stephen Perlmutter *Park:* Local garage. *Loc:* 1 block from Massachusetts Ave at the corner of Newbury & Hereford Sts.

LESLIE'S ANTIQUES & COLLECTIBLES
49 Charles St 2nd fl, 02114
(617)227-1882 36 47

Collection of small furniture, period lamps & custom lampshades, mirrors, prints, jewelry, Oriental porcelain & decorative accessories from the 19th & early 20th C. *Pr:* $10–1000. *Est:* 1987. *Serv:* Purchase estates, custom lampshades. *Hours:* Tue-Sat 11-5 & by chance/appt. Leslie Weinstein *Park:* Local garage. *Loc:* On Charles St 2 blocks from the Public Garden.

LINDERMAN SCHENCK
49A River St, 02108
(617)227-0338 46 63

Majolica pottery. *Est:* 1985. *Serv:* Interior design. *Hours:* Mon-Fri 10-5. Mrs Robert P Linderman III *Loc:* 1 block W of Charles Street between Chestnut & Lime St.

LONDON LACE
167 Newbury St 2nd fl, 02116
(617)267-3506 48 80

Specializing in fine linens, lace windowcoverings, bedspreads & pillowcases. *Pr:* $25–200. *Serv:* Brochure. *Hours:* Mon-Sat 10-5:30. *Size:* Medium. *CC:* MC/V. Diane Jones Judy Godfrey *Park:* Copley Place parking lot. *Loc:* Between Dartmouth & Exeter Sts.

SAMUEL L LOWE JR ANTIQUES INC
80 Charles St, 02114
(617)742-0845 1 56 59

Nation's leading marine dealer of fine Americana with a large selection of museum-quality American marine paintings & prints, ship models, scrimshaw, china, instruments, marine books, steamship memorabilia, China trade items, furniture & folk art. *Est:* 1964. *Serv:* Consultation, marine interior design. *Hours:* Sep-Jun Mon-Fri 10:30-5 Sat 10:30-4, Sum: CLOSED WEEKENDS. *Size:* Medium. *Park:* In front. *Loc:* On Charles St between Mt Vernon & Pinckney Sts.

THE MARCH HARE, LTD
170 Newbury St, 02116
(617)536-7525   29

Antique furniture, mirrors & decorative accessories. *Est:* 1983. *Serv:* Interior design. *Hours:* Tue-Fri 11-5. Rosemary Giglia *Park:* Nearby. *Loc:* Between Dartmouth & Exeter Sts.

MARCOZ ANTIQUES & JEWELRY
177 Newbury St, 02116
(617)262-0780   29 39

Fine selection of English formal furniture & accessories. *Serv:* Antiques & estates purchased. *Hours:* Mon-Sat 10-6. Marc S Glasberg *Park:* Nearby.

MARIKA'S ANTIQUE SHOP, INC
130 Charles St, 02114
(617)523-4520   29 59 77

General line of antiques & collectibles. *Est:* 1945. *Serv:* Purchase antiques. *Hours:* Daily 10-5 & BY APPT, Jul,Aug CLOSED SAT. *CC:* DC/MC/V. *Park:* Nearby. *Loc:* At the N end of Charles St on Beacon Hill.

NELSON-MONROE, ANTIQUES
PO Box 8863, 02114
(617)492-1368   63 77

18th & early 19th C English & Continental pottery & porcelain, China trade porcelain & silver, old Sheffield plate. *Pr:* $100–5000. *Serv:* Appraisal. *Hours:* BY APPT. *Assoc:* AADLA. *Shows:* ELLIS. James M Labaugh

NEWBURY STREET JEWELRY & ANTIQUE
255 Newbury St, 02116
(617)236-0038   46 63 77

Estate jewelry, Tiffany, art nouveau, antique furniture, old silver, Rose Medallion, porcelain, china, clocks & lamps. *Est:* 1986. *Hours:* Daily 10-5. *CC:* MC/V. Doris Nichols *Park:* Nearby lot. *Loc:* Between Fairfield & Gloucester Sts.

THE NOSTALGIA FACTORY
144 Kneeland St, 02111
(617)482-8803   1 13 33

Original old advertising: posters, signs, tins, trade cards, an extensive selection of ephemera: catalogs, programs, post cards, rare books, royalty collectibles & movie memorabilia. *Pr:* $15–1200. *Serv:* Appraisal, interior design. *Hours:* Daily 11-5. *Size:* Large. *CC:* AX/DC/MC/V. Rudy Franchi *Park:* Local garage. *Loc:* From I-90 Downtown Exit. From SE Expressway Kneeland St Exit: located between South Station & Chinatown.

JAMES F O'NEIL
PO Box 326, 02114
(617)266-2412   13

Antiquarian books: literary first editions, art, architecture & sets. *Assoc:* ABAA.

O'REILLY/EINSTADTER, LTD
186 South St, 02116
(617)423-0919   60 63 82

Fine Asian antiques in a museum setting. Folk art, tribal art, furniture & jewelry. *Serv:* Appraisal. *Hours:* Mon-Fri 9:30-6:30 Sat 10-6 Sun 12-6.

Leon Ohanian and Sons Co.
Incorporated

SINCE 1919

NEW ENGLAND'S DIAMOND CUTTERS

EXPERT APPRAISERS

ANTIQUE & ESTATE JEWELRY

STONES

Upstairs at 387 Washington Street Suite 703

Boston

(617) 426 - 0558

We are always interested in buying
antique and estate jewelry and stones.

Monday through Friday 9:00 - 5:00

Saturday 9:00 - 3:00

Ara Ohanian		Eric Ohanian
Haig Ohanian	Roseen Ohanian	Gregg Ohanian

LEON OHANIAN & SONS CO INC
387 Washington St Suite 703, 02108
(617)426-0558   **4 47**

Antique & estate jewelry & stones. *Est:* 1919. *Serv:* Diamond cutting, jewelry appraisal, purchase estates. *Hours:* Mon-Fri 9-5 Sat 9-3. *CC:* AX/MC/V. Ara Ohanian *Park:* Nearby lot. *Loc:* In the heart of the business district in downtown Boston.

PERIOD FURNITURE HARDWARE CO
123 Charles St, 02114
(617)227-0758   **50 70**

Located in historic Beacon Hill, a storehouse of brass hardware & accessories for the discriminating dealer or homeowner. Highest quality reproduction furniture & door hardware, light fixtures, bath accessories, fireplace equipment & weather vanes. *Pr:* $5-2500. *Serv:* Catalog ($4.50), reproduction. *Hours:* Mon-Fri 8:30-5 Sat 10-2, Jul-Aug CLOSED SAT. *CC:* MC/V. *Park:* Local garage. *Loc:* At the N end of Charles St on famed Beacon Hill.

THE PRINTERS' DEVIL
729 Boylston St, 02116
(617)646-6762   **13 72**

Unique shop specializing in antique medical instruments, books & prints dealing with the history of medicine. *Est:* 1973. *Serv:* Appraisal, catalog, consultation, purchase estates. *Hours:* Tue-Fri 1-6 Sat 10-2 or BY APPT. *Size:* Medium. *CC:* AX/MC/V. *Assoc:* ABAA MRIAB. Barry A Wiedenkeller *Park:* Local garage. *Loc:* In Copley Sq near Boston Public Library & Hynes Convention Ctr.

RERUNS ANTIQUES
125B Charles St, 02114   **36 50 53**

Reasonably-priced antiques & furniture from Beacon Hill & greater Boston. *Pr:* $1-500. *Serv:* Purchase estates. *Hours:* Mon-Sat 1:30-5:30. *CC:* MC/V. Sarah Gorman *Park:* Local garage. *Loc:* MBTA Red Line to Charles St stop.

ROSE & CLEAVES
488 Harrison Ave, 02118
(617)742-7887   **4 8**

Scheduled auctions of 18th, 19th & 20th C furniture & decorations assembled from homes throughout New England. *Est:* 1987. *Serv:* Auction, appraisal, real estate. Robert E Cleaves *Loc:* Call for information.

RUE DE FRANCE
215 Newbury St, 02118
(617)536-5974   **48**

Country lace of France including curtains, tablecloths, pillows & placemats. Also French linens, glassware & pottery. *Est:* 1988. *Serv:* Custom orders accepted. *Hours:* Mon-Sat 10-6. *Loc:* Between Exeter & Fairfield Sts.

C A RUPPERT
121 Charles St, 02114
(617)523-5033   **29 39 63**

18th, 19th & early 20th C English, Continental & American furniture & decorative accessories. *Est:* 1988. *Hours:* Mon-Sat 10-6. *CC:* MC/V. *Park:* Nearby lot.

SHER-MORR ANTIQUES
82 Charles St, 02114
(617)227-4780   **13 60 66**

General line with emphasis on the Oriental. Featuring decorative prints, used & antiquarian books. Specialize in dance material. *Pr:* $4-2000. *Hours:*

Mon-Sat 9-5 Sun 10-4. *Size:* Medium.
CC: MC/V. Jack Sherman *Loc:*
Boston's Antique Shop Row just off
Storrow Dr.

SHOP ON THE HILL
81A West Cedar St, 02114
(617)523-0440   **29 41 45**

Trompe l'oeil furniture, garden ornaments, decorative accessories in a
charming shop on a side street of Beacon Hill. *Hours:* Wed-Sun 12-6:30 call
ahead. Paul F MacDonald *Park:*
Nearby garage. *Loc:* 1 block E of
Charles St & S of Cambridge St.

SHREVE, CRUMP & LOW
**Antiques Dept 330 Boylston St,
02116**
(617)267-9100   **39 63 66**

Large selection of fine English, American & Chinese export, 18th & early
19th C furniture, ceramics, glass,
prints & paintings. *Pr:* $50–30000.
Est: 1865. *Serv:* Purchase estates, 1-
800-225-7088. *Hours:* Sep-Jun Mon-
Sat 9:30-5:30, Jul-Aug CLOSED SAT.
Size: Medium. *CC:* AX/MC/V. *Shows:*
ELLIS. Kevin Jenness *Park:* Local garage. *Loc:* I-90 Copley Sq Exit: across
from the Public Garden at Boylston &
Arlington Sts.

ROBERT W SKINNER INC
2 Newbury St, 02116
(617)236-1700   **8**

Boston office specializing in jewelry
auctions. *Serv:* Auction & appraisal.
Karen Keane

SLENSKA'S ANTIQUES &
INTERIORS
29 Newbury St, 02116
(617)437-0822   **29 38 53**

A carefully-chosen selection of Continental furniture, mirrors & decorative

accessories. *Serv:* Interior design.
Hours: Mon-Sat 11-5. *Size:* Medium.
Linda Slenska *Park:* Nearby. *Loc:* 1.5
blocks W of the Public Garden.

SOTHEBY'S
101 Newbury St, 02116
(617)247-2851   **8**

Boston office of the famous auction
house. *Est:* 1744. *Serv:* Auctioneer.
Hours: Please call ahead. Patricia E
Ward

TERI ANTIQUES
**PO Box 163 Hanover St Station,
02113**
(617)569-9465   **50 61**

Specializing in Tiffany, Handel.
Pairpoint & other fine lamps & accessories. Also quality glass paperweights, pottery & fountain pens. *Pr:*
$50–15,000. *Est:* 1968. *Serv:* Ap-
praisal, consultation, restoration, purchase estates, repairs. *Hours:* BY
APPT ONLY. Dan McNamara *Park:*
In front.

TIGER LILY
70 Charles St, 02114
(617)723-8494   **5 36 38**

A large inventory of antique Continental furnishings, garden statuary & furniture, textiles & objets d'art. *Pr:*
$250–10000. *Hours:* Sep 15-Jun 15
Mon-Sat 12-5, Jun 16-Sep 14 by
chance/appt. *Size:* Medium. Libby H
Holsten *Park:* Local garage.

VOSE GALLERIES OF BOSTON,
INC.
238 Newbury St, 02116
(617)536-6176   **59**

19th C American & 20th C American
Impressionist paintings up to 1925.
Est: 1841. *Serv:* Referrals for restora-

tion services. *Hours:* Mon-Fri 8-5:30
Sat 9-4. *Shows:* ELLIS. Abbot W Vose
Park: Nearby.

ALFRED J WALKER FINE ART
158 Newbury St, 02116
(617)247-1319   59

19th & 20th C American paintings
specializing in the Boston School. *Est:*
1978. *Serv:* Appraisal, consultation,
restoration. *Hours:* Tue-Sat 10-5.
Park: Nearby. *Loc:* Dartmouth & Exeter Sts above the Copley Society.

WEINER'S ANTIQUE SHOP
22 Beacon St, 02108
(617)227-2894   **29 36 63**

One of Boston's most interesting shops

featuring a large selection with variety
& quality. Continuous family ownership for 93 years. *Pr:* $25-15000. *Est:*
1896. *Serv:* Appraisal, brochure, purchase estates. *Hours:* Mon-Fri 9-4 Sat
11-4. *Size:* Medium. *CC:* MC/V.
Assoc: AAA NAWCC. Paul Weiner
Park: Local garage. *Loc:* Directly
across the street from the Gold Dome
of State House on Beacon Hill.

WENHAM CROSS ANTIQUES
232 Newbury St, 02116
(617)236-0409   **29 36 63**

18th & 19th C furniture & decorative
objects - featuring Quimper of the period. *Pr:* $25-10000. *Est:* 1979. *Serv:*
Appraisal, consultation, purchase es-

tates. *Hours:* Tue-Sat 10-5:30 Mon 10-4. Emily Lampert *Park:* Nearby lot. *Loc:* Between Exeter & Fairfield Sts.

CHARLES B WOOD, III INC
116 Commonwealth Ave, 02116
(617)247-7844   13

Antiquarian books: science & technology, architecture, photography, decorative arts, landscape gardening & book arts. *Hours:* BY APPT ONLY. *Assoc:* ABAA. *Park:* Nearby.

THE YANKEE MERCHANT GROUP
15 Court Sq, 02108
(617)742-0470   47 77

Sterling flatware, pattern matching,

hollowware & antique jewelry. *Serv:* Purchase estates. *Hours:* Mon-Fri 9-5. Benjamin Lambert

Brewster

ANTIQUES ETC
2759 Main St, 02631
(508)896-5782   40 42

Turn-of-the-century golden oak & English scrubbed pine. *Est:* 1987. *Hours:* Mon-Fri 9-6 Sat 10-5. *CC:* AX/MC/V. *Park:* On site. *Loc:* Near the Ocean Edge Resort Complex.

WILLIAM M BAXTER ANTIQUES
3439 Main St, 02631
(508)896-3998　　　　　**21 37 38**

American, English, Oriental & Continental furniture, rugs, paintings & accessories of the 18th & early 19th C. *Pr:* $100–60000. *Est:* 1960. *Hours:* Jun-Thanksgiving Mon-Sat 10-5, else BY APPT. *Size:* Medium. *Park:* On site. *Loc:* On Rte 6A in Brewster opposite Nickerson State Park.

BAYBERRY ANTIQUES
3799 Main St Rte 6A, 02631
(508)255-9251　　　　　**27 32 67**

Quality country antiques, furniture, toys, paper & quilts. *Est:* 1987. *Hours:* Sum: daily 10-5, else BY APPT. *CC:* MC/V. *Assoc:* CCADA. *Park:* Nearby. *Loc:* On Brewster-Orleans line.

BRETON HOUSE
1222 Stoney Brook Rd, 02631
(508)896-3974　　　　　**32**

Eclectic selection focusing on children's toys, memorabilia & furniture. *Est:* 1956. *Hours:* Daily 11:30-5. *CC:* MC/V. *Park:* On site. *Loc:* At Jct of Stoney Brook Rd & 6A.

BARBARA GRANT - ANTIQUES
1793 Main St Rte 6A, 02631
(508)896-7198　　　　　**13**

Old & out-of-print books, furniture, primitives, old kitchenware, glass, porcelain, prints, linen, decorative accessories, jewelry, collectibles & nostalgia. *Pr:* $1–1000. *Est:* 1980. *Serv:* Purchase estates. *Hours:* Apr-Dec daily 10-5, Jan-Mar BY APPT ONLY. *Size:* Medium. *Assoc:* CCADA. *Park:* On site. *Loc:* On Rte 6A between Rte 137 & Rte 124.

THE HOMESTEAD ANTIQUES
2257 Main St Rte 6A, 02631
(508)896-2917　　　　　**6 33 56**

Weapons, Victorian canes, nautical items, paintings, prints, scrimshaw, early tobacco advertising tins & signs. *Est:* 1983. *Hours:* Sum: Daily 9-5, Oct 15-May 15: Thu-Mon 9-5. *CC:* MC/V. *Park:* On site. *Loc:* .5 MI W of Chillingsworth Restaurant.

DONALD B HOWES - ANTIQUES
1424 Main St Rte 6A, 02631
(508)896-3502　　　　　**36 59 66**

Paintings, prints, books, documents & furniture. *Hours:* BY APPT. *Assoc:* CCADA. *Loc:* Almost opposite Fire Museum.

KINGS WAY BOOKS & ANTIQUES
774 Main St Rte 6A, 02631
(508)896-3639　　　　　**13**

Old & out-of-print books & smalls. *Est:* 1988. *Hours:* Thu-Sun 10-6. *CC:* MC/V. Ella Socky *Park:* On site. *Loc:* Across from the Drummer Boy Museum.

THE PFLOCK'S-ANTIQUES
598 Main St Rte 6A, 02631
(508)896-3457　　　　　**2 16 36**

Furniture, fireplace equipment, copper, brass, nautical & primitives. *Serv:* Metal restorations, furniture refinishing. *Hours:* Apr-Nov daily 10-5, Dec-Mar daily 10-4:30. *Assoc:* CCADA. Anne Pflock

THE PUNKHORN BOOKSHOP
672 Main St, 02631
(508)896-2114　　　　　**13 66**

Antiquarian books: American literature, history, limited editions, natural history, prints, publisher's covers &

first editions. *Serv:* Appraisal, search service. *Hours:* May 15-Sep 15 daily 10-5, else BY APPT. *Assoc:* MRIAB. David L Luebke

ROCKING CHAIR ANTIQUES
1379 Main St, 02631
(508)896-7389   **33 52**
Ephemera & doll house miniatures. *Hours:* BY APPT ONLY. *Assoc:* CCADA. Bill Nielsen *Loc:* On Rte 6A.

EDWARD SNOW HOUSE ANTIQUES
2042 Main St Rte 6A, 02631
(508)896-2929   **37 59 80**
American formal & country furniture, paintings, textiles in a 1700 Cape Cod house. *Hours:* Call ahead. *Assoc:* CCADA. Karen Etsell

SUNSMITH HOUSE - ANTIQUES
2926 Main St Rte 6A, 02631
(508)896-7024   **32 65 85**
Quilts, linens, toys, dolls, games, primitives, jewelry, country furniture & accessories, vintage clothing, china & glass, used, rare & out-of-print books. *Pr:* $5-1200. *Est:* 1978. *Serv:* Free catalog, purchase estates. *Hours:* Apr-Oct Mon-Sat 10-5 Sun 12-5 by chance/appt. *Size:* Medium. *Assoc:* CCADA. Wendell Smith *Park:* On site. *Loc:* Diagonally across from Ocean Edge Conference Center.

TALIN BOOKBINDERY
1990 Main St Rte 6A, 02631
(508)896-6444   **12 25 71**
Fine bindings, paper conservation &

marble papers. *Est:* 1976. *Serv:* Restoration of books, paper conservation. *Hours:* Mon-Fri 9-5. *Park:* Nearby. *Loc:* Rte 6 or Rte 124N to Rte 6A, turn R, 3 buildings on the R.

J. OGDEN TYLDSLEY, JR
PO Box 353, 02631
(508)896-5823   **21**
Professional cleaning of Oriental rugs only. *Est:* 1971. *Serv:* Appraisal, repairs. *Hours:* BY APPT ONLY.

YANKEE TRADER
2071 Main St Rte 6A, 02631
(508)896-7822
Ancient to antique - always the unusual. *Est:* 1958. *Hours:* Daily 10-5, CLOSED Christmas. *CC:* AX/MC/V. Stephen Rosen *Park:* Nearby. *Loc:* Downtown Brewster.

YORKSHIRE HOUSE
Rte 6A & Crosby Ln, 02631
(508)896-6570   **{GR8}**
Elegant Victorian carriage house featuring period formal & country furniture, marine antiques, Orientalia, kitchenalia, Victoriana, fireplace antiques, Staffordshire & Worcester china & Americana. *Pr:* $10-10000. *Est:* 1985. *Serv:* Appraisal, brochure, interior design. *Hours:* Jun-Sep Tue-Sun 10-5, Oct-May Thu-Sun 10-5. *Size:* Large. *CC:* MC/V. *Assoc:* CCADA. Jeffrey Bairstow *Park:* On site. *Loc:* Mid-Cape Hwy Rte 6 Exit 12: W on 6A for 2 MI shop is on R opposite Nickerson State Park Entrance.

Brighton

DERBY DESK COMPANY
140 Tremont St, 02135
(617)787-2707 37
19th C American desks & tables.
Hours: Mon-Sat 9-5. Carl Unger *Loc:*
I-90 Exit 17: 1 min.

DINING ROOM SHOWCASE
379 Washington St, 02135
(617)254-6647 36
Quality estate dining room sets specializing in mahogany, walnut, china cabinets, credenzas, lamps, rugs, chandeliers & paintings. *Serv:* Purchase antiques. *Hours:* Mon-Sat 10-6 Thu til 7. *Park:* On site. *Loc:* I-90 Exit 17: 2 MI, 3 blocks from St Elizabeth's Hospital.

Brimfield

BRIMFIELD ANTIQUES
Haynes Hill Rd, 01010
(413)245-3350 2 16 59
Offering one of the finest selections of antique fireplace equipment, specializing in fine Federal furniture, paintings & accessories. *Serv:* Conservation, appraisal. *Hours:* BY APPT. *Assoc:* AAA ADAA. *Shows:* ELLIS. Richard N Raymond *Loc:* 8 MI W of Old Sturbridge Village.

Brockton

BEN GERBER & SON, INC.
386 Pleasant St, 02401
(508)586-2547
China, glass, silver & jewelry. *Est:* 1946. *Serv:* Appraisal for estates. *Hours:* Mon-Sat 9-3:30. *Assoc:* AAA.

Brookline

ANTIQUERS III
171 Harvard St, 02146
(617)738-6718 7
Specializing in art deco. *Pr:* $25–2500. *Est:* 1972. *Serv:* Appraisal. *Hours:* Mon-Sat 10-5. *Size:* Medium. *CC:* AX/DC/MC/V. Mark Fellman *Park:* In front. *Loc:* Next to Stop & Shop.

APPLETON ANTIQUES
195 Harvard St, 02146
(617)482-4910 7 50 83
Victorian & art deco, furniture, lighting & decorative accessories. *Est:* 1978. *Serv:* Appraisal, consultation, purchase estates, repairs, restoration of lamps. *Hours:* Mon-Sat 10-6 Sun By Appt. *Size:* Medium. *CC:* MC/V. Loukas Deimezis *Park:* On site. *Loc:* 1 block up from Coolidge Corner.

AUTREFOIS II
130 Harvard St, 02146
(617)566-0113 35 38 50
Large selection of country French & Continental furniture, Oriental porcelains, decorative accessories, garden statuary & lighting. *Serv:* Custom mounted lamps. *Size:* Medium. *CC:* AX/DC/MC/V. *Park:* Nearby.

BEAZE OF BROOKLINE
1362 Beacon St, 02146
(617)566-7636 50 59 60
Oriental art, oil paintings, mirrors & lighting. *Est:* 1937. *Serv:* Purchase estates. *Hours:* Daily 10-5. *CC:* MC/V. *Park:* Nearby. *Loc:* MBTA Green Line to Cleveland Circle, get off at Coolidge Corner.

BROOKLINE ANTIQUES
8 Cypress St, 02146
(617)731-5557   **37 38 71**

European & American furniture. *Pr:* $500–3500. *Est:* 1968. *Serv:* Restoration, repair, appraisal. *Hours:* Mon-Sat 9-6 Sun 12-6. *Size:* Large. *CC:* AX/DC/MC/V. Gabriel Davis *Park:* Nearby lot. *Loc:* 1 block from Town Hall at Cypress & Washington Sts.

CYPRESS TRADING POST
144 Cypress St, 02146
(617)566-5412   **17 60 63**

Large selection of porcelain, furniture, bronzes & Oriental art. *Est:* 1970. *Hours:* Mon-Sat 10:30-5. *Size:* Medium. Dick Maccini *Park:* On site. *Loc:* Corner of Rte 9 & Cypress St in a blue house.

JERRY FREEMAN LTD
1429 Beacon St, 02146
(617)731-6720   **29 37 53**

18th, 19th & 20th C furniture, decorative accessories, paintings & mirrors. *Est:* 1978. *Serv:* Interior design, purchase estates. *Hours:* Mon-Sat 11-5. *Size:* Medium. *CC:* MC/V. *Park:* In front. *Loc:* 3 blocks from Coolidge Corner on the Green Line (C Route).

TIM GALLAGHER ANTIQUES
Arcade Bldg 318 Harvard Ave #7, 02146
(617)566-2555   **29 36 59**

19th C American & European antiques, including furniture, art work, framed engravings, decorative accessories & collectibles. *Serv:* Purchase estates, restoration. *Hours:* Tue-Sat 10-5 Mon BY APPT. *CC:* MC/V. *Park:* Nearby lot.

EMANUAL GENOVESE
50 Littel Rd, 02146
(617)738-6367   **68 70**

Repair & restoration of stained & lead glass: windows, lamps & period pieces. Reframing & sizing of old panels. Brass, zinc, wood, glass etching & protective shields (lexan) installed. *Est:* 1982. *Serv:* Free estimates, pick up & delivery available. *Hours:* By chance/appt. *Park:* In front. *Loc:* In the heart of Brookline at Coolidge Corner, 3 blocks S on Harvard St, L on Alton Pl, 1 block, L on Littel Rd.

ROSINE GREEN ASSOCIATES, INC.
45 Bartlett Crescent, 02146
(617)277-8368   **25 68 71**

Experts in the restoration of Oriental lacquer, paintings, frames, art objects, metals, porcelain & glass & in the design of pedestals & cases for display. *Est:* 1955. *Serv:* Brochure upon request. *Hours:* BY APPT. Mrs Rosine Green *Loc:* Off Washington St between Beacon St & Commonwealth Ave.

RENOVATORS SUPPLY
1624 Beacon St, 02146
(617)739-6088   **50 70 74**

Period hardware, plumbing & lighting supplies. *Serv:* Reproduction. *Hours:* Mon-Sat 10-6 Thu 10-8 Sun 12-5. *Size:* Medium. *CC:* MC/V. *Park:* In front. *Loc:* Between Coolidge Corner & Cleveland Circle.

ROBERT H RUBIN, BOOKS
Box 267, 02146
(617)277-7677   **13**

Antiquarian books: economics, law, Americana, philosophy & social sciences. *Assoc:* ABAA.

NANCY A SMITH APPRAISAL ASSOC
7 Kent St, 02146
(617)566-1339   **4 26**

An association of personal property appraisers specializing in furniture, clocks, silver, metals, rugs, textiles, ceramics & glass, fine arts & architectural interior elements, reports prepared for insurance/estate planning, estate taxation, gift values. *Serv:* Appraisal, brochure, consultation. *Hours:* Daily 9-5. *Assoc:* ASA CPPC. *Loc:* Brookline Village T stop on Green Line.

THE STRAWBERRY PATCH
12 Cypress St, 02146
(617)566-0077   **40**

Quality refinished oak furniture & brass accessories. *Pr:* $200–800. *Est:* 1981. *Hours:* Thu-Sat 8:30-5:30 Sun 12-3. *Size:* Medium. *CC:* AX/MC/V. Myrna Aschenbrand *Park:* In front. *Loc:* 3 blocks from Rte 9.

Brookline Village

A ROOM WITH A VIEUX
220 Washington St, 02146
(617)227-2700   **35 50 53**

French furniture, mirrors, lamps & sconces. *Est:* 1988. *Hours:* Mon-Sat 10-6. *Park:* In front. *Loc:* 1 block from Rte 9.

THE ANTIQUE COMPANY
311 Washington St, 02146
(617)738-9476   **29 47 77**

Antique jewelry & silver, 19th & 20th C fine & decorative arts. *Pr:* $5–15000. *Est:* 1978. *Serv:* Purchase estates. *Hours:* Mon-Sat 10-5. *Size:* Medium.

CC: AX/MC/V. Toby Langderman *Park:* Nearby lot. *Loc:* 1 block from Rte 9.

BECKERMAN NEAL ANTIQUES
31 Harvard St, 02146
(617)232-6414   **7 38 73**

Continental furniture, fine paintings, sculpture, deco, tapestries, folk art & garden statuary. *Pr:* $100–25000. *Est:* 1973. *Serv:* Purchase estates, appraisal. *Hours:* Mon-Fri 9:30-5:30 Sat,Sun 12-5:30. *Size:* Medium. Ellen Carlino *Park:* In front. *Loc:* 3 blocks from stop on MBTA Green Line.

BROOKLINE VILLAGE ANTIQUES
18 Harvard St, 02146
(617)734-6071   **38 39 53**

18th & 19th C English, Continental & American furniture, paintings & restored lighting. *Hours:* Mon-Sat 10-6 Sun 11-7. Herb Hough *Loc:* 2 blocks from Rte 9.

BROOKLINE VILLAGE BOOKSHOP
23 Harvard St, 02146
(617)734-3519   **13 14**

Americana, biography, children's, local history, & nautical all covered in 30,000 books. *Pr:* $5–1000. *Hours:* Mon-Sat 10-6 Thu til 9. *Size:* Medium. *CC:* AX/MC/V. *Assoc:* ABAA MRIAB. James Lawton *Loc:* I-95 to Rte 9E: to Washington St in Brookline Village, L on Washington by taking R around Fire Station, R at 1st fork.

THE COLLECTOR
135 Cypress St, 02146
(617)734-1037   **55 62 82**

Five rooms full of cameras, antique & vintage furniture, African & ethnic art, paintings, rugs, coins, photographs, mission, oak, musicals, wicker & pottery. *Pr:* $5–5000. *Serv:* Appraisal, conservation, consultation, purchase estates, repair, restoration. *Hours:* Mon-Sat 11-5 Sun BY APPT. *Size:* Large. *CC:* AX/MC/V. Steven Berkovitz *Park:* In front. *Loc:* Corner of Rte 9, Brookline Hills stop on Green Line.

TOWNE ANTIQUES
256 Washington St, 02146
(617)731-3326   **37 38 39**
Large selection of mahogany, cherry, & walnut furniture & mirrors. *Pr:* $500–5000. *Est:* 1970. *Serv:* Purchase estates, appraisal, auctioneers. *Hours:* Mon-Sat 9-6. *Size:* Huge. *CC:* DC/MC/V. Francis J O'Boy *Park:* Nearby. *Loc:* Brookline Village on the MBTA Green line, 1 block off Rte 9.

Buzzards Bay

THE ANTIQUE MART
61 Main St, 02532
(508)759-7556   **{GR20}**
Full line of decorative accessories, jewelry, furniture, glass & china. *Est:* 1973. *Hours:* Jun-Oct daily 9:30-5, Nov-May Tue-Sun 9:30-5. *CC:* MC/V. Donna De Felice *Park:* Behind. *Loc:* Across from RR station.

THE OLD HOUSE
291 Head of Bay Rd, 02532
(508)759-4942   **44 63**
Six rooms of early American pressed glass including blown & cut glass, china & porcelain. *Est:* 1935. *Serv:* Annual brochure. *Hours:* Apr-Dec Mon-Sat 9:30-5, Sun BY APPT ONLY. *CC:* MC/V. Pearl B Henshaw *Loc:* .9 MI from Belmont Circle (Grandma's Restaurant).

Cambridge

JAMES R BAKKER ANTIQUES INC.
370 Broadway, 02139
(617)864-7067   **8 59 66**
Cambridge's only fine arts auction & appraisal service featuring regular sales of paintings, prints & sculpture. *Serv:* Appraisal, auction, catalog, purchase estates. *Hours:* Mon-Fri 10-5 Sat BY APPT. *Size:* Medium. *Assoc:* ADA MSAA. *Loc:* Walking distance from Central & Harvard Sqs in Cambridge.

BERNHEIMER'S ANTIQUE ARTS
52 C Brattle St, 02138
(617)547-1177   **3 47 60**
Like a museum - featuring rare & unusual art objects from around the world, including ancient, European, Asian, Islamic & Pre-Columbian art & antique jewelry - a family tradition since 1864. *Est:* 1963. *Serv:* Appraisal. *Hours:* Mon-Sat 10-5. *Size:* Medium. *CC:* AX/DC/MC/V. *Assoc:* AAA. G. Max Bernheimer *Park:* Nearby lot. *Loc:* On Brattle St, 1 block from the center of Harvard Sq & the Harvard MBTA stop.

ROBIN BLEDSOE
1640 Massachusetts Ave (rear), 02138
(617)576-3634   **13**
Antiquarian books: horses, graphic design, women artists, photographs, sporting art, archaeology, architecture, fine arts & gardening. *Serv:* Appraisal, catalog, search service. *Hours:* Tue-Fri 10-5 Sat 10-6 & BY APPT. *Assoc:* ABAA MRIAB.

SHARON BOCCELLI & CO ANTIQUES
358 Broadway, 02139
(617)354-7919   **29 63 83**
General line of antiques - wholesale. *Est:* 1978. *Serv:* Appraisal, auction. *Hours:* Sat 10-6. *Size:* Medium. *Park:* In front.

CITY LIGHTS
2226 Massachusetts Ave, 02140
(617)547-1490   **50**
Large selection of fine restored lighting. *Pr:* $500–4500. *Est:* 1976. *Serv:* Appraisal, brochure, catalog. *Hours:* Tue-Sat 10-6 Thu til 7:30. *Size:* Medium. *CC:* MC/V. Chris Osbourne *Park:* In front. *Loc:* Int Rte 2 & Alewife Brook Pkwy OR Red Line to Davis Sq.

DOWN UNDER
1132 Massachusetts Ave, 02138
(617)354-5352   **29 47**
Specializing in affordable vintage & antique jewelry & accessories, glassware, china & home furnishings. *Est:* 1985. *Hours:* Tue-Sat 11-6. Leslie Z Salerno *Park:* In front. *Loc:* Across from Dolphin Seafood.

EASY CHAIRS
375 Huron Ave, 02138
(617)491-2131   **27 40 50**
Vintage oak, wicker & rattan, brass lamps & country store items. *Pr:* $2–4000. *Est:* 1980. *Serv:* Purchase estates. *Hours:* Tue-Sat 10-5:30. *Size:* Medium. Lee Joseph *Park:* In front. *Loc:* 1 MI N of Harvard Sq.

FLEUR DE LIS GALLERY
52C Brattle St, 02138
(617)864-7738   **44 47 63**
Antique jewelry, colored glass, European hand-painted china, classic furniture, Quimper, Victorian frames,

Oriental art & old Victorian plate. *Est:* 1981. *Hours:* Tue-Sat 11:30-4:30 call ahead. *Size:* Medium. Silvia Burger *Park:* Nearby lot. *Loc:* At the ground floor next to Bernheimer's.

F B HUBLEY & CO
364 Broadway, 02139
(617)876-2030   **4 8**
Auctioneers & estate appraisers since 1935; specializing in estate liquidation & consignments of antiques, fine arts, & custom furniture or furnishings. No buyers premium. *Serv:* Appraisal, auction, purchase estates. *Hours:* Mon-Fri 8:30-5. *Assoc:* AAA. *Loc:* Midway between Harvard University & Kendall Sq.

HURST GALLERY
53 Mt Auburn St, 02138
(617)491-6888   **3 4 82**
In a sun-lit gallery 3 blocks from Harvard's Fogg Museum antiquities & ethnographic art: African, American Indian, Oceanic, Pre-Columbian, Asian & Classical. Special exhibitions & catalog sales. *Pr:* $50–50000. *Est:* 1977. *Serv:* Appraisal, conservation & mounting, restoration, catalog, free newsletter. *Hours:* Tue-Sat 12-6 Thu til 8. *Size:* Medium. *CC:* AX/DC/MC/V. *Assoc:* ASA ISA. Norman Hurst *Park:* Nearby lot. *Loc:* 4 blocks off JFK St Harvard Sq.

KEEZER'S HARVARD COMMUNITY EXCH
140 River St, 02139
(617)547-2455   **85**
Reasonably priced classic clothing, traditional styles, tuxedos & overcoats. *Est:* 1895. *Hours:* Daily 10-6. *Size:* Large. *Park:* On site. *Loc:* I-90 Cambridge Exit: .25 MI from Memorial Dr.

LAMP GLASS
2230 Massachusetts Ave, 02140
(617)497-0770   **50 70**

Large selection of glass shades & antique reproductions. *Est:* 1984. *Serv:* Reproduction. *Hours:* Wed,Fri,Sat 10-6 Thu 10-7:30. *Size:* Medium. *CC:* MC/V. Tania Maxwell *Park:* In front.

MARC J MATZ
366B Broadway, 02139
(617)661-6200   **29 37 59**

Period American, English & Continental furniture, paintings & decorative accessories. *Pr:* $50–20000. *Est:* 1976. *Serv:* Appraisal, consultation, interior design, purchase estates, repairs. *Hours:* Daily 10-5. *Size:* Medium. *CC:* MC/V. Heidi M Pribell *Park:* In front.

H MENDELSOHN FINE EUROPEAN BOOKS
1640 Massachusetts Ave, 02138
(617)576-3634   **13**

Antiquarian books: architecture, decorative arts, gardening, & printing history. *Serv:* Catalog. *Hours:* Tue-Sat 10-5. *Assoc:* MRIAB. Harvey L Mendelsohn *Park:* Nearby.

THE MUSIC EMPORIUM
2018 Massachusetts Ave, 02140
(617)661-2099   **25 55**

Vintage guitars, banjos, mandolins, concertina, wooden flutes, stringed instruments & dulcimers. *Pr:* $10–15000. *Est:* 1977. *Serv:* Appraisal, conservation, repair, restoration. *Hours:* Mon-Sat 11-5:30 Th 11-8. *Size:* Medium. *CC:* MC/V. *Park:* Nearby lot. *Loc:* Red Line to Porter Sq, 3 block walk.

CARL R NORDBLOM
Harvard Square, 02138
(617)491-1196   **8**

Auctioneers whose specialty sales include an Americana auction every Fall. 10% buyer's premium. *Serv:* Appraisal of American antiques.

KARIN J PHILLIPS ANTIQUES
348 Broadway, 02139
(617)547-9433   **36 60**

Eclectic selection of furniture & accessories ranging from early 19th C to fabulous 50s. *Pr:* $20–8000. *Est:* 1978. *Serv:* Appraisal, purchase estates. *Hours:* Mon-Fri 11-6 Sat 11-4. *Park:* In front. *Loc:* From Harvard, take Massachusetts Ave under the underpass and bear R on Broadway.

POSTAR ANTIQUES
356 Broadway, 02139
(617)576-0463

Buying & selling quality antiques for over 60 years. *Est:* 1917. *Serv:* Appraisal, consultation, purchase estates. *Hours:* By chance. *Size:* Medium. Henry Postar *Park:* In front. *Loc:* Between Central & Inman Sqs, 10 min from downtown Boston.

THE STARR BOOK SHOP
29 Plympton St, 02138
(617)547-6864   **13**

Antiquarian books: literary criticism & biography, literature, philosophy, sets & scholarly remainders. *Serv:* Catalog. *Hours:* Mon-Sat 10-6 Sun 12-6. *Assoc:* MRIAB.

A TOUCH OF CLASS
1309 Cambridge St, 02139
(617)491-7000   **36 83**

Specializing in Victorian antiques. *Serv:* Appraisal, auction, purchase estates, restoration. *Hours:* Daily 9:30-6.

Size: Large. *CC:* MC/V. *Assoc:* AAA
NEAA. *Park:* In front. *Loc:* .5 MI from
Harvard Sq.

Centerville

FOR OLDE TIME'S SAKE
168 Longview Dr, 02632
(508)771-2089   **65 67**

Formal & country furniture, primitives
& quilts. *Hours:* BY APPT ONLY.
Assoc: CCADA. Belle Dienes

Charlestown

BUNKER HILL RELICS
207 Main St, 02129
(617)241-9534   **17 60 63**

Orientalia, Oriental rugs, porcelains,
bronzes, marble busts, furniture & silver pieces. *Serv:* Purchase estates.
Hours: Tue-Fri 11-5:30 Sat 9:30-5:30
& BY APPT.

THE FISKE HOUSE
81 Warren St, 02129
(617)242-2837   **1 37 60**

Four rooms of 18th & 19th C American formal & country furniture located
in an 1808 Federal period home. Accessories include Chinese export
stoneware & candlesticks. *Pr:* $50–
5000. *Est:* 1987. *Hours:* By
chance/appt. Thomas H Slaman *Park:*
In front. *Loc:* From North Station,
over Charlestown Bridge, City Sq to
Warren St.

Chatham

BACKYARD ANTIQUES
10 Bearse's ByWay, 02633
(508)945-2232   **27 65**

Five rooms of American country furniture & primitives - some in paint &
childhood antiques. *Hours:* Apr-Dec
daily, Jan-Mar Sat & BY APPT. *Assoc:*
CCADA. *Loc:* Off Main St near Puri-
tan.

CHAPDELAINE ANTIQUES
585 Main St rear, 02633
(508)945-1511   **27 44 67**

Country furniture, accessories, quilts
& glass. *Est:* 1986. *Hours:* Mon-Sat
10-5, Dec 20-Apr weekends only. *CC:*
MC/V. *Park:* Nearby. *Loc:* Next to
Chatham T's.

HOUSE ON THE HILL
17 Seaview St, 02633
(508)945-2290   **11 33 64**

Post cards, baseball cards, paper Amer-
icana, political memorabilia, old adver-
tising items, toys, primitives & glass.
Hours: Summer daily 10-5. *Assoc:*
CCADA. Richard Soffey *Loc:* At Main
St.

OLD HARBOR HOUSE
ANTIQUES
400 Main St, 02633
(508)945-4669

An eclectic mix of American antiques
from the late 19th - early 20th C. *Est:*
1985. *Hours:* Mon-Sun 10-4
CLOSED WED. *CC:* AX/DC/MC/V.
Bob Peterson *Loc:* Toward the lighthouse.

OLDE VILLAGE COUNTRY BARN
432 Main St, 02633
(508)945-4931   **23 42 56**

Specializing in English pine furnishings & accessories, English & American clocks, grandfather clocks, carved pub signs & nautical paintings. *Hours:* Thu-Sat 10-5 Sun 12-4 or by appt. Robb Sequin

PAPYRUS BOOKS
Rte 28 Main St, 02633
(508)945-5903   **13**

Antiquarian books: biography, detective fiction, literature, psychology & travel. *Serv:* Search service. *Hours:* Apr-Oct Thu-Mon 12-5. *Assoc:* MRIAB. Katherine Dalton

SIMPLER PLEASURES
393 Main St, 02633
(508)945-4040   **27**

Country furniture & decorative accessories. *Est:* 1984. *Hours:* Mon-Sat 10-5. *CC:* AX/MC/V. *Park:* On site. *Loc:* On the way to the lighthouse.

THE SPYGLASS
618 Main St, 02633
(508)945-9686   **10 56**

Antique nautical instruments - telescopes, mercurial & aneroid barometers, charts, half-models, lap desks, captains desks, shadow boxes. *Est:* 1981. *Serv:* Telescope repair, reconditioning. *Hours:* Mon-Sat 9-5. *CC:* AX/MC/V. *Assoc:* CCADA. Daniel J Vaughn *Park:* Nearby. *Loc:* Rte 6 Exit 11: Rte 137S to Rte 28, turn L, straight thru rotary on Main St, 1 block on L.

SHIRLEY WALKER ANTIQUES
400 Main St, 02633
(508)896-8138   **27 34**

Distinctive American country antiques & folk art. *Hours:* Mon-Sat 10-4 & BY APPT. *Assoc:* CCADA.

Chesterfield

CHESTERFIELD ANTIQUES
Rte 143, 01012
(413)296-4252   **1 37**

A large stock of American 18th & 19th C furniture & accessories. *Hours:* Daily (a call ahead advised). *Assoc:* BCoADA NHADA PVADA. Jack Geishen *Park:* On site. *Loc:* 20 min W of Northampton, I-91 Exit 9W, between Pittsfield & Northampton.

Chestnut Hill

SONIA PAINE
616A Hammond St, 02167
(617)566-9669   **47 60 77**

French & Oriental estate jewelry, silver, porcelain, Russian & French enamel. Promoter of major antique shows. *Est:* 1968. *Serv:* Purchase estates, appraisal, promoter of major antiques shows. *Hours:* Tue-Sat 12-4 & BY APPT. *Assoc:* AAA SADA. *Park:* Nearby. *Loc:* Corner of Rte 9 & Hammond St.

DALE POLLOCK APPRAISAL SERVICES
Box 193, 02167
(617)277-4962   **4**

Appraisals of jewelry & silver for insurance, probate, property division, donations & sale. *Est:* 1979. *Serv:* Appraisal, consultation. *Hours:* BY APPT ONLY. *Assoc:* AR ASA GIA.

MAGDA TISZA RARE BOOKS
130 Woodchester Dr, 02167
(617)527-5312   13
Antiquarian books: foreign languages & literature, illustrated, Judaica, philosophy & psychology. *Serv:* Appraisal, catalog. *Hours:* BY APPT. *Assoc:* ABAA MRIAB.

Concord

THE BARROW BOOKSTORE
79 Main St, 01742
(508)369-6084   13
Antiquarian books: transcendentalism, Concord & its writers, Thoreau, Alcotts, literature, children's books, local history & nature. *Serv:* Search service. *Hours:* Mon-Sat 9:30-5. *Assoc:* MRIAB. Claiborne Dawes

BOOKS WITH A PAST
17 Walden St, 01742
(508)371-0180   13
Antiquarian books: Concord authors, Thoreau, Alcotts, Hawthorne, Concord history, transcendentalism, natural history & music. *Serv:* Search service. *Hours:* Mon-Sat 10-5. *Assoc:* MRIAB. Bonnie Bracker

CANTERBURY ANTIQUES
490 Cambridge Tnpk, 01742
(508)369-0197   27 28 67
Country & formal furniture, stoneware, porcelain, quilts & baskets. *Hours:* Fri-Mon 11-4 or by chance/appt. *Assoc:* SADA. Margaret Goud

CONCORD ANTIQUES
32 Main St Basement Level, 01742
(508)369-8218   {GR8}
Furniture, paintings, quilts, laces, linens, sterling silver & books. *Hours:* Mon-Sat 10-5 Sun 1-5. *CC:* MC/V. *Assoc:* SADA. MaryAnn Boynton

CONCORD PATRIOT ANTIQUES
1595 Main St Rte 62, 01742
(617)263-0105   36 44 77
Large selection of early antiques, including Chippendale, East Lake, Victorian, Gothic country & oak. Glassware includes Chelsea, Staffordshire, Bohemian, Limoges, Nippon/Noritake & Bisque. Also carry jade, ivory, silver & cloisonne. *Hours:* Weekdays BY APPT, weekends & holidays 9-4. Tom Gorham

JOSLIN HALL RARE BOOKS
Box 516, 01742
(508)371-3101   13 14
Specialists in scarce & out-of-print books on the decorative arts & American fine arts, especially references on American decorative fine arts of the 18th & 19th C. *Pr:* $25-2500. *Est:* 1981. *Serv:* Brochure, catalog (free), purchase libraries, search service. *Hours:* BY APPT ONLY.

BERNICE JACKSON
Box 1188, 01742
(508)369-9088   66
Vintage European & American posters & poster-related graphics 1895-1950. *Est:* 1976. *Serv:* Appraisal, fine arts consultant. *Hours:* BY APPT. *CC:* MC/V. *Loc:* Call for directions.

Conway

CONWAY HOUSE
Rte 116 Ashfield Rd, 01341
(413)369-4660   16 50 65

All 18th & 19th C samplers, primitives, paintings, lighting devices, copper, brass, iron, Staffordshire, textiles & furniture. *Est:* 1963. *Serv:* Appraisal. *Hours:* Appt advised. *Assoc:* ADA NHADA VADA. Jack Van Gelder *Park:* On site. *Loc:* I-91N Exit 25: I-91S Exit 24: take Rte 116 to Conway, 6.5 MI.

ROBERT L MERRIAM
Newhall Rd, 01341
(413)369-4052   13

10,000 out-of-print books on a wide variety of subjects, specializing in bibliography, decorative arts & Americana. This bed & breakfast in an attractive country setting permits evening browsing. *Serv:* Appraisal, catalog. *Hours:* Sun 1-5 or by chance/appt. *Size:* Medium. *Assoc:* MRIAB. *Park:* In front. *Loc:* From S: Rte 91 Exit 24 to Rtes 5 & 10 to Rte 116 to Conway. In Conway Shelburne Falls Rd to Newhall Rd.

Cummaquid

CUMMAQUID FINE ARTS
4275 Main St Rte 6A, 02637
(508)362-2593   29

Fine decorative antiques & arts for the table, bar & conservatory, including crystal, porcelain & silver. *Hours:* Jul-Labor Day Tue-Sat 10-5 Spring & Fall Wed-Sun or BY APPT. *CC:* MC/V.

Assoc: CCADA. Jim Hinkle Roy Hammer *Park:* On site. *Loc:* Rte 6 Exit 7: to Yarmouthport, L on Rte 6A for .6 MI.

THE OWL'S NEST ANTIQUES
4083 Main St, 02637
(508)362-4054   27 32 65

Country furniture, primitives, dolls & textiles. *Serv:* Furniture refinishing. *Hours:* In season daily 10-5. *Assoc:* CCADA. Nancy Galloni *Park:* In front. *Loc:* On Rte 6A, 4th house E of the post office.

THE PICKET FENCE
Rte 6A, 02637
(508)362-4865   44 63

Furniture, depression glass, pottery, porcelain, mirrors & lighting fixtures. *Est:* 1987. *Hours:* Daily 10-5 CLOSED JAN-FEB. *CC:* MC/V. Mary Ann Windsor *Park:* On site. *Loc:* 1.7 MI from Barnstable Village lights.

Cummington

B SHAW ANTIQUES
Rte 9 At The Green Bridge, 01026
(413)634-2289   36

Large stock of furniture - oak, walnut, Victorian, wicker, early pine, primitives, desks, round tables, sets of chairs, rockers & brass beds - primarily to the trade. *Pr:* $25–500. *Hours:* By chance/appt.

Danvers

SPRAGUE HOUSE ANTIQUES
59 Endicott St, 01923
(508)774-3944   37

Period & fine custom furniture of investment quality in original or professionally restored condition. *Hours:* By chance/appt. *Loc:* Just off Rte 128 at Exit 24.

Dedham

CENTURY SHOP
626 High St, 02026
(617)326-1717   **4 8**
A general line of antiques. *Serv:* Purchase estates, appraisal, auctions. *Hours:* Daily 11-4:30 CLOSED FRI,SUN. *Assoc:* SADA. Eleanor Woodward *Loc:* Near Court House.

DEDHAM ANTIQUE SHOP
622 High St, 02026
(617)329-1114   **1 37**
Large stock of authentic American furniture & accessories - fourth generation in American antiques. *Serv:* Private & trade enquiries invited. *Hours:* By chance/appt. *Assoc:* SADA. Simon Nager

HENRY HORNBLOWER III
176 Court St, 02026
(617)329-3226   **36 59 66**
Paintings, prints & furniture. *Est:* 1965. *Serv:* Purchase estates, appraisal. *Hours:* BY APPT ONLY, primarily to the trade. *Loc:* Call for directions.

Deerfield

ELLIE'S ANTIQUE CENTER
Rtes 5 & 10, 01342
(413)774-5692   **{GR35}**
Antiques & collectibles. *Pr:* $5–1000. *Est:* 1987. *Serv:* Brochure. *Hours:* Tue-Sun 10-5. *Size:* Large. *CC:* MC/V. *Assoc:* PVADA. *Park:* On site. *Loc:* 1.25 MI S of Historic Deerfield.

Dennis

ANTIQUES 608
608 Rte 6A, 02638
(508)385-2755
American, English & Oriental antiques from the 19th & early 20th C. *Hours:* Daily 11-5 CLOSED WED. Tom Cardaropoli

LESLIE CURTIS ANTIQUES
838 Main St, 02638
(508)385-2921   **63 86**
Distinctive early wicker furniture, Quimper pottery, faux & Brighton bamboo. *Hours:* Seasonal. *Assoc:* CCADA. *Loc:* Rte 6A at Corporation Rd.

DOVETAIL ANTIQUES
543 Rte 6A, 02638
(508)385-2478   **27 81**
Old woodworking & sailmakers tools & country furniture. *Est:* 1984. *Hours:* Fri-Tue 10-5 CLOSED WED,THU. *Park:* On site. *Loc:* .25 MI from Dennis post office.

ELLIPSE ANTIQUES
427 Main St, 02638
(508)385-8626   **1 44 50**
Specializing in colored Sandwich & early American glass & lighting, fine line of country Americana including furniture & folk art accessories & period items. *Pr:* $100–3000. *Est:* 1980. *Serv:* Interior design. *Hours:* Apr-Oct daily 9:30-Dusk, Nov-Mar by chance/appt. *Size:* Medium. *CC:* MC/V. *Assoc:* CCADA. Vince Hinman *Park:* On site. *Loc:* Rte 6A corner of Black Ball Hill Rd, 1 MI W of Dennis town center, Exit 7 from Rte 6 to Rte 6A, R 4 MI on R.

HYLAND GRANBY ANTIQUES
528 Main St Rte 6A, 02638
(508)771-3070 **56**

Large inventory of museum-quality 18th & 19th C marine antiques, ship models, scrimshaw, paintings & navigational instruments. *Est:* 1980. *Serv:* Appraisal, consultation. *Hours:* Daily 11-5, CLOSED WED. *Loc:* Call for directions.

KING'S GRANT ANTIQUES
620 Main St, 02638
(508)385-4903 **47 59 66**

Antique furniture, paintings, prints, antique & estate jewelry, china, rugs, quilts, miniature lamps, glass & country. *Hours:* Apr-Dec daily 10-5:30. *Assoc:* CCADA. Ronald A Gray *Park:* Nearby.

THE LEANING TREE
632 Main St, 02638
(508)385-8826 **47 59 67**

18th - 20th C American antiques, formal & country furniture, paintings, jewelry, art glass, Orientalia, clocks & Shaker quilts. *Hours:* Sum: 10-5, Win: 11-4. *Assoc:* CCADA. Linda M Sharp

OLD TOWNE ANTIQUES
593 Main St, 02638
(508)771-1915 **{GR8}**

Country furniture & accessories, period furnishings, toy soldiers & paintings. *Hours:* Variable. *Assoc:* CCADA. Claire M Guiney *Park:* In front.

VILLAGE PEDLAR CLOCK SHOP
623 Main St, 02638
(508)385-7300 **23 59**

Antique clocks & old paintings. *Est:* 1979. *Serv:* Clock repair, appraisal. *Hours:* Mon-Sat 9:30-5:30. *CC:*

MC/V. *Assoc:* NAWCC. John Anderson *Loc:* 2 doors down from the Dennis Public Market.

Dennis Village

ANOTHER TIME & PLACE
766 Main St, 02638
(508)385-3877 **13 51**

Antiquarian book dealer specializing in old books in nice condition: 19th C maps of Massachusetts localities, steel engravings, the sea, women's fiction & theatre. *Pr:* $3–300. *Est:* 1988. *Serv:* Purchase estates, search service. *Hours:* Mon-Wed 10-5:30 Thu-Sun 10-6:30 or BY APPT. Dave Drolet *Park:* On site. *Loc:* In the upper gallery of The Mercantile behind the red post office near the Cape Playhouse.

BOSTON BRASS WORKS
Theatre Marketplace Rte 6A, 02638
(508)385-5089 **50**

Custom & antique lighting & chandeliers. *Est:* 1978. *Hours:* Sum: Mon-Sat 10-4, Sept 15-May 30 Tue-Sat 10-4. *CC:* AX/MC/V. Bill Block *Park:* Nearby. *Loc:* Next to the post office.

RED LION ANTIQUES
601 Main St, 02633
(508)385-4783 **{GR10}**

Imported English & European antique furniture & decorative accessories. Handmade Windsor chairs a specialty. *Serv:* Appraisal, interior design, purchase estates. *Hours:* Year round Mon-Sat 10-5 Sun 11-4. *CC:* AX/MC/V. *Park:* On site.

Dennisport

THE SIDE DOOR
103 Main St Rte 28, 02639
(508)394-7715 **33 44 64**
Large selection of paper collectibles,
post cards, sheet music, photographs,
books, china & glass. *Pr:* $1–500. *Est:*
1973. *Serv:* Flow blue matching service. *Hours:* Sum: daily 10-5 Sun 12-4.
Win: Fri,Sat 10-5 Sun 12-4. *CC:*
AX/MC/V. *Assoc:* CCADA. Frank R
Lewy *Park:* In front.

Dorchester

OLDE BOSTONIAN
135 Buttonwood, 02125
(617)282-9300 **5 44 74**
Architectural antiques - newel posts,
mouldings, fireplace mantels, brackets,
brass work, unusual doors, old bathtubs, balasters, floor registers, stained
glass, wainscoting & columns. *Est:*
1980. *Serv:* Stripping. *Hours:* Mon-
Sat 8-5 Sun 9-4. *CC:* MC/V. *Park:* On
site. *Loc:* Exit 15 off the SE Expressway.

Dover

INTERIOR MOTIVES, INC.
*Springdale Crossing 14 Dedham St,
02030*
(508)785-1959 **27 38 67**
American & European country furniture with appropriate accessories:
quilts, textiles, pottery & New England folk art. *Est:* 1983. *Serv:* Interior
design, consultation, custom woodwork. *Hours:* Tue-Fri 10-4 Sat,Sun 12-
4 by chance/appt. *Size:* Medium. *CC:*

AX/MC/V. *Assoc:* NHADA SADA.
Gary Gardner-Glynn *Park:* Nearby
lot. *Loc:* From 128W on Rte
109/Westwood, R on Summer St to
end, L on Dedham St to Dover Ctr @
light R on Springdale Ave to Crossing.

Dracut

**THE ANTIQUARIAN
SCIENTIST**
Box 367, 01826
(508)957-5267 **13**
Antiquarian books: history of science,
medicine, natural history, science,
technology & scientific instruments.
Serv: Appraisal, catalog. *Hours:* BY
APPT. *Assoc:* MRIAB. Raymond
Giordana

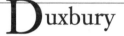Duxbury

ANTIQUES AT MILLBROOK
St George St, 02332
(617)934-0635 **{GR2}**
A small, year-round country shop with
an ever-changing inventory of collectibles & antiques. Furniture, primitives, linens, china, glass & silver. *Pr:*
$5–1000. *Est:* 1985. *Serv:* Appraisal,
consultation, purchase estates. *Hours:*
Tue-Sat 10-5 Sun,Mon by
chance/appt. *Size:* Medium. *CC:*
MC/V. *Assoc:* SSADA. Lya J Fait *Park:*
In front. *Loc:* Rte 3 Duxbury/Rte 14
Exit: E for 2 MI, .3 MI from Rte 3A
lights on R.

**LOWY FRAME & RESTORING
COMPANY**
667 Union St, 02332
(617)834-2929 **25 68 70**
Handcrafted reproduction picture

frames - all styles & periods & period frames. *Pr:* $300–30000. *Serv:* Conservation, consultation, repairs, reproduction, replication, restoration. *Hours:* Appt suggested. Edward P LaBlue *Park:* On site.

East Bridgewater

ANTIQUES AT FORGE POND
35 N Bedford St Rte 18, 02333
(508)378-3057   **{GR5}**
Multi-dealer shop featuring glass, china, dolls, furniture & post cards. *Est:* 1974. *Serv:* Brochure, purchase estates. *Hours:* Daily 11-5. *Size:* Medium. *Assoc:* HAAD SADA SSADA. Marie A Davis *Park:* In front. *Loc:* On Rte 18.

East Dennis

ROBERT C ELDRED CO, INC
1483 Main St Rte 6A, 02641
(508)385-3116   **4 8**
Summer auctions weekly, variety of special auctions - Americana, European, Oriental items. July collectors sale. Sep-May general auctions held twice weekly. 10% buyer's premium. *Est:* 1950. *Serv:* Fine arts auction & appraisal. *Hours:* Office daily 8:30-5. *Assoc:* AAA. *Park:* On site. *Loc:* Rte 6 Exit 9: L onto Rte 134, to Int of Rte 6A, turn L again, .25 MI on L.

East Longmeadow

W D HALL
99 Maple St, 01028
(413)525-3064   **13 33**
Antiquarian books: Americana, ephemera, fine arts, nautical, Western Americana & prints. *Serv:* Catalog. *Hours:* Mail order only. *Assoc:* MRIAB. W. Douglas Hall

East Orleans

COUNTRYSIDE ANTIQUES
6 Lewis Rd, 02643
(508)240-0525   **39**
Fine English & Irish antiques accompanied by collectibles & unusual gift items. *Pr:* $25–4500. *Hours:* Mar-Dec Mon-Sat 11-5 Sun 12-5. *Size:* Medium. *CC:* AX/MC/V. *Assoc:* CCADA. Deborah R Rita *Park:* On site. *Loc:* Rte 6 Exit 12 (Orleans): R at light, thru next light, R at 3rd light , approx 1.2 MI to Lewis Rd (on R), 1st driveway on R.

East Otis

LYMAN BOOKS - THEATRE
PO Box 853, 01029
(413)269-6311   **13**
Antiquarian books: theater literature, American & foreign plays, theater histories & criticism & theater biographies. *Assoc:* ABAA. Samuel N Freedman

East Sandwich

HENRY THOMAS CALLAN FINE ANTIQUE
162 Quaker Meeting House Rd, 02537
(508)888-5372
American samplers & Chinese export porcelain. **Hours:** BY APPT ONLY. **Assoc:** NEAA.

THE GILDED SWAN
685 Rte 6A, 02537
(508)362-2301   **29 47 63**
Fine antique & estate jewelry, export porcelain, Russian, African & European decorative accessories. **Serv:** Unconditional guarantee of authenticity. **Hours:** Daily 10:30-5:30. **Assoc:** CCADA. Ronald A Gray **Park:** In front. **Loc:** On Sandwich/Barnstable line.

HEATHER HOUSE
350 Rte 6A, 02537
(508)888-2034   **42**
Country pine furniture, crocks, tinware, kitchen items & quilts. **Est:** 1977. **Hours:** May-Dec daily 10-5, Jan-Apr Thu-Sun. **CC:** MC/V. **Park:** On site. **Loc:** Rte 6E Exit 3: turn L, R on Rte 6A, 2nd bldg on R.

HORSEFEATHERS ANTIQUES
454 Rte 6A, 02537
(508)888-5298   **32 48 83**
Specializing in linens & lace, Victorian accessories & childhood antiques. **Est:** 1982. **Hours:** Year round. **CC:** MC/V. **Assoc:** CCADA. Jeanne Gresham **Park:** In front. **Loc:** Next to East Sandwich fire station.

JESSE CALDWELL LEATHERWOOD
39 Discovery Hill Rd, 02537
(508)888-8076   **37 45 56**
American & European furniture & decorative arts, marine items especially ship wool embroideries, exceptional campaign furniture, garden furniture & sculpture. **Pr:** $100–25000. **Hours:** BY APPT. **Size:** Medium. **Assoc:** AADLA. **Shows:** WAS. **Park:** On site. **Loc:** Rte 6 Exit 3: N 1 MI to Rte 6A, turn L (W), .6 MI to Discovery Hill Rd, turn L, .3 MI up dirt Rd to #39.

TITCOMB'S BOOKSHOP
432 Rte 6A, 02537
(508)888-2331   **13**
Two floors of rare & out-of-print books located in charming barn attached to 1790 restored 3/4 Cape Cod home located on historic Old King's Highway. **Serv:** Appraisal, catalog. **Hours:** Daily 10-5 Sun 12-5. **Size:** Medium. **CC:** MC/V. **Assoc:** MRIAB. Ralph Titcomb **Park:** On site. **Loc:** 7 MI E of the Sagamore Bridge on Rte 6A, statue of Ben Franklin in front.

Eastham

QUAIL SONG ANTIQUES
RR 1 Box 261, 02642
(508)255-4968   **16 63 65**
Primitives, tin, woodenware, molds, lamps & china. **Hours:** Daily 10-5. **Assoc:** CCADA. Irma D Smith

Easthampton

PETER FRANKLIN CABINETMAKERS
1 Cottage St, 01027
(413)527-4004   **19 43 70**
Handcrafted reproductions of Windsor chairs, custom reproductions of other furniture done by request. *Pr:* $200–1500. *Est:* 1984. *Serv:* Catalog $3, custom woodwork, reproduction. *Hours:* Mon-Fri 9-5 appt suggested. *Park:* On site. *Loc:* I-91 Exit 17B (Rte 141W): 6 MI to Central Easthampton, large 19th C factory located on Rte 141 at 1st light.

GLASKOWSKY & COMPANY
180 Main St, 01027
(413)527-2410   **37**
Connecticut spun glass kettles, American chairs, including Windsor, Hitchcock, Shaker, Hepplewhite & Victorian. *Serv:* Polaroids $1, appraisal for insurance & estates. *Hours:* By chance/appt. *Assoc:* PVADA. *Loc:* On Rte 10.

Edgartown

AUNTIES ATTIC ANTIQUES
224 Edgartown Rd, 02539
(508)627-9833   **{GR5}**
A diverse collection of reasonably-priced Americana, furniture, rugs, books, bottles, brass, decoys, glass, linens, porcelain, prints, quilts, jewelry, tools, toys, silver, baskets & lamps. *Pr:* $25–1500. *Est:* 1983. *Serv:* Appraisal. *Hours:* Jun 10-Sep 20 Mon-Sat 10-5, Sep 21-Jun 9 Fri-Sat 10-5. *Size:* Medium. *CC:* MC/V. *Park:* In front. *Loc:* In Red General Stores Building on

Edgartown Vineyard Haven Rd, Upper Main St Edgartown Triangle Area.

Elmwood

DOING ANTIQUES AT ELMWOOD
734 Bedford St, 02337
(508)378-2063   **{GR7}**
Large selection of Royal Doulton including figurines, character jugs, series ware, flambe. Also Royal Bayreuth, Orientalia, jewelry, paintings, prints, pottery & porcelain, displayed in a 19th C general store with the oldest working post office in NE. *Pr:* $25–700. *Est:* 1985. *Serv:* Appraisal, brochure, purchase estates. *Hours:* Tue-Fri 10:30-4 Sat,Sun 10-5. *Size:* Large. *Assoc:* SNEADA. Paul Dewing *Park:* On site. *Loc:* Rte 24N or S to Rte 106E, Int of Rtes 18 & 106 to East Bridgewater.

Essex

AMERICANA ANTIQUES
48 Main St, 01929
(508)768-6006   **40 42 50**
Country pine & walnut with Victorian oak furniture & brass lighting a specialty. *Pr:* $25–2500. *Est:* 1969. *Hours:* Daily 10-5. *CC:* AX/MC/V. *Assoc:* NSADA. Kenneth Monroe *Park:* On site. *Loc:* Rte 128N Exit 15: to Essex.

ANNEX ANTIQUES
69 Main St, 01929
(508)768-7704   **{GR3}**
A general line of antiques featuring furniture, decorative accessories, pottery & porcelain. *Est:* 1958. *Serv:* Pur-

chase estates. *Hours:* Mon-Sat 10-5 Sun 11-5. *Size:* Large. *CC:* MC/V. Barbara Dyer-Reymond *Park:* In front. *Loc:* On Causeway overlooking Essex River.

AS TIME GOES BY ANTIQUES
163 Main St, 01929
(508)768-7479

Furniture particularly dining room tables. *Hours:* Daily 11-5 CLOSED WED. *CC:* MC/V. *Park:* On street. *Loc:* Downtown Essex.

BLACKWOOD MARCH
3 Southern Ave, 01929
(508)768-6943   8

Auctions of fine arts & antiques. 10% buyer's premium. *Serv:* Auction & appraisal. Michael March

BRICK HOUSE ANTIQUES
166 Main St Rte 133, 01929
(508)768-6617   36 59 63

Antique furniture, textiles paintings, jewelry, china & collectibles displayed in a 200-year-old brick house. *Hours:* Wed-Sun 10:30-4:30. Cathie Beattie Susan Stella *Park:* In front.

CHEBACCO ANTIQUES
38 Main St Rte 133, 01929
(508)768-7371   {GR10}

Featuring American pine & country furniture & related accessories, including quilts, textiles, pottery, porcelain & stoneware. *Pr:* $25-500. *Est:* 1981. *Hours:* Daily 10:30-4:30. *Size:* Medium. *CC:* AX/MC/V. *Assoc:* SADA. Jane Adams *Park:* In front. *Loc:* Rte 128N Exit 15 (School St): turn L toward Essex, At Int Rte 133, go L, 1 MI on R.

CHRISTIAN MOLLY ANTIQUES
Rte 133, 01929
(508)768-6079   44 47 77

American & European antiques, furniture, porcelain, glass, silver & jewelry. *Hours:* Mon-Sat 10-5 Sun 12-5. *Assoc:* NSADA. *Park:* In front. *Loc:* Rte 128 Exit 15.

COUNTRY CORNER ANTIQUES
57R John Wise Ave, 01929
(617)768-7702   27

Country & cottage furniture, accessories & collectibles. *Hours:* Tue-Sat 10-5. Paul Schroeter *Park:* On site. *Loc:* On Rte 133.

JOHN CUSHING ANTIQUE RESTORATION
113 Martin St, 01929
(508)768-7356   68 71

Antique furniture restoration: repairs, hand stripping, veneer work, hand-rubbed oil finishes, varnishes & shellac finishes. *Serv:* Consultation, custom woodwork, repairs, restoration. *Hours:* APPT ESSENTIAL. *Assoc:* NSADA. *Park:* In front. *Loc:* Rte 22 from ctr of Essex: .5 MI from Jct of Rtes 22W & 133 on R side of road, sign in front.

FRIENDSHIP ANTIQUES
Rte 133, 01929
(617)468-2248   21 36

Furniture, art, rugs & accessories. *Serv:* Appraisal, Purchase estates. *Hours:* Tue-Sat 10-5. William S Friend *Park:* On site.

HOTEL ESSEX ANTIQUES
67 Main St, 01929
(508)768-7716   {GR4}

Three floors of fine quality 18th, 19th, & 20th C antiques & collectibles attractively displayed in a restored Victorian hotel. *Pr:* $25-3000. *Est:*

1983. *Serv:* Appraisal, consultation, interior design, purchase estates, repairs. *Hours:* Daily 10-5. *Size:* Large. *CC:* AX/MC/V. Robert C Coviello *Park:* In front. *Loc:* Rte 128N from Boston Exit 15: toward Essex 3 MI, turn L onto Main St, .25 MI up on L.

HOWARD'S FLYING DRAGON ANTIQUES
136 Main St Rte 133, 01929
(508)768-7282 **44 45**

A general line of antiques, handcrafts & statuary. *Est:* 1972. *Hours:* Daily 10:30-6. *CC:* AX/MC/V. Laura Howard *Park:* Nearby. *Loc:* Rte 128N Exit 15: 4 MI, in the ctr of town.

L A LANDRY ANTIQUES
164 Main St, 01929
(508)768-6233 **4 8 58**

Buying, selling, appraising & auctioning fine antiques on the North Shore of Boston for over fifty years. *Pr:* $25–150000. *Est:* 1938. *Serv:* Appraisal, auction, conservation, consultation, interior design, repairs. *Hours:* By chance/appt suggested. *Assoc:* AAA AR. Robert E Landry *Park:* Nearby lot. *Loc:* Rte 128N to Rte 133W, on Rte 133 on Burnham's Corner in South Essex.

MAIN STREET ANTIQUES
44 Main St, 01929
(508)768-7039 **{GR5}**

Three floors of fine quality 18th, 19th & 20th C antiques & collectibles attractively displayed in a restored, Victorianized 18th C New England home. *Pr:* $1–3000. *Est:* 1983. *Serv:* Appraisal, consultation, interior design, purchase estates, repairs. *Hours:* Daily 10-5. *Size:* Large. *CC:* AX/MC/V. Robert C Coviello *Park:* On site. *Loc:*

Rte 128N from Boston Exit 15: toward Essex, 3 MI, turn L onto Main St, .25 MI up on R.

NORTH HILL ANTIQUES
155 Main St, 01929
(508)768-7716 **37 46 59**

Located on the 1st floor of a restored 19th C house, featuring a collection of quality 18th & 19th C European & American furniture & accessories. *Pr:* $100–5000. *Est:* 1988. *Serv:* Appraisal, consultation, interior design, purchase estates, repairs. *Hours:* Daily 10-5. *Size:* Medium. *CC:* MC/V. Sylvia G Kaplan *Park:* In front. *Loc:* Rte 128N from Boston Exit 15: toward Essex, 3 MI, turn L onto Main St, 200 yds up on R.

RIDER & CLARKE ANTIQUES
165 Eastern Ave Rte 133, 01929
(508)768-7441 **21 39 59**

Fine period, formal & decorative furniture, paintings, Oriental rugs & works of art from the 18th & 19th C. *Pr:* $500–50000. *Serv:* Appraisal, conservation, consultation, purchase estates, restoration. *Hours:* Tue-Sun. *Size:* Large. Jon Rider *Park:* On site. *Loc:* Rte 128N Exit 14: Rte 133 toward Essex, 2 MI on L.

STEPHEN SCORE
159 Main St, 01929
(508)768-6252 **34 41 65**

American primitive paintings, painted furniture, folk art & decorative accessories. *Hours:* Weekends 12-5 & BY APPT. *Park:* Nearby. *Loc:* At Burnham's Corner in Essex.

THE SCRAPBOOK
34 Main St Rte 133, 01929
(508)768-7404 **51 66**

Antique paper, prints, maps & botani-

cals - from the 15th through 19th C.
Hours: By chance/appt. *Assoc:*
NSADA.

Fairhaven

SOUTH ESSEX ANTIQUES
166 Eastern Ave, 01929
(508)768-6373   {GR6}
A variety of decorative & unusual items
from all periods & cultures, jewelry,
ethnography, furniture & decorative
objects & paintings. *Pr:* $25–7000. *Est:*
1982. *Serv:* Appraisal, purchase estates. *Hours:* Mon-Sat 11-5 Sun 12-5.
Size: Medium. *Assoc:* NEAA. William
Taylor *Park:* On site. *Loc:* Rte 128N
Exit 14: L 2.5 MI to Essex, on R, low
white building surrounded by parking
lot.

SUSAN STELLA ANTIQUES
166 Main St, 01929
(508)768-6617   {GR4}
18th & 19th C furniture, paintings,
quilts, antique garden furniture, porcelains, period accessories & marine antiques. *Pr:* $25–5000. *Est:* 1978. *Serv:*
Appraisal. *Hours:* Daily 10:30-5. *Size:*
Medium. *CC:* MC/V. *Assoc:* NEAA.
Susan Stella *Park:* On site. *Loc:* Rte
128N Exit 15: toward Essex, 3 MI,
across from SS entering Essex, white
brick building.

THE WHITE ELEPHANT SHOP
32 Main St, 01929
(508)768-6901   27 44 63
One of New England's oldest consignment shops featuring collectibles,
china, books & furniture. *Pr:* $1–1500.
Est: 1953. *Serv:* Appraisal, auction,
brochure, conservation, custom woodworking, repairs. *Hours:* Mon-Sat 10-
5 Sun 12-5. *Size:* Large. Thomas Ellis
Park: On site. *Loc:* Rte 128 Exit 14: to
Essex, from NH: Rte 95 to Rte 133 to
Essex.

FANTASY HOUSE ANTIQUES
32 Cedar St, 02719
(508)993-8558   50 63
Pairpoint, Limoges, silver plate &
lamps. *Serv:* Appraisal, purchase estates. *Hours:* BY APPT ONLY. *Assoc:*
SNEADA. Kenneth L Tobergta Sr

HARE & TORTOISE
ANTIQUES/COLLECT
92 Washington St, 02719
(508)994-2408   44 63 64
Glass, brass, china, woodenware, post
cards, books, lace, linen & miniatures.
Assoc: SNEADA. Essjay Foulkrod

EDWARD J LEFKOWICZ INC
43 Fort St, 02719
(508)997-6839   13 51 56
Specialize exclusively in rare & antiquarian books, manuscripts, charts &
prints relating to ships & the sea, voyages, naval history & science, naviga-
tion & shipbuilding, whaling & marine
art. *Pr:* $25–10000. *Est:* 1974. *Serv:*
Appraisal, catalog. *Hours:* BY APPT
ONLY. *CC:* MC/V. *Assoc:* ABAA
MRIAB. *Park:* On site. *Loc:* E on Rte
6 from New Bedford, 2nd R after
bridge onto Main St, Follow Main St
to End, L, 1st R is Fort St.

BARRY SCOTT
PO Box 630, 02719
            9 13
Antiquarian books: first editions, in-
scribed & illustrated books, fine print-
ing & art. *Serv:* Catalog. *Hours:* BY
APPT ONLY. *Assoc:* ABAA.

Fall River

COLLECTORS JUNCTION
791 Plymouth Ave, 02721
(508)674-9586   **{GR}**

Four large rooms featuring furniture, clocks, glass, paintings, lamps, old toys & dolls, country store advertising & old jewelry. *Est:* 1986. *Serv:* Appraisal, brochure, purchase estates. *Hours:* Apr-Dec Mon-Sat 10-4. *Size:* Large. Faith Wong *Park:* On site. *Loc:* I-195 Exit 7: halfway between Providence RI & Cape Cod MA.

DORCAS BOOKS
133 Keeley St, 02723
(508)675-1904   **13**

Antiquarian books: biography, Civil War, illustrated, American & English first editions, detective fiction, children's literature, exploration & voyages. *Serv:* Appraisal, catalog, search service. *Assoc:* MRIAB. Stanley Kay

Falmouth

AURORA BOREALIS ANTIQUES
Historic Queens Byway, 02540
(508)540-3385   **44 63 72**

Pattern glass, historic glass, cut glass, Staffordshire pottery, metalware, paintings, jewelry, porcelain, scientific instruments, ephemera, books, wooden articles, furniture & Orientalia. *Serv:* Appraisal, consultation, purchase estates. *Hours:* May-Oct daily 11-4 CLOSED WED,SUN, Oct-Dec by chance/appt. *Size:* Medium. *Assoc:* CCADA. Maureen E

Northern *Park:* On site. *Loc:* 1.5 hrs from Boston on the way to/from Martha's Vineyard or Nantucket.

Fitchburg

JOHN CLEMENT FINE ART
52 Buttrick Ave, 01420
(508)345-5863   **59 60 66**

Small but carefully chosen selection of decorative & historical prints, drawings & maps of all periods. Occasional offerings of master prints, drawings & paintings from a lifetime collection. *Pr:* $25–5000. *Est:* 1985. *Serv:* Purchase estates & collections. *Hours:* BY APPT ONLY TO THE TRADE ONLY. *Loc:* Call for appt & directions.

Foxboro
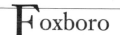

POND HOUSE WOODWORKING
39 Main St, 02035
(508)543-8633   **25 68**

Conservation of furniture, gilt frames & wooden artifacts, specializing in French & American veneered furniture, marquetry & parquetry. Located in a carriage house attached to an old Victorian. *Est:* 1975. *Serv:* Conservation, custom woodwork, repairs, restoration, gilding. *Hours:* Mon-Fri 9-6 Sat,Sun BY APPT. *Size:* Medium. *Assoc:* AIC NTHP SPNEA. John Philibert *Park:* On site. *Loc:* I-95 approx 20 MI N of Providence RI, take Rte 140 to Foxboro, 7 houses beyond Foxboro Ctr on R (Rte 140 is Main St).

SILVER LADY ANTIQUES
PO Box 27, 02035
(508)784-9184 **4 77**
Sterling silver flatware matching service, patterns produced by American silver companies from ca 1880 to the present with special focus on patterns manufactured around the turn-of-the-century. Flatware by Georg Jensen a specialty. *Serv:* Appraisal. *Hours:* Shows & mail order. *Assoc:* ISA SADA.

Framingham

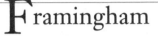

AVERY'S ANTIQUES
74 Franklin St, 01701
(508)875-4576 **37 65**
Early American furniture & accessories, beds, primitives & Victorian upholstered furniture. *Hours:* Mon-Fri 8-5 Sat 8-12. *Assoc:* SADA.

FRANKLIN STREET ANTIQUE MALL
10 Franklin St, 01701
(508)875-8948 **{GR}**
Two floors of furniture, primitives, linens, china, depression era glass & pottery, books, paper & prints. *Serv:* Purchase estates, moving sale services. *Hours:* Mon-Sat 10-5 or BY APPT. *Size:* Large. *Assoc:* SADA. Dorothy M Fitch

Franklin

JOHNSTON ANTIQUES
789 W Central St, 02038
(508)528-0942 **24 51 79**
Formal furniture & accessories, china, brass, copper, pottery, jewelry, Orientalia, paintings, prints, maps, early

paper, Shaker, coins, stamps & primitives. *Serv:* Appraisal. *Hours:* Daily 10-5 or BY APPT. *Assoc:* SADA. *Loc:* Rte 495W Exit 17: to Rte 140.

Gardner

IRENE'S BOOK SHOP
49 W Broadway, 01440
(508)632-5574 **13**
Collectable & rare books in all categories. Lists issued six times a year. *Est:* 1967. *Serv:* Appraisal, catalog. *Hours:* Mon-Sun 1-5 & BY APPT. *Assoc:* MRIAB. Irene M Walet *Park:* In front. *Loc:* On Rte 2A, 5 houses down from ctr of S Gardner.

PAUL C RICHARDS AUTOGRAPHS
16 Woodland Ave, 01440
(508)630-1228 **9 13 33**
Wide range of original autographs of historically important personages, 15th C to the present, including presidents, historical, military, literary, scientific, music & the arts, world leaders, offered in letters, documents & signed images. *Pr:* $25–300000. *Serv:* Appraisal, catalog $5, consultation. *Hours:* Year round daily 10-5 Sat BY APPT. *Size:* Large. *Assoc:* ABAA MRIAB. *Park:* On site. *Loc:* Approx 1 MI off Rte 2 in northern Worcester County, call for specific directions.

Georgetown

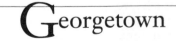

THOMAS A EDISON COLLECTION
51 W Main St, 01833
(508)352-9830 **55**
Wind-up phonographs, disc & cylin-

der records, piano rolls & music boxes. *Pr:* $100–3800. *Est:* 1978. *Serv:* Repairs. *Hours:* Daily 10-5, CLOSED MON,THU. *CC:* MC/V. Ralph Woodside *Loc:* I-95, Rte 133, 1.5 MI into Georgetown, located in Sedler's Antique Village.

JANE FIELD BOOKS
14 North St, 01833
(508)352-6641   13

Antiquarian books: biography, military & general. *Serv:* Search service. *Hours:* BY APPT. *Assoc:* MRIAB. Marcia Jane

PHEASANT HILL ANTIQUES
Nelson St, 01833
(508)352-9818   36 66 67

Offering country & formal American furniture, textiles & graphics, particularly those related to the American South. Extensive stock of Harvardiana. *Pr:* $100–10000. *Est:* 1986. *Serv:* Purchase estates. *Hours:* BY APPT ONLY.

SCALA'S ANTIQUES
28 W Main St, 01833
(508)352-8614   {GR}

A general line shop featuring furniture & china. *Serv:* Insurance & estate appraisal. *Hours:* Tue-Sun 11-5. *Size:* Large.

SEDLER'S ANTIQUE VILLAGE
51 W Main St, 01833
(508)887-5123   {GR30}

Furniture, quilts, glass, pottery, porcelain & folk art. *Est:* 1977. *Hours:* Tue-Sun 10-5. *CC:* MC/V. *Park:* On site. *Loc:* I-95, Rte 133 Exit: through town 1.5 MI in Georgetown.

Gloucester

BANANAS
78 Main St, 01930
(508)283-8806   47 85

A large selection of vintage clothing, accessories & costume jewelry ranging from the turn of the century to the 60s. *Pr:* $5–250. *Est:* 1975. *Hours:* Mon-Sat 10-5 Sun 1-5. *Size:* Medium. *CC:* MC/V. Richard A Leonard *Park:* In front. *Loc:* Rte 128N to end, Exit to downtown Gloucester.

BEAUPORT ANTIQUES
45 Main St, 01930
(508)281-4460   29 36 63

Furniture, china & decorative accessories. *Hours:* Mon-Sat 10:30-3:30. Lois Derrick *Park:* Nearby. *Loc:* Downtown.

BURKE'S BAZAAR-POET'S ANTIQUES
Rte 133, 01930
(508)283-4538   59

Fine paintings. *Hours:* Tue-Sat 10-5. *Size:* Medium. Edward Leaman *Park:* On site. *Loc:* On the border between Gloucester & Essex.

CAPE ANN ANTIQUES & ORIENTALS
108 Main St, 01930
(508)281-3444   21 36 59

Orientals, furniture, paintings, jewelry, china & glass. *Pr:* $5–5000. *Serv:* Appraisal, purchase estates. *Hours:* Mon-Sat 10-5, Sum: Sun 1-5. *Size:* Large. *CC:* AX/MC/V. Mark Longval *Park:* Nearby. *Loc:* Opposite Cape Ann Savings Bank.

GLOUCESTER FINE ARTS & ANTIQUARI
PO Box 133, 01930
(508)281-3638   **4 37 59**

American furniture, decorative & fine arts of the 18th, 19th & 20th C. Emphasis on the Gloucester-Rockport area artist masters old & contemporary. *Est:* 1978. *Serv:* Appraisal, auctions, conservation & research services, estate liquidation. *Hours:* BY APPT. *Assoc:* ISA NEAA NSADA SPNEA. John MacFarlane

WILLIAM N GREENBAUM
179 Concord St, 01930
(508)281-2376   **51 66**

Art prints - old masters, early English mezzotints, 20th C American, British, European & Japanese woodblocks, fine drawings & watercolors. *Pr:* $50–2000. *Hours:* BY APPT ONLY.

MAIN STREET ARTS & ANTIQUES
124 Main St, 01930
(508)281-1531   **{GR10}**

Paintings, jewelry, ephemera, post cards, wicker, textiles, second-hand furniture, china, glass & books. *Est:* 1988. *Serv:* Appraisal, auction, consultation, purchase estates, restoration of frames. *Hours:* Mon-Sat 10:30-5 Sun 12:30-5. *Size:* Medium. *Assoc:* ISA NADA NEAA. David B Cox *Park:* On street.

TEN POUND ISLAND BOOK CO
3 Center St, 01930
(508)283-5299   **4 13**

Old & rare books of all kinds, with specialties in maritime, local history & fine & decorative arts. *Pr:* $5–5000. *Est:* 1976. *Serv:* Appraisal, catalog, consultation, purchase estates. *Hours:* Year round Mon-Fri 12-5 Sat 10-5.

Size: Medium. *CC:* MC/V. *Assoc:* ABAA MRIAB NEAA. Gregory Gibson *Loc:* Corner of Center & Main St in downtown Gloucester.

Grafton

PEGGY PLACE ANTIQUES
119 George Hill Rd, 01519
(508)839-2703   **27 65**

Country pieces, primitives, cubbies & cupboards, toys & lighting. *Hours:* Thu-Sun 11-5 Mon-Wed By Chance. *Assoc:* SADA. Peggy Marshall *Loc:* Off Rte 140 1 MI from Common.

Great Barrington

ANTHONY'S ANTIQUES
597 S Main St, 01230
(413)528-0414   **36 63 77**

Antique & reproduction Oriental porcelain, furniture, silver plate & custom lamp bases. *Est:* 1987. *Hours:* Wed-Mon 11-4. Anthony Bonadies *Park:* In front. *Loc:* On Rte 7.

BY SHAKER HANDS
14 Lake Ave, 01230
(413)528-5560   **27 37**

Shaker & fine country furniture. *Est:* 1987. *Serv:* Appraisal, consultation. *Hours:* BY APPT. Jim Johnson *Park:* On site. *Loc:* 5 blocks W of Int of Rte 7 & Taconic Ave in Great Barrington.

BYGONE DAYS
969 Main St Rte 7S, 01230
(413)528-1870   **42**

A large collection of used, antique & country pine furniture & round oak. *Pr:* $5–1000. *Est:* 1981. *Serv:* Repairs.

Hours: Mon-Sun 10:30-5. **CC:** MC/V. Ted Portnoff **Park:** On site. **Loc:** S of the fairgrounds.

COMPASS ANTIQUES
224 State Rd, 01230
(413)528-1353   **16**
Dealers in fine 18th & 19th C metalware & scales. **Pr:** $25–5000. **Est:** 1968. **Serv:** Interior design. **Hours:** Daily 11-6. **Size:** Medium. **Assoc:** BCoADA NADA. Edward P Lotz Jr **Park:** In front. **Loc:** I-90 Lee Exit: at Int of Rtes 7 & 23.

CORASHIRE ANTIQUES
Rtes 7 & 23 @ Belcher Sq, 01230
(413)528-0014   **27 29 37**
American country furniture & accessories in the red barn. **Hours:** Daily 9-5. **Assoc:** BCoADA. Nancy Dinan **Park:** Nearby.

THE EMPORIUM
319 Main St, 01230
(413)528-2731   **{GR20}**
Glassware, rare books, prints, silver, primitives, country furniture, art deco, advertising & jewelry. **Hours:** Daily 10-5 Sun 12-4 CLOSED TUE. Terry Whitcomb **Park:** Nearby. **Loc:** In the ctr of town.

JONESES ANTIQUES
740 S Main St, 01230
(413)528-0156   **36 45 81**
Huge collection of everything from garden statuary to china. **Hours:** Daily 8:30-5. **Park:** On site. **Loc:** Across from Barrington Fair.

KAHNS ANTIQUE & ESTATE JEWELRY
38 Railroad St, 01230
(413)528-9550   **47 77**
Antique & estate jewelry of all periods, silver smalls & vintage wrist watches. **Pr:** $25–10000. **Est:** 1987. **Serv:** Appraisal, purchase estates, repairs. **Hours:** May-Dec Mon-Sat 10-5 & Jun-Labor Sun 11-4. **Assoc:** BCoADA. Steven Kahn **Park:** Nearby. **Loc:** 1 block W of Rte 7.

PAUL & SUSAN KLEINWALD INC
578 S Main St, 01230
(413)528-4252   **29 37 53**
18th & 19th C American furniture, paintings & decorative accessories. **Serv:** Insurance & estate appraisals. **Hours:** Daily 10-5 CLOSED TUE,WED. **Assoc:** BCoADA. **Park:** In front. **Loc:** On Rte 7.

J & J LUBRANO ANTIQUARIAN BOOKS
39 Hollenbeck Ave, 01230
(413)528-5799   **9 13 66**
Antiquarian booksellers specializing in music, dance & theatre arts including early & rare printed music & musical literature, autographs & manuscripts of important composers, early & rare material relating to theatre arts, books, prints & paintings. **Pr:** $100–10000. **Est:** 1977. **Serv:** Appraisal, catalog, purchase library estates. **Hours:** BY APPT ONLY. **Assoc:** ABAA MRIAB. John Lubrano **Loc:** Call for directions.

GEORGE R MINKOFF, INC
RFD 3 Box 147, 01230
(413)528-4575   **9 13 66**
Antiquarian books: 19th & 20th C English & American literature, signed & presentation copies, illustrated books, manuscripts, letters & original drawings. **Est:** 1967. **Serv:** Appraisal, catalog $5, purchase estates. **Hours:** Year

round Mon-Fri 9-5 weekends BY APPT. *Size:* Large. *CC:* MC/V. *Assoc:* ABAA. *Park:* On site.

MULLIN-JONES ANTIQUITIES
525 Main St, 01230
(413)528-4871   35 38 41
17th, 18th & 19th C country antiques direct from France, emphasis on armoires, buffets, tables, rush chairs, some marble, colorful faience, French lace & fabrics, ironwork & tiles. *Pr:* $25–10000. *Est:* 1986. *Serv:* Custom woodworking, interior design, repairs, restoration. *Hours:* Wed-Mon 10-5 Tue BY APPT. *Assoc:* BCoADA. Patrice Mullin *Park:* On site. *Loc:* Rte 7 (S Main St) between fairgrounds & Int of Rtes 7, 41 & 23, .5 MI S of downtown business district.

RED HORSE ANTIQUES
Rtes 7 & 23, 01230
(413)528-2637   27 36
Two floors of furniture & accessories of all periods. *Est:* 1966. *Hours:* Daily 10-5 CLOSED TUE. April Ehrenman *Park:* On site.

SNYDER'S STORE
945 S Main St, 01230
(413)528-1441   27 65 67
Country, oak & rustic furniture, tramp art, primitives, quilts, linen, jewelry, architectural details & garden pieces. *Hours:* Apr-Dec 20 daily 12-5, Jan-Mar weekends & BY APPT. *Assoc:* BCoADA. Shirley Snyder *Park:* Nearby. *Loc:* On Rte 7.

Groton

THE ANNEX
Main St, 01450
(508)448-3330   27 42
Refinished pine furniture & country antiques. *Est:* 1986. *Hours:* Daily 10-5 Sun 12-5. *Loc:* Behind Groton Antiques.

BOSTON ROAD ANTIQUES
498 Boston Rd Rte 119, 01450
(508)448-9433   1 27 34
American country furniture & decorative accessories, featuring primitives, folk art & Shaker. *Hours:* Tue-Sun 10-5. *Assoc:* NHADA. Richard Walker

PAM BOYNTON
82 Pleasant St Rtes 111 & 225, 01450
(508)448-5031   29 36
18th & 19th C furniture & accessories. *Est:* 1948. *Hours:* Daily. *Assoc:* NHADA. *Park:* On site. *Loc:* 2 blocks off Main St.

GROTON ANTIQUES
Main St, 01450
(508)448-3330   {MDS20}
A large multi-dealer shop of fine Americana & country. *Est:* 1980. *Hours:* Daily 10-5 Sun 12-5. *Park:* On site. *Loc:* On Rte 119, behind Joseph Kilbridge.

JOS KILBRIDGE CHINA TRADE ANTIQU
Main St, 01450
(508)448-3330   1 39 60
Antiques of early America & the China trade, Americana & English furniture. *Est:* 1974. *Hours:* Daily 10-5 Sun 12-5. *Assoc:* NADA. *Park:* On site. *Loc:* On Rte 119.

JAMES MATTOZZI & MARILYN BURKE
Main St, 01450
(508)448-3038 **29 36**
18th & 19th C period furniture & accessories. *Hours:* By Chance/Appt. *Assoc:* NHADA SADA. *Park:* In front. *Loc:* On Rte 119 in center of town.

OLD FASHIONED MILK PAINT COMPANY
436 Main St, 01450
(508)448-6336 **46 70 74**
The only authentic early paint available. Manufacturer & distributor of genuine milk paint in powder form. For restoration or reproduction of furniture, walls & woodwork. Eight authentic colors. Wholesale & retail. *Est:* 1974. *Serv:* Brochure (3 stamps). *Hours:* Year round Mon-Sat 9-5. Charles E Thibeau *Park:* On site. *Loc:* Rte 495 Exit 31W: 8 MI on Rte 119, 1 MI W of Groton on Rte 119 take driveway on R just before railroad bridge.

Hadley

HADLEY ANTIQUES CENTER
Rte 9, 01035
(413)586-4093 **{GR70}**
Antiques & collectibles. *Hours:* Daily 10-5 CLOSED WED. Sue Allen *Loc:* From I-91N Exit 19, from I-91S Exit 20.

HOME FARM ANTIQUES
206 Russell St, 01035
(413)584-8810 **50 71**
General line of mostly 19th C furniture & accessories featuring electrified lamps & custom-made lamp shades. *Pr:* $10–1000. *Est:* 1976. *Serv:*

Custom woodwork, repairs, proper & careful restoration. *Hours:* Tue-Fri 10-5:30 Sat 10-4:30. *Assoc:* PVADA. Bob Berra *Park:* On site. *Loc:* On Rte 9, 3 MI E of Jct with I-95 (Exit 19).

KEN LOPEZ BOOKSELLER
51 Huntington Rd, 01035
(413)584-4827 **13**
Antiquarian books: detective fiction, first editions, modern literature, poetry, science fiction & fantasy & Vietnam War literature. *Serv:* Appraisal, catalog, search service. *Hours:* Call ahead. *Assoc:* ABAA MRIAB.

MOUNTAIN CREST ANTIQUES
45 Lawrence Plain Rd Rte 47S, 01035
(413)586-0352 **37**
Early American & country furniture & accessories. *Hours:* Tue-Sun 10-5. *Size:* Large. *Assoc:* NEAA. Marian Szala *Park:* In front. *Loc:* I-91N Exit 19: R 3 MI to shop OR I-91S Exit 20: L 4 MI to shop.

OLDE HADLEY FLEA MARKET
Rte 47 S, 01035
(413)586-0352 **{GR100}**
Furniture, crafts & collectibles. *Est:* 1980. *Serv:* Free admission. *Hours:* Sun 8-5. *Park:* Free. *Loc:* I-91N Exit 19: 2 MI from Hadley ctr on Rte 47 S.

Halifax

JOAN F CADDIGAN
598 Monponsett St Rte 58, 02338
(617)826-8648 **8**
Antiques & collectibles auctions, estate liquidations. No buyer's premium. *Serv:* Auctioneer, mailing list. *CC:* MC/V. *Assoc:* MSAA NAA.

WILLEM & INGER LEMMENS ANTIQUES
394 Plymouth St Rte 106, 02338
(617)293-2292   1 4 37
Period American furniture & appropriate accessories from the 17th, 18th & early 19th C. All items guaranteed as represented. *Pr:* $25–20000. *Est:* 1970. *Serv:* Appraisal, auction, purchase estates. *Hours:* By chance/appt, call if coming from a distance. *Size:* Medium. *Assoc:* ADA NEAA SADA. *Park:* On site. *Loc:* .5 MI W of the Int of Rtes 106 & 58 on Rte 106 in Halifax.

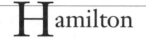

Hamilton

ELMCRESS BOOKS
161 Bay Rd Rte 1A, 01982
(508)468-3261   13 33 64
Antiquarian books: books about books, ephemera, natural history, nautical, prints, royalty & Third World. *Serv:* Appraisal, catalog, search service. *Hours:* Tue-Sat 12-5. *Assoc:* MRIAB. Cheever Cressy

RO-DAN ANTIQUES
18 Bay Rd, 01982
(508)468-7427   37 38 63
Oriental porcelain, 18th & 19th C American & European furniture. *Hours:* Tue-Sat 10-5 Sun 12-5. *Loc:* Rte 128N Exit 20N: 3 MI on Rte 1A, on Hamilton/Wenham line.

Hancock

MOUNTAIN ROAD ANTIQUES
Brodie Mountain Rd & Rte 43, 01237
(413)738-5194   27 34 37
American country furniture, folk art &

accessories. *Hours:* BY APPT. *Assoc:* BCoADA. Robert Bach *Loc:* Opposite Jiminy Peak.

Hanover

RESTORATION RESOURCES
200 Webster St Rte 123, 02339
(617)878-3794   5 74
Authentic & reproduction items for the home including architectural pieces, hardware & collectibles: unusual mantels, moldings, doors, stained glass, classic pedestal sinks, claw foot tubs, bath fixtures & accessories, woodwork & ornamental plaster. *Est:* 1987. *Serv:* Restoration, reproduction. *Hours:* Daily 10-6:30 Sun 4-7. *CC:* MC/V. *Park:* On site. *Loc:* 150 yds from the Barnside Restaurant.

Harvard

CORNUCOPIA, INC
PO Box 44SG, 01451
(508)772-0023   43
Handcrafted Windsors & dining furniture in pine, cherry & curly maple. *Est:* 1972. *Serv:* 24-page catalog ($2), reproductions to order. *Hours:* BY APPT. *Loc:* Call for directions.

THREE BAGS FULL
Hickory Hill, 01451
(508)456-3712   29 41
Quality painted furniture & accessories in original condition. *Serv:* Consultant for period interiors. *Hours:* Appt suggested. *Assoc:* NHADA. Paula T McColgan

Harwich

PATTI SMITH
51 Parallel St, 02645
(508)432-0851 **28**
Specializing in antique decorated blue stoneware. **Pr:** $200–2000. **Hours:** BY APPT ONLY.

Harwich Center

ANTIQUES AT THE BARN AT WINDSONG
243 Bank St, 02645
(508)432-8281 **{GR7}**
Furniture, pattern glass, small primitives, old wicker, prints, early 19th C furniture. **Est:** 1988. **Hours:** Mon-Sat 10-5 Sun 12-5. **CC:** AX/MC/V. **Park:** On site. **Loc:** Between Harwich & Harwichport.

STATEN HOOK BOOKS
705 Main St, 02645
(508)432-2155 **13**
Antiquarian books - marine, Cape Cod, fishing & a general stock. **Hours:** Sum: Mon-Sat 11-5, else Mon-Fri 3-5 Sat 11-5. William Mc Caskie

Harwichport

HARWICH BOOKSTORE
390 Main St, 02646
(508)432-0798 **13 14**
A general stock of antiquarian books. **Hours:** Sum: Mon-Sun 10-5, Win: Tue-Sat 10-5. Lee Tighe **Loc:** On Rte 28.

MAGGIE'S ANTIQUES & COLLECTIBLES
2 Cross St, 02646
(508)432-4299 **47 48 85**
Specializing in kitchen collectibles, cookbooks, children's books, jewelry, linens & vintage clothing. **Hours:** Tue-Sun 10-6. **Loc:** Just off Rte 28 in the center of Harwichport.

SEVEN SOUTH STREET ANTIQUES
7 South St, 02646
(508)432-4366 **47 63 77**
Silver, jewelry, china & glass. **Est:** 1976. **Hours:** Wed-Sat 1-5, Jul-Labor Day Mon-Sat 10:30-5. **Park:** Nearby. **Loc:** Around the corner from the post office, just off Rte 28.

Haverhill

CONSTANCE MORELLE BOOKS
1282 Broadway, 01830
(508)374-7256 **13 33**
Antiquarian books: American literature, biography, children's books, ephemera, Massachusetts history, natural history, cookery, embroidery, needlework, literature & sheet music. **Serv:** Catalog, search service. **Hours:** Call ahead. **Assoc:** MRIAB.

Haydenville

BRASSWORKS ANTIQUES CENTER
132 Main St, 01039
(413)268-7985 **{GR}**
Fine quality antiques. **Hours:** Mon-Sat 10-5 Sun 12-5. Susan Kostek **Loc:** On Rte 9, 6 MI from downtown Northampton.

THE MILLER'S DAUGHTER
9 Poplar Hill Rd, 01039
(413)665-4464   13

Reference books on antiques & collectibles. *Hours:* At shows & by mail order. *Assoc:* PVADA. Grace M Dickinson

Hingham

ONE TEN NORTH
110 North St, 02043
(617)740-4333   27

Country antiques & accessories. *Hours:* Tue-Sat 10-4. Pam Geissler

PIERCE GALLERIES INC
721 Main St, 02043
(617)749-6023   4 59

Paintings of the American Impressionists of Hudson River School, 1840-present. *Est:* 1968. *Serv:* Consultant to corporations & individuals on American art. *Hours:* BY APPT ONLY. *Assoc:* AAA. Patricia J Pierce *Loc:* Rte 3 to Rte 228 which is Main St.

Holden

DAVIDIAN AMERICANA
4 Boyden Rd, 01520
(508)829-9222   27 28 32

Specializing in country furniture & accessories, pantry boxes, stoneware, baskets & early toys. *Est:* 1970. *Hours:* Wed-Fri 10-4 Sat,Sun by chance/appt. *Assoc:* SADA. Peter Davidian *Park:* On site. *Loc:* Just off 122A in the center of town.

VILLAGE ANTIQUES
1 Zottoli Rd Rte 122A, 01520
(508)829-6708   44 48 50

Furniture, glass, baskets, oil lamps, frames & linens. *Est:* 1984. *Hours:* Tue-Fri 10-5:30 Sat 10-2, Sum: CLOSED SAT. *Park:* In front. *Loc:* Behind Luddy Chevrolet.

Holliston

WILDER SHOP
400 Washington St, 01746
(508)429-4836   50 87

Antiques, refinished furniture & accessories, handcrafted lighting & weather vanes. *Hours:* Mon-Sat 10-5 Sun 1-5. *Assoc:* SADA. The Brighams *Loc:* Jct of Rtes 16 & 126.

Hopkinton

HERITAGE ANTIQUES
216 Wood St, 01748
(508)435-4031   21 36 58

Quality antiques, furniture & accessories, rugs & objets d'art. *Hours:* Tue-Fri 9-5 weekend evenings by chance/appt. *Assoc:* SADA. Clifton L Gilson *Loc:* Rte 135.

Hudson

THE NEW ENGLAND ANTIQUE TOY MALL
65 Main St, 01749
(508)568-0856   32 33 54

Wind-ups, battery ops, lead & cast playsets, character items, space toys, Disneyana, premiums, advertising, games, trains, tv-related ephemera, vehicles, models, Beatles & puzzles. *Serv:* Always buying. *Hours:* Daily 12-5:30. *CC:* AX. *Park:* Free. *Loc:* Jct Rtes 62 & 85, 1 MI from Rtes 495 & 290.

Huntington

PAULSON'S ANTIQUARIAN PAPER/BOOK
Allen Coit Rd, 01050
(413)667-3208   14 33 36

A two-floor country shop of antiquarian paper, old prints, Victorian greeting cards, trade cards & scraps, collectibles, old post cards & used books. *Pr:* $1–1000. *Est:* 1981. *Serv:* Appraisal, custom woodwork, purchase estates, repairs, restoration. *Hours:* May-Nov daily 10-5, Dec-Apr BY APPT ONLY. *Size:* Medium. *Assoc:* MRIAB. Barbara C Paulson *Park:* On site. *Loc:* Off Rte 66 near Westhampton/Huntington line, follow signs to bookshop.

Hyannis

ALBERT ARTS & ANTIQUES
645 Main St, 02601
(508)771-3040   17 50 63

American & European antiques including furniture, paintings, porcelains, bronzes & lighting. *Hours:* Year round 10-5. *Assoc:* CCADA NEAA. Albert L Watson

RICHARD A BOURNE CO INC
Corporation St, 02601
(508)775-0797   4 8

Auctioning general merchandise, marine items, decoys, antique weapons & glass. Two or three auctions per month year round. Special auctions:

Decoy Auction - early July; Marine Sale - August; Americana - Thanksgiving Weekend. 10% buyer's premium. *Serv:* Estate appraisers, catalogs, absentee & phone bidding arranged. Marie Bagley *Loc:* .5 MI W of Airport Rotary Circle on Rte 28.

HYANNIS AUCTION
379 Iyanough Rd, 02601
(508)790-1112   4 8

A weekly consignment auction house offering expert appraisal service & prompt payment. Handling complete estates & single items. *Serv:* Appraisal, accept mail/phone bids, catalog, consultation. *Hours:* Mon,Wed,Fri,Sat 10-5 Tue 2-11 Sun 12-5. *Size:* Medium. Donna Johnson *Park:* Nearby lot. *Loc:* Rte 6E Exit 6: R on Rte 132 to rotary, 3rd R onto Rte 28E, .25 MI on R across from Grossman's behind Bank of New England.

RICHARD J O'MALLEY
319 Ocean St, 02601
(508)775-3968   54

Authentic shipmodels, fully-rigged, museum quality - intricately built by a Cape Cod craftsman. *Hours:* BY APPT. *CC:* MC/V.

PRECIOUS PAST
315 Iyanough Rd Rte 28, 02601
(508)771-1741   21 44 48

Nippon, fiesta, Noritake, Limoges, depression, Pairpoint, cut glass & early American pattern glass. Linens, Oriental rugs, paintings & prints, old dolls & accessories, collectibles, ephemera, toys & furniture. *Hours:* Daily 10-4 CLOSED TUE,SUN. *Park:* On site.

STARTING OVER LTD
1336 Phinney's Ln, 02601
(508)775-5088 71
Furniture restoration, custom work &
fine antiques. *Est:* 1964. *Serv:* Restoration, free pick-up & delivery. *Loc:* At
Harborside Landing.

STONE'S ANTIQUE SHOP
659 Main St, 02601
(508)775-3913 16 36 44
One of the oldest antiques shops on
Cape Cod. *Est:* 1923. *Serv:* Appraisal,
interior design. *Hours:* Mon-Sat 9-5
CLOSED SUN. *Size:* Large. E Stone
Park: On site. *Loc:* W end of Main St.

Ipswich

ESSEX ANTIQUE CO-OP
145 High St Rte 1A, 01938
(508)356-4770 {GR10}
Furniture, primitives, glass & china.
Hours: Tue-Sun 10:30-5. *CC:* MC/V.
Assoc: NSADA. *Loc:* Rtes 1A & 133E.

HILDA KNOWLES ANTIQUES
207 High St Rte 1A, 01938
(508)356-4561 32 44 63
Glass, china & dolls. *Hours:* By
chance/appt. *Assoc:* NSADA.

Lancaster

ANTIQUES TOOLS &
CATALOGS
Box 400, 01523
(508)368-8468 81
Fine American antique tools & related
catalogs. Author of "Patented Transitional Metallic Planes in America
1827-1927". *Serv:* Appraisal, auction,

catalog $5 annually, purchase estates.
Hours: Year round BY APPT. Roger K
Smith *Loc:* Call for directions.

Lanesborough

AMBER SPRING ANTIQUES
Main St Rt 7, 01237
(413)442-1237 33 37 81
American furnishings, tools, pottery &
advertising. *Hours:* Daily call ahead.
Assoc: BCoADA. Gae Elfenbein *Loc:* 5
MI N of Pittsfield.

MAPLE COURT ANTIQUES
14 S Main St, 01237
(413)442-9343
General line of antiques. *Est:* 1980.
Hours: Fri-Sun, else by chance/appt.
Loc: On Rte 7, 20 min from Lee Exit
on MA Pike.

SAVOY BOOKS
Bailey Rd, 01237
(413)499-9968 13
Antiquarian books: horticulture, agriculture, domestic arts, Americana,
American & English literature before
1900. *Serv:* Appraisal, catalog. *Hours:*
BY APPT. *Assoc:* ABAA MRIAB. Robert Fraker

SECOND LIFE BOOKS
Quarry Rd, 01237
(413)447-8010 13
Antiquarian books: agriculture, first
editions, literature, women, signed &
fine press books. *Serv:* Appraisal, catalog. *Hours:* BY APPT. *Assoc:* ABAA
MRIAB. Russell Freedman

WALDEN'S ANTIQUES & BOOKS
Main St Rte 7, 01237
(413)442-5346 **13**
General line of antiques & 1000's of books. *Serv:* Estate liquidation. *Hours:* Apr-Nov daily by chance/appt. *Assoc:* BCoADA. William C Walden

Lee

AARDENBURG ANTIQUES
144 W Park St, 01238
(413)243-0001 **29 37**
Early 19th C American furniture & accessories. *Hours:* Weekends by chance, else BY APPT. *Assoc:* BCoADA. David Hubregsen *Park:* Nearby.

CAROPRESO GALLERY
136 High St, 01238
(413)243-3424 **4 8**
Specializing in estate liquidation & 18th & 19th C Americana auctions. *Est:* 1962. *Serv:* Auction, appraisal, brochure. *Hours:* Mon-Fri 9-5. *Assoc:* BCoADA NEAA. Louis E Caropreso

FERRELL'S ANTIQUES & WOODWORKING
67A Center St, 01238
(413)243-0041 **1 41 71**
Fine line of country furniture & accessories in original condition. Shaker furniture. *Serv:* Repair, restoration, custom woodwork, replication, reproduction. *Hours:* Mon-Sat 9-5. *Size:* Medium. *CC:* AX/MC/V. *Assoc:* BCoADA. Glenn Ferrell *Park:* On site. *Loc:* I-90 Exit 2: R on Rte 20 to Town Green, R on Main to end, R & immediate L into parking lot, shop at rear.

HENRY B HOLT INC
Golden Hill, 01238
(413)243-3184 **4 25 59**
Dealer in 19th & early 20th C American paintings will advise on the disposal of individual paintings or estates. *Serv:* Appraisal, restoration, purchase estates, conservation. *Hours:* BY APPT ONLY. *Assoc:* AAA BCoADA NEAA. *Loc:* Rte 20N from Lee to Golden Hill Rd, opposite Black Swan Motel follow Golden Hill Rd to 1st T Int, L.

THE KINGSLEIGH 1840
32 Park St Rte 20, 01238
(413)243-3317 **47 53 83**
Jewelry, small furniture, mirrors & collectibles - all part of a unique 1840 Victorian house & bed & breakfast. *Pr:* $5–500. *Est:* 1985. *Serv:* Purchase estates, repairs, restoration. *Hours:* Jun-Sep daily 10-6, Oct-May Fri,Sat 10-5 Sun 11-4. *Size:* Medium. *CC:* AX/MC/V. *Assoc:* BCoADA. Linda Segal *Park:* On site. *Loc:* I-90 Exit 2: Rte 2W for .75 MI.

PEMBROKE ANTIQUES
28 Housatonic St Rte 20, 01238
(413)243-1357 **34 37 59**
Shaker furniture & accessories, 18th & 19th C folk art, paintings & furniture. *Hours:* Weekdays BY APPT. *Assoc:* BCoADA. Morton B Dobson Jr *Park:* Nearby.

Lenox

CHARLES L FLINT
64 Housatonic, 01240
(413)637-1634 **34 37 38**
American & European furniture, oil paintings, folk art, accessories &

Shaker. *Serv:* Appraisal & consultations on Shaker. *Hours:* Mon-Sat 10-5 Sun by chance, anytime BY APPT. *Assoc:* BCoADA. *Park:* Nearby.

HAMLET ANTIQUES
116 East St, 01240
(413)637-2309   **63**

Victorian Staffordshire including figures, cottages, castles & bocages. *Pr:* $300–800. *Hours:* BY APPT ONLY. *Assoc:* BCoADA. F. Brooks Butler *Park:* Nearby.

OCTOBER MOUNTAIN ANTIQUES
136 East St, 01240
(413)637-0439   **27 34 37**

Country & Shaker furniture & 18th & 19th C folk art. *Hours:* May-Dec 10 by chance/appt. *Assoc:* BCoADA. Betty Fleishman *Park:* Nearby.

STONE'S THROW ANTIQUES
57 Church St, 01240
(413)637-2733   **36 63 77**

19th C American, English & French furniture, china, glass, inkstands, frames, prints, perfumes, silver & Orientalia. *Hours:* May-Oct daily 10-5, Nov-Apr Fri,Sat,Sun 10-5. *Size:* Medium. *CC:* AX/MC/V. *Assoc:* BCoADA. Sydelle S Shapiro *Park:* On site.

MARY STUART COLLECTION
81 Church St, 01240
(413)637-0340   **77**

Silver, silver smalls & occasional pieces of furniture. *Est:* 1980. *Hours:* Mon-Sat 10:30-5 Sun 11-4. *CC:* AX/MC/V. *Park:* Ample. *Loc:* 2 blocks N of Walker St.

Lexington

EVA AROND
52 Turning Mill Rd, 02173
(617)862-6379   **13**

Antiquarian books specializing in juveniles (including foreign languages), fine literature, fine & performing arts, cookbooks & general out-of-print. *Est:* 1978. *Serv:* Appraisal, catalogs, purchase estates. *Hours:* BY APPT ONLY. *Assoc:* MRIAB. *Loc:* Rte 128/I-95 Exit 31B: 1.5 MI from Exit, call for directions.

ON CONSIGNMENT GALLERIES
32 Waltham St, 02173
(617)861-3800

Furniture, china, sterling, jewelry, paintings, lamps, mirrors, glassware, objets d'art & collectibles. *Est:* 1987. *Hours:* Mon-Sat 10-5. *CC:* MC/V. *Park:* In front. *Loc:* In the center of town.

GALLERY ON THE GREEN LTD
1837 Massachusetts Ave, 02173
(617)861-6044   **59**

American & European oils & works on papers. *Est:* 1980. *Serv:* Referrals on framing & restoration. *Hours:* Tue-Sat 10-5. *Park:* On street. *Loc:* Just short of the Minuteman statue.

PATRIOT ANTIQUARIAN BOOKS
28 Woodcliffe Rd, 02173
(617)862-6837   **13**

Antiquarian books: Americana, history, literary criticism, biography, local history, university & small press books. *Serv:* Search service. *Hours:* Call ahead. *Assoc:* MRIAB. Howard Quinn

RAINY DAY BOOKS
44 Bertwell Rd, 02173
(617)861-8656   13 33 66

Antiquarian booksellers specializing in old, rare & out-of-print books & paper, including early science & technology, travel, exploration, ephemera, European royalty, textile history, women's studies, cookbooks & children's books. *Pr:* $10–500. *Serv:* Appraisal, catalog, search service, purchase estates. *Hours:* BY APPT. *Assoc:* ESA MRIAB. Frank Bequaert *Park:* In front. *Loc:* 4 blocks from Rte 128 at the Lexington Exit Rte 4-225.

Lincoln

BROWN-CORBIN FINE ART
Sandy Pond Rd, 01773
(617)259-1210   26 40 59

Specializing in fine 19th & early 20th C American paintings, watercolors & drawings, with emphasis on Luminists, American Pre-Raphaelites & Impressionists selected with a view toward quality & importance. *Pr:* $2000–250000. *Serv:* Appraisal, consultation. *Hours:* BY APPT. Jeffrey Brown Kathryn Corbin

WILKERSON BOOKS
31 Old Winter St, 01773
(617)259-1110   13

Antiquarian books: gardening, landscape design & decorated trade bindings. *Serv:* Appraisal, catalog, search service. *Hours:* Call ahead. *Assoc:* ABAA MRIAB. Robin Wilkerson

Littleton

ANTIQUES AT SIGN OF THE BLUEBIRD
287 Great Rd, 01460
(508)486-3067
General line of quality antiques. *Pr:* $10–10000. *Est:* 1971. *Serv:* Appraisal. *Hours:* Tue,Wed 12-5 Thu-Sat 10-5. *CC:* MC/V. *Assoc:* SADA. James Baird *Park:* On site. *Loc:* I-495 Exit 31, to Rte 2A/119, E to Littleton Ctr, continue thru lights for .25 MI, on L.

BLUE CAPE ANTIQUES
Rte 119, 01460
(508)486-4709
Eclectic assortment of antiques. *Est:* 1963. *Hours:* Wed-Sat 11-5. *Park:* On site. *Loc:* 495 Exit 31: 1 MI W.

HAMLET ANTIQUES
256 Great Rd Rte 2A, 01460
(508)486-4976   27 41
Danish country antiques & painted furniture. *Hours:* Mon-Sat 10-6 Sun 12-6. *Loc:* 6.7 MI W of Concord Rotary on Rte 2A.

P & J ANTIQUES
655 Great Rd, 01460
(508)486-9049   50
Kerosene lamps, works of art & Victorian & country items. *Est:* 1986. *Hours:* Wed-Sun 10-5 Mon-Tue by chance/appt. *CC:* MC/V. Joseph J Incatasciato *Park:* In front. *Loc:* 495 Exit 31: Rte 119W is Great Rd.

UPTON HOUSE ANTIQUES
275 King St Rte 2A-110, 01460
(508)486-3367   27
Antiques in the country manner, featuring furniture & smalls in original condition - some with paint. *Est:* 1981.

Serv: Early interiors decorating service with room consultation & written proposal. *Hours:* Tue,Thu,Fri 10-3 Sat 10-4 Sun by chance. *CC:* MC/V. Eileen Poland *Loc:* Rte 495 Exit 30: R, 1000 ft.

Longmeadow
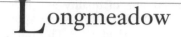

LE PERIGORD
805 Williams St, 01106
(413)567-0262   **35**
French antiques & decorations, 18th C country, art deco & architectural items. *Hours:* Tue-Sat 10-5 or BY APPT. *Size:* Medium. *Loc:* Just off I-91 Exit 49: next to post office.

Lowell

R P DURKIN & COMPANY INC
44 Stedman St Unit 12, 01851   **4 8**
Divorce & estate litigation appraisal. Provide valuation services for personal property, real estate, M&E & business valuation. *Est:* 1968. *Serv:* Appraisal, auction. *Hours:* Mon-Sat 10-5 appt suggested. *Assoc:* ASA GIA NEAA. Roger P Durkin, ASA

Malden

EXCALIBUR HOBBIES
63 Exchange St, 02148
(617)322-2959   **6 49**
Lead soldiers & toys, military items & strategic games. *Hours:* Mon-Sat 10-6 Fri til 8. *CC:* MC/V. *Loc:* I-93 exit 32: Rte 60E for 1.5 MI, L on Commercial Ave, R on Exchange St, 1.5 blocks.

FLIGHTS OF FANCY ANTIQUES
106 Dexter St, 02148
(617)322-7372   **48 63 85**
Vintage clothing, accessories, linens, china & glassware. *Hours:* Tue 10-8, Sat 10-4, else BY APPT. Sandy Katz *Loc:* Driveway off Clifton St.

Mansfield
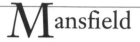

FROG HOLLOW ANTIQUES
82 Stearns Ave, 02048
(508)339-8066
A country shop of antiques, vintage collectibles, curiosities & newer good things from area homes & estates. *Serv:* Appraisal, consultation. *Hours:* Thu-Sat 10-4:30 BY APPT. *Size:* Medium. *Assoc:* SADA. Cal Vizedom *Park:* On site. *Loc:* I-95 Exit 7A (Mansfield): Rte 140 to Rte 106, L on 106 to Stearns Ave, L on Stearns Ave to #82 on L.

Marblehead

LORRAINE ALLISON
235 Washington St, 01945
(617)631-0341   **13**
Antiquarian books: old cookbooks, Massachusetts history, New England, nautical & folklore. *Serv:* Appraisal, search service. *Hours:* Mail order only. *Assoc:* MRIAB.

THE ANTIQUE SHOP
92 Washington St, 01945
(617)639-0413   **44 60 63**
Orientalia, cut glass & hand painted china, furniture & silver. *Hours:* Mon-Thu 1-5 Fri,Sat 12-5. *CC:* AX/MC/V.

Edith Harris Eleanor Meyers **Park:** Nearby. **Loc:** Across from The Town House.

ANTIQUEWEAR
82 Front St, 01945
(617)631-4659 **18**

Antique buttons of the 1800s fashioned to jewelry. **Pr:** $25–300. **Est:** 1970. **Serv:** Appraisal, consultation, purchase estates, repairs. **Hours:** May-Dec Thu-Sun, else BY APPT. **CC:** AX/DC. Jerry Fine **Loc:** Across from the Landing Restaurant, 1 block from Marblehead Antique Exchange on the harbor front.

THE BLACK GOOSE
28 Atlantic Ave, 01945
(617)639-0465

Antiques, used furniture, glass, dolls & gifts. **Pr:** $10–600. **Hours:** Year round daily 1:30-5:30. **Size:** Large. **CC:** MC/V. Jean A Lee **Park:** Nearby. **Loc:** Across from Marblehead Savings.

BRASS & BOUNTY
68 Front St, 01945
(617)631-3864 **50 56**

Nautical antiques, restored gas & electric chandeliers. **Serv:** Restoration. **Hours:** Daily 9-5:30. **Size:** Medium. **CC:** MC/V. Maryanne Dermody **Park:** Nearby. **Loc:** Just across from The Landing on the harbor.

E R BUTLER & SONS
25 Mugford St, 01945
(617)631-4031 **75**

Packing & crating of antique & other items, shipping arranged for, phone estimates subject to inspection of item. **Est:** 1948. **Hours:** Mon-Sat 10-4. **CC:** MC/V. Wayne Butler **Park:** On site. **Loc:** Go to end of Pleasant St (Rte 114),

L, L again at Old Town House (yellow bldg in middle of st) across from church.

CROWN & EAGLE ANTIQUES
235 Washington St, 01945
(617)631-0198

Antiques & unusual collectibles. **Hours:** Daily 10-5. **CC:** MC/V. Egea Branscombe

EVIE'S CORNER
96 Washington St, 01945
(617)639-0007 **5 17 74**

Architectural bronzes & marble, featuring antique leaded glass & period furniture. **Est:** 1978. **Hours:** Weekends 12-5 or BY APPT. **Park:** Nearby street.

FIVE HONEST LADIES
120 Pleasant St, 01945
(617)631-7555

Furniture & decorative accessories. **Hours:** Mon-Sat 10-5:30. **CC:** MC/V. **Park:** Nearby.

HEELTAPPERS ANTIQUES
134 Washington St, 01945
(617)631-7722 **36 63 77**

18th & 19th C country & formal furniture, silver, glass, porcelains & accessories. **Serv:** Consultation, appraisal. **Hours:** Tue-Sat 11-5. **Size:** Medium. **CC:** MC/V. **Assoc:** NSADA. **Park:** Nearby. **Loc:** In the Historic District.

MARBLEHEAD ANTIQUES
118 Pleasant St, 01945
(617)631-9791 **29 36 63**

Formal & country furniture, American & Continental decorative accessories. **Est:** 1968. **Serv:** Appraisal, consultations. **Hours:** Mon-Sun 12-5 CLOSED THU. **Size:** Medium. **CC:**

MC/V. *Assoc:* NSADA. Harriet Norman *Park:* In front. *Loc:* Across from the movie theatre.

MUCH ADO
7 Pleasant St, 01945
(617)639-0400   13

Two floors of old, out-of-print & rare books including children's books, women's literature, nautical & first editions. *Serv:* Appraisal, catalog, search service. *Hours:* Mon-Fri 9:30-6 Sat,Sun 10:30-6 & BY APPT. *Assoc:* MRIAB. Nash Robbins

OLD TOWN ANTIQUE CO-OP
108 Washington St, 01945
(617)631-9728   {GR6}

Delightful assortment of American antiques & accessories, concentrating on wicker, quilts, oak & pine furniture, prints & jewelry. *Est:* 1979. *Serv:* Appraisal, catalog, interior design, purchase estates, restoration. *Hours:* Daily 10-5 Jul-Sep CLOSED TUE. *Size:* Medium.

ON CONSIGNMENT GALLERIES
27 Atlantic Avenue, 01945
(617)639-1337

Furniture, china, sterling, jewelry, lamps, mirrors, chandeliers, glass, objets d'art, pottery, bronzes, copper & brass. *Serv:* Consignments accepted daily. *Hours:* Mon-Sar 10-5 Sun 1-5. *CC:* MC/V.

S & S GALLERIES
231 Washington St, 01945
(617)631-7595   2 27 36

Estate furniture, country & formal, antiques, jewelry & fireplace equipment. *Hours:* Tue-Sat 10:30-4. *Size:* Medium. *CC:* MC/V. *Park:* Nearby.

SACKS ANTIQUES
38 State St @ Front St, 01945
(617)631-0770   39 63 77

Marblehead's oldest antique shop, fine English furniture & china, large collection of silver objects of art. *Pr:* $25–5000. *Est:* 1912. *Serv:* Appraisal, purchase estates. *Hours:* Daily CLOSED SUN. *CC:* AX/DC/MC/V. Stanley S Sacks *Park:* Nearby lot (side). *Loc:* 17 MI N of Boston, located opposite the Town Landing, look for famous gold eagle.

THREE SEWALL STREET ANTIQUES
3 Sewall St @ Spring St, 01945
(617)631-3601   47 48 63

Featuring a decorative array of furniture, glass, jewelry, pottery, linens & vintage clothing from all periods. *Est:* 1988. *Hours:* Daily 10-5 Sun 12-5. *CC:* MC/V. *Park:* Nearby.

Marlboro

DOWER HOUSE
124 Hosmer St #11, 01752
(508)480-0764   13

Antiquarian books including children's & gardening. *Serv:* Appraisal, catalog, search service. *Assoc:* MRIAB. Ann G Swindells

WAYNE PRATT & CO
257 Forest St, 01752
(508)481-2917   32 36 37

A large selection of fine American 18th & early 19th C furniture, both country & formal - specializing in Windsor chairs & featuring a toy showroom for the collector. *Serv:* Appraisal. *Hours:* Appt suggested. *Size:* Large. *Assoc:* ADA NHADA. *Park:* In front. *Loc:*

From Boston, I-90W to 495N Exit Rte 20W, from Hartford, Rte 84 to I-90 to 495N Exit Rte 20W.

WAYSIDE ANTIQUES
1015 Boston Post Rd, 01752
(508)481-9621   **40 42 86**
Quality Victorian, walnut, mahogany, oak, wicker, pine, early furniture & accessories in an historic setting. *Serv:* Appraisal. *Hours:* Mon-Sat 10-5. *Assoc:* SADA. Buck Colaianni *Loc:* Next to Wayside Country Store.

Marshfield

WILLIS HENRY AUCTIONS
22 Main St, 02050
(617)834-7774   **4 8**
Nation's only auction gallery featuring annual sales of Shaker furniture & accessories, specializing in American Indian & African art, Americana & estate sales. 10% buyers premium. *Serv:* Appraisal, accept mail/phone bids, catalog, consultation, purchase estates. *Hours:* Mon-Fri 9-5 appt suggested. *Loc:* Call for directions to specific auctions.

LORD RANDALL BOOKSHOP
22 Main St, 02050
(617)837-1400   **13**
A general stock of 15,000 of antiquarian books with an emphasis on New England & literature, art & children's books, housed in a 100-year-old heated barn. *Pr:* $1–500. *Est:* 1972. *Serv:* Appraisal, purchase estates, search service. *Hours:* Mon-Sat 11-5. *Size:* Medium. *Assoc:* MRIAB. Gail Wills *Park:* On site. *Loc:* Rte 3S from Boston Exit Marshfield: R onto Rte 139, 1.5 MI to 1st light, L on Rte 3A, 1st bldg on R.

Maynard

CHIPPENDALES ANTIQUES
99 Main St, 01754
(508)897-5600   **{GR}**
American & European furniture, accessories, Oriental rugs, fine jewelry & costume jewelry. Gene Davey *Loc:* Directly across from Digital World Headquarters.

MOLLY'S VINTAGE CLOTHING PROMO'N
PO Box 191, 01754
(508)877-8863   **48 67 85**
Produce vintage clothing shows. *Est:* 1984. *Serv:* Consultation, purchase estates, mailing service. *Assoc:* PSMA. Debbie Regan

Medway

MARJORIE PARROTT ADAMS BOOKS
396 Village St, 02053
(508)533-5677   **13 33 66**
Antiquarian books: Victoriana, natural history, gardening, children's literature, fine arts, prints, ephemera & textiles. *Serv:* Appraisal, catalogs issued, search service. *Hours:* BY APPT. *Assoc:* ABAA MRIAB.

Melrose

ANOTHER ERA
954 Main St, 02176
(617)665-9452
One of the North Shore's oldest stores, offering varied sampling of personal property from attic to cellar. Monthly auctions. *Est:* 1968. *Serv:* Appraisal,

auction, accept phone bids, consultation, purchase estates. *Hours:* Mon-Sat 9:30-4:30. *CC:* MC/V. *Assoc:* MSAA NAA NEAA. Florence M Lionetti *Park:* In front. *Loc:* Rte 1N or S Melrose Exit: Essex St, R on Main St, 1 MI.

ROBINSON MURRAY III, BOOKSELLER
150 Lynde St, 02176
(617)665-3094   13
Rare & unusual books: 18th & 19th C Americana, early American imprints, pamphlets, broadsides, American literature, Black history. *Serv:* Appraisal, catalogs. *Hours:* BY APPT. *Assoc:* MRIAB.

STARR BOOK CO INC
44 W Wyoming Ave, 02176
(617)662-2580   13
Antiquarian books: American literature, Americana, English literature, first editions, literary criticism & biography, fiction, translations & nonfiction. *Serv:* Appraisal, search service. *Hours:* Mon-Fri 9:30-5 Sat 9:30-4. *CC:* MC/V. *Assoc:* MRIAB. Norman Starr *Park:* On site. *Loc:* 10 Min N of Boston.

Middleboro

CHARLES & BARBARA ADAMS
15 Prospect St, 02346
(508)947-7277   63
Bennington pottery & quality baskets. *Assoc:* ADA.

Milford

DUNBAR'S GALLERY
76 Haven St, 01757
(508)473-5771   32 34
Old toys, advertising, banks, folk art & automobilia. *Hours:* Mon-Fri 8-5 BY APPT. Howard Dunbar *Park:* On site. *Loc:* I-95 Exit 21B.

Millis

BIRCHKNOLL ANTIQUES
Millis, 02054
(508)376-8808   16 21 59
18th & 19th C period furniture & appropriate accessories in paintings, brass, silver, porcelains & Oriental rugs. *Serv:* Appraisal for insurance & probate. *Hours:* BY APPT. *Assoc:* SADA. Carole Greco *Loc:* Call for directions.

Montague

PETER L MASI BOOKS
17 Central St, 01351
(413)367-2628   13
Antiquarian books: Americana, architecture, science, technology & trade catalogs. *Serv:* Catalog. *Hours:* BY APPT. *Assoc:* ABAA MRIAB.

KARL SCHICK
15 Depot St, 01351
(413)367-9740   13
Antiquarian books: science & medicine, philosophy, psychiatry, psychology & rare books. *Hours:* BY APPT ONLY. *Assoc:* ABAA.

Nantucket

JANICE ALDRIDGE INC
7 Centre St, 02554
(508)228-6673 **66**

17th-19th C decorative engravings, botanical, architectural & natural history. English & Continental furnishings & accessories. *Hours:* Late May-Sep.

AMERICAN PIE
42-44 Main St Upstairs, 02554
(508)228-2700 **27 45**

A unique collection of colorful country furniture & accessories including hooked rugs & garden statuary. *Est:* 1982. *Hours:* Apr-Dec daily 10-5, Jan-Mar BY APPT. *CC:* MC. Emily Lennett *Park:* Nearby. *Loc:* Above the camera shop.

ARKELYAN RUGS
72 Orange St, 02554
(508)228-4242 **21**

Specializing in Portuguese needlepoint rugs. A fine selection of elegant handmade wool rugs in stock at all times. *Serv:* Shop offers a custom design service. *Hours:* Jun 15-Sep 15th by appt. In Boston: Sep 16-Jun 14 by appt. Cindy Lydon

AVANTI ANTIQUE JEWELRY
Four Federal St, 02554
(508)228-5833 **47**

European & American antique & estate jewelry. *Est:* 1986. *Hours:* Apr-Dec daily 10-5, Win: BY APPT (508/228-4952). *CC:* AX/MC/V. Kathryn Kay *Park:* Nearby. *Loc:* Across from the post office.

FORAGER HOUSE COLLECTION
22 Broad St, 02554
(508)228-5977 **1 34 45**

Folk art, Americana, rugs, quilts, historical, decorative & American master prints, garden accessories for the discriminating collector. *Pr:* $50–10000. *Est:* 1975. *Serv:* Appraisal, conservation, consultation, interior design, repairs. *Hours:* May 15-Dec 15 Mon-Sun 10-6, Dec 16-May 14 BY APPT ONLY. *CC:* AX/MC/V. George Korn *Park:* In front. *Loc:* Located in the ctr of the Historic District.

FOUR WINDS CRAFT GUILD
6 Great Wharf, 02554
(508)228-9623 **30 54 56**

Authentic lightship baskets, scrimshaw, ivory carvings, hand-carved decoys & shore birds, bone ship models & ditty boxes, paintings, prints & nautical items. *Est:* 1948. *Hours:* Mon-Sat 9-6. *CC:* AX/MC/V. *Park:* Nearby lot.

NINA HELLMAN
22 Broad St, 02554
(508)228-4677 **1 34 56**

Fine selection of nautical antiques, including ship models, navigational instruments, scrimshaw, marine paintings, whaling items, Americana & folk art. *Pr:* $10–10000. *Serv:* Nautical appraisals. *Hours:* Jul-Sep daily 10-10, call for hours. *CC:* AX/MC/V.

ISLAND ATTIC INDUSTRIES INC
Miacomet Ave, 02554
(508)228-9405 **1 36 42**

American & European period furniture, Nantucket memorabilia. *Pr:* $25–25000. *Est:* 1976. *Serv:* Appraisal, auction, brochure, consultation, purchase estates, repair. **Hours:** May-Dec Mon-Sat 9-5, Jan-Apr Mon-Sat 10-5. **Size:** Large. **CC:** MC/V. **Assoc:** NEAA. Anne B Wilson **Park:** On site. **Loc:** From Town: Main to Pleasant St to Five Corners, R on Atlantic Ave toward Surfside Rd for .8 MI, R onto Miacomet.

VAL MAITINO ANTIQUES
31 N Liberty St, 02554
(508)228-2747 **39 50 56**

English & American furniture, marine items, old hooked rugs, lighting fixtures, weather vanes, Nantucket lightship baskets & decorative accessories. **Est:** 1958. **Hours:** Year round. **Loc:** At the end of Liberty St.

NANTUCKET HOUSE ANTIQUES
1 South Beach St, 02554
(508)228-4604 **29 34 37**

English & American country furniture, decorative accessories & folk art. **Serv:** Interior design, furniture repair, appraisal, off island delivery service. **Hours:** Year round.

NANTUCKET LIGHTSHIP BASKETS
9 Old South Wharf, 02554
(508)228-2326

Lightship baskets in traditional oak construction. **Est:** 1964. **Serv:** Custom orders, repair. **Hours:** May-Oct daily 10-5 & 7-10, else call for appt. **CC:** AX/MC/V. Richard Anderson **Loc:** 1 block over from Main St.

NANTUCKET NEEDLEWORKS
11 S Water St, 02554
(508)228-1913 **57**

100% virgin wool hand-hooked rugs in original design. **Est:** 1986. **Serv:** Complete kits, catalog ($5-refundable with

order). **Hours:** Mon-Sat 9-6 Sun 10-4 during season, else CLOSED SUN,MON. **CC:** AX/MC/V. Claire Murray **Loc:** Between the ferries off Main St.

RAFAEL OSONA AUCTIONEER
American Legion Washington St, 02554
(508)228-3942 **4 8**

General merchandise sales approximately once a month year round. Special auctions include: major marine & special items - first weekend in August; Nantucket memorabilia & quilts - mid-August. No buyer's premium. **Est:** 1980. **Serv:** Auction, appraisal. **Hours:** Daffodil Weekend to Christmas Stroll.

PETTICOAT ROW
19 Centre St, 02554
(508)228-5900 **35 41 48**

English & French antiques, painted furniture & linens. **Est:** 1988. **Hours:** Year round. Liza Dyche

PUSS-N-BOOTS
20 Old South Wharf, 02554
(508)228-5787 **47 77**

18th & 19th C antiques, antique jewelry & sterling decorative accessories. **Hours:** May-Oct.

SABOL AND CROSS, LTD
1 Windy Way, 02554
(508)228-3777 **51 66**

Maps & prints: botanical, nautical, whaling, Nantucket, birds & fish. **Serv:** Custom picture framing. **Hours:** Year round. **Loc:** Off Surfside Rd.

FRANK F SYLVIA ANTIQUES
6 Ray's Court, 02554
(508)228-0960 **56 63 77**

Period furniture, scrimshaw, paintings, silver & porcelain. **Est:** 1927. **Serv:** Appraisal, consultation. *Hours:* Year round BY APPT. *CC:* AX. *Loc:* 1 block from Int of Fair & Main Sts.

TILLER ANTIQUES
Easy St, 02554
(508)228-1287   36 39 63

One of Nantucket's oldest & finest antique shops featuring museum-quality porcelains, American & European furniture, paintings & decorative accessories. *Est:* 1972. *Hours:* May 25-Oct 10 Mon-Sat 10-4. *Size:* Medium. Howard Chadwick, Mgr *Loc:* Just a few feet from Steamboat Wharf, overlooking Nantucket Harbor.

TONKIN OF NANTUCKET
33 Main St, 02554
(508)228-9697   56 72

English furniture with a large selection of silver, Staffordshire, marine & scientific instruments, long case clocks, brass & copper accessories, marine paintings & English prints, ship models, fishing equipment & Nantucket lightship baskets. *Hours:* Year round Mon-Sat 9-5 Sun during summer. *Size:* Large. *CC:* AX/DC/MC/V. *Park:* On site.

TRANQUIL CORNERS ANTIQUES
49 Sparks Ave Sanford Boat Bldg, 02554
(508)228-6000   37 56 67

Country & formal, American, Canadian & English Furniture, accessories, antique, estate jewelry, scrimshaw & quilts. *Hours:* Easter-Columbus Day.

THE WICKER PORCH
13 N Water St, 02554
(508)228-1052   37 86

Wicker furniture, American & English

accessories in a 7-room Victorian house. *Assoc:* NEAA. Frank McNamee

LYNDA WILLAUER ANTIQUES
2 India St, 02554
(508)228-3631   37 60 67

English & American furniture, Chinese export porcelain, paintings, watercolors, samplers, folk art, quilts, Quimper, majolica, brass & papier mache'. *Est:* 1974. *Hours:* Late Jun-Early Oct Mon-Sat 10-5:30. *CC:* MC/V. *Loc:* 1 block from Main St.

Natick

VANDERWEG ANTIQUES
77 Worcester Rd Rte 9, 01760
(508)651-3634   **38 39 63**
Interesting mix of furniture & decorative accessories, emphasizing European items. *Pr:* $25–1000. *Est:* 1988. *Hours:* Mon-Sat 10-5 Sep-May Sun 1-5. *Size:* Medium. *CC:* MC/V. *Assoc:* SADA. Dini Zevitas *Park:* On site. *Loc:* Rte 128 Exit 20BW: 5 MI on Rte 9, just over Wellesley line.

Needham

GEORGE A DOWNER FINE ARTS
Box 905, 02192
(617)449-0971   **59**
Investment-quality oil paintings, primarily American Impressionists & watercolors. *Est:* 1978. *Serv:* Appraisal, buying/selling. *Hours:* BY APPT. *Loc:* Call for directions.

GOLDEN FLEECE ANTIQUES
PO Box 29, 02192
(617)444-8767   **37 63 77**
Furniture & early decorative accessories with emphasis on our American past. *Pr:* $25–5000. *Est:* 1968. *Serv:* Consultation, interior design, purchase estates. *Hours:* BY APPT. *Assoc:* SADA.

HORST KLOSS
1200 Great Plain Ave, 02192
(617)444-4383   **4**
Musical instrument appraisals. *Hours:* BY APPT.

ON CONSIGNMENT GALLERIES
1090 Great Plain Avenue, 02192
(617)444-4783
Furniture, glass, china, sterling, jewelry, lamps, mirrors, chandeliers, glass, objets d'art, pottery, bronzes, copper & brass. *Serv:* Accept consignments. *Hours:* Mon-Sat 10-5:30 Fri til 8 Sun 1-5. *CC:* MC/V.

STEWARTS OF NEEDHAM
190 Nehoiden St, 02192
(617)444-0124
Antiques for amateur & expert in a simple country setting - general line of furniture, china, glass, ironware & quilts. *Est:* 1927. *Hours:* BY APPT please. *Assoc:* SADA. Mrs Sidney Stewart *Loc:* Off Rte 135.

ESTHER TUVESON
30 Brookside Rd, 02192
(617)444-5533   **13**
Antiquarian books: Americana, children's, fine arts, first editions, illustrated & nonfiction special interests. *Serv:* Search service. *Hours:* Call ahead. *Assoc:* MRIAB.

THE WICKER LADY INC
925 Webster St, 02192
(617)449-1172   **68 71 86**
Nationally-recognized resource for expert restoration of wicker furniture - antique or new. *Est:* 1980. *Serv:* Refinishing, repair, free appraisal on repair estimates, restoration. *Hours:* Mon-Fri 7:30-4, please call ahead. Charlie Wagner *Park:* In front. *Loc:* Rte 128 Exit 17 (Rte 135): toward Needham Ctr, approx 1 MI from Rte 128 turn L on Webster, driveway between Texaco & 1st hse.

New Bedford

BROOKSIDE ANTIQUES
44 N Water St, 02741
(508)993-4944 **44**

New England's finest collection of 19th C art glass & a large collection of New Bedford glass. *Serv:* Appraisal, consultation, purchase estates. *Hours:* Jun-Dec Mon-Sat 10-5, Jan-May Tue-Sat 10:30-4:30. *Size:* Medium. *CC:* MC/V. Louis O St Aubin Jr *Park:* In front. *Loc:* Directly E of the Whaling Museum.

NEW BEDFORD ANTIQUES COMPANY
85 Coggeshall St, 02746
(508)993-7600 **{GR200}**

One of New England's largest group shops with a wide selection of jewelry, silver, glass, furniture, clocks & toys. *Pr:* $50–2000. *Est:* 1986. *Serv:* Purchase estates. *Hours:* Year round Mon-Sat 10-5 Sun 12-5. *Size:* Huge. *CC:* DC/MC/V. *Park:* On site. *Loc:* I-95 Exit 16E or 17W.

New Salem

THE COMMON READER BOOKSHOP
Old Main St, 01355
(508)544-3002 **13**

Antiquarian books: American literature, literary criticism, biography, women, theatre, ephemera, history & Americana. *Serv:* Appraisal, search service. *Hours:* May-Oct 15 Wed-Sun 10-5. *Assoc:* MRIAB. Dorothy Johnson *Loc:* Just off Rte 202.

Newburyport

JOHN J COLLINS, JR.
74A Water St, 01950
(508)462-7276 **21**

Specializing in Oriental rugs. *Hours:* Daily, call ahead CLOSED SUN. *Assoc:* ADA NHADA.

PETER EATON
39 State St, 01950
(508)465-2754 **37**

Fine New England 18th C furniture selected for knowledgeable collectors. *Est:* 1970. *Serv:* Appraisal, consultation, photography. *Hours:* Daily 10-5. *Assoc:* NHADA. *Shows:* ELLIS. *Park:* Nearby. *Loc:* In the heart of downtown Newburyport.

ELIZABETH'S 20TH CENTURY
98 Water St, 01950
(508)465-7421 **7 47 85**

A large assortment of art deco & designer 50s furniture & furnishings - Russell Wright, Frankart, Saarinen & Bertoia. Large assortment of costume jewelry & small assortment of precious metals & stones. Vintage clothing from turn of the century - 50s. *Pr:* $25–8000. *Est:* 1979. *Hours:* Apr-Dec 24 Mon-Sat 11:30-6 Sun 2-6, Jan-Mar Fri-Tue 11:30-6. M. Elizabeth Baratelli *Loc:* I-95N Exit 57 (Newburyport): R onto High St, 3 MI L onto Lime, at corner of Water & High Sts.

LEPORE FINE ARTS
2 Federal St, 01950
(508)462-1663 **59**

American & European paintings from the 19th & 20th C with a focus on the years 1870-1930. Works by such artists as: Laura Hills, C H Davis, Theresa

Bernstein, Theodore Wendel & Gertrude Fiske. *Serv:* Appraisal, conservation, interior design, purchase estates. *Hours:* May-Oct Tue-Fri 11-5 Sat 10-5, Nov-Apr Thu,Fri 11-5 Sat 10-5.

ON CONSIGNMENT GALLERIES
1 Merrimac St, 01950
(508)462-3127   **50 53 58**
Furniture, china, sterling, jewelry, lamps, mirrors, chandeliers, glass, objets d'art, pottery bronzes, copper & brass. *Serv:* Consignments accepted daily. *Hours:* Mon-Sat 10-5 Fri til 8 Sun 12-5. *CC:* MC/V.

CHRISTOPHER L SNOW ASSOCIATES
Two Inn St, 01950
(508)465-8872   **4 8**
Twenty-eight years experience with antiques, fine arts, Americana & paintings offering accurate, confidential & professional appraisal service for insurance companies, private collectors, executors, individuals, corporate trustees & banks. *Est:* 1960. *Serv:* Appraisal, auction, purchase estates. *Hours:* Mon-Fri 10-4, appt suggested. *Assoc:* AAA. *Park:* Nearby lot. *Loc:* Located in the heart of Newburyport's historic Market Sq on Inn St.

Newton

THE BOOK COLLECTOR
375 Elliot St, 02164
(617)964-3599   **13 14**
Antiquarian books: American literature, general history, Massachusetts history, science & theatre. *Pr:* $1–500. *Serv:* Appraisal, search service. *Hours:* Mon-Sat 10-5. *Size:* Medium. *Assoc:* MRIAB. Theodore Berman *Park:*

Nearby lot. *Loc:* Rte 9E .25 MI, W Newton/Woburn Exit: R at SS on Ellis St, R at SS up hill to Chestnut St, R at light to Elliot, 50 ft to lot.

BRASS BUFF ANTIQUES
977 Chestnut St, 02164
(617)964-9388   **16 71 72**
Polish brass & copper, iron & metals restored, specialize in scientific & medical instruments, nautical items, lighting, sconces, candlesticks, cannons, fireplace equipment, tools, kitchenware, copper, selected furniture, armor, hardware & doorknobs. *Pr:* $3–10000. *Est:* 1973. *Serv:* Polish brass & copper, iron & metals restored, conservation, repairs. *Hours:* Tue-Sun 1-5, call first. *Size:* Medium. *Assoc:* SADA. Mel Rosenburg *Park:* In front. *Loc:* Rte 9W Chestnut St Exit: L under Rte 9, 1st shop on R at top of hill.

PETER D COWEN
Box 181, 02168
(617)965-5135   **59**
Fine 19th & early 20th C American paintings, 1850-1930. *Est:* 1977. *Serv:* Appraisal, consultation, framing. *Hours:* BY APPT. *Loc:* Call for directions.

GIVE & TAKE CONSIGNMENT SHOP
799 Washington St, 02160
(617)964-4454
Consignment furniture, jewelry, china & glass. *Est:* 1981. *Serv:* Accept consignments. *Hours:* Mon-Sat 10:30-5. *CC:* MC/V. *Park:* On street. *Loc:* Just below Walnut St.

HARD-TO-FIND NEEDLEWORK BOOKS
96 Roundwood Rd, 02164
(617)969-0942   **13 57**

Embroidery & needlework, lace, quilting, knitting, crocheting & textiles. *Serv:* Appraisal, catalog, search service. *Hours:* Call ahead. *Assoc:* MRIAB. Bette S Feinstein

PAST TENSE
284 California St, 02158
(617)244-5725

A general line of antiques featuring jewelry & furniture. *Hours:* Tue-Sat 10-5.

KENNETH W RENDELL, INC
154 Wells Ave, 02159
(617)969-7766   **9 13**

Antiquarian bookseller featuring autograph letters, manuscripts, ancient writing & medieval manuscripts, Western Americana, fine bindings, classical western antiquities. *Serv:* Appraisal, cable "Autographs Boston". *Hours:* Appt preferred. *Assoc:* ABAA.

Newton Centre

EDWARD MORRILL & SON
27 Country Club Rd, 02159
(617)527-7448   **13**

Antiquarian books: science, sports & nature, reference, travel & Americana. *Hours:* BY APPT ONLY. *Assoc:* ABAA. Samuel R Morrill

SUZANNE SCHLOSSBERG BOOKS
529 Ward St, 02159
(617)964-0213   **13**

Antiquarian books: children's, first editions & illustrated. *Serv:* Appraisal, catalog, search service. *Assoc:* ABAA MRIAB.

Newton Highlands

BENCHMARK ANTIQUES
25 Lincoln St, 02161
(617)969-6800   **40 71 83**

Fine American, Victorian & turn-of-the-century furniture & accessories. Complete restoration services, including revitalization of original finishes, veneer work, carving of missing parts, caning, metal polishing/plating & mirror resilvering. *Pr:* $25-3500. *Est:* 1983. *Serv:* Appraisal, auction, conservation, custom woodworking, consultation. *Hours:* Mon-Sat 10-4 by chance/appt. *Size:* Medium. Colman N Herman *Park:* Nearby lot. *Loc:* I-95 to Rte 9E, 1st L at lights onto Woodward, 2nd R is Lincoln.

MARCIA & BEA ANTIQUES
One Lincoln St, 02161
(617)332-2408   **27 40 67**

19th C American country furniture, pine, oak, mirrors, quilts, baskets, rugs & accessories. *Hours:* Mon-Sat 10-5 Thu til 8 Sun 1-5. *Assoc:* SADA.

TREFLER ANTIQUE RESTORING STUDIO
177 Charlemont St, 02161
(617)965-3388   **25 68 71**

Master restorers - crystal, porcelain, jade, ivory, wood, paintings, objets d'art & metal. *Est:* 1948. *Serv:* Restoration, repair, conservation. *Hours:* Mon-Fri 9-5 Sat 10-2 or BY APPT. *Assoc:* AIC IIC. Leon Trefler *Park:* On site. *Loc:* Rte 128 Exit 19A (Newton Highlands): .7 MI, R after Federal Express Grey bldg, 100 yds up on L.

Newton Lower Falls

ARTHUR T GREGORIAN INC
2284 Washington St, 02162
(617)244-2553   **21**
6000 new & antique Oriental rugs. *Hours:* Mon,Tue,Thu,Fri 9-6 Wed 9-9 Sat 9-5. *Park:* In front.

Newton Upper Falls

THE MALL @ ECHO BRIDGE
381 Eliot St, 02164
(617)965-8141   **{GR12}**
American furniture including oak, arts & crafts, art nouveau, art deco, porcelain & pottery, jewelry, sterling silver flatware, prints & glass. *Est:* 1975. *Serv:* Purchase estates, repair silver. *Hours:* Mon-Sat 11-4, CLOSED SUN. *CC:* MC/V. Steve Nelson *Park:* In front. *Loc:* Rte 128 Exit Rte 9E (1st Exit): Chestnut St, R at 2nd SS, R at light onto Eliot.

NORTH WIND FURNISHINGS INC
1005 Chestnut St, 02164
(617)527-7724   **40 67 86**
Distinctive turn-of-the-century furnishings, oak, wicker, quilts, brass & iron beds & accessories. *Serv:* Restoration, repair. *Hours:* Tue-Sat 10-5. *Assoc:* SADA. Neil Friedman

Newtonville

AROUND THE CORNER ANTIQUES
10 Austin St, 02160
(617)964-1149   **36 44 47**
Furniture, textiles, jewelry & glassware. *Hours:* Mon-Sat 10-4. *Loc:* Across from Star Market.

VIRGINIA S CLARK
76 Highland Ave, 02160
(617)527-1807   **56**
Marine antiques, nautical instruments, whaling items, ship's appurtenances & memorabilia of seafaring. *Hours:* BY APPT ONLY. *Assoc:* SADA. Roy Wires

Norfolk

ROBERT F. GRABOWSKY
87 Cleveland St, 02056
(508)528-5140   **7**
Interior arts: art deco, art moderne & fine antiques from the 18th-20th C.

NORFOLK ANTIQUES
14 Carson Circle, 02056   **27**
Specializing in country furnishings. *Hours:* Wed-Sat 10-6. Peter J Kane *Loc:* Rte 115, behind Post Office.

North Adams

STATIONHOUSE ANTIQUES CENTER
Rte 8 Heritage State Pk, 01247
(413)662-2961   **{GR50}**
A full line of antiques & collectibles displayed in a restored freightyard

building. *Est:* 1987. *Hours:* Daily 10:30-5. *Size:* Large. *CC:* AX/MC/V. Barbara Foster *Park:* Nearby lot. *Loc:* Rte 8, just S of Main St & Rte 2, follow signs to Heritage Park.

North Amherst

PIONEER AUCTION OF AMHERST
Jct Rtes 116N & 63, 01059
(413)253-9914   **8**

Antique & estate auctions. Call for specific information. 10% buyer's premium. Bruce Smebakken *Loc:* Jct of Rtes 116N & 63.

North Andover

COUNTRY IN ANDOVER
58 Osgood St, 01845
(508)689-3550   **27 35**

Exceptional quality 18th & 19th C English & French country furniture with a wide selection of unusual accessories, all gathered in England. *Est:* 1983. *Serv:* Appraisal, consultation, interior design. *Hours:* BY APPT ONLY. *CC:* AX/MC/V. *Loc:* Call for directions.

ROLAND B HAMMOND INC
169 Andover St, 01845
(508)682-9672   **37 59 77**

American silver, furniture & paintings. *Est:* 1951. *Serv:* Estate appraisals. *Hours:* Appt suggested. *Shows:* ELLIS. *Loc:* Call for directions.

North Attleboro

RYAN'S ANTIQUES &
REFINISHING
585 E Washington St, 02760
(508)695-6464   {GR15}

Reasonably priced formal & country furniture & accessories including glass, porcelain, pottery, jewelry, paintings, prints, maps & ephemera. Furniture restoration & repair, cane, natural rush & wicker repair & custom framing. *Pr:* $5–3000. *Est:* 1985. *Serv:* Appraisal, auction, conservation, consultation, custom woodwork. *Hours:* Tue-Sat 10-6 Sun 12-4. *Size:* Medium. *CC:* MC/V. *Assoc:* MAA NAA NEAA SNEADA.

Park: On site. **Loc:** I-95 to Rte 495S to Rte 1N Attleboro Exit: approx 3 MI from Exit on L.

North Brookfield Ctr

PAUL R LANGEVIN AUCTIONEER
Rte 67, 01506
(508)867-8020   8
Diversified auctions of antiques & collectibles. **Park:** On site. **Loc:** From Rte 20 take Rte 148 12 MI N of Sturbridge Village.

North Eastham

EASTHAM AUCTION HOUSE
Box 1114 Holmes Rd, 02651
(508)255-9003   8 58
On Cape Cod, bi-monthly auctions from 1st Saturday in May thru last Saturday in November. 1st Saturday is a general (household) auction & the last Saturday of the month is a good antiques auction. **Pr:** $1–3000. **Est:** 1985. **Serv:** Appraisal, auction, purchase estates, real estate auction. **Hours:** May-Nov Mon-Fri 10-4 Sat 2-11. **Assoc:** NAA. Bill Fidalgo **Loc:** From Orleans rotary, 4 MI N to lights (Brackett Rd), R, .1 MI, R (Holmes Rd).

North Orange

ARMCHAIR BOOKS
107 Main St, 01364
(508)575-0424   13
A general stock of antiquarian books:

New England town histories, genealogy & cookery. **Hours:** Daily 10-4 or BY APPT. **Assoc:** MRIAB. Ed Rumrill

North Randolph

MIKE MIHAICH
12 Edwin St, 02368
(617)961-1643   74
Specialize in laying intricate parquet floors & special color & dye treatments for wood floors. **Hours:** BY APPT.

Northampton

AMERICAN DECORATIVE ARTS
9 3/4 Market St, 01060
(413)584-6804   7 40
Modern design from 1890 - 1960 including mission oak, art deco & fifties modern, furniture & accessories. **Pr:** $25–5000. **Est:** 1977. **Serv:** Appraisal, consultation, purchase estates. **Hours:** Thu-Tue 10-6 Sun 12-5. **Size:** Medium. **CC:** MC/V. **Assoc:** PVADA. **Park:** In Front. **Loc:** I-91 Exit 18: to light in ctr of town, R, then 1st L. In the Antique Center of Northampton.

ANTIQUE CENTER OF NORTHAMPTON
9 1/2 Market St, 01060
(413)584-3600   {GR40}
Three floors in a restored historic building featuring mission furniture & accessories, art deco & art nouveau, country & formal furniture, lighting, books, 50s modern jewelry, American Indian items, toys, pottery & wrist watches. **Pr:** $10–10000. **Est:** 1987. **Serv:** Appraisal, purchase estates.

Hours: Mon-Sat 10-6 Sun 12-5 CLOSED WED. *Size:* Large. *CC:* MC/V. *Assoc:* PVADA. *Park:* In front. *Loc:* From S: I-91 Exit 18: N on Rte 5 to 1st light, R, L at next light(Market St), from N: I-91 Exit 20: S on Rte 5, L on Market.

BARBARA L FERET, BOOKSELLER
136 Crescent St, 01060
(413)586-0384   13

Antiquarian books on cookery, wine & gastronomy. *Serv:* Appraisal, catalog, search service. *Hours:* BY APPT. *Assoc:* MRIAB.

GLOBE BOOKSHOP
38 Pleasant St, 01060
(413)584-0374   13

Antiquarian books: fine arts, literature, local history, philosophy, poetry, classical literature, fine printing, first editions, limited editions & children's. *Serv:* Appraisal, search service. *Hours:* Mon-Sat 9-9 Sun 10-5. *Assoc:* MRIAB. Mark Brumberg

ELEANOR KOCOT ANTIQUES
323 Bridge St, 01060
(413)584-7275   44 63

Fine glass, china, furniture & jewelry. *Hours:* Mon-Sat 9-5. *Loc:* On Rte 9 across from Mobil Station.

L & M FURNITURE
1 Market St, 01060
(413)584-8939   28 32 40

Oak furniture, toys, Roseville pottery, crocks, wicker, glassware & graniteware. *Hours:* Mon-Sat 11-5. *Assoc:* PVADA. Marge Farrick

RUMPLESTILTSKIN
Rte 9, 01060
(413)268-7604   5 50 74

Extensive inventory of architectural originals, including doors, fireplace mantels, stained glass, beveled glass, lighting fixtures, hardware, columns, handrails, spindles, wrought iron fencing, gates, church pews & cobblestone. *Hours:* Mon-Sat 9:30-6 Sun 12-6. *Loc:* On Northampton/Williamstown line.

SCHOEN & SON BOOKSELLERS
66 Massasoit St, 01060
(413)584-0259   13

Antiquarian books specializing in psychoanalysis, Judaica, scholarly works, American imprints & sermons. *Est:* 1983. *Serv:* Catalog, purchase estates, search service. *Hours:* BY APPT ONLY. *Assoc:* MRIAB. Kenneth Schoen *Loc:* A few blocks from Smith College.

Norton

DUBOIS' OLD HOUSE
9 Smith St, 02766
(508)285-4747   36 63 81

Furniture, primitives, paintings, prints, china, glass, pottery, books & early tools. *Hours:* By chance/appt. *Assoc:* SADA. Blanche DuBois *Loc:* Rte 140 at the Reservoir.

Norwood

COUNTRY TURTLE
1101 Washington St, 02062
(617)769-3848   {GR3}

Furniture, accessories, linens, tools, glass, textiles & primitives. *Est:* 1986. *Serv:* Appraisal, custom woodwork,

purchase estates. *Hours:* Tue-Sat 11-4.
CC: DC/MC/V. *Assoc:* SADA. Barbara
Cohen *Park:* Nearby lot. *Loc:* I-95 to
Rte 1 to Norwood, Dean St, L onto
Washington, 1.5 blocks.

Old Deerfield

ANTIQUE CENTER OF OLD
DEERFIELD
Rte 5, 01341
(413)773-3620   **{GR18}**
Antiques & collectibles. *Est:* 1979.
Hours: Daily 10-5 CLOSED MON.
Arthur N Breuer *Loc:* I-95 exit 24: Rte
5 for 7 MI.

Onset

JOSEPH A DERMONT,
BOOKSELLER
Box 654, 02255
(508)295-4760   **9 13 66**
Fine & rare books & autographs in
American & English literature, book
fairs. *Pr:* $25–500. *Serv:* Appraisal,
catalog, search service. *Hours:* BY
APPT ONLY. *CC:* MC/V. *Assoc:*
ABAA MRIAB.

Orange

BLDG 38 ANTIQUE CENTER
57 S Main St, 01364
(508)544-3800   **{GR30}**
Two floors of dealers in a renovated
brick building on the river with a wide
variety of quality antiques. *Est:* 1987.
Hours: Mon-Thu 9-6 Fri,Sat 9-8 Sun
10-6. *Size:* Large. *CC:* MC/V. *Assoc:*
AAA NEAA. Robin Martin *Park:*

Nearby lot. *Loc:* Rte 2 to Rte 122 Orange Exit: located on Main St in downtown Orange.

ORANGE TRADING COMPANY
57 S Main St, 01364
(508)544-6683   **33 55**
A unique shop specializing in
jukeboxes, slot machines, arcade
games, coke machines & advertising.
Est: 1980. *Serv:* Appraisal, restoration.
Hours: Daily 9-6 Fri,Sat til 8. *Size:*
Large. *CC:* MC/V. *Assoc:* AAA NEAA.
Gary H Moise *Park:* In front. *Loc:* Rte
2 to Rte 122 Orange Exit: located in
the ctr of Orange.

EDGAR STOCKWELL
DECORATING/ANTIQ
80 New Athol Rd Rte 2A, 01364
(508)575-0340   **50**
Small antiques, custom lamps, silk
shades & lamp conversions. *Serv:* Decorating service, custom draperies.
Hours: Daily CLOSED WED,SUN.
Assoc: PVADA. Jerome Willard

Orleans

CONTINUUM
#7 Rte 28, 02653
(508)255-8513   **36 50 69**
A small shop specializing in restored
electric lighting. Approximately 200
old lamps of all types, original lead
crystal shades by Holophane, Gillin-
der, Cambridge, Gill, Franklin are fea-
tured. Annual sale New Year's Day. *Pr:*
$100–3000. *Serv:* Appraisal, consulta-
tion, repairs, replication, restoration,
buy old parts. *Hours:* Jul 5-Sep Mon-
Sat 10:30-5 Sun 12-5, else Thu-Mon
10:30-5. *Size:* Medium. *CC:*

AX/MC/V. Dan Johnson *Park:* On site. *Loc:* Across from the Christmas Tree Shop.

HAUNTED BOOK SHOP
14 Cove Rd, 02653
(508)255-3780 **13**

Used & rare books & prints. *Hours:* Mon-Thu 9-5 Fri,Sat 10-5. Drucilla Meany

FRANK H HOGAN FINE ARTS INC
PO Box 1829, 02653
(508)255-2676 **4 59**

Fine arts dealer specializing in paintings of the Rockport & Provincetown Schools. *Pr:* $500–15000. *Serv:* Appraisal, consultation, purchase estates. *Hours:* Year round appt suggested. *Assoc:* ISA. *Park:* On site. *Loc:* Mid-Cape Hwy Exit 12: to Ctr of Orleans, then call for directions.

LILAC HEDGE ANTIQUES
12 West Rd, 02653
(508)255-1684 **1 47 63**

American antiques including furniture, china, pottery, glass, rugs, paintings, kitchenalia, estate & costume jewelry. *Hours:* Daily 10-5. *Assoc:* CCADA. *Loc:* Just off Rte 6A at light across from Angelo's.

Osterville

FERRAN'S INTERIORS
Farmhouse 1340 Main St, 02655
(508)428-4222 **29 36**

Unusual American, English & European pieces from the 18th-20th C. *Est:* 1988. *Serv:* Interior design, consultation. *Hours:* Mon-Sat 10-5 Sun after-

noons by chance. *CC:* AX/MC/V. *Park:* On site. *Loc:* In the farmhouse next to Appleseeds Clothing.

OAK & IVORY
12 Fire Station Rd, 02655
(508)428-9425 **47**

Custom Nantucket lightship baskets & fine ivory jewelry. *Est:* 1985. *Hours:* Mon-Sat 10-5. *CC:* AX/MC/V. *Assoc:* JBT. Robert Marks *Park:* On site. *Loc:* Rte 6 Exit 5: to Osterville, by the fire station.

ELDRED WHEELER
857 Main St, 02655
(508)428-9049 **43**

Handcrafters of fine 18th C furniture reproductions. *Serv:* Catalog ($4). *Hours:* Mon-Sat 10-5 or BY APPT.

Palmer

FURNITURE BARN
Meadowbrook Acres, 01069
(413)283-4094 **40 83**

Victorian & oak furniture. *Hours:* Wed-Mon 10-4. Art Corbett *Loc:* At Jct of Rtes 32 & 20.

QUABOAG VALLEY ANTIQUE CENTER
10 Knox St, 01069
(413)283-3091 **{GR50}**

Two floors of fine glass, pottery, toys, clocks, jewelry, books & furniture, including over 500 pieces of oak, mahogany, walnut & country. *Pr:* $1–5000. *Est:* 1983. *Serv:* Appraisal, brochure, consultation, custom woodwork, purchase estates. *Hours:* Mon-Sat 9-5 Sun 12-5. *Size:* Huge. David Braskie *Park:*

On site. *Loc:* I-90 Exit 8: 1 MI, take Rte 32 thru 2 sets of lights on to Main St, .25 MI up to Knox St.

axton

THE SHOP AT BLACK HILL
460 West St, 01612
(508)754-1659   {GR10}

Country, toys & folk art. *Hours:* Wed-Sun 10-4:30. *Loc:* 15 min from Sturbridge: Rte 20E to Rte 49 to Rte 9W to Rte 31N. From Worcester: Rte 9 to Rte 122 to Rte 31S in Paxton Ctr.

Peabody

AMERICANA ANTIQUES
South Ln Rte 1, 01960
(508)535-1042   **36 83**

Furniture only - period, Federal, Empire & Victorian. *Pr:* $25–25000. *Est:* 1968. *Hours:* Fri,Sat 9-5. M Meehan *Park:* On site.

HERITAGE CANING
28 Foster St, 01960
(508)531-5094   **22 68 71**

Press & hand cane, fiber rush, porch weave, herringbone, Shaker tape, seat weaving of all kinds, stripping & refinishing. *Est:* 1969. *Serv:* Appraisal, consultation, conservation, chair repairs a specialty. *Hours:* Year round Mon-Fri 8:30-4. John Newman *Park:* On site. *Loc:* In Peabody Sq 1.5 blocks from Monument, across from Bank of New England branch.

Pembroke

ENDLESS ANTIQUES
95 Church St, 02359
(617)826-7177   {GR6}

Refinished pine & oak furniture, jewelry, linens, fine glass & china. Dolls & doll supplies a specialty. *Pr:* $2–2000. *Est:* 1987. *Serv:* Doll hospital, purchase estates. *Hours:* Daily 11-5. *Size:* Medium. *CC:* MC/V. *Assoc:* SSADA. Marie A Davis *Park:* In front. *Loc:* Rte 3S Exit 12: R on Rte 139S, .25 MI on L.

Pepperell

GODWIN GALLERY
High Meadow Farm, 01463
(508)433-6205   **59**

Specializing in 19th & 20th C American women artists. *Hours:* BY APPT.

etersham

GROUND FLOOR ATTIC ANTIQUES
West St, 01366
(508)724-3297   **28 81 83**

Country & Victorian furniture, tools, china, prints, lamps, kitchenware, stoneware & glass located in an 1860s building. *Hours:* Wed-Sun 10:30-5:30. *Assoc:* PVADA. Hank Sherwood *Loc:* Off the Common.

Pittsfield

BERKSHIRE ANTIQUES
1716 W Housatonic St Rte 20, 01201
(413)447-9044   **5 37 59**

A general of line American & European furniture - always a large inventory - in a converted greenhouse. *Est:* 1985. *Serv:* Appraisal, consultation, purchase estates. *Hours:* Apr 16-Dec 20 Thu-Sun 10-5. *Size:* Large. Paul Fenwick *Park:* On site. *Loc:* On Rte 20, .25 MI E of the Hancock Shaker Museum.

FONTAINE'S AUCTION GALLERY
20 Keeler St, 01201   **8**

Antique & estate liquidation. John Fontaine *Loc:* Directly of Rte 7, 1 MI N of downtown Pittsfield.

GREYSTONE GARDENS
436 North St, 01201
(413)442-9291   **47 48 85**

A full line of ladies' & men's clothing & jewelry set in an environment of country ease & Victorian elegance. *Pr:* $1-500. *Serv:* Brochure. *Hours:* Jun-Dec Mon-Sat 11-6 Thu 11-9. *Size:* Medium. *CC:* MC/V. *Park:* In front. *Loc:* N of the town green on North St (Rte 7).

RUNNING FENCE BOOKS
148 North St, 01201
(413)442-6876   **13**

Antiquarian books specializing in western Massachusetts & the Berkshire County. *Hours:* Mon-Sat 10-5 Thu til 9. Eric Wilska

Plainfield

DICK HALE ANTIQUES
Main St Rte 116, 01070
(413)634-5317   **36 42**

Barn full of as-found & refinished antiques & accessories - specializing in pine & cherry. *Pr:* $25–3000. *Serv:* Purchase estates. *Hours:* Apr-Dec daily 11-4:30, Jan-Mar Tue-Sun 11-4:30. *Size:* Medium. *Assoc:* BCoADA PVADA. *Park:* On site. *Loc:* I-91 to Rte 116W to Plainfield OR Rte 9 to Rte 116N to Plainfield, OR Rte 2 to Rte 112S to Rte 116, then W.

Plainville

BRIAR PATCH ANTIQUES & COLLECTIB
62 Spring St, 02762
(508)695-1950   **1 28 65**

Shop located in 19th C barn, featuring country furniture & smalls, stoneware, quilts, baskets, toys, dolls, tinware & woodenware. *Pr:* $5–600. *Serv:* Appraisal, purchase estates. *Hours:* By chance/appt. *Assoc:* SADA. Marie Oldread *Park:* On site. *Loc:* I-495 Exit 15: Rte 1A to Plainville, 2.2 MI, L on Broad St, R on Spring St.

Plymouth

ANTIQUE CENTER OF PLYMOUTH
32 Hedges Pond Rd, 02360
(508)888-8342   **{GR70}**

Furniture, collectibles, pottery, clocks, paintings, prints, Orientalia & coins. *Hours:* Daily 10-5, Thu,Fri til 9. *Loc:*

Rte 3S Exit 2: follow arrows to Rte 3A, L onto 3A, L at firehouse, 5th building on L.

ANTIQUES UNLIMITED INC
96 Long Pond Rd, 02360
(508)746-4100   37 38
An extensive selection of cabinet pieces. *Pr:* $250–12000. *Serv:* Search service, purchase estates. *Hours:* MON-SAT 10-5:30 SUN 12-4 or by appt. *Size:* 0. *CC:* MC/V. Lawrence B Bill *Park:* On site. *Loc:* Rte 3 Exit 5: .25 MI W.

THE YANKEE BOOK & ART GALLERY
10 North St, 02360
(508)747-2691   13
A quaint rare & out-of-print bookshop with an attached art gallery specializing in local history, fine bindings, children's books & antique & contemporary art, originals & prints. *Est:* 1981. *Serv:* Appraisal, catalog, purchase estates, search service. *Hours:* Mon-Sat 10-5. *Size:* Medium. *CC:* AX/DC/MC/V. *Assoc:* MRIAB. Charles F Purro *Park:* Nearby lot. *Loc:* SE Expressway to Rte 3S Exit 6(Rte 44): R on Rte 44 to traffic light, R at light, L on North St.

Provincetown

JULIE HELLER GALLERY
2 Gosnold St, 02657
(508)487-2169   1 34 59
Featuring work by early Provincetown artists, fine estate jewelry, folk art, Americana & 19th & 20th C decorative arts. *Hours:* Sum: daily 12-11, Win: daily 12-4. *Assoc:* CCADA. *Loc:* On the beach Town Landing across from Adams Pharmacy.

INTERIOR ARTS GALLERY
208 Bradford St, 02657
(508)487-0483   7
Bakelite jewelry, Chase chrome & art deco advertising, furniture & lighting. *Pr:* $15–2500. *Est:* 1988. *Hours:* Thu-Sun 3-11 Mon-Wed by chance/appt. Robert F Grabosky *Park:* In front. *Loc:* In the E end of Provincetown.

REMEMBRANCES OF THINGS PAST
376 Commercial St, 02657
(508)487-9443   7 33 55
An unusual shop of remembrances, both old & new, from turn-of-the-century to 1950s with emphasis on nostalgia from the 20s & 30s, including art deco, jewelry, neon, juke boxes & pin-

AMERICAN & EUROPEAN FURNITURE

96 Long Pond Road
Plymouth, Mass. 02360
(508) 746-4100
Lawrence B. Bill ~ President

HOURS:
10 - 5:30 DAILY, 12 - 4:00 SUNDAY
OR BY APPOINTMENT

ball machines. *Pr:* $25–5000. *Serv:* Brochure. *Hours:* May 15-Oct 15 daily 11-11, Oct 16-Jan Mon-Thu 11-4. *Size:* Large. *CC:* AX/DC/MC/V. Helene Lyons *Park:* Nearby lot. *Loc:* Corner of Pearl & Commercial Sts at the end of Cape Cod's Rte 6.

Randolph

B & B AUTOGRAPHS
PO Box 465, 02368
(617)986-5695   **9**

Specializing in presidential signers, letters & documents authenticity guaranteed. *Pr:* $250–20000. *Est:* 1976.

Serv: Appraisal, purchase estates. *Hours:* BY APPT ONLY. Barry Bernstien

Rehoboth

MENDES ANTIQUES
52 Blanding Rd Rte 44, 02769
(508)336-7381   **37**

Large selection of American furniture & beds. *Hours:* Daily 9-6 Sun 11-6. *Loc:* 7 MI E of Providence.

JIM NEARY ANTIQUES
11 New St, 02769
(508)252-4292   **22**

Cane & wicker supplies, replacement

hardware, shipping, mail orders welcome. *Hours:* By chance/appt. *CC:* MC/V. *Loc:* Off Rte 44.

Richmond

WYNN SAYMAN
Old Fields Rossiter Rd, 01254
(413)698-2272   63
A large & comprehensive selection of fine 18th & 19th C English ceramics - primarily for collectors - shown in a Federal period country home. *Pr:* $500–29000. *Est:* 1980. *Hours:* BY APPT ONLY. *Size:* Medium. *Assoc:* AADLA. *Park:* On site. *Loc:* Call for directions.

Rockland

YE PRINTERS' ANTIQUES
267 Union St, 02370
(617)878-3440   {GR8}
Glass, china, linens & used furniture. *Pr:* $2–500. *Est:* 1984. *Serv:* Brochure, purchase estates. *Hours:* Mon-Sat 11-5. *Size:* Medium. *Assoc:* SSADA. Marie A Davis *Park:* In front. *Loc:* Rte 123, Union St at K-Mart Plaza, 1 MI on R.

Rockport

ELIOT ANTIQUES
153 Main St, 01966
(508)546-1090   21 36 47
Important furniture, 18th C New England artists, estate jewelry & rare Oriental rugs. *Hours:* By chance/appt. Michael M Eliot

FIVE CORNERS ANTIQUES
At Five Corners, 01966
(508)546-7063   67
Quilts & collectibles. *Hours:* By chance/appt. *Assoc:* NSADA.

MOUNT VERNON ANTIQUES
Box 66, 01966
(508)546-2434   21 48 80
Patchwork & appliqued quilts, hooked rugs, calico day dresses, embroidery, tapestry, lace & unusual textiles. *Pr:* $25–20000. *Est:* 1973. *Serv:* Appraisal, conservation, consultation, interior design, repairs, restoration. *Hours:* By chance/appt. *CC:* V. Elizabeth Enfield *Park:* In front.

RECUERDO
20 Main St #11, 01966
(508)546-9471   7 47 77
Small shop featuring estate & antique jewelry dating from Georgian thru 1940s, silver & smalls. *Pr:* $5–7500. *Serv:* Appraisal, purchase estates. *Hours:* May-Dec Wed-Mon 11-5, Jan-Apr by chance/appt. *CC:* MC/V. *Assoc:* GIA. Arlene Vincent *Park:* In front.

YE OLDE LANTERN ANTIQUES
28 Railroad Ave, 01966
(508)546-6757   36 44 63
An exceptional selection of fine furniture & accessories from the 18th, 19th & 20th C. Specialize in glass & porcelains from the early Victorian period thru the 20th C. Nice selection of estate jewelry. *Pr:* $10–5000. *Est:* 1970. *Serv:* Appraisal, consultation, purchase estates. *Hours:* Apr-Dec Mon-Sat 10-5, Jan-Mar BY APPT ONLY. *Size:* Medium. Matt Jackson *Park:* On site. *Loc:* Rte 128N to Rockport, from 5 Corners, L to Railroad Ave (Rte 127), across from RR station.

Rowley

FRANK D'ANGELO INC
53 Bradford St, 01969
(508)948-2137
17th, 18th & 19th C country & formal
furniture, paintings & accessories in
original as found condition & finish.
Serv: Appraisal, purchase estates, shipping. *Hours:* Mon-Sat by chance/appt.
Assoc: NEA NSADA SADA. *Loc:* In
The Isaac Kilbourne House off Rte
133.

NORTH FIELDS
RESTORATIONS
Rowley, 01969
(508)948-2722   **5 74**
Dismantled houses & barns - a complete line of building materials from
the 17th & 18th C through the Victorian period. Post & beam frames, wide
pine flooring, old doors, mantels, paneled room ends, barns, out buildings,
louvers & entrance ways. *Serv:* Reconstruction on site, buy and sell. Mark
Phillips

ROWLEY ANTIQUE CENTER
Rtes 1A & 133, 01969
(508)948-2591   **{GR35}**
Furniture, glass, china, quilts, jewelry
& metalwork. *Hours:* Tue-Sun 10-4:30
& Mon holidays. *Assoc:* NSADA.

SALT MARSH ANTIQUES
224 Main St Rte 1A, 01969
(508)948-7139   **{GR11}**
Two full floors in a restored 1805 barn,
packed with furniture paintings, Oriental rugs & decorative items. *Pr:* $25–
3000. *Est:* 1985. *Serv:* Purchase
estates, repairs, restoration. *Hours:*
Year round daily 9:30-4:30PM. *Size:*
Large. *CC:* AX/MC/V. *Assoc:* NADA

SPNEA. Robert Cianfrocca *Park:* On
site. *Loc:* Rte 93N Exit Rtc 133E: to
Rte 1A, L at lights Rte 1AN, 1 MI on
L.

TODD FARM
Rte 1A, 01969
(508)948-2217   **{GR31}**
A general line of antiques with furniture & collectibles. *Hours:* Year round
Thu-Sun & Mon holidays. *Assoc:*
NSADA. *Loc:* 1 MI N of Jct of Rtes
133 & 1A.

VILLAGE ANTIQUES
201 Main St Rte 1A, 01969   **{GR30}**
Furniture, Hummels, glass & china.
Hours: Wed-Sun 10:30-4:30. *CC:*
MC/V. *Assoc:* NSADA.

Roxbury

SOUTHPAW BOOKS
57 Beechglen St, 02119
(617)442-5524   **13**
Antiquarian books: first editions,
women, labor & radical studies & photography. *Serv:* Catalog, search service. *Assoc:* MRIAB. Eugene Povirk

Salem

AMERICAN MARINE MODEL
GALLERY
12 Derby Sq, 01970
(508)745-5777   **4 54 56**
Representing the finest in the art of
marine models, antique models &
models to order. *Serv:* Restoration, appraisal. *Hours:* Tue-Sat 10-4 or BY
APPT. *CC:* AX/MC/V. *Assoc:* ICMM

ISFAA USNRG. R. Michael Wall *Park:* In front. *Loc:* 2 blocks W of Peabody Museum.

ANTIQUES GALLERY
Pickering Wharf Derby Bldg, 01970
(508)741-3113   {GR35}

Furniture, paintings, glass, china, jewelry, silver, textiles, country furniture & Oriental rugs. *Est:* 1984. *Serv:* Appraisal, purchase estates, shipping. *Hours:* Win: daily 10-5 Sun 12-5, Sum: daily 10-6 Sun 12-6 Fri til 8. *Size:* Huge. *CC:* AX/MC/V. *Assoc:* NSADA. Nancy Denzler *Park:* On site. *Loc:* At the corner of Derby & Congress Sts.

ASIA HOUSE
18 Washington Sq W, 01970
(508)745-8257   60 63 77

Fine Oriental antiques from Japan, China & Southeast Asia & books on related subjects. *Pr:* $100–15000. *Est:* 1977. *Serv:* Appraisal. *Hours:* Mon-Sat 12-5, Win: CLOSED MON. *CC:* AX/MC/V. Emile Dubrule *Park:* On site. *Loc:* On Rte 1A in the Hawthorne Hotel on the Salem Common.

CANAL STREET ANTIQUES
266 Canal St, 01970
(508)744-0123

Weekly market of antiques & collectibles. Admission cost of $.50. *Serv:* Admission $.50. *Hours:* Every Sun 8:30-4. *Assoc:* NSADA.

JER-RHO ANTIQUES
4 Bridge St, 01970
(508)745-9891   4 44 47

China, glass, estate jewelry, extensive art glass, furniture, prints & paintings. *Serv:* Buy & sell estates, appraisal. *Hours:* Tue-Sun 10-6. *Size:* Medium.

CC: AX/MC/V. *Assoc:* NEAA NSADA. *Park:* Nearby. *Loc:* Rte 128 Exit 20S: into Salem, on R.

MARCHAND'S LAFAYETTE ANTIQUES
159 Lafayette St, 01970
(508)744-7077   29 36 60

Oriental china, paintings, decorative accessories & furniture. *Pr:* $25–500. *Serv:* Appraisal, purchase estates. *Hours:* BY APPT ONLY. *Assoc:* NSADA.

MARINE ARTS GALLERY
135 Essex St, 01970
(508)745-5000   4 56 59

Largest dealer in fine marine paintings in the Northeast displaying on 3 floors. *Serv:* Appraisal, framing, consultation, restoration. *Hours:* Mon-Sat 9-4. *Size:* Large. *Assoc:* AADLA NEAA. *Shows:* ELLIS. Russell Kiernan *Park:* Nearby. *Loc:* Directly across from the Peabody Museum.

ROBERT A MURPHY BOOKSELLER
14 Derby Sq, 01970
(508)745-7170   13

Antiquarian books: genealogy & local history. *Pr:* $3–180. *Serv:* Catalog, search service. *Hours:* Mail order only. *CC:* MC/V. *Assoc:* MRIAB.

UNION STREET ANTIQUES
Pickering Wharf, 01970
(508)745-4258   23 47 63

Porcelains, furniture, jewelry, collectibles, restored clocks & watches. *Hours:* Year round daily. *Assoc:* NSADA.

Salisbury

FORT HILL ANTIQUES
258 Main St Rte 286W, 01950
(508)465-5739   **27 63 67**
Country furniture, quilts, ironstone, china & accessories. *Hours:* Most days 10-5. *Assoc:* NHADA.

Sandwich

THE BROWN JUG
155 Main St @ Jarves, 02563   **7 44 50**
Smalls & primitives. *Est:* 1935. *Hours:* Daily 9:30-5:30. Dorothy L Haines *Loc:* 3 doors from Daniel Webster Inn.

DEN OF ANTIQUITY SLAVID INC
Box 1450, 02563
(508)477-4047   **63**
Specializing in fine English & Oriental pottery & porcelain. *Est:* 1953. *Serv:* Brochure. *Hours:* BY APPT. *Assoc:* CCADA. Stuart Slavid

FAULCONNER HOUSE ANTIQUES
193 Main St, 02563   **16 27 63**
Metalware, country accessories, pottery & porcelain. *Hours:* By chance/appt. *Park:* On site. *Loc:* On Rte 6A.

PAUL MADDEN ANTIQUES
146 Main St, 02563
(508)888-6434   **34 56 59**
Americana in great variety - paintings, scrimshaw, Nantucket baskets, folk art, furniture & decorative accessories - for the collector & dealer. *Pr:* $25-25000. *Serv:* Appraisal. *Hours:* Year round mornings by appt, afternoons by

chance. *Assoc:* CCADA. *Loc:* Rte 6 Exit 2: N on Rte 130 for 1.25 MI. Across from the Daniel Webster Inn.

MAYPOP LANE
161 Old King's Hwy Rte 6A, 02563
(508)888-1230   **{GR7}**
Tools, kitchen collectibles, furniture, jewelry, baskets, quilts, rugs, glass, pottery, china & country collectibles. *Hours:* Daily 10-4. *CC:* MC/V. *Park:* In front. *Loc:* On Rte 6A.

SANDWICH AUCTION HOUSE
15 Tupper Rd, 02563
(508)888-1926   **8**
General merchandise auctions every Saturday night September-May, Wednesday nights June-August. Special auctions include: Americana sale - late November; Antiques Auction - late September; Antiques & Victoriana sale - late May.

SHAWME POND ANTIQUES
13 Water St Rte 130, 02563
(508)888-2603   **2 44 48**
Andirons & tools, Sandwich glass, fine linens & accessories. *Hours:* Year round by chance/appt. *Assoc:* CCADA. Beverly Turnbull *Park:* In front.

THE STITCHERY IN SANDWICH
179 Old Main St, 02563
(508)888-4647   **27 44 77**
Country accessories, furniture, glass & silver. *Est:* 1976. *Hours:* Mon-Sat 10-5. *CC:* MC/V. *Park:* On site. *Loc:* 2 blocks E of Daniel Webster Inn.

H RICHARD STRAND FINE ANTIQUES
Rte 130 Town Hall Sq, 02563
(508)888-3230   **29 36 44**
An authentic collection of antique fur-

niture, lamps, china, paintings - including an outstanding selection of American glass - shown period room settings. *Hours:* All year daily 9-5. *Assoc:* CCADA. *Park:* On site. *Loc:* Opposite the Sandwich Glass Museum.

TOBEY HOUSE ANTIQUES
44 Water St, 02563
(508)888-1690   **21 50 67**
Braided rugs, baskets, quilts, country items, early lighting fixtures & accessories. *Est:* 1978. *Hours:* BY APPT ONLY. *Assoc:* CCADA. Stephanie Palmer *Loc:* Call for directions.

Santuit

BARRETT ANTIQUES
Rtes 28 & 130, 02635
(508)428-5374
18th-20th C furniture & accessories. *Est:* 1981. *Hours:* By chance/appt. *CC:* MC/V. *Park:* Nearby.

Scituate

GREENHOUSE ANTIQUES
182 First Parish Rd, 02066
(508)545-1964   **23 50 81**
Two rooms of interesting, varied antiques & collectibles. *Est:* 1987. *Serv:* Appraisal, purchase estates, repairs. *Hours:* May-Sep Tue-Sat 11-4 Sun 1-4, Oct-Jun Wed-Sat 11-4 Sun 1-4. *CC:* MC/V. *Assoc:* AAA. Jim Conover *Park:* On site. *Loc:* Rte 3A to First Parish Rd at Police Station, E 1.5 MI, past the Common on L.

Seekonk

ANTIQUES AT HEARTHSTONE HOUSE
15 Fall River Ave, 02771
(508)336-6273   **27 29 36**
Unusually large selection of American, English & Continental 18th & 19th C country & formal furniture & accessories displayed in 18th C farmhouse & barn. Furniture available in original, as found, & restored condition. *Pr:* $2–20000. *Est:* 1974. *Serv:* Purchase estates. *Hours:* Mon-Sat 10-5 Sun 12-5 or BY APPT. *Size:* Huge. *CC:* MC/V. *Assoc:* SNEADA. Bob Woods *Park:* On site. *Loc:* I-95 from N or S to Rte 195 at Providence RI Rte 195E to MA Exit 1, Rte 114A N across Rte 44, around bend on L.

RUTH FALKINBURG'S DOLL SHOP
208 Tauton Ave, 02771
(508)336-6929   **32**
Antique dolls, toys & other small items. *Hours:* Weekdays 11-3 Sat 12-4 Sun 2-4 CLOSED WED. *Assoc:* SNEADA. Nancy Fredricks

LEONARD'S ANTIQUES, INC.
600 Taunton Ave Rte 44, 02771
(508)336-8585   **4 36 43**
Two large floors of fine antique furniture specializing in American four poster beds. Classic reproduction furniture by Eldred Wheeler, Jenkins Plaud & other fine local craftsmen is on display in the Tudor-style house. *Pr:* $200–10000. *Est:* 1933. *Serv:* Appraisal, brochure $1, catalog $4, consultation, custom woodwork, repairs. *Hours:* Mon-Sat 8-5 Sun 1-5. *Size:* Huge. *CC:* MC/V. *Assoc:* NEAA. Jeffrey L Jenkins *Park:* On site. *Loc:* 295

Exit 1: N on Rte 114A, bear R at Old Gristmill Tavern, R at next light onto Rte 44, on L at top.

PENNY LANE ANTIQUES & GIFTS INC
288 Fall River Ave, 02771
(508)336-5070   **35 71 83**

Elegant showrooms featuring French country & Victorian furniture - restoration a specialty. *Pr:* $25–500. *Est:* 1986. *Serv:* Appraisal, consultation, interior design, purchase estates, repairs. *Hours:* Wed-Sun 11-5. *Size:* Medium. *Assoc:* NEAA. David M Murray *Park:* On site. *Loc:* Rte 195E to RI/MA line Exit 1N: on Rte 114A, R at York, .1 MI on R.

Sharon

ANTIQUARIAN BOOKWORM
22 Sentry Hill Rd, 02067
(617)784-9411   **13 66**

Antiquarian books: Americana, architecture, Civil War, medicine, Western Americana & hand colored prints. *Serv:* Appraisal, catalog. *Assoc:* ABAA MRIAB. Billie Weetall

BLAND'S BOOK BIN
37 Glendale Rd, 02067
(617)784-8303   **13**

Antiquarian books: American literature, Americana, children's, cookery, poetry & a general stock. *Serv:* Search service. *Hours:* Mail order only. *Assoc:* MRIAB. Frances E Memoe

MICHAEL GINSBERG BOOKS INC
60 Lincoln Rd, 02067
(617)784-8181   **13 51**

Antiquarian books: Americana, bibli-ography, Civil War, explorations & voyages, Indians, maps, atlases, religion, theology, travel & Western Americana. *Serv:* Appraisal, catalog, search service. *Hours:* By appt. *Assoc:* MRIAB ABAA. *Loc:* 25 MI S of Boston.

PEPPER & STERN RARE BOOKS, INC
Box 357, 02067
(617)784-7618   **9 13**

Antiquarian books: American literature, autographs & manuscripts, detective fiction, English literature, modern literature & rare cinema material. *Serv:* Appraisal, catalog. *Hours:* BY APPT. *Assoc:* ABAA MRIAB. Peter L Stern

Sheffield

1750 HOUSE ANTIQUES
S Main St, 01257
(413)229-6635   **23 44 55**

American, French & European clocks, music boxes & phonographs, fine glass, china, furniture & decorative accessories. *Serv:* Expert clock repairs. *Hours:* Always open. *Assoc:* BCoADA. Frances Leibowitz *Park:* On site.

ANTIQUE CENTER OF SHEFFIELD
Rte 7, 01257
(413)229-3400   **{GR}**

Broad range of antiques & collectibles. *Est:* 1982. *Hours:* Thu-Sun 10-5, else by chance. K J Cooper *Park:* On site. *Loc:* Across from Sheffield Library.

BRADFORD GALLERIES, LTD
N Main St Rte 7, 01257
(413)229-6667   8

Monthly estate auctions. *Serv:* Appraisal for insurance & estates. *Assoc:* BCoADA. William Bradford *Park:* On site.

CARRIAGE HOUSE ANTIQUES
Sheffield Plain Rte 7, 01257
(413)229-3367   71

Furniture restoration. *Serv:* Restoration. *Hours:* Daily 10-5. *Park:* On site.

CENTURYHURST ANTIQUES
Main St Rte 7, 01257
(413)229-8131   23 27 63

Two large rooms in a ca 1800 Colonial specializing in antique American clocks & a large selection of early Wedgwood, Jasperware, china & country furniture. *Est:* 1980. *Hours:* Daily 9-5 by chance/appt. *Size:* Medium. *CC:* AX/MC/V. *Assoc:* BCoADA. Judith Timm *Park:* On site. *Loc:* From NYC: I-95 Rte I-287 to Taconic Pkwy to Rte 23 Exit: R (E) on Rte 23 to Rte 7, Great Barrington, R (S) to Sheffield.

CORNER HOUSE ANTIQUES
Main St & Old Mill Pond Rd,
01257
(413)229-6627   27 86

Specializing in antique wicker furniture & accent pieces. Traditional wicker sets as well as rare & unusual collector's items. Full line of styles in natural, original paint or custom finish. Also a diverse selection of American country furniture. *Est:* 1977. *Serv:* Repairs, restoration, custom painting. *Hours:* Year round, most days 10-5, please call if coming a distance. *Size:*

Medium. *Assoc:* BCoADA. Kathleen Tetro *Park:* On site. *Loc:* 1 MI N of Sheffield Ctr, on L.

COVERED BRIDGE ANTIQUES
N Main St, 01257
(413)229-2816   29 36 50

Furniture, lighting, decorative accessories, jewelry, folk art & ethonographic items. *Hours:* Daily 9-5. *Assoc:* BCoADA. Thomas C Carpentier *Park:* On site. *Loc:* On Rte 7.

CUPBOARDS & ROSES
Rte 7, 01257
(413)229-3070   34

Exclusive importers of superb replicas of 17th & 18th C historic folk art. *Hours:* Sum: daily 10-5 CLOSED TUE, Win: Daily 10-5, CLOSED TUE,WED. Edith Gilson *Loc:* On Rte 7 N of Sheffield.

DARR ANTIQUES AND INTERIORS
S Main St, 01257
(413)229-7773   37 50 63

Seven showcase rooms full of fine period furniture of the Federal, Empire & Regency periods, including paintings, lamps, porcelains, textiles & accessories. *Pr:* $10–85000. *Serv:* Consultation, interior design. *Hours:* May-Oct daily 9-5, Nov-Apr Thu-Mon. *Assoc:* BCoADA. Robert R Stinson *Park:* On site. *Loc:* On Route 7.

DOVETAIL ANTIQUES
N Main St Rte 7, 01257
(413)229-2628   23 37

Always a large selection of 18th & 19th C American wall, shelf & tall case clocks compatible with country interiors. Country furniture mostly in old paint or finish, redware, spongeware, stoneware & tools. *Pr:* $250–12500.

Est: 1976. *Hours:* Wed-Mon 11-5 Tue by chance/appt. *Size:* Medium. *CC:* MC/V. *Assoc:* BCoADA NAWCC. Judith Steindler *Park:* On site. *Loc:* On Rte 7, .75 MI N of the ctr of Sheffield on E side of road.

FALCON ANTIQUES
176 Undermountain Rd, 01257
(413)229-7745   16 36 81

Two floors of American & English smalls, copper, brass, pewter & treen, American & English country furniture, plus a fine selection of woodworking tools for the collector, decorator or user. Custom furniture made to order on the premises. *Pr:* $10–2500. *Est:* 1973. *Serv:* Custom woodwork. *Hours:* Daily 10-5. *Size:* Medium. *CC:* MC/V. *Assoc:* BCoADA. *Park:* On site. *Loc:* Rte 41, 5 MI N of Int of Rtes 41 & 44, 7 MI from Rte 7 Sheffield Ctr, follow signs @ Berkshire School Rd.

GOOD & HUTCHINSON ASSOCIATES
Main St Rte 7, 01257
(413)229-8832   39 60 63

Specializing in American, English & Continental furniture, paintings, fine pottery, china & silver for museums & antiquarians. *Serv:* Appraisal. *Hours:* Mon-Sat 10-5 Sun 1-5. *Assoc:* AADLA BCoADA. *Shows:* ELLIS. David Good *Park:* On site. *Loc:* On The Green, near Tanglewood & Jacob's Pillow.

FREDERICK HATFIELD ANTIQUES
S Main St Rte 7, 01257
(413)229-7986   29 47 59

18th, 19th & 20th C antiques & accessories, jewelry, silver, paintings & Oriental rugs. *Hours:* Daily 10-5 & BY APPT. *Assoc:* BCoADA. *Park:* On site.

KUTTNER ANTIQUES
Rte 7, 01257
(413)229-2955   29 37 39

Specializing in elegant country English & American furniture & decorative accessories. *Est:* 1987. *Hours:* May-Oct Wed-Mon 11-5:30, Nov-Apr Fri-Mon 11-5. *Size:* Medium. *Park:* In front. *Loc:* Rte 7 on L side travelling N of Sheffield.

MAY'S ANTIQUES
Main St Rte 7, 01257
(413)229-2037

Furniture, hall stands, china closets, clocks, jewelry, glassware, wicker & dolls. *Hours:* Fri-Mon 10-5. *CC:* MC/V. *Park:* On site.

HOWARD S MOTT INC
Main St Rte 7S, 01257
(413)229-2019   9 13 33

Antiquarian book dealers in rare books & first editions, broadsides, 18th C British pamphlets, English & American literature (16th-20th C), juveniles, autographs, West Indies to 1860, golf & tennis before 1900. Located in a ca 1780 Federal house. *Est:* 1936. *Serv:* Appraisal, catalog, restoration. *Hours:* We strongly urge prospective visitors to have an appointment. *Size:* Large. *Assoc:* ABAA BCoADA MRIAB. Donald N Mott *Park:* In front. *Loc:* On Rte 7.

OLE T J'S ANTIQUE BARN
S Main St Rte 7, 01257
(413)229-8382   27 29 36

Two floors of antiques & collectibles from around the world - Oriental, African, European & early American -

including jewelry, furniture, paintings, rugs, lamps & art objects. *Est:* 1985. *Serv:* Purchase estates, consultation, custom woodwork, interior design. *Hours:* Daily 10-dark, call Tue,Wed before coming. *Size:* Medium. *CC:* MC/V. Theodore J Fuchs *Park:* On site. *Loc:* Rte 7, 1.5 MI S of Sheffield, 6 MI S of Gt Barrington, 3.5 MI from Canaan CT.

EGH PETER AMERICAN ANTIQUES
Rte 7, 01257
(413)229-8881   41
Folk art, painted furniture & objects of the 18th & 19th C. *Est:* 1976. *Hours:* Open every weekend, mid-week by appt (203)824-1112. *Assoc:* ADA. Evan G Hughes *Park:* On site. *Loc:* On Rte 7 between Susan Silver & the Bradford galleries.

SUSAN SILVER ANTIQUES
N Main St Rte 7, 01257
(413)229-8169   **39 53 63**
Specializing in 18th & 19th C fine formal furniture & accessories. *Pr:* $100–50000. *Hours:* Daily 10-5 CLOSED TUE. *Size:* Large. *Assoc:* BCoADA. *Park:* In front. *Loc:* On Rte 7.

LOIS W SPRING
Ashley Falls Rd Rte 7A, 01257
(413)229-2542   **27 37**
18th & 19th C American furniture - country & formal. *Hours:* Sat Sun 10-5 weekdays by chance/appt. *Assoc:* BCoADA. *Park:* On site. *Loc:* Between Ashley Falls & Sheffield.

DAVID M WEISS
Rte 7, 01257
(413)229-2716   **1 29 37**
A small shop with quality 18th & 19th C formal & country furniture, china,

paintings & select accessories. *Hours:* Daily 10-5 appt advised. *Size:* Medium. *Assoc:* BCoADA. *Park:* On site. *Loc:* From Boston: I-90 to Rte 7 in Sheffield, From NY: Taconic Pkwy to Rte 23 to Rte 7.

Shelburne

ORCHARD HILL ANTIQUES
Colrain Rd, 01370
(413)625-2433   **16 27 81**
Shop & barn annex containing a collection of country furniture, lamps, tools, brass & copper accessories. *Pr:* $5–3000. *Serv:* Appraisal, interior design. *Hours:* Fri 3-6 Sat,Sun 10-6 else by chance/appt. *Size:* Medium. Jeffrey C Bishop *Park:* On site. *Loc:* From Greenfield, Rte 2W, 4 MI, R at Duck Pond Inn onto Colrain Rd, .5 MI of Rte 2 (Mohawk Trail).

Shelburne Falls

LUELLA MC CLOUD ANTIQUES
Ashfield Rd Rte 112, 01370
(413)625-2215   **27 34**
Country furniture, accessories & folk art. *Hours:* By chance/appt. *Loc:* 10 MI W of Greenfield.

Sherborne

KENNETH W VAN BLARCOM
Five Butler St, 01770
(508)653-7017   **8**
Individual antiques & estates appraised, purchased or sold on consignment. *Assoc:* AR.

Somerville

A-1 ANTIQUE PLUMBING FIXTURES
30 Prospect St, 02143
(617)625-6140 74
Large inventory of antique bath fixtures, claw footed bathtubs, pedestal & marble top lavatories, new, used & period radiators. *Pr:* $50–800. *Serv:* Consultation, repairs. *Hours:* Sep-May daily 8-5, Jun-Oct Mon-Fri 8-5. *Size:* Medium. Francis X Fahey *Park:* On site. *Loc:* In Union Sq across from Dunkin Donuts.

EMBELLISHMENTS
99 Beacon St, 02143
(617)547-9232 29
Antiques & fine decorative accessories. *Est:* 1988. *Hours:* Tue-Sat 10-6 Sun 12-5. Gilbert Stancourt *Loc:* 1/2 way between Inman & Porter Sqs.

FAUX-ARTS ASSOCIATES
40 Dartmouth St, 02145
(617)666-3965 70
Special finishes for floors, walls & furniture including wall glazes, murals, marbleizing, stenciling, gilding & trompe l'oeil. *Serv:* Reproduction. *Hours:* BY APPT. Diana Thayer

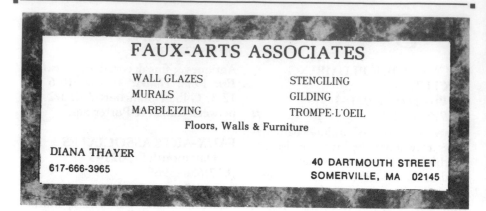

LONDONTOWNE GALLERIES
380 Somerville Ave, 02143
(617)625-2045   **5 42 45**
Warehouse of fine antiques, country pine, classical garden ornamentation, French country & architectural artifacts. *Est:* 1979. *Serv:* Financing available, appraisal, restoration, modification. *Hours:* Mon-Sat 10-4:30 Sun 12-4. *Size:* Large. *CC:* MC/V. *Assoc:* NEAA. William J Herbert Sr *Park:* On site. *Loc:* In Union Sq, .75 MI from Harvard Sq.

ROBERT E SMITH
20 Vernon St, 02145
(617)625-3992   **19 43 70**
Period furniture design & reproductions. *Est:* 1973. *Serv:* Brochure, furniture restoration. *Hours:* Mon-Fri 8-5 weekends. *Park:* On site. *Loc:* From McGrath Hwy, W on Broadway, L on Central, R on Vernon, 1 MI from Int of Broadway & McGrath Hwy.

South Ashfield

RUSS LOOMIS JR
West Rd, 01330
(413)628-3813   **19 43 70**
Fine furniture & cabinetmaking - in all styles, but specializing in Queen Anne & Chippendale periods. Each piece individually crafted. *Est:* 1974. *Serv:* Catalog ($2), custom woodwork, reproduction. *Hours:* BY APPT. *Park:* On site. *Loc:* Call for appt and directions.

South Bellingham

COYLE'S AUCTION GALLERY
21 Westminster Ave, 02019
(508)883-1659   **8**

Permanent antique auction gallery. *Serv:* Accept consignments. *Hours:* Daily 9-5. Michael Coyle *Loc:* 495 Exit 16: follow signs to Woonsocket RI, stay on King St to Rte 126S, S 300 yds to Old Colony Gas.

South Brewster

SMITH ANTIQUES
157 S Orleans Rd, 02631
(508)255-8659   **16 44 77**

Glass, silver, furniture, porcelain, pottery, brass, copper, iron & decorative items. *Hours:* By chance/appt. *Assoc:* CCADA. Shirley Smith *Loc:* On Rte 39.

South Deerfield

DOUGLAS AUCTIONEERS
Rte 5, 01373
(413)665-2877   **4 8**

Western New England's largest auction gallery, two auctions a week year round. 10% buyer's premium. *Est:* 1968. *Serv:* Appraisal, brochure, consultation, purchase estates. *Hours:* Mon-Fri 8-4:30 Sat 9-12. *Assoc:* CAI NAA. Douglas P Bilodeau *Park:* On site. *Loc:* I-91 Exit 24: 2 MI N.

INTERNATIONAL AUCTION SCHOOL
Rte 5, 01373
(413)665-2877   **8**

New England's only auction school. Licensed by the Commonwealth of Massachusetts, Department of Education. *Est:* 1978. *Serv:* Auction, brochure. *Hours:* Mon-Fri 8-4:30 Sat 9-12. *Size:* Huge. Douglas P Bilodeau *Park:* On site. *Loc:* I-91 Exit 24: 2 MI N.

South Egremont

ANTIQUES & VARIETIES
Main St, 01258
(413)528-0057   **33 34 47**

Antiques & a variety of figures, animals & toys personally picked with an eye for humor, the unusual, whimsy, folk art; precisely organized in well-lighted display cases in a most interesting store. *Hours:* Jul-Aug Mon-Sun 10-5:30, else Fri-Sun 10-5:30. *CC:* AX/MC/V. Geffner Schatzky *Park:* On site. *Loc:* In ctr of town at the Sign of the Juggler.

BIRD CAGE ANTIQUES
Main St Rte 23, 01258
(413)528-3556   **1 36 77**

18th-20th C eclectic stock includes jewelry, silver, country accessories & old collector's items from local homes. *Pr:* $10–5000. *Est:* 1958. *Serv:* Purchase estates. *Hours:* Daily 9-5:30 or BY APPT. *Size:* Medium. *CC:* AX/MC/V. *Assoc:* BCoADA. Arnold Baseman *Park:* On site. *Loc:* NYS Thruway Exit 21: Rte 23E past Hillsdale, on R in white building, from I-90 Lee Exit: to Rte 7, Rte 23W, 3 MI.

COUNTRY LOFT ANTIQUES
Rte 23, 01258
(413)528-5454   **36 44 47**

Furniture, glass, rockers, jewelry, pottery & quilts. *Hours:* Wed-Sun 10-5. *CC:* MC/V. Tom Millot

DALZELL HOUSE ANTIQUES
Rte 23, 01258
(413)528-4967   **32 33**

Dolls, collectibles & ephemera dealers are a speciality. *Est:* 1973. *Serv:* Doll repairs. *Hours:* By chance/appt. D D Zigmand *Park:* On site. *Loc:* 500 ft from the post office on Rte 23.

DOUGLAS ANTIQUES
Rte 23, 01258
(413)528-1810   **40 67 83**
Victorian oak furniture, quilts 1820-1940, rolltop & flat top desks, Hoosiers, tables & chests. *Hours:* Wed-Mon 10-5:30 Tue by chance. *Assoc:* BCoADA. Douglas Levy *Park:* On site.

BRUCE & SUSAN GVENTER, BOOKS
Tyrrell Rd Rte 23, 01258
(413)528-2327   **13 66**
Antiquarian books - specializing in 19th C hand-colored prints, authentic manuscript leaves from the 13th to the 15th C, rare & unique books, fashion, costume, cookbooks, calligraphy & a large general stock. *Pr:* $1–2500. *Est:* 1980. *Serv:* Purchase estates. *Hours:* Wed-Sun 10:30-5 or BY APPT. *Size:* Medium. *Assoc:* MRIAB. *Park:* On site. *Loc:* 1 MI E of NY state border; 2.25 MI W of S Egremont Ctr on Rte 23.

HOWARD'S ANTIQUES
Hillsdale Rd Rte 23, 01258
(413)528-1232   **27 37 50**
18th & 19th C American country furniture, chandeliers, brass lamps & accessories. *Serv:* Furniture refinishing. *Hours:* Daily 10-5 CLOSED TUE. *Assoc:* BCoADA. Lynda Howard *Park:* On site.

LITTLE HOUSE STUDIO
Old Sheffield Rd, 01258
(413)528-9517   **27 34**
American country furniture, collectibles, decorative accessories & folk art.

Serv: Custom painted & cut lampshades. *Hours:* Wed-Sat 10-5 Sun 1-5. *Assoc:* BCoADA. Libby Fett *Park:* On site.

RED BARN ANTIQUES
Rte 23, 01258
(413)528-3230   **29 36 50**
Furniture, glass, accessories & large selection of early lighting - electric, gas & kerosene. *Est:* 1943. *Serv:* Appraisal, restoration, auction. *Hours:* Daily 9-5. *CC:* MC/V. *Assoc:* NAA. John Walther *Park:* On site. *Loc:* At the Int of Rtes 23 & 41.

GLADYS SCHOFIELD ANTIQUES
Rtes 23 & 41, 01258
(413)528-0387   **36 44 50**
Furniture, china, glass & lamps. *Est:* 1949. *Serv:* Appraisal. *Hours:* Fri-Mon 10-5 Sun 1-5. *Park:* On site.

ELLIOTT & GRACE SNYDER
Undermountain Rd Rte 41, 01258
(413)528-3581   **16 37 80**
18th & 19th C American furniture & folk art, with emphasis on textiles & metalwork. *Hours:* Appt suggested. *Assoc:* ADA BCoADA. *Park:* On site. *Loc:* Rte 41 .5 MI S of Rte 23.

SPLENDID PEASANT
Rte 23 & Old Sheffield Rd, 01258
(413)528-5755   **27 34**
Specializing in 18th & 19th C country furniture, folk art, decorative smalls, whimsy & kitchenalia. *Est:* 1987. *Serv:* Consultation. *Hours:* Daily 9:30-5. *Assoc:* BCoADA. Martin Jacobs *Park:* In front. *Loc:* 1 block from Egremont.

South Harwich

CAPE COLLECTOR
1012 Main St Rte 28, 02661
(508)432-3701   13
Antiquarian books: children's, Cape
Cod, maritime & a general stock.
Hours: Daily 12:30-6. H Jewel
Geberth

South Natick

COMING OF AGE ANTIQUES
22 Elliot St Rte 16, 01760
(508)653-9789   3 29 58
In the John Eliot historic district: glass,
china, furniture, tools, handcrafts &
jewelry. *Pr:* $5–1500. *Est:* 1981. *Serv:*
Consultation. *Hours:* Tue-Sat 11-4
Sun 1-4. *CC:* AX/MC/V. *Assoc:* SADA.
Rosamond H Haley *Park:* In front.
Loc: Rte 128 Wellesley Exit: Rte 16, 6
MI.

South Orleans

PLEASANT BAY ANTIQUES
540 Chatham Rd Rte 28, 02662
(508)255-0930   1 30 59
Early American furniture & accessories, decoys & paintings. *Hours:* Year
round daily 10-5. *Assoc:* CCADA.
Steve Tyng *Park:* In front.

South Weymouth

DANA R JOHNSEN
182 Pine St, 02190
(617)337-2143   81
Antique tools. *Hours:* BY APPT.

Southampton

SOUTHAMPTON ANTIQUES
172 College Hwy Rte 10, 01073
(413)527-1022   29 40 87
Three large barns filled with a large
selection of quality oak & Victorian
furniture - as found & restored. *Hours:*
Thu-Sat 10-5 Sun 12-5, CLOSED
AUG. *Size:* Huge. *CC:* DC/MC/V.
Meg Cummings *Park:* On site. *Loc:*
I-90 Exit 3: L onto Rte 10N, 7 MI.

Southborough

GOLDEN PARROT
22 E Main St, 01772
(508)485-5780   36 44
Furniture, glass, collectibles & consignment items. *Hours:* Mon-Fri 1-5
Sat,Sun by chance/appt. *Assoc:* SADA.
Glen Urquhart

GOLDEN PONY ANTIQUES
184 Cordaville Rd, 01772
(508)485-8455   36
Antiques, collectibles & furniture.
Hours: Tue-Fri 1-4 Sat 12-5. *Assoc:*
SADA. Barbara Sullivan *Loc:* Rte 85
head S Off Rte 9, shop 4th house on L.

MAPLEDALE ANTIQUES
224 Boston Rd, 01772
(508)485-5947   29 36
Furniture, accessories & collectibles.
Hours: Daily 2-5 CLOSED SUN.
Assoc: SADA. Eleanor J Hamel

TEN EYCK BOOKS
PO Box 84, 01772
(508)481-3517   13
Antiquarian books: children's, fishing

& hunting, illustrated & literature.
Serv: Catalog. *Assoc:* MRIAB. Arthur
Ten Eyck

TOOMEY'S HAVEN ANTIQUES
89 Framingham Rd, 01772
(508)485-6910   **36**
Antiques, collectibles & furniture.
Hours: Thu-Sat 11-5 Sun-Wed by
chance/appt. *Assoc:* SADA. Helen L
Toomey *Loc:* Down by Willow Brook
Farm.

Southbridge

STEEPLE BOOKS
62 Elm St, 01550
(508)765-0370   **13**
A general stock of antiquarian books.
Serv: Appraisal, search service. *Assoc:*
MRIAB. Rev. Roland Boutwell

SUN GALLERIES
299 South St, 01550
(508)765-5540   **59**
19th & early 20th C American Impressionists, social realists & abstract art.
Hours: BY APPT ONLY. Eric Glass

Southfield

ANTIQUES @ BUGGY WHIP
FACTORY
Main St, 01259
(413)229-2433   **{GR32}**
Specializing in country antiques. *Serv:*
Lunch in Boiler Room Cafe. *Hours:*
Jun-Dec daily 10-4, Jan-May Fri-Mon
10-4. Don Coffman *Loc:* 8 MI from Int
of Rtes 44 & 272 in Norfolk. Across
from the new Marlboro Fire Station.

Southwick

THE TOY SHOP
350 College Hwy, 01077
(413)569-3291   **11 32**
Toys from turn-of-the-century to 80s -
antiques & collectible, comic toys,
transportation toys & games, a selection of baseball cards & memorabilia.
Pr: $5–5000. *Est:* 1982. *Serv:* Ap-
praisal. *Hours:* Fri 9-4 Sat,Sun 10-4 or
by chance/appt. John Cammisa *Park:*
On site. *Loc:* I-91, Rte 57W to Rte 202,
S for 3 MI OR I-90 Exit 3 (Westfield):
Rte 202S.

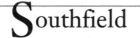
Spencer

QUABOAG USED BOOKS
152 Main St, 01562
(508)568-2186   **13 33**
Used books, town histories, ephemera,
pamphlets, children's books, magazines & trade catalogs. *Serv:* Catalog.
Hours: Sat 10-5 BY APPT. *Assoc:*
MRIAB. Donald D Hunter

Springfield

ANTIQUARIA
60 Dartmouth St, 01109
(413)781-6927   **83**
Specializing in American Victorian antiques. *Serv:* Catalog $3, packing &
shipping. Dan Cooper

JOHNSON'S SECONDHAND
BOOKSHOP
1379 Main St, 01103
(413)732-6222   **13**
A general stock of antiquarian books,

remainders & local history. *Serv:* Search service. *Hours:* Mon-Sat 9-5:30 Thu til 9. *Assoc:* MRIAB.

TROTTING HILL PARK BOOKS
Box 1324, 01101
(413)567-6466   **13**
Antiquarian books: Americana, explorations & voyages, medicine, moutaineering, science & true crime. *Serv:* Catalog. *Hours:* Mail order only. *Assoc:* MRIAB. Barbara Verrilli

Sterling

PUDDLE DUCK ANTIQUES
1 Lake Shore Dr, 01564
(508)835-3825   **37 40 42**
Choice selection of American furniture: oak, mahogany, pine & interesting collectibles. *Hours:* BY APPT. Walt Gunderman *Park:* On site.

Stockbridge

TOM CAREY'S PLACE
Sergeant St, 01262
(413)298-3589   **23 27 50**
American clocks, 18th & 19th C country furniture, lamps, glass & unusual accessories. *Hours:* Daily BY APPT. *Assoc:* BCoADA. Lucille Nickerson *Park:* Nearby. *Loc:* Behind Mission House, off Main St.

OVERLEE FARM BOOKS
PO Box 1155, 01262
(413)637-2277   **13**
Antiquarian books: explorations & voyages, history, literature, nautical & Herman Melville. *Serv:* Catalog. *Hours:* BY APPT. *Assoc:* MRIAB. Martin Torodash

REUSS GALLERIES
Pine & Shamrock Sts, 01262
(413)298-4074   **66**
Two floors of art & antiques, specializing in Audubon & nature prints & antiques in pine, cherry & walnut in a restored 1855 house. *Serv:* Appraisal, repair. *Hours:* May-Jan daily 10-4. *Size:* Large. *CC:* MC/V. Vern Reuss *Park:* On site. *Loc:* 1 block N of Red Lion Inn.

JOHN R SANDERSON
West Main St, 01262
(413)274-6093   **13**
Select stock of rare books from the 16th C onward - including literary 1st editions, science, medicine, economics, inscribed & signed books, children's literature, art reference, travel & Americana. *Pr:* $35–1500. *Est:* 1976. *Serv:* Appraisal, catalog, purchase estates. *Hours:* Visitors welcomed by appt. *Size:* Medium. *CC:* MC/V. *Assoc:* ABAA MRIAB. *Park:* In front. *Loc:* Call for directions.

Stoneham

FRANK C KAMINSKI
193 Franklin St, 02180
(617)438-7595   **8**
Auctioneer dealing in early American & European antiques, paintings, furniture, rugs, silver, clocks, glass, porcelain, sculpture, photography, jewelry, militaria, Indian items, toys & automobiles. Historic real estate a specialty. *Est:* 1978. *Serv:* Appraisal, accept mail/phone bids, brochure, consultation, purchase estates. *Hours:* Appt suggested. *Park:* On site. *Loc:* I-93 Exit 36: Montvale Rd to R on Main, 2 blocks, L onto Franklin, 2 MI on L, 10 min from Boston.

Stoughton

WESTERN HEMISPHERE INC
144 West St, 02072
(617)344-8200   **13**
Antiquarian books: business, economics, government documents, Americana & periodicals. *Hours:* BY APPT ONLY. *Assoc:* ABAA. Eugene L Schwaab Jr

Sturbridge

THE COPPERSMITH
Main St Rte 20, 01566
(508)347-7038   **50 70**
Handcrafted lighting in copper, tin & brass, Colonial lanterns, weather vanes, chandeliers, sconces & cupolas. *Est:* 1982. *Serv:* Custom-made lighting fixtures. *Hours:* Weekends 10-5 & Mon holidays. *CC:* MC/V. *Park:* On site. *Loc:* .25 MI past Sturbridge Village entrance, opposite the Sturbridge Yankee Workshop.

THE GREEN APPLE
On the Common Rte 131, 01566
(508)347-7921   **27 34**
American folk art & country furnishings. *Est:* 1975. *Hours:* Mon-Sat 10-9 Sun 10-6. *CC:* MC/V. Elaine Cook *Park:* In front. *Loc:* Next door to the Publick house.

R "N" G ANTIQUES & COLLECTIBLES
Rte 131, 01566
(508)347-2245   **{GR}**
Furniture, glass, country, linens, dolls, toys, china & silver. *Hours:* Thu-Tue

11-5:30. Richard George *Loc:* On-the-Common next to the Publik House, .25 MI from Rte 20.

STURBRIDGE ANTIQUE SHOPS
200 Charlton Rd Rte 20, 01566
(508)347-2744   **{GR75}**
Furniture, decorative accessories, glass, china & porcelain. *Hours:* Mon-Fri 9-5 Sat,Sun 10-5. *CC:* MC/V. Robert Hopfe *Park:* On site. *Loc:* 6 MI E of Brimfield & 2 MI E of Old Sturbridge Village & .5 MI E of I-84 & I-90.

YESTERDAYS ANTIQUE CENTER
Rte 20, 01566
(508)347-9339   **{GR45}**
Furniture & decorative accessories. *Hours:* Daily 10-5. Ken Boland *Park:* On site. *Loc:* Located in the heart of Sturbridge, 200 yds from Old Sturbridge Village.

Sudbury

ADAMS ANTIQUES USA
361 Boston Post Rd, 01776
(508)443-8756   **27 42 43**
Direct importers of 18th & 19th C pine furniture & decorative items from all parts of the United Kingdom, Ireland, Scandinavia & Austria featuring fine quality armoires, dressers, cupboards, chiffoniers, tables, chairs & mirrors. *Pr:* $50–3000. *Hours:* Daily 10-5 Sun 12-5 CLOSED MON. *Size:* Medium. *CC:* MC/V. Peter H Bissett *Park:* On site. *Loc:* On Rte 20 in Sudbury.

THE ANTIQUE EXCHANGE OF SUDBURY
236 Concord Rd, 01776
(508)443-8175　　　**29 44 63**

Armoires, Royal Doulton, Shaker, Dresden, steins, Wedgwood, majolica, 18th & 19th C porcelains, Oriental items, Oriental rugs, mirrors, cut glass, silver, Staffordshire, flow blue, Minton, prints & frames, decoys & tapestries. *Est:* 1987. *Serv:* Appraisal, restoration, consignments accepted. *Hours:* Tue-Sat 10:30-5 Sun 12-5. *Size:* Large. Jeanie Quirk *Park:* On site. *Loc:* .5 MI S of Rte 27.

FARMHOUSE COLLECTIBLES
170 Hudson Rd, 01776
(508)443-6593　　　**1 29 27**

In a converted old barn - vintage home accessories, furniture, clothing & jewelry. *Est:* 1986. *Hours:* Wed-Sat 10-4 Sun 12-4, CLOSED JUL. *Size:* Medium. Jane Bramberg *Park:* In front. *Loc:* Rte 20 in Wayland,to Rte 27 N to Sudbury Ctr, straight to Hudson, 1 MI on R.

MAGGIE FLOOD
357 Boston Post Rd, 01776
(508)443-7324　　　**85**

Romantic dresses created from antique fabrics & laces & an assortment of folk art. *Pr:* $20–1000. *Est:* 1985. *Serv:* Dresses to order. *Hours:* Wed,Thu 12-8 Fri,Sat 10-5:30. *CC:* AX/MC/V. *Park:* On site. *Loc:* From the Wayside Inn, E on Rte 20 for 5 MI.

Sunderland

RICHARD E OINONEN
9 School St, 01375
(413)665-3253　　　**13**

A general stock of antiquarian books. *Serv:* Periodic book auctions, appraisal, catalog, mailing list. *Assoc:* MRIAB.

SALT BOX ANTIQUES
168 N Main St, 01375
(413)665-2421　　　**65**

18th C country primitives, iron, hardware & doors. *Hours:* BY APPT. Dan Fleming

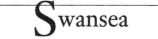

Swansea

AMERICAN ART & ANTIQUES, INC
11 Maiden Ln, 02777
(508)678-9563　　　**59 66 71**

A diverse inventory of American paintings from early 19th to mid 20th C. *Pr:* $500–50000. *Serv:* Conservation, restoration. *Hours:* BY APPT. Mel Davey *Park:* On site. *Loc:* I-95, 15 min from Fall River, or Providence, call for directions.

FERGUSON & D'ARRUDA
1 Main St, 02777
(508)674-9186　　　**5 36**

Diverse line of furniture, textiles, architectural elements & garden accessories. *Hours:* By chance/appt. *Assoc:* NHADA. *Loc:* 5 min from I-95.

Taunton

JO-ANN E ROSS
1679 Somerset Ave Rte 138, 02780
(508)824-8255   **34 59**

Folk art paintings, country period furniture & lampshades. *Serv:* Design lampshades. *Hours:* BY APPT. *Assoc:* SADA.

Templeton

1800 HOUSE ANTIQUES, LTD
Templeton, 01468
(508)939-8073   **27 44 63**

Small country antiques attractively displayed in a bright new shop - part of a large, yellow, restored Federal farmhouse. Companion barn loft offers furniture in the rough & collectibles. *Pr:* $10–2000. *Est:* 1986. *Hours:* Daily 10-5, CLOSED Thanksgiving, Christmas, New Year's Day. June Poland *Park:* On site. *Loc:* Rte 2 Petersham Exit: Proceed toward Petersham, go L at Rte 101 toward Templeton, approx 6 MI, yellow Federal house on L.

CHETWOOD ANTIQUES
Rte 2A, 01468
(508)939-8641

Victorian, early primitive, custom & formal antiques. *Hours:* Wed-Sat 9-5 & BY APPT.

WRIGHT TAVERN ANTIQUES
The Common, 01468
(508)939-8879   **16 27 50**

Country furniture, primitives, brass, iron, tin, wooden accessories & lighting of kerosene era. *Hours:* Year round by chance/appt. *Assoc:* PVADA. George Pushee *Loc:* Next to the library.

Townsend

MARTHA BOYNTON ANTIQUES
1 Greeley Rd, 01469
(508)597-6794   **41**

Furniture in original paint, doorstops & a bit of everything. *Hours:* By chance/appt. *Loc:* Corner Rte 119 & Greeley Rd.

THE COUNTRY GENTLEMAN
354 Main St, 01469
(508)597-5566 **36 44 63**

Collectibles, furniture, glassware & china. *Hours:* Wed-Mon 10-5. Richard Aghababian *Loc:* On Rte 119.

FRANK J TAMMARO
11 Brookline St, 01469
(508)597-8044 **36**

17th, 18th & 19th C furniture & accessories. *Hours:* Daily by chance/appt. *Loc:* 4.4 MI S of NH at Jct of Rte 13N & 119, at N end of town common.

Townsend Harbor

THE GRIST MILL ANTIQUES
2 South St & Rte 119, 01469
(508)597-2025

Specializing in late 18th & early 19th C American country antiques in original condition. *Hours:* Daily 10-5 Sun 1-5. Gwen Bentley

HARBORSIDE ANTIQUES
Rte 119 & Spaulding St, 01469
(508)597-8558 **{GR14}**

New stock daily from private homes. *Hours:* Wed-Sun 10-5. *Loc:* I-495 to Rte 119.

Upton

DAVID ROSE ANTIQUES
36 W Main St, 01568
(508)529-3838 **1 29 36**

American furniture of the 18th & 19th C, appropriate smalls & paintings. Trade inquiries invited. *Serv:* Purchase estates. *Hours:* Daily 10-5, call ahead. *Size:* Medium. *CC:* MC/V. *Assoc:*

NTHP SADA. *Park:* In front. *Loc:* 495 Exit 21B: 4 MI to Rte 140, R on 140, approx 1 MI on L.

Vineyard Haven

EARLY SPRING FARM ANTIQUES
93 Lagoon Pond Rd, 02568
(508)693-9141 **34 36 65**

18th & 19th C country furniture, quilts, hooked rugs, folk art, iron, copper, woodenware & children's items. *Pr:* $5-3000. *Serv:* Brochure, consultation, some restoration. *Hours:* Jun-Oct 15 Mon-Sun 10-4 Sat 2-5 CLOSED WED else Mon-Sun 10-4. Allen Hanson *Park:* On site. *Loc:* Boat to Vineyard Haven, Lagoon Pond Rd at 5 Corners to Hine's Point, on R.

Waban

ANTIQUE RESEARCHERS
PO Box 79, 02168
(617)969-6238 **26**

Quality antique research on the provenance & genealogy of one item or a collection. *Hours:* BY APPT, call after 7:30 weekday evenings.

PRIPET HOUSE ANTIQUE PRINTS
PO Box 90, 02168
(617)235-7557 **66**

A fine collection featuring natural history prints with decorative french mats & museum standard framing. *Est:* 1984. *Hours:* BY APPT. Elizabeth King

DIANA J RENDELL, INC
177 Collins Rd, 02168
(617)969-1774   **9 13**
Antiquarian bookseller featuring autograph letters, manuscripts, antiquities & illuminated pages. *Hours:* BY APPT ONLY. *Assoc:* ABAA.

Waltham

HAROLD M BURSTEIN & CO
36 Riverside Dr, 02154
(617)893-7494   **13 33 66**
Antiquarian books: Rare & scholarly Americana, bibliography & reference, literary first editions, juveniles, fine prints & graphics. *Serv:* Appraisal, catalog, search service. *Hours:* BY APPT. *Assoc:* ABAA MRIAB. Eunice K Burstein

FIREMATIC SPECIALTIES
148 Overland Rd Unit 2-8, 02154
(617)647-5820   **8**
Specializing in firefighting antiques & related items exclusively. Unique, hard-to-find firefighting items a specialty. *Pr:* $25–2500. *Serv:* Appraisal, auction, brochure, consultation, purchase estates. *Hours:* BY APPT ONLY. Paul Klaver

MISTER BIG TOYLAND
399 Moody St, 02154
(617)893-8582   **32**
A collection of very special toys, dolls & baseball cards. *Hours:* Mon-Sat 10-5. Mrs Sandberg

RESTORATION SERVICES
621 Main St #3, 02154
(617)647-7865   **25 71**
Highest quality conservation & invisible restoration of antiques - specializ-

ing in porcelain, glass & lacquer, as well as pottery gold leaf, sculpture & ivory - the full range of objets d'art. *Serv:* Conservation, restoration. *Hours:* Mon-Fri 7:30-5 appt suggested. *Assoc:* AIC NECA. Neil Dale *Park:* Nearby lot. *Loc:* Directly across from Waltham City Hall on Main St (Rte 20).

SPNEA CONSERVATION CENTER
Lyman Estate 185 Lyman St, 02154
(617)891-1985   **25 26 74**
Preservation plans for architectural preservation & furniture restoration. Archival collection of photographs, prints, architectural drawings, advertising matter, manuscripts & other documentation. *Est:* 1972. *Serv:* Analytical research, conservation services, refinishing, reproduction. *Hours:* By appt. *Park:* On site. *Loc:* .5 MI off Rte 20.

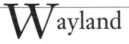

Wayland

GREAT MEADOWS JOINERY
Box 392, 01778
(508)358-4370   **19 43 70**
Creating & designing Shaker & American country furniture reproductions, selecting the finest examples of the genre. Repetoire prominently features Shaker designs. *Pr:* $800–5000. *Est:* 1986. *Serv:* Catalog $2, custom woodwork, reproduction. *Hours:* Year round daily 9-5 BY APPT. *Size:* Medium. Gene Cosloy *Park:* On site. *Loc:* 5 min from Wayland Ctr, call for specific directions.

WAYLAND ANTIQUE EXCHANGE
303A Boston Post Rd, 01778
(508)358-7452
Consignment shop offering old & antique furniture, rugs, oils, china, glass, jewelry & toys. *Hours:* Tue-Sat 10-4. *Assoc:* SADA. Ruth Newell *Loc:* Wayland Village.

YANKEE CRAFTSMAN
357 Commonwealth Rd Rte 30, 01778
(508)653-0031   **36 50 71**
Antique lighting & furniture, featuring one of the country's most extensive collections of antique lighting fixtures. *Est:* 1968. *Serv:* Appraisal, consultation, restoration, repair. *Hours:* Year round daily 10-5. *Assoc:* NEAA SADA. Bill Sweeney *Loc:* Near The Villa.

Wellesley

EUROPEAN MANOR
566 Washington St, 02181
(617)235-8660   **38 80**
European furniture, French Provencal cottons, handpainted marbleized papers, ceramics & accessories. *Serv:* Custom fabrication.

MARCUS & MARSHALL ANTIQUES
184 Worcester Rd Rte 9, 02181
(617)239-0611   **38 66**
Three floors of European furniture & accessories. One of the largest collections of botanical prints in the Boston area, custom dried flower arranging. *Pr:* $50–10000. *Serv:* Framing, furniture painting. *Hours:* Mon-Sat 10-5, CLOSED last 2 weeks of AUG. *Size:* Large. *CC:* MC/V. Beth Marcus *Park:* On site. *Loc:* Rte 128 Exit Rte 9W: 2nd

Cedar St Exit (Needham/Dover), bear R, over bridge, 1st L at light, on R next to "The Wok".

LINDA RICKLES INTERIORS INC
277 Linden St, 02181
(617)237-6262   **29 58**
Objets d'art & accessories. *Hours:* Mon-Sat 9-5 Wed 9-9.

SPIVACK'S ANTIQUES
54 Washington St, 02181
(617)235-1700   **29 37 39**
One of New England oldest & largest shops, direct importers of European furniture & accessories. Also carry American furniture & accessories. *Pr:* $25–2500. *Hours:* Mon-Fri 8:30-5:30 Wed 8:30-9. *Size:* Huge. *CC:* AX/MC/V. *Park:* On site. *Loc:* I-90 to Rte 128S to Rte 16, .5 MI on Rte 16 to Washington St, on the L.

D B STOCK PERSIAN CARPETS
555 Washington St, 02181
(617)237-5859   **21**
Specializing in selected antique & old Oriental carpets. *Pr:* $2000–40000. *Serv:* Appraisal, purchase estates, repairs, restoration. *Hours:* Sep-Jun 14 Wed-Sat 11-5, Jun 15-Aug by chance/appt. *Size:* Medium. *Park:* In front. *Loc:* I-90, Rte 128S to Rte 16W, in Wellesley Sq, past Town Hall.

TERRAMEDIA BOOKS
19 Homestead Rd, 02181
(617)237-6485   **13**
Antiquarian books: travel & exploration, Africa, Asia, Americana, natural history, art & architecture, sporting, literature & science. *Serv:* Appraisal, catalog, search service. *Hours:* BY APPT. *Assoc:* MRIAB. Elias N Saad

Wellesley Hills

COUNTRY INTERIORS
402 Washington St Rte 16, 02181
(617)237-9340   **36 63 67**

Two rooms filled with country pine furniture & decorative accessories, carefully arranged. Specializing in American furniture, old lamps with pierced & cut shades, quilts, majolica & folk art. *Serv:* Interior design. *Hours:* Tue-Fri 11-4 Sat 12-4. CLOSED AUG. *Size:* Medium. *CC:* MC/V. *Assoc:* SADA. Virginia Fernald *Park:* On site. *Loc:* On Rte 16, off Rt 9.

ERNEST S KRAMER FINE ARTS
PO Box 37, 02181
(617)237-3635   **59 66**

Quality oils, watercolors & prints. *Hours:* BY APPT.

LACES UNLIMITED
339 Washington St, 02181
(617)235-6812   **48**

Imported laces: valances, tablecloths, panels, curtains & spreads. *Hours:* Mon-Sat 10-5. *Park:* Nearby. *Loc:* In the Wellesley Hills train depot.

Wellfleet

THE FARMHOUSE
RR 2 & Village Ln, 02667
(508)349-1708   **{GR6}**

Antique & collectible ephemera, oak, pine, glass, china, early American objects of all kinds & paintings. *Pr:* $1–5000. *Est:* 1988. *Serv:* Purchase estates. *Hours:* Daily 10-6. *Size:*

Large. *CC:* AX/MC/V. *Park:* On site. *Loc:* 5 MI N of Orleans Rotary, Rte 6, Opposite Wellfleet Drive-In.

MORTAR & PESTLE ANTIQUES
Rte 6, 02667
(508)349-2574   **27 42 72**

Country furniture & accessories, pine, cherry, mortar & pestles, pharmacy items, microscopes & decoys. *Hours:* May-Sep daily 10-6. *Assoc:* CCADA. Larry Keane *Park:* In front. *Loc:* Next to Bay Sails.

H B & DOROTHY WATSON
17 School St, 02667
(508)349-9207   **47 50 63**

Antique & estate jewelry, lamps, silver, small furniture, porcelain & glass. *Serv:* Estate liquidation & appraisal. *Hours:* Mon-Fri 10-5 & BY APPT. *Assoc:* CCADA NEAA. *Park:* In front. *Loc:* Off Rte 6 at Yum Yum Tree traffic lights.

Wellfleet Ctr

FINDERS KEEPERS
Briar Ln, 02667
(508)349-7627   **50 83**

Period, Victorian & second-hand furniture & lighting. *Hours:* Fri-Mon 10-5 & BY APPT.

Wenham

FIREHOUSE ANTIQUES
148 Main St Rte 1A, 01984
(508)468-9532   **36**

Fine furniture & antiques, including the largest selection of brass & iron beds in New England. *Hours:* Daily 10-5.

HENDERSON'S
300 At Main St, 01984
(508)468-4245 **29 63 77**
Furniture, accessories, silver & Oriental porcelains. *Hours:* Mon-Sat 9-5:30 Sun by chance.

West Barnstable

BARNSTABLE STOVE SHOP
Rte 149, 02668
(508)362-9913 **74**
Several hundred stoves in stock - genuine Victorian ranges & parlor stoves, ranging from 1850s-1940s. *Serv:* Parts inventory, brochure $1, restoration. *Hours:* Year round.

THE CLOCK SHELF
1549 Rte 6A, 02668
(508)362-3577 **23**
18th-20th C American, German & Austrian clocks. *Hours:* Year round weekdays 10-4. *Assoc:* CCADA.

LUDWIG'S ANTIQUES
1595 Main St, 02668
(508)362-2791 **27**
18th & 19th C English & American furniture, pottery & Staffordshire. *Hours:* Year round.

PACKET LANDING IRON
1022 Rte 6A, 02668
(508)362-2697 **70**
Handmade reproductions of 18th C wrought iron lamps. *Hours:* Tue-Sun 11-5. *Loc:* Between Rtes 132 & 149.

SALT & CHESTNUT
WEATHERVANES
651 Rte 6A at Maple St, 02668
(508)362-6085 **5 74 87**
Exclusively devoted to weather vanes -

antique & new, miniature replicas. *Pr:* $200–30000. *Est:* 1978. *Serv:* Appraisal, catalog ($2), consultation, repairs, restoration, replication. *Hours:* Mon-Sat 11-5 CLOSED Tue Sun BY APPT. *CC:* MC/V. *Assoc:* CCADA NTHP SPNEA. Marilyn Strauss *Park:* On site. *Loc:* Rte 6A, .5 MI past Int of Rtes 6A & 149.

THE WHIPPLETREE
660 Main St Rte 6A, 02668
(508)362-3320 **27 34 81**
A 200 year-old barn with country, folk art, tools & linen. *Hours:* Jun-Dec daily 10-5, Jan-May Wed-Sat 10-5. *Assoc:* CCADA. Merrill Davis

West Boylston

A & G ANTIQUES
277 W Boylston St, 01583
(508)835-4945 **{GR20}**
Furniture, jewelry, art & collectibles. *Hours:* Tue-Sat 11-5 Sun 1-5. Ann Gardner *Loc:* On Rte 12.

THE DEACONS BENCH
18 N Main St Rte 140, 01583
(508)835-3858 **{GR16}**
Furniture, art, stoneware, tools, pottery, glass, china, prints, lamps, linens, jewelry & reference books. *Hours:* Daily 11-5 CLOSED WED. *Size:* Large. Cynthia A Secord

OBADIAH PINE ANTIQUES
160 W Boylston St Rte 12, 01583
(508)835-4656 **23 27 40**
Country furniture, oak, walnut, baskets, lamps, clocks, jewelry & glass. *Hours:* By chance/appt. Linda Toppin

PUDDLE DUCK ANTIQUES
9 Maple St Rte 140, 01583
(508)835-3825   **37 40**

American furniture, including oak & mahogany. *Est:* 1982. *Hours:* Tue-Sun 10-5. Walt Gunderman *Loc:* .25 MI from Int of Rtes 12 & 140 at Parker's Barn.

THE ROSE COTTAGE
24 Worcester St Rtes 12 & 140, 01583
(508)835-4034   **{GR8}**

A turn of the century barn featuring primitives, toys, Black memorabilia, costume & fine jewelry, linens, large & small furniture, collectibles & some reproduction pieces. *Pr:* $1–1000. *Est:* 1970. *Serv:* Purchase estates, repairs, restoration. *Hours:* Apr-Feb Tue-Sun 11-5, Mar Fri-Sun 11-5. Loretta Kittredge *Park:* On site. *Loc:* I-90, 495N to Rte 290 to Rte 140N.

YANKEE HERITAGE ANTIQUES
44 Sterling St Rtes 12-110, 01583
(508)835-2010   **36 44**

Collectibles, furniture & glass specializing in oak. *Serv:* Purchase estates. *Hours:* Mon-Fri 9:30-5:30 Sun 9-6. Rod Reams

West Brewster

SENTIMENTAL JOURNEY
424 Main St, 02631
(508)385-6388   **44 47 65**

Quality period & turn-of-the-century furniture, glassware, unusual & unique collectibles, country items, primitives, clocks & jewelry. *Hours:* Apr-Nov Daily 11-5 & BY APPT. *Assoc:* CCADA. Linda Cadarette

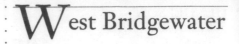

West Bridgewater

SHUTE AUCTION GALLERY
50 Turnpike St, 02379
(508)588-0022   **4 8**

Liquidation of estates & fine antiques. *Serv:* Auction, appraisal. *Assoc:* SSADA. Philip C Shute

WILLOWBROOK
Rte 106, 02379
(508)580-1019   **36**

Fine quality formal furniture & accessories for discriminating tastes. *Serv:* Interior design. *Hours:* Daily 10-5 Sun 12-5, CLOSED MON.

West Brookfield

BOOK BEAR
W Main St Rte 9, 01585
(508)867-8705   **13**

A general stock of antiquarian books: psychology, anthropology, military, religion, theology & technology. *Serv:* Appraisal, catalog. *Hours:* Wed-Sun 10-6. *Assoc:* MRIAB. Al Navitski

West Chatham

1736 HOUSE ANTIQUES
1731 Main St, 02669
(508)945-5690   **41 42**

Large inventory of cupboards, chests, primitives, old paint, old pine cupboards, trunks & dressers. *Hours:* May-Dec daily 10-5. *Assoc:* CCADA. John Miller *Loc:* On Rte 28.

West Chesterfield

TIMOTHY GORHAM, CABINET MAKER
1 Ireland St, 01084
(413)296-4061   **19**
One-man shop specializing in reproductions using traditional joinery & methods. Casework, tables, chairs, turnings & carving made from air-dried native woods including tiger maple, cherry, walnut & pine. *Pr:* $300–5000. *Est:* 1980. *Serv:* Custom woodwork, repairs, reproduction, restoration. *Hours:* Most days. *Loc:* In West Chesterfield at the corner of Rte 143 & Ireland St.

SUSAN K RILEY, SEAT WEAVER
1 Ireland St, 01084
(413)296-4061   **68 70 71**
Specializing in natural rush seat replacement - also splint & fiber. *Hours:* By chance/appt.

TEXTILE REPRODUCTIONS
666 Worthington Rd, 01084
(413)296-4437   **46 57 74**
Goods for 18th & 19th C textile furnishings, needlework & clothing reproductions. Wide assortment of fabrics, threads, tapes, hardware & other supplies for replicating textile goods. Finished goods also available. *Est:* 1983. *Serv:* Catalog ($3/$12), minor conservation, consultation, interior design, repair. *Hours:* BY APPT ONLY. *CC:* MC/V. *Assoc:* NTHP SPNEA. Kathleen Smith

West Dennis

RUMFORD ANTIQUES
218 Main St, 02670
(508)394-3683   **44 50**
Depression & pressed pattern glass, oil lamps & books on antiques. *Serv:* Appraisal, textile conservation. *Hours:* Summer daily 10-5. *Assoc:* CCADA. Edna F Anness

West Falmouth

APROPOS
636 Rte 28A, 02574
(508)457-0045
18th-20th C American & English furniture & accessories attractively displayed in our cottage buildings.. *Hours:* Daily, CLOSED TUE WED in winter.

VILLAGE BARN ANTIQUE COOP
606 Rte 28A, 02574
(508)540-3215   **{GR8}**
American & European antiques in a Cape Cod barn. *Hours:* Daily 10-5. *Loc:* Next to the Ideal Spot Motel.

West Granville

IVES HILL ANTIQUES
Ives Hill Main Rd Rte 57, 01034
(413)357-8703   **37 67**
Large barn showroom nestled in the Berkshire hills featuring American country & period furnishings & accessories. *Pr:* $25–6000. *Hours:* May-Oct Wed-Sun 10-5, else BY APPT. *Size:* Medium. *CC:* MC/V. Dee Bates *Park:* On site. *Loc:* 1 MI W of West Gran-

ville Ctr, on Rte 57 opposite the Granville State Forest Rd. 13 MI W of Westfield.

West Harwich

RALPH DIAMOND ANTIQUES
103 Main St Rte 28, 02671
(508)432-0634   **59**
Specializing in 19th & early 20th C American oil & watercolor paintings. *Hours:* BY APPT. *Assoc:* CCADA.

HOOKED RUG RESTORATION
11 North Rd Professional Ctr, 02671
(508)432-0897   **71**
Restoration of hooked rugs done with expert care. *Serv:* Conservation, consultation. *Hours:* Year round BY APPT ONLY. *Size:* Medium. *Assoc:* AIC. Charles J Quigley *Park:* On site. *Loc:* 1 MI E of Dennisport on Rte 128, 2nd 3-story building on L after Bishops Terrace Restaurant.

West Newbury

HELIGE ANDE ARTS
85 Church St, 01985
(508)363-2253   **26 46 71**
19th C decorative arts techniques, both custom & restoration work, early paint matching in restoration a specialty. Painting techniques include: stenciling, graining, marbleizing, wall glazing & dragging & reverse painting on glass. *Serv:* Consultation, interior design, restoration. *Hours:* BY APPT. Ingrid Sanborn *Park:* On site. *Loc:* I-95N Exit Rte 113 (Newburyport/W Newburyport): W 5 MI to ctr of West Newbury, R on Church St.

MOODY-RIDGEWAY HOUSE
803 Main St, 01985
(508)465-8046   **13 51 66**
Books, maps & prints. *Hours:* BY APPT ONLY. *Assoc:* NSADA.

VALYOU AUCTIONS
PO Box 132, 01985
(508)363-2946   **8**
Country consignment auction almost every Wednesday. *Est:* 1973. *Serv:* Consultation, purchase estates. *Hours:* BY APPT. *CC:* MC/V. *Assoc:* MSAA NAA. LeRoy N Valyou *Park:* On site. *Loc:* 495 Exit 53 (Broad St): N .25 MI to Horizons Function Hall in Merrimac.

West Newton

AUCTION INDEX INC
30 Valentine Pk, 02165
(617)964-2876   **26**
Publisher's of Leonard's Price Index of Art Auctions. Susan Theran

ON CONSIGNMENT GALLERIES
1276 Washington Avenue, 02165
(617)965-6131
Furniture, china, sterling, jewelry, lamps, mirrors, chandeliers, glass, objets d'art, pottery, bronzes, copper & brass. *Serv:* Accept consignments. *Hours:* Mon-Sat 9:15-5 Fri til 9. *CC:* MC/V.

West Stockbridge

DOROTHY ELSBERG BOOKS
PO Box 178, 01266
(413)232-8560   **13 55**
Music & sheet music. *Serv:* Catalog.
Hours: Mail order only. *Assoc:*
MRIAB.

SAWYER ANTIQUES
Shaker Mill Depot St, 01266
(413)232-7062   **37**
Early American furniture & accessories - formal, Shaker & country. *Serv:*
Appraisal. *Hours:* Fri-Sun 10-5 BY
APPT. *Assoc:* ASA BCoADA. Edward
S Sawyer *Park:* On site.

West Townsend

ANTIQUE ASSOC AT WEST TOWNSEND
473 Main St, 01474
(508)597-8084   **{MDS80}**
Eighty quality dealers specializing in
Americana, period, country & formal
furniture, decorative arts & accessories
displayed in an 18th C Colonial house.
Pr: $25–25000. *Est:* 1984. *Serv:* Ship
worldwide, 800# ="1(800)562-SALE",
financing available. *Hours:* Daily 10-5.
Size: Large. *CC:* MC/V. Lynne C Hillier *Park:* On site. *Loc:* On Rte 119 in
West Townsend.

ANTIQUE ASSOC AT JOSLIN TAVERN
519 Main St, 01474
(508)597-2330   **{MDS80}**
Fine antiques & Americana displayed
in a colonial tavern by more than 90
carefully-selected, quality dealers. *Pr:*
$25–25,000. *Est:* 1987. *Serv:* Ship

worldwide, 800# = "1(800)562-
SOLD", financing available. *Hours:*
Daily 10-5. *Size:* Large. *CC:* MC/V.
Park: In front. *Loc:* In a historic grey
& white tavern on Rte 119 W of Antique Associates at West Townsend.

JOHN & BARBARA DELANEY CLOCKS
435 Main St, 01474
(508)597-2231   **23 26 37**
Largest collection of American tall
case clocks for sale in the country. *Pr:*
$500–250000. *Serv:* Auction, consultation, purchase estates. *Hours:* Sat-Sun 9-5 Mon-Fri by chance/appt.
Size: Medium. *Park:* On site. *Loc:* On
Rte 119, 50 MI W of Boston.

GARY SULLIVAN ANTIQUES
435 Main St, 01474
(508)597-2680   **37**
Specializing in American furniture of
the Federal period, with emphasis on
formal furniture, at affordable prices
for collectors & dealers. *Hours:* Sat-Sun 10-5 weekdays by chance/appt.
Assoc: SADA. *Park:* On site. *Loc:* Next
to John Delaney.

Westborough

THE BAYBERRYSHOP ANTIQUES
114 W Main St Rte 30, 01581
(508)366-2554   **32 65**
Toys & primitives. *Hours:* Apr-Dec
Thu 10-4 CLOSED JUL.

MAYNARD HOUSE
11 Maynard St, 01581
(508)366-2073   **27 43**
Country shop featuring cupboards, tables, baskets, herb loft & exclusive line

of upholstered country sofas & wing chairs representing 1750-1820. *Serv:* Catalog. *Hours:* Thu-Sun 10-5 BY APPT. *Assoc:* SADA. Betty Urquhart *Loc:* Off Rte 135.

OLD SCHOOLHOUSE
ANTIQUES
196 E Main St Rte 30, 01581
(508)366-1752   **16 27 65**
Country furniture, primitives, decorative items in brass, copper & tin. *Hours:* Year round. *Assoc:* SADA. Doris A Dall

PUSHCART PLACE
86 E Main St, 01581
(508)366-6116   **34 50 63**
Folk art, pottery, lamps, tin, iron & old tools displayed in pushcarts & stalls. *Hours:* Daily 10-5:30 Thu til 8. *Assoc:* SADA. Bunnie Cummings *Loc:* Rte 30 at Water St near Rte 9.

SALT-BOX HOUSE ANTIQUES
9 Maynard St, 01581
(508)366-4951   **27 41**
Early, painted country furniture & accessories, cupboards & a full line of custom upholstered sofa & wing chairs. *Serv:* Reproduction. *Hours:* Thu-Sun 10-5 or BY APPT. *Assoc:* SADA. Margaret M Gure *Loc:* I-495 Exit 23B: W to Rte 9W to Rte 135E, R on Rte 135, 3rd R.

Westfield

ANTIQUE MARKETPLACE
One Broad St, 01085
(413)562-9562   **{GR68}**
Three floors of antiques & collectibles located in a unique, restored post office, ca 1912. *Est:* 1986. *Serv:* Ap-

praisal, purchase estates. *Hours:* Daily 10-5 Sun 12-5. *Size:* Huge. *CC:* MC/V. Paul R Tuller *Park:* On site. *Loc:* I-90 Exit 3: 18 MI S of Northampton, located at Jct of Rtes 10-202 & 20.

Westford

ANTIQUES ORCHARD
83 Boston Rd, 01886
(508)692-7161   **{GR50}**
Furniture, toys, clocks, export porcelain, linens & accessories on 2 floors. *Hours:* Daily 10-5 Sun 11-5. *Assoc:* SADA. Sally Cady *Loc:* Rte 495 Exit 32.

WESTFORD VALLEY
ANTIQUES
434 Littleton Rd, 01886
(508)486-4023   **{GR}**
Country, Victorian & period furniture, paintings, brass, copper, sterling & jewelry. *Hours:* Daily 10-4:30 CLOSED MON.

Weston

JANE CHORAS, BOOKS
225 Winter St, 02193
(617)237-9828   **13 33**
Antiquarian books: children's, ephemera, first editions, illustrated, science fiction & fantasy. *Serv:* Search service. *Hours:* BY APPT. *Assoc:* MRIAB.

HOLLYDAY HOUSE
55 Chestnut St, 02193
(617)894-4361   **29 59 74**
Consultants in 18th C period rooms, specializing in early bed hangings & interior wood paneling. Computerized database on early wood panelling

sites. Carrying antiques, accessories & paintings. *Est:* 1986. *Serv:* Consulting on non-structural aspects of 18th C homes. *Hours:* BY APPT. Thomas Hollyday *Loc:* Call for directions.

M & S RARE BOOKS, INC
45 Colpitts Rd, 02193
(617)891-5650   **9 13**

Antiquarian books: American literature, Americana, broadsides & posters, first editions, history of science, Judaica, medicine, philosophy, Western Americana & Black history. *Serv:* Appraisal, catalog. *Hours:* BY APPT. *Assoc:* ABAA MRIAB. Daniel G Siegel

Westport

WING CARRIAGE HOUSE
1151 Main Rd, 02790
(508)636-2585   **{GR3}**

Fine antique & estate jewelry & carefully chosen selection of furnishings including primitives, quilts & silver. *Est:* 1971. *Serv:* Purchase estates. *Hours:* Jan-May Wed-Sat 12-5, Jun-Dec Mon-Sat 12-5. *CC:* MC/V. F Travis *Park:* In front. *Loc:* 195 to Rte 88, L at Hixbridge Rd & L onto Main Rd.

Westwood

THE APPRAISERS' REGISTRY
Box 261, 02090
(617)329-4680

Appraisals of fine arts, jewelry, rare books, guns, Asian art, coins & stamps for insurance & estates purposes. *Est:*

1979. *Serv:* Photographic inventories. *Hours:* Mon-Sat BY APPT. Michael F Wynne-Willson

GABRIEL'S AUCTION CO INC.
PO Box 390, 02090
(617)329-7484

Estate, antique, and consignment auctions 10% buyer's premium. *Serv:* Appraisal. *Assoc:* CAI NEAA. Evan N Gavrilles

PEG WILLIS ANTIQUES
117 Oak St, 02090
(617)762-6684   **36 56 67**

American antiques for country or townhouse, furniture, Dedham & Dorchester pottery, hooked rugs, quilts, Indian & nautical items - always a good supply of items for decorators. *Serv:* Purchase estates. *Hours:* BY APPT. *Assoc:* SADA. *Loc:* Turn Off Rte 109 at Pond St then 1 MI to Oak St.

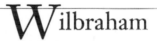

Wilbraham

MURRAY BOOKS
473 & 477 Main St, 01095
(413)596-9372   **13 33 66**

Stock of old & rare books for collectors & dealers & ephemera of all sorts. *Serv:* Appraisal, purchase estates. *Hours:* BY APPT ONLY. *Size:* Medium. *Assoc:* ABAA MRIAB. Paul M Murray *Park:* On site. *Loc:* 8 MI E of Springfield, 2 MI S of N Wilbraham on 20, phone for directions.

Williamsburg

COUNTRY FINE ANTIQUES
25 South St, 01096
(413)268-3298   **36 42 65**
Changing stock of 18th & 19th C country primitives & accessories, including some textiles, some finer quality pieces of the period, pine furniture with painted & unpainted woods. *Pr:* $25–500. *Est:* 1986. *Serv:* Appraisal, consultation, interior design. *Hours:* Sat-Sun 12-5:30 Thu,Fri by chance/appt. Susan Netto *Park:* In front. *Loc:* In Williamsburg, turn at Williamsburg General Store onto South St, .25 MI on L.

GEORGE THOMAS LEWIS
78 Old Goshen Rd, 01096
(413)268-7513   **4 8**
Estate appraisers & liquidators. *Assoc:* NEAA.

Williamstown

CARRIAGE BARN BOOKS
839 Cold Spring Rd, 01267
(413)458-5534   **13**
Antiquarian books - scholarly, quaint & rare - subjects include: Americana, New England, social sciences, the arts & children's. *Serv:* Appraisal, catalog, search service. *Hours:* Jun-Oct Mon-Sat 10-5 & by appt, Nov-May by appt only. *Assoc:* MRIAB. Martha Mercer

COLLECTORS WAREHOUSE
105 North St, 01267
(413)458-9686
A general line of antiques & collectibles. *Est:* 1985. *Hours:* Wed-Sat 12-5.

CC: MC/V. *Park:* On site. *Loc:* Off Rte 7 next to Le Country Restaurant in the Mc Clelland Press Building.

COUNTRY PEDLAR ANTIQUES
1 Main St, 01267
(413)458-5566   **{GR15}**
Sterling silver flatware, jewelry, stained glass, furniture, rugs, china, vintage clothing, porcelain, dolls & crystal. *Est:* 1953. *Serv:* Doll repair. *Hours:* Mon-Sat 9-5 Sun 11-5. *Size:* Huge. *CC:* AX/MC/V. Sanford Plumb *Park:* On site. *Loc:* On Rte 2 E of Williamstown/North Adams town line.

LIBRARY ANTIQUES
70 Spring St, 01267
(413)458-3436   **29 36**
Furniture & decorative accessories. *Est:* 1986. *Hours:* Mon-Sat 10-5 Sun BY APPT. *CC:* MC/V. *Park:* Nearby. *Loc:* 2 doors from the post office.

SETH NEMEROFF, ANTIQUARIAN BOOKS
35 Spring St 2nd fl, 01267
(413)458-9212   **13**
Antiquarian books - scholarly & general - classical & medieval studies, Oriental studies, art history & theory, philosophy, theology, science, folklore, psychoanalysis, music, travel, illustrated books & selected objets d'art. *Serv:* Appraisal, catalog, search service. *Hours:* Thu-Sun 9-3 by chance APPT STRONGLY SUGGESTED. *Assoc:* MRIAB.

Winchester

ACQUIS LTD
7 Stratford Rd, 01890
(617)729-3576   **26 74**

Consultants to the trade & private individuals, offering personalized search & buying service, dealing with highly reputable dealers, full details & photographs supplied by mail. *Serv:* Brochure, consultation. *Hours:* BY APPT ONLY. L Gail Macneill

KOKO BOODAKIAN & SONS
1026 Main St, 01890
(617)729-5566   **21 26 71**

Experts in Oriental rugs offering fine quality rugs for sale or trade to the discriminating collector.   Complete

restoration a specialty. *Est:* 1938. *Serv:* Consultation, appraisal, cleaning, complete restoration, repair. *Hours:* Tue-Sat 9:30-5 Thu til 9 CLOSED SUN,MON.

Woburn

PATRICK J GILL & SONS
9 Fowle St, 01801
(617)933-3275   **68 71**

Complete restoration of silver, pewter, brass & copper including repairing, refinishing & plating. Over 75 years experience - specializing in plating (gold, silver & rhodium) all work performed on premises. *Est:* 1911. *Serv:* Repairs, restoration. *Hours:* Mon-Sat 9-5. *CC:*

MC/V. Joe Gill *Park:* On site. *Loc:* I-93 Montvale Ave Exit: to Woburn Ctr rotary, take Rte 38S, 1st lights take L onto Fowle.

Worcester
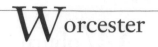

J & N FORTIER INC
484 Main St, 01608
(508)757-3657   **24 79**
Worcester's largest antique coin & stamp store. *Serv:* Appraisal, purchase estates. *Hours:* Mon-Sat 10-5 Wed til 8. *Size:* Medium. *CC:* MC/V. Naomi Fortier *Park:* Nearby lot.

HAMMERWORKS
6 Freemont St, 01603
(508)755-3434   **50**
Handmade Colonial lighting including chandeliers, sconces, hardware, andirons, candlestands in copper, brass, iron & tin. *Serv:* Lighting catalog $3, ironware catalog $1.

JEFFREY D MANCEVICE INC
PO Box 413 West Side Station, 01602
(508)755-7421   **13**
Antiquarian books: early printing, history of science, incunabula, medicine, early religion, theology, early mathematics, Renaissance & humanism. *Serv:* Catalog. *Hours:* BY APPT. *Assoc:* ABAA MRIAB.

ISAIAH THOMAS BOOKS & PRINTS
980 Main St, 01603
(508)754-0750   **13 66**
50,000+ books from paperbacks to rare books in all fields, located in a Victorian house near Clark University. *Serv:* Appraisal, search service. *Hours:* Tue,Thu,Fri,Sun 12-5 Wed 12-8 Sat

9-5 call ahead Sun. *CC:* MC/V. *Assoc:* ABAA MRIAB. Jim Visbeck *Park:* In front. *Loc:* Near Clark University, 1 MI from Worcester's City Hall.

Worthington

COUNTRY CRICKET VILLAGE INN
Huntington Rd Rte 112, 01098
(413)238-5366   **1 36 50**
Furniture, lighting & collectibles displayed in a charming country restaurant. *Pr:* $10–1000. *Est:* 1980. *Serv:* Purchase estates. *Hours:* Daily 10-6 CLOSED TUE. *Size:* Medium. *CC:* AX/MC/V. *Assoc:* PVADA. Donald F Bridgeman *Park:* On site. *Loc:* Northampton Rte 9W to Rte 143 to Worthington Rte 112S.

Wrentham
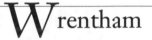

WRENTHAM ANTIQUE COMPANY
505 South St, 02093
(508)384-3740   **{GR15}**
Fine antiques & collectibles. *Est:* 1987. *Serv:* Appraisal, consultation, custom woodwork, interior design, purchase estates. *Hours:* Mon-Fri 10-7 Sat 10-5 Sun 12-5. *Size:* Medium. *CC:* AX/DC/MC/V. *Park:* On site. *Loc:* 495 Exit 15: Rte 1A to Wrentham.

Yarmouth Port

CC CANCER CONSIGNMENT EXCHANGE
133 Rte 6A, 02675
(508)362-3416   **44 63**

American, European & Oriental furniture, accessories & jewelry. *Hours:* Mon-Sat 10-4. *Park:* In front.

COLLECTOR'S CORNER
161 Main St Rte 6A, 02675
(508)362-9540   **27 47 65**

Country accessories, china, glass jewelry, linens & primitives. Leona Feistel

DESIGN WORKS
159 Main St, 02675
(508)775-3075   **41 42 63**

Scandinavian country antiques & accessories with a scattering of American & Continental majolica. *Pr:* $5–25000. *Serv:* Appraisal, custom woodwork, interior design, repairs, replication. *Hours:* Daily 10-5 Sun 12-5. *Size:* Large. *CC:* AX/MC/V. Jack Hill *Park:* On site. *Loc:* Rte 6 Exit 7N: to Rte 6A, .75 MI on R.

STEPHEN H GARNER
161 Main St Rte 6A, 02675
(508)362-8424   **36 59**

Early American 18th & 19th C furniture & accessories & paintings. *Hours:* By chance/appt, please call ahead. *Assoc:* CCADA.

CONSTANCE GOFF
161 Main St Rte 6A, 02675
(508)362-9540   **21 44 63**

19th C furniture & related accessories, flow blue, ironstone, hooked rugs & glass. *Hours:* Year round daily 10-5 Sun 11-4. *Assoc:* CCADA.

BETSY HEWLETT
PO Box 191, 02675
(508)362-6875   **44**

Early American pattern glass. *Serv:* Mail order. *Hours:* BY APPT ONLY. *Loc:* Call for directions.

LIL-BUD ANTIQUES
142 Main St Rte 6A, 02675
(508)362-8984   **44**

Specializing in early American pattern glass - including flint & colored - goblets, wines, tumblers & table sets. *Est:* 1968. *Serv:* Appraisal, catalog ($1). *Hours:* By chance/appt. *Assoc:* CCADA. Walter L Marchant Jr *Park:* In front. *Loc:* Rte 6A, to Ctr of Yarmouth Port.

NICKERSON'S ANTIQUES
162 Rte 6A, 02675
(508)362-6426   **16 27 63**

Country furniture, china, decorative accessories & metalware. *Hours:* Year round. *Park:* Nearby.

PARNASSUS BOOK SERVICE
Route 6A, 02675
(508)362-6420   **13**

A complete bookstore, carrying new & old books in many specialties including art, maritime affairs, antiques, ornithology, Americana, Slavia, Latin America, Caribbean, Central America, crafts & literary history. *Pr:* $1–5000. *Est:* 1951. *Serv:* Appraisal, catalog, purchase estates, search services. *Hours:* May-Sep 15 Mon-Sat 9-9 Sun 12-5, Sep 16-Apr Mon-Sat 9-5. *Size:* Medium. *Park:* On site. *Loc:* Rte 6A, across from the Yarmouth Port post office.

TOWN CRIER ANTIQUES
151 Main St, 02675   **32 44 63**

China, glassware, decorative accessories, dolls & toys. Marion Crewsdon

YARMOUTHPORT ANTIQUES
431 Main St, 02675
(508)362-3599   {GR}

Formal & country furniture, folk art, glass, china, linens, paintings & decorative accessories. *Hours:* Daily 10-5 BY APPT. *Assoc:* CCADA. Lillian Mc Kinney *Park:* On site. *Loc:* On Rte 6A.

New Hampshire

Alexandria

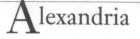

ALEXANDRIA WOOD JOINERY
Plumer Hill Rd, 03222
(603)744-8243 **19 68 70**

Expert antique furniture reproduction, chair seating, cane & splint. Custom designed & manufactured cabinets & furniture. *Serv:* Custom woodwork. *Hours:* Tue-Fri 10-5 Sat 10-3, please call first. *Size:* Large. George G Whittaker *Park:* In front. *Loc:* Willow St from Rte 3A in Bristol across from town offices, take L fork 1 MI up, 1st set of bldgs on R after fork.

COLE HILL FARM ANTIQUES
Alexandria, 03222
(603)744-8768 **16 39**

English period furniture & pewter. *Assoc:* NHADA. H S Bennett *Loc:* In Alexandria Village, N of Bristol, follow antique signs to Cole Hill Farm.

Alstead

PAPERMILL VILLAGE ANTIQUES
Rtes 12A & 123, 03602
(603)835-6414 **{GR}**

Quality American furniture, paintings, smalls, folk art & toys located in a picturesque mill on Cold River. *Serv:* Furniture restoration. *Hours:* Fri,Sat,Sun or BY APPT. *Assoc:* NHADA. R W Viegener *Park:* On site. *Loc:* On Cold River, 30 min from Keene, 10 min from Bellows Falls, VT.

Alton

FLEUR-DE-LIS ANTIQUES
Rte 11, 03809
(603)875-6555 **44 63**

Early American pattern glass, cup plates, china & art glass. *Serv:* Clocks bought & sold, repair. *Hours:* Jun-Sep 15 Daily 10-5 CLOSED WED. *Assoc:* NHADA. Audrey S Ritchie

Amherst

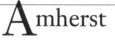

AMHERST VILLAGE ANTIQUE SHOP
101 Boston Post Rd, 03031
(603)673-5946 **37 38 83**

Diversified stock of American & Continental furniture & decorative accessories; specializing in refinished trunks. *Pr:* $25–5000. *Est:* 1974. *Hours:* By chance/appt. *Size:* Medium. Ralph Bolnick *Park:* On site. *Loc:* In the village center just off the Village Green.

CARRIAGE SHED ANTIQUES
Walnut Hill Rd, 03031
(603)673-4243 **27**

Country antiques. *Hours:* May-Oct Thu-Sun 10-5 Nov-Dec 15 Sat-Sun 10-4. *Assoc:* NHADA. Gladys Pestana *Loc:* Off Rte 101.

Andover

THE CILLEYVILLE BOOKSTORE
Box 127, 03216
(603)735-5667   **13**

Ireland & cookbooks. *Hours:* Tue-Sat 10-4 or BY APPT. *Assoc:* NHABA. E. Leslie

Antrim

BACKWARD LOOK ANTIQUES
Rte 9, 03440
(603)588-2751   **{GR10}**

Primitives, furniture, horsedrawn vehicles, tools, folk art, sandwich glass & tole painting. *Hours:* Year round daily 10:30-5:30. *Assoc:* GSAAA NHADA. Bob McNeil *Loc:* At entrance to Hawthorne College.

COURT'S CUPBOARD ANTIQUES
Rtes 202 & 31, 03440
(603)588-2455   **40 42**

Refinished pine, Victorian oak furniture & accessories. *Hours:* Usually open. *CC:* MC/V. *Assoc:* NHADA. Dick Court *Loc:* Just S of Antrim.

GRIST MILL ANTIQUES
Rte 202, 03440
(603)588-2378   **32 67**

Old dolls, doll furniture & china, iron door stops, banks, quilts, miniature animals, pink & copper luster, Windsor chairs & paintings. *Hours:* May-Nov. *Assoc:* NHADA. M Millard

Barnstead (North)

COOPER SHOP ANTIQUES
Peachem Rd, 03225
(603)776-7191   **27 65**

Featuring country furniture, primitives & carefully selected accessories that stress the unusual. *Hours:* Jun-Oct 15 Wed-Sat 10-5 Sun 12-5. *Assoc:* NHADA. Bea Nelson *Loc:* 1 MI off Rte 28.

Bedford

BEDFORD CENTER ANTIQUES
7 Meeting House Rd, 03102
(603)472-3557   **27 36 44**

Furniture, glass, china, silver, paintings & country antiques. *Serv:* Appraisal, video taping. *Hours:* Mon-Fri 10-6 CLOSED JAN,FEB. *Assoc:* GSAAA NEAA NHADA. Elaine Tefft

BELL HILL ANTIQUES
Rte 101 & Bell Hill Rd, 03012
(603)472-5580   **{GR20}**

Country furniture, primitives, folk art, quilts & textiles, rugs, hearth accessories, prints, toys, silver, glass & china. *Est:* 1974. *Hours:* Daily 10-5. *CC:* MC/V. *Assoc:* GSAAA NIIADA. Sharon S Kace *Loc:* In Houck Realty Bldg; 1/2 way between Townsend, MA & Rte 4 in NH.

CLOAK & DAGGER BOOKS
9 Eastman Ave, 03102
(603)668-1629   **13**

Out-of-print & rare books relating to nonfiction espionage, intelligence, true spy, codes & ciphers, guerrilla, terrorism & POW escapes. *Serv:* Catalog. *Hours:* BY APPT ONLY. *Assoc:* NHABA. Dan D Halpin, Jr

DRUMMER BOY ANTIQUES
278 Wallace Rd, 03102
(603)472-3172   **1 6 65**

Primitives, Americana, general antiques, Civil War & military & early photography. *Hours:* BY APPT. *Assoc:* NHADA. Hank Ford

RICHARDSON BOOKS, LTD
47 Old Farm Rd, 03102
(603)472-3117   **13**

Interesting books in all subjects, including works by Jane Austen, Virginia Woolf, the Bloomsbury Group & Sarah Orne Jewett. *Hours:* BY APPT ONLY. *Assoc:* NHABA. Jon Richardson

LILLIAN WIENER
20 Stonehenge Rd, 03102
(603)472-2313   **27**

Selective stock of small quality antiques, country & primitives. *Hours:* All year BY APPT. *Assoc:* GSAAA NHADA.

Bradford

KALONBOOKS
Rte 114, 03221
(603)938-2380   **13**

Antiquarian books: American & European history, biography & autobiography, literature, New England & literary criticism. *Serv:* Catalog. *Hours:* Sat-Sun 1-5, Jul & Aug Wed-Sun 1-5. *Assoc:* NHABA. Rod Jones

JEF & TERRI STEINGRIBE
Hogg Hill Rd, 03221
(603)938-2748   **27**

Country furniture & accessories. *Hours:* All year BY APPT. *Assoc:* NHADA.

Bridgewater

IDLE-A-WHILE COUNTRY ANTIQUES
Bridgewater, 03222
(603)744-8310   **6 64 65**

Old guns, swords, knives, military & hunting items, primitives, flow blue & other dishes, furniture & post cards. *Hours:* May-Oct by chance/appt. *Assoc:* NHADA. Bill Weir *Loc:* 6 MI N of Bristol on Rte 3A on Newfound Lake.

Brookline

1786 HOUSE ANTIQUES
274 Milford Rd Rte 13, 03033
(603)673-1918   **23 36 77**

Formal & country furniture, clocks, silver, glass, paintings & other early American accessories. *Serv:* Clock restoration. *Hours:* Sat-Mon 11-4 & BY APPT. *Assoc:* NHADA. Jan Messner *Loc:* 3 MI S of Rte 101 on Rte 13.

BROOKLINE VILLAGE ANTIQUES
Rte 130, 03033
(603)673-0081   **40 42 48**

Antique cooperative featuring oak, pine, linens, kitchen items, glass, mahogany, china & jewelry. *Hours:* Daily 10-5 CLOSED TUE. Ron Pelletier *Loc:* 1 hr from Boston.

Canaan

AMERICAN CLASSICS
Canaan St Lake, 03741
(603)523-7139   **34 37 67**
American country furniture, paintings, quilts, hooked rugs & folk art. *Hours:* Jun-Aug BY APPT. *Assoc:* NHADA. Meryl Weiss *Loc:* Just past Cardigan Mt School.

ERNIE'S ANTIQUES
RR 1 Box 106, 03741
(603)523-4226   **27 40 65**
Two floors of country pine & oak furniture, cupboards & accessories located in a large barn. *Pr:* $25–3000. *Est:* 1987. *Hours:* May-Sep Tue-Sun 9-5, Oct-Jun by chance/appt. *Size:* Medium. Ernest R Eastman *Park:* On site. *Loc:* Take rd at blinking light to Canaan St, 3 MI on R.

Canterbury

CRABTREE'S COLLECTION
310 Baptist Rd, 03224
(603)783-9394   **13**
A general stock of antiquarian books as well as those relating to nature studies & the outdoors. *Hours:* By chance/appt. *Assoc:* NHABA. Penny Crabtree

Center Harbor

ACCENTS FROM THE PAST
Rte 25, 03226
(603)253-4088   **36 50 63**
Specializing in refinished furniture, American art pottery & early electric lamps. Carriage house & barn open for browsing. *Hours:* Sum: Tue-Sun 10-5. *Assoc:* NHADA. Anna Miller *Loc:* Across from Longwood Farms.

HOLIDAY HOUSE ANTIQUES
Bean Rd at Center Harbor, 03226
(603)253-6891   **36 63 77**
Antiques, furniture, china, silver & glass. *Hours:* Apr-Oct daily 9-5 CLOSED MON. *Assoc:* NHADA. Edith L Murphy *Loc:* Off Rte 25.

THE ROYALE MESS
Lake Shore Dr, 03226
(603)253-6338   **44 47 63**
Quality glassware, china, jewelry, unusual accessories & lamps. *Hours:* Sat-Sun 9-5. *Assoc:* NHADA. Jean Hazeltine

Center Sandwich

HILL COUNTRY BOOKS
Box 268, 03227
(603)284-7008   **13**
Literature & biography. *Hours:* May 15-Columbus Day Weekend Tue-Sat 10-5 else by appt. *Assoc:* NHABA. John E Perkins *Loc:* In the village Historic District.

Center Strafford

HALF THE BARN
Rte 126, 03815
(603)664-9808   **21 67**
Country furniture & accessories, quilts, clothes, baskets, hooked & braided rugs. *Hours:* All year. Bonnie Inglis

BERT & GAIL SAVAGE
Rte 126, 03815
(603)269-7411   **27 34**

Early 19th C country furniture, folk art & accessories, Adirondack-type items & Indian clubs. *Hours:* All year BY APPT. *Assoc:* AADA NHADA.

Charlestown

ANTIQUES CENTER
Main St, 03603
(603)826-3639   **33 36 44**

China & glass, primitive & formal furniture & ephemera. *Est:* 1973. *Hours:* Mon-Sat 10:30-4:30 Sun 1-4:30. *Assoc:* NHADA. William Orcutt

Chester

OLDE CHESTER ANTIQUES
Raymond Rd Rte 102, 03036
(603)887-4778   **16 27 28**

Early country furniture with emphasis on paint, early smalls, wooden primitives, stoneware, copper & iron. *Hours:* By chance/appt. *Assoc:* NHADA.

WALNUT HILL ANTIQUES
Walnut Hill, 03036
(603)887-2627   **27**

18th & 19th C American country furniture & accessories - most in original surface & condition. *Hours:* By chance/appt. *Assoc:* NHADA. Bob Leonard *Loc:* 3 MI S of Chester Center on Rte 121.

Chesterfield

HEMLOCK HILL ANTIQUES
Cross Rd, 03466
(603)256-3281   **28 30 42**

Country furniture, especially pine, quilts, crocks, decoys & accessories. *Hours:* Year round by chance/appt. *Assoc:* NHADA. Shiela Kinnare *Loc:* Off Rte 9.

Chichester

DOUGLAS H HAMEL
RFD 10 Box 100, 03301
(603)798-5912   **37**

Shaker furniture & accessories for the serious collector. *Est:* 1966. *Hours:* BY APPT. *Assoc:* NHADA.

Concord

ART RUG
74 N Main St, 03301
(603)224-3099   **21**

Superior selection of hand knotted Orientals with a constantly changing stock of nearly 1000 rugs, ranging from antiques to new. *Pr:* $100–15000. *Est:* 1968. *Serv:* Appraisal, consultation, purchase estates, repairs, restoration. *Hours:* Mon-Sat 9-5. *Size:* Medium. *CC:* MC/V. *Assoc:* NHADA. *Park:* Local garage. *Loc:* 1 block S of State Capitol Building.

BOOKSHELF SHOP
3 Pleasant St, 03301
(603)224-8496 13
Cookbooks, children's books & general stock. *Hours:* Tue-Sat 10:30-5. *Assoc:* NHABA. Polly Powers

CARR BOOKS
51 N Spring St, 03301
(603)225-3109 13
General stock of antiquarian books & paper. *Hours:* BY APPT ONLY. *Assoc:* NHABA. Roberta Carr

VERNA H MORRILL
River Rd, 03301
(603)224-0163 1 80
American antiques & textiles. *Hours:* By appt/chance. *Assoc:* NHADA. *Loc:* 4 MI S of Concord on Rte 3A.

THE OLD ALMANACK SHOP
5 S State St, 03301
(603)225-5411 13 33 51
Antiquarian, out-of-print, & rare books from the 18th to the 20th C, prints, maps & ephemera. *Pr:* $1–500. *Est:* 1975. *Hours:* Win: Sat 12-5 else by chance Sum: Mon-Fri 11-5 Sat 12-5. *Assoc:* NHABA. Craig B Holmes

C WALLENSTEIN AUCTIONWORLD INC
5 S State St, 03301
(603)224-4390 8
Auctioning antiques from early New England homes. No buyer's premium. *Serv:* Auction, brochure, 800 # = 1-800-SOLD. Ckristopher L Wallenstein

Contoocook

THE ARNOLDS
Maple St, 03229
(603)746-3624 13
Americana, art & illustrated books. *Hours:* By chance/appt. *Assoc:* NHABA. Don Arnold

CHURCHILLBOOKS
Burrage Rd, 03229
(603)746-5606 13
Sir Winston S. Churchill - books by, about, or related to his life & times. *Hours:* Mon-Fri 9-5 or by chance/appt. *Assoc:* NHABA. Richard Langworth

EMERY'S BOOKS
Duston Rd Rte, 03229
(603)746-5787 13 51
Early books, travel, atlases, literature & Americana. *Hours:* By chance/appt. *Assoc:* NHABA. Ron Emery

GOLD DRAGON ANTIQUES
Rte 127, 03229
(603)746-3466 23 44 63
Art & pattern glass, Oriental porcelains, pottery, cloisonne & clocks. *Pr:* $5–2000. *Hours:* Daily 11-5 appt suggested. *Size:* Medium. *Assoc:* NHADA. Philip B Cole *Park:* On site. *Loc:* I-89 Exit 6: 1 MI to Contoocook, follow Rte 127 thru village to Park Ave Shopping Ctr, 3rd house on R.

PIATT'S COPPER COW
Briar Hill Rd, 03229
(603)746-4568 27 80
Country furniture, cupboards, early accessories & textiles. *Hours:* By chance. *Assoc:* NHADA. Gail Piatt

SHIRLEY D QUINN ANTIQUES
Putney Hill Rd, 03229
(603)746-5030   **27 67 80**
Country furniture & accessories, quilts, textiles & children's things. *Hours:* BY APPT. *Assoc:* NHADA.

Cornish

NATHAN SMITH HOUSE
RR 2 Rte 12A, 03745
(603)675-2951   **37 41 65**
A country shop in an historic 1791 Federal house on the Connecticut River. Specializing in unusual, high-quality American furniture & accessories, including Shaker, brass, copper, items in original paint, paintings, redware & early lighting. *Pr:* $25–2000. *Hours:* Apr 15-Oct 15 Mon-Sat 8-7. *Assoc:* NHADA. Daniel B Eastman *Park:* On site. *Loc:* I-91 Exit 8: L on Rte 12A for 4.5 MI.

Deerfield

DAVID OTTINGER
Deerfield, 03037
(603)463-7451   **5 74**
Early architectural materials, barn & house frames, outbuildings, doorstones, brick, beams, flooring & doors. *Hours:* BY APPT. *Assoc:* NHADA.

Derry

BERT BABCOCK BOOKSELLER
9 E Derry Rd, 03038
(603)432-9142   **13**
Modern first editions, signed & association copies, poetry broadsides & rare books. *Assoc:* ABAA NHABA.

FARMER'S MARKET ANTIQUES
173 Rockingham Rd Rte 28, 03038
(603)432-4138   **{GR42}**
Primitives, paper, china, glass, advertising, dolls, collectibles, vintage clothing, furniture, toys, painting & jewelry. *Hours:* Daily.

HILLTOP ANTIQUES
179 Rockingham Rd, 03038
(603)434-9277   **{GR}**
Furniture & glass - including Quezal & Lutz. *Hours:* Thu-Sun 10-5. *Loc:* Mins N of MA border on Rte 28.

Dover

MICHAEL G BENNETT AUCTIONS
Pickering Rd, 03820
(603)335-1694   **8**
Antique & estate auctions held at Seaboard Auction Gallery, Eliot ME. *Serv:* Auctioneer.

Dublin

WM LARY-THOMAS SEAVER ANTIQUES
Gold Mine Rd, 03444
(603)563-8603   **30 34**
18th & 19th C country & formal furni-

ture, quality accessories including art, Shaker, paint, decoys & folk. *Hours:* Tue-Sat 10-5. *Assoc:* GSAAA NHADA. *Loc:* 3 MI W of Peterborough on Rte 101, R on Gold Mine Rd, 1st house on R.

ANN & DAN WALSH
Snow Hill Rd, 03444
(603)563-8542 **16 63**

Accessory items, pewter, brass, porcelains & soft paste. *Hours:* All year by chance/appt. *Assoc:* GSAAA NHADA. *Loc:* Rte 101, S on Upper Jaffrey Rd, 1 MI, R on Snow Hill Rd to marked driveway.

Durham

WISWALL HOUSE
Wiswall Rd, 03824
(603)659-5106 **36**

Country & formal furniture. *Hours:* Wed-Sat 10-6. *Assoc:* NHADA. Joan Carter *Loc:* From Durham, Rte 108S toward Newmarket, 1.1 MI, R on Bennett Rd, go to end, R then next L onto Wiswall Rd.

East Lempster

PETER HILL INC
Maplewood Manor, 03605
(603)863-3656 **37 50 83**

Significant 19th C American furniture, fine & decorative arts for collectors & museums. *Est:* 1961. *Serv:* Appraisal, conservation, purchase estates, consultation. *Hours:* BY APPT. *Park:* On site. *Loc:* Call for directions.

East Swanzey

PINE GROVE ANTIQUES
Rte 12, 03446
(603)357-7922 **{GR40}**

Country & Victorian furniture, collectibles & restored antique trunks. *Est:* 1977. *Hours:* Daily 9-4:30 Sun 10-4. *CC:* MC/V. James Jackson, Jr *Park:* On site. *Loc:* 6 MI S of Int of Rtes 9,10,12 & 101, 4 MI S of Keene.

Enfield

THE CLOCK SHOP
Enfield, 03748
(603)632-7461 **23**

Antique clocks, country furniture, accessories & books. *Hours:* Sat by chance or call for appt. June Rock

DANA ROBES WOOD CRAFTSMEN
Rte 4A, 03748
(603)632-5385 **19 43 70**

Shaker reproduction furniture & crafts. Workshop & showroom in former creamery & laundry building of the Enfield Shaker community, custom furniture in Shaker tradition is also created on a special order basis. *Pr:* $20000–30000. *Serv:* Catalog ($1), custom woodwork, reproduction. *Hours:* Mon-Fri 8-5 Sat 9-3. *Size:* Medium. *CC:* MC/V. Ronald Boehm *Park:* On site. *Loc:* I-89 Exit 17: 6 MI from Int of I-91/I-89 in VT, 5.25 MI E on Rte 4A.

Epping

PLEASANT HILL ANTIQUES
7 Pleasant St, 03042
(603)679-5447   **27**

Early American country furniture & quality accessories. *Hours:* Jun-Oct by chance/appt. *Assoc:* NHADA. Marcha R Latwen *Loc:* Rte 127 .50 MI W of Rte 125.

Epsom

BOB & RITA BECKER
Rte 4, 03234
(603)736-8115   **29 34 36**

Furniture, accessories, folk art & collectibles. *Hours:* Year round. *Assoc:* NHADA. *Loc:* Brown barn 1.5 MI E of Epsom Circle.

THE BETTY HOUSE
North Rd, 03234
(603)736-9087   **36 81**

Four barns full of a general assortment of antiques including furniture, household items of wood, tin or iron & large collection of tools. *Assoc:* NHADA. Charles Yeaton *Loc:* .5 MI off Rte 4 on North Rd.

COPPER HOUSE
Rte 4, 03234
(603)736-9798   **50 70 87**

Copper & brass lighting in traditional styles, copper weather vanes & cupolas. *Est:* 1976. *Serv:* Reproductions. *Hours:* Thu-Sat 12-5 Sun 10-5 or BY APPT. *Size:* Medium. *CC:* MC/V. *Loc:* Located on Rte 4, approx 15 min E of Concord, .75 MI E of Epsom Traffic Circle.

Exeter

A THOUSAND WORDS
65 Water St, 03833
(603)778-1991   **13 66**

Antiquarian books: scholarly non-fiction, modern literary first editions, Western Americana & natural history prints. *Hours:* Mon-Sat 10-6. *Assoc:* NHABA. Jennifer Segal

HOLLIS & TRISHA BRODRICK
Box 40, 03838
(603)778-8842   **15 37 63**

18th C decorative accessories, English ceramics, iron, brass, lighting, Delft, combware, bottles, textiles & American furniture. *Hours:* BY APPT. *Assoc:* ADA NHADA.

HERSCHEL B BURT
93 Linden St, 03833
(603)778-8633   **23**

American clocks & timepieces. *Est:* 1958. *Serv:* Appraisal. *Hours:* BY APPT. *Loc:* Call for directions.

COLOPHON BOOK SHOP
117 Water St, 03883
(603)772-8443   **13**

19th & 20th C literary first editions, literary bibliographies, press books & books about books. *Hours:* Mon-Sat 9-5. *Assoc:* ABAA NHABA. Robert Liska

DECOR ANTIQUES
11 Jady Hill Circle, 03833
(603)772-4538   **36 63 77**

Furniture, glass, china, silver, books, prints & paintings. *Assoc:* NHADA. *Loc:* From 101/108 S (Portsmouth Ave) Exeter, take R at lights, next L.

SANDY ELLIOTT, COUNTRY ANTIQUES
Pickpocket Rd, 03833
(603)772-2248　　　　　　**27**
Country furniture & accessories. *Hours:* BY APPT ONLY. *Assoc:* NHADA.

EXETER OLD BOOK BARN
200 High St, 03833
(603)772-0618　　　　　　**13**
Scholarly general stock of antiquarian books; Asia, Scotland, music & gardening. *Hours:* Daily 10-5. *Assoc:* NHABA. Anthony M Tufts

LANDSCAPE BOOKS
Box 483, 03833
(603)964-9333
Books on gardening, landscape & horticulture. *Hours:* Mail order. Jane Robe

OCTOBER STONE ANTIQUES
56 Jady Hill Ave, 03833
(603)772-2024　　　　　　**27**
Country furniture & unusual accessories. *Hours:* Daily 10-4. *Assoc:* NHADA. Linda J Rogers *Loc:* Next to Exeter Country Club.

JANE ROBIE - LANDSCAPE BOOKS
PO Box 483, 03833
(603)964-9333　　　　　　**13**
Books on landscape architecture, garden history & design. *Hours:* MAIL ORDER ONLY. *Assoc:* NHABA.

Farmington

THE BOOKERY
62 N Main St Rte 153, 03835
(603)755-4471　　　　　　**13**
Antiquarian books: military, other nonfiction & selected fiction. *Hours:* Fri 10-6 or by chance. *Assoc:* NHABA. Robert M Colpitt

Fitzwilliam

ANTIQUES PLUS & STRAWBERRY ACRES
Rte 12, 03447
(603)585-6517　　　　　　**{GR55}**
Primitives, glass, furniture, dolls & toys. *Est:* 1979. *Serv:* Restaurant open Fri-Sun 11-3. *Hours:* Daily 10-5. *Park:* On site. *Loc:* 3 MI from MA line, 2 MI S of Jct of Rte 119.

BLOOMIN' ANTIQUES
On The Village Green, 03447
(603)585-6688　　　　　**27 37**
American country furniture & related accessories. *Hours:* All year by chance/appt. *Assoc:* NHADA. Gary Taylor *Park:* Nearby.

CLOCKS ON THE COMMON
Village Common, 03447
(603)585-3321　　　　　　**23**
Antique clocks. *Serv:* Repairs. *Hours:* Most afternoons by chance/appt. John H Fitzwilliam

DAVIS HOMESTEAD
Old Rte 12, 03447
(603)585-7759　　　　　**27 29**
Period & country furniture & their accessories. *Hours:* Year round by chance/appt. *Loc:* Off Rte 12.

DENNIS & DAD ANTIQUES
Rte 119, 03447
(603)585-9479   **36 44 63**
Glass, china & furniture. *Hours:* Mon-Sat after 1pm by chance/appt CLOSED SUN. *Assoc:* NHADA. Dennis Berard *Loc:* Off Rte 12 heading E, 5th house on L.

EXPRESSIONS
Rte 12, 03447
(603)585-6586   **24 44 83**
Victorian furniture, stained glass, Oriental rugs, country, bells, fans, bottles, coins, vintage clothing & oak. *Hours:* Daily 10-5. *Assoc:* NHADA. JoAnn Champion

FITZWILLIAM ANTIQUE CENTER
Jct Rtes 12 & 119, 03447
(603)585-9092   **{GR42}**
18th & 19th C country furniture & accessories, folk art & antique reference books. *Hours:* Mar-Oct Mon-Sat 10-5 Sun 11-5, Nov-Feb Mon-Sat 10-4 Sun 11-4. *Size:* Large. *Assoc:* GSAAA NHADA. Warren Legsdin

WILLIAM LEWAN ANTIQUES
Old Troy Rd, 03447
(603)585-3365   **1 27 41**
Actively changing inventory of early & country furniture, art, folk art & appropriate accessories. *Pr:* $25–5000. *Est:* 1972. *Serv:* Appraisal, purchase estates. *Hours:* All year daily 10-5 by chance/appt. *Size:* Medium. *Assoc:* NHADA. *Park:* On site. *Loc:* 4.5 MI from Fitzwilliam Village, W on Rte 119 look for sign for turn.

RED BARN ANTIQUES
Old Richmond Rd, 03447
(603)585-3134   **28 44 59**
Art, decorated stoneware, cut glass, American primitives, paintings, some Victorian & country items. *Hours:* Thu-Mon 10-4 or BY APPT. *Assoc:* NHADA. Arlene Rich *Loc:* .25 MI W of Fitzwilliam Inn, 5th House on R, red barn on the hill.

Francestown

THE FRANCESTOWN GALLERY
Main St, 03043
(603)547-6635   **34 59**
Early 19th & late 18th C New England antiques, folk art, paintings & textiles. *Hours:* By Chance/Appt. Ann Stewart

BERT MC CLEARY AUCTIONEER
Turnpike Rd, 03043
(603)547-2796   **4 8**
Auctioneers & appraisers buying/selling single items or whole estates.

MILL VILLAGE ANTIQUES
Rte 136E New Boston Rd, 03043
(603)547-2050   **23 30 65**
Duck & fish decoys, clocks, country furniture, primitives, glass, china, collector items & ice cream & chocolate molds. *Est:* 1982. *Hours:* Year round by chance/appt. *Assoc:* GSAAA. Barbara Radtke *Park:* On site. *Loc:* .5 MI E of Francestown Town Hall.

NAN SHEA ANTIQUES
PO Box 129, 03043
(603)547-3523   **63**
Majolica & Chinese export porcelain. *Est:* 1984. *Hours:* BY APPT ONLY. *Assoc:* GSAAA. Nancy Shea *Loc:* Call for directions.

STONEWALL ANTIQUES
New Boston Rd Rte 136, 03043
(603)547-3485   **36 41 44**
Selected formal, country & painted furniture, glass, china, paintings, primitives, decorator & collector items. *Hours:* Year round by chance/appt. *Assoc:* GSAAA NHADA. Elsie E Mikula *Park:* Off street. *Loc:* 1 MI E of Village.

THE TYPOGRAPHEUM
BOOKSHOP
The Stone Cottage-Bennington Rd,
03043   **13**
Choice selection of modern first editions with a special emphasis on British & European literature, the private press & fine bindings. *Est:* 1976. *Serv:* Catalog - quarterly (free). *Hours:* By chance/appt. R T Risk *Park:* On site. *Loc:* Rte 47, 1 MI N of village of Francestown.

WOODBURY HOMESTEAD
ANTIQUES
1 Main St, 03043
(603)547-2929   **47 50**
Specializing in kerosene lamps & jewelry of the Victorian era. *Pr:* $25–5000. *Est:* 1983. *Serv:* Appraisal, consultation, interior design, purchase estates, repairs. *Hours:* Year round by chance/appt suggested. *Assoc:* GIA GSAAA NHADA NTHP. Alan R Thulander *Park:* In front. *Loc:* On the Town Common at Jct of Rtes 136 & 47.

Franconia

COLONIAL COTTAGE
Blake Rd, Sugar Hill, 03580
(603)823-5614   **16 53 63**
Six rooms brimming with formal decorative accessories including brass, copper, pottery & porcelain including Canton & Rose Medallion, glass, mirrors & furniture all charmingly displayed. *Hours:* Daily 9-5. *Size:* Medium. Lauren Howard *Park:* On site. *Loc:* 1.5 MI up Blake Rd.

ELEANOR M
LYNN/ELIZABETH MONAHAN
Rte 117, Sugar Hill, 03585
(603)823-5550   **21 37 63**
Fine American period furniture & decorative accessories, paintings, Oriental rugs & fine porcelain. *Hours:* BY APPT. *Assoc:* NHADA. *Shows:* ELLIS. *Park:* On site. *Loc:* W of Franconia on Rte 117.

Franklin

EVELYN CLEMENT
45 Central St, 03235
(603)934-5496   **13**
Antiquarian books featuring some unusual subjects & a general stock including early technical, New Hampshire & White Mountains. *Hours:* By chance/appt. *Assoc:* NHABA.

Freedom

FREEDOM BOOKSHOP
Maple St, 03836
(603)539-7265   **13 33**
Antiquarian books: books, magazine
& ephemera of the 1920-1970 period.
poetry & books on books, large selec-
tion of literary magazines, English &
American. Special collections of an
earlier period in the arts & agriculture.
Hours: Jun-Sep Sun-Wed 10-6, Win:
BY APPT (Unheated Barn). *Assoc:*
MABA. George L Wrenn

Gilford

LOUISE FRAZIER, BOOKS
380 Morrill St, 03246
(603)524-2427   **13**
A general stock of antiquarian books.
Hours: By chance/appt. *Assoc:*
NHABA.

Gilford Village

VISUALLY SPEAKING
778 Gilford Ave Rte 11A, 03246
(603)524-6795   **13 66**
General stock of antiquarian books

with emphasis on nonfiction, prints & paper. *Hours:* By chance/appt. *Assoc:* NHABA. Barbara French

Gilmanton Iron Works

STEPHEN P BEDARD
Durrell Mountain Farm, 03837
(603)528-1896   **43 46 69**
Windsor chair replications using the same procedures and locally grown woods as those utilized by 18th C chairmakers. Authentic to their period in every detail, including line, form & technique. *Est:* 1980. *Serv:* Catalog $3. *Hours:* BY APPT.

Goffstown

SACRED & PROFANE
New Boston Rd Rte 13, 03752
(603)645-6282   **13**
Antiquarian books with an emphasis on art/illustrated, leatherbound, theology & religion from 17th-20th C. *Hours:* Mon 6-8 Sat,Sun 1-4. *Assoc:* NHABA. H. Donley Wray

Goshen

NELSON CRAFTS & USED BOOKS
Brook Rd, 03752
(603)863-4394   **13**
Large collection of antiquarian books: fiction, nonfiction & children's. *Hours:* May-Sep daily, else by chance/appt. *Assoc:* NHABA. Audrey Nelson

Greenland

DANIEL OLMSTEAD ANTIQUES/AUCTION
1119 Portsmouth Ave, 03840
(603)431-1644   **8**
Antiques & estate liquidations. *Serv:* Appraisal, purchase estates. *Hours:* By chance/appt. *Assoc:* NHAA.

WM THOMPSON, ANTIQUARIAN BKSELLR
10 Tide Mill Rd, 03840
(603)431-2369   **13**
Antiquarian books: Americana, natural history & sporting. *Hours:* Daily 12-5 BY APPT, Win: call ahead. *Assoc:* NHABA. *Loc:* I-95 Exit 3: 2.5 MI on Rte 101.

Guild

PAUL & MARIE MAJOROS
Sunapee Rd Rtes 11 & 103, 03754
(603)863-3165   **13**
General stock of books & paper. *Hours:* By chance/appt. *Assoc:* NHABA.

Hampton

RONALD BOURGEAULT ANTIQUES
694 Lafayette Rd Rte 1, 03842
(603)926-8222   **1 4 39**
Formal & country Americana, English & Oriental objects from estates. *Serv:* Consultant to museums, auction, appraisal. *Hours:* BY APPT ONLY. *Assoc:* NHADA. *Shows:* ELLIS WAS. *Park:* In front.

GARGOYLES & GRIFFINS
Old Rte 1 On The Moors, 03842
(603)926-3744   **5 36 83**
Specializing in heavily carved furniture, Victoriana, stained glass & architectural antiques. *Est:* 1984. *Serv:* Appraisal, purchase estates. *Hours:* Daily 10-5. T A Bennett *Park:* On site. *Loc:* Just S of Rte 51.

HEYDAY ANTIQUES OF HAMPTON
418 Lafayette Rd, 03842
(603)926-4249   **1 27 59**
Diverse stock of country & formal accessories, Americana & 18th & 19th C paintings. *Serv:* Expert shipping guaranteed. *Hours:* Year round. *Assoc:* NEAA NHADA. Tony K Pescosolido *Loc:* 1 hr N of Boston on I-95.

HISTORIC HARDWARE LTD
821 Lafayette Rd, 03842
(603)926-8315   **50 70**
Restoration-quality period hardware, lighting & decorative accessories - including Leforte reproduction furniture. *Serv:* Catalog ($2), custom woodwork, reproduction, restoration. *Hours:* Mon-Sat 9-5. *CC:* MC/V. *Assoc:* NTHP SPNEA. John R DeWaal *Park:* On site. *Loc:* I-95N Exit 2 in NH: L after toll, Rte 51, 1st R (Rte 101), top of Exit turn R, L at light, 1 MI N on R.

GUS JOHNSON ANTIQUES
21 Fern Rd, 03842
(603)964-9752   **37**
American country & formal furniture. *Hours:* BY APPT.

NORTHEAST AUCTIONS
PO Box 363, 03842
(603)926-9200   **4 8**
Regular auctions of antique formal & country American & European furniture, clocks, paintings, decorative arts & oriental carpets. 10% buyer's premium. *Est:* 1987. *Serv:* Appraisal, accept mail/phone bids, consultation. Ronald Bourgeault *Loc:* Many auctions held at Center of New Hampshire Holiday Inn, Manchester NH but always call for directions.

THE RED BARN ANTIQUES
418 Lafayette Rd, 03842
(603)926-2142   **36 44 47**
Specializing in rare & unusual trunks, chests, furniture, glass, china & jewelry. *Serv:* Photographs & delivery available. *Hours:* All year Tue-Sat 10-5. *Assoc:* NEAA NHADA. Nicholas J Wood *Park:* On site. *Loc:* On Rte 1.

H G WEBBER
Rte 1, 03842
(603)926-3349   **21 23 44**
Furniture, rugs, clocks, glass & china. *Est:* 1950. *Serv:* Appraiser, auctioneer. *Hours:* Tue-Sat 9-5 Sun 1-5. *Assoc:* NAA NAWCC. Robert S Webber *Park:* On site. *Loc:* I-95 Exit 2: follow Rte 51E to Rte 1, turn L, 1 block on R.

Hampton Falls

AMERICAN PRIDE
Rtes 1 & 84, 03844
(603)926-3087   **27 34**
Country & folk art in original paint & as-found condition. *Hours:* All year Mon-Sat 9:30-4:30. *Assoc:* NHADA. Barbara Merriman

ANTIQUES AT HAMPTON FALLS
Lafayette Rd Rtes 1 & 88, 03844
(603)926-1971   {GR35}
Antiques in a 3-story barn including fine furniture, primitives, smalls & collectibles. *Est:* 1987. *Hours:* Mon-Sat 10-5 Sun 12-5. *Size:* Large. *Park:* On site. *Loc:* I-95 Exit 1: 2 MI N on Rte 1.

ANTIQUES NEW HAMPSHIRE
Rte 1, 03844
(603)926-9603   {GR50}
Antiques in a large restored late Victorian house & barn. *Est:* 1987. *Hours:* Daily 10-5 Sun 12-5. *Size:* Large. *Assoc:* NHADA. Bob Hudson *Park:* On site. *Loc:* I-95 Exit 1 or 2.

ANTIQUES ONE
80 Lafayette Rd Rte 1, 03844
(603)926-5332   {GR50}
A two-story house, carriage house & barn filled with a diversified selection of smalls & furniture. *Serv:* Reference books on antiques. *Hours:* Mon-Sat 10-5 Sun 12-5. Alma Libby *Park:* On site. *Loc:* I-95 Exit 1:Rte 1N, 2 MI.

APPLE COUNTRY ANTIQUES
286 Exeter Rd Rte 88, 03844
(603)772-0624   22
Chairs: reed, rush, cane & splint. *Hours:* Tue-Sat 10-4.

THE BARN AT HAMPTON FALLS
44 Lafayette Rd Rte 1, 03844
(603)926-9003   {GR}
Specializing in fine American & European antique furniture & accessories. *Est:* 1977. *Serv:* Consultation, interior design, delivery service available. *Hours:* Year round daily 10-5. *Size:* Huge. Barry Welker *Park:* On site. *Loc:* On Rte 1, approx 1 MI from I-95.

PAUL MC INNIS, INC.
356 Exeter Rd, 03844
(603)778-8989   8
Auctions of antiques & Americana. 10% buyers premium. *Assoc:* NAA. *Loc:* I-95 Exit 2: Rte 51 for 1.2 MI to exit for 101D, L to SS, R onto 101W for 1.2 MI, L onto Rte 88.

Hancock

THE BARN OF HANCOCK VILLAGE
Main St, 03449
(603)525-3529   21 36 59
Quality 19th C antiques, china, paintings, furniture, Oriental rugs, glass & decorative accessories. *Hours:* Nov-Apr BY APPT, CLOSED MON. *Size:* Medium. *Assoc:* GSAAA NHADA. Helen M Pierce *Loc:* Across from John Hancock Inn.

CROOKED ONION FARM ANTIQUE
North Elmwood Rd, 03449
(603)525-3558   27 47 63
Country goods, small furniture, early pottery & porcelain, metals, rugs, jewelry & miniatures. *Hours:* May-Oct Thu-Sun 10-5, else BY APPT ONLY. *Assoc:* GSAAA. Bradford Daniels *Park:* In front. *Loc:* N Elmwood is off Rte 202, 7 MI N of Peterborough.

HARDINGS OF HANCOCK
Depot St, 03449
(603)525-3518   16 27
Country furniture, woodenware, ironware, lighting, tin, brass, copper & primitive accents. *Hours:* By chance. *Assoc:* GSAAA NEAA NHADA. Vince Harding *Loc:* Red house.

OLD BENNINGTON BOOKS
Box 142, 03449
(603)525-4035   **13**

Antiquarian books - literary first editions, poetry, detective fiction, Americana, fine & rare books. *Pr:* $5000–25000. *Est:* 1982. *Serv:* Appraisal, purchase estates, search service. *Hours:* BY APPT ONLY. *Assoc:* GSAAA NHABA. Alan Lambert *Park:* In front. *Loc:* .25 MI from ctr of Hancock on Old Bennington Road.

Hanover

COUNTRY LOOK ANTIQUES
Main St, 03755
(603)643-4553   **27**

Country furniture & accessories. *Hours:* BY APPT. *Assoc:* NHADA. Constance Campion

G B MANASEK, INC
35 S Main St Suite 22, 03755
(603)643-2227   **13 51 66**

Antiquarian books: science & medicine, astronomy, maps, atlases & cartography, manuscripts & prints. *Hours:* Wed-Fri 10-4 Sat 11-3. *Assoc:* ABAA NHABA. Francis J Manasek

MARIE-LOUISE ANTIQUES
Rte 10, 03755
(603)643-4276   **47 63 77**

Fine silver, china, glass & jewelry. *Serv:* Flatware matching service. *Hours:* BY APPT ONLY. *Assoc:* AAA NHADA. Paul J Fredyma *Loc:* 3 MI N of Hanover on Rte 10.

TAKE YOUR LIFE IN YOUR HANDS
80 Lebanon St, 03755
(603)643-4382   **13**

Antiquarian books. *Hours:* By chance/appt. *Assoc:* NHABA. Wayne Van Voorhees

Harrisville

BEN'S OLD BOOKS
PO Box 162, 03450
(603)827-3639   **13**

Antiquarian books specializing in Colonial, Revolutionary, New England & local history, biographies, children's history. *Hours:* Call for appt. *Assoc:* NHABA. Craig Brown

Haverhill

SUZANNE BRUCKNER 1812 HOUSE
Rte 10, 03765
(603)989-5575   **27**

Country furniture & accessories. *Hours:* All year by chance/appt. *Assoc:* NHADA. *Park:* On site. *Loc:* S of the Village Green, across from the Victorian on Main St.

THE VICTORIAN ON MAIN STREET
Rte 10, 03765
(603)989-3380   **48 85**

A Victorian house brimming with vintage clothing, linens, antiques & curiosities in 4 large rooms. *Hours:* Sum: most days 10-5 CLOSED MON. *Size:* Large. Ann Hayden *Park:* In front. *Loc:* S of the Village Green on Rte 10.

Henniker

OLD NUMBER SIX BOOK DEPOT
26 Depot Hill Rd, 03242   **13**

Antiquarian books: history, science, medicine, New England, social sciences, psychiatry, psychology & psychoanalysis. *Serv:* Appraisal, catalog. *Hours:* May-Oct daily 12:30-5:30 or BY APPT. *Assoc:* NHABA. Helen Morrison

RONALD J ROSENBLEETH INC
28 Western Ave, 03242
(603)428-7686   **4 8**

Auctioneer & appraiser specializing in fine estates, antiques & real estate. *Serv:* Appraisal. *Hours:* Mon-Fri 8-5 & BY APPT. *Assoc:* NAA NEAA.

Hillsboro

APPLEYARD ANTIQUES
Rte 9, 03244
(603)478-5344   **36**

Large shop displaying a wide variety of furniture dating from late 1700s - some refinished - & a large variety of smalls. *Pr:* $25–3500. *Est:* 1983. *Serv:* Brochure, refinishing. *Hours:* Daily 10-6. *Size:* Medium. *CC:* MC/V. *Assoc:* NHADA. Wally Appleyard *Park:* On site. *Loc:* On Rte 9 halfway between Keene & Concord at the W end of Hillsboro.

BARBARA'S ANTIQUES
Bridge St Rte 149, 03244
(603)464-3451   **27 44 63**

Refinished country furniture, accesso-ries, glass, china & primitives. *Hours:* Mar 15-Dec 15 by chance/appt. *Assoc:* NHADA. Joe Murphy

BEAR TRACK FARM ANTIQUES
Hillsboro, 03244
(603)478-3263   **23 65**

Clocks, watches, country furniture, primitives, toys & smalls. *Hours:* All year by chance/appt. *Assoc:* NHADA. Pat McLaughlin *Loc:* 2 MI past Hillsboro Ctr toward E Washington.

LOON POND ANTIQUES
School St, 03244
(603)464-5647   **29 36**

Country & formal furniture & accessories. *Est:* 1980. *Hours:* Thu-Mon 10:30-5:30. Dean Lowry *Park:* On site. *Loc:* 4 MI N of Rtes 202 & 9.

OLD DUNBAR HOUSE
PO Box 150 Amoskeag Bank, 03105
(603)464-3937   **16 37 63**

Early American furniture, pewter & fine porcelain. *Hours:* By chance/appt. Ralph C Stuart

STEPHEN SANBORN CLOCK REPAIR
Bridge St, 03244
(603)464-5382   **68 71**

Clocks. *Serv:* Repair & restoration. *Hours:* BY APPT. *Assoc:* NHADA.

CHERYL & PAUL SCOTT ANTIQUES
Bear Hill Rd, 03244
(603)464-3617   **29 36**

18th & 19th C furniture & appropriate accessories. *Hours:* BY APPT. *Assoc:* NHADA.

THE SHADOW SHOP
Preston St, 03244
(603)464-4038 **9 13 33**

Antiquarian books & ephemera, stereo views, manuscripts, business graphics & children's books. *Hours:* Tue-Sat 10-5 by chance/appt, Win: BY APPT ONLY. *Assoc:* GSAAA NHABA. Lois Meredith *Loc:* Rtes 202 & 9, turn N at Reade & Woods Insurance Co, 3rd house on R.

TATEWELL GALLERY
Jct Rtes 9 & 31, 03244
(603)478-5755 **36 50 63**

Early lighting, glass, china, 18th & 19th C furniture, fine art & accessories. *Hours:* May 3-Labor Day & Sep 20-Oct Tue-Sun 10-5, else by chance. *Assoc:* GSAAA NHADA. Jack H Tate *Loc:* Next to Pierce homestead.

WELL SWEEP ANTIQUES
RD 2 Box 441, 03244
(603)464-3218 **34 36 50**

Country & formal furniture, accessories, hooked rugs, woodenware, early iron, lighting, folk art, yellow ware & early china. *Hours:* All year by chance/appt. *Assoc:* NHADA. Richard S Withington, Jr *Loc:* In Hillsboro Ctr 3 MI N of Hillsboro.

RICHARD W WITHINGTON AUCTIONEER
RD 2 Box 440, 03244
(603)464-3232 **4 8**

Forty years experience in selling antiques & fine furnishing - mostly estate auctions & doll auctions. 10% buyer's premium. *Est:* 1948. *Serv:* Appraisal. *Assoc:* NAA. Richard W Withington

WYNDHURST FARM ANTIQUES
Rte 2, 03244
(603)464-5377 **44**

A variety of antiques specializing in pattern glass. *Hours:* By chance/appt. *Assoc:* NHADA. Rosa Webb

Holderness

WILLIAM F DEMBIEC ANTIQUES
Squamm Lakes Rd Rtes 3 & 25, 03245
(603)968-7170 **30**

General line of antiques & collectibles. *Hours:* Apr-Oct daily 10-5, Nov-Mar by chance/appt. *Assoc:* NHADA. *Loc:* I-93 Exit 24: 3 MI.

SQUAM LAKE GALLERY
Rtes 3 & 25, 03245
(508)887-8996 **29 59**

Specializing in paintings of the White Mountain School & American decorative arts. Jeanne A Demers

Hollis

THE BLUE LANTERN ANTIQUES
28 Pine Hill Rd, 03049
(603)465-2624 **16 44 56**

Marine antiques, country furniture, early glass, brass & copper. *Hours:* May-Dec Fri,Sat 10-5 or BY APPT, CLOSED AUG. *Assoc:* NHADA. Martha Davis *Loc:* Off Rte 130.

THE COOPERAGE
Rte 130, 03049
(603)465-3322 **27 29 36**

Antiques & select wares in a restored

1830 setting in Hollis village. *Pr:* $20–2000. *Est:* 1988. *Serv:* Consultation, purchase estates. *Hours:* Tue-Sun 10-5, please call ahead. *Size:* Medium. *CC:* MC/V. *Park:* On site. *Loc:* Directly opposite post office.

COUGHLIN ANTIQUE/ESTATE APPRAISA
34 Flagg Rd, 03049
(603)465-7351   **4**

Appraisal for insurance & estates with special emphasis on American country & folk art. Including furniture, rugs, china, glass, prints, paintings, toys & folk arts of all kinds. *Est:* 1971. *Serv:* Will travel for large collections. *Hours:* BY APPT. *Assoc:* ISA NEAA. Patricia P Coughlin

GEORGE LABARRE
GALLERIES, INC.
Box 746, 03049
(800)842-7000   **9**

Early stocks & bonds, autographs & collectibles. *Hours:* Daily 9-5. *Assoc:* NADA.

Hopkinton

ANDERSON'S ANTIQUES, INC.
South Rd, 03229
(603)746-3364   **37 59 63**

Fine New England furniture, lamps, china, glass, Chinese export porcelain & decorative accessories for the discriminating & knowledgeable collector. *Est:* 1948. *Hours:* BY APPT. *Size:* Medium. *Shows:* ELLIS. Mabel A Lomas *Park:* On site. *Loc:* Just S of Int of Rtes 103 & 202.

MEADOW HEARTH
Briar Hill Rd Rte 3, 03229
(603)746-3947   **29 37 67**

Early American furniture, diverse stock, quilts & general line of decorative accessories. *Pr:* $5–3000. *Est:* 1938. *Hours:* Apr 15-Nov Appt suggested, Dec-Apr 14 BY APPT ONLY. *Size:* Medium. *Assoc:* NHADA. John Howe *Park:* On site. *Loc:* From Hopkinton Village, rd opposite Cracker Barrel, to L of church is Briar Hill, 1 MI up rd, L onto dirt rd, house on R.

THE SOULES-ANTIQUES
Blaze Hill Rd, 03229
(603)746-4527   **16 42 57**

Refinished furniture, samplers, brass, lamps & other decorative accessories. *Pr:* $10–1000. *Est:* 1970. *Hours:* Year round by chance/appt, please call ahead. *Assoc:* NHADA. Bob Soule *Park:* On site. *Loc:* Off Rte 103 between Hopkinton & Contoocook, N on Gould Hill Rd 3/4 MI. L on Blaze Hill, 2nd Driveway on R.

WOMEN'S WORDS BOOKS
Straw Rd, 03229
(603)228-8000   **13**

Specializing in all areas of women's studies. *Est:* 1976. *Serv:* Search service, special collections development, catalog, purchase estates. *Hours:* BY APPT. *CC:* MC/V. *Assoc:* NHABA. Nancy Needham

WAYNE & PEGGY WOODARD ANTIQUES
Hopkinton Rd Rte 103, 03229
(603)746-3313   **16 36 57**

18th & 19th C American, French & English country & formal furniture & accessories, blue & white spongeware, brass & samplers. *Pr:* $45–5000. *Est:*

1972. *Serv:* Guarantee merchandise in writing, crating/shipping of merchandise. *Hours:* May-Oct daily 9-5, Nov-Jun Wed-Sun 9-5 or by chance. *Size:* Large. *Assoc:* NHADA. *Park:* On site. *Loc:* On Rte 103, N of Rte 202.

Hudson

COLONIAL SHOPPE
20 Old Derry Rd, 03051
(603)882-2959   **2 22 27**
Country furniture, fireplace accessories, treenware, chair caning & rushing. *Serv:* Refinishing, repairs. *Hours:* By chance/appt. *Assoc:* GSAAA NHADA. Carol Murray *Loc:* Rte 102, turn onto Old Derry Rd at Hudson Motor Inn.

Jackson

RED SHED ANTIQUES
Rte 16, 03846
(603)383-9267   **65 81**
Primitives, tools, kitchenware & a general line. *Pr:* $25–800. *Hours:* Jun-Oct 15 Mon-Sat 10:30-5 CLOSED SUN. *CC:* MC/V. *Assoc:* NADA NHADA. *Park:* On site. *Loc:* .5 MI N of Covered Bridge, on rd to Mt Washington.

Jaffrey

AT THE SIGN OF THE FOX
3 Blackberry Ln, 03452
(603)532-6897   **37 66 67**
Fine early American & country furniture, accessories, paintings, prints, hooked rugs & quilts. *Hours:* BY APPT ONLY. *Assoc:* NHADA.

INDIAN SUMMER ANTIQUES
54 Main St, 03452
(603)532-4401   **30 34**
Folk art, fish decoys, woodenware, cast iron doorstops & ashwood baskets. *Est:* 1960. *Serv:* Appraisal. *Hours:* Thu-Sat 9-5. *Park:* Nearby. *Loc:* Across from the bandstand.

THE TOWNE HOUSE
30 Ellison St, 03452
(603)532-7118   **50**
Antiques, lamps, lamp parts & shades. *Hours:* All year daily 10-5 CLOSED SUN. *Assoc:* NHADA. Tat Duval *Loc:* Off E Main St.

Keene

ANDERSON GALLERY
21 Davis St, 03431
(603)352-6422   **48 77**
A sophisticated collection of Victorian silver & estate linens with emphasis on tea services, trays & formal table linens. *Hours:* BY APPT. *Assoc:* GSAAA NADA. Thelma E Anderson

BEECH HILL GALLERY
109 Washington St, 03431
(603)352-2194   **36 67**
Quilts, furniture, paintings & prints. *Hours:* By Chance/Appt. *Assoc:* NHADA. Harold Goder

HAYS SCULPTURE STUDIO
RFD 1 #399, 03431
(603)352-0572   **71**
Restoration of carousel figures & woodcarvings. *Serv:* Pick up & delivery. *Hours:* BY APPT.

PETER PAP ORIENTAL RUGS INC
21 Roxbury St, 03431
(603)357-4695 **21 80 82**
An internationally recognized gallery featuring antique carpets, textiles & tribal weavings. *Serv:* Appraisal, repairs, restoration. *Hours:* Tue-Sat 10-5. *CC:* MC/V. *Assoc:* NHADA VADA. *Park:* In front. *Loc:* Just off Central Sq.

THE YARD SALE
276 West St, 03431
(603)352-3331 **32 44 48**
Dolls, linens, jewelry, art deco & glassware. *Hours:* Mon-Fri 10-6 Sat,Sun 10-5. *Loc:* 3 doors down from Colony Mill Marketplace.

Kensington

PETER SAWYER ANTIQUES
50 Moulton Ridge Rd, 03833
(603)772-5279 **23 37**
Specializing in American clocks from tall case to Connecticut shelf & wall clocks & New England furniture. *Hours:* By chance/appt. *Assoc:* NHADA. *Loc:* 1 hr N of Boston, 10 min off I-95.

Kingston

THE PEDDLER'S CART
Carriage Towne Plaza, 03848
(603)642-6005 **{GR}**
A general line of antiques & accessories featuring reproduction furniture. *Est:* 1988. *Serv:* Custom services. *Hours:* Open daily. Audrey Peverley *Loc:* Just off Rte 125.

RED BELL ANTIQUES
Rte 125, 03848
(603)642-5641 **{GR10}**
China, furniture, jewelry, quilts, tools & primitives. *Hours:* Daily 10-5. *CC:* MC/V.

Laconia

1893 ANN-TEEKS
373 Court St, 03246
(603)524-0129 **32 36**
Dolls & furniture a specialty. *Serv:* Doll & toy hospital. *Hours:* All year. *Assoc:* NEAA NHADA. Bob Dearborn

BARN LOFT BOOKSHOP
96 Woodland Ave, 03246
(603)524-4839 **13**
Antiquarian books specializing in children's & New England. *Hours:* By chance/appt. *Assoc:* NHABA. Lee Burt

COTTON HILL BOOKS
RFD #6 Box 298, 03246
(603)524-4967 **13**
Antiquarian books: New England, art & garden. *Hours:* BY APPT ONLY. *Assoc:* NHABA. Elizabeth K Emery

THE HOFFMANS
Union Rd, 03246
(603)528-2792 **16 27 28**
Early American country furniture & accessories, pewter, baskets, quilts & crocks. *Hours:* All year, call ahead. *Assoc:* NHADA. *Loc:* I-93 Exit 20: 5.3 MI N on Rte 3, R on Union Rd at Double Decker Restaurant, 2.4 MI on R.

Lancaster

BRETTON HALL ANTIQUITIES
12 Cottage St, 03584
(603)788-2202   13
Specializing in White Mountain material & books. **Hours:** BY APPT ONLY. **Assoc:** NHADA. Richard C Force

ELM STREET & STOLCRAFT BOOKS
20 Elm St, 03584
(603)788-4844   13
Used & out-of-print books. **Hours:** Mid May-Mid Oct Mon-Sat 10-5, Win: BY APPT ONLY. **Assoc:** NHABA. Albert Tetreault

GRANARY ANTIQUES
North Rd, 03584
(603)788-2790   36 63 67
Quilts, furniture, china & miniature lamps. **Hours:** Apr 15-Jan 19 daily 8-6. **Assoc:** NHADA. Louise Martin **Loc:** 1 MI N from town.

LANCASTER MALL & ANTIQUES MARKET
18 Middle St, 03584
(603)788-2421   {GR9}
In the White Mountains, reproduction Shaker furniture & an art gallery. **Pr:** $1–3500. **Est:** 1987. **Hours:** Tue-Thu 9-5 Fri,Sat 9-8 & BY APPT. **Size:** Large. **CC:** MC/V. **Loc:** From St Johnsbury VT: Rte 2E, from ME: Rte 2W, from Concord NH: Rte 93N to Rte 3N at Franconia.

THE SHOP IN THE BARN
7 Prospect St, 03584
(603)788-2313   32 36 50
Furniture, china, glass, jewelry, lamps, lampshades, toys & books. **Hours:** Jun-

Oct 15 daily 9-5 Sat 9-4 CLOSED SUN. **Assoc:** NHADA. **Park:** On site. **Loc:** Opposite Soldier's Park.

Lincoln

MILLSIDE ANTIQUES
Millfront Market Pl Main St, 03251
(603)745-8937   {GR}
Fine antiques & collectibles, furniture, primitives, silver, glass, paintings, textiles, estate jewelry, lighting, ephemera & Orientalia. **Hours:** All year daily 10-9, Sun 10-6. **CC:** AX/MC/V. J C Hughes **Loc:** I-93N Exit 32.

Lisbon

EARTH BOOKS
78 Water St, 03585
(603)838-6016   13
Antiquarian books: geology, mineralogy, mines & mining. **Assoc:** NHABA. Andrew Gutterman

HOUSTON'S FURNITURE BARN
Rtes 302 & 117, 03585
(603)838-5920   36
Used furniture, antiques & collectibles. **Hours:** All year.

Littleton

THE BEAL HOUSE INN & ANTIQUES
18 Main St, 03561
(603)444-2661   {GR}
Furniture & smalls. **Serv:** Intimate country inn. **Hours:** Daily 10-4 or BY

APPT, CLOSED WED. *Assoc:*
GSAAA NHADA. Doug Clickenger
Loc: Jct of Rtes 302 & 10.

NILA PARKER
17 Redington St, 03561
(603)444-5628 **63**
Flow blue china. *Hours:* By
chance/appt.

Londonderry

LONDONDERRY ANTIQUES
130 Rockingham Rd, 03053
(603)432-8514 **40**
Refinished oak furniture. *Hours:* Wed-
Mon 10-5 CLOSED TUE. Paul
O'Connell *Loc:* 300 yds S of Exit 5 off
Rte 93.

THE TATES ANTIQUES
449 Mammoth Rd Rte 128, 03053
(603)434-0272 **27 37**
Specializing in New England country
furniture & accessories. *Hours:* All
year by chance/appt. *Assoc:* NHADA.
Loc: 2 MI from Exit 5 I-93.

Loudon

CHIMES & TIMES CLOCK SHOP
RFD 8 Box 225C Rte 129, 03301
(603)435-7900 **23**
Quality antique clocks. *Pr:* $75–15000.
Est: 1980. *Serv:* Appraisal, consulta-
tion, repairs, restoration. *Hours:* Appt
suggested. *Size:* Medium. *Assoc:*
NAWCC. Ralph J Dickerson *Park:*
On site. *Loc:* Int Rtes 106 & 129, take
Rte 129 4 MI E, located at sharp curve
in the road.

COUNTRY ANTIQUES
Rte 129E, 03263
(603)435-6615 **27 34 59**
Country formal furniture, folk art,
paintings & quality accessories. *Hours:*
All year. *Assoc:* NHADA. Fred Cadarette *Loc:* 12 MI from Concord on Rte
129E off Rte 106N.

GODIVA ANTIQUES
Rte 129 Ext in Loudon Village, 03263
(603)798-5729 **29 63**
Staffordshire & European china &
porcelain, small pieces of furniture &
fine accessories. *Hours:* Year round
weekday afternoons & all day weekends. *Assoc:* NHADA. Pat Smith

Loudon Village

LOUDON VILLAGE ANTIQUE
SHOP
Oak Hill Rd, 03263
(603)783-4741
A general line of antiques. *Hours:* All
year by chance/appt. *Assoc:* NHADA.
Richard Malfait *Park:* On site. *Loc:*
Loudon Village Exit off Rte 106 at Jct
Rte 129, then 1st R, 2nd L.

Lyme

MARJORIE BARRY ANTIQUE
SHOW PROM
RFD 1 Box 18, 03768
(603)795-4641
Antique show promotion.

FALCON'S ROOST ANTIQUES
River Rd, 03768
(603)353-9815 **37**
Fine American 18th C & early 19th C
formal & country furniture & accesso-

ries located in a restored 18th C cape & barn. *Pr:* $25–7500. *Serv:* Bed & breakfast, appraisal, consultation, purchase estates. *Hours:* Apr 1-Nov 15 by chance/appt, Nov 16-Mar 31 BY APPT ONLY. *Assoc:* CADA NEAA NHADA VADA. Marilyn Bierylo *Park:* On site. *Loc:* I-91 Exit 14 to Lyme: 1st L after crossing CT River Bridge 2.5 MI on river side.

SOMEWHERE IN TIME ANTIQUES
Rte 10, 03768
(603)795-4641   **29 36**

Furniture, accessories & childhood treasures. *Hours:* May 15-Oct 15 call ahead. *Assoc:* NHADA. Marjorie A Barry *Loc:* 9 MI N of Hanover.

Lyme Center

JOAN & GAGE ELLIS
The Village Farm, 03796
(603)795-4170   **5 30 36**

18th & early 19th C furniture & decorative accessories, quilts, working decoys & architectural pieces. *Hours:* Call ahead. *Assoc:* NHADA. Joan Ellis *Park:* On site. *Loc:* 12 MI N of Hanover on the Village Green in Lyme on Rte 10.

Manchester

ANITA'S ANTIQUARIAN BOOKS
1408 Elm St, 03101
(603)669-7695   **13**

Antiquarian books specializing in New Hampshire, most stock pre-1920. *Hours:* Mon-Sat 9:30-5. *Assoc:* NHABA. Michael Danello

VICTORIAN BARN ANTIQUES
1029 Elm St, 03101
(603)622-1524   **1 37**

A fine selection of American furnishings & accessories 1800-1920. *Est:* 1982. *Serv:* Appraisal, purchase estates. *Hours:* Wed-Sat 11-4. *Size:* Medium. *CC:* MC/V. *Park:* Nearby lot. *Loc:* I-93 Exit 8: follow Bridge St & signs to downtown Manchester.

Marlborough

1836 GRANITE HOUSE
Main St Rte 101, 03455
(603)876-4218

Antiques & collectibles. *Hours:* By chance/appt. Reva Fields *Loc:* 5 MI E of Keene.

HOMESTEAD BOOKSHOP
Rte 101, 03455
(603)876-4213   **12 13**

Children's books, Americana, regional, printing & printing history, cookery, gastronomy, naval & marine. *Serv:* Appraisal, bookbinding. *Hours:* Apr 15-Oct 15 daily 9-5, Oct 16-Apr 14 CLOSED SUN. Harry E Kenney Jr

THOMAS R LONGACRE
628 Jaffrey Rd Rte 124, 03455
(603)876-4080   **29 37 59**

American country & formal furniture including early New England pieces & appropriate accessories. *Est:* 1971. *Hours:* All year appt advisable. *Assoc:* NEAA NHADA. *Loc:* 3.5 MI E on Rte 124, off Rte 101.

BETTY WILLIS ANTIQUES, INC
Jaffrey Rd Rte 124, 03455
(603)876-3983   **29 37 39**

American, English & European formal

& country furniture & accessories of the 18th & 19th C. *Hours:* By chance/appt. *Assoc:* NHADA. Betty Barenholtz

WOODWARDS ANTIQUES
166 Main St Rte 101, 03455
(603)876-3360   **27**
Country furniture refinished & in the rough. *Hours:* All year by chance/appt. *Assoc:* NHADA. Terry Woodward

M arlow

PEACE BARN ANTIQUES
Forest Rd Rte 123N, 03456
(603)446-7161   **16 27 65**
A country home, barn & herb garden offering early furniture, decorative accessories & pewter. *Hours:* Apr-Oct by chance/appt. *Assoc:* GSAAA NHADA. Ace Ells *Loc:* Red barn & cape at edge of village.

M eredith

ALEXANDRIA LAMP SHOP
Main St & Marketplace Ln, 03253
(603)279-4234   **50**
Antique kerosene, gas & electric lighting, lamp supplies, brass lighting, fabric shades, country-style pine & oak furniture, prints, jewelry, glassware, tools, reference books & collectibles. *Hours:* Mon-Sat 11-6 Sun 1-5 CLOSED WED (except Summer). *Assoc:* NHADA. Fran Governanti

BURLWOOD ANTIQUE CENTER
Jct Rtes 3 & 104, 03253
(603)279-6387   **[GR120]**
Two floors of smaller antiques, 1 floor

of furniture, displayed in a converted 18th C barn. *Est:* 1983. *Hours:* May-Oct daily 10-5. *Size:* Huge. *CC:* MC/V. *Assoc:* NHADA. Thomas Lindsey *Park:* On site. *Loc:* I-93 Exit 23: to Rte 104E, 9 MI to Jct of Rte 3, turn R, 100 yds up on R.

GORDONS ANTIQUES
Rte 3, 03253
(603)279-5458   **44 48 63**
Turn-of-the century antiques including porcelains, linens, jewelry, art glass, pottery, vintage clothing, lamps, sterling silver, clocks, furniture & decorative objects. *Pr:* $1–3000. *Est:* 1981. *Serv:* Purchase estates. *Hours:* May-Oct Mon-Sat 10-5, Nov-Dec 24 Mon,Sat 10-4. *Size:* Medium. *CC:* AX/MC/V. *Assoc:* NHADA. Marlene Gordon *Park:* In front. *Loc:* Rte 93N Exit 23: to Rte 104E to end, turn R on Rte 3, 1.5 MI S on L after Harpers Boat Yard.

THE OLD PRINT BARN
Winona Rd, 03253
(603)279-6479   **66**
Antiques & modern prints, etchings, engravings, serigraphs, mezzotints. 18th, 19th, & 20th C prints from New Hampshire, America, Europe & Japan. *Est:* 1976. *Serv:* Framing, restoration. *Hours:* May 15-Oct 15 daily 10-6, Oct 16-May 14 BY APPT ONLY. *Size:* Large. *CC:* MC/V. *Assoc:* NHADA. Sophia Lane *Park:* On site. *Loc:* From Hart's Restaurant on Rte 3, 1.5 MI on Rte 104 to blinking light, R on Winona Rd, 1.5 MI.

MARY ROBERTSON - BOOKS
Rte 3 & Parade Rd, 03253
(603)279-8750   **13**
Specializing in old/new children's &

needlework & craft books. *Hours:* Sum: daily 10-5, Spring/Fall most days 12-4. *Assoc:* NHABA.

Meriden

WATERCRESS ANTIQUES
Stage Rd & Rte 120, 03770
(603)469-3229 **27 65**
Country furniture, primitives & accessories. *Hours:* By chance/appt. Stephanie Thompson

Merrimack

JEANNINE DOBBS COUNTRY FOLK
PO Box 1076, 03054
(603)424-7617 **34 41 67**
18th & 19th C painted furnishings & accessories, baskets, samplers, quilts, hooked rugs, folk art & woodenware. *Hours:* BY APPT. *Assoc:* NHADA.

Milford

MILFORD ANTIQUES
14 Nashua St, 03055
(603)672-2311 **47**
Jewelry, general antiques & furniture. *Est:* 1955. *Serv:* Appraisal, evaluations. *Hours:* Wed-Sun 10-5. Mary Dugan *Park:* On site. *Loc:* Opposite the library.

NEW HAMPSHIRE ANTIQUE CO-OP, INC
Rte 101-A, 03055
(603)673-8499 **{GR100}**
Furniture, china, collectibles, Oriental rugs & sterling. *Est:* 1983. *Hours:*

Daily 10-5. *Size:* Huge. *CC:* MC/V. *Assoc:* GSAAA. Sam Hackler *Park:* On site. *Loc:* Rte 3 Exit 7W: Rte 101A into Milford 1.5 MI W of ctr of Milford.

THE RENAISSANCE MAN
275 Elm St Rte 101-A, 03055
(603)673-5653 **19 70 71**
Custom woodworking, museum-quality restoration, specializing in hand-rubbed oil finished reproduction true to early American design & technique, wood carving & parts reproduced. *Serv:* Consultation, interior design, repairs, replication, reproduction. *Hours:* Wed-Mon 10-5. *Assoc:* NHADA. Walter Haney MFA *Park:* On site. *Loc:* Rte 3 Exit 101A: to Milford, approx 9 MI, 1.5 MI past Milford Town Green, located at NH Antique Co-op.

VICTORIA PLACE
88 Nashua St Rte 101A, 03055
(603)673-7101 **39**
Imported English furniture, antiques & accessories. *Loc:* Rte 3 Exit 7W.

Mont Vernon

CANDLEWICK ANTIQUES
Main St Rte 13N, 03057
(603)673-1941 **34 63 80**
Country furniture, folk art, early china & glass, toys, textiles & Christmas ornaments. *Hours:* Sat,Sun 11-5, else by chance/appt. *Assoc:* NHADA. Jessie Anderson

Moultonboro

ANTIQUES AT MOULTONBORO
Old Rte 109S, 03254
(603)476-8863　　　**1 36**
In a restored 1840 New England cape 3 rooms of quality country & formal furniture, folk art, glass & other accessories. Barn is stocked with Americana, collectibles & furniture - refinished or rough. *Pr:* $10–2000. *Serv:* Refinishing. *Hours:* Daily 9-6 appt suggested. *Size:* Medium. *Assoc:* NHADA. Jack May *Park:* In front. *Loc:* Just off Rte 25, on Old Rte 109, Moultonboro Ctr.

BENCHMARK ANTIQUES
Rte 25, 03254
(603)253-6362　　　**27**
Country furniture & accessories. *Hours:* All year daily 10-5 by chance/appt. *Assoc:* NHADA. Gene Kincaid *Loc:* Opposite the Red Hill Motel.

CARL & BEVERLY SHELDRAKE
Stone Crop Farm, 03254
(603)544-9008　　　**29 36**
18th C country furniture & related accessories. *Hours:* By chance/appt. *Loc:* S of Moultonboro on Severance Rd btw Rtes 109 & 171 located near Lake Winnipesaukee.

Mt Sunapee

RED SLEIGH
Rte 103, 03782　　　**34 42 65**
Country pine, primitives, folk art & smalls. *Pr:* $10–1500. *Serv:* Consultation, purchase estates, repairs, restoration. *Hours:* Jun-Oct Mon-Sat 11-4:30. Joan Pirozzoli *Loc:* Rte 103E to base of Mt Sunapee, located at E end of traffic circle.

Nashua

PAUL HENDERSON
50 Berkeley St, 03060
(603)883-8918　　　**13**
Antiquarian books: genealogies, local history & Kansas. *Serv:* Catalog, search services. *Hours:* By chance/appt. *Assoc:* NHABA.

RALPH KYLLOE
288 Stone Bridge, 03063
(603)595-2992　　　**37**
Specializing in old hickory, Adirondack, twig, antler & rustic furnishings. *Serv:* Purchase single items or sets. *Hours:* BY APPT ONLY.

RUSTIC ACCENTS, INC.
69 Main St, 03060
(603)882-4112　　　**27 65**
Country, primitives & decorative accessories. *Hours:* Mon-Fri 9-5 weekends by chance/appt. *Assoc:* NHADA. Ken Pike

UNICORN ANTIQUES
523 Broad St Rte 130, 03063
(603)882-4118　　　**{GR30}**
Furniture, glass, ephemera & crafts. *Hours:* Wed-Mon 10-4 CLOSED TUE. *Loc:* Rte 3 Exit 6: Rte 130 W.

New Ipswich

ESTELLE M GLAVEY, INC.
Rte 124, 03071
(603)878-1200   **21 36 59**
Two brick Colonials with rooms of quality stock including country & formal furniture, paintings & rugs. *Est:* 1964. *Hours:* All year by chance/appt. *Assoc:* NHADA.

New London

THE BLOCK HOUSE
Hominy Pot Rd, 03257
(603)927-4623   **30 78**
Decoys, sporting artifacts, sporting prints & paintings. *Hours:* All year by chance/appt. Doug Knight

LEE BURGESS ANTIQUES
Little Sunapee Rd, 03257
(603)526-4657   **27**
Fine country furniture & accessories. *Hours:* BY APPT. *Assoc:* NHADA.

MOSES BURPEE FARM ANTIQUES
Burpee Hill Rd, 03257
(603)526-6315   **27**
Country furniture & accessories & lithographs. *Hours:* Jun-Aug by chance/appt. *Assoc:* NHADA. Elaine Robar *Loc:* Off Rte 11.

BURPEE HILL BOOKS
Burpee Hill Rd, 03257
(603)526-6654   **13**
General Americana, early printed books, books on art & collecting & paper. *Serv:* Catalog. *Hours:* By chance/appt. *Assoc:* NHABA. Alf E Jacobson

PRISCILLA DRAKE ANTIQUES
Main St, 03257
(603)526-6514   **36 44 63**
Furniture, glass, china & accessories. *Hours:* Jul-Aug Tue-Sat 10-4, May Jun & Sep by chance/appt. *Assoc:* NHADA.

MAD EAGLE INC FINE ANTIQUES
Rte 11, 03257
(603)526-4880   **16 37 63**
Fine early American furniture & choice accessories - both country & formal - & Oriental rugs. *Pr:* $1–16000. *Est:* 1961. *Hours:* May 15-Oct 15 Mon-Sat 1-5 appt suggested. *Size:* Large. *Assoc:* NHADA. *Park:* In front. *Loc:* I-89 Exit 11: 2 MI E.

Newington

NEWINGTON STAR CENTER
25 Fox Run Rd,
(603)431-9403
Antique fair & giant flea market. *Hours:* Sundays. *Park:* Ample. *Loc:* I-95: Portsmouth rotary to Spaulding Tnpk to Fox Run Rd.

Newport

JUNIPER HILL BOOKS
PO Box 119, 03773
(603)863-3919   **13**
Antiquarian books: Americana, biography, children's, travel & first editions. *Hours:* BY APPT ONLY. *Assoc:* NHABA. Anne D Purnell

Newton

STEVEN J ROWE
One N Main St, 03858
(603)382-4618   **27**
Country furniture & fine accessories in
original condition. *Hours:* All year BY
APPT. *Assoc:* NHADA. *Loc:* I-495
Exit 53: 4 MI.

North Conway

**ANTIQUES & COLLECTIBLES
BARN**
Rtes 16 & 302, 03860
(603)356-7118   **{GR40}**
Antiques & collectibles, including jew-
elry, silver, rugs, ephemera, linens,
quilts & period lighting. *Serv:* Consul-
tation, search service. *Hours:* Daily 10-
5. *Size:* Large. *CC:* AX/MC/V. *Assoc:*
NHADA. Mardy Friary *Park:* On site.
Loc: 1.5 MI N of lights in N Conway
Village.

GRALYN ANTIQUES, INC
Main St, 03860
(603)356-5546   **59**
19th C American art of the White
Mountain School. *Hours:* By
chance/appt. *Assoc:* NHADA. Robert
A Goldberg *Park:* In front. *Loc:* Rte
16S & 302 across from the Red Jacket
Motor Lodge.

**RICHARD M PLUSCH
ANTIQUES**
Main St Rtes 6 & 302, 03860
(603)356-3333   **29 59 63**
A diverse selection of fine period furnishings & accessories, glass, china,
silver, Orientalia, rugs, clocks, 19th C
paintings & prints, country & some

formal furniture. Always an interesting
collection of quality antiques. *Pr:* $5-
5000. *Serv:* Appraisal, consultation,
purchase estates. *Hours:* Daily Jun-
Oct 10-5 Sun 12-5 Nov-May Sat 10-5
Sun 12-5. *Size:* Medium. *Assoc:*
NHADA. *Loc:* In the heart of the
White Mountains 3 hrs N of Boston.

North Hampton

**NORTH HAMPTON ANTIQUE
CENTER**
One Lafayette Rd Rte 1, 03862
(603)964-6615   **{GR22}**
Antiques & collectibles. *Hours:* Year
round Mon-Sat 10-4 Sun by
chance/appt. *Assoc:* NHADA.

North Weare

**NEW HAMPSHIRE BOOK
AUCTIONS**
c/o Sykes Gallery Woodbury Rd, 03281
(603)529-1700   **8 13**
Auctions of books, prints, maps &
ephemera held May to November. Ex-
perienced cataloguers in rare Americana, early printed books, plate books
& modern first editions. *Est:* 1985.
Serv: Catalog ($15 sub), accept con-
signments, appraisal, purchase estates.
Hours: May-Nov BY APPT on non-
auction days. *Size:* Medium. Richard
Sykes *Park:* On site. *Loc:* 12 MI W of
Concord, Rte 13 to Rte 77, 20 MI W
of Manchester, Rte 114 to 77 at corner
of Rte 77 & Woodbury Ave.

Northwood

COUNTRY TAVERN OF NORTHWOOD
Rte 4, 03261
(603)942-7630   {GR50}

Quality American antiques in an 18th C tavern & barn, room settings, early country furniture, folk art, quilts & textiles, toys, rugs, baskets, distinctive smalls & primitives. *Hours:* All year Mon-Sat 10-5 Sun 12-5. *Size:* Large. *CC:* MC/V. *Assoc:* NHADA. Fern D Eldridge

DRAKE'S HILL ANTIQUES
Rte 202A, 03261
(603)942-5958   63

Soft paste, flow blue, Mulberry, Staffordshire, transferware & country furniture. *Hours:* All year by chance/appt. *Assoc:* NHADA. James Boyd

HARTLEY'S ANTIQUES
Jenness Pond, 03261
(603)942-7734   4 26

18th & 19th C furniture, decorative accessories, primitives, antique jewelry & silver. *Est:* 1940. *Serv:* Appraisal, consultation, purchase estates. *Hours:* BY APPT ONLY. *Assoc:* AAA NHADA. Helena Hartley

HAYLOFT ANTIQUE CENTER
Rte 4, 03261
(603)942-5153   {GR120}

Clocks, tools, treen, rugs, early bottles, silver, copper, lanterns, jewelry & furniture. *Hours:* Daily 10-5. Marie Hay *Loc:* Located on New Hampshire's famous Antique Alley.

JUNCTION ANTIQUE CENTER
Rtes 4 & 202, 03261
(603)942-5756   {GR}

Fine formal & country furniture & accessories. *Hours:* Mon-Fri 10-5 Sun 12-5.

NORTHWOOD INN ANTIQUE CENTER
454A Route 4A, 03261
(603)942-5611   {GR}

A general line of antiques. *Serv:* Purchase estates. *Hours:* Daily year round. *CC:* MC/V. Stuart Frye

PARKER FRENCH ANTIQUE CENTER
Rte 4, 03261
(603)942-8852   {GR110}

Oldest group shop in Northwood, featuring jewelry, silver, paintings & furniture. *Est:* 1974. *Serv:* Appraisal, purchase estates. *Hours:* Daily 10-5. *Size:* Huge. *Assoc:* NHADA. *Park:* In front. *Loc:* Midway between Concord & Portsmouth, 12 MI W of Lee traffic circle, 6 MI E of Epsom traffic circle.

PIONEER AMERICA
Rte 4 & Upper Bow St, 03261
(603)942-8588   63 65 66

Early country furniture, unique prints, primitives & pottery, glass, kitchenware, jewelry, lamps. *Hours:* Daily 9-5. *Size:* Medium. *CC:* MC/V. *Loc:* On antique alley.

TOWN PUMP ANTIQUES
Rte 4, 03261
(603)942-5515   {GR}

Three spacious floors of furniture, glass & collectibles. *Est:* 1986. *Serv:* Packing & shipping, restoration service. *Hours:* Mon-Sat 9-5 Sun 10-5. *Size:* Large. Joanie Ebberson

THE WHITE HOUSE ANTIQUES
Rte 4, 03261
(603)942-8994   {GR}

Signs & ephemera. *Serv:* Purchase estates. *Hours:* Daily 10-5. Joe Trovato

WILLOW HOLLOW ANTIQUES
Rte 4, 03261
(603)942-5739   {GR50}

Small antiques, primitives, advertising, paper, china, glass, toys & jewelry. *Serv:* Catalog. *Hours:* Daily 10-5. *CC:* MC/V. *Assoc:* NHADA. Nancy Winston

Ossipee

FLAG GATE FARM ANTIQUES
Rte 28, 03864
(603)539-2231   44 50

Two large floors furnished with period antiques, Irish pine, antique lighting & glassware, cut glass, pattern glass, art glass, lace & miniature lamps. *Pr:* $25–6600. *Serv:* Bed & breakfast. *Hours:* Daily 12-7, call for hours in April. *Size:* Large. *CC:* MC/V. *Assoc:* AAA NHADA. Marion M Ingemi *Park:* On site. *Loc:* On Rte 28 in Ossipee .25 MI S off Rte 16, N of Portsmouth.

GREEN MOUNTAIN ANTIQUE CENTER
Rte 16, 03864
(603)539-2236   {GR75}

Glass, china, primitives, tools, furniture, books, linens, vintage clothing, jewelry & coins. *Est:* 1982. *Hours:* Year round daily 9-5. *Size:* Huge. *Assoc:* NHADA.

THE STUFF SHOP
Box 5 Rte 171, 03864
(603)539-7715

Diverse selection of antiques & collectibles. *Pr:* $10–1000. *Est:* 1960. *Serv:* Appraisal, lamp repair. *Hours:* May 20-Oct 12 daily 10-6 BY APPT ONLY. *Size:* Medium. *CC:* MC/V. *Assoc:* AAA NEAA. Len Wenant *Park:* In front. *Loc:* Rte 16 to Rte 28W on Rte 171, 6th house on L from Rte 28.

Pelham

CARTER'S BARN ANTIQUES
Mammoth Rd Rte 128, 03076
(603)883-3269   {GR}

Early pine, oak, mahogany & walnut furniture. *Serv:* Stripping, refinishing. *Hours:* Wed-Sun 10-5. *Size:* Large. *CC:* MC/V.

Peterborough

BRENNANS ANTIQUES
130 Hunt Rd, 03458
(603)924-3445   65 81

Country furniture, primitives, woodenware, tin, iron, early tools & decorative accessories. *Hours:* BY APPT. *Assoc:* GSAAA. Judy Brennan

THE COBBS ANTIQUES
83 Grove St, 03458
(603)924-6361   21 34 41

Quality primitive, country, formal & painted furniture, paintings, rugs, fabrics, folk art, porcelains, glass & silver. *Serv:* Appraisal. *Hours:* Mon-Sat 9:30-5. *Assoc:* NHADA. Charles M Cobb *Loc:* 1 block N of Int of Rtes 202 & 101.

OLD TOWN FARM ANTIQUES
121B Old Town Farm Rd, 03458
(603)924-3523   **21 27 59**

Period & country furniture, Oriental rugs, decorative accessories, paintings & smalls. **Hours:** Daily 10-5 Sun & Holidays call ahead. **Size:** Large. **Assoc:** NHADA. Robert Taylor **Loc:** From 101W, S on Rte 202 1 MI R on Old Jaffrey Rd, R on Old Town Farm Rd, big red barn on R.

PARTRIDGE REPLICATIONS
83 Grove St, 03458
(603)924-3002   **46 69 80**

18th C handcrafted replicas, documented fabrics & decorative accessories. **Serv:** Interior design. **Hours:** Mon-Sat 10-4:30. **CC:** MC/V. Ted Partridge

PETERBOROUGH USED BOOKS & PRINTS
105 Grove St, 03458
(603)924-3534   **13 51 66**

Rare & unusual books & prints, as well as maps, manuscripts & ephemera. **Pr:** $1–500. **Est:** 1987. **Serv:** Appraisal, consultation, purchase estates. **Hours:** Mon-Sat 9:30-4:30. **Size:** Medium. **Assoc:** GSAAA. **Park:** In front. **Loc:** From Int of Rtes 101 & 202, E on Grove St (Rte 202).

PETERBOROUGH ANTIQUE ASSOCIATES
76 Grove Street, 03458
(603)924-7297   **{GR}**

Offering a large & varied selection of 18th, 19th & 20th C furniture, art & accessories. **Hours:** Mon-Sat 9:30-5 Sun 12:30-4:30. **Loc:** Just off Rte 101 headed N.

Plainfield

PLAINFIELD AUCTION GALLERY
Plainfield, 03781
(603)675-2549   **4 8**

Auctioneer specializing in fine antiques. **Serv:** Auction, appraisal, purchase single items or complete estates. William A Smith **Loc:** I-89 Exit 20: S on Rte 12-A from West Lebanon Plaza 7 MI.

Plymouth

PAULINE CHARON ANTIQUES
Texas Hill Rd, 03264
(603)968-7975   **27 65**

Country furniture & primitives. **Hours:** All year by chance. **Assoc:** NHADA. **Loc:** I-93 Exit 24 (Ashland): 3.5 MI, N on Rte 3, after bridge.

SUSAN B LARSEN ANTIQUES
Texas Hill Rd, 03264
(603)968-7510   **20 23 47**

Jewelry, daguerreotypes & clocks. **Hours:** By chance/appt. **Assoc:** NHADA. **Loc:** Next house on R after Pauline Charon.

Portsmouth

BOOK GUILD OF PORTSMOUTH
58 State St, 03801
(603)436-1758   **13**

Antiquarian books: maritime history, New England, Civil War & Confederacy, voyages, travels & explorations, children's & illustrated. **Serv:** Catalogs, search service. **Hours:** Mon-Fri 10-5 Sat 11-3. **Assoc:** NHABA. Martin Held

NANCY BORDEN
PO Box 4381, 03801
(603)436-4284   **74 80**
Replicas of 17th, 18th & mid-19th C textile furnishings, wall coverings, bedhangings, period slip covers & upholstery using museum-documented textile reproductions in their historic context. **Est:** 1968. **Serv:** Period interior consultant, brochure upon request. **Hours:** BY APPT & scheduled consultation.

MARGARET SCOTT CARTER, INC.
175 Market St, 03801
(603)436-1781   **16 27 57**
Needlework, furniture & country accessories, old woodworking tools, decoys & folk art. **Hours:** Daily 10-5 CLOSED SUN. **Assoc:** NHADA. **Park:** Nearby. **Loc:** I-95 Exit 7: 2 min E.

COBBLESTONES OF MARKET SQUARE
10 Market St, 03801
(603)436-4468   **29 37 39**
English & American antiques, collectibles & accessories. **Hours:** Memorial Day Weekend-Dec Daily, Win: CLOSED SUN. **Assoc:** NHADA.

THE DOLL CONNECTION
117 Market St, 03801
(603)431-5030   **32**
Dolls ranging from 1820-1950, doll accessories - including clothes, doll house furniture. **Est:** 1973. **Serv:** Doll restoration service, appraisal, consultation. **Hours:** Mon-Sat 10-4. Helen Jarvis **Loc:** I-95N Exit 7: .75 MI.

GARAKUTA COLLECTION
65 Bow St, 03801
(603)433-1233   **60**
Japanese woodblocks, Tansu & Mingei, Asian arts, textiles & antiques. **Est:** 1986. **Serv:** Consultation. **Hours:** Jun-Sep 6 Tue-Thu 11-6 Fri 11-9 Sat 11-6 Sun 11-5. Sylvia Chaplain

MILL POND ANTIQUES
Box 4298, 03801
(603)481-5508   **34**
English & American antiques & folk art. Bill Renner

W MORIN FURNITURE RESTORATION
871 Islington St, 03801
(603)431-7418   **25 68 71**
Careful restoration of antique furniture paying particular attention to original construction details with an eye to making as few alterations as possible. **Serv:** Conservation, consultation, repairs, custom finishes. **Hours:** Mon-Fri 9:30-5 Sat 10-2 appt suggested. Will Morin **Park:** On site. **Loc:** I-95 Exit 3: Rte 101, R at SS, .25 MI, L on Islington, .75 MI on L in an old mill building.

PARTRIDGE REPLICATIONS
63 Penhallow St, 03801
(603)431-8733   **46 69 80**
18th C handcrafted replicas, documented fabrics & decorative accessories. **Est:** 1978. **Serv:** Interior design. **Hours:** Mon-Sat 10-4:30. **CC:** MC/V. Ted Partridge **Loc:** 1 block N of Market Square.

PORTSMOUTH BOOKSHOP
110 State St, 03801
(603)433-4406   **13**
General stock of fine antiquarian & children's illustrated books. **Hours:**

Tue-Sun 10-6, expanded hours in Summer. *Assoc:* NHABA. Brian DiMambro

SAUNDERS & COOKE INC
Box 1459, 03801
(603)436-0011   **10 70**
Reproductions of handcrafted stick barometers. *Serv:* Reproductions, brochure ($2). *Hours:* MAIL ORDER ONLY.

TRUNKWORKS
68 State St, 03801
(603)431-3310   **13 40 81**
Specializing in tools, rare books, jewelry, golden oak furniture & trunks. *Serv:* Restoration, refinishing. *Hours:* Mon-Sat 11-5 Sun 12-5. *Assoc:* NEAA NHADA. Julie Bickerstaff

ED WEISSMAN
110 Chapel St, 03801
(603)431-7575   **16 29 37**
Pre-1840 American furniture, American, European & Oriental 15th-early 19th C accessories. *Est:* 1956. *Hours:* May-Sep daily 10-5, else BY APPT. *Assoc:* ISA NHADA. *Loc:* In town, near the wharf.

WISTERIA TREE
18 Ladd St, 03801
(603)431-8920   **47**
Antique & estate jewelry. *Est:* 1978. *Hours:* Jan-Apr Wed-Sat 10-5, May-Oct Mon-Sat 10-5, extended Xmas hr. *CC:* MC/V. Oreen Audette *Park:* Nearby. *Loc:* Across from "In Town" parking garage - elevator side.

Raymond

BURT DIAL COMPANY
Rte 107, 03077
(603)895-2879   **23 31 71**
Refinish & restoration of reverse paintings & restoration of tall clock dials. *Est:* 1917. *Hours:* Mon-Fri 8-5.

CALOUBAR COLLECTABLES
25 Scribner Rd, 03077
(603)895-3634   **21 36**
Rugs, furniture, baskets & yellow ware. *Hours:* By chance/appt. *Assoc:* NHADA. Cathy Cosentino

Richmond

NORTH COUNTRY BOOKSHOP
Rte 119 Four Corners, 03470
(603)239-6547   **13 33**
General rare books, first editions, children's books, Americana & ephemera. *Serv:* Catalog. *Hours:* BY APPT/MAIL. *Assoc:* NHABA. Alan S Harvey *Loc:* Jct of Rtes 119 & 32.

SPINNING WHEEL ANTIQUES
Rte 32, 03470
(603)239-6208   **27**
Country furniture & accessories. *Hours:* All year by chance/appt. *Assoc:* NHADA. Ron Frazier *Loc:* .7 MI from Int of Rtes 32 & 119.

Rindge

SCOTT BASSOFF/SANDY JACOBS
Robbins Rd, 03461
(603)899-3373   **37**

Early American furniture & accessories. *Hours:* Appt advisable. *Assoc:* NHADA. *Loc:* Rte 202 to Thomas Rd, 3 MI, brown cape with red picket fence.

Rochester

PETER CARSWELL ANTIQUES
293 Pond Hill Rd, 03867
(603)332-4264   **1 36 65**

Wide selection from New England homes with emphasis on country & formal furniture & accessories in as-found condition. *Pr:* $25–10000. *Serv:* Appraisal, auction, purchase estates. *Hours:* Daily by chance/appt. *Size:* Medium. *Assoc:* NHADA. *Park:* On site. *Loc:* W of Rochester approx 3 MI watch for sign on Rte 202.

Rumney

JOHN F HENDSEY -BOOKSELLER
Quincy Rd, 03266
(603)786-2213   **13**

Fine & rare books in all fields, New Hampshire's oldest rare book auction firm. *Serv:* Appraisal. *Hours:* BY APPT ONLY. *Assoc:* ABAA NHABA.

ELIZABETH OLCOTT BOOKS
Quincy Rd, 03266
(603)786-9898   **13**

Antiquarian books: modern first editions, detective fiction, cookbooks & biography. *Hours:* By chance/appt. *Assoc:* NHABA.

VILLAGE BOOKS
Main St, 03266
(603)786-9300   **13 33**

Antiquarian books: general New England Americana, White Mountains, hunting, fishing & ephemera. *Hours:* Jun-Oct & Dec-Mar daily. *Assoc:* ABAA NHABA. George Kent

Salem

SANDERS ANTIQUES
101 Main St, 03079
(603)893-2763   **23 29**

Period furnishing & early American clocks. *Serv:* Shipping, all descriptions guaranteed. *Hours:* Wed-Fri 12-5. *CC:* MC/V.

Salisbury Heights

BARKER'S OF SALISBURY HEIGHTS
Rte 4, 03268
(603)648-2488   **36 44 81**

Furniture, tools & glass. *Hours:* Daily 9-5. *Loc:* Opposite the library.

Sandwich

ANTIQUES & AUCTIONS, LTD
Rtes 113 & 113A, 03270
(603)284-6600 **65 67**
Primitives, quilts, tin, furniture, china, glass & baskets. *Hours:* Mid Jun-Mid Oct daily 10-5 CLOSED WED,SUN. *Assoc:* NHADA. Harold Bonnyman *Loc:* 4 MI from Ctr Sandwich.

THE CENTER ANTIQUES
Sandwich, 03270
(603)284-6828
General line of antiques & collectibles. *Hours:* May-Jun Wed-Sat 10-5 Jul 4-Oct 12 Mon-Sat 10-5. *Assoc:* NHADA.

Seabrook

STONE HOUSE ANTIQUES
855 Lafayette Rd Rte 1, 03874
(603)474-3668 **21 37 59**
Early New England furniture, paintings, hooked rugs & accessories. *Hours:* All year daily 10-5 CLOSED MON. *Assoc:* NHADA. Edwin Page *Loc:* I-95 Exit 1: 1 MI.

Shelburne

CROW MOUNTAIN FARM ANTIQUES
North Rd, 03581
(603)466-2509 **65 81**
American primitives, tools, paintings, prints, furniture, tinware & accessories. *Hours:* May-Oct daily, Nov-Apr call ahead. *Assoc:* NHADA. *Loc:* 1 MI E of Philbrook Farm Inn.

Snowville

SLEIGH MILL ANTIQUES
Snow Rd, 03832
(603)447-6791 **28 50 83**
A mill full of antiques, accessories & authentic 19th C lighting. *Est:* 1982. *Serv:* Shipping. *Hours:* By chance/appt. Edith Dashnau *Park:* On site. *Loc:* 6 MI S of Conway NH off Rte 153.

South Hampton

R G BETTCHER RESTORATIONS
Rte 107A, 03827
(603)394-7546 **5 16 74**
Quality 18th C architectural materials, early braced frame buildings & early ironware. *Hours:* By chance/appt. *Assoc:* NHADA. Bob Bettcher

Spofford

FINE ANTIQUES
Spofford, 03462
(603)363-4363 **36 59 65**
Quality period formal furniture, primitives, oil paintings, glass, copper lustre & silver resist. *Hours:* BY APPT ONLY. *Assoc:* NHADA. William W Lewis

Springfield

THE COLONEL'S SWORD
Four Corners Rd, 03284
(603)763-2112 **39 44 63**
English & American furniture, glass,

china, paintings, Oriental export porcelain & military items. *Hours:* May-Jun, Sep-Oct weekends, Jul & Aug Thu-Sat 10-5 BY APPT. *Assoc:* NHADA. Caye Currier

LAZY FOX ANTIQUES ET GALLERIE
Springfield, 03284
(603)763-2122   **32 38 63**

English, European & American furniture, porcelain, attic treasures, dolls & child-related items. *Hours:* Jun-Oct daily 10-5 or BY APPT. *Assoc:* NHADA. Jacki Beam

SPRING HILL FARM ANTIQUES
Four Corners Rd, 03284
(603)763-2292   **44 63 77**

China, glass, silver, country things, linens, prints & baskets. *Hours:* May-Oct daily 10-4. *Assoc:* NHADA. Robert E Moore *Loc:* I-89 Exit 12A.

Stratham

COMPASS ROSE ANTIQUES
17 Winnicut Rd, 03885
(603)778-0163   **1 6 32**

Diverse selection of general antiques, with accent on country smalls & fine furniture. *Pr:* $10–5000. *Est:* 1981. *Serv:* Appraisal, consultation, purchase estates. *Hours:* Apr-Dec daily 10-4 CLOSED THU, else Sat,Sun 10-4:30. *Size:* Medium. *Assoc:* GSAAA. NHADA. Laurie Clark *Park:* In front. *Loc:* From Portsmouth: Rte 101W toward Exeter to ctr of Stratham, L on Winnicut Rd, 1 block from Rte 101.

THE COURTYARD EMPORIUM
Portsmouth Ave, 03885
(603)772-6835   **{GR}**

Furniture, glass, prints, linens, dolls, trunks, rugs, baskets, lamps & books. *Hours:* Apr-Dec 25 Mon-Sat 10-5 Sun 12-5. *Assoc:* NHADA. *Loc:* Next to Carriage Stall Restaurant.

JOHN PIPER HOUSE
Sandy Point Rd, 03885
(603)778-1347   **1 27 65**

Early American, country furniture & accessories pre-1860 in an 18th C barn. *Pr:* $25–2000. *Est:* 1980. *Hours:* Apr-Dec 24 by chance/appt, Dec 26-Mar BY APPT ONLY. *Size:* Medium. *Assoc:* NHADA. Barbara Mann *Park:* On site. *Loc:* I-95 to Rte 101W to Stratham approx 5.5 MI, R onto Sandy Point Rd, opposite Stratham Hill Park.

Sunapee

FRANK & BARBARA POLLACK
Box 344, 03782
(603)763-2403   **34 37 65**

American country furniture, primitive paintings, folk art, art deco jewelry, toleware, textiles & decorative arts of the 20th C. *Hours:* Jun-Aug 15 BY APPT. *Assoc:* NHADA. *Loc:* Call for directions.

Swanzey

O'BRIEN ENTERPRISES
Rte 121, 03431
(603)357-0679   **{GR40}**

Country, Victorian, glassware, dolls, tools, vintage clothing, jewelry & tin. *Hours:* Daily 10-5. Jim O'Brien *Loc:* At Cheshire County Fairgrounds.

Tamworth

SANDERS & MOCK, ASSOCIATES
Box 37, 03886
(603)323-8749   **8**
Specializing in fine antiques, Americana, & fine arts, large modern gallery, offices in New London & Tamworth, NH & Portland, ME. *Est:* 1972. *Serv:* Appraisal, auction, brochure, catalog, consultation, purchase estates. *Hours:* Mon-Fri 8:30-4:30 Sat,Sun BY APPT. *Assoc:* CAI. Wayne Mock

Troy

RED SHED
Central Sq, 03465
(603)242-6473   **40 42 81**
Pine & oak furniture, clocks, iron & brass beds, cast iron stoves, tools & collectibles. *Hours:* Daily 10-5 CLOSED SUN,MON. *Loc:* On Rte 12.

Tuftonboro

LOG CABIN ANTIQUES
Rte 109A & Ledge Hill Rd, 03816
(603)569-1909   **1 48 64**
Small shop off the beaten path with a general line of antiques & collectibles including linens & post cards. *Pr:* $5–250. *Est:* 1968. *Serv:* Purchase estates. *Hours:* Memorial Day-Labor Day Fri-Sun 9-5. *Size:* Medium. *Assoc:* NHADA. Betty Buttrick *Park:* On site. *Loc:* From Wolfeboro, Rte 109A, 6 MI to Int of 109A & Ledge Hill Rd, on corner opposite Ctr Tuftonboro School.

Tuftonboro Center

GOLDEN PAST ANTIQUE MARKET
Rte 109A, 03816
(603)569-4024   **{GR10}**
Primitives, linen, sterling, furniture, china, political items, paper, post cards, books, gold & jewelry. *Assoc:* NHADA. *Loc:* Between General Store & school.

Tuftonboro Corner

DOW'S CORNER SHOP
Rte 171 & Ledge Hill Rd, 03864
(603)539-4790   **7**
An old-fashioned shop in a well-stocked, large barn, specializing in art deco. *Est:* 1948. *Hours:* Apr-Nov daily 10-5, else BY APPT. *Size:* Large. *Assoc:* NHADA. *Loc:* Rte 171 between Rtes 16 & 25.

Twin Mountain

BRETTON HALL ANTIQUITIES
At the Big Red Store, 03595
(603)846-2226   **13**
Antiquarian books relating to the White Mountains. *Hours:* Jun-Oct, Dec-Mar daily. *Assoc:* NHABA. Richard Force

Farquhar Antiques

Prospect Hill Road
Walpole, NH 03608
603/756-4871

*Rope Bed in Original
Vermillion Paint*

Union

CARSWELL'S ANTIQUES
Rte 153, 03887
(603)473-2304   **23 27 47**
Country furniture, primitives, yellow ware, baskets, clocks & jewelry. *Hours:* All year by chance/appt. *Assoc:* NHADA. Kippy Carswell

Walpole

FARQUHAR ANTIQUES
Prospect Hill Rd, 03608
(603)756-4871   **28 36 44**
Period, Empire, Victorian & country furniture, art glass, decorated stoneware, coverlets, quilts & accessories. *Est:* 1986. *Serv:* Purchase estates. *Hours:* Daily 9-5 by chance/appt. *Assoc:* NHADA VADA. Mary E Farquhar *Park:* On site. *Loc:* Off S Main St.

GOLDEN PAST OF WALPOLE
Rte 12, 03608
(603)756-3974   **23 37 59**
Fine collection of oil paintings, stained glass windows, American & Victorian furniture, Oriental rugs, china, quilts

& clocks. *Hours:* Apr 15-Dec 15 daily 9:30-5:30. *Assoc:* NHADA. Woody Boynton

RHODES OF WASHINGTON SQUARE
Washington St, 03608
(603)756-3980   **36 59**
18th & 19th C furniture, paintings & collectibles. *Hours:* Weekends & Summer evenings. Robert H Rhodes *Loc:* On the Town Green 1 block W of Main St.

Warner

LINDA L DONOVAN
Melvin Mills Rd, 03278
(603)456-3718   **25**
Conservation & restoration of oil paintings. *Hours:* BY APPT. *Assoc:* AIC. *Loc:* I-89N Exit 9: W on Rte 103 for 4.5 MI to Melvin Mills Rd.

HILLSIDE BOOKS
Rte 103, 03278
(603)456-3338   **13**
Antiquarian books: Americana, science, paper & magazines. *Hours:* By chance/appt. *Assoc:* NHABA. Christopher Stotler *Loc:* 2 MI W of I-89.

SCOTT'S ANTIQUES
Main St, 03278
(603)456-3960   **27 37**

American & country furniture & accessories in as-found condition. *Hours:* Apr-Dec daily til 5 or by chance. *Assoc:* NHADA. Harriet Scott *Loc:* I-89 Exit 9 (Warner): 3rd house on L.

Warren

WM MERRIFIELD MERTSCH ANTIQUES
Rtes 25 & 118, 03279
(603)764-9945   **59 65**

Early American furniture, accessories, small paintings & primitives in the Obadiah Clement homestead. *Hours:* All year by chance/appt. *Assoc:* NHADA.

KEN MOSHOLDER
Rte 25, 03279
(603)764-5838

Early pine country cupboards & furniture. *Hours:* Call ahead.

Washington

HALF-MOON ANTIQUES
Half-Moon Pond Rd, 03280
(603)495-3663   **29 36**

Furniture & accessories. *Hours:* Year round. *CC:* AX. *Assoc:* NHADA.

TINTAGEL ANTIQUES
Rte 31, 03280
(603)495-3429   **27 63 81**

Country furniture & accessories, tools, frames, flow blue china & hooked rugs. *Serv:* Pewter repair. *Assoc:* NHADA. Sally Krone *Loc:* 1 MI N of village on Rte 31.

Weare

SYKES & FLANDERS ANTIQUARIAN BKS
92 Woodbury Rd, 03281
(603)529-7432   **13 51 66**

A collector's stock of general fine & rare books, maps & prints with emphasis on 19th & 20th C first editions, Americana, White Mountains, modern first editions including detective fiction, New Hampshire, illustrated books, travel & exploration. *Pr:* $25–5000. *Est:* 1975. *Serv:* Appraisal, free catalog, purchase estates. *Hours:* Apr-Dec BY APPT. *Size:* Medium. *Assoc:* ABAA NHABA NHADA. Richard Sykes *Park:* On site. *Loc:* 12 MI W of Concord via Rte 13 to Rte 77, 20 MI W of Manchester via Rte 114 to Rte 77, at Jct of Woodbury Ave & Rte 77.

FRED P WHITTIER III
Greenleaf Farm, 03281
(603)529-2936   **8**

Auctions of antique furniture & furnishings from area estates. No buyer's premium or reserves. *Serv:* Auctioneer. Jeffrey Wigsten

Wentworth

THE RE-STORE ANTIQUES
Rtes 25 & 25A, 03282
(603)764-9395   **71**

Restored turn-of-the-century furniture, specializing in rolltop desks. *Hours:* Daily 10-5.

RETOUCH THE PAST
Rte 25, 03282
(603)764-5851   **1 22 71**

Refinished trunks & lamps with assorted smalls. *Serv:* Repairs, restoration. *Hours:* By chance/appt. Robert Stover *Park:* In front. *Loc:* I-93 Exit 26: Rte 25 to Wentworth (15 MI), across from Town Common on Rte 25.

West Lebanon

COLONIAL PLAZA ANTIQUES
Rte 12A, 03784
(603)298-7712   {GR90}

Giant flea market with antiques, furniture, old books, old clothes, estate jewelry, paintings & bottles. *Hours:* Daily 9-5 Sun Outside May-Oct. *Loc:* I-89 Exit 20.

PARTRIDGE REPLICATIONS
The Power House Rte 12A, 03784
(603)298-6066   46 69 80

18th C handcrafted replicas, documented fabric & decorative accessories. *Est:* 1978. *Serv:* Interior design. *Hours:* Mon-Sat 10-4:30. *CC:* MC/V. Ted Partridge

WINDHAM ANTIQUES
PO Box 401, 03784
(603)298-8352   36 63

Fine 18th & 19th C furniture & accessories, including fireplace accessories, early soft paste & porcelain, early flint glass, exceptional woodenware, including items in good old paint, Shaker items, early brass & iron, anything unusual or of merit. *Pr:* $20–4000. *Serv:* Appraisal, consultation. *Hours:* BY APPT ONLY. *Assoc:* GSAAA. Andrew Katz *Loc:* Several group shop locations including the Windsor Antiques Market, call for appt and directions.

West Nottingham

MERRY HILL FARM
Rte 4 & Merry Hill Rd, 03291
(603)942-5370   {GR}
Antiques & folk art. *Hours:* Daily 10-5.

West Swanzey

KNOTTY PINE ANTIQUE MARKET
Rte 10, 03469
(603)352-5252   {GR300}
China, glass, metalware, jewelry, furniture, pottery, primitives, rugs, quilts, art glass, pewter, dishes, toys & advertising. Non-dealer admission $2. *Hours:* Year round daily 9-5. Joan E Pappas *Park:* On site. *Loc:* 5 MI S of Keene.

FREDERICK MAC PHAIL ANTIQUES
Rte 10, 03469
(603)357-7257   24 40 83
Large selection of antiques featuring oak & Victorian furniture, collectibles, coins & toys. *Est:* 1982. *Serv:* Auctions, appraisal. *Hours:* Sat,Sun 10-5 or BY APPT, weekdays by chance/appt. *Assoc:* ANA NHAA NHNA. *Park:* On site. *Loc:* From Keene: 4 MI S of Ramada Inn. From S: just past Swanzey Historical Museum.

Westmoreland

THE ANTIQUES SHOPS
Rte 12, 03467
(603)399-7039   {GR40}

Decorative accessories, glass, pottery & porcelain, linens & metalware. *Est:* 1987. *Hours:* Daily 10-5. *Size:* Large. *CC:* MC/V. *Assoc:* NHADA. Larry Muchmore *Park:* On site. *Loc:* Rte 12N, 7 MI N of Keene.

CELTIC CROSS BOOKS
Rte 12, 03467
(603)399-4342   13

Specializing in Catholic books - especially liturgy, spirituality & Thomistic philosophy. *Pr:* $10–500. *Est:* 1981. *Serv:* Catalog $1. *Hours:* By chance/appt. *Size:* Medium. *Assoc:* NHABA. Henry Hurley *Park:* In front. *Loc:* Rte 12, 10 MI W of Keene.

HURLEY BOOKS
Rte 12, 03467
(603)399-4342   13

Specializing in Protestant religion, farming & horticulture, miniature books, printing & early imprints. *Pr:* $1–1000. *Est:* 1966. *Serv:* Catalog $1. *Hours:* By chance/appt. *Size:* Medium. *Assoc:* NHABA. Henry Hurley *Park:* In front. *Loc:* Rte 12, 10 MI W of Keene.

Whitefield

THE FAIRWEATHER SHOP
Rte 116 65 Jefferson Rd, 03598
(603)837-9806   44 63

Specializing in glass & china, featuring quality antiques only. *Assoc:* NHADA. *Loc:* .5 MI from blinking light in Whitefield.

Wilmot Flat

PLEASANT ACRES ANTIQUES ETC
Campground Rd, 03287
(603)526-4662   27

Country accessories. *Loc:* Off Rte 11.

YE OLDE SHAVEHORSE WORKSHOP
Kearsarge Valley Rd, 03287
(603)927-4900   {GR11}

A variety of antiques & collectibles located on one floor in a gambrel building, with an adjoining restoration shop. *Est:* 1986. *Serv:* Custom woodwork, repairs, restoration. *Hours:* Daily 9-5. *Size:* Medium. *CC:* MC/V. *Assoc:* GSAAA. Dick H Bacon *Park:* In front. *Loc:* I-89 Exit 11: 5 MI E on Rte 11, 1 MI from Rte 11 on R.

Winchester

FAT CHANCE ANTIQUES
102 N Main St, 03470
(603)239-6423   24 64 79

Post cards, maps, prints, sheet music, wicker, coins & stamps. *Hours:* Most Sat,Sun,Mon 11-4 CLOSED WIN. Robert Evans

GOOD OLD DAYS ANTIQUES
Main St Rte 10, 03470
(603)239-8818   {GR15}

Historical flasks, bottles, insulators, furniture, collectibles, art glass, china, clocks, jugs & toys. *Serv:* Appraisal.

Hours: Year round daily 9-5. Joseph Pillarella **Park:** On site. **Loc:** Corner of Rtes 10 & 119.

RICHARD WHITE ANTIQUES
98 N Main St, 03470
(603)239-4445   **1 21 23**

Fine 18th & early 19th C furniture & accessories including clocks & Oriental rugs. **Pr:** $5–25000. **Serv:** Appraisal, purchase estates. **Hours:** Mon-Fri 1-4 by chance/appt. **Size:** Medium. **Park:** On site. **Loc:** Rte 10.

Wolfeboro

AREA CODE 603 ANTIQUES
Rte 28, 03894
(603)569-3101   **27 51 64**

Country furniture & accessories, silver, maps & post cards. **Hours:** Jun-Sep by chance/appt.

AUCTIONS BY BOWERS & MERENA, INC
Box 1224, 03894
(603)569-5095   **8 24**

Numismatic auctions. **Est:** 1953. **Serv:** Catalog. Q. David Bowers

RICHARD G MARDEN
Elm St, 03894
(603)569-3209   **34 44 63**

Staffordshire historical china, spatterware, gaudy Dutch, Leeds & other early china for the American market, small folk art items & early American glass. **Pr:** $10–10000. **Serv:** Appraisal, auction, free catalog, consultation, purchase estates. **Hours:** By chance/appt. **Park:** On site. **Loc:** 100 MI N of Boston.

MONIQUE'S ANTIQUES
4 Brummitt Ct, 03894
(603)569-4642   **44 77 85**

Glass, china, silver, jewelry, furniture & vintage clothing. **Hours:** By chance/appt. **Assoc:** NHADA. Jean Radetzky

NEW ENGLAND GALLERY
RR 2 Box 959, 03894
(603)569-3501   **14 59**

19th & 20th C American paintings, watercolors & small antique collectibles. **Pr:** $200–10000. **Serv:** Free catalog of art reference books & price guides, appraisal, consultation. **Hours:** May-Oct 15 BY APPT. Arthur Fraumeni

RALPH K REED ANTIQUES
Pleasant Valley Rd, 03894
(603)569-1897   **10 39 56**

Furniture - mainly English campaign chests, boxes & sea chests in camphorwood, teak, mahogany & pine. Old mercury barometers a specialty. **Pr:** $50–5000. **Est:** 1965. **Hours:** All year by chance/appt. **Assoc:** NHADA. **Park:** On site. **Loc:** 3 MI off Rte 28 on Pleasant Valley Rd, 2 MI S of Wolfeboro.

TOUCHMARK ANTIQUES
S Main St, 03894
(603)569-1386   **27 42 65**

Country barn on Rust Pond specializing in country primitives, pine furniture & decorative items. **Pr:** $25–1000. **Est:** 1974. **Serv:** Appraisal, purchase estates, restoration. **Hours:** May-Oct daily 10-5 BY APPT ONLY. **Size:** Medium. **CC:** MC/V. **Assoc:** NHADA. Anne Roome **Park:** On site. **Loc:** From downtown Wolfeboro, 2.5 MI S on Rte 28 on L.

▼

Rhode Island

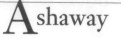shaway

ASHAWAY ANTIQUES STORE
20 High St Rte 216, 02804
(401)377-8116   **16 37 67**
1850 country store with early American furniture in old finish & paint, quilts, coverlets, hooked rugs, needlework, Staffordshire, coin silver, brass, copper, tin, iron, paintings, folk art, kitchenware & wood. *Pr:* $1–2500. *Est:* 1978. *Serv:* Appraisal, consultation, interior design. *Hours:* By chance/appt. *Size:* Medium. Sally Van Den Bossche *Park:* In front. *Loc:* I-95 CT Exit 93: 1 MI E on Rte 216 to ctr of Ashaway Village, on L after crossing river.

BRIGGS HOUSE ANTIQUES
18 High St Rte 216, 02804
(401)377-4464   **44 59 63**
Rhode Island & New England artist paintings, glass, porcelain, furniture. *Hours:* Weekends 10-5 & BY APPT. Carol Prendergast

STEPHEN P MACK
Chase Hill Farm, 02804
(401)377-8041   **5 71 74**
A selection of fine historic structures - including houses, barns, farms and period rooms - ready for reconstruction on the owner's site. *Hours:* By appt. *Park:* On site. *Loc:* S of I-95 at the CT-RI line.

arrington

STOCK EXCHANGE
57 Maple Ave, 02806
(401)245-4170
Fine quality used home furnishings.

Hours: Tue-Sat 10-4. Jan Hess *Park:* On site. *Loc:* From I-95, Rte 114S to Barrington, R at red light at Town Hall, 5 bldgs down on R.

ristol

ALFRED'S
331-327 Hope St, 02809
(401)253-3465   **29 36 44**
Mahogany furniture, cut glass, flow blue, decorative accessories. *Est:* 1971. *Serv:* Appraisal. *Hours:* Mon-Sat 10-5. *CC:* AX/MC/V. *Assoc:* SNEADA. Alfred Brazil *Park:* In front. *Loc:* On Rte 114.

ROBERT BARROW, CABINETMAKER
412 Thames St, 02809
(401)253-4434   **43 71**
Traditional & contemporary handmade Windsor poster beds & tables. *Est:* 1978. *Serv:* Catalog ($3), restoration. *Hours:* Tue-Sat 8-5 BY APPT. *Loc:* I-95E Exit 7: Rte 114S to Bristol, on Thames St along the water.

Carolina

JAMES E SCUDDER
Rte 112, 02812
(401)364-7228   **36 44 63**
Furniture, glass, china & decorative accessories. *Hours:* By chance/appt.

Charlestown

ARTIST'S GUILD & GALLERY
Post Rd Rte 1, 02813
(401)322-0506 **59**
Specializing in 19th & 20th C art.
Serv: Conservation, frame repair &
gilding. **Hours:** Thu-Sun 10-5 appt
suggested. Ruth Gulliver

BUTTERNUT SHOP
Old Post Rd Rte 1A, 02813
(401)364-6121 **27 65**
Primitives & country accessories.
Hours: May-Nov daily. Florence S Ide

**FOX RUN COUNTRY
ANTIQUES**
Cross St, 02813
(401)364-3160 **27 44 65**
Country & primitives, furniture, jewelry, glassware, china & Orientalia.
Hours: Wed-Sun 10-4. Irene Larsen
Loc: Jct of Rtes 1 & 2, down Cross St,
across from the Charlestown Village.

LION'S MANE ANTIQUES
Jct of Rtes 1 & 2, 02813
(401)364-9104 **36 53 77**
Desks, chests, armoires, tables, chairs,
silver, mirrors, watercolors & engravings. **Serv:** Monthly mailings - call for
listing. Kyle Barnett Tello

SALT BOX ANTIQUES
Rte 1 at 216, 02813
(401)789-6106 **1 37 34**
Fine 18th & 19th C American country
furniture & decorative accessories,
specializing in folk art, iron & unique
items. **Pr:** $15–3500. **Est:** 1985. **Serv:**
Appraisal, consultation, purchase estates. **Hours:** May-Oct Tue-Sun 11-5,
Nov-Apr Fri-Sun 11-5 & BY APPT.

Size: Large. **CC:** MC/V. **Assoc:** NEAA
SNEADA. Dean Anslow **Park:** On
site. **Loc:** I-95 Exit 1: S on Rte 216 to
Rte 1, turn L go .2 MI.

Chepachet

CHESTNUT HILL ANTIQUES
One Victory Highway, 02814
(401)568-4365 **40 64**
Fiesta, azalea, refinished oak furniture,
jewelry, post cards & country. **Loc:** 1
block N of Chepachet Ctr on Rte 102.

JADED LION
8 Main St, 02814
(401)568-6005 **27 29 65**
Antiques & collectibles. **Hours:** Daily
11-5 Mon & Holidays by chance/appt.
Park: In front. **Loc:** In the center of
Chepachet.

**KIMBALL HOUSE
1753/REMINGTON ANT**
Main St, 02814
(401)568-0416 **{GR2}**
Country antiques offered in natural
surroundings. **Est:** 1987. **Serv:** Consignments accepted. **Hours:** Thu-Sun
12-5 By Chance. **Park:** On street. **Loc:**
I-395 Exit 97: Rte 44E or Rte 295
Greenville Exit, Rte 44W.

**OLD CHEPT VILLAGE
ANTIQUE CENTER**
Rtes 44 & 102, 02814
(401)568-2455
Outdoor market every Saturday Sunday & Monday Holidays. Admission
50c. **Serv:** Dealer space $15. **Hours:**
Sat, Sun & Mon Holidays 9-5. **Size:**
Large. **Park:** On site. **Loc:** 150 yards N
of Rte 44 on Rte 102 between Purple
Cat Restaurant & Chepachet Pharmacy.

Coventry

CANDLE SNUFFER
28 Maple Root Rd, 02816
(401)397-5565   **50 71**
A complete lamp shop - specialists in restored lighting, oil & electric, large inventory of lamp parts, over 5000 glass & fabric lampshades. *Pr:* $25–1500. *Est:* 1968. *Serv:* Repairs, restoration. *Hours:* Tue-Sat 9-5. *Size:* Medium. Letha Sodergren *Park:* On site. *Loc:* I-95 Exit 6: N for 1 MI, L at Maple Root Inn, 1st L, red bldg with white picket fence.

Cranston

JEFFREY HERMAN
Box 3599, 02910
(401)461-3156   **71 77**
Restoration & hand finishing of sterling, coin, pewter, brass & mixed metal holloware, flatware & dresserware. Full line of silver polishing supplies. Fully equipped & insured silversmithing studio with a central alarm system. *Est:* 1984. *Serv:* Catalog, price list, conservation, restoration, repairs. *Assoc:* JBT MJSA.

East Greenwich

CONSTANTINE'S FINE FURNITURE
110 Main St, 02818
(401)884-5441   **43 59 60**
Reproduction & antique European & Oriental decorative accessories & paintings. *Serv:* Appraisal. *Hours:* Mon-Sat 9-5. *CC:* AX. *Park:* Plenty. *Loc:* I-95 Exit 8.

HARBOUR GALLERIES
253 Main St, 02818
(401)884-6221   **47 71**
Fine antique and estate jewelry & large selection of cameos. *Serv:* Appraisal, consultation, purchase estates, repairs, restoration. *Hours:* Tue-Sat 11-5 Fri 11-8. *CC:* AX/DC/MC/V. *Assoc:* GIA NEAA. *Park:* Nearby lot. *Loc:* I-95 E Greenwich Exit (Division St): to Main St (1 MI from I-95).

Hope Valley
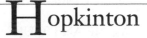

DUKSTA'S ANTIQUES
40 Arcadia Rd, 02898
(401)539-2095   **36**
Furniture & collectibles. *Hours:* Daily 10-5. Cindy Duksta

Hopkinton

THE ELEGANT DRAGON
Thurston-Wells House Rte 3, 02833
(401)377-9059   **31 60**
Exotic Orientalia - unusual & unique Far Eastern antique treasures from China, Japan, Korea, Malaysia, Tibet, bronzes, porcelains, root, wood, hardstone & soapstone carvings, baskets, weapons, elegant rosewood display stands & cabinets. *Pr:* $1–400000. *Hours:* All year by chance/appt. *Size:* Large. *CC:* MC/V. Norma H Schofield *Park:* On site. *Loc:* I-95 Exit 1 to RI: N at top of ramp (sign for Hopkinton), .75 MI on L.

Little Compton

BLUE FLAG ANTIQUES
601 West Main Rd, 02837
(401)635-4733   **27 59 62**
Paintings, drawings, 19th C furniture, photographs & a broad range of curious & wonderful things, from primitive to industrial design, emphasize unusual items of good design & condition. *Pr:* $5–2500. *Est:* 1983. *Serv:* Appraisal, custom woodwork, repairs, replication, reproduction, restoration. *Hours:* May-Nov Daily 11-4 Dec-Jun Fri-Sun 11-4, call first. *Size:* Medium. *Assoc:* SNEADA. Sarah Harkness *Park:* On site. *Loc:* Rte 77 2 MI below turn off to Little Compton Ctr & 2 MI above Harbor.

THE GALLERY ON THE COMMONS
PO Box 932,
(401)635-8935   **21**
Antique & semi-antique Oriental rugs, country & formal furniture & accessories. *Serv:* Appraisal. *Hours:* Sat,Sun 11-4 or BY APPT. *Assoc:* ASA. Nancy Walker

Newport

AARDVARK ANTIQUES
475 Thames St, 02840
(401)849-7233   **5 45 50**
Architectural antiques, garden statuary, ornaments, iron fence, gates, stained glass & decorative lighting. *Est:* 1967. *Serv:* Appraisal, conservation, restoration, repairs. *Hours:* Mon-Sat 10-5. *CC:* MC/V. Arthur Grover *Park:* On site.

ANCHOR & DOLPHIN BOOKS
30 Franklin St, 02840
(401)846-6890   **13**
Select stock of old & rare books with emphasis on works relating to the history of design, especially books on gardens, landscape architecture, early horticulture & the decorative arts. *Pr:* $5–5000. *Est:* 1979. *Serv:* Appraisal, catalog $1, purchase estates. *Hours:* Year round by chance/appt. *Assoc:* ABAA MRIAB. Ann Marie Wall *Park:* On site. *Loc:* Downtown Newport between Thames & Spring Sts, 1 block N of Memorial Blvd, near post office in the ctr of Antique District.

ANTIQUES AT FIFTY NINE BELLEVUE
59 Bellevue Ave, 02840
(401)846-7898   **41 48 63**
Fine furniture, accessories, painted furniture, porcelain & lace. *Hours:* By chance.

BELLEVUE GOLD
129 Bellevue Ave, 02840
(401)849-3734   **4 24 47**
Gold, silver, antiques, estate jewelry & coins. *Est:* 1980. *Serv:* Appraisal, repairs. *Hours:* Tue-Sat 10-5. *Park:* Nearby.

BLACK SHEEP ANTIQUES
99 Spring St, 02840
(401)846-6810   **44 48 67**
Antiques & collectibles, featuring glassware, quilts, linens, baskets, furniture & nautical antiques. *Serv:* Restoration. *Hours:* By chance. Ken Gates

ARAKEL H BOZYAN STORE
140 Bellevue Ave, 02840
(401)847-0012　　　　　　　**21 58**

Antiques, Oriental rugs & objets d'art.
Est: 1880. *Hours:* Afternoons. *Park:*
Nearby.

C & T LAMP SHOP/ANTIQUE DEALERS
42 Spring St, 02840
(401)461-3130　　　　　　　**50**

Antique furniture, lamps & accessories. *Serv:* Restoration. *Hours:* Tue-Sat 12-5 BY APPT. John Clayton

THE CLASSIC TOUCH
One Casino Terr, 02840
(401)849-1717　　　　　　　**23 41**

Eclectic collections of international antiques, entertaining accessories, specializing in fine 19th C clocks. *Pr:* $10–10000. *Est:* 1984. *Serv:* Custom painted furniture, art of the painted finish. *Hours:* Daily 10-5 by chance/appt. *Size:* Medium. Diane Beaver *Park:* On site. *Loc:* Bellevue Ave, L on Casino Terrace, Bellevue Plaza.

COUNTRY PLEASURES LTD
15 Mill St, 02840
(401)849-6355　　　　　　　**39 42**

Antique British & Irish cut pine furniture, antique farmhouse pine, British & American collectibles & accessories. *Est:* 1985. *Hours:* Mon-Sat 11-5 Sun 12-5. *CC:* MC/V. *Park:* On site. *Loc:* Between Tower, Thames & Spring Sts.

THE DOLL MUSEUM
481 Thames St, 02840
(401)849-0405　　　　　　　**32 52**

A fine collection of antique & modern dolls on permanent display & collectible miniatures. *Pr:* $10–5000. *Serv:*

Doll hospital, appraisals, repairs. *Hours:* Wed,Mon 10-5 Sun 12-5. *CC:* MC/V. Linda Edward *Park:* In front.

THE DRAWING ROOM ANTIQUES
221 Spring St, 02840
(401)841-5060　　　　　　　**37 46**

Large collection of 19th C furniture & decorative arts - including American Empire & Gothic - for the serious collector. *Pr:* $100–10000. *Serv:* Appraisal, brochure, consultation, purchase estates, restoration. *Hours:* Mon,Thu-Sat 11-5 Sun 12-5. *Size:* Medium. *CC:* MC/V. Federico Santi *Loc:* From Boston: Rte 24 onto Island to Rte 138 or Rte 114 to Newport, from NYC: I-95N follow signs to Newport Bridge.

FAIR DE YORE
170 Spring St, 02840
(401)849-5582　　　　　　　**34 47 48**

Linens, folk art crafts, old & new jewelry. *Est:* 1982. *Hours:* Thu-Tue 12-5 CLOSED SUN. *CC:* DC/MC/V. Hazel Pharis *Park:* Nearby. *Loc:* 1 block from Thames St.

CHRISTOPHER FOSTER GLASS WORKS
10 Marlboro St, 02840
(401)847-4178　　　　　　　**50 70 71**

Restoration of stained glass. Will design & build windows to specification. Restoration of leaded lamp shades. Custom leaded lamp shades made to order. *Hours:* By chance/appt. *Park:* Nearby. *Loc:* 1.5 blocks NE of Brick Market.

FULL SWING
474 Thames St, 02840
(401)849-9494　　　　　　　**7 46 80**

Furnishings & accessories 1920s to

1950s. Extensive collection of vintage yardage & draperies, wicker, bamboo & rattan (seasonal), re-covered in vintage fabrics. From art deco bedrooms to atomic modern living rooms. *Pr:* $25–1500. *Serv:* Nationally recognized source for vintage textiles. *Hours:* Jun-Sep Mon-Sat 10-6, Oct-May Mon-Sat 11-6. *Size:* Medium. *CC:* AX/MC/V. Michele Mancini *Park:* In front. *Loc:* Heart of shopping district, on 1st st parallel to Harbor.

A & A GAINES
40 Franklin St, 02840
(401)849-6844　　　　**23 56 60**

Period furniture, clocks, China trade porcelain, nautical items & Oriental silver. *Serv:* All pieces guaranteed. *Hours:* Tue-Sat 11-5 or BY APPT. Alan Gaines *Park:* Nearby. *Loc:* Just off Thames St on Antique Row.

GALLERY '76 ANTIQUES INC
83 Spring St, 02840
(401)847-4288　　　　**36 63 77**

Period furniture, accessories, silver, porcelain, jewelry, fine 19th C export & European porcelain & clocks. *Hours:* Daily 10-5:30 CLOSED SUN. *CC:* AX/MC/V. *Assoc:* NADA. Barbara Leis *Park:* Nearby. *Loc:* Between Colony House & Trinity Church.

JOHN GIDLEY HOUSE
22 Franklin St, 02840
(401)846-8303　　　　**36 50 58**

Fine furniture, lighting fixtures & decorative arts. *Pr:* $75–5000. *Hours:* Tue-Sat 11-5. *Size:* Medium. *Assoc:* AAA. Carl Ritorno *Loc:* Across Franklin St from main post office just off America's Cup Ave.

HARRY GREW
PO Box 172, 02840
(401)846-7372　　　　**36 59 63**

American paintings, British ceramics, Staffordshire & furniture. *Est:* 1977. *Hours:* BY APPT. *Loc:* Call for directions.

JB ANTIQUES
33 Franklin St, 02840
(401)849-0450　　　　**58 59 63**

Furniture, paintings, large selection of china & high style decorative arts. *Serv:* Appraisal. *Hours:* Daily 10-5. *CC:* AX/MC/V. *Assoc:* NADA. Jacqueline Barratt *Park:* Nearby. *Loc:* .5 block E of Thames St.

JENNIFERS
119 Bellevue Ave, 02840
(401)849-8857

Eclectic second-hand shop featuring quality used furniture, art, household items, costume jewelry & lamps. *Hours:* Mon-Sat 10-5 Sun 12-5. *CC:* AX/MC/V. *Park:* Nearby.

ETHEL M KALIF ANTIQUES
233 Spring St, 02840
(401)846-0454　　　　**63 65**

Fine furniture, furnishings, porcelain, decorative accessories & primitives.

R KAZARIAN
35 Franklin St, 02840
(401)846-3563　　　　**1 5 34**

Primitives, furniture, architectural & garden details & folk art. *Hours:* Daily 11-5. *CC:* MC/V. *Assoc:* NADA. *Park:* Nearby.

ROGER KING GALLERY OF FINE ART
21 Bowen's Wharf 2nd fl, 02840
(401)847-4359　　　　**4 59 71**

Fine paintings of the 19th & early 20th

C. *Pr:* $200–and up. *Est:* 1973. *Serv:* Appraisal, conservation, consultation, purchase estates, restoration. *Hours:* Year round daily 12-5 (extended summer hours) appt suggested. *Size:* Medium. *CC:* AX/MC/V. *Assoc:* NEAA. Roger King *Park:* Nearby lot. *Loc:* Opposite the Clarke Cooke House.

LAMP WORKS
626 Lower Thames St, 02840
(401)847-0966   **37 39 50**

Antiques, restored antique lighting, antique shades, English & American furniture. *Serv:* Custom & lighting repair. *Hours:* Tue-Sat 10-5 Sun 1-5. *CC:* AX/DC/MC/V. *Loc:* By the Boat House Pub.

LAMPLIGHTER ANTIQUES
42 Spring St, 02840
(401)849-4179   **23 37 50**

Specializing in oil lamps, clocks, American furniture & Currier & Ives prints. *Est:* 1976. *Hours:* Mon-Sat 11-5. Al Lozito

MAINLY OAK LTD
489 Thames St, 02840
(401)846-4439   **40 53 86**

Oak furniture, mirrors & wicker. *Serv:* Refinishing. *Hours:* Mon-Sat 10-5. *CC:* MC/V. *Assoc:* NADA. John Majewski *Park:* On street. *Loc:* Downtown.

NEW ENGLAND ANTIQUES
60 Spring St, 02840
(401)849-6646   **27 63 65**

Country, English transfer china, glass, paintings, flow blue, primitives & items in original paint. *Pr:* $20–2000. *Hours:* Mon-Sat 11-5 & BY APPT. *CC:* MC/V. *Loc:* Int of Spring & Touro Sts in the heart of 18th C Newport, across from Touro Synagogue.

NEWELL'S CLOCK/CHINA RESTORATION
79 Thames St, 02840
(401)849-6690   **71**

Restoration of fine antique pendulum clocks only, restoration of fine porcelains & pottery. *Est:* 1972. *Serv:* Repairs, restoration. *Hours:* Mon-Sat 10-1 2:30-5:30 appt suggested. *Assoc:* AWI NAWCC. A F Newell *Park:* In front. *Loc:* .5 block N of Marlborough St on W side of Thames St.

NEWPORT FINE ARTS INVESTMENT CO
23 Bowens Wharf, 02840
(401)846-4096   **4 59 71**

Specializing in important works by American artists - investment & museum quality. *Pr:* $25000–and up. *Serv:* Appraisal, conservation, consultation, restoration. *Hours:* Year round daily & by chance/appt. *Size:* Medium. *Assoc:* NEAA. Roger H King, Jr *Loc:* Across from the Clarke Cooke House located above Roger King Gallery on Bowens Wharf.

THE NEWPORT GALLERY LTD
Suite 4 337 Thames St, 02840
(401)849-8218   **56 59**

Fine 19th & 20th C marine paintings & selections of coastal fine art. *Hours:* Mon-Sat 10-6 Sun 11-6 BY APPT (849-8218). *CC:* AX/MC/V. *Assoc:* NADA. *Loc:* Perry Mill Market, at st level of Bay Club Hotel.

NEWPORT SCRIMSHAW COMPANY
337 Thames St, 02840
(401)846-8666   **56 58**

Antique American scrimshaw, quality American Oriental & European antique ivory carvings. *Serv:* Appraisal, repairs. *Hours:* Daily 10-5 Sun 12-5.

CC: MC/V. *Assoc:* NADA. Chet Gotauco *Park:* Nearby. *Loc:* Perry Mill Market.

OLD FASHION SHOP
38 Pelham St, 02840
(401)847-2692   1 21 63

Americana, furniture, accessories, Oriental rugs & porcelains. *Est:* 1959. *Hours:* Mon-Sat 1-5. *Assoc:* NADA. *Park:* Nearby. *Loc:* At sign of the Hand, 3 houses down from corner of Pelham & Spring sts.

PETTERUTI ANTIQUES
105 Memorial Blvd W, 02840
(401)849-5117   58 59 86

Unique antique wicker, fine paintings, 19th C bronzes, quality furniture & objets d'art. *Serv:* Appraisal, consultation. *Hours:* May-Nov daily 10-5 Sun 12-5. *CC:* AX/MC/V. *Assoc:* NADA. Carmine Petteruti Jr *Park:* Off street. *Loc:* Below Int of Memorial Blvd & Spring St.

RAMSON HOUSE ANTIQUES
36 Franklin St, 02840
(401)847-0555   43 50 63

Antiques & fine reproductions of furniture, desks, lamps, Oriental porcelains & decorative accessories. *Est:* 1978. *Serv:* Repair lamps. *Hours:* Mon-Sat 10-5:30. *CC:* MC/V. *Assoc:* NADA. Joan DeDionisio *Loc:* On Antique Row.

SIMMONS & SIMMONS
223 Spring St, 02840
(401)849-7281   13 33 66

Books, prints, paper, curios, Arctic material, advertising, paper theatres & modern 1st editions. *Hours:* By chance/appt. Eric Simmons

ALICE SIMPSON ANTIQUES
40 1/2 Franklin St, 02840
(401)849-4252   47 77 80

Victorian silver plate, textiles & jewelry. *Serv:* Appraisal. *Hours:* Mon-Sat 11-5. *CC:* MC/V. *Assoc:* NADA. *Loc:* .5 block from Newport post office.

SMITH MARBLE LTD
44 Franklin St, 02840
(401)846-7689   36 44 63

Specializing in fine antiquities, works of art, objects of vertu, silver, porcelains, glass, furniture, tapestries & rugs. *Est:* 1970. *Serv:* Appraisal, consultation, interior design. *Hours:* May-Nov Mon-Sat 10-5 Sun 12-5 BY APPT (617)838-2019. *CC:* AX/MC/V. *Assoc:* NADA. Ada V Smith *Park:* Nearby. *Loc:* Corner of Franklin & Spring.

TIGER LILY
26 Franklin St, 02840
(401)849-5259   38 41

Smaller version of Boston store, mostly Continental furniture & accessories. *Pr:* $25–5000. *Est:* 1983. *Serv:* Decorating service. *Hours:* May 15-Oct Mon-Sat 12-5 or by chance/appt. *Size:* Medium. Libby H Holsten *Park:* In front.

TRITON ANTIQUES
160 Spring St, 02840   27 29

American country furniture & accessories. *Hours:* Fri-Wed 11:30-4:30 CLOSED THU. Herbert Motz

UNIQUE ANTIQUES
473 Thames St, 02840
(401)846-4439   36

Antique furnishings, custom mahogany furniture, walnut, cherry, pictures

& glass. *Est:* 1982. *Hours:* Daily 12-4. *CC:* MC/V. *Park:* On street. *Loc:* Downtown Newport.

WILLIAM VAREIKA FINE ARTS
212 Bellevue Ave, 02840
(401)849-6149   **59 66**
Offering 18th, 19th & early 20th C American paintings, drawings & prints by important artists, i.e., Bierstadt, Church, Gifford & Kensett. Two large floors in a museum-like setting, located on Newport's historic Bellevue Ave.. *Pr:* $500–500000. *Serv:* Appraisal, brochure, catalog, conservation, consultation, restoration. *Hours:* Mon-Sat 10-6 & BY APPT. *Size:* Large. *Assoc:* NEAA. *Park:* Nearby lot. *Loc:* From N: Rte 124S to Rte 114 to central Newport. From W: Rte 138 & Newport Bridge, 1 block S of Int'l Tennis Hall of Fame.

MICHAEL WESTMAN FINE ARTS
Box 3562, 02840
(401)847-3091   **29 59 66**
20th C decorative arts, paintings & prints. *Serv:* Appraisal. *Hours:* BY APPT. *Assoc:* NADA.

GUSTAVES J.S. WHITE
37 Bellevue Ave, 02840
(401)849-3000   **8 29 36**
Auctions of antique & estate furniture, decorative accessories. 10% buyer's premium. *Hours:* Daily 9-4. Michael R Corcoran

North Kingstown

LAFAYETTE ANTIQUES
814 Ten Rod Rd Rte 102, 02852
(401)295-2504   **37 83**
Early American & Victorian furniture. *Hours:* Tue-Sun 11-5. Chet Chandronnet

LILLIAN'S ANTIQUES
7442 Post Rd Rte 1, 02852
(401)885-2512   **44 47 86**
Antique jewelry, china, glass, paintings, furniture, wicker & general line. *Serv:* Purchase estates. *Hours:* Thu-Sun 1-5 or BY APPT. Lillian Anderson

MENTOR ANTIQUES
7512 Post Rd Rte 1, 02852
(401)294-9412   **39 45**
Fine furniture & accessories from England & garden statuary. *Hours:* Mon-Sun 10-6. *CC:* MC/V. *Park:* On site. *Loc:* I-95, on Rte 1 in North Kingston.

North Scituate

VILLAGE ANTIQUES
Main St, 02857
(401)647-3243   **37**
18th & 19th C American furniture & accessories. *Hours:* Wed-Sat 10:30-5 Sun 11-4. David Guilmain *Park:* On site. *Loc:* In town.

Pawtucket

SUZANNE'S BOOK SHOPPE
PO Box 3502, 02861
(401)724-3350   **13**
Children's books, detective fiction, history, literature, science fiction & fantasy & paperbacks. *Serv:* Catalog, search service. *Hours:* By mail order. *Assoc:* MRIAB. Suzanne Riendeau

Peace Dale

ANTIQUITY RESTORATIONS & REPRO'S
53 Green St, 02883
(401)789-2370   **68 70 71**
Antique sales, repair & refinishing, furniture & game board reproductions, carriage & sleigh restoration. *Est:* 1984. *Serv:* Repairs, reproduction, restoration. *Hours:* Mon-Fri 8-5 Sat 9-5. Jim Harmon *Park:* On site. *Loc:* 2 MI from Univ of RI off Rte 108.

SIGN OF THE UNICORN BOOKSHOP
1187 Kingstown Rd, 02883
(401)295-7867   **13 26**
15,000 volumes of antiquarian & out-of-print books. "Scarce, medium rare & well done". *Pr:* $5–3000. *Est:* 1978. *Serv:* Appraisal, consultation, search service. *Hours:* Jun 20-Aug Mon-Sat 10-5, Sep-Jun 19 Sat 10-5 BY APPT. Mary Jo Munroe *Park:* In front.

Portsmouth

COUNTRY CUPBOARD
934 E Main Rd Rte 138, 02871
(508)379-9780   **28 37 67**
Fine crocks, stoneware, quilts & American furniture. *Est:* 1985. Anthony Travis *Park:* Nearby. *Loc:* Rte 138 2 doors from Historical Society.

BENJAMIN FISH HOUSE ANTIQUES
934 East Main Rd, 02871
(401)683-0099   **37 60 63**
Dedham pottery, Dorchester, early American furniture, accessories, Heisey & Oriental porcelain. *Est:* 1980. *Hours:* Mon-Sat 10-5 Sun 12-4. *Assoc:* SNEADA. Charles Crouch *Park:* Nearby. *Loc:* On Rte 138 2 doors from Portsmouth Historical Society.

Providence

ASSOCIATES APPRAISERS INC
915 Industrial Bank Building, 02903
(401)331-3211   **4 8**
Appraisers for probate family division & insurance & estate auctions. *Serv:* Brochure, purchase estates. *Hours:* BY APPT.

BERT GALLERY
Biltmore Hotel Kennedy Plaza, 02903
(401)751-2628   **59**
19th & early 20th C oil paintings by American artists. *Hours:* Sum: Tue-Fri 10-5.

BRASSWORKS
379 Charles St, 02904
(401)421-5815   **68 71**

Repair, restoration & polishing of brass, copper, pewter & silver. *Hours:* Mon-Fri 9-5 Sat 9-3.

CELLAR STORIES BOOKS
190 Mathewson St, 02903
(401)521-2665   **13 14**

One of the largest used & antiquarian bookshops in Rhode Island. *Pr:* $1-2000. *Serv:* Appraisal, purchase estates, repair. *Hours:* Mon-Fri 11-6 Sat 10-6. *Size:* Medium. *Assoc:* MRIAB. Michael K Chandley *Park:* Nearby lot.

CHAMBERLAIN ANTIQUES LTD
188 Wayland Ave, 02906
(401)273-4040   **4 58 77**

A fine selection of antiques, estate jewelry, accessories, pottery & porcelain, objets d'art, silver, paintings & Oriental rugs. *Pr:* $25-4500. *Est:* 1986. *Serv:* Appraisal, purchase estates. *Hours:* Mon-Sat 10-5. *Size:* Medium. *CC:* MC/V. *Assoc:* AAA. Francesca Erice *Park:* On site. *Loc:* Rte 195E Gano St Exit: R on Gano, thru 2 sets of lights, R on Waterman, L onto Wayland.

MARTIN CONLON AMERICAN ANTIQUES
PO Box 3070, 02906
(401)831-1810   **37**

Fine American furniture & accessories of the 18th & 19th C. *Est:* 1986. *Serv:* Auction, consultation, conservation. *Hours:* BY APPT. *Loc:* 3 min from I-95, call for directions.

CAROL LOMBARDI ANTIQUES
PO Box 5954, 02903   **1 38 47**

American & European decorative art & furnishings, antique jewelry & pe-riod & custom furniture. *Serv:* Appraisal, interior design, purchase estates. *Hours:* BY APPT TO THE TRADE. Carol Lombardi

METACOMET BOOKS
Box 2479, 02906
(401)861-7182   **13**

Americana, literature, scientific & general antiquarian books. *Serv:* Appraisal, catalog, search service. *Hours:* BY APPT. *Assoc:* MRIAB. James Sanford *Loc:* 2 min from I-95, call for directions.

MY FAVORITE THINGS
Arcade Building, 02903
(401)831-3332   **18 48 77**

Specializing in antique lace & linen, sewing items, buttons & buckles, sterling silver smalls & jewelry. *Pr:* $25-500. *Hours:* Dec 27-Nov 24 Mon-Sat 10-6, Nov 25-Dec 24 daily 10-9. *Size:* Medium. *CC:* AX/MC/V. Patricia Mc Garty *Park:* Nearby lot. *Loc:* In Historic Arcade Bldg, between Westminster & Weybosset sts in downtown Providence.

QUE ANTIQUES
Box 2367A, 02906
(401)751-7991   **62 66**

Specializing in prints: botonicals, horticulturals, early advertising & photographs. *Hours:* By appt. Kathie Florsheim

THE RATHBUN GALLERY-SHAKER
75 Burlington St, 02906
(401)861-8043   **37**

A complete line of Shaker antiques for the beginning or established collector. *Pr:* $35-30000. *Serv:* Consultation. *Hours:* Jun-Sept Wed-Sun 11-5, Oct-May Tue-Fri 11-5 & BY APPT. *Size:*

Medium. Richard Schneider **Park:** In front. **Loc:** I-95 & 146 Branch Ave Exit: E on Branch Ave, L on N Main St, E on Rochambeau Ave, L on Hope St, R on Burlington, 1st on R.

THE REEL MAN
PO Box 752 Annex Station, 02901
(401)941-6853 **78**

Antique fishing tackle including complete vintage outfits - rod, reel, line & lure - creels, nets, bobbers, tackle boxes, angling paraphernalia, artwork, shadow boxes & framed displays. **Serv:** Consultation, appraisal, repair, refinishing, restoration, interior design. **Hours:** By appt.

SEWARDS' FOLLY, BOOKS
139 Brook St, 02906
(401)272-4454 **13**

First editions, literary criticism & biography, philosophy, poetry & Rhode Island history. **Pr:** $1–2000. **Est:** 1976. **Serv:** Purchase estates, search services. **Hours:** Wed-Fri 12-7 Sat 9-7 Sun 12-6 Mon, Tue by chance/appt. **Size:** Medium. **Assoc:** MRIAB. Schuyler Seward **Park:** In front. **Loc:** 8-10 blocks S of Brown Univ, on E side of Providence.

SUNNY DAYS
287 Thayer St, 02906
(401)274-5570 **47 85**

Antique clothing & jewelry, 1900-1960. **Est:** 1981. **Hours:** Mon-Sat 11-6 Sun 12-5. **CC:** MC/V. **Assoc:** SNEADA. Lois Hollingsowth **Park:** On street. **Loc:** On the E side of Providence, in the heart of the college area.

TYSON'S OLD & RARE BOOKS
334 Westminster St, 02903
(401)421-3939 **13**

American literature, Americana, first editions, travel, Rhode Island history,

better books in all fields. **Est:** 1935. **Serv:** Appraisal, catalog, search service. **Hours:** Mon-Fri 11-5 most Sat 11-4. **Assoc:** MRIAB. Mariette P Bedard **Park:** Behind building. **Loc:** 5 min from I-95.

VAN DALE GALLERY
140 Wickendon St, 02903
(401)861-3883 **43 59**

Antique oil paintings & reproduction furniture. **Est:** 1987. **Serv:** Sponsor annual Rhode Island artists show. **Hours:** Tue-Fri 10-5 Sat 11-4. **CC:** AX. **Loc:** I-95 Exit 2.

BARBARA WALZER, BOOKSELLER
175 Ontario St, 02907
(401)785-2277 **13**

Women's history, general antiquarian & collection development. **Hours:** By appt. **Assoc:** ABAA.

Rumford

ANTIQUES BEAUTIFUL
337 N Broadway, 02916
(401)434-0275 **{GR4}**

Five rooms featuring period furniture, custom mahogany, cherry, pine & oak, Oriental rugs, paintings, glassware, antique jewelry & country items. **Pr:** $25–2500. **Serv:** Appraisal, consultation, interior design, purchase estates, repair. **Hours:** Mon-Fri 9:30-5. **Assoc:** SNEADA. Dennis Vieira **Park:** On site. **Loc:** I-95E Exit 6: R onto Warren Ave, R at light onto Broadway, 1.4 MI on L, I-95W Exit 6: R onto Broadway, 1.3 MI on L.

Saunderstown

STEPHANIE ADAMS WOOD
PO Box 444, 02874
(401)294-2787   **59 73 80**
American furniture, textiles, paintings, sculptural objects & accessories. *Hours:* BY APPT. *Assoc:* NHADA.

Smithfield

MARTY'S ANTIQUE AUCTION SERVICE
RFD 4 Mountainside Rd, 02917
(401)231-8246   **8**
Auctions of antiques & estate liquidations. *Hours:* Please call. Marty Austin

Tiverton

METAL RESTORATION SERVICES
43 Wm S Canning Blvd Rte 81S, 02878
(401)624-6486   **25 68 71**
Conservation, restoration, refinishing & spray coating of metal antiques made of gold, silver, bronze, copper, brass, pewter & tin. Lighting fixture work from lamps to chandeliers. No work done on jewelry. *Est:* 1980. *Serv:* Conservation, consultation, repair, restoration. *Hours:* Mon-Fri 8:30-4:30 Sat 8-12. *Size:* Large. Peter M Pflock *Park:* In front. *Loc:* From Rte 24 S of Fall River, MA, take Exit for Rte 81 S Adamsville RI, take 2nd driveway on R marked Canning Pl Bus Condos.

Wakefield

DOVE AND DISTAFF ANTIQUES
365 Main St, 02879
(401)783-5714   **29 37**
Early American furniture & accessories. *Serv:* Restoration, refinish, upholstery & drapery workshop, lampshades. *Hours:* Mon-Fri 8-5 Sat 8-12. Caleb Davis

JIGGER'S ANTIQUES
12-14 Columbia St, 02879
(401)783-5460   **14**
Antiques, collectibles & collector's books. *Hours:* Tue-Sat 10-4. Don Southwick

OLDE TOWNE SHOPPE
406 Main St, 02879
(401)294-4226
Antiques & collectibles. *Hours:* Tue-Sat 10-4. Bob Anderson

JANET L THOMPSON
130 Silver Lake Ave, 02879
(401)783-0958   **27**
General line of antiques emphasizing country. *Hours:* BY APPT. Janet Thompson

Warren

CHRISTIE & HADLEY ANTIQUES
160 Water St, 02885
(401)245-2711   **29 47**
Eclectic decorative accessories, smalls, jewelry & small furniture. *Est:* 1987. *Hours:* Tue-Sat 1-5. *Assoc:* SNEADA. Suzanne Christie *Park:* On street. *Loc:* Just off Rte 114.

Warwick

THE EMPORIUM
1629 Warwick Ave, 02889
(401)738-8824   **47 64 77**

Fine jewelry, costume jewelry, kitchen collectibles, glassware, furniture, silver, paintings, china & post cards. *Est:* 1983. *Hours:* Daily 11-5 CLOSED WED,SUN. *CC:* MC/V. *Assoc:* SNEADA. *Park:* In front. *Loc:* In back of Green Airport.

FORTUNATE FINDS BOOKSTORE
16 W Natick Rd, 02886
(401)737-8160   **13**

Antiquarian books- Rhode Island, genealogies, documents, general books, travel, children, fiction & nonfiction. *Pr:* $5–500. *Est:* 1958. *Serv:* Appraisal, auction, catalog. *Hours:* Fri-Sat 9-5 & BY APPT. *Park:* On site. *Loc:* .5 MI from the Warwick Mall on Bald Hill Rd & Lambert Lind Hwy Rte 195/95.

Watch Hill

A TO Z ANTIQUES
Watch Hill Rd, 02891
(401)348-8775

Barn full of interesting items. *Hours:* All year by chance/appt. Adelaide S Zanke

THE BOOK & TACKLE SHOP
7 Bay St, 02891
(401)596-0700   **13 64 66**

Antiquarian books - rare science & medical books, sea voyages, exploration, cookery, children's, music & rare post cards, fine bindings, early printings & engravings. *Pr:* $5–10000. *Est:*

1955. *Serv:* Appraisal, auction, purchase estates, search service. *Hours:* May-Oct daily 9-5, Nov-Apr BY APPT. *Size:* Large. *CC:* MC/V. *Assoc:* ABAA MRIAB. Bernard Gordon *Park:* In front. *Loc:* 10 MI from CT/RI border on US Rte 1, 7 MI from Westerly RI, accessible by boat on Watch Hill RI Harbor.

FINITNEY & COMPANY
Bay St, 02891
(401)596-6210   **48 58**

Antiques, fine arts & linens. *Hours:* May-Oct daily 10-5. Barbara B Eyre

OCEAN HOUSE ANTIQUES/CURIOSITIES
Ocean House, Lanphere Rd, 02891
(401)596-1605   **44**

Heisey & general line. *Hours:* Late Jun-Labor Day nights only 6:30-9:30. Carole B Lacey

West Greenwich

MARTONE'S GALLERY
699 New London Tnpk, 02816
(401)885-3880   **8 44**

Auctioneer of antique furniture, rugs & glassware 10% buyer's premium. *Serv:* Appraisal, mailing. *CC:* AX/MC/V. Jack Martone *Park:* On site. *Loc:* Rte 95 Exit 7. 20 min from CT border.

West Kingston

PETER POTS AUTHENTIC AMERICANA
101 Glen Rock Rd, 02892
(401)783-2350 **28 29**

Stoneware, period furniture, decorative & collectible items. *Hours:* Mon-Sat 10-4 Sun 1-4. Oliver Greene

West Kingstown

G R CLIDENCE, 18TH C WOODWORKS
Box 272 James Trial, 02892
(401)539-2558 **19 70**

Reproductions of Colonial beds, adapting antique beds to modern uses, featuring cannonballs, pencil posts, canopy field beds, law posts & variations, tavern tables & tea tables. *Est:* 1984. *Serv:* Custom woodwork. *Hours:* Mon-Fri 9-5 Sat BY APPT. *Park:* On site. *Loc:* From U of RI: 3 MI W off Rte 138, from I-95 Exit 3: E to West Kingstown.

Westerly

HERITAGE ANTIQUES
46 School St, 02891
(401)596-0540 **23 36 83**

Victorian furniture & selection of mahogany, including pineapple beds, grandfather clocks & desks. *Serv:* Purchase estates. *Hours:* Wed-Sat 10-4. Sandra Avery

LAUREL LEDGE ANTIQUES
107 Post Rd Rte 1, 02891
(401)596-2671 **27**

Country furnishings. *Hours:* All year, please call for appt. Sherry L Bowen

WESTERLY ENTERPRISES
28 Canal St, 02891
(401)596-2298 **24 47**

Rare coins, jewelry, art, antiques & collectibles. *Hours:* Tue-Sat 10-5. George Champlin

MANFRED R WOERNER
Westerly, 02891
(401)596-7280 **71**

Specializing in fine antique period upholstered pieces. *Est:* 1953. *Serv:* References available. *Hours:* Phone for consultation & appt.

Wickford

THE BALL & CLAW
4 Brown St, 0
(401)295-1200 **30 59 67**

Period oils & watercolors, quilts, pewter, decoys, weather vanes & pottery. *Serv:* Brochure ($2). *Hours:* Mon Wed Sat 10-5 Sun 12-5.

Woonsocket

THE CORNER CURIOSITY SHOPPE
25 Crawford St, 02895
(401)766-7678 **36 44 65**

Quality antiques, collectibles, furniture, primitives & glassware. *Est:* 1988. *Hours:* Thu 11-8 Fri-Sun 11-5. *Loc:* Rte 146A to Park Ave to Crawford St.

Wyoming

BRAD SMITH
Jct Rtes 112 & 138, 02898
(401)539-2870   **29 36 59**
Furniture, paintings & decorative accessories.

Vermont

Adamant

ADAMANT BOOKS
Box 46, 05640
(802)223-2951   **13 33**

Antiquarian books: Vermont, New England, agriculture, gardening & ephemera. **Serv:** Search service. **Hours:** BY MAIL & PHONE ONLY. **Assoc:** VABA. Weston A Cate Jr

Addison

OLD STONE HOUSE ANTIQUES
Old Stone House Rd Rte 22A, 05491
(802)759-2134   **36 44 63**

Choice furniture, glass, china, Orientals & primitives. Large selection of glazed pottery. **Hours:** All year 9-5 by chance/appt. **Assoc:** VADA. Walter Washburn **Park:** On site. **Loc:** 1 MI N of Addison 4 Corners.

Barre

ARNHOLM'S ANTIQUES
891 N Main St, 05641
(802)476-5921   **47**

Antique & estate jewelry. **Est:** 1940. **Hours:** BY APPT ONLY. **Assoc:** AAA VADA. Rachel Arnholm **Park:** On site. **Loc:** On Rte 302 between Barre & Montpelier.

Bellows Falls

ARCH BRIDGE BOOKSHOP
142 Westminster St 2nd fl, 05101
(802)463-9395   **13**

5,000 volumes, specializing in WW II, American West, Civil War, biographies & history. **Hours:** By chance/appt. **Assoc:** VABA. Barbara Whitehead **Park:** Nearby. **Loc:** Westminster St is Rte 5, S end of Bellows Falls Village.

Bennington

AISLINN BOOK & RESEARCH
Box 589, 05201
          13

Ireland & other Celtic countries, Japan, poetry & women. **Hours:** MAIL ORDER ONLY. **Assoc:** VABA. J M Hays

BRADFORD BOOKS
West Rd Rte 9, 05201
(802)447-0387   **13**

Antiquarian books: children's, Vermont & history. **Serv:** Search service. **Hours:** May-Oct Wed-Sat 11-5 Sun 1-5 BY APPT. **Assoc:** VABA. Brad Craig **Loc:** Opposite Fairdale Farms.

FOUR CORNERS EAST, INC
307 North St, 05201
(802)442-2612   **37 38 59**

Country & formal American & Continental furniture, accessories & paintings. **Est:** 1973. **Serv:** Appraisal, shipping. **Hours:** Mon-Sun 10-5. **CC:** AX/MC/V. **Assoc:** AADLA VADA. Douglas L Millay **Park:** On site.

NEW ENGLANDIANA
121 Benmont Ave, 05201
(802)447-1695   **13**
Antiquarian books dealing with Americana, biography & autobiography, genealogies, history, religion, theology & social sciences. *Pr:* $1–100. *Est:* 1961. *Serv:* Catalog $2 for 4 issues. *Hours:* Mon & most weekdays 8-4:30. *Size:* Medium. *Assoc:* VABA. Roger D Harris *Park:* In front. *Loc:* From US Rte 7 take River St between A&P & Mazda dealer 2 blocks to shop on corner of Benmont Ave.

NOW AND THEN BOOKS
439 Main St, 05201
(802)447-1470   **13**
General line of used & out-of-print books. *Hours:* Wed-Sat 11-4 Mon, Tue by chance. *Assoc:* VABA. Frances Stockman *Loc:* 1 block E of US Rte 7.

Bethel

OLD BOOKS & EPHEMERA
Rte 107, 05032
(802)234-9505   **13 33**
Vermont material, ephemera & collectibles. *Hours:* Daily afternoons. *Assoc:* VABA. Patricia S Smith *Loc:* On highway at Rtes 107 & 12S, 3 MI off I-89.

Brandon

BRANDON ANTIQUES
Rte 73E, 05733
(802)247-3026   **34 37 80**
19th C American formal & country furniture, specializing in cannonball beds, textiles, chests & cupboards. Folk art for the knowledgeable. *Est:* 1963.

Hours: Most days 10-5, call ahead. *Assoc:* VADA. Warren Kimball *Park:* On site. *Loc:* 1.4 MI from ctr of town, across from 2nd hole of Neshobe Golf Course.

H GRAY GILDERSLEEVE ANTIQUES
57 Park St, 05733
(802)247-6684   **34 65**
Primitives, folk art & the unusual. *Est:* 1960. *Hours:* BY APPT. *CC:* MC/V. *Loc:* Park St-Rte 73, .5 block from the Brandon Inn.

NUTTING HOUSE ANTIQUES
40 Park St Rte 73E, 05733
(802)247-3302   **27 34 80**
Country & early American furniture - refinished or original surface, folk art, textiles & decorative accessories. *Pr:* $60–3000. *Est:* 1984. *Serv:* Appraisal, restoration, shipping. *Hours:* Most days by chance/appt. *CC:* MC/V. *Assoc:* VADA. Pamela Laubscher *Park:* On site. *Loc:* Rte 7 to 73E.

Brattleboro

BLACK MOUNTAIN ANTIQUE CENTER
Rte 30, 05301
(802)254-3848   **{GR50}**
Furniture, glassware, china, stoneware, milk bottles, books, ephemera, tools & jewelry. *Hours:* Daily 10-5. *Park:* On site. *Loc:* 2 MI N of downtown Brattleboro on Rte 30.

PAUL LAWTON & SON
PO Box 551, 05301
(802)254-8969   **4 8**
Twice weekly sales in the gallery Wednesday evening & Saturday except

when Saturday sale is on sight. Annual antique auction on Labor Day. No buyers' premium. *Est:* 1951. *Serv:* Appraisal, auction house, accept mail/phone bids. Terry W Lawton

Bristol

TERRY HARPER, BOOKSELLER
120 North St Apt D, 05443
(802)453-5088   13

Americana, historical, rare & scarce books with emphasis on condition. *Serv:* Appraisal, purchase estates. *Hours:* BY APPT. *Size:* Medium. *CC:* MC/V. *Assoc:* VABA. *Park:* On site. *Loc:* Shop at Jct of Rtes 7 & 116, call for directions to home.

Brownsville

SCHOOLHOUSE TEN ANTIQUES
Brownsville, 05037
(802)484-3396

A general line of antiques. *Hours:* May-Oct daily 10-5. *Assoc:* VADA. Kim Stapleton *Loc:* From Brownsville take the Brownsville Hartland Rd for 2.2 MI.

Burlington

ASHLEY BOOK COMPANY
PO Box 534, 05402
(802)863-3854   13

Press books & fine printing, illustrated books, American & English literature, books about books, biography & ski-

ing. *Serv:* Catalog. *Hours:* BY APPT ONLY. *Assoc:* VABA. George C Singer

BYGONE BOOKS
91 College St, 05401
(802)862-4397   13 66

General stock of 10,000 used & out-of-print books & some prints. *Serv:* Appraisal, search service. *Hours:* Mon-Sat 9:30-5:30. *Assoc:* VABA. S Soule *Loc:* Between Pine & Champlain Sts.

CODEX BOOKS
30 Elmwood Ave, 05401
(802)862-6413   13

15,000 books specializing in out-of-print & scarce books in philosophy, theology, the classics, foreign languages, history of science & books printed pre-1700. *Serv:* Appraisal, catalog, search service. *Hours:* Tue-Sat 9-5 Sun,Mon BY APPT. *Size:* Medium. *Assoc:* VABA. Paul S McDonald *Park:* On site. *Loc:* Downtown Burlington, across from post office.

CONANT CUSTOM BRASS
270 Pine St, 05401
(802)658-4482   16 50 71

A mix of fine brass & copper antiques & unusual one-of-a-kind treasures all set in a bustling workshop. Stock three hundred restored antique light fixtures & hundreds of glass shades. *Pr:* $5–5000. *Est:* 1979. *Serv:* Custom brass, brochure, consultation, repairs, reproduction, restoration. *Hours:* Mon-Fri 9-5 Sat BY APPT. *Size:* Large. *CC:* MC/V. Stephen W Conant *Park:* On site. *Loc:* From Rte 89N, Exit 14W, W on Rte 2 into Burlington, cross Church St, St. Paul St & turn L on Pine St, 2 blocks down.

COLIN & ELIZABETH DUCOLON
41 University Terr, 05401
(802)863-1497 **44 80**

Early textiles, flint glass & rural paint.
Hours: BY APPT. *Assoc:* VADA.

JAMES FRASER
PO Box 494, 05402
(802)658-0322 **13**

Antiquarian books: Stock Market & Wall Street, economics, business, political, social & cultural history. *Hours:* BY APPT ONLY. *Assoc:* ABAA. James Fraser

TAILOR'S ANTIQUES
68 Pearl St, 05401
(802)862-8156 **44 65**

Primitives, glass, china & art. *Est:* 1958. *Hours:* Mon-Fri 8-5 Sat 8-4. *Assoc:* VADA. *Park:* In front. *Loc:* Near the post office.

WEBB & PARSONS NORTH
545 S Prospect St, 05401
(802)658-5123 **34**

Contemporary, folk & outsider art. *Hours:* BY APPT.

Castleton Corners

OLD HOMESTEAD ANTIQUES
Rte 4A, 05732
(802)468-2425 **21 44 65**

Lamps, Oriental rugs, glass, china, primitives, vintage clothing, choice linens, some furniture & early Americana. *Est:* 1963. *Serv:* Consultation. *Hours:* May-Nov appt suggested. *Assoc:* VADA. Alma G Donchian

Cavendish

SIGOURNEYS' ANTIQUES
Rte 131, 05142
(802)226-7713 **16 32 49**

English copper & brass, Quimper, biscuit tins, children's books, toy soldiers, Schoenhut circus & other toys. *Hours:* Apr-Oct BY APPT ONLY. *Assoc:* VADA. Doris Sigourney *Loc:* .75 MI E of Cavendish on Rte 131.

Chelsea

BOOKS AT CHELSEA
Main St, 05038
(802)685-3115 **13**

General stock of hardcover used & out-of-print books. *Hours:* Afternoons BY APPT. *Assoc:* VABA. John Hickman

Chester

1828 HOUSE
Rte 103 N of Chester, 05143
(802)875-3075 **27 29 39**

Specializing in English 18th & 19th C country furniture & accessories. *Hours:* May 15-Oct 15 daily 10-5. *CC:* MC/V. *Assoc:* VADA. Jane W Thrailkill *Park:* On site. *Loc:* Between Chester & Ludlow.

WILLIAM AUSTIN'S ANTIQUES
Rte 103 Maple St, 05143
(802)875-3032 **40**

Large selection of quality country oak & Victorian pieces. *Serv:* Shipping. *Hours:* Daily 9-7. William Smith *Loc:* Int of Rtes 103 & 11.

Chester Depot

**STONE VILLAGE
ANTIQUARIAN BOOKS**
Crowhill Rd, 05144
(802)875-2297   **13**
Antiquarian books: history of Vermont & Polish paper cut-outs. **Serv:** Appraisal, estates purchased. **Hours:** BY APPT. **Assoc:** VABA. Edward Pell

Clarendon Springs

**CLARENDON HOUSE
ANTIQUES**
Clarendon Springs Rd, 05777
(802)438-2449   **23 28 85**
Country furniture, vintage clothing, clocks, paintings, rugs & stoneware. **Est:** 1973. **Serv:** Appraisal, purchase estates. **Hours:** All year by chance/appt. Tony Costantino **Loc:** 3 MI S of West Rutland off Rte 133.

Colchester

MATTESON GALLERY OF ARTS
Prim Rd Rte 127, 05446
(802)862-3422   **36 59 67**
Antiques & art: deco furniture, paintings, prints, quilts, glass, silver, jewelry, tools, clocks & watches, decoys, folk art & collectibles. **Pr:** $25–50000. **Est:** 1971. **Serv:** Appraisal, conservation, custom woodwork, purchase estates, restoration. **Hours:** By chance/appt. **Size:** Medium. **Assoc:** VADA. David Matteson **Park:** Nearby lot. **Loc:** From Burlington, take Rte 127N into Colchester, to Prim Rd. From I-89, Exit 16, N on Rtes 2 & 7 to Rte 127 to Prim Rd.

Corinth

ROBERT CHAMBERS
Corinth, 05039
(802)439-6232   **43 69**
Maker of Windsor chairs - to order. **Serv:** Catalog ($3). **Hours:** BY APPT. **Loc:** Call for directions.

Coventry

YESTERYEAR SHOP
Box 58, 05825
(802)754-2129
Antiques & collectibles. **Hours:** May 15-Oct 15 Mon-Sat 10-5 Sun 1-5 & BY APPT. **Assoc:** VADA. Marion C Conway **Park:** On site. **Loc:** Rte 5 Coventry Village.

Craftsbury Common

**CRAFTSBURY COMMON
ANTIQUARIAN**
Box 69, 05827
                                   13
Antiquarian books: maritime, Americana & illustrated. **Hours:** BY APPT. **Assoc:** VABA. Ralph Lewis

Cuttingsville

**HAUNTED MANSION
BOOKSHOP**
Rte 103, 05738
(802)492-3462   **13**
Two floors of an 1880s Victorian: Vermontania, Americana, art, travel, Eu-

rope, cookbooks, natural history, antiques, Civil War, New Englandiana, illustrated books & juveniles. *Pr:* $3–300. *Est:* 1968. *Serv:* Appraisal, brochure, purchase estates. *Hours:* May-Oct Mon-Sat 9-5 (Jul,Aug Sun 11-5). *Size:* Huge. *Assoc:* VABA. Clint Fiske *Park:* On site. *Loc:* Rte 103, 10 MI S of Rutland.

Danby

DANBY ANTIQUES CENTER
S Main St, 05739
(802)293-9984 {GR20}
Eleven rooms & barn filled with 18th & 19th C American country & formal furniture & related accessories, accent on stoneware, folk art, textiles & some architectural pieces. *Pr:* $25–10000. *Est:* 1982. *Serv:* Appraisal, brochure. *Hours:* Apr-Oct Daily 10-5, Nov-Mar Thu-Mon 10-5. *CC:* AX/MC/V. *Assoc:* VADA. Agnes Franks *Park:* On site. *Loc:* 13 MI N of Manchester, .25 MI off Rte 7, watch for state signs.

MAIN STREET ANTIQUES CENTER
Main St, 05739
(802)293-9919 {GR10}
18th, 19th & 20th C furniture, decorative accessories, antique linens & lace, & collectibles. *Est:* 1987. *Hours:* Daily 10-5. *CC:* MC/V. *Park:* In front. *Loc:* On old Rte 7 in Danby.

Derby Line

CARRIAGE HOUSE ANTIQUES
29 Main St, 05830
(802)873-3606 16 36 81
Furniture, glass, Oriental rugs, china, paintings, prints, copper, tools, primitives & treen. *Est:* 1987. *Hours:* Sum: daily 10-7, Win: daily 12-5. James J Noble *Park:* On site. *Loc:* In the house.

TRANQUIL THINGS
43 Main St, 05830
(802)873-3454 13
General stock of used & out-of-print books. *Hours:* By chance/appt. *Assoc:* VABA. Richard Wright

Dorset

AMERICAN SPORTING ANTIQUES
Rte 30, 05251
(802)867-2271 6 30 78
Specializing in antique & classic fishing tackle, classic shotguns, decoys & sporting art. *Est:* 1976. *Serv:* Appraisal, consultation, repairs. *Hours:* Wed-Sun 10-5. *CC:* MC/V. *Assoc:* NLCC NRA VADA. Harold Smith *Park:* On site. *Loc:* 1 MI S of Dorset Village.

THE ANGLOPHILE ANTIQUES
The Old Schoolhouse Rte 30, 05251
(802)362-1621 52 63 77
Large stock of authentic English antiques in an old schoolhouse, emphasis on 18th & 19th C china, jewelry, amber, tortoise, silver, brass & copper, tea caddies & boxes & large selection of miniature china. *Pr:* $20–2000. *Hours:* May 15-Oct daily. *Size:* Medium. *Assoc:* VADA. Dorothy R Jones *Park:* On site. *Loc:* Rte 30, 4 MI N of Manchester Ctr, to Jct of Rte 7A (Main St), 2 MI S of Dorset Village Green.

VIRGINIA POPE, INC.
Box 537, 05251
(802)867-5314   **29 34 59**

American & European folk art, portraits & decorative arts. *Hours:* BY APPT. *Assoc:* NHADA.

East Arlington

EAST ARLINGTON ANTIQUE CENTER
Old Mill Rd, 05252
(802)375-9607   **{GR25}**

Country & formal furniture, primitives, Oriental rugs, paintings, jewelry, china & glass. *Est:* 1987. *Serv:* Appraisal, purchase estates. *Hours:* Year round daily 9-5. *CC:* MC/V. Phil Elwell *Park:* On site. *Loc:* Located in the Post Office Building across from the Candle Mill Village.

GEBELEIN SILVERSMITHS
Box 157, 05252
(802)375-6307   **77**

Silver: American, arts & crafts. *Hours:* BY APPT. *Park:* Nearby.

East Barre

FARR'S ANTIQUES
Rte 110, 05641
(802)476-4308   **27 44 65**

Country & Victorian furniture, glass, china, primitives, baskets, tools & clocks. *Est:* 1967. *Hours:* All year by chance. *CC:* MC/V. *Assoc:* VADA. Edward Farr *Loc:* 4 MI E of Barre on Rte 302, turn R, .25 MI on Rte 110.

East Middlebury

BREADLOAF BOOKS
Main St Rte 125, 05740
(802)388-3502   **13**

General stock of used & out-of-print books, including foreign languages - particularly German. *Pr:* $2–15. *Serv:* Search service. *Hours:* May-Oct Mon-Sat 10-5, Nov-Apr Mon-Sat 11-4. *Assoc:* VABA. Lawrence M Washington *Park:* On site. *Loc:* In the ctr of town.

MIDDLEBURY ANTIQUE CENTER
Rtes 7 & 116, 05740
(802)388-6229   **{GR50}**

Furniture, glass, metalwork, quilts, crocks, jewelry & oil paintings. *Hours:* Year round daily 9-6. *CC:* MC/V. Francis Stevens Jr *Loc:* On corner of Rtes 7 & 116.

East Montpelier

JEFFREY R CUETO ANTIQUES
Murray Rd RD 1 Box 125, 05651
(802)223-5175   **1 37**

Early American country & formal furniture, clocks & decorative accessories located on a farm. *Pr:* $50–5000. *Serv:* Appraisal, purchase estates. *Hours:* By chance/appt. *Size:* Medium. *Assoc:* NAWCC VADA. *Park:* On site. *Loc:* Take R on Towne Hill Rd at top of Main St, .7 MI, L on Murray Rd for .7 MI, red farmhouse.

East Poultney

RIVERS EDGE ANTIQUES
RD 2 Box 182, 05764
(802)287-9553 **66 59 78**

Paintings, American & European sporting & miscellaneous prints, books, china, linen, quilts, jewelry & furniture. *Hours:* May-Oct Wed-Sat 10-5 else by chance/appt. Charlotte Osbourne *Loc:* On the Gorge in E Poultney.

Essex Junction

ALL THINGS CONSIDERED
16 Lincoln St Rte 2A, 05452
(802)878-8166 **40**

Antiques & collectibles including a selection of oak furniture. *Hours:* Mon-Sat 10-6. *Size:* Large. *Loc:* On Rte 2A.

YANKEE PEDLAR'S ANTIQUES
86 Pearl St, 05452
(802)878-4360 **36 44 63**

Furniture, collectibles, glass, china & accessories. *Hours:* Mon-Sat 10-5 Sun by chance. Linda McNulty *Park:* On site. *Loc:* Across from Champlain County fairgrounds.

Fair Haven

FOUNDATION ANTIQUES
148 N Main St, 05743
(802)265-4544 **34 65**

Specializing in Quimper, graniteware & kitchenware in period room settings. *Pr:* $1–10000. *Serv:* Appraisal, consultation, purchase estates, brochure, catalog. *Hours:* Apr 15-Jan 15 Daily 9-5

appt advised. *Size:* Large. *Assoc:* VADA. Stephen G Smith *Park:* On site. *Loc:* Approx 300 yds N of Village Green.

Fairfax

THE BOOKSTORE
223 Main St, 05454
(802)849-2209 **13**

General stock of used books & paperbacks, some rare & out-of-print. *Est:* 1979. *Hours:* May 15-Oct 15 Tue-Fri 1-5 Sat 10-4 or by chance/appt. *Assoc:* VABA. The Wolds *Park:* In front. *Loc:* I-89 Exit 18: 6 MI.

THE CAT'S MEOW ANTIQUES
Rte 104, 05454
(802)849-6065 **7 47 85**

Small, friendly shop specializing in art deco, vintage clothing & accessories, costume jewelry, small collectibles - Oriental, cat collectibles, kitchen things, lamps & prints. *Pr:* $10–500. *Est:* 1984. *Hours:* Most weekdays, weekends & winter by chance/appt. Bonnie Groves *Park:* On site. *Loc:* I-89 Exit 18: Rte 7 to Rte 104A, 6 MI turn R toward Fairfax Village, 2 MI at bottom of hill on R, watch for sign.

GLENORTON COUNTRY ANTIQUES
Rte 104, 05454
(802)849-6103 **16 37 50**

American country furniture, iron, tin, primitives & early lighting. *Hours:* May-Nov by chance/appt. *Assoc:* VADA. Stuart Orton *Loc:* Next to Village Bridge.

Fairlee

EDITH M ACKERMAN
4 Woodland Terr, 05045
(802)333-4457   **44**
Depression, Heisey, Fostoria & Cambridge glass. *Serv:* Mail order. *Hours:* By chance/appt. *Assoc:* Nat'l Heisey. *Loc:* Off Lake Morey Rd.

Ferrisburg

TWIN MAPLES ANTIQUES
RR 1 Box 167, 05456
(802)877-3486   **63**
China, glass & prints - specialize in Buffalo Pottery. *Est:* 1980. *Hours:* By chance/appt. Roger Northon *Loc:* .75 MI S of Dakin Farm on Rte 7.

Grafton

GABRIELS' BARN ANTIQUES
Inn @ Woodchuck Hill Farm,
05146
(802)843-2398   **1 28 36**
A carefully selected inventory of country furniture & unusual decorative accessories: decorated stoneware, pottery, decoys, treen, pewter & copper, paintings, gameboards, porcelain & china - Canton, flow blue, yellow ware & spongeware. *Pr:* $25–3000. *Serv:* Appraisal, purchase estate, country inn on premises. *Hours:* May-Oct daily 9-5. *Size:* Medium. *CC:* MC/V. *Assoc:* VADA. Anne Gabriel *Park:* In front. *Loc:* I-91 Exit 5: W on Rte 121 to Grafton, located 2 MI W of village on Middletown Rd.

GRAFTON GATHERING PLACE
Sylvan Rd, 05146
(802)875-2309   **27 36**
Specializing in period furniture, country pieces & the appropriate accessories. *Hours:* Daily by chance/appt. Best to call ahead in winter. Mary Pill *Loc:* I-91 Exit 6: Rte 103 8 MI to Sylvan Rd, 2.5 MI to shop.

PICKLE STREET ANTIQUES
Rte 121, 05146
(802)843-2533   **27 28 67**
Country furniture, primitives, stoneware, tinware, porch rockers & quilts. *Hours:* All year by chance. *Assoc:* VADA. Obe McMahon *Loc:* .25 MI E of the Village.

WOODSHED ANTIQUES
Rte 121, 05146
(802)843-2365   **27 44 81**
Country furniture, tools, primitives, glass, china, lamps & parts, ox yokes & phonographs. *Est:* 1978. *Serv:* Estate appraisal, bed & breakfast. *Hours:* May-Oct daily. *Assoc:* VADA. Ernestine Lake *Park:* On site. *Loc:* .5 MI E of Grafton.

Grand Isle

BACK DOOR ANTIQUES
Lakeside Rd, 05458
(802)372-5832   **78**
Sporting collectibles & interesting country smalls. *Hours:* BY APPT, CLOSED Deer Season. *Assoc:* VADA. Jean Tudhope

Greensboro

RECOVERY BOOKS
Box 232, 05841
(802)586-2846   13

Antiquarian books including works by Robert Frost, Gladys Taber & Dorothy Canfield Fisher. *Hours:* BY APPT. *Assoc:* VABA. John M Jeffrey

Groton

STEPHEN JONES ANTIQUES
N End of Lake Groton, 05046
(802)584-3858   27 33 64

Country furniture, paintings, accessories, paper goods & post cards. *Hours:* By chance or call ahead. *Assoc:* VADA.

OLD BOOKS
Box 7, 05046
(802)584-3748   13

A general stock of antiquarian books. *Hours:* By chance/appt. *Assoc:* VABA. Faye Jordan

Hardwick

WILLIAM F HILL
Box 15, 05843
(802)472-6308   8

Auctions of all types - including antiques. *Est:* 1957. *Serv:* Accept mail/phone bids, brochure, consultation, purchase estates. *Hours:* Year round daily. *Assoc:* NAA.

OLD FIREHOUSE ANTIQUES
Old Mill St, 05843
(802)472-6166   {GR10}

Pine furniture & quilts restored in old fire house. *Est:* 1985. *Hours:* Daily 9:30-5 Mon, Sat til 4 Sun 12-4. Jean Hanzl *Park:* On site. *Loc:* .5 block from downtown Int.

Hartland

18TH CENTURY DESIGN
Hartland, 05048
(802)436-2299   70 74

Preservation, reproduction & reconstruction of traditional architecture of the early American periods. *Serv:* Building/site design, antique procurement, project supervision. *Hours:* Call for appt & directions.

ANTIQUES CENTER AT HARTLAND
Rte 5, 05048
(802)436-2441   {MDS52}

Fine antiques of the 18th & early 19th C, displayed in two restored 18th C houses & "the little shop", choice furniture & decorative accessories for beginning & advanced collectors & trade. *Est:* 1981. *Hours:* May-Oct daily 9-5, Nov-Apr Wed-Sun 10-4. *Size:* Large. *CC:* MC/V. *Assoc:* VADA. Barbara E Mills *Park:* On site. *Loc:* From S: I-91 Exit 9: L onto Rte 5 2 MI N to Ctr, From N: I-91 Exit 10: White River Jct turn R onto Rte 5, S 10 MI.

Hinesburg

HAWK'S NEST ANTIQUES & DECOYS
Silver St, 05461
(802)482-2076 **27 30 41**

Specializing in fine decoys by well-known carvers, early & paint decorated furniture, country accessories, quilts & folk art. *Hours:* By chance/appt. *Assoc:* NHADA. *Loc:* 1 MI S of village.

Hinesburg Village

WALKER HOUSE ANTIQUES
Rte 116 Charlotte Rd, 05461
(802)482-3410 **27 65**

Country furniture & accessories, primitives & collectibles. *Hours:* Apr-Oct Sat,Sun, else by chance/appt. Daphne Walker

Jamaica

ANTIQUES ANONYMOUS
Rte 30, 05343
(802)874-4207 **24 28 67**

Furniture, crocks, quilts, coins, toys, advertising, political, photos, books & Vermont memorabilia. *Est:* 1979. *Serv:* Appraisal, conservation, purchase estates, repairs. *Hours:* By chance/appt. Andrew Avery *Loc:* 2 houses S of bank.

Jeffersonville

1829 HOUSE ANTIQUES
Rte 15, 05464
(802)644-2912 {GR20}

Country antiques in a turn-of-the-century barn. *Est:* 1976. *Serv:* Purchase estates, shipping. *Hours:* Mon-Sat 9-5. *Size:* Large. *CC:* MC/V. Richard Haver *Loc:* 2.5 MI E of Jeffersonville on Rte 15.

MARY'S GLASS & COLLECTIBLES
RR 1 Box 249, 05464
(802)644-8878 **16 44 48**

Small shop featuring depression & collectible glass, kitchen collectibles, linens, old books, tinware & some small furniture. *Hours:* By chance/appt. Mary Edwards *Park:* On site. *Loc:* Int Rtes 15 & 108, N on Rte 108 .25 MI, Rte 109, 1st house on L.

Johnson

MEL SIEGEL ANTIQUES
Rte 15 W of Johnson Village, 05656
(802)635-7838 **1 40 63**

Country antiques, refinished pine & oak furniture, primitives, majolica, spongeware, Quimper, jewelry, glass, china, tools, advertising & general line. *Pr:* $10–2000. *Est:* 1959. *Serv:* Purchase estates. *Hours:* May-Oct 12 daily 9-5:30. *Size:* Medium. *Assoc:* VADA. *Park:* On site. *Loc:* From Burlington: E on Rte 15.

Ludlow

LUDLOW ANTIQUE & GIFT CENTER
Rte 103, 05149
(802)228-7335   {GR12}
Furniture, wood stoves, tools, tin books, china, glass silverware, period clothing & jewelry. *Est:* 1986. *Hours:* Year round daily 10-5. *CC:* MC/V. *Park:* On site. *Loc:* 2 MI S of Ludlow.

RED CLOVER ANTIQUES
119 Main St, 05149
(802)228-4333   **27 28 81**
Farmhouse furniture, glass, tools, stoneware & quilts. *Serv:* Repairs. *Hours:* Mon-Sun 9-5. *CC:* MC/V. *Park:* On site. *Loc:* .5 MI S of Okemo Mountain Ski Area.

Lyndonville

GREEN MOUNTAIN BOOKS & PRINTS
100 Broad St, 05851
(802)626-5051   **13 66**
Antiquarian books: Americana, history, art & antiques. *Serv:* Catalog. *Hours:* Mon-Thu 10-4 Fri 10-6 Sat 10-1. *Assoc:* VABA. Ralph Secord *Loc:* Corner of Depot & Broad St.

Manchester

THE CLOCK EMPORIUM
Rte 7A, 05254
(802)362-3328   **23 32 55**
A choice selection of antique clocks & music boxes on display. *Pr:* $25-4000. *Est:* 1976. *Serv:* One year guarantee,

repairs, old toy trains bought & repaired. *Hours:* Tue-Sat 10-5. *CC:* MC/V. Edward H Voigt *Park:* On site. *Loc:* On Rte 7A, 1 MI S of the blinking light in Manchester Ctr.

HOOKED RUG RESTORATION
Box 542, 05254
(802)867-2252   **21 71**
Restoration of hooked rugs, including, backing, binding, repair of tears & holes. *Serv:* Restoration, free estimates. *Hours:* BY APPT ONLY. Linda Eliason

PARAPHERNALIA ANTIQUES
Rte 7A, 05254
(802)362-2421   **17 38 77**
Continental antiques, collectibles, jewelry, furniture, bronzes, silver bibelots & perfume bottles. *Est:* 1967. *Serv:* Appraisal. *Hours:* Jun-Oct 11:30-6 by chance/appt. *Assoc:* VADA. Anne Alenick *Park:* On site. *Loc:* .5 MI S of Manchester Village.

STEVENSON GALLERY
Union St, 05254
(802)362-3668   **34 59**
Fine art: specializing in American artists & American folk art. *Hours:* Thu-Tue 10-5 never at lunch. *CC:* MC/V. Timothy J Stevenson *Park:* In front. *Loc:* Across from the Equinox.

Manchester Center

1812 HOUSE ANTIQUE CENTER
Rte 7N, 05255
(802)362-1189   {GR}
Items from kitchen, bedroom & parlor to shop, barn & sugarhouse - rag rugs,

copper molds, American antiques, pictures, oil paintings, crocks, collectibles, tools, guns & trade cards. *Est:* 1984. *Hours:* Apr-Dec daily 10-5, Jan-Mar Thu-Mon 10-5. *CC:* MC/V. Sara H Symons *Park:* On site. *Loc:* 2.3 MI N of Manchester on Rte 7, next to Enchanted Doll House.

BELLWETHER GALLERY
Rte 30 Bonnet St, 05255
(802)362-4811   **21 43 50**
18th & 19th C country furniture & accessories, quality scrubbed pine, fine reproduction furniture, decorative accessories, dhurries, kilims, rag rugs, baskets & lighting. *Hours:* Mon-Sat 10-5:30 Sun 12-5. Barbara Geldbaugh

BREWSTER ANTIQUES
Corner Bennett & School Sts, 05255
(802)362-1579   **44 47 77**
Antique & estate jewelry, sterling flatware, glass small furniture, silver, oddments & paintings. *Est:* 1945. *Hours:* May-Jan Mon-Sat 10-5 call ahead, else by chance. *Assoc:* VADA. *Park:* Nearby. *Loc:* 1 block W of Rte 7 on Rte 30.

CARRIAGE TRADE ANTIQUES CENTER
Rte 7, 05255
(802)362-1125   **{GR31}**
Decorative glass, porcelain, Victorian & country furniture. *Hours:* Apr-Dec Daily 10-5, Jan-Mar Thu-Mon 10-5 & BY APPT. *CC:* MC/V. Carmen Kingery *Park:* On site. *Loc:* 2.5 MI N of Manchester Ctr on Rte 7.

CENTER HILL PAST & PRESENT ANTIQ
Center Hill, 05255
(802)362-3211   **{GR}**
Country furniture, folk art, collectibles & crafts. *Hours:* Daily 10-5. *CC:* MC/V. Jeff Metzger *Park:* On site. *Loc:* Off Rte 7, 1 block from Manchester.

BARBARA B TRASK, APPRAISALS
PO Box 1752 Rte 7N, 05255
(802)362-2214   **4 34 59**
Personal property appraisals for insurance, estate settlement, property division, sale. Commission sales on selected items, personal advisory service for purchasers & for sellers. *Serv:* Appraisal, consultation. *Hours:* Apr-Dec by chance/appt. *Assoc:* ASA VADA. *Loc:* Rte 7, N of Manchester Ctr, opposite post office.

Manchester Village

EQUINOX ANTIQUES
Rte 7A, 05254
(802)362-3540   **29 36**
Carefully selected stock of 18th & early 19th C formal furniture & related decorative accessories selected for discriminating collectors. *Serv:* All pieces backed by a written guarantee. *Hours:* Tue-Sun 10-5. *CC:* MC/V. *Assoc:* VADA. Charles E Dewey *Park:* In front. *Loc:* Opposite Equinox Hotel in Equinox Shops Building.

JOHNNY APPLESEED BOOKSHOP
Main St, 05254
(802)362-2458 **13**

Regional Americana, fine & rare bindings, first editions, American history, hunting, fishing & angling & rare books. *Hours:* Daily 9:30-5. *Assoc:* VABA. Frederic F Taylor

Middlebury

BIX ANTIQUES
Rte 116, 05753
(802)388-2277 **27 44 81**

Country furniture in as-found condition & refinished, some glass, woodenware & tools. *Hours:* Mon-Sat 8-5. *Assoc:* VADA. John Wetmore *Loc:* 1.5 MI N of E Middlebury on Rte 116.

REBA BLAIR SALES
Middlebury, 05753
(802)388-2970 **32 52**

Miniature furniture, doll house furnishings, salesmen's samples, toys & collectors items. *Hours:* BY APPT ONLY. *Assoc:* VADA.

BRADY GALLERIES, INC.
88 Main St, 05753
(802)388-3350 **29 37 59**

19th & 20th C paintings, 18th & 19th C American furniture & accessories. *Hours:* All year Tue-Sat 1-5 & BY APPT. *Assoc:* VADA. Rosemary Brady

HOBNOB ANTIQUES
Rte 7, 05753
(802)388-6813 **37 44 51**

American furniture, stoneware, pressed glass, lamps, maps & prints.

Hours: Year round by chance/appt. *Assoc:* VADA. Bunny Templeton *Loc:* 5 MI S of Middlebury.

POOR RICHARDS USED BOOKS
52 Main St, 05753
(802)388-3241 **13**

12,000 used & out-of-print books. *Hours:* Jan-May Tue-Sat 12-5, Jun-Dec Mon-Sat 10-5, MAR BY APPT. *Assoc:* VABA. Lois B Craig

C. TILEY ANTIQUES
91 Court St Rte 7, 05753
(802)388-7569 **32 53**

Toys & looking glasses. *Hours:* Apr-Nov by chance/appt. *Assoc:* VADA. Candy Tiley

VILLAGE STORE OF MIDDLEBURY
Rte 7, 05753
(802)388-6476 **16 30 80**

Country furniture, primitives, decoys, baskets, wood, iron, brass, tin, linens & textiles. *Hours:* All year by chance/appt. *Assoc:* VADA. Jean Panicucci *Loc:* 4 MI S of Middlebury.

Middletown Springs

CLOCK DOCTOR
South St Rte 133, 05757
(802)235-2440 **23**

European & American mechanical clocks; mixture of tall clocks, wall clocks & shelf clocks. *Est:* 1976. *Serv:* Restoration, repairs. *Hours:* Year round by chance/appt. *Assoc:* VADA. Alan L Grace *Loc:* .25 MI from Int of Rtes 133 & 140.

THE LAMPLIGHTER
South St Rte 133, 05757
(802)235-2306   **50**

A large selection of old oil lamps & hanging lamps. *Est:* 1976. *Hours:* Jun-Oct Tue-Sun 10-5, else by chance/appt. *Assoc:* VADA. Jim Webber *Park:* On site.

NIMMO & HART ANTIQUES
South St, 05757
(802)235-2388   **29 39 63**

17th & 18th C furniture & decorations, pottery & porcelains, oak, walnut, fruitwoods, nice selection of drop leaf tables, chests & chairs. *Est:* 1965. *Serv:* Appraisal. *Hours:* By chance/appt. *Shows:* WAS, ELLIS. *Loc:* 1 block from crossroads of village.

OLD SPA SHOP ANTIQUES
Rte 133 & 140 On Village Green, 05757
(802)235-2366   **23 36 83**

Specializing in the Victorian styles & 19th C formal furniture & diverse accessories. *Est:* 1978. *Hours:* All year 10-5 by chance/appt. *Size:* Medium. *Assoc:* NAWCC VADA. Janna Rupprecht *Park:* On site. *Loc:* From Rutland: Rte 4 to W Rutland then Rte 133W into Middletown Springs.

Milton

BARSALOW AUCTIONS
15 Main St, 05468
(802)893-2660   **8**

Estate auctions conducted on site throughout Vermont. *Est:* 1958. *Serv:* Appraisal, brochure, consultation, purchase estates, mailing list. *Hours:* Jun-Oct. *Assoc:* NAA VAA. Charles M Barsalow *Park:* On site. *Loc:* Approx 15 MI N of Burlington.

Montpelier

GREAT AMERICAN SALVAGE COMPANY
3 Main St, 05602
(802)223-7711   **5 74**

Nation's largest architectural antiques dealer with 5 showrooms on East Coast. Computerized inventory of over 25,000 pieces in more than 100 categories. Showroom, warehouses & workshops in Montpelier, VT. *Serv:* Custom woodwork, newsletter. *Hours:* Year round Mon-Sat 9-5. *Size:* Huge. *CC:* AX/MC/V. *Park:* On site.

Morrisville

BRICK HOUSE BOOKSHOP
RFD #3, Box 3020, 05661
(802)888-4300   **13**

A wide selection of hardcovers & paperbacks in all subjects - 25,000 books. *Pr:* $1–200. *Est:* 1977. *Serv:* Appraisal, brochure, search services. *Hours:* Tue-Sun 10-5 Mon BY APPT. *Size:* Huge. *CC:* MC/V. *Assoc:* VABA. Alexandra Heller *Park:* On site.

New Haven

COLLECTOR'S EMPORIUM ANTIQUE CTR
Rte 7, 05472
(802)877-2853   **{GR33}**

Furniture, primitives, baskets & collectibles. *Est:* 1985. *Serv:* Purchase estates. *Hours:* Daily 10-5. *Size:* Medium. *Park:* On site. *Loc:* 2 MI S of Vergennes on Rte 7.

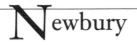

Newbury

OXBOW BOOKS
Rte 5, 05051
(802)866-5940   **13 64**
Vermontania, literature, old post cards, books & paper antiques. *Hours:* Jul 4-Sep 6 by chance/appt. *Assoc:* VABA. Peter Keyes

Newfane

NEWFANE ANTIQUES CENTER
Old Rte 30, 05345
(802)365-4482   **{GR20}**
Three floors of quality antiques & collectibles from the 19th & early 20th C. *Pr:* $50–2000. *Est:* 1985. *Hours:* Thu-Tue 10-5, Jan-Mar CLOSED WED. *Size:* Large. *CC:* MC/V. *Assoc:* VADA. Anne M King *Park:* In front. *Loc:* 10 MI from Brattleboro, Rte 30, 1st R past Rick's Tavern.

NU-TIQUE SHOP
Box 35, 05345
(802)365-7677   **13**
Town histories, poetry, novels, medical, Civil War & genealogy. *Hours:* Sat-Wed 10:30-4:30. *Assoc:* VABA. Don Kent

SCHOMMER ANTIQUES
Rte 30 N Of Village Common, 05345
(802)365-7777   **36 44 66**
19th C furniture, china, glass, prints, table settings & paintings, displayed in a white Victorian listed in the National Register of Historic Houses. *Est:* 1967. *Hours:* May-Dec daily 9:30-5:30, else by chance/appt. *Assoc:* VADA. William Schommer *Loc:* Next to Vermont National Bank.

SIBLEYS VILLAGE WORKSHOP
Rte 30, 05345
(802)365-4653   **27**
Fine classic & country antiques, featuring tin of the 1800s. *Pr:* $25–500. *Est:* 1982. *Serv:* Custom woodwork, purchase estates, repairs, restoration. *Hours:* Year round Mon-Sun 10:30-4:30. *Size:* Medium. *CC:* MC/V. Alta Sisley *Park:* In front. *Loc:* 2 MI S of Newfane Village on Rte 30.

Newport

MICHAEL DUNN - BOOKS
PO Box 436, 05855
(802)334-2768   **13**
Antiquarian books: Americana, Canada & Canadiana, Vermont, hunting & fishing, angling, mountaineering & bibliography. *Serv:* Catalog. *Hours:* BY APPT & MAIL ORDER ONLY. *Assoc:* VABA.

North Bennington

NATURAL HISTORY BOOKS
RD 1, 05257
(802)442-6738   **13**
Antiquarian books relating to natural history, birds, botany, zoology, travels & explorations. *Hours:* BY APPT ONLY. *Assoc:* ABAA. John Johnson

North Ferrisburg

MARTIN HOUSE ANTIQUE CENTER
Corner of Rte 7 & Hollow Rd, 05473
(802)425-2874   **{GR15}**
Eleven rooms & 3 barns country: furniture, primitives, art glass, sporting collectibles, country Irish pine furniture, linens, toys, jewelry, folk art & architectural antiques. *Serv:* Full time cabinet maker, dismantle homes/barns. *Hours:* Apr-Oct Daily 10-6, Win: Tue-Sun 10-5 CLOSED JAN 1-15. *Size:* Huge. Carol Anderson *Park:* On site. *Loc:* 4 MI N of Vergennes, 12 MI S of Shelburne.

North Hero

DORWALDT'S ANTIQUES
Lakeview Dr, 05474
(802)372-4444   **27 65**
Country furniture, primitives & accessories. *Hours:* May 15-Sep 15 Fri-Wed, else by chance/appt. *Assoc:* VADA. Louis Dorwaldt *Loc:* 3.5 MI N of Village off Rte 2 toward state camp grounds.

North Pomfret

RICHARD H ADELSON ANTIQUARIAN BK
Cloudland Rd, 05053
(802)457-2608   **13**
Antiquarian books: voyages, travels & explorations, Pacific region Americana, Africa & children's. *Serv:* Appraisal, catalog. *Hours:* BY APPT ONLY. *Assoc:* ABAA VABA.

Norwich

LILAC HEDGE BOOKSHOP
Main St, 05055
(802)649-2921   **13**
9,000 volumes, many in arts & literature. *Hours:* Thu-Sat 10-5 Mon,Wed by chance/appt. *Assoc:* VABA. Katherine Ericson *Loc:* 1 MI from Dartmouth College, across from the Norwich Inn.

F J MANASEK
Box 705, 05055
(802)649-3962   **9 13 51**
Rare maps, rare books, medieval & Oriental manuscripts. *Hours:* BY APPT ONLY. *Assoc:* VABA.

Old Bennington

ANTIQUARIAN
39 West Rd off VT 9, 05201
(802)442-4614   **38 59**
Fine European period furniture, paintings & unique decorative accessories. A gallery specializing in antiques of distinction. *Hours:* Mon-Sun 10-5. *CC:* MC/V. *Park:* On site. *Loc:* .5 MI W of Old First Church.

ANTIQUE CENTER AT OLD BENNINGTON
60 West Rd Rte 9, 05201
(802)447-0039   **{GR26}**
From Oriental to country: furniture, china, glass, paintings, pottery, porcelain, brass, primitives & folk art. *Hours:* Daily 9:30-5. *CC:* AX/MC/V. RoseMary Valentine *Loc:* .5 MI from Bennington Museum at Camelot Village.

Orwell

HISTORIC BROOKSIDE FARMS ANTIQUE
Rte 22A, 05760
(802)948-2727   {GR}

Country furnishings, accessories, folk art, pewter, china, crystal, tin ware, depression glass, wooden ware, prints, quilts, farm tools, paintings, 17th, 18th & early 19th C English furniture & early lighting. Est: 1983. Serv: Appraisal, purchase estates. Hours: Always open. Assoc: VADA. Joan Korda Park: On site. Loc: 1.25 MI S of Rte 73.

Pawlet

EAST WEST ANTIQUES
Rte 30, 05761
(802)325-3466   36 42

Indonesian & Dutch colonial furniture & wood carvings & Irish pine furniture. *Est:* 1986. *Hours:* Daily 9-5 Sun BY APPT. *CC:* MC/V. *Loc:* 5 MI N of Dorset.

Pittsford

ART INTERIORS ANTIQUES-PITTSFORD
Rte 7, 05763
(802)483-6766   59 80 81

Featuring a wide selection of paintings, furniture, Orientalia, tools, glass, fabric & accessories. *Hours:* Thu-Sun 10-5 or by chance/appt. *Loc:* Just N of Rutland on Rte 7, across from the library.

COUNTRY BARN ANTIQUE CENTER
Rte 7, 05763
(802)483-9409   {GR35}

Authentic 18th C post & beam barn with glass, used furniture, china, primitives & collectibles. *Hours:* Daily 9-6. *CC:* MC/V. Jim Owen *Park:* On site. *Loc:* Furnace Brook Marketplace, 7 MI N of Rutland.

IRON HORSE ANTIQUES, INC
RFD 2 Box 245 B, 05763
(802)483-2111   8 65 81

Specializing in antique tools & books on tools, hold 2 absentee auctions per year. *Pr:* $5–3000. *Est:* 1970. *Serv:* Appraisal, auction, publisher of The Fine Tool Journal. *Hours:* Jun-Dec Mon-Sat 10-5 Sun 12-5, Jan-May Fri-Sun 10-5. *Size:* Medium. *CC:* MC/V. *Assoc:* MADA. *Park:* On site. *Loc:* Rte 7, 4 MI N of Rutland at Int Rte 4 E & 7, opposite Sawdi's Steak House.

NOSTALGIA NOOK
Rte 7, 05763
(802)483-6826   33 55 64

Collectibles, post cards, sheet music, paper, advertising, ladies' accessories, jewelry & furniture. *Hours:* Apr-Dec daily 9-5, else BY APPT. *Assoc:* VADA. Betty Cormier

PITTSFORD GREEN ANTIQUES
Box 428, 05763
(802)483-6221   {GR}

Porcelain, glass, paintings, prints, linens, jewelry, silver, books & furniture. *Serv:* Purchase estates. *Hours:* Mon-Sat 9:30-5:30 Sun 12-5 CLOSED WED. *CC:* MC/V. Lynne Cleveland *Park:* On site. *Loc:* Call for directions.

Plainfield

THE COUNTRY BOOKSHOP
RFD #2, 05667
(802)454-8439 13

Out-of-print & scarce books, books on bells & folk culture. *Serv:* Appraisal, catalogs. *Hours:* By chance/appt. *Assoc:* VABA. Benjamin Koenig

Poultney

DEN OF ANTIQUITY
Furnace St, 05764
(802)287-9914 40 53 63

Oak furniture, mirrors, glass, china & oil lamps. *Est:* 1985. *Hours:* Mar-Dec Mon-Sun 10-6 CLOSED JAN,FEB. Ted Bachman *Loc:* On Rte 30 in Poultney.

THINGS OF YESTERYEAR
63 Main St, 05764
(802)287-5202

Antiques & collectibles. *Est:* 1984. *Hours:* Jul-Labor Day Mon-Sat 9-5 else Tue-Sat 9-5 CLOSED JAN-MAR 15. *CC:* MC/V. Jo Trombley *Park:* On site. *Loc:* Rte 30 into Poultney, R at light, on the R.

Putney

UNIQUE ANTIQUE
Main St Rte 5, 05346
(802)387-4488 9 33 51

Ephemera including bookplates, autographs, catalogs, letters, post cards, dance programs, political advertising. Old & rare books, maps, drawings, prints & 19th C paintings in a yellow Victorian house. *Est:* 1977. *Hours:*
Daily 9-6 by chance/appt. *Assoc:* VABA VADA. Jonathan Flaccus *Park:* On site.

Quechee

ANTIQUE MALL AT TIMBER RAIL VIL.
Rte 4, 05059
(802)295-1550 {GR200}

Antiques, collectibles, furniture, glass, china, porcelain, primitives, paintings, prints & quilts. *Est:* 1985. *Hours:* Year round daily 9-6. *CC:* MC/V. *Park:* On site. *Loc:* On scenic Rte 4 at Quechee Gorge.

PEDLER'S ATTIC
Rte 4, 05059
(802)296-2422 40 42 84

Oak & pine furniture, glass, wagon wheels, sleighs & cupboards. *Serv:* Stripping & refinishing. *Hours:* Tue-Sun 9-6. *Loc:* By Quechee Gorge.

QUECHEE BOOKS
Rte 4, 05059
(802)295-1681 13

17,500 volumes, including Americana, militaria, sciences, history, social science & New England. *Hours:* Daily 9:30-5:30, evenings & in summertime. *CC:* MC/V. *Assoc:* VABA. Ian Morisson *Park:* On site. *Loc:* I-89N Exit 1: 1 MI, I-89S Exit 1: 100 yds.

Randolph Center

PAGE JACKSON ANTIQUE GALLERY
Ridge Rd, 05061
(802)728-5303 27 63 66

Country & formal furniture & accessories, original prints, Navajo rugs, American art pottery. *Hours:* All year by chance. *Assoc:* VADA. *Loc:* I-89 Exit 4: 2 MI N of Randolph Ctr on Ridge Road.

RED BRICK HOUSE
Randolph Center, 05061
(802)728-5843   **23**
Specializing in antique clocks of all types. *Hours:* BY APPT. *Assoc:* VADA. Bill Mather *Loc:* .5 MI off I-89.

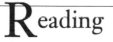

Reading

LIBERTY HILL ANTIQUES
Rte 106, 05062
(802)484-7710   **27 81**
Country furniture refinished or as-found, accessories & woodworking tools. *Hours:* May 15-Oct. *Assoc:* VADA. James Mulder *Loc:* S of Mill Brook Antiques.

MILL BROOK ANTIQUES
Rte 106, 05062
(802)484-5942   **28 36 65**
Country shop & barn filled with furniture, primitives, stoneware & china. *Hours:* May-Oct daily Tue by chance. *Assoc:* VADA. Nancy Stahura *Loc:* 10 MI S of Woodstock.

YELLOW HOUSE ANTIQUES
Rte 106, 05062
(802)484-7799   **1 4 67**
A small shop of fine Shaker, 18th & early 19th C Americana furniture, decorative & folk art, with an emphasis on provincial New England forms & museum-quality community Shaker pieces. *Serv:* Consultation, purchase estates. *Hours:* By chance/appt. *Size:* Medium. *Assoc:* VADA. Elizabeth

Harley *Park:* On site. *Loc:* 10 MI S of the Woodstock Green, on the E side of Rte 106.

Richmond

VINCENT J FERNANDEZ ORIENTAL RUG
Rte 2, 05477
(802)434-3626   **21**
Handwoven Orientals from all weaving areas & a general line of antiques. *Pr:* $50–9000. *Est:* 1976. *Serv:* Appraisal, conservation, interior design, purchase estates, restoration. *Hours:* Appt suggested. *Size:* Medium. *Assoc:* NEAA ORRA VADA. *Park:* On site. *Loc:* On Rte 2, 2.7 MI E of Richmond Ctr.

Rockingham Village

STEPHEN-DOUGLAS ANTIQUES
Meetinghouse Rd, 05101
(802)463-4296   **1 37**
18th & early 19th C American furniture & decorative accessories from country homes for collectors who appreciate quality. Interesting smalls. *Hours:* APPT PREFERRED. *Assoc:* NHADA. Stephen Douglas *Park:* On site. *Loc:* Rte 91 Exit 6: 1 MI.

Rutland

ANTIQUES CENTER & SPECIALTY SHOP
67 Center St, 05701
(802)775-3215   {GR40}

Collectibles & country accessories. *Est:* 1986. *Hours:* Mon-Sat 9:30-5:30 Sun 12-5. *CC:* AX/DC/MC/V. *Park:* On site. *Loc:* Close to Jct of Rtes 4 & 7 in downtown Rutland.

CONWAY'S ANTIQUES & DECOR
90 Center St, 05701
(802)775-5153   21 37 63

American, Chinese & English furniture, Oriental rugs & porcelain. *Est:* 1956. *Serv:* Appraisal, conservation, repair, refinish upholstery. *Hours:* Mon-Fri 9:30-5 CLOSED NOON Sat 'til 12pm or BY APPT. *CC:* MC/V. Tom Brown *Loc:* 1 block W of Rte 7.

EAGLE'S NEST ANTIQUES
53 Prospect St, 05701
(802)773-2418   32 52 65

Primitives, fine china, lamps, dolls, kettles, jewelry, silver, bottles, copper & miniatures. *Hours:* All year Sat,Sun by chance. *Assoc:* NEAA VADA. James Lemmo *Loc:* 2 short blocks from Rte 7.

PARK ANTIQUES
75 Woodstock Ave, 05701
(802)775-4184   28 36 65

Period furniture, primitives, jugs, crocks, glass, china, jewelry, quilts, paintings & folk art. *Est:* 1982. *Serv:* Purchase estates. *Hours:* Tue-Sun 10-5. *CC:* AX/MC/V. *Assoc:* VADA. John Smart *Park:* On site. *Loc:* .5 MI from Rte 7, on Rte 4E on the way to Killington.

RUTLAND ANTIQUES
Rte 7, 05701
(802)775-6573   {GR}

In a 150-year-old Vermont farmhouse on the northern outskirts of Rutland an interesting variety of reasonably priced, locally acquired antiques. *Pr:* $5–10000. *Serv:* Appraisal, consultation, purchase estates. *Hours:* Tue-Sat 9-5 Sun 10-5. *Size:* Medium. *CC:* MC/V. *Assoc:* NEAA. Joanna Seward *Park:* On site. *Loc:* Approx 3 MI N of the Jct of Rtes 4 & 7, on Rte 7, red farmhouse on the R.

SOPHIE'S COLLECTIQUES
71 Wales St, 05701
(802)775-5041   47 80 85

Furniture, collectibles, textiles, jewelry, vintage clothing & accessories. *Serv:* Textile restoration, alterations, dressmaking. *Hours:* Mon,Sat 10-4:30 Fri 11-5:30. Denise Byers *Park:* Nearby. *Loc:* In the city: Rte 7S to Washington St, to Wales St.

SUGAR HOUSE ANTIQUES
Rte 4E, 05701
(802)775-0547   27 40 63

Country furniture & accessories, oak & Victorian furniture, glass & china. *Hours:* Year round daily 9-6. *Assoc:* VADA. Ron Sweet

TRULY UNIQUE ANTIQUES
Rte 4E, 05701
(802)773-7742   27 84

Country furniture & accessories, horse drawn wagons & sleighs. *Hours:* Year round daily 9-6. *CC:* AX/MC/V. Joanne Fratrich *Loc:* 2.5 MI E of Jct of Rtes 4 & 7 in Rutland.

TUTTLE ANTIQUARIAN BOOKS INC
28 S Main St, 05701
(802)773-8930   **13 51**
Antiquarian books: genealogies, general & New England Americana, maps & atlases & Orientalia. *Hours:* Mon-Fri 8-5 Sat 8-4. *Assoc:* ABAA VABA. Charles E Tuttle

WALDRON & RHODES FINE JEWELERS
10 Stratton Rd, 05701
(802)747-4500   **4 47**
Fine antique jewelry, master jeweler on premises for repair & restoration of jewelry. *Serv:* Appraisal, purchase estates, repair, restoration. *Hours:* Fri-Tue 9-6 Wed,Thu 9-9 Sun BY APPT. *Assoc:* GIA ISA NEAA. John A Walron, Jr, CG

Ryegate Corner

RYEGATE CORNER ANTIQUES
Ryegate Corner, 05042
(802)584-3538   **44 63**
Fine china & glass. *Assoc:* VADA. Melve Zuccaro *Loc:* 2 MI W of Rte 5.

Saxtons River

SCHOOLHOUSE ANTIQUES
Rte 121, 05154
(802)869-2332   **1 27 65**
Two floors of country furniture, some refinished & a nice selection of accessories. *Pr:* $10–2000. *Hours:* Daily 9-5 or by chance. *Size:* Medium. *Assoc:* VADA. Faith Boone *Park:* On site. *Loc:* 2.2 MI W of Saxtons River on Rte 121.

SIGN OF THE RAVEN
Main St Rte 121, 05154
(802)869-2500   **1 59**
Big red barn with fine early American antiques & new gallery showing early & contemporary fine oils, watercolors & prints with exceptional assortment of decorative accessories. *Pr:* $25–25000. *Est:* 1968. *Serv:* Appraisal, brochure, consultation, custom woodwork, interior design. *Hours:* Jun-Oct daily 9-5 by chance/appt. *Assoc:* VADA. Mary Ellen Warner *Park:* On site. *Loc:* 5 MI W of 91 & Bellows Falls on Rte 121.

The Gallery at the

SIGN OF THE RAVEN ANTIQUES
ESTABLISHED · 1968

SAXTONS RIVER · VERMONT 05154
(802) 869·2500

Shaftsbury

THE CHOCOLATE BARN ANTIQUES
Rte 7A, 05262
(802)375-6928   **29 36**

Two floors of antiques, 200 antique chocolate molds used to form Swiss chocolate figures; furniture, decorative accessories in period room settings in 1842 sheep barn. *Est:* 1976. *Hours:* Daily 9:30-5:30. *CC:* MC/V. Lucinda D Gregory *Park:* On site. *Loc:* 8 MI N of Bennington on historic Rte 7A.

Shelburne

GADHUE'S ANTIQUES
Rte 7, 05482
(802)985-2682   **44 65 80**

Early furniture, glassware, china, textiles & primitives. *Hours:* Win: by chance/appt. *Assoc:* VADA. Rene Gadhue

HARRINGTON HOUSE 1800
Rte 7, 05482
(802)985-2313   **1**

Americana - glass, primitives & books. *Hours:* Jun-Oct by chance. *Assoc:* VADA. Henrietta Panetieri *Loc:* .5 MI N of the Shelburne Museum.

WILLIAM L PARKINSON BOOKS
RR 1 Box 1330, 05482
(802)482-3113   **13 33 51**

Specializing in Vermontiana, books, maps, broadsides, ephemera. Anything printed having to do with Vermont. *Pr:* $2–500. *Est:* 1977. *Serv:* Catalog (free), purchase estates. *Hours:* BY APPT ONLY. *Assoc:* VABA.

Shelburne Village

UNDERBRIDGE ANTIQUES
Falls Rd, 05482
(802)985-3666   **30 34 59**

Paintings, American Indian items, decoys & folk art. *Hours:* Year round by chance/appt. Jason Miles

Shoreham

LAPHAM & DIBBLE GALLERY, INC.
Main St, 05770
(802)897-5531   **51 59 66**

19th & early 20th C American paintings, prints & maps. *Serv:* Painting conservation. *Hours:* Year round Tue-Sat 9-5. *Assoc:* VADA. Rick Lapham

Shraftsbury

NORMAN GRONNING ANTIQ/ARCH ITEMS
Rte 7A, 05262
(802)375-2202   **2 5 21**

18th & 19th C American country & formal furniture, paintings, carpets, weapons, fireplace accessories, 18th & 19th C architectural items such as beams, hinges, cranes, flooring, doors & moldings, post & beam frames. *Hours:* Wed-Sun 11-5, Apr-Oct BY APPT.

South Barre

COUNTRY LOFT ANTIQUES
Middle Rd, 05670
(802)476-8439　　　**27**
Country furnishings & accessories in as-found or refinished condition. *Est:* 1984. *Hours:* All year by chance. *Assoc:* VADA. Marilyn J Carbonneau *Park:* On site. *Loc:* 2.25 MI S on Rte 14 from Barre.

South Burlington

ETHAN ALLEN ANTIQUE SHOP INC
1625 Williston Rd, 05403
(802)863-3764　　**27 63 66**
American period & country furniture & accessories, china & prints. *Est:* 1939. *Hours:* Daily 10-4:30 Sun BY APPT. *Assoc:* VADA. Nathan E Merrill *Loc:* I-89 Exit 14E: E of Burlington.

SIMPLY COUNTRY
185 Dorset St, 05403
(802)862-9626　　　**40 53**
Refinished furniture, oak, pine & wicker, roll top desks, plant stands, mirrors, floor lamps & country decorating items. *Hours:* Year round Mon-Sat 10-5, May-Dec Sun 12-4. *Size:* Medium. *CC:* MC/V. Audrey Chetti *Park:* On site. *Loc:* 1-89 Exit 14E: .5 MI S.

South Hero

FRANCES L ROBINSON
RR 1 Box 238, 05486
(802)372-4343　　　**13**
Used & collectible books. *Hours:* Mon-Sat 8-5. *Assoc:* VABA.

Springfield

PASTIMES ANTIQUES
218 River St, 05156
(802)885-5819　　**16 28 81**
Furniture, tinware, baskets, advertising items, lamps, crocks & jugs, quilts, toys, miniatures, tools, brass & copper. *Hours:* Year round Tue-Sat 10-5 Mon by chance. *Loc:* Jct Rtes 11 & 106, next to McDonald's.

SUMMER HILL SHOP
80 Summer Hill, 05156
(802)885-3294　　　**32**
Specializing in dolls, toys & related items. *Hours:* May-Nov 10-5 BY APPT ONLY. *Assoc:* VADA. Julia Currie

St Albans

PAULETTE'S ANTIQUES/COLLECTIBL
Fairfield Hill, 05478
(802)524-5664　　**16 40 44**
Furniture, Victorian, country & oak; cut glass, china, brass - including a variety of candlesticks - iron, clocks, art quilts & linens.. *Hours:* Daily 9-5 Sun BY APPT. Marge Paulette *Loc:* I-89 Exit 19: Rte 36E.

St George

A J BELLIVEAU BOOKS
Rte 2A Goose Creek Farms, 05495
(802)482-2540   **13**

Antiquarian books: Vermontiana, military & Americana. *Hours:* BY APPT. *Assoc:* VABA.

St Johnsbury

SIGN OF THE DIAL CLOCK SHOP
63 Eastern Ave, 05819
(802)748-2193   **23 71**

Specializing in antique American & European clocks, pocket watches & older wristwatches. *Pr:* $100–5000. *Est:* 1967. *Serv:* Appraisal, repairs, restorations. *Hours:* Mon-Fri 9-5 Sat 8-12. *Size:* Medium. *CC:* MC/V. *Assoc:* AWI NAWCC VADA. Richard Diefenbach *Park:* In front. *Loc:* Easter Ave is in the center of St Johnsbury & connects the upper & lower levels.

St Johnsbury Ctr

UNA GALLERIES
62 Main St, 05863
(802)748-5034   **13**

History & children's collections. *Hours:* Jun-Dec Thu-Sun 9-6. *Assoc:* VABA. Jeanne M Douglas *Loc:* I-91 Exit 22.

Stowe

ENGLISH COUNTRY ANTIQUES
Pond St, 05672
(802)253-7850   **16 42 48**

Country pine furniture, copper & brass, wooden boxes, linens, prints & toys. *Hours:* Daily 10:30-4 CLOSED TUE. *Assoc:* VADA. Louise Reed

GREEN MOUNTAIN ANTIQUES
Main St, 05672
(802)253-4369   **36 67 77**

Fine line of selected antiques, furniture, primitives, quilts, silver & decorative accessories. *Hours:* Jul-Oct 10-5 Daily, Nov-Jun 11-5 CLOSED WED. *Assoc:* VADA. Judy Foregger

Swanton

RAY & AL'S ANTIQUES
41 Liberty St, 05488
(802)868-4715   **32 48**

Linens, hand lamps, small primitives, flow blue, doll stands, dolls & accessories. *Hours:* Mon-Sat Sun by chance. E. Letourneau

TANSY FARM ANTIQUES
Rte 7, 05488
(802)868-2340   **40 42 67**

Pine, oak, primitives, quilts & folk art. Lorraine Raleigh *Loc:* On Rte 7, 1 MI S of Swanton.

Taftsville

FRASER'S ANTIQUES
Happy Valley Rd, 05073
(802)457-3437   27 32 34
Village barn filled with country antiques. **Pr:** $25–6000. **Serv:** Show management. **Hours:** All year by chance/appt. **Size:** Medium. Bob Fraser **Park:** On site. **Loc:** 3 MI E of Woodstock, just off Rte 4, turn at Country Store.

Townshend

COLT BARN ANTIQUES
Peaked Mountain Rd, 05353
(802)365-7574   1 34 65
A small barn, filled with country furniture & accessories, cupboards, drop leaf tables, chairs, mirrors & unusual folk art & iron tools. **Hours:** Year round daily 8-5. **Size:** Medium. **Assoc:** VADA. Howard Graff **Park:** In front. **Loc:** 2 MI N of Townshend toward Grafton on Rte 35 follow state signs 2 MI.

Vergennes

EIGHTH ELM FARM ANTIQUES
Rte 7, 05491
(802)877-3218   40 42 86
Oak, wicker, pine & walnut furniture, refinished & as-found, quilts, glassware, china & accessories. **Hours:** Year round daily. Paulette McNary

FACTORY MARKETPLACE ANTIQUES
Rte 22A At Kennedy Brothers, 05491
(802)877-2975   {GR50}
Antiques & collectibles in a renovated Vermont creamery. **Pr:** $10–1000. **Est:** 1987. **Hours:** Apr-Dec daily 9-6, else 10-5. **Size:** Huge. **CC:** MC/V. Edwin R Grant **Park:** On site. **Loc:** 22 MI S of Burlington, Rte 7 to Rte 22A, .5 MI S on Rte 22A to Kennedy Bros on L.

FITZ-GERALDS' ANTIQUES
Rte 7, 05491
(802)877-2539   23 36 81
Barn with furniture as-found, tools & clocks. **Hours:** Mon-Sat CLOSED SUN. **Assoc:** VADA. G M Fitz-Gerald

Waitsfield
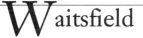

ROSIE BOREL'S L'ESCALIER
Sugarbush Village, 05673
(802)583-2666   52 67 80
Small selection of furniture, miniatures, quilts & textiles. **Hours:** BY APPT. **Assoc:** VADA.

RARE & WELL DONE BOOKS
Rte 100, 05674
(802)496-2791   13
19th & 20th C first editions, natural history & evolution. **Hours:** BY APPT. **Assoc:** VABA. Cathleen G Miller

THE STORE, INC
Rte 100, 05673
(802)496-4465   29 37 66
19th C English & American country furniture, prints & decorative accessories. **Hours:** Daily 10-5. **Assoc:** VADA. Jacqueline Rose

Wallingford

COUNTRY HOUSE ANTIQUES
Rte 7, 05773
(802)446-2344   **28 37 65**
American country & formal furniture
& accessories, primitives & stoneware.
Hours: All year. *Assoc:* VADA. Wayne
Santwire *Loc:* 1 MI S of Village.

TOM KAYE ANTIQUES LTD
Mooney Rd, 05773
(802)446-2605   **39 56 72**
Importers of fine quality 18th C English formal & country furniture, specializing in library & office furnishings,
with marine, medical & scientific instruments. *Assoc:* VADA.

WALLINGFORD ANTIQUE CENTER
Main St Rte 7, 05773
(802)446-2450   **{GR}**
Country primitives, oak, European,
paintings, dolls & collectibles. *Serv:*
Shipping. *Hours:* May 1-Oct 31 Daily
10-5, else Thu-Sun 10-5. *Assoc:*
VADA. Richard Savery *Loc:* Next door
to shops at 16 S Main.

YANKEE MAID ANTIQUES
Rte 7, 05773
(802)446-2463   **27 65 80**
Early country furniture in original
condition & refinished, primitives,
baskets, textiles & appropriate accessories. *Hours:* By Chance. *Assoc:* VADA.
Lynne N Gallipo

Waltham

C J HARRIS ANTIQUES
Maple St Extension, 05491
(802)877-3961   **36 65**
Furniture in old paint, primitives, bas-
kets, Shaker & folk art. *Hours:* BY
APPT. *Assoc:* VADA. *Loc:* 2.2 MI S of
Vergennes.

Warren

WARREN ANTIQUES
Rte 100, 05674
(802)496-2864   **32 36 66**
Large selection of furniture on two full
floors, iron toys, banks, prints, kitchen
collectibles, fiesta & Victorian furniture. *Hours:* Year round daily. *Assoc:*
VADA. Carl Lobel

Waterbury

CABELL ANTIQUES
Waterbury Shopping Ctr, 05676
(802)244-6959   **16 63 77**
China, glass, silver, brass, prints &
small furniture. *Hours:* Daily 10-4.
Assoc: VADA. Mary Cabell

EARLY VERMONT ANTIQUES
Rte 100N, 05676
(802)244-5373   **{GR20}**
American country furniture & decorative accessories. *Est:* 1985. *Hours:* Year
round daily 10-5. *CC:* MC/V. *Loc:*
Across from Ben & Jerry's.

UPLAND ACRES ANTIQUES
RD #1, Box 1455, 05676
(802)244-7197　　　　　**16 36 44**

Early country furniture, glass, china, iron, brass, pewter & copper in a big red barn. *Pr:* $25–2500. *Serv:* Appraisal. *Hours:* Jun-Nov Tue-Sat BY APPT ONLY. *Assoc:* VADA. Rebecca T Higgins *Loc:* I-89 Exit 10 in Waterbury: N toward Stowe, L up Blush Hill, beyond Holiday Inn follow signs, across from Country Club.

West Brattleboro

THE BEAR BOOK SHOP
RFD #4, Box 446, 05301
(802)464-2260　　　　　**13 55**

25,000 volumes of used & rare books, academic books on music & musicians a specialty. *Pr:* $1–600. *Est:* 1975. *Serv:* Purchase estates, search services. *Hours:* May-Labor Day daily 10-5, Fall & Spring by chance/appt. *Size:* Large. *CC:* MC/V. *Assoc:* VABA. John Greenberg *Park:* On site. *Loc:* I-91 Exit 2: Rte 9W, pass turnoff to Marlboro, 3 MI after this, up steep hill, .5 MI by sign, .25 MI L on dirt rd, .5 MI.

West Rupert

AUTHENTIC DESIGNS
36 The Mill Rd, 05776
(802)394-7713　　　　　**68 69 70**

Meticulously crafted reproduction lighting fixtures of Colonial & early American design. Solid brass, maple, pewter & tin. Over 300 models displayed in room settings. *Pr:* $100–5000. *Serv:* Appraisal, repairs, replication, reproduction, restoration. *Hours:* Daily 9-5 Sat BY APPT. *Size:*

Large. *CC:* MC/V. *Assoc:* NEAA. Dan Krauss *Park:* On site. *Loc:* Follow state directional signs.

Westminster

LARSON'S CLOCK SHOP
Main St, 05158
(802)722-4203　　　　　**23**

Hundreds of antique clocks in many styles. *Serv:* Shipping, catalog (send SASE). *Hours:* By chance/appt suggested. *Assoc:* NAWCC VADA. Lindy Larson

Weston

GAY MEADOW FARM ANTIQUES
Trout Club Rd, 05161
(802)824-6386　　　　　**27**

Country & period furniture & accessories. *Hours:* May 15-Oct. *Assoc:* VADA. Harriet Sisson *Park:* In back. *Loc:* Turn at post office on Rte 100, follow signs to the 2nd L, look for decoy in front.

Wilder

STANLEY BOOKS
29 Gillette St, 05088
(802)295-9058　　　　　**13**

A general stock of antiquarian books. *Hours:* BY APPT. *Assoc:* VABA. Thomas Stanley

Williamstown

CLELAND E SELBY
PO Box 362, 05679
(802)433-6787 **21**
Original hooked rugs. *Hours:* Evenings. *Loc:* I-89 Exit 5: 1.5 on Rte 64.

Williston

GREEN MOUNTAIN CLOCK SHOP
73 Essex Rd Rte 2A N, 05495
(802)879-4971 **23 55 71**
Specialize in antique, tower & grandfather clocks & cylinder & disk musical boxes. *Pr:* $100–10000. *Est:* 1974. *Serv:* Appraisal, custom woodwork, repairs, restoration, locator service. *Hours:* Jan-Dec Mon-Fri 9-5 Sat 9-1. *Size:* Medium. *CC:* AX/MC/V. *Assoc:* GMTS NAWCC VADA. Pat Boyden *Park:* On site. *Loc:* I-89 Exit 12 (Williston-Essex Jct), 2.7 MI N.

DUANE E MERRILL
27 James Brown Dr, 05401
(802)878-2625 **8**
Specializing in estate, antique, fine household & real estate auctions. *Assoc:* NAA, VAA.

Wilmington

DEERFIELD VALLEY ANTIQUES
Rte 9 & Lake Raponda Rd, 05363
(802)464-8221 **23 44 63**
Clocks, china, glass & period furniture.

Hours: Apr 20-Oct 25 9:30-5, Win: weekends 10-4 & BY APPT. *Assoc:* VADA. Henri Logcher

WILMINGTON FLEA MARKET
Rtes 9 & 100, 05363
(802)464-3345
10 acre flea market, vendor space $10. *Hours:* Sat,Sun through Oct. The Gores *Park:* Free.

Windsor

WINDSOR ANTIQUES MARKET
53 N Main St, 05089
(802)674-9336 **{GR32}**
In a Gothic-Revival Church: American furniture, folk art, paintings, accessories, Orientalia, American Indian & military items, textiles & art pottery. *Pr:* $25–10000. *Est:* 1984. *Serv:* Appraisal, consultation. *Hours:* May-Oct Mon-Sun 9:30-5:30, Nov-Apr Thu-Mon 10-5. *Size:* Large. *CC:* MC/V. *Assoc:* NEAA VADA. L T Hall *Park:* On site. *Loc:* I-91 Exit 9: 3 MI S on Rte 5. 5 MI from Antiques Ctr at Hartland.

Woodstock

SHEILA BARTON ANTIQUES
53 Central St, 05091
(802)457-1320
Fine antiques & accessories. *Hours:* Jun-Oct daily 9-5. *Assoc:* VADA.

CHURCH STREET GALLERY
4 Church St Rte 4, 05091
(802)457-2628 **36 53 63**
Fine antiques, carefully chosen & arranged - period furniture, mirrors,

lamps, porcelain, crystal, art work, accessories, majolica & Quimper. *Pr:* $10–10000. *Est:* 1916. *Hours:* Daily 9:30-5:50, Sun 12:30-5. *Size:* Medium. *CC:* AX/MC/V. *Assoc:* VADA. Lillian C Phelan *Park:* On site. *Loc:* Just W of the Woodstock Green, on Rte 4, near the churches.

COUNTRY WOODSHED
Rte 12N, 05091
(802)457-2490   **36 65**
New England country furniture, both refinished & original condition & related accessories. *Pr:* $25–1000. *Est:* 1966. *Hours:* Mon-Sat 9-5 by chance/appt. *Size:* Medium. *Assoc:* VADA. *Park:* On site. *Loc:* 2.5 MI N from the ctr of town on Rte 12.

LOFTY IDEAS
Rte 4, 05091
(802)457-1922   **27**
Country things. *Hours:* May-Oct daily 10-5 Wed by chance. *Assoc:* VADA. Pia Nichols

PLEASANT STREET BOOKS
48 Pleasant St, 05091
(802)457-4050   **9 13 33**
Rare used books including arts, music, sports, US history, children's, historic newspapers, autographs, coins & greeting cards. *Hours:* Thu-Sun 11-4, else by chance/appt. *Assoc:* VABA. Harry Saul Jr *Loc:* 20 min from Dartmouth College.

Indexes

ALPHABETICAL INDEX OF BUSINESS NAMES

1736 HOUSE ANTIQUES, *West Chatham, MA* 272
1750 HOUSE ANTIQUES, *Sheffield, MA* 253
1774 HOUSE ANTIQUES, *Wells, ME* 153
1784 HOUSE ANTIQUES, *Canton, CT* 49
1786 HOUSE ANTIQUES, *Brookline, NH* 286
1800 HOUSE ANTIQUES, LTD, *Templeton, MA* 266
1812 HOUSE ANTIQUE CENTER, *Manchester Center, VT* 359
1828 HOUSE, *Chester, VT* 351
1829 HOUSE ANTIQUES, *Jeffersonville, VT* 358
1836 GRANITE HOUSE, *Marlborough, NH* 308
1840 HOUSE, *Norwich, CT* 86
1847 HOUSE ANTIQUES, *Pine Meadow, CT* 88
1860 HOUSE OF ANTIQUES, *Darien, CT* 54
1893 ANN-TEEKS, *Laconia, NH* 305
1895 SHOP, *Bernard, ME* 119
18TH CENTURY DESIGN, *Hartland, VT* 357
5 CHURCH STREET ANTIQUES, *Mystic, CT* 76
A & G ANTIQUES, *West Boylston, MA* 271
A R M ASSOCIATES, *Beverly, MA* 166
A ROOM WITH A VIEUX, *Brookline Village, MA* 194
A SUMMER PLACE, *Guilford, CT* 66
A THOUSAND WORDS, *Exeter, NH* 292
A TO Z ANTIQUES, *Watch Hill, RI* 343
A-1 ANTIQUE PLUMBING FIXTURES, *Somerville, MA* 257
AARDENBURG ANTIQUES, *Lee, MA* 223
AARDVARK ANTIQUES, *Newport, RI* 333
DON ABARBANEL, *Ashley Falls, MA* 164
ABCDEF BOOKSTORE, *Camden, ME* 123
ABINGTON AUCTION GALLERY, *Abington, MA* 162
ABLE TO CANE, *Warren, ME* 153
THE ACADIA MEWS ANTIQUE CENTER, *Trenton, ME* 152
ACAMPORA ART GALLERY, *New Canaan, CT* 77
ACCENTS FROM THE PAST, *Center Harbor, NH* 287
EDITH M ACKERMAN, *Fairlee, VT* 356
ACQUIS LTD, *Winchester, MA* 279
ADAMANT BOOKS, *Adamant, VT* 348
ADAMS ANTIQUES USA, *Sudbury, MA* 264
MARJORIE PARROTT ADAMS BOOKS, *Medway, MA* 229
CHARLES & BARBARA ADAMS, *Middleboro, MA* 230
RICHARD H ADELSON ANTIQUARIAN BK, *North Pomfret, VT* 364
ARNE E AHLBERG, *Guilford, CT* 66
EDWIN C AHLBERG, *New Haven, CT* 79

AISLINN BOOK & RESEARCH, *Bennington, VT* 348
ALBERT ARTS & ANTIQUES, *Hyannis, MA* 221
ALBERTS-LANGDON, INC., *Boston, MA* 167
EBENEZER ALDEN HOUSE, *Union, ME* 152
JANICE ALDRIDGE INC, *Nantucket, MA* 231
ALEXANDRIA LAMP SHOP, *Meredith, NH* 309
ALEXANDRIA WOOD JOINERY, *Alexandria, NH* 284
ALFRED TRADING COMPANY, *Alfred, ME* 116
ALFRED'S, *Bristol, RI* 330
ALL THINGS CONSIDERED, *Essex Junction, VT* 355
ALLINSON GALLERY INC, *Coventry, CT* 53
LORRAINE ALLISON, *Marblehead, MA* 226
AMBER SPRING ANTIQUES, *Lanesborough, MA* 222
SHIELA B AMDUR - BOOKS, *Mansfield Center, CT* 73
AMERICA'S PAST, *Stratford, CT* 100
AMERICAN ART & ANTIQUES, INC, *Swansea, MA* 265
AMERICAN CLASSICS, *Canaan, NH* 287
AMERICAN DECORATIVE ARTS, *Northampton, MA* 240
AMERICAN MARINE MODEL GALLERY, *Salem, MA* 249
AMERICAN PIE, *Nantucket, MA* 231
AMERICAN PRIDE, *Hampton Falls, NH* 298
AMERICAN SPORTING ANTIQUES, *Dorset, VT* 353
AMERICAN TRADITION GALLERY, *Greenwich, CT* 63
AMERICAN WORLDS BOOKS, *Hamden, CT* 66
AMERICANA ANTIQUES, *Essex, MA* 207
AMERICANA ANTIQUES, *Peabody, MA* 244
AMERICANA, *Lakeville, CT* 70
AMHERST ANTIQUARIAN MAPS, *Amherst, MA* 162
AMHERST VILLAGE ANTIQUE SHOP, *Amherst, NH* 284
ANCHOR & DOLPHIN BOOKS, *Newport, RI* 333
ANCHOR FARM ANTIQUES, *Thomaston, ME* 151
A MATHEWS ANDERSON ANTIQUES, *Essex, CT* 59
BRUCE W ANDERSON ANTIQUES, *New Milford, CT* 81
FRANCESCA ANDERSON GALLERY, *Boston, MA* 167
ANDERSON GALLERY, *Keene, NH* 304
KENNETH ANDERSON, *Auburn, MA* 165
ANDERSON'S ANTIQUES, INC., *Hopkinton, NH* 303

ANDOVER ANTIQUARIAN BOOKS, *Andover, MA* 163

ANDREWS & ANDREWS, *Belfast, ME* 118

ANGLER'S & SHOOTER'S BOOKSHELF, *Goshen, CT* 63

THE ANGLOPHILE ANTIQUES, *Dorset, VT* 353

ANITA'S ANTIQUARIAN BOOKS, *Manchester, NH* 308

ANN MARIE'S VINTAGE BOUTIQUE, *New Haven, CT* 79

ANNEX ANTIQUES, *Essex, MA* 207

THE ANNEX, *Groton, MA* 216

ANOTHER ERA, *Melrose, MA* 229

ANOTHER TIME & PLACE, *Dennis Village, MA* 203

ANTAN ANTIQUES LTD, *Greenwich, CT* 63

ANTHONY'S ANTIQUES, *Great Barrington, MA* 214

ANTIQUARIAN BOOKSELLERS INC, *Boston, MA* 167

ANTIQUARIAN BOOKWORM, *Sharon, MA* 253

THE ANTIQUARIAN SCIENTIST, *Dracut, MA* 204

ANTIQUARIAN, *Old Bennington, VT* 364

ANTIQUARIA, *Springfield, MA* 262

THE ANTIQUARIUM, *Bethany, CT* 45

ANTIQUE ASSOC AT JOSLIN TAVERN, *West Townsend, MA* 275

ANTIQUE ASSOC AT WEST TOWNSEND, *West Townsend, MA* 275

ANTIQUE BOOKS, *Hamden, CT* 66

ANTIQUE CENTER OF NORTHAMPTON, *Northampton, MA* 240

ANTIQUE CENTER AT OLD BENNINGTON, *Old Bennington, VT* 364

ANTIQUE CENTER OF OLD DEERFIELD, *Old Deerfield, MA* 242

ANTIQUE CENTER OF PLYMOUTH, *Plymouth, MA* 245

ANTIQUE CENTER OF SHEFFIELD, *Sheffield, MA* 253

ANTIQUE CENTER OF WALLINGFORD, *Wallingford, CT* 101

ANTIQUE CLOCK SHOP, *Brookfield Center, CT* 49

THE ANTIQUE COMPANY, *Brookline Village, MA* 194

ANTIQUE CORNER, *New Haven, CT* 79

ANTIQUE DE-LIGHTS, *Coventry, CT* 53

THE ANTIQUE EXCHANGE OF SUDBURY, *Sudbury, MA* 265

ANTIQUE FURNITURE RESTORATION, *Woodbury, CT* 109

ANTIQUE MALL AT TIMBER RAIL VIL., *Quechee, VT* 366

ANTIQUE MARKETPLACE, *Westfield, MA* 276

THE ANTIQUE MART, *Buzzards Bay, MA* 195

ANTIQUE PORCELAINS LTD, *Boston, MA* 167

ANTIQUE RESEARCHERS, *Waban, MA* 267

THE ANTIQUE SHOP, *Marblehead, MA* 226

ANTIQUE WICKER, *Bernard, ME* 119

ANTIQUERS III, *Brookline, MA* 192

ANTIQUES & AUCTIONS, LTD, *Sandwich, NH* 320

ANTIQUES & COLLECTIBLES BARN, *North Conway, NH* 313

ANTIQUES & INTERIORS AT THE MILL, *Greenwich, CT* 63

ANTIQUES & THINGS, *Willimantic, CT* 107

ANTIQUES & VARIETIES, *South Egremont, MA* 259

ANTIQUES 608, *Dennis, MA* 202

ANTIQUES AND HERBS OF RIVERTON, *Riverton, CT* 91

ANTIQUES ANONYMOUS, *Jamaica, VT* 358

ANTIQUES AT FIFTY NINE BELLEVUE, *Newport, RI* 333

ANTIQUES AT THE BARN AT WINDSONG, *Harwich Center, MA* 219

ANTIQUES AT CANTON VILLAGE, *Canton, CT* 50

ANTIQUES AT FORGE POND, *East Bridgewater, MA* 205

ANTIQUES AT HAMPTON FALLS, *Hampton Falls, NH* 299

ANTIQUES AT HEARTHSTONE HOUSE, *Seekonk, MA* 252

ANTIQUES AT THE HILLMANS, *Searsport, ME* 149

ANTIQUES AT MADISON, *Madison, CT* 72

ANTIQUES AT MILLBROOK, *Duxbury, MA* 204

ANTIQUES AT MOULTONBORO, *Moultonboro, NH* 311

ANTIQUES AT NINE, *Kennebunkport, ME* 134

ANTIQUES AT SIGN OF THE BLUEBIRD, *Littleton, MA* 225

ANTIQUES BEAUTIFUL, *Rumford, RI* 341

ANTIQUES CENTER & SPECIALTY SHOP, *Rutland, VT* 368

ANTIQUES CENTER AT HARTLAND, *Hartland, VT* 357

ANTIQUES CENTER, *Charlestown, NH* 288

ANTIQUES ETC, *Woolwich, ME* 158

ANTIQUES ETC, *Brewster, MA* 189

ANTIQUES FROM POWDER HOUSE HILL, *Farmington, ME* 129

ANTIQUES GALLERY, *Salem, MA* 250

THE ANTIQUES MARKET, *New Haven, CT* 79

ANTIQUES NEW HAMPSHIRE, *Hampton Falls, NH* 299

ANTIQUES OF TOMORROW, *Milford, CT* 75

ANTIQUES ON THE GREEN, *Woodbury, CT* 109

ANTIQUES ONE, *Hampton Falls, NH* 299

ANTIQUES ORCHARD, *Westford, MA* 276

ANTIQUES PLUS & STRAWBERRY ACRES, *Fitzwilliam, NH* 293

THE ANTIQUES SHOPS, *Westmoreland, NH* 326

ANTIQUES TOOLS & CATALOGS, *Lancaster, MA* 222

ANTIQUES UNLIMITED, *Darien, CT* 55

ANTIQUES UNLIMITED INC, *Plymouth, MA* 246

ANTIQUEWEAR, *Marblehead, MA* 227

ANTIQUITY RESTORATIONS & REPRO'S, *Peace Dale, RI* 339

APEX ANTIQUES, *Belfast, ME* 118

APPLE COUNTRY ANTIQUES, *Hampton Falls, NH* 299

APPLETON ANTIQUES, *Brookline, MA* 192

APPLEYARD ANTIQUES, *Hillsboro, NH* 301

APPRAISAL ASSOCIATES, *Trumbull, CT* 101

THE APPRAISERS' REGISTRY, *Westwood, MA* 277

APROPOS, *West Falmouth, MA* 273

ARABY RUG, *Boston, MA* 168

ARCH BRIDGE BOOKSHOP, *Bellows Falls, VT* 348

ARCHIVES HISTORICAL AUTOGRAPHS, *Wilton, CT* 107

AREA CODE 603 ANTIQUES, *Wolfeboro, NH* 327

ARK ANTIQUES, *New Haven, CT* 79

ARKELYAN RUGS, *Boston, MA* 168
ARKELYAN RUGS, *Nantucket, MA* 231
ARMAN ABSENTEE AUCTION, *Woodstock, CT* 114
ARMCHAIR BOOKS, *North Orange, MA* 240
ARNHOLM'S ANTIQUES, *Barre, VT* 348
THE ARNOLDS, *Contoocook, NH* 289
EVA AROND, *Lexington, MA* 224
AROUND THE CORNER ANTIQUES, *Newtonville, MA* 238
THE ARRINGTONS, *Wells, ME* 153
ARS ANTIQUA BOOKS, *Bloomfield, CT* 46
ARS LIBRI, *Boston, MA* 168
ART INTERIORS ANTIQUES-PITTSFORD, *Pittsford, VT* 365
ART RUG, *Concord, NH* 288
ARTIST'S GUILD & GALLERY, *Charlestown, RI* 331
ARTISTIC VENTURES GALLERY, *West Haven, CT* 103
ARUNDEL ANTIQUES, *Arundel, ME* 116
AS TIME GOES BY ANTIQUES, *Essex, MA* 208
ASHAWAY ANTIQUES STORE, *Ashaway, RI* 330
ASHLEY BOOK COMPANY, *Burlington, VT* 350
ASHLEY FALLS ANTIQUES, *Ashley Falls, MA* 164
ASIA HOUSE, *Salem, MA* 250
ASSOCIATES APPRAISERS INC, *Providence, RI* 339
AT THE SIGN OF THE FOX, *Jaffrey, NH* 304
ATTIC OWL BOOKS, *New Sharon, ME* 139
ATTIC TREASURES, *Ridgefield, CT* 90
AUBURN FLEA MARKET, *Auburn, MA* 165
AUCTION BARN, *New Milford, CT* 82
AUCTION INDEX INC, *West Newton, MA* 274
AUCTIONS BY BOWERS & MERENA, INC, *Wolfeboro, NH* 327
AUNTIE BEA'S ANTIQUES, *Caribou, ME* 124
AUNTIES ATTIC ANTIQUES, *Edgartown, MA* 207
AURORA BOREALIS ANTIQUES, *Falmouth, MA* 211
WILLIAM AUSTIN'S ANTIQUES, *Chester, VT* 351
AUTHENTIC DESIGNS, *West Rupert, VT* 375
AUTHENTIC REPRODUCTION LIGHTING, *Avon, CT* 44
AUTREFOIS II, *Brookline, MA* 192
AUTREFOIS, *Boston, MA* 168
AUTUMN POND ANTIQUES, *Bolton, MA* 46
AVANTI ANTIQUE JEWELRY, *Nantucket, MA* 231
AVERY'S ANTIQUES, *Framingham, MA* 212
B & B AUTOGRAPHS, *Randolph, MA* 247
BERT BABCOCK BOOKSELLER, *Derry, NH* 290
BACK DOOR ANTIQUES, *Grand Isle, VT* 356
BACKWARD LOOK ANTIQUES, *Antrim, NH* 285
BACKYARD ANTIQUES, *Chatham, MA* 198
BACON ANTIQUES, *Hartford, CT* 67
BAD CORNER ANTIQUES & DECORATION, *Lakeville, CT* 70
F O BAILEY ANTIQUARIANS, *Portland, ME* 144
JAMES R BAKKER ANTIQUES INC., *Cambridge, MA* 195
BALCONY ANTIQUES, *Canton, CT* 50
THE BALL & CLAW, *Wickford, RI* 344
BANANAS, *Gloucester, MA* 213
BANCROFT BOOK MEWS, *Newtown, CT* 84
BANKSVILLE ANTIQUES, *Greenwich, CT* 64
ROBERT T BARANOWSKY, *Plainville, CT* 88
BARBARA'S ANTIQUES, *Hillsboro, NH* 301
BARBARA'S BARN ANTIQUES, *Monroe, CT* 76

PATRICIA BARGER, *Fairfield, CT* 60
BARKER'S OF SALISBURY HEIGHTS, *Salisbury Heights, NH* 319
THE BARN AT CAPE NEDDICK, *Cape Neddick, ME* 123
THE BARN AT HAMPTON FALLS, *Hampton Falls, NH* 299
THE BARN DOOR, *Caribou, ME* 124
BARN LOFT BOOKSHOP, *Laconia, NH* 305
THE BARN OF HANCOCK VILLAGE, *Hancock, NH* 299
THE BARN ON 26 ANTIQUE CENTER, *Gray, ME* 131
BARN STAGES BOOKSHOP, *Newcastle, ME* 139
BARNSTABLE STOVE SHOP, *West Barnstable, MA* 271
BARNSTABLE VILLAGE ANTIQUES, *Barnstable Village, MA* 165
BARRETT ANTIQUES, *Santuit, MA* 252
BARRIDOFF GALLERIES, *Portland, ME* 144
THE BARROW BOOKSTORE, *Concord, MA* 200
ROBERT BARROW, CABINETMAKER, *Bristol, RI* 330
AMABEL BARROWS ANTIQUES, *Wilton, CT* 107
MARJORIE BARRY ANTIQUE SHOW PROM, *Lyme, NH* 307
BARSALOW AUCTIONS, *Milton, VT* 362
BARTER SHOP, *Norwalk, CT* 85
SHEILA BARTON ANTIQUES, *Woodstock, VT* 376
SCOTT BASSOFF/SANDY JACOBS, *Rindge, NH* 319
FREDERICK BAUER, *New Sharon, ME* 139
JOHN BAUER SONIA SEFTON ANTI, *Newfield, ME* 141
WILLIAM M BAXTER ANTIQUES, *Brewster, MA* 190
BAY STREET ANTIQUES, *Boothbay Harbor, ME* 120
THE BAY TREE ANTIQUES, *Woodbury, CT* 109
BAYBERRY ANTIQUES, *Brewster, MA* 190
THE BAYBERRYSHOP ANTIQUES, *Westborough, MA* 275
BEACON HILL FINE ARTS/ANTIQUES, *Boston, MA* 168
THE BEAL HOUSE INN & ANTIQUES, *Littleton, NH* 306
FRANCIS BEALEY AMERICAN ARTS, *Essex, CT* 59
RICHARD & PATRICIA BEAN, *Winterport, ME* 156
THE BEAR BOOK SHOP, *West Brattleboro, VT* 375
BEAR TRACK FARM ANTIQUES, *Hillsboro, NH* 301
BEAUFURN INC, *South Norwalk, CT* 94
BEAUPORT ANTIQUES, *Gloucester, MA* 213
BEAUPORT INN ANTIQUES, *Ogunquit, ME* 142
BEAZE OF BROOKLINE, *Brookline, MA* 192
BOB & RITA BECKER, *Epsom, NH* 292
BECKERMAN NEAL ANTIQUES, *Brookline Village, MA* 194
STEPHEN P BEDARD, *Gilmanton Iron Works, NH* 297
BEDELLE INC, *Boston, MA* 170
BEDFORD CENTER ANTIQUES, *Bedford, NH* 285
BEECH HILL GALLERY, *Keene, NH* 304
BELCHER'S ANTIQUES, *Deer Isle, ME* 126
BELGRAVIA ANTIQUES INC, *Boston, MA* 170

GERALD W BELL AUCTIONEER, *Yarmouth, ME* 158
BELL HILL ANTIQUES, *Bedford, NH* 285
BELLEVUE GOLD, *Newport, RI* 333
A J BELLIVEAU BOOKS, *St George, VT* 372
BELLTOWN TRADING POST, *East Hampton, CT* 57
BELLWETHER GALLERY, *Manchester Center, VT* 360
BEN'S OLD BOOKS, *Harrisville, NH* 300
BENCHMARK ANTIQUES, *Newton Highlands, MA* 237
BENCHMARK ANTIQUES, *Moultonboro, NH* 311
MICHAEL G BENNETT AUCTIONS, *Dover, NH* 290
ROGER & BEE BENNETT, *Damariscotta, ME* 125
DEBORAH BENSON BOOKSELLER, *West Cornwall, CT* 102
BERDAN'S ANTIQUES, *Hallowell, ME* 131
THE BERGERON'S ANTIQUES, *Killingworth, CT* 69
BERKSHIRE ANTIQUES, *Pittsfield, MA* 245
BERNARDSTON BOOKS, *Bernardston, MA* 166
BERNHEIMER'S ANTIQUE ARTS, *Cambridge, MA* 195
BERT GALLERY, *Providence, RI* 339
BESCO PLUMBING, *Boston, MA* 170
MILLICENT RUDD BEST, *Weston, CT* 104
R G BETTCHER RESTORATIONS, *South Hampton, NH* 320
BETTER DAY'S ANTIQUES, *Searsport, ME* 149
BETTERIDGE JEWELERS INC, *Greenwich, CT* 64
THE BETTY HOUSE, *Epsom, NH* 292
BETTY'S TRADING POST, *Lincolnville Beach, ME* 137
BIBLIOLATREE, *East Hampton, CT* 57
BIDDEFORD ANTIQUE CENTER, *Biddeford, ME* 120
BIG CHICKEN BARN - BOOKS, *Ellsworth, ME* 127
JAMES BILLINGS, *Boston, MA* 170
BIRCHKNOLL ANTIQUES, *Millis, MA* 230
BIRD CAGE ANTIQUES, *South Egremont, MA* 259
BIT OF COUNTRY, *New Milford, CT* 82
BITTERSWEET SHOP, *Gaylordsville, CT* 62
BIX ANTIQUES, *Middlebury, VT* 361
THE BLACK GOOSE, *Marblehead, MA* 227
BLACK MOUNTAIN ANTIQUE CENTER, *Brattleboro, VT* 349
BLACK SHEEP ANTIQUES, *Newport, RI* 333
BLACK SWAN ANTIQUES, *New Preston, CT* 82
BLACKWOOD MARCH, *Essex, MA* 208
REBA BLAIR SALES, *Middlebury, VT* 361
DAVID & DALE BLAND ANTIQUES, *Hebron, CT* 68
BLAND'S BOOK BIN, *Sharon, MA* 253
RICHARD BLASCHKE, *Bristol, CT* 48
BLDG 38 ANTIQUE CENTER, *Orange, MA* 242
ROBIN BLEDSOE, *Cambridge, MA* 195
THE BLOCK HOUSE, *New London, NH* 312
BLOOMIN' ANTIQUES, *Fitzwilliam, NH* 293
BLUE CAPE ANTIQUES, *Littleton, MA* 225
BLUE FLAG ANTIQUES, *Little Compton, RI* 333
THE BLUE LANTERN ANTIQUES, *Hollis, NH* 302
BLUE UNICORN, *Boothbay, ME* 120
BLUE WILLOW FARM, *Manchester, ME* 138
BLUEBERRY HILL FARM, *Rangeley, ME* 146
THE BLUEBERRY PATCH, *Hope, ME* 132

MR & MRS JEROME BLUM, *Lisbon-Jewett City, CT* 70
BO & CO, *Pomfret, CT* 88
BO-MAR HALL, *Wells, ME* 153
SHARON BOCCELLI & CO ANTIQUES, *Cambridge, MA* 196
JAMES BOK ANTIQUES, *Fairfield, CT* 60
BONSAL-DOUGLAS ANTIQUES, *Essex, CT* 59
KOKO BOODAKIAN & SONS, *Winchester, MA* 279
THE BOOK & TACKLE SHOP, *Watch Hill, RI* 343
BOOK ADDICT, *Sanford, ME* 148
THE BOOK BARN, *Wells, ME* 153
BOOK BEAR, *West Brookfield, MA* 272
THE BOOK BLOCK, *Cos Cob, CT* 52
BOOK CELLAR, *Freeport, ME* 129
THE BOOK COLLECTOR, *Newton, MA* 236
THE BOOK EXCHANGE, *Plainville, CT* 88
BOOK GUILD OF PORTSMOUTH, *Portsmouth, NH* 316
BOOK MARKS, *Amherst, MA* 162
BOOK PEDLARS, *Cundys Harbor, ME* 125
BOOK STORE, *Canton, CT* 50
BOOKCELL BOOKS, *Hamden, CT* 67
THE BOOKERY, *Farmington, NH* 293
BOOKLOVER'S ATTIC, *Belfast, ME* 118
BOOKS & AUTOGRAPHS, *Eliot, ME* 127
BOOKS & BIRDS, *Manchester, CT* 73
BOOKS ABOUT ANTIQUES, *Woodbury, CT* 109
BOOKS AT CHELSEA, *Chelsea, VT* 351
BOOKS BOUGHT AND SOLD, *Madison, ME* 138
BOOKS BY THE FALLS, *Derby, CT* 56
BOOKS WITH A PAST, *Concord, MA* 200
BOOKSHELF SHOP, *Concord, NH* 289
THE BOOKSTORE, *Fairfax, VT* 355
NANCY BORDEN, *Portsmouth, NH* 317
ROSIE BOREL'S L'ESCALIER, *Waitsfield, VT* 373
BORSSEN ANTIQUES, *Belgrade, ME* 119
THOMAS G BOSS-FINE BOOKS, *Boston, MA* 171
BOSTON ANTIQUE COOPERATIVE I/, *Boston, MA* 171
BOSTON BOOK ANNEX, *Boston, MA* 171
BOSTON BRASS WORKS, *Dennis Village, MA* 203
THE BOSTON HAMMERSMITH, *Boston, MA* 171
BOSTON ORNAMENT COMPANY, *Boston, MA* 171
BOSTON ROAD ANTIQUES, *Groton, MA* 216
RONALD BOURGEAULT ANTIQUES, *Hampton, NH* 297
RICHARD A BOURNE CO INC, *Hyannis, MA* 221
MARTHA BOYNTON ANTIQUES, *Townsend, MA* 266
PAM BOYNTON, *Groton, MA* 216
BERT & PHYLLIS BOYSON, *Brookfield, CT* 48
ARAKEL H BOZYAN STORE, *Newport, RI* 334
BRADFORD BOOKS, *Bennington, VT* 348
BRADFORD GALLERIES, LTD, *Sheffield, MA* 254
BRADY GALLERIES, INC., *Middlebury, VT* 361
BRANDON ANTIQUES, *Brandon, VT* 349
BRANFORD RARE BOOK & ART GALLERY, *Branford, CT* 47
BRASS & BOUNTY, *Marblehead, MA* 227
BRASS BUFF ANTIQUES, *Newton, MA* 236
THE BRASS BUGLE, *Cornwall Bridge, CT* 52
BRASSWORKS ANTIQUES CENTER, *Haydenville, MA* 219
BRASSWORKS, *Providence, RI* 340
BRATTLE BOOK SHOP, *Boston, MA* 171
BREADLOAF BOOKS, *East Middlebury, VT* 354
BRENNANS ANTIQUES, *Peterborough, NH* 315

BRETON HOUSE, *Brewster, MA* 190
BRETTON HALL ANTIQUITIES, *Lancaster, NH* 306
BRETTON HALL ANTIQUITIES, *Twin Mountain, NH* 322
BREWSTER ANTIQUES, *Manchester Center, VT* 360
BRIAR PATCH ANTIQUES & COLLECTIB, *Plainville, MA* 245
BRICK HOUSE ANTIQUES, *Stockton Springs, ME* 151
BRICK HOUSE ANTIQUES, *Essex, MA* 208
BRICK HOUSE BOOKSHOP, *Morrisville, VT* 362
BRIDGTON BOOK HOUSE, *Bridgton, ME* 121
BRIGER FAIRHOLME JONES, *Old Lyme, CT* 86
BRIGGS HOUSE ANTIQUES, *Ashaway, RI* 330
BRIMFIELD ANTIQUES, *Brimfield, MA* 192
·BRITANNIA BOOKSHOP, *New Preston, CT* 82
BRITISH COUNTRY ANTIQUES, *Woodbury, CT* 109
BRODNEY INC, *Boston, MA* 171
HOLLIS & TRISHA BRODRICK, *Exeter, NH* 292
BROMER BOOKSELLERS INC, *Boston, MA* 171
MAURY A BROMSEN ASSOCIATES, INC, *Boston, MA* 173
BROOKLINE ANTIQUES, *Brookline, MA* 193
BROOKLINE VILLAGE ANTIQUES, *Brookline Village, MA* 194
BROOKLINE VILLAGE ANTIQUES, *Brookline, NH* 286
BROOKLINE VILLAGE BOOKSHOP, *Brookline Village, MA* 194
BROOKMEAD FARM, *Damariscotta, ME* 125
BROOKS, GILL & CO INC., *Boston, MA* 173
BROOKSIDE ANTIQUES, *New Bedford, MA* 235
BARBARA WOOD BROWN, *Colchester, CT* 51
THE BROWN JUG, *Sandwich, MA* 251
BROWN-CORBIN FINE ART, *Lincoln, MA* 225
SUZANNE BRUCKNER 1812 HOUSE, *Haverhill, NH* 300
BRUSH FACTORY ANTIQUES, *Essex (Centerbrook), CT* 60
BRYN MAWR BOOK SHOP, *New Haven, CT* 79
BUCKLEY & BUCKLEY ANTIQUES, *Salisbury, CT* 92
BUDDENBROOKS, *Boston, MA* 173
ANTIQUES @ BUGGY WHIP FACTORY, *Southfield, MA* 262
BUNKER HILL ANTIQUES, *Jefferson, ME* 133
BUNKER HILL RELICS, *Charlestown, MA* 198
BUNKHOUSE BOOKS, *Gardiner, ME* 129
LEE BURGESS ANTIQUES, *New London, NH* 312
T J BURKE ORIENTAL RUGS, *Bangor, ME* 117
BURKE'S BAZAAR-POET'S ANTIQUES, *Gloucester, MA* 213
BURLWOOD ANTIQUE CENTER, *Meredith, NH* 309
MOSES BURPEE FARM ANTIQUES, *New London, NH* 312
BURPEE HILL BOOKS, *New London, NH* 312
J R BURROWS & COMPANY, *Boston, MA* 173
HAROLD M BURSTEIN & CO, *Waltham, MA* 268
BURT DIAL COMPANY, *Raymond, NH* 318
HERSCHEL B BURT, *Exeter, NH* 292
E R BUTLER & SONS, *Marblehead, MA* 227
BUTTERNUT SHOP, *Charlestown, RI* 331
BY SHAKER HANDS, *Great Barrington, MA* 214
BYGONE BOOKS, *Burlington, VT* 350
BYGONE DAYS, *Great Barrington, MA* 214

C & T LAMP SHOP/ANTIQUE DEALERS, *Newport, RI* 334
CABELL ANTIQUES, *Waterbury, VT* 374
CACKLEBERRY FARMS ANTIQUES, *Canterbury, CT* 49
JOAN F CADDIGAN, *Halifax, MA* 217
STEPHEN CALCAGNI, *Washington Depot, CT* 102
CALISTA STERLING ANTIQUES, *Ellsworth, ME* 127
HENRY THOMAS CALLAN FINE ANTIQUE, *East Sandwich, MA* 206
CALOUBAR COLLECTABLES, *Raymond, NH* 318
CANAL STREET ANTIQUES, *Salem, MA* 250
CANDLE SNUFFER, *Coventry, RI* 332
CANDLEWICK ANTIQUES, *Mont Vernon, NH* 310
CANTERBURY ANTIQUES, *Concord, MA* 200
CANTON BARN AUCTIONS, *Canton, CT* 50
CAPE ANN ANTIQUES & ORIENTALS, *Gloucester, MA* 213
CAPE COD SHOPPER, *Barnstable Village, MA* 165
CAPE COLLECTOR, *South Harwich, MA* 261
THE CAPTAIN STANNARD HOUSE, *Westbrook, CT* 104
THE CAPTAIN'S HOUSE ANTIQUES, *Searsport, ME* 149
TOM CAREY'S PLACE, *Stockbridge, MA* 263
CARLSON AND TURNER BOOKS, *Portland, ME* 144
CARNIVAL HOUSE ANTIQUES, *Danbury, CT* 54
CAROPRESO GALLERY, *Lee, MA* 223
CARR BOOKS, *Concord, NH* 289
RUSSELL CARRELL, *Salisbury, CT* 92
CARRIAGE BARN BOOKS, *Williamstown, MA* 278
CARRIAGE HOUSE ANTIQUES, *Woodbury, CT* 109
CARRIAGE HOUSE ANTIQUES, *Sheffield, MA* 254
CARRIAGE HOUSE ANTIQUES, *Derby Line, VT* 353
CARRIAGE HOUSE, *Round Pond, ME* 147
CARRIAGE SHED ANTIQUES, *Amherst, NH* 284
CARRIAGE TRADE ANTIQUES CENTER, *Manchester Center, VT* 360
PETER CARSWELL ANTIQUES, *Rochester, NH* 319
CARSWELL'S ANTIQUES, *Union, NH* 323
MARGARET SCOTT CARTER, INC., *Portsmouth, NH* 317
CARTER'S BARN ANTIQUES, *Pelham, NH* 315
EDWARD & ELAINE CASAZZA, *Limington, ME* 136
CASTLE ANTIQUE IMPORTERS, *Wilton, CT* 107
THE CAT'S MEOW ANTIQUES, *Fairfax, VT* 355
CATTAILS ANTIQUES, *Kennebunkport, ME* 134
CC CANCER CONSIGNMENT EXCHANGE, *Yarmouth Port, MA* 281
CELLAR STORIES BOOKS, *Providence, RI* 340
CELTIC CROSS BOOKS, *Westmoreland, NH* 326
THE CENTER ANTIQUES, *Sandwich, NH* 320
CENTER FOR ANTIQUES CONSERVATION, *Boston, MA* 173
CENTER HILL PAST & PRESENT ANTIQ, *Manchester Center, VT* 360
CENTERPIECE ANTIQUES, *East Haddam, CT* 57
CENTURY SHOP, *Dedham, MA* 202
CENTURYHURST ANTIQUES, *Sheffield, MA* 254
HOWARD CHADWICK ANTIQUES, *Boston, MA* 173

CHAMBERLAIN ANTIQUES LTD, *Providence, RI* 340

BARBARA CHAMBERS RESTORATIONS, *Branford, CT* 47

ROBERT CHAMBERS, *Corinth, VT* 352

DONALD CHANDLER - BOOKS, *New Gloucester, ME* 139

CHAPDELAINE ANTIQUES, *Chatham, MA* 198

CHARLES GALLERY, *Bozrah, CT* 47

CHARLOTTE'S DOLLS & COLLECTIBLES, *Caribou, ME* 124

PAULINE CHARON ANTIQUES, *Plymouth, NH* 316

CHEBACCO ANTIQUES, *Essex, MA* 208

CHECKERED PAST ANTIQUES CENTER, *Belfast, ME* 118

CHELSEA ANTIQUES OF GREENWICH, *Greenwich, CT* 64

CHELSEA ANTIQUES, *Southport, CT* 96

SAMUEL S T CHEN, *West Hartford, CT* 103

CHESTERFIELD ANTIQUES, *Chesterfield, MA* 199

CHESTNUT & COMPANY, *Boston, MA* 174

CHESTNUT HILL ANTIQUES, *Chepachet, RI* 331

CHETWOOD ANTIQUES, *Templeton, MA* 266

CHILDS GALLERY, *Boston, MA* 174

CHIMES & TIMES CLOCK SHOP, *Loudon, NH* 307

CHIPPENDALES ANTIQUES, *Maynard, MA* 229

CHISWICK BOOK SHOP INC, *Sandy Hook, CT* 92

CHISWICK BOOK SHOP, INC., *Southbury, CT* 95

THE CHOCOLATE BARN ANTIQUES, *Shaftsbury, VT* 370

JANE CHORAS, BOOKS, *Weston, MA* 276

CHOREOGRAPHICA, *Boston, MA* 174

CHRISTIAN MOLLY ANTIQUES, *Essex, MA* 208

CHRISTIE & HADLEY ANTIQUES, *Warren, RI* 342

CHURCH STREET GALLERY, *Woodstock, VT* 376

CHURCHILLBOOKS, *Contoocook, NH* 289

CIDER MILL ANTIQUE MALL, *Windham, ME* 156

CIDERPRESS BOOKSTORE, *Poland Spring, ME* 144

THE CILLEYVILLE BOOKSTORE, *Andover, NH* 285

CINDY'S ANTIQUES, *Ellsworth, ME* 127

CIRCA, *Ashley Falls, MA* 164

CITY LIGHTS, *Cambridge, MA* 196

CITY POINT ANTIQUES, *New Haven, CT* 79

CLAPP AND TUTTLE, *Woodbury, CT* 109

CLARENDON HOUSE ANTIQUES, *Clarendon Springs, VT* 352

MARIANNE CLARK FINE ANTIQUES, *Southwest Harbor, ME* 150

VIRGINIA S CLARK, *Newtonville, MA* 238

THE CLASSIC TOUCH, *Newport, RI* 334

CLASSICS IN WOOD, *Ashford, CT* 44

CLEARING HOUSE AUCTION GALLERIES, *Wethersfield, CT* 106

CLELAND E SELBY, *Williamstown, VT* 376

EVELYN CLEMENT, *Franklin, NH* 295

JOHN CLEMENT FINE ART, *Fitchburg, MA* 211

G R CLIDENCE, 18TH C WOODWORKS, *West Kingstown, RI* 344

CLOAK & DAGGER BOOKS, *Bedford, NH* 285

CLOCK DOCTOR, *Middletown Springs, VT* 361

THE CLOCK EMPORIUM, *Manchester, VT* 359

THE CLOCK SHELF, *West Barnstable, MA* 271

THE CLOCK SHOP, *Enfield, NH* 291

THE CLOCKERY, *East Norwalk, CT* 58

CLOCKS ON THE COMMON, *Fitzwilliam, NH* 293

COACH HOUSE ANTIQUES, *Wiscasset, ME* 156

RUTH COATES ANTIQUES, *Ridgefield, CT* 90

COBBLESTONES OF MARKET SQUARE, *Portsmouth, NH* 317

THE COBBS ANTIQUES, *Peterborough, NH* 315

COCK HILL FARM, *Albion, ME* 116

CODEX BOOKS, *Burlington, VT* 350

CODFISH ANTIQUES, *Newtown, CT* 84

LILLIAN BLANKLEY COGAN ANTIQUARY, *Farmington, CT* 61

THE R COGSWELL COLLECTION, *New Preston, CT* 83

HAROLD E COLE ANTIQUES, *Woodbury, CT* 110

CHRISTOPHER & KATHLEEN COLE, *Stonington, CT* 98

COLE HILL FARM ANTIQUES, *Alexandria, NH* 284

COLEBROOK BOOK BARN, *Colebrook, CT* 52

COLLECTOR SHOP, *Boothbay Harbor, ME* 120

COLLECTOR'S CORNER, *Yarmouth Port, MA* 281

COLLECTOR'S EMPORIUM ANTIQUE CTR, *New Haven, VT* 362

COLLECTOR'S SHOP, *Boston, MA* 174

THE COLLECTOR, *Brookline Village, MA* 194

COLLECTORS JUNCTION, *Fall River, MA* 211

COLLECTORS WAREHOUSE, *Williamstown, MA* 278

COLLECTORS, *Salisbury, CT* 92

BRUCE D COLLINS FINE ART, *Denmark, ME* 126

JOHN J COLLINS, JR., *Newburyport, MA* 235

ISABELLE COLLINS OF LONDON, *Boston, MA* 175

JACK COLLINS WOODWORKING, *Mansfield Center, CT* 73

THE COLONEL'S SWORD, *Springfield, NH* 320

COLONIAL COTTAGE, *Franconia, NH* 295

COLONIAL PLAZA ANTIQUES, *West Lebanon, NH* 325

COLONIAL SHOPPE, *Hudson, NH* 304

COLOPHON BOOK SHOP, *Exeter, NH* 292

COLT BARN ANTIQUES, *Townshend, VT* 373

THOMAS COLVILLE FINE ART, *New Haven, CT* 79

COMENOS FINE ARTS, *Boston, MA* 175

COMING OF AGE ANTIQUES, *South Natick, MA* 261

THE COMMON READER BOOKSHOP, *New Salem, MA* 235

COMPASS ANTIQUES, *Great Barrington, MA* 215

COMPASS ROSE ANTIQUES, *Stratham, NH* 321

COMSTOCK HSE ANTIQUE RESTORATION, *Ivoryton, CT* 68

CONANT CUSTOM BRASS, *Burlington, VT* 350

CONCORD ANTIQUES, *Concord, MA* 200

CONCORD PATRIOT ANTIQUES, *Concord, MA* 200

MARTIN CONLON AMERICAN ANTIQUES, *Providence, RI* 340

CONNECTICUT ANTIQUE WICKER, *Newington, CT* 83

CONNECTICUT BOOK AUCTION, *Fairfield, CT* 60

CONNECTICUT CANE & REED CO, *Manchester, CT* 73

CONNECTICUT FINE ARTS, INC, *Westport, CT* 105
THE CONNECTICUT GALLERY, *Marlborough, CT* 74
CONNECTICUT RIVER BOOKSHOP, *East Haddam, CT* 57
CONNIE'S ANTIQUES, *Rumford, ME* 148
CONSIGN IT, *Greenwich, CT* 64
CONSIGNMART, *Westport, CT* 105
CONSTANTINE'S FINE FURNITURE, *East Greenwich, RI* 332
CONTINUUM, *Orleans, MA* 242
CONWAY HOUSE, *Conway, MA* 201
CONWAY'S ANTIQUES & DECOR, *Rutland, VT* 368
THE COOLEY GALLERY, *Old Lyme, CT* 86
RYAN M COOPER, *Limerick, ME* 136
COOPER SHOP ANTIQUES, *Barnstead (North), NH* 285
COOPER'S RED BARN, *Damariscotta, ME* 125
THE COOPERAGE, *Hollis, NH* 302
COPPER HOUSE, *Epsom, NH* 292
THE COPPERSMITH, *Sturbridge, MA* 264
CORASHIRE ANTIQUES, *Great Barrington, MA* 215
THE CORNER CURIOSITY SHOPPE, *Woonsocket, RI* 344
CORNER HOUSE ANTIQUES, *Sheffield, MA* 254
CORNUCOPIA ANTIQUE CONSIGNMENTS, *Guilford, CT* 66
CORNUCOPIA, INC, *Harvard, MA* 218
JANE COTTINGHAM ANTIQUES, *Newtown, CT* 84
COTTON HILL BOOKS, *Laconia, NH* 305
COUGHLIN ANTIQUE/ESTATE APPRAISA, *Hollis, NH* 303
COUNTRY ANTIQUES, *South China, ME* 150
COUNTRY ANTIQUES, *Loudon, NH* 307
COUNTRY ANTIQUES AT MIDDLETOWN, *Middletown, CT* 74
COUNTRY AUCTION SERVICE, *Torrington, CT* 100
COUNTRY BARN, *South Windsor, CT* 94
COUNTRY BARN, *Wells, ME* 154
COUNTRY BARN ANTIQUE CENTER, *Pittsford, VT* 365
COUNTRY BED SHOP, *Ashby, MA* 164
THE COUNTRY BOOKSHOP, *Plainfield, VT* 366
COUNTRY CORNER ANTIQUES, *Essex, MA* 208
COUNTRY COTTAGE ANTIQUES, *Pomfret Center, CT* 89
COUNTRY CRICKET VILLAGE INN, *Worthington, MA* 280
COUNTRY CUPBOARD, *Portsmouth, RI* 339
COUNTRY FINE ANTIQUES, *Williamsburg, MA* 278
THE COUNTRY GENTLEMAN, *Townsend, MA* 267
COUNTRY HOUSE ANTIQUES, *Wallingford, VT* 374
COUNTRY HOUSE CONSIGNMENTS, *Litchfield, CT* 70
COUNTRY IN ANDOVER, *North Andover, MA* 239
COUNTRY INTERIORS, *Wellesley Hills, MA* 270
COUNTRY LANE BOOKS, *Collinsville, CT* 52
COUNTRY LOFT ANTIQUES, *Woodbury, CT* 110
COUNTRY LOFT ANTIQUES, *South Egremont, MA* 259

COUNTRY LOFT ANTIQUES, *South Barre, VT* 371
COUNTRY LOOK ANTIQUES, *Hanover, NH* 300
COUNTRY PEDLAR ANTIQUES, *Williamstown, MA* 278
COUNTRY PLEASURES LTD, *Newport, RI* 334
COUNTRY SQUIRE ANTIQUES, *Gorham, ME* 130
THE COUNTRY STORE, *Presque Isle, ME* 146
COUNTRY SWEDISH ANTIQUES, *Westport, CT* 105
COUNTRY TAVERN OF NORTHWOOD, *Northwood, NH* 314
COUNTRY TURTLE, *Norwood, MA* 241
COUNTRY VILLAGE ANTIQUES, *Ridgefield, CT* 90
COUNTRY WOODSHED, *Woodstock, VT* 377
COUNTRYSIDE ANTIQUES, *East Orleans, MA* 205
COURT'S CUPBOARD ANTIQUES, *Antrim, NH* 285
THE COURTYARD EMPORIUM, *Stratham, NH* 321
COVENTRY ANTIQUE CENTER, *Coventry, CT* 53
COVENTRY BOOK SHOP, *Coventry, CT* 53
COVERED BRIDGE ANTIQUES, *Sheffield, MA* 254
PETER D COWEN, *Newton, MA* 236
MICHAEL COX ANTIQUES, *Salisbury, CT* 92
COYLE'S AUCTION GALLERY, *South Bellingham, MA* 258
CRABTREE'S COLLECTION, *Canterbury, NH* 287
CRAFTSBURY COMMON ANTIQUARIAN, *Craftsbury Common, VT* 352
CRANBERRY HILL ANTIQUES/LIGHTING, *Cape Neddick, ME* 124
CRANE COLLECTION, *Boston, MA* 175
CRANE'S ANTIQUES, ETC, *Portland, CT* 89
CRICKET HILL CONSIGNMENT, *New Milford, CT* 82
CROOKED ONION FARM ANTIQUE, *Hancock, NH* 299
CROSS & GRIFFIN, *Belmont, MA* 166
CROSS HILL BOOKS, *Brunswick, ME* 122
CROSSWAYS ANTIQUES, *Woodbury, CT* 110
CROW MOUNTAIN FARM ANTIQUES, *Shelburne, NH* 320
CROWN & EAGLE ANTIQUES, *Marblehead, MA* 227
KIRT & ELIZABETH CRUMP, *Madison, CT* 72
JEFFREY R CUETO ANTIQUES, *East Montpelier, VT* 354
CUMMAQUID FINE ARTS, *Cummaquid, MA* 201
CUNNINGHAM BOOKS, *Portland, ME* 144
CUPBOARDS & ROSES, *Sheffield, MA* 254
LESLIE CURTIS ANTIQUES, *Dennis, MA* 202
JOHN CUSHING ANTIQUE RESTORATION, *Essex, MA* 208
NATHAN D CUSHMAN INC, *Yarmouth, ME* 158
CUSTOM HOUSE, *Cromwell, CT* 54
CYPRESS TRADING POST, *Brookline, MA* 193
D & R ANTIQUES, *Hallowell, ME* 131
FRANK D'ANGELO INC, *Rowley, MA* 249
THE CHARLES DALY COLLECTION, *Ridgefield, CT* 90
DALZELL HOUSE ANTIQUES, *South Egremont, MA* 259
DANBY ANTIQUES CENTER, *Danby, VT* 353

COREY DANIELS, *Wells, ME* 154
DARIA OF WOODBURY, *Woodbury, CT* 111
DARR ANTIQUES AND INTERIORS, *Sheffield,
MA* 254
DAVIDIAN AMERICANA, *Holden, MA* 220
DAVIS ANTIQUES, *Woodbury, CT* 111
DAVIS HOMESTEAD, *Fitzwilliam, NH* 293
JOHN M DAVIS INC, *Harwinton, CT* 67
NANCY DAVIS, *West Simsbury, CT* 104
THE DEACONS BENCH, *West Boylston, MA* 271
FREDERICA DEBEURS - BOOKS, *Garland, ME*
130
DECOR ANTIQUES, *Exeter, NH* 292
DEDHAM ANTIQUE SHOP, *Dedham, MA* 202
DEERFIELD VALLEY ANTIQUES, *Wilmington,
VT* 376
JOHN & BARBARA DELANEY CLOCKS, *West
Townsend, MA* 275
WILLIAM F DEMBIEC ANTIQUES, *Holderness,
NH* 302
DEN OF ANTIQUITY SLAVID INC, *Sandwich,
MA* 251
DEN OF ANTIQUITY, *Poultney, VT* 366
VICTOR A DENETTE BOOKS/EPHEMERA,
Yalesville, CT 114
DENNIS & DAD ANTIQUES, *Fitzwilliam, NH* 294
DERBY DESK COMPANY, *Brighton, MA* 192
JOSEPH A DERMONT, BOOKSELLER, *Onset,
MA* 242
DESIGN WORKS, *Yarmouth Port, MA* 281
NIKKI & TOM DEUPREE, *Suffield, CT* 100
RALPH DIAMOND ANTIQUES, *West Harwich,
MA* 274
DICK'S ANTIQUES, *Bristol, CT* 48
DIERINGERS ARTS & ANTIQUES, *Bethel, CT* 46
DIFFERENT DRUMMER ANTIQUES, *Newcastle,
ME* 139
ELAINE DILLOF, *Greenwich, CT* 64
DINING ROOM SHOWCASE, *Brighton, MA* 192
RONALD & PENNY DIONNE, *West Willington,
CT* 104
THE DITTY BOX, *North Edgecomb, ME* 141
DIVINE DECADENCE, *Boston, MA* 175
DIXON'S ANTIQUES, *Norway, ME* 142
JEANNINE DOBBS COUNTRY FOLK,
Merrimack, NH 310
BARBARA DOHERTY, *Kennebunkport, ME* 134
DOING ANTIQUES AT ELMWOOD, *Elmwood,
MA* 207
THE DOLL CONNECTION, *Portsmouth, NH* 317
DOLL FACTORY, *Newington, CT* 83
THE DOLL MUSEUM, *Newport, RI* 334
THE DOLL ROOM, *Bridgewater, CT* 48
GWENDOLYN DONAHUE, *Trumbull, CT* 101
LINDA L DONOVAN, *Warner, NH* 323
MICHAEL C DOOLING, *Middlebury, CT* 74
DORCAS BOOKS, *Fall River, MA* 211
DORWALDT'S ANTIQUES, *North Hero, VT* 364
DOUGLAS ANTIQUES, *South Egremont, MA* 260
DOUGLAS AUCTIONEERS, *South Deerfield, MA*
259
DOVE AND DISTAFF ANTIQUES, *Wakefield, RI*
342
DOVETAIL ANTIQUES, *Dennis, MA* 202
DOVETAIL ANTIQUES, *Sheffield, MA* 254
DOW'S CORNER SHOP, *Tuftonboro Corner, NH*
322
DOWER HOUSE, *Marlboro, MA* 228
DOWN UNDER, *Cambridge, MA* 196

DOWNEAST ANTIQUE CENTER, *Ellsworth,
ME* 128
GEORGE A DOWNER FINE ARTS, *Needham,
MA* 234
DOWNSTAIRS AT HARBOR VIEW, *Stonington,
CT* 98
PRISCILLA DRAKE ANTIQUES, *New London,
NH* 312
DRAKE'S HILL ANTIQUES, *Northwood, NH* 314
THE DRAWING ROOM ANTIQUES, *Newport,
RI* 334
DRUMMER BOY ANTIQUES, *Bedford, NH* 286
DUBOIS' OLD HOUSE, *Norton, MA* 241
DUCK TRAP ANTIQUES, *Lincolnville, ME* 137
COLIN & ELIZABETH DUCOLON, *Burlington,
VT* 351
WILLIAM CORE DUFFY, *Kittery, ME* 136
DUKSTA'S ANTIQUES, *Hope Valley, RI* 332
DUNBAR'S GALLERY, *Milford, MA* 230
MICHAEL DUNN - BOOKS, *Newport, VT* 363
DUNN'S MYSTERIES OF CHOICE, *Meriden, CT*
74
DAVID DUNTON/ANTIQUES, *Woodbury, CT* 111
R P DURKIN & COMPANY INC, *Lowell, MA* 226
DYNAN FINE ARTS, *Kennebunk, ME* 133
ROBERT E DYSINGER - BOOKS, *Brunswick, ME*
122
EAGLE'S NEST ANTIQUES, *Rutland, VT* 368
EAGLES LAIR ANTIQUES, *Norwalk, CT* 85
EAGLES NEST, *Avon, CT* 44
EARLY NEW ENGLAND ROOMS, *South Windsor,
CT* 95
EARLY SPRING FARM ANTIQUES, *Vineyard
Haven, MA* 267
EARLY VERMONT ANTIQUES, *Waterbury, VT*
374
EARTH BOOKS, *Lisbon, NH* 306
EAST ARLINGTON ANTIQUE CENTER, *East
Arlington, VT* 354
EAST COAST BOOKS, *Wells, ME* 154
EAST WEST ANTIQUES, *Pawlet, VT* 365
EASTHAM AUCTION HOUSE, *North Eastham,
MA* 240
HARLAND EASTMAN - BOOKS, *Springvale, ME*
150
EASY CHAIRS, *Cambridge, MA* 196
PETER EATON, *Newburyport, MA* 235
EDGECOMB BOOK BARN, *North Edgecomb, ME*
141
THOMAS A EDISON COLLECTION, *Georgetown,
MA* 212
EIGHTH ELM FARM ANTIQUES, *Vergennes, VT*
373
ROBERT C ELDRED CO, INC, *East Dennis, MA*
205
ERNEST ELDRIDGE AUCTIONEER,
Willimantic, CT 107
THE ELEGANT DRAGON, *Hopkinton, RI* 332
THE ELEPHANT TRUNK, *Old Lyme, CT* 86
ELFAST'S ANTIQUES, *Spruce Head, ME* 151
ELI THE COBBLER ANTIQUES, *Biddeford, ME*
120
ELIOT ANTIQUES, *Rockport, MA* 248
ELIZABETH'S 20TH CENTURY, *Newburyport,
MA* 235
ELLIE'S ANTIQUE CENTER, *Deerfield, MA* 202
JAS E ELLIOTT ANTIQUES, *Winthrop, CT* 108
SANDY ELLIOTT, COUNTRY ANTIQUES,
Exeter, NH 293

ELLIPSE ANTIQUES, *Dennis, MA* 202
JOAN HARTMAN ELLIS ANTIQUE PRINT,
Rockport, ME 147
JOAN & GAGE ELLIS, *Lyme Center, NH* 308
ELM STREET & STOLCRAFT BOOKS, *Lancaster,
NH* 306
ELMCRESS BOOKS, *Hamilton, MA* 218
DOROTHY ELSBERG BOOKS, *West Stockbridge,
MA* 275
GARY F ELWELL ANTIQUES, *Hallowell, ME* 131
EMBELLISHMENTS, *Somerville, MA* 257
R & D EMERSON, BOOKSELLERS, *Falls Village,
CT* 61
EMERSON'S ANTIQUES, *Blue Hill, ME* 120
EMERY'S BOOKS, *Contoocook, NH* 289
THE EMPORIUM, *Great Barrington, MA* 215
THE EMPORIUM, *Warwick, RI* 343
ENCORES, *Acton, MA* 162
ENDLESS ANTIQUES, *Pembroke, MA* 244
ENFIELD MALL INTERNATIONAL, *Enfield, CT*
58
ENGLISH COUNTRY ANTIQUES, *Stowe, VT* 372
ENGLISH HERITAGE ANTIQUES, INC, *New
Canaan, CT* 77
ENSINGER ANTIQUES LTD, *Fairfield, CT* 61
EQUINOX ANTIQUES, *Manchester Village, VT* 360
ERNIE'S ANTIQUES, *Canaan, NH* 287
ESSEX ANTIQUE CO-OP, *Ipswich, MA* 222
ESSEX ANTIQUES CENTER, *Essex, CT* 59
ESSEX AUCTION & APPRAISAL, *Essex, CT* 59
ESSEX COLONY ANTIQUES, *Essex, CT* 59
THE ESSEX FORGE, *Essex, CT* 59
ESSEX-SAYBROOK ANTIQUES VILLAGE, *Old
Saybrook, CT* 87
ESTATE TREASURES, *Riverside, CT* 91
THE ETCETERA SHOPPE, *Lebanon, CT* 70
ETHAN ALLEN ANTIQUE SHOP INC, *South
Burlington, VT* 371
EUGENE GALLERIES, *Boston, MA* 176
EUROPEAN COUNTRY ANTIQUES, *Brookfield,
CT* 48
EUROPEAN MANOR, *Wellesley, MA* 269
NEIL B EUSTACE, *Stonington, CT* 98
WILLIAM EVANS, CABINETMAKER, *Waldoboro,
ME* 152
EVIE'S CORNER, *Marblehead, MA* 227
EXCALIBUR HOBBIES, *Malden, MA* 226
EXETER OLD BOOK BARN, *Exeter, NH* 293
EXPRESSIONS, *Fitzwilliam, NH* 294
FACTORY MARKETPLACE ANTIQUES,
Vergennes, VT 373
FAIENCE, *South Norwalk, CT* 94
FAIR DE YORE, *Newport, RI* 334
FAIR WEATHER ANTIQUES, *Meriden, CT* 74
THE FAIRWEATHER SHOP, *Whitefield, NH* 326
FALCON ANTIQUES, *Sheffield, MA* 255
FALCON'S ROOST ANTIQUES, *Lyme, NH* 307
BARBARA FALK - BOOKSELLER, *Castine, ME*
124
P HASTINGS FALK SOUND VIEW PRESS,
Madison, CT 72
RUTH FALKINBURG'S DOLL SHOP, *Seekonk,
MA* 252
FALLS BOOK BARN, *Farmington Falls, ME* 129
THE FAMILY ALBUM, *Westport, CT* 105
FANTASY HOUSE ANTIQUES, *Fairhaven, MA*
210
FARMER'S MARKET ANTIQUES, *Derry, NH* 290
FARMHOUSE COLLECTIBLES, *Sudbury, MA* 265

THE FARMHOUSE, *Wellfleet, MA* 270
THE FARM, *Wells, ME* 154
BARBARA FARNSWORTH, *West Cornwall, CT* 103
FARQUHAR ANTIQUES, *Walpole, NH* 323
FARR'S ANTIQUES, *East Barre, VT* 354
CRAIG FARROW CABINETMAKER, *Woodbury,
CT* 111
FAT CHANCE ANTIQUES, *Winchester, NH* 326
FAULCONNER HOUSE ANTIQUES, *Sandwich,
MA* 251
FAUX-ARTS ASSOCIATES, *Somerville, MA* 257
FENDELMAN & SCHWARTZ, *Stamford, CT* 97
BARBARA L FERET, BOOKSELLER, *Northampton,
MA* 241
FERGUSON & D'ARRUDA, *Swansea, MA* 265
ROBIN FERN GALLERY, *West Hartford, CT* 103
VINCENT J FERNANDEZ ORIENTAL RUG,
Richmond, VT 367
FERRAN'S INTERIORS, *Osterville, MA* 243
FERRELL'S ANTIQUES & WOODWORKING,
Lee, MA 223
JANE FIELD BOOKS, *Georgetown, MA* 213
FINDERS KEEPERS, *Wellfleet Ctr, MA* 270
FINE ANTIQUES, *Spofford, NH* 320
FINE TIME VINTAGE TIMEPIECES, *Boston, MA*
176
THE FINEST HOUR, *Boston, MA* 176
FINITNEY & COMPANY, *Watch Hill, RI* 343
FIREHOUSE ANTIQUES, *Wenham, MA* 270
FIREMATIC SPECIALTIES, *Waltham, MA* 268
FIRESTONE AND PARSON, *Boston, MA* 176
BENJAMIN FISH HOUSE ANTIQUES,
Portsmouth, RI 339
THE FISKE HOUSE, *Charlestown, MA* 198
FITZ-GERALDS' ANTIQUES, *Vergennes, VT* 373
FITZWILLIAM ANTIQUE CENTER, *Fitzwilliam,
NH* 294
FIVE CORNERS ANTIQUES, *Rockport, MA* 248
FIVE HONEST LADIES, *Marblehead, MA* 227
FLAG GATE FARM ANTIQUES, *Ossipee, NH* 315
FLEUR DE LIS GALLERY, *Cambridge, MA* 196
FLEUR-DE-LIS ANTIQUES, *Alton, NH* 284
FLIGHTS OF FANCY ANTIQUES, *Malden, MA*
226
CHARLES L FLINT, *Lenox, MA* 223
MAGGIE FLOOD, *Sudbury, MA* 265
FLYNN BOOKS, *Portland, ME* 144
FONTAINE'S AUCTION GALLERY, *Pittsfield,
MA* 245
FOR OLDE TIME'S SAKE, *Centerville, MA* 198
FORAGER HOUSE COLLECTION, *Nantucket,
MA* 231
LAWRENCE FORLANO, *York, ME* 159
THE FORRER'S, *Kent, CT* 68
FORT HILL ANTIQUES, *Salisbury, MA* 251
J & N FORTIER INC, *Worcester, MA* 280
THE FORTRESS CORPORATION, *Boston, MA*
176
FORTUNATE FINDS BOOKSTORE, *Warwick, RI*
343
CHRISTOPHER FOSTER GLASS WORKS,
Newport, RI 334
FOSTER'S AUCTION GALLERY, *Newcastle, ME*
140
FOUNDATION ANTIQUES, *Fair Haven, VT* 355
FOUR CORNERS EAST, INC, *Bennington, VT* 348
FOUR WINDS CRAFT GUILD, *Nantucket, MA*
231

GEORGE & PATRICIA FOWLER, BOOKS, *Brooklin, ME* 121

FOX RUN COUNTRY ANTIQUES, *Charlestown, RI* 331

FRAN & DEAN'S ANTIQUES, *Brewer, ME* 121

THE FRANCESTOWN GALLERY, *Francestown, NH* 294

PETER FRANKLIN CABINETMAKERS, *Easthampton, MA* 207

FRANKLIN STREET ANTIQUE MALL, *Framingham, MA* 212

JAMES FRASER, *Burlington, VT* 351

FRASER'S ANTIQUES, *Taftsville, VT* 373

LOUISE FRAZIER, BOOKS, *Gilford, NH* 296

FREEDOM BOOKSHOP, *Freedom, NH* 296

F BARRIE FREEMAN ANTIQUES, *West Bath, ME* 155

JERRY FREEMAN LTD, *Brookline, MA* 193

FREEPORT ANTIQUE MALL, *Freeport, ME* 129

R & R FRENCH ANTIQUES, *Amherst, MA* 162

FRIEDMAN GALLERY, *Westport, CT* 105

FRIENDSHIP ANTIQUES, *Essex, MA* 208

FROG HOLLOW ANTIQUES, *Mansfield, MA* 226

FROM HERE TO ANTIQUITY, *New Haven, CT* 80

FULL SWING, *Newport, RI* 334

FURNITURE BARN, *Palmer, MA* 243

FUSCO & FOUR ASSOCIATES, *Boston, MA* 176

G G G ANTIQUES, *Fairfield, CT* 61

GABRIEL'S AUCTION CO INC., *Westwood, MA* 277

GABRIELS' BARN ANTIQUES, *Grafton, VT* 356

GADHUE'S ANTIQUES, *Shelburne, VT* 370

PATTY GAGARIN ANTIQUES, *Fairfield, CT* 61

A & A GAINES, *Newport, RI* 335

TIM GALLAGHER ANTIQUES, *Brookline, MA* 193

GALLERY '76 ANTIQUES INC, *Newport, RI* 335

GALLERY 4, *Hamden, CT* 67

GALLERY FORTY FOUR, *New Hartford, CT* 78

THE GALLERY ON THE COMMONS, *Little Compton, RI* 333

GALLERY ON THE GREEN LTD, *Lexington, MA* 224

THE GALLERY SHOP, *Sebago, ME* 149

GAMAGE ANTIQUES, *Bangor, ME* 117

GARAKUTA COLLECTION, *Portsmouth, NH* 317

AVIS & ROCKWELL GARDINER, *Stamford, CT* 97

GARGOYLES & GRIFFINS, *Hampton, NH* 298

STEPHEN H GARNER, *Yarmouth Port, MA* 281

GAY MEADOW FARM ANTIQUES, *Weston, VT* 375

GEBELEIN SILVERSMITHS, *East Arlington, VT* 354

EMANUAL GENOVESE, *Brookline, MA* 193

GEORGIAN ANTIQUES, *Greenwich, CT* 64

PEG GERAGHTY-BOOKS, *Westbrook, ME* 155

BEN GERBER & SON, INC., *Brockton, MA* 192

GIAMPIETRO ANTIQUES, *New Haven, CT* 80

GIBRAN ANTIQUE GALLERY, *Kennebunkport, ME* 134

JOHN GIDLEY HOUSE, *Newport, RI* 335

GILANN SUMMER BOOK SHOP, *Darien, CT* 55

GILDAY'S ANTIQUES, *Woodbury, CT* 111

THE GILDED SWAN, *East Sandwich, MA* 206

H GRAY GILDERSLEEVE ANTIQUES, *Brandon, VT* 349

PATRICK J GILL & SONS, *Woburn, MA* 279

KENT & YVONNE GILYARD ANTIQUES, *Bantam, CT* 45

MICHAEL GINSBERG BOOKS INC, *Sharon, MA* 253

GIORDANO GRAZZINI, *Ridgefield, CT* 90

GIVE & TAKE CONSIGNMENT SHOP, *Newton, MA* 236

GLASKOWSKY & COMPANY, *Easthampton, MA* 207

ROBERT H GLASS AUCTIONEERS, *Sterling, CT* 98

J. GLATTER BOOKS, *South Portland, ME* 150

ESTELLE M GLAVEY, INC., *New Ipswich, NH* 312

GLEASON FINE ART AT MCKOWN ST, *Boothbay Harbor, ME* 120

GLENORTON COUNTRY ANTIQUES, *Fairfax, VT* 355

GLOBE BOOKSHOP, *Northampton, MA* 241

GLOUCESTER FINE ARTS & ANTIQUARI, *Gloucester, MA* 214

GODIVA ANTIQUES, *Loudon, NH* 307

GODWIN GALLERY, *Pepperell, MA* 244

MARIE PLUMMER GOETT, *Kennebunkport, ME* 134

CONSTANCE GOFF, *Yarmouth Port, MA* 281

GOLD COAST ANTIQUES, *Searsport, ME* 149

GOLD DRAGON ANTIQUES, *Contoocook, NH* 289

GOLDEN FLEECE ANTIQUES, *Needham, MA* 234

GOLDEN PARROT, *Southborough, MA* 261

GOLDEN PAST ANTIQUE MARKET, *Tuftonboro Center, NH* 322

GOLDEN PAST OF WALPOLE, *Walpole, NH* 323

GOLDEN PONY ANTIQUES, *Southborough, MA* 261

GOLDEN SALES & AUCTIONS, *Plainville, CT* 88

GOLDEN THISTLE ANTIQUES, *Kent, CT* 69

LAWRENCE GOLDER, RARE BOOKS, *Collinsville, CT* 52

GOOD & HUTCHINSON ASSOCIATES, *Sheffield, MA* 255

GOOD OLD DAYS ANTIQUES, *Winchester, NH* 326

GOODE HILL ANTIQUES, *North Kent, CT* 84

SALLY GOODMAN ANTIQUES, *New Haven, CT* 80

GOODSPEED'S BOOK SHOP INC, *Boston, MA* 176

LOUISA GOODYEAR ANTIQUES, *West Brooklin, ME* 155

THE GOOSE HANGS HIGH, *Kennebunkport, ME* 135

GOOSE RIVER EXCHANGE, *Lincolnville Beach, ME* 137

GOOSEBORO BROOK ANTIQUES, *Bantam, CT* 45

GORDON'S BOOKSHOP, *Brunswick, ME* 122

GORDONS ANTIQUES, *Meredith, NH* 309

GORGEANA ANTIQUES, *York, ME* 159

TIMOTHY GORHAM, CABINET MAKER, *West Chesterfield, MA* 273

GOSHEN ANTIQUE CENTER, *Goshen, CT* 63

W B GOTTLEIB - BOOKS, *Deep River, CT* 56

ROBERT F. GRABOWSKY, *Norfolk, MA* 238

GRAFTON GATHERING PLACE, *Grafton, VT* 356

GRALYN ANTIQUES, INC, *North Conway, NH* 313

GRAMS & PENNYWEIGHTS, *Putnam, CT* 89

GRANARY ANTIQUES, *Lancaster, NH* 306

HYLAND GRANBY ANTIQUES, *Dennis, MA* 203
GRANBY ANTIQUES EMPORIUM, *Granby, CT* 63
GRAND ILLUSIONS, *East Hampton, CT* 57
GRAND TROUSSEAU, *Boston, MA* 176
BARBARA GRANT - ANTIQUES, *Brewster, MA* 190
GRASS ROOTS ANTIQUES, *Woodbury, CT* 111
GEORGE I GRAVERT ANTIQUES, *Boston, MA* 178
GRAY MATTER SERVICE, *South China, ME* 150
THE GRAY'S ANTIQUES, *Moody, ME* 138
GRAYNOOK ANTIQUES & INTERIORS, *Bridgeport, CT* 48
GREAT AMERICAN SALVAGE COMPANY, *Montpelier, VT* 362
GREAT MEADOWS JOINERY, *Wayland, MA* 268
THE GREEN APPLE, *Sturbridge, MA* 264
ROSINE GREEN ASSOCIATES, INC., *Brookline, MA* 193
THE GREEN DOOR ANTIQUE SHOP, *Orono, ME* 143
GREEN MOUNTAIN ANTIQUE CENTER, *Ossipee, NH* 315
GREEN MOUNTAIN ANTIQUES, *Stowe, VT* 372
GREEN MOUNTAIN BOOKS & PRINTS, *Lyndonville, VT* 359
GREEN MOUNTAIN CLOCK SHOP, *Williston, VT* 376
GREEN'S CORNER ANTIQUES, *Troy, ME* 152
WILLIAM N GREENBAUM, *Gloucester, MA* 214
GREENHOUSE ANTIQUES, *Scituate, MA* 252
GREENWILLOW ANTIQUES, *Ridgefield, CT* 90
ARTHUR T GREGORIAN INC, *Newton Lower Falls, MA* 238
HARRY GREW, *Newport, RI* 335
GREYSTONE GARDENS, *Pittsfield, MA* 245
THE GRIST MILL ANTIQUES, *Townsend Harbor, MA* 267
GRIST MILL ANTIQUES, *Amherst, MA* 162
GRIST MILL ANTIQUES, *Antrim, NH* 285
GROGAN & COMPANY, *Boston, MA* 178
NORMAN GRONNING ANTIQ/ARCH ITEMS, *Shraftsbury, VT* 370
RENE GROSJEAN ANTIQUES, *Greenwich, CT* 64
H GROSSMAN, *Boston, MA* 178
GROTON ANTIQUES, *Groton, MA* 216
GROUND FLOOR ATTIC ANTIQUES, *Petersham, MA* 244
GROVE FARM ANTIQUES, *Rumford Center, ME* 148
GERALD GRUNSELL & ASSOCIATES, *Ridgefield, CT* 90
C E GUARINO, *Denmark, ME* 126
GUIDO, *Boston, MA* 178
GUILD ANTIQUES, *Greenwich, CT* 64
GUTHMAN AMERICANA, *Westport, CT* 105
PAT GUTHMAN ANTIQUES, *Southport, CT* 96
BRUCE & SUSAN GVENTER, BOOKS, *South Egremont, MA* 260
GWS GALLERIES, *Southport, CT* 96
HADLEY ANTIQUES CENTER, *Hadley, MA* 217
HADSELL'S ANTIQUES, *Burlington, CT* 49
HAILSTON HOUSE INC, *Bolton, CT* 47
DICK HALE ANTIQUES, *Plainfield, MA* 245
HALEY & STEELE INC, *Boston, MA* 178
HALF THE BARN, *Center Strafford, NH* 287
HALF-MOON ANTIQUES, *Washington, NH* 324
MICHAEL HALL ANTIQUES, *Gaylordsville, CT* 62

JOSLIN HALL RARE BOOKS, *Concord, MA* 200
W D HALL, *East Longmeadow, MA* 205
HALLOWELL & CO, *Greenwich, CT* 65
DOUGLAS H HAMEL, *Chichester, NH* 288
HAMLET ANTIQUES, *Lenox, MA* 224
HAMLET ANTIQUES, *Littleton, MA* 225
HAMMERWORKS, *Worcester, MA* 280
KENNETH HAMMITT ANTIQUES, *Woodbury, CT* 111
ROLAND B HAMMOND INC, *North Andover, MA* 239
HANDS OF TIME, *Coventry, CT* 53
HANSEN & CO, *Southport, CT* 96
HANSON'S CARRIAGE HOUSE, *Cape Elizabeth, ME* 123
HARBORSIDE ANTIQUES, *Townsend Harbor, MA* 267
HARBOUR GALLERIES, *East Greenwich, RI* 332
HARD CIDER FARM ORIENTAL RUGS, *Falmouth, ME* 128
HARD-TO-FIND NEEDLEWORK BOOKS, *Newton, MA* 237
HARDINGS BOOK SHOP, *Wells, ME* 154
HARDINGS OF HANCOCK, *Hancock, NH* 299
HARE & TORTOISE ANTIQUES/COLLECT, *Fairhaven, MA* 210
HAROLD'S LTD INC, *New Haven, CT* 80
HARPER & FAYE INC, *Boston, MA* 178
TERRY HARPER, BOOKSELLER, *Bristol, VT* 350
HARRINGTON HOUSE 1800, *Shelburne, VT* 370
C J HARRIS ANTIQUES, *Waltham, VT* 374
HARTLEY'S ANTIQUES, *Northwood, NH* 314
HARWICH BOOKSTORE, *Harwichport, MA* 219
HASTINGS ART, LTD, *New Canaan, CT* 77
HASTINGS HOUSE, *Essex, CT* 60
FREDERICK HATFIELD ANTIQUES, *Sheffield, MA* 255
HAUNTED BOOK SHOP, *Orleans, MA* 243
HAUNTED BOOKSHOP, *Paris, ME* 143
HAUNTED MANSION BOOKSHOP, *Cuttingsville, VT* 352
HAWK'S NEST ANTIQUES & DECOYS, *Hinesburg, VT* 358
HAYLOFT ANTIQUE CENTER, *Northwood, NH* 314
HAYS SCULPTURE STUDIO, *Keene, NH* 304
ELLIOTT HEALY PHOTOGRAPHICA, *Damariscotta, ME* 125
HEATHER HOUSE, *East Sandwich, MA* 206
NORMAN C HECKLER & CO, *Woodstock Valley, CT* 114
HEELTAPPERS ANTIQUES, *Marblehead, MA* 227
HEIRLOOM ANTIQUES, *Brooklyn, CT* 49
HELIGE ANDE ARTS, *West Newbury, MA* 274
JULIE HELLER GALLERY, *Provincetown, MA* 246
NINA HELLMAN, *Nantucket, MA* 231
HEMLOCK HILL ANTIQUES, *Chesterfield, NH* 288
PAUL HENDERSON, *Nashua, NH* 311
HENDERSON'S, *Wenham, MA* 271
JOHN F HENDSEY -BOOKSELLER, *Rumney, NH* 319
HENRI-BURTON FRENCH ANTIQUES, *Greenwich, CT* 65
WILLIS HENRY AUCTIONS, *Marshfield, MA* 229
HER MAJESTY'S ANTIQUES, *New Haven, CT* 80
HERITAGE ANTIQUES, *Hopkinton, MA* 220
HERITAGE ANTIQUES, *Westerly, RI* 344
HERITAGE ART, *Boston, MA* 178

HERITAGE CANING, *Peabody, MA* 244
JEFFREY HERMAN, *Cranston, RI* 332
BETSY HEWLETT, *Yarmouth Port, MA* 281
HEY-DAY ANTIQUES, *Clinton, CT* 51
HEYDAY ANTIQUES OF HAMPTON, *Hampton, NH* 298
HICKORY STICK BOOKSHOP, *Washington Depot, CT* 102
HIGHGATE GALLERIES, *Boston, MA* 180
PETER G HILL & ASSOCIATES, *New Haven, CT* 80
CATHERINE HILL ANTIQUES, *West Southport, ME* 155
HILL COUNTRY BOOKS, *Center Sandwich, NH* 287
PETER HILL INC, *East Lempster, NH* 291
WILLIAM F HILL, *Hardwick, VT* 357
HILLSIDE BOOKS, *Warner, NH* 323
HILLTOP ANTIQUES, *Derry, NH* 290
HISTORIC BROOKSIDE FARMS ANTIQUE, *Orwell, VT* 365
HISTORIC HARDWARE LTD, *Hampton, NH* 298
HOBNOB ANTIQUES, *Middlebury, VT* 361
MARY HODES, *Newcastle, ME* 140
HODGE PODGE LODGE, *Durham, CT* 57
THE HOFFMANS, *Laconia, NH* 305
FRANK H HOGAN FINE ARTS INC, *Orleans, MA* 243
HOLIDAY HOUSE ANTIQUES, *Center Harbor, NH* 287
HOLLYDAY HOUSE, *Weston, MA* 276
HARRY HOLMES ANTIQUES, *Kent, CT* 69
HOLMES RESTORATIONS, *Kent, CT* 69
THE HOLMES, *Round Pond, ME* 147
HENRY B HOLT INC, *Lee, MA* 223
HOME FARM ANTIQUES, *Hadley, MA* 217
HOMER'S JEWELRY & ANTIQUES, *Boston, MA* 180
THE HOMESTEAD ANTIQUES, *Brewster, MA* 190
HOMESTEAD BOOKSHOP, *Marlborough, NH* 308
THE HONEY POT, *Southbury, CT* 95
HOOKED RUG RESTORATION, *West Harwich, MA* 274
HOOKED RUG RESTORATION, *Manchester, VT* 359
HENRY HORNBLOWER III, *Dedham, MA* 202
HORSEFEATHERS ANTIQUES, *East Sandwich, MA* 206
HORTON BRASSES, *Cromwell, CT* 54
HOTEL ESSEX ANTIQUES, *Essex, MA* 208
THE HOUSE OF CLOCKS, *Canton, CT* 50
THE HOUSE OF PRETTY THINGS, *Old Saybrook, CT* 87
HOUSE ON THE HILL, *Chatham, MA* 198
THE HOUSE THAT JACK BUILT, *Greenwich, CT* 65
HOUSTON'S FURNITURE BARN, *Lisbon, NH* 306
HOWARD'S ANTIQUES, *South Egremont, MA* 260
HOWARD'S FLYING DRAGON ANTIQUES, *Essex, MA* 209
AVIS HOWELLS ANTIQUES, *Belfast, ME* 119
DONALD B HOWES - ANTIQUES, *Brewster, MA* 190
STEPHEN & CAROL HUBER INC, *East Lyme, CT* 58
F B HUBLEY & CO, *Cambridge, MA* 196
HULLS COVE TOOL BARN, *Hulls Cove, ME* 133

HUNT COUNTRY ANTIQUES, *Tolland, CT* 100
HUNTER'S CONSIGNMENT, *Ridgefield, CT* 90
JOSEPHINE HURD ANTIQUES, *Boothbay Harbor, ME* 121
HURLEY BOOKS, *Westmoreland, NH* 326
CONSTANCE H HURST, *Newcastle, ME* 140
HURST GALLERY, *Cambridge, MA* 196
HYANNIS AUCTION, *Hyannis, MA* 221
IDLE-A-WHILE COUNTRY ANTIQUES, *Bridgewater, NH* 286
IMAGES, HEIRLOOM LINENS/LACE, *Wallingford, CT* 101
IMPERIAL DECORATING & UPHOLSTERY, *Avon, CT* 44
INDIAN LANE FARM, *West Cornwall, CT* 103
INDIAN SUMMER ANTIQUES, *Jaffrey, NH* 304
INTERIOR ARTS GALLERY, *Provincetown, MA* 246
INTERIOR MOTIVES, INC., *Dover, MA* 204
INTERNATIONAL AUCTION SCHOOL, *South Deerfield, MA* 259
IRENE'S BOOK SHOP, *Gardner, MA* 212
IRON HORSE ANTIQUES, INC, *Pittsford, VT* 365
IRREVERENT RELICS, *Arlington, MA* 164
ISLAND ATTIC INDUSTRIES INC, *Nantucket, MA* 231
ISLAND HOUSE ANTIQUES, *Ridgefield, CT* 91
ISLAND TO ISLAND ANTIQUES, *Peaks Island, ME* 143
IVES HILL ANTIQUES, *West Granville, MA* 273
RAYMOND IZBICKI, *Stonington, CT* 98
PAGE JACKSON ANTIQUE GALLERY, *Randolph Center, VT* 366
BERNICE JACKSON, *Concord, MA* 200
JADED LION, *Chepachet, RI* 331
JANDRA'S WOODSHED, *Fort Fairfield, ME* 129
JASMINE, *New Haven, CT* 80
JB ANTIQUES, *Newport, RI* 335
JENNIFERS, *Newport, RI* 335
FRANK C JENSEN ANTIQUES, *Woodbury, CT* 111
JER-RHO ANTIQUES, *Salem, MA* 250
JEWETT CITY EMPORIUM, *Jewett City, CT* 68
JIGGER'S ANTIQUES, *Wakefield, RI* 342
JOHNNY APPLESEED BOOKSHOP, *Manchester Village, VT* 361
DANA R JOHNSEN, *South Weymouth, MA* 261
GUS JOHNSON ANTIQUES, *Hampton, NH* 298
JOHNSON'S SECONDHAND BOOKSHOP, *Springfield, MA* 262
JOHNSTON ANTIQUES, *Franklin, MA* 212
EMY JANE JONES ANTIQUES, *Darien, CT* 55
STEPHEN JONES ANTIQUES, *Groton, VT* 357
JONESES ANTIQUES, *Great Barrington, MA* 215
JERALD PAUL JORDON GALLERY, *Ashford, CT* 44
R JORGENSEN ANTIQUES, *Wells, ME* 154
TOM JOSEPH & DAVID RAMSAY, *Limerick, ME* 136
JOSKO & SONS AUCTIONS, *Southport, CT* 96
JUDY'S ANTIQUES, *Caribou, ME* 124
JULIA & POULIN ANTIQUES, *Fairfield, ME* 128
JOHN D JULIA ANTIQUES, *Fairfield, ME* 128
JAMES D JULIA AUCTIONEERS, *Fairfield, ME* 128
THE JUMPING FROG, *Hartford, CT* 67
JUNCTION ANTIQUE CENTER, *Northwood, NH* 314
JUNIPER HILL BOOKS, *Newport, NH* 312
PRISCILLA JUVELIS INC, *Boston, MA* 180

KAHNS ANTIQUE & ESTATE JEWELRY, *Great Barrington, MA* 215
KAJA VEILLUX ART & ANTIQUES, *Newcastle, ME* 140
ETHEL M KALIF ANTIQUES, *Newport, RI* 335
KALONBOOKS, *Bradford, NH* 286
FRANK C KAMINSKI, *Stoneham, MA* 263
MARIE LOUISE KANE, *Newtown, CT* 84
MILTON H KASOWITZ, *New Haven, CT* 80
KAY BEE FURNITURE COMPANY, *Boston, MA* 180
TOM KAYE ANTIQUES LTD, *Wallingford, VT* 374
KAYES CONSIGNMENTS, *Milford, CT* 75
R KAZARIAN, *Newport, RI* 335
J J KEATING INC, *Kennebunk, ME* 133
JUDITH A KEATING, GG, *Kennebunk, ME* 133
JOYCE B KEELER - BOOKS, *North Monmouth, ME* 142
KEEZER'S HARVARD COMMUNITY EXCH, *Cambridge, MA* 196
KENNISTON'S ANTIQUES, *Pittsfield, ME* 143
KENT ANTIQUES CENTER, *Kent, CT* 69
JOS KILBRIDGE CHINA TRADE ANTIQU, *Groton, MA* 216
KIMBALL HOUSE 1753/REMINGTON ANT, *Chepachet, RI* 331
ROGER KING GALLERY OF FINE ART, *Newport, RI* 335
KING'S GRANT ANTIQUES, *Dennis, MA* 203
KINGS WAY BOOKS & ANTIQUES, *Brewster, MA* 190
THE KINGSLEIGH 1840, *Lee, MA* 223
KINGSMILL BOOK SHOP, *South Willington, CT* 94
PAUL & SUSAN KLEINWALD INC, *Great Barrington, MA* 215
HORST KLOSS, *Needham, MA* 234
KNOLLWOOD ANTIQUES, *Boston, MA* 180
KNOTTY PINE ANTIQUE MARKET, *West Swanzey, NH* 325
HILDA KNOWLES ANTIQUES, *Ipswich, MA* 222
ELEANOR KOCOT ANTIQUES, *Northampton, MA* 241
JEFF KOOPUS, *Harrison, ME* 132
LYNNE KORTENHAUS, *Boston, MA* 180
ERNEST S KRAMER FINE ARTS, *Wellesley Hills, MA* 270
RALPH KRISTIANSEN BOOKSELLER, *Boston, MA* 180
ALICE KUGELMAN, *West Hartford, CT* 103
KUTTNER ANTIQUES, *Sheffield, MA* 255
RALPH KYLLOE, *Nashua, NH* 311
L & M FURNITURE, *Northampton, MA* 241
L'OBJET D'ART LTD, *Westport, CT* 105
LA CALECHE, *Darien, CT* 55
GEORGE LABARRE GALLERIES, INC., *Hollis, NH* 303
LACE BROKER, *Boston, MA* 180
LACES UNLIMITED, *Wellesley Hills, MA* 270
LAFAYETTE ANTIQUES, *North Kingstown, RI* 338
LAKESIDE ANTIQUES, *East Winthrop, ME* 127
LAMB HOUSE FINE BOOKS, *Guilford, CT* 66
LAMP GLASS, *Cambridge, MA* 197
LAMP WORKS, *Newport, RI* 336
LAMPLIGHTER ANTIQUES, *Newport, RI* 336
THE LAMPLIGHTER, *Middletown Springs, VT* 362
LANCASTER MALL & ANTIQUES MARKET, *Lancaster, NH* 306
L A LANDRY ANTIQUES, *Essex, MA* 209
LANDSCAPE BOOKS, *Exeter, NH* 293

PAUL R LANGEVIN AUCTIONEER, *North Brookfield Ctr, MA* 240
LAPHAM & DIBBLE GALLERY, INC., *Shoreham, VT* 370
SUSAN B LARSEN ANTIQUES, *Plymouth, NH* 316
LARSON'S CLOCK SHOP, *Westminster, VT* 375
WM LARY-THOMAS SEAVER ANTIQUES, *Dublin, NH* 290
LEIF LAUDAMUS, RARE BOOKS, *Amherst, MA* 163
LAUREL LEDGE ANTIQUES, *Westerly, RI* 344
DAVID LAWRENCE GALLERY, *Boston, MA* 181
PAUL LAWTON & SON, *Brattleboro, VT* 349
LAZY FOX ANTIQUES ET GALLERIE, *Springfield, MA* 226
JAMES H. LE FURGY BOOKS & ANT., *Hallowell, ME* 131
LE PERIGORD, *Longmeadow, MA* 226
THE LEANING TREE., *Dennis, MA* 203
JESSE CALDWELL LEATHERWOOD, *East Sandwich, MA* 206
PATRICIA LEDLIE-BOOKSELLER ABAA, *Buckfield, ME* 122
JOHN LEEKE, PRESERVATION CONSULT, *Sanford, ME* 148
JENNY LEES ANTIQUES, *Milford, CT* 75
EDWARD J LEFKOWICZ INC, *Fairhaven, MA* 210
ANN LEHMANN ANTIQUES, *Stonington, CT* 98
LEMANOIR COUNTRY FRENCH ANTIQUES, *Fairfield, CT* 61
WILLEM & INGER LEMMENS ANTIQUES, *Halifax, MA* 218
LEON-VANDERBILT, *New Milford, CT* 82
LEONARD'S ANTIQUES, INC., *Seekonk, MA* 252
LEONE'S AUCTION GALLERY, *Jewett City, CT* 68
LEPORE FINE ARTS, *Newburyport, MA* 235
LES TROIS PROVINCES, *Colchester, CT* 51
LESLIE'S ANTIQUES & COLLECTIBLES, *Boston, MA* 181
LEVETT'S ANTIQUES, *Camden, ME* 123
WILLIAM LEWAN ANTIQUES, *Fitzwilliam, NH* 294
LEWIS & WILSON, *Ashley Falls, MA* 165
GEORGE THOMAS LEWIS, *Williamsburg, MA* 278
LIBERTY HILL ANTIQUES, *Reading, VT* 367
LIBERTY WAY ANTIQUES, *Greenwich, CT* 65
LIBRARY ANTIQUES, *Williamstown, MA* 278
LIL-BUD ANTIQUES, *Yarmouth Port, MA* 281
LILAC COTTAGE, *Wiscasset, ME* 156
LILAC HEDGE ANTIQUES, *Orleans, MA* 243
LILAC HEDGE BOOKSHOP, *Norwich, VT* 364
LILLIAN'S ANTIQUES, *North Kingstown, RI* 338
LIMEROCK FARMS ANTIQUES, *Marble Dale, CT* 73
LINDERMAN SCHENCK, *Boston, MA* 181
D W LINSLEY INC, *Litchfield, CT* 70
LION'S HEAD BOOKS, *Salisbury, CT* 92
LION'S MANE ANTIQUES, *Charlestown, RI* 331
LIPPINCOTT BOOKS, *Bangor, ME* 117
LIROS GALLERY, *Blue Hill, ME* 120
LISA C INC, *Lakeville, CT* 70
LISSARD HOUSE, *New Canaan, CT* 77
LITCHFIELD AUCTION GALLERY, *Litchfield, CT* 71
LITTLE HOUSE OF GLASS, *Old Saybrook, CT* 87

LITTLE HOUSE STUDIO, *South Egremont, MA* 260

NATHAN LIVERANT & SON, *Colchester, CT* 51

THE LOFT ANTIQUES, *Richmond, ME* 146

LOFTY IDEAS, *Woodstock, VT* 377

LOG CABIN ANTIQUES, *Tuftonboro, NH* 322

LOMBARD ANTIQUARIAN MAP/PRINTS, *Cape Elizabeth, ME* 123

CAROL LOMBARDI ANTIQUES, *Providence, RI* 340

LONDON LACE, *Boston, MA* 181

LONDONDERRY ANTIQUES, *Londonderry, NH* 307

LONDONTOWNE GALLERIES, *Somerville, MA* 258

THOMAS R LONGACRE, *Marlborough, NH* 308

LONGVIEW ANTIQUES, *Gorham, ME* 130

RUSS LOOMIS JR, *South Ashfield, MA* 258

LOON POND ANTIQUES, *Hillsboro, NH* 301

KEN LOPEZ BOOKSELLER, *Hadley, MA* 217

LORD RANDALL BOOKSHOP, *Marshfield, MA* 229

LORD SEAGRAVE'S, *Northport, ME* 142

LOUDON VILLAGE ANTIQUE SHOP, *Loudon Village, NH* 307

SAMUEL L LOWE JR ANTIQUES INC, *Boston, MA* 181

LOWY FRAME & RESTORING COMPANY, *Duxbury, MA* 204

J & J LUBRANO ANTIQUARIAN BOOKS, *Great Barrington, MA* 215

A. LUCAS, BOOKS, *Fairfield, CT* 61

ROBERT F LUCAS, *Blandford, MA* 166

LUDLOW ANTIQUE & GIFT CENTER, *Ludlow, VT* 359

LUDWIG'S ANTIQUES, *West Barnstable, MA* 271

GARY LUNDIN, *Southbury, CT* 96

LYMAN BOOKS - THEATRE, *East Otis, MA* 205

ELEANOR M LYNN/ELIZABETH MONAHAN, *Franconia, NH* 295

RUSSELL LYONS, *Ashley Falls, MA* 165

LYONS' DEN ANTIQUES, *Hanover, ME* 132

M & S RARE BOOKS, INC, *Weston, MA* 277

FREDERICK MAC PHAIL ANTIQUES, *West Swanzey, NH* 325

MACDONALD'S MILITARY, *Eustis, ME* 128

STEPHEN P MACK, *Ashaway, RI* 330

MAD EAGLE INC FINE ANTIQUES, *New London, NH* 312

PAUL MADDEN ANTIQUES, *Sandwich, MA* 251

MAGGIE'S ANTIQUES & COLLECTIBLES, *Harwichport, MA* 219

MAGIC HORN LTD, *East Haddam, CT* 57

STEFANO MAGNI ANTIQUES/FINE ART, *Greenwich, CT* 65

M.A.H. ANTIQUES, *North Edgecomb, ME* 141

MARY MAHLER ANTIQUES, *Stonington, CT* 99

MAIN STREET ANTIQUES CENTER, *Danby, VT* 353

MAIN STREET ANTIQUES, *Essex, MA* 209

MAIN STREET ARTS & ANTIQUES, *Gloucester, MA* 214

MAIN(E)LY BOOKS, *Skowhegan, ME* 150

MAINE ANTIQUE MERCHANTS LTD, *Lincolnville Beach, ME* 137

MAINELY ANTIQUES, *Hallowell, ME* 131

MAINLY OAK LTD, *Newport, RI* 336

MAISON AUCTION COMPANY INC, *Wallingford, CT* 102

VAL MAITINO ANTIQUES, *Nantucket, MA* 232

PAUL & MARIE MAJOROS, *Guild, NH* 297

THE MALL @ ECHO BRIDGE, *Newton Upper Falls, MA* 238

F J MANASEK, *Norwich, VT* 364

G B MANASEK, INC, *Hanover, NH* 300

JEFFREY D MANCEVICE INC, *Worcester, MA* 280

ELIZABETH S MANKIN ANTIQUES, *Kent, CT* 69

KENNETH & IDA MANKO, *Moody, ME* 138

MANOR ANTIQUES, *New Canaan, CT* 77

DORVAN L MANUS, *Westport, CT* 106

MAPLE AVENUE ANTIQUES, *Farmington, ME* 129

MAPLE COURT ANTIQUES, *Lanesborough, MA* 222

MAPLEDALE ANTIQUES, *Southborough, MA* 261

THE MAPLES, *Damariscotta, ME* 125

MARBLEHEAD ANTIQUES, *Marblehead, MA* 227

MARC THE 1ST ANTIQUES, *Bridgeport, CT* 48

THE MARCH HARE, LTD, *Boston, MA* 182

MARCHAND'S LAFAYETTE ANTIQUES, *Salem, MA* 250

MARCIA & BEA ANTIQUES, *Newton Highlands, MA* 237

MARCOZ ANTIQUES & JEWELRY, *Boston, MA* 182

MARCUS & MARSHALL ANTIQUES, *Wellesley, MA* 269

RICHARD G MARDEN, *Wolfeboro, NH* 327

MARIE-LOUISE ANTIQUES, *Hanover, NH* 300

MARIKA'S ANTIQUE SHOP, INC, *Boston, MA* 182

MARINE ANTIQUES, *Wiscasset, ME* 156

MARINE ARTS GALLERY, *Salem, MA* 250

MARITIME AUCTIONS, *York, ME* 159

MARITIME MUSEUM SHOP, *Kennebunkport, ME* 135

DOUGLAS MARSHALL, *Holden, ME* 132

MARSTON HOUSE AMERICAN ANTIQUES, *Wiscasset, ME* 156

MARTIN HOUSE ANTIQUE CENTER, *North Ferrisburg, VT* 364

MARTINGALE FARM ANTIQUES, *Morris, CT* 76

MARTONE'S GALLERY, *West Greenwich, RI* 343

MARTY'S ANTIQUE AUCTION SERVICE, *Smithfield, RI* 342

MARY'S GLASS & COLLECTIBLES, *Jeffersonville, VT* 358

PETER L MASI BOOKS, *Montague, MA* 230

MATHOM BOOKSHOP & BINDERY, *Dresden, ME* 126

MATTESON GALLERY OF ARTS, *Colchester, VT* 352

JAMES MATTOZZI & MARILYN BURKE, *Groton, MA* 217

MARC J MATZ, *Cambridge, MA* 197

MAURER & SHEPHERD, JOYNERS, *Glastonbury, CT* 62

MAVIS, *North Kent, CT* 85

TIMOTHY MAWSON BOOKS & PRINTS, *New Preston, CT* 83

MAY'S ANTIQUES, *Sheffield, MA* 255

MAYNARD HOUSE, *Westborough, MA* 275

MAYO ANTIQUES GALLERY, *Trenton, ME* 152

MAYPOP LANE, *Sandwich, MA* 251

THOMAS MC BRIDE ANTIQUES, *Litchfield, CT* 71

MC CAFFREY BOOTH ANTIQUES, *Brookfield, CT* 48

BERT MC CLEARY AUCTIONEER, *Francestown,
NH* 294
LUELLA MC CLOUD ANTIQUES, *Shelburne
Falls, MA* 257
PAUL MC INNIS, INC., *Hampton Falls, NH* 299
PHILL A MC INTYRE & DAUGHTERS, *Anson,
ME* 116
JEAN S MC KENNA BOOK SHOP, *Beverly, MA*
166
H P MC LANE ANTIQUES INC, *Darien, CT* 55
MCBLAIN BOOKS, *Hamden, CT* 67
KEVIN B MCCLELLAN, *Norwalk, CT* 85
MCKAY'S ANTIQUES, *Gardiner, ME* 130
MCLEOD MILITARY ANTIQUES, *Brewer, ME*
121
MCMORROW AUCTION COMPANY, *Mechanic
Falls, ME* 138
MEADOW HEARTH, *Hopkinton, NH* 303
MEADOW ROCK FARM ANTIQUES, *Pomfret
Center, CT* 89
MECHANICAL MUSIC CENTER INC, *South
Norwalk, CT* 94
MELLIN'S ANTIQUES, *Redding, CT* 89
J THOMAS MELVIN, *Bethel, CT* 46
MEMORY LANE ANTIQUE CENTER, *Coventry,
CT* 53
H MENDELSOHN FINE EUROPEAN BOOKS,
Cambridge, MA 197
MENDES ANTIQUES, *Rehoboth, MA* 247
MENTOR ANTIQUES, *North Kingstown, RI* 338
ROBERT L MERRIAM, *Conway, MA* 201
DUANE E MERRILL, *Williston, VT* 376
MERRIMAC'S ANTIQUES, *Orrington, ME* 143
MERRY HILL FARM, *West Nottingham, NH* 325
MERRYMEETING ANTIQUES, *Topsham, ME* 152
MERRYTHOUGHT, *Ashford, CT* 44
WM MERRIFIELD MERTSCH ANTIQUES,
Warren, NH 324
BETTY MESSENGER, *Barkhamsteud, CT* 45
METACOMET BOOKS, *Providence, RI* 340
THE METAL MENDER, *Ridgefield, CT* 91
METAL RESTORATION SERVICES, *Tiverton, RI*
342
MEURS RENEHAN, *Clinton, CT* 51
MICKLESTREET RARE BOOKS/MOD 1STS,
East Lebanon, ME 126
MIDDLE HADDAM ANTIQUES, *Middle Haddam,
CT* 74
MIDDLEBURY ANTIQUE CENTER, *East
Middlebury, VT* 354
MIKE MIHAICH, *North Randolph, MA* 240
MILFORD ANTIQUE CENTER, *Milford, CT* 75
MILFORD ANTIQUES, *Milford, NH* 310
MILFORD EMPORIUM, *Milford, CT* 75
MILFORD GREEN ANTIQUES GALLERY,
Milford, CT 75
MILK STREET ANTIQUES, *Portland, ME* 145
GEORGE E MILKEY BOOKS, *Springvale, ME* 151
MILL BROOK ANTIQUES, *Reading, VT* 367
MILL HOUSE ANTIQUES, *Woodbury, CT* 111
MILL POND ANTIQUES, *Portsmouth, NH* 317
MILL VILLAGE ANTIQUES, *Francestown, NH* 294
THE MILLER'S DAUGHTER, *Haydenville, MA*
220
MILLING AROUND, *Newcastle, ME* 140
MILLSIDE ANTIQUES, *Lincoln, NH* 306
GEORGE R MINKOFF, INC, *Great Barrington,
MA* 215
MISTER BIG TOYLAND, *Waltham, MA* 268

LEE MOHN ANTIQUES AND ART, *Wallingford,
CT* 102
MOLLY'S VINTAGE CLOTHING PROMO'N,
Maynard, MA 229
MONIQUE'S ANTIQUES, *Wolfeboro, NH* 327
MOODY-RIDGEWAY HOUSE, *West Newbury, MA*
274
CONSTANCE MORELLE BOOKS, *Haverhill, MA*
219
W MORIN FURNITURE RESTORATION,
Portsmouth, NH 317
MORIN'S ANTIQUES, *Auburn, ME* 116
MORRELL'S ANTIQUES, *Gardiner, ME* 130
EDWARD MORRILL & SON, *Newton Centre, MA*
237
VERNA H MORRILL, *Concord, NH* 289
THE MORRIS HOUSE, *New Canaan, CT* 78
MORTAR & PESTLE ANTIQUES, *Wellfleet, MA*
270
WOODY MOSCH CABINETMAKERS, *Bethlehem,
CT* 46
KEN MOSHOLDER, *Warren, NH* 324
MOTHER GOOSE ANTIQUES, *Hallowell, ME* 131
HOWARD S MOTT INC, *Sheffield, MA* 255
MOUNTAIN CREST ANTIQUES, *Hadley, MA*
217
MOUNTAIN ROAD ANTIQUES, *Hancock, MA*
218
MOUNT VERNON ANTIQUES, *Rockport, MA*
248
MUCH ADO, *Marblehead, MA* 228
J MUENNICH ASSOCIATES, INC, *Cheshire, CT*
50
BRYCE GEORGE MUIR, *Higganum, CT* 68
MULLIN-JONES ANTIQUITIES, *Great
Barrington, MA* 216
GERALD MURPHY ANTIQUES LTD, *Woodbury,
CT* 112
ROBERT A MURPHY BOOKSELLER, *Salem, MA*
250
ROBINSON MURRAY III, BOOKSELLER,
Melrose, MA 230
MURRAY BOOKS, *Wilbraham, MA* 277
MUSEUM GALLERY BOOK SHOP, *Fairfield, CT*
61
THE MUSIC EMPORIUM, *Cambridge, MA* 197
MUSICAL WONDER HOUSE, *Wiscasset, ME* 157
MY FAVORITE THINGS, *Providence, RI* 340
MYSTIC FINE ARTS, *Mystic, CT* 76
MYSTIC RIVER ANTIQUES MARKET, *Mystic,
CT* 76
JOSEPH LOUIS NACCA, *West Haven, CT* 104
NADEAU'S AUCTION GALLERY, *Colchester, CT*
52
NANTUCKET HOUSE ANTIQUES, *Nantucket,
MA* 232
NANTUCKET LIGHTSHIP BASKETS,
Nantucket, MA 232
NANTUCKET NEEDLEWORKS, *Nantucket, MA*
232
NATURAL HISTORY BOOKS, *North Bennington,
VT* 363
NATURAL SELECTION BOOKS, *Avon, CT* 44
NAUTICAL ANTIQUES, *Kennebunkport, ME* 135
NANCY NEALE TYPECRAFT, *Bernard, ME* 119
JIM NEARY ANTIQUES, *Rehoboth, MA* 247
NELSON CRAFTS & USED BOOKS, *Goshen, NH*
297
PETER A NELSON, *Woodbury, CT* 112

RANDALL NELSON, *West Willington, CT* 104
NELSON RARITIES, INC, *Portland, ME* 145
NELSON-MONROE, ANTIQUES, *Boston, MA* 182
SETH NEMEROFF, ANTIQUARIAN BOOKS, *Williamstown, MA* 278
NEVILLE ANTIQUES, *Cushing, ME* 125
NEW BEDFORD ANTIQUES COMPANY, *New Bedford, MA* 235
NEW CANAAN ANTIQUES, *New Canaan, CT* 78
THE NEW ENGLAND ANTIQUE TOY MALL, *Hudson, MA* 220
NEW ENGLAND ANTIQUES, *Newport, RI* 336
NEW ENGLAND FIREBACKS, *Woodbury, CT* 112
NEW ENGLAND GALLERY INC, *Andover, MA* 163
NEW ENGLAND GALLERY, *Wolfeboro, NH* 327
THE NEW ENGLAND SHOP, *Bethlehem, CT* 46
NEW ENGLAND SHOP, *Old Greenwich, CT* 86
NEW ENGLANDIANA, *Bennington, VT* 349
NEW HAMPSHIRE ANTIQUE CO-OP, INC, *Milford, NH* 310
NEW HAMPSHIRE BOOK AUCTIONS, *North Weare, NH* 313
NEWBURY STREET JEWELRY & ANTIQUE, *Boston, MA* 182
NEWCASTLE ANTIQUES, *Newcastle, ME* 140
NEWELL'S CLOCK/CHINA RESTORATION, *Newport, RI* 336
NEWFANE ANTIQUES CENTER, *Newfane, VT* 363
NEWINGTON STAR CENTER, *Newington, NH* 312
STEVE NEWMAN FINE ARTS, *Stamford, CT* 97
NEWPORT FINE ARTS INVESTMENT CO, *Newport, RI* 336
THE NEWPORT GALLERY LTD, *Newport, RI* 336
NEWPORT SCRIMSHAW COMPANY, *Newport, RI* 336
NICKERSON'S ANTIQUES, *Yarmouth Port, MA* 281
GORDON NICOLL, *Newcastle, ME* 140
NIMMO & HART ANTIQUES, *Middletown Springs, VT* 362
NININGER & COMPANY LTD, *Woodbury, CT* 112
NOBODY EATS PARSLEY, *Norfolk, CT* 84
RONALD NOE ANTIQUES, *Stonington, CT* 99
NONESUCH HOUSE, *Wiscasset, ME* 157
CARL R NORDBLOM, *Cambridge, MA* 197
NORFOLK ANTIQUES, *Norfolk, MA* 238
NORMAN'S ANTIQUES, *Torrington, CT* 101
NORTH COUNTRY BOOKSHOP, *Richmond, NH* 318
NORTH FIELDS RESTORATIONS, *Rowley, MA* 249
NORTH HAMPTON ANTIQUE CENTER, *North Hampton, NH* 313
NORTH HILL ANTIQUES, *Essex, MA* 209
NORTH HOUSE FINE ANTIQUES, *Lincolnville Beach, ME* 137
NORTH WIND FURNISHINGS INC, *Newton Upper Falls, MA* 238
NORTHEAST AUCTIONS, *Hampton, NH* 298
NORTHWOOD INN ANTIQUE CENTER, *Northwood, NH* 314
NORWICHTOWN ANTIQUE CENTER, *Norwich, CT* 86
NOSEY GOOSE, *Madison, CT* 72
THE NOSTALGIA FACTORY, *Boston, MA* 182
NOSTALGIA NOOK, *Pittsford, VT* 365

NOW AND THEN BOOKS, *Bennington, VT* 349
C RUSSELL NOYES, *Simsbury, CT* 93
NU-TIQUE SHOP, *Newfane, VT* 363
MARILYN NULMAN, BOOK REPAIR, *Brunswick, ME* 122
NUTMEG BOOKS, *Torrington, CT* 101
NUTTING HOUSE ANTIQUES, *Brandon, VT* 349
F M O'BRIEN-ANTIQUARIAN BOOKS, *Portland, ME* 145
O'BRIEN ENTERPRISES, *Swanzey, NH* 321
RICHARD J O'MALLEY, *Hyannis, MA* 221
JAMES F O'NEIL, *Boston, MA* 182
O'REILLY/EINSTADTER, LTD, *Boston, MA* 182
OAK & IVORY, *Osterville, MA* 243
OCEAN HOUSE ANTIQUES/CURIOSITIES, *Watch Hill, RI* 343
MOLL OCKETT, *Bryant Pond, ME* 122
OCTAVIA'S ANTIQUES, *Portland, ME* 145
OCTOBER MOUNTAIN ANTIQUES, *Lenox, MA* 224
OCTOBER STONE ANTIQUES, *Exeter, NH* 293
MARGARET B OFSLAGER, *Wiscasset, ME* 157
LEON OHANIAN & SONS CO INC, *Boston, MA* 185
RICHARD E OINONEN, *Sunderland, MA* 265
ELIZABETH OLCOTT BOOKS, *Rumney, NH* 319
THE OLD ALMANACK SHOP, *Concord, NH* 289
OLD BANK ANTIQUES, *East Hampton, CT* 58
OLD BANK HOUSE GALLERY, *East Haddam, CT* 57
OLD BENNINGTON BOOKS, *Hancock, NH* 300
OLD BOOKS & EPHEMERA, *Bethel, VT* 349
OLD BOOKS, *Brunswick, ME* 122
OLD BOOKS, *Groton, VT* 357
OLD CHEPT VILLAGE ANTIQUE CENTER, *Chepachet, RI* 331
OLD COUNTRY STORE ANTIQUES, *Coventry, CT* 53
OLD DUNBAR HOUSE, *Hillsboro, NH* 301
OLD ENGLISH ANTIQUES & TEA ROOM, *Scotland, CT* 93
OLD FASHIONED MILK PAINT COMPANY, *Groton, MA* 217
OLD FASHION SHOP, *Newport, RI* 337
OLD FIREHOUSE ANTIQUES, *Hardwick, VT* 357
OLD FORT INN & ANTIQUES, *Kennebunkport, ME* 135
OLD HARBOR HOUSE ANTIQUES, *Chatham, MA* 198
OLD HICKORY ANTIQUES, *Somers, CT* 93
OLD HOMESTEAD ANTIQUES, *Castleton Corners, VT* 351
THE OLD HOMESTEAD, *Lille, ME* 136
THE OLD HOUSE, *Buzzards Bay, MA* 195
OLD LIBRARY BOOKSTORE, *Waldoboro, ME* 153
OLD LISBON SCHOOLHOUSE ANTIQUES, *Lisbon, ME* 137
OLD MYSTIC FLEA MARKET, *Old Mystic, CT* 87
OLD NUMBER SIX BOOK DEPOT, *Henniker, NH* 301
THE OLD PRINT BARN, *Meredith, NH* 309
THE OLD RED STORE, *Bernard, ME* 119
OLD SCHOOLHOUSE ANTIQUES, *Westborough, MA* 276
OLD SOUTHPORT BOOKS, *Southport, CT* 96
OLD SPA SHOP ANTIQUES, *Middletown Springs, VT* 362
OLD STONE HOUSE ANTIQUES, *Addison, VT* 348

OLD THYME SHOP, *Freeport, ME* 129
OLD TOWN ANTIQUE CO-OP, *Marblehead, MA* 228
OLD TOWN FARM ANTIQUES, *Peterborough, NH* 316
OLD TOWNE ANTIQUES, *Dennis, MA* 203
OLD WELL ANTIQUES, *South Norwalk, CT* 94
OLDE BOSTONIAN, *Dorchester, MA* 204
OLDE CHESTER ANTIQUES, *Chester, NH* 288
OLDE HADLEY FLEA MARKET, *Hadley, MA* 217
OLDE STATION ANTIQUES, *Kent, CT* 69
OLDE TOWNE SHOPPE, *Wakefield, RI* 342
OLDE VILLAGE COUNTRY BARN, *Chatham, MA* 199
OLE T J'S ANTIQUE BARN, *Sheffield, MA* 255
RICHARD W OLIVER AUCTIONEERS, *Kennebunk, ME* 133
SANDI OLIVER FINE ART, *Weston, CT* 105
DANIEL OLMSTEAD ANTIQUES/AUCTION, *Greenland, NH* 297
ROSE W OLSTEAD, *Bar Harbor, ME* 117
ON CONSIGNMENT OF MADISON, *Madison, CT* 72
ON CONSIGNMENT GALLERIES, *Lexington, MA* 224
ON CONSIGNMENT GALLERIES, *Marblehead, MA* 228
ON CONSIGNMENT GALLERIES, *Needham, MA* 234
ON CONSIGNMENT GALLERIES, *Newburyport, MA* 236
ON CONSIGNMENT GALLERIES, *West Newton, MA* 274
ONCE UPON A TIME, *Bernard, ME* 119
ONE TEN NORTH, *Hingham, MA* 220
ONE-OF-A-KIND INC, *Chester, CT* 50
OPERA HOUSE ANTIQUES, *East Hampton, CT* 58
OPUS I, *Stonington, CT* 99
ORANGE TRADING COMPANY, *Orange, MA* 242
ORCHARD HILL ANTIQUES, *Shelburne, MA* 257
ORDNANCE CHEST, *Madison, CT* 72
ORIENTAL RUGS LTD, *Mystic, CT* 77
ORKNEY & YOST ANTIQUES, *Stonington, CT* 99
ORPHAN ANNIE'S, *Auburn, ME* 116
ORPHEUS BOOKS, *Danbury, CT* 54
ORUM SILVER CO, *Meriden, CT* 74
RAFAEL OSONA AUCTIONEER, *Nantucket, MA* 232
DAVID OTTINGER, *Deerfield, NH* 290
OUT-OF-PRINT SHOP, *Portland, ME* 145
OVERLEE FARM BOOKS, *Stockbridge, MA* 263
THE OWL'S NEST ANTIQUES, *Cummaquid, MA* 201
OXBOW BOOKS, *Newbury, VT* 363
OXFORD COMMON ANTIQUE CENTER, *Oxford, ME* 143
P & J ANTIQUES, *Littleton, MA* 225
PACKET LANDING IRON, *West Barnstable, MA* 271
PADDY'S COVE ANTIQUES, *Cape Porpoise, ME* 124
THE PAGES OF YESTERYEAR, *Newtown, CT* 84
SONIA PAINE, *Chestnut Hill, MA* 199
PETER PAP ORIENTAL RUGS INC, *Keene, NH* 305
PAPERMILL VILLAGE ANTIQUES, *Alstead, NH* 284
ART & PEGGY PAPPAS ANTIQUES, *Woodbury, CT* 112

PAPYRUS BOOKS, *Chatham, MA* 199
PARAPHERNALIA ANTIQUES, *Manchester, VT* 359
PARC MONCEAU, *Westport, CT* 106
PARK ANTIQUES, *Rutland, VT* 368
PARK PLACE ANTIQUES, *West Hartford, CT* 103
AARON & HANNAH PARKER ANTIQUES, *Wiscasset, ME* 157
PARKER FRENCH ANTIQUE CENTER, *Northwood, NH* 314
NILA PARKER, *Littleton, NH* 307
WILLIAM L PARKINSON BOOKS, *Shelburne, VT* 370
PARNASSUS BOOK SERVICE, *Yarmouth Port, MA* 281
GARY R PARTELOW REPRODUCTIONS, *Old Lyme, CT* 86
JACK PARTRIDGE, *North Edgecomb, ME* 141
PARTRIDGE REPLICATIONS, *Peterborough, NH* 316
PARTRIDGE REPLICATIONS, *Portsmouth, NH* 317
PARTRIDGE REPLICATIONS, *West Lebanon, NH* 325
GARLAND AND FRANCES PASS, *Avon, CT* 44
PAST TENSE ANTIQUES, *Portland, ME* 145
PAST TENSE, *Newton, MA* 237
PAST TIME BOOKS, *Sherman, CT* 93
PASTIMES ANTIQUES, *Springfield, VT* 371
PATRICIAN DESIGNS, *Alfred, ME* 116
PATRIOT ANTIQUARIAN BOOKS, *Lexington, MA* 224
BARBARA PATTERSON'S ANTIQUES, *Belmont, ME* 119
PAULETTE'S ANTIQUES/COLLECTIBL, *St Albans, VT* 371
A DAVID PAULHUS BOOKS, *Wells, ME* 154
PAULINE'S PLACE, *Kent, CT* 69
PAULSON'S ANTIQUARIAN PAPER/BOOK, *Huntington, MA* 221
PAYSON HALL BOOKSHOP, *Belmont, MA* 166
PEACE BARN ANTIQUES, *Marlow, NH* 309
THE PEDDLER'S CART, *Kingston, NH* 305
PEDLER'S ATTIC, *Quechee, VT* 366
PEMBROKE ANTIQUES, *Lee, MA* 223
PENNY LANE ANTIQUES & GIFTS INC, *Seekonk, MA* 253
PEPPER & STERN RARE BOOKS, INC, *Sharon, MA* 253
PERIOD FURNITURE HARDWARE CO, *Boston, MA* 185
PERIOD LIGHTING FIXTURES, *Chester, CT* 50
EGH PETER AMERICAN ANTIQUES, *Sheffield, MA* 256
PETERBOROUGH USED BOOKS & PRINTS, *Peterborough, NH* 316
PETERBOROUGH ANTIQUE ASSOCIATES, *Peterborough, NH* 316
JONATHAN PETERS, *New Preston, CT* 83
PETTERUTI ANTIQUES, *Newport, RI* 337
PETTICOAT ROW, *Nantucket, MA* 232
THE PFLOCK'S-ANTIQUES, *Brewster, MA* 190
PHEASANT HILL ANTIQUES, *Georgetown, MA* 213
KARIN J PHILLIPS ANTIQUES, *Cambridge, MA* 197
PHIPPS OF PITTSTON, *Pittston, ME* 143
KATRIN PHOCAS LTD, *Rockport, ME* 147

PHOENIX ANTIQUE RESTORATION, *New Milford, CT* 82
PIATT'S COPPER COW, *Contoocook, NH* 289
THE PICKET FENCE, *Cummaquid, MA* 201
PICKLE STREET ANTIQUES, *Grafton, VT* 356
PICKWICK HOUSE ANTIQUES, *Bethel, CT* 46
PIERCE GALLERIES INC, *Hingham, MA* 220
PIERCE-ARCHER ANTIQUES, *Cos Cob, CT* 52
OBADIAH PINE ANTIQUES, *West Boylston, MA* 271
PINE BOUGH, *Northeast Harbor, ME* 142
THE PINE CHEST, INC., *Wilton, CT* 107
PINE CHESTS & THINGS, *Damariscotta, ME* 125
PINE GROVE ANTIQUES, *East Swanzey, NH* 291
PINE MEADOW ANTIQUES, *Pine Meadow, CT* 88
PINE TREE STABLES ANTIQUES, *Augusta, ME* 117
PINE WOODS ANTIQUES, *Woodbury, CT* 112
WILLIAM & LOIS M PINKNEY, *Granby, CT* 63
PIONEER AMERICA, *Northwood, NH* 314
PIONEER AUCTION OF AMHERST, *North Amherst, MA* 239
JOHN PIPER HOUSE, *Stratham, NH* 321
PITTSFORD GREEN ANTIQUES, *Pittsford, VT* 365
PEGGY PLACE ANTIQUES, *Grafton, MA* 214
PLAINFIELD AUCTION GALLERY, *Plainfield, NH* 316
PLEASANT ACRES ANTIQUES ETC, *Wilmot Flat, NH* 326
PLEASANT BAY ANTIQUES, *South Orleans, MA* 261
PLEASANT HILL ANTIQUES, *Epping, NH* 292
PLEASANT STREET BOOKS, *Woodstock, VT* 377
RICHARD M PLUSCH ANTIQUES, *North Conway, NH* 313
THE POLISHED SNEAKER, *Woodbury, CT* 112
POLISSACK ANTIQUE JEWELRY, *Amherst, MA* 163
FRANK & BARBARA POLLACK, *Sunapee, NH* 321
DALE POLLOCK APPRAISAL SERVICES, *Chestnut Hill, MA* 199
POMEROY ANDERSON, *Southport, CT* 96
POMFRET ANTIQUE WORLD, *Pomfret, CT* 89
POMFRET BOOK SHOP, *Pomfret Center, CT* 89
POND HOUSE ANTIQUES, *Winter Harbor, ME* 156
POND HOUSE WOODWORKING, *Foxboro, MA* 211
POOR RICHARDS USED BOOKS, *Middlebury, VT* 361
VIRGINIA POPE, INC., *Dorset, VT* 354
PORRINGER & BRUCE MARCUS ANTIQUE, *Wiscasset, ME* 157
PORT 'N STARBOARD, *Portland, ME* 145
PORT ANTIQUES, *Kennebunkport, ME* 135
PORT OF GARDINER ANTIQUES, *Gardiner, ME* 130
HORACE PORTER ANTIQUES, *South Windsor, CT* 95
PORTSMOUTH BOOKSHOP, *Portsmouth, NH* 317
POST ROAD ANTIQUES & BOOKS, *York, ME* 159
POSTAR ANTIQUES, *Cambridge, MA* 197
POTPOURRI ANTIQUES, *Ogunquit, ME* 142
PETER POTS AUTHENTIC AMERICANA, *West Kingston, RI* 344
POVERTY HOLLOW ANTIQUES, *Newtown, CT* 84

STEVE POWELL, *Bar Harbor, ME* 118
WAYNE PRATT & CO, *Marlboro, MA* 228
ALDEN PRATT, BOOKS, *East Livermore, ME* 127
PRECIOUS PAST, *Hyannis, MA* 221
PRESENCE OF THE PAST, *Old Saybrook, CT* 87
PRICE HOUSE ANTIQUES, *Beverly, MA* 166
PRIMROSE FARM ANTIQUES, *Searsport, ME* 149
PRINCE OF WALES, *Westport, CT* 106
THE PRINTERS' DEVIL, *Boston, MA* 185
PRIPET HOUSE ANTIQUE PRINTS, *Waban, MA* 267
PROVINCES DE FRANCE, *Greenwich, CT* 65
PUDDLE DUCK ANTIQUES, *Sterling, MA* 263
PUDDLE DUCK ANTIQUES, *West Boylston, MA* 272
PUMPKIN PATCH ANTIQUE CENTER, *Searsport, ME* 149
THE PUNKHORN BOOKSHOP, *Brewster, MA* 190
PURPLE DOOR ANTIQUES, *Darien, CT* 55
PUSHCART PLACE, *Westborough, MA* 276
PUSS-N-BOOTS, *Nantucket, MA* 232
QUABOAG USED BOOKS, *Spencer, MA* 262
QUABOAG VALLEY ANTIQUE CENTER, *Palmer, MA* 243
QUAIL SONG ANTIQUES, *Eastham, MA* 206
QUAKER LADY ANTIQUES, *Bolton, CT* 47
QUE ANTIQUES, *Providence, RI* 340
QUECHEE BOOKS, *Quechee, VT* 366
QUESTER GALLERY, *Stonington, CT* 99
QUIMPER FAIENCE, *Stonington, CT* 99
SHIRLEY D QUINN ANTIQUES, *Contoocook, NH* 290
R & J GLASSWARE, *Milford, CT* 75
R "n" G ANTIQUES & COLLECTIBLES, *Sturbridge, MA* 264
EMILIE J RAHHAL, *Woodbury, CT* 112
RAINBOW BOOKS, *Storrs, CT* 100
RAINY DAY BOOKS, *Lexington, MA* 225
RAMASE, *Woodbury, CT* 113
RAMSON HOUSE ANTIQUES, *Newport, RI* 337
RANDALL AND KOBLENZ, *Sharon, CT* 93
RANDS ANTIQUES ON RAND GREEN, *Kennebunkport, ME* 135
RAPHAEL'S ANTIQUE RESTORATION, *Stamford, CT* 97
RARE & WELL DONE BOOKS, *Waitsfield, VT* 373
THE RATHBUN GALLERY-SHAKER, *Providence, RI* 340
RAY & AL'S ANTIQUES, *Swanton, VT* 372
THE RE-STORE ANTIQUES, *Wentworth, NH* 324
READING TREASURES BOOKSHOP, *Augusta, ME* 117
RECENT PAST, *Bath, ME* 118
RECOVERY BOOKS, *Greensboro, VT* 357
RECUERDO, *Rockport, MA* 248
RED BARN ANTIQUES, *Fitzwilliam, NH* 294
THE RED BARN ANTIQUES, *Hampton, NH* 298
RED BARN ANTIQUES, *South Egremont, MA* 260
RED BELL ANTIQUES, *Kingston, NH* 305
RED BRICK HOUSE, *Randolph Center, VT* 367
RED CLOVER ANTIQUES, *Ludlow, VT* 359
RED HORSE ANTIQUES, *Great Barrington, MA* 216
RED KETTLE ANTIQUES, *Searsport, ME* 149
RED LION ANTIQUES, *Dennis Village, MA* 203
THE RED PETTICOAT, *Ridgefield, CT* 91
RED SHED ANTIQUES, *Jackson, NH* 304
RED SHED, *Troy, NH* 322
THE RED SHED, *Yarmouth, ME* 158

RED SLEIGH, *Easton, CT* 58
RED SLEIGH, *Mt Sunapee, NH* 311
PATRICIA ANNE REED ANTIQUES, *Damariscotta, ME* 125
RALPH K REED ANTIQUES, *Wolfeboro, NH* 327
THE REEL MAN, *Providence, RI* 341
WILLIAM REESE COMPANY, *New Haven, CT* 81
MARY ALICE REILLEY, *Portland, ME* 145
CATHERINE SYLVIA REISS, *Darien, CT* 55
REMEMBER WHEN, *Portland, ME* 145
REMEMBRANCES OF THINGS PAST, *Provincetown, MA* 246
THE RENAISSANCE MAN, *Milford, NH* 310
DIANA J RENDELL, INC, *Waban, MA* 268
KENNETH W RENDELL, INC, *Newton, MA* 237
RENOVATORS SUPPLY, *Brookline, MA* 193
RERUNS ANTIQUES, *Boston, MA* 185
RESTORATION RESOURCES, *Hanover, MA* 218
RESTORATION SERVICES, *Waltham, MA* 268
RETOUCH THE PAST, *Wentworth, NH* 324
REUSS GALLERIES, *Stockbridge, MA* 263
RHODES OF WASHINGTON SQUARE, *Walpole, NH* 323
RIBA AUCTIONS, *South Glastonbury, CT* 93
THE RICHARDS ANTIQUES, *Camden, ME* 123
PAUL C RICHARDS AUTOGRAPHS, *Gardner, MA* 212
PETER/JEAN RICHARDS FINE ANTIQUE, *Damariscotta, ME* 126
RICHARDSON BOOKS, LTD, *Bedford, NH* 286
RICHARDSON BOOKS LTD, *New Harbor, ME* 139
J B RICHARDSON GALLERY, *Southport, CT* 97
LINDA RICKLES INTERIORS INC, *Wellesley, MA* 269
SHEILA & EDWIN RIDEOUT, *Wiscasset, ME* 157
RIDER & CLARKE ANTIQUES, *Essex, MA* 209
RIDGEFIELD ANTIQUE SHOPS, *Ridgefield, CT* 91
SUSAN K RILEY, SEAT WEAVER, *West Chesterfield, MA* 273
RINHART GALLERIES, *Colebrook, CT* 52
MARGUERITE RIORDAN, *Stonington, CT* 99
RIVER CROFT, *Madison, CT* 72
RIVER OAKS BOOKS, *Jay, ME* 133
RIVERBANK ANTIQUES, *Wells, ME* 154
RIVERGATE ANTIQUES MALL, *Kennebunk, ME* 133
RIVERS EDGE ANTIQUES, *East Poultney, VT* 355
RIVERWIND ANTIQUE SHOP, *Deep River, CT* 56
RO-DAN ANTIQUES, *Hamilton, MA* 218
FRED ROBBINS, *Gardiner, ME* 130
MARY ROBERTSON - BOOKS, *Meredith, NH* 309
DANA ROBES WOOD CRAFTSMEN, *Enfield, NH* 291
JANE ROBIE - LANDSCAPE BOOKS, *Exeter, NH* 293
CEDRIC L ROBINSON-BOOKSELLER, *Windsor, CT* 108
FRANCES L ROBINSON, *South Hero, VT* 371
CHARLES ROBINSON RARE BOOKS, *Manchester, ME* 138
ROCKING CHAIR ANTIQUES, *Brewster, MA* 191
ROSE & CLEAVES, *Boston, MA* 185
DAVID ROSE ANTIQUES, *Upton, MA* 267
THE ROSE COTTAGE, *West Boylston, MA* 272
ROSE D'OR, *Darien, CT* 56
RONALD J ROSENBLEETH INC, *Henniker, NH* 301

ROSENTHAL PAPER RESTORATION, *Amherst, MA* 163
JO-ANN E ROSS, *Taunton, MA* 266
ROUND POND ANTIQUES, *Round Pond, ME* 147
STEVEN J ROWE, *Newton, NH* 313
ROWLEY ANTIQUE CENTER, *Rowley, MA* 249
THE ROYALE MESS, *Center Harbor, NH* 287
ROBERT H RUBIN, BOOKS, *Brookline, MA* 193
RUE DE FRANCE, *Boston, MA* 185
RUMFORD ANTIQUES, *West Dennis, MA* 273
RUMPLESTILTSKIN, *Northampton, MA* 241
RUNNING FENCE BOOKS, *Pittsfield, MA* 245
C A RUPPERT, *Boston, MA* 185
HANES RUSKIN, *Westbrook, CT* 104
RUSSIAN BEAR ANTIQUES, *Thompson, CT* 100
RUSTIC ACCENTS, INC., *Nashua, NH* 311
RUTLAND ANTIQUES, *Rutland, VT* 368
RYAN'S ANTIQUES & REFINISHING, *North Attleboro, MA* 239
RYAN'S ANTIQUES, *Harwinton, CT* 68
RYEGATE CORNER ANTIQUES, *Ryegate Corner, VT* 369
S & S GALLERIES, *Marblehead, MA* 228
SOUTH WILLINGTON ANTIQUES, *South Willington, CT* 94
SABOL AND CROSS, LTD, *Nantucket, MA* 232
SACKS ANTIQUES, *Marblehead, MA* 228
SACRED & PROFANE, *Goffstown, NH* 297
SAGE AUCTION GALLERIES, *Chester, CT* 51
SAIL LOFT, *Newcastle, ME* 140
SALISBURY ANTIQUES CENTER, *Salisbury, CT* 92
SALLEA ANTIQUES, *New Canaan, CT* 78
SALT & CHESTNUT WEATHERVANES, *West Barnstable, MA* 271
SALT BOX ANTIQUES, *Charlestown, RI* 331
SALT BOX ANTIQUES, *Sunderland, MA* 265
SALT MARSH ANTIQUES, *Rowley, MA* 249
SALT-BOX HOUSE ANTIQUES, *Westborough, MA* 276
SAMUS STAIRS ANTIQUES, *Kennebunkport, ME* 135
STEPHEN SANBORN CLOCK REPAIR, *Hillsboro, NH* 301
LINCOLN & JEAN SANDER INC, *West Redding, CT* 104
SANDERS & MOCK, ASSOCIATES, *Tamworth, NH* 322
SANDERS ANTIQUES, *Salem, NH* 319
JOHN R SANDERSON, *Stockbridge, MA* 263
SANDWICH AUCTION HOUSE, *Sandwich, MA* 251
SAUNDERS & COOKE INC, *Portsmouth, NH* 318
BERT & GAIL SAVAGE, *Center Strafford, NH* 288
SAVOY BOOKS, *Lanesborough, MA* 222
PETER SAWYER ANTIQUES, *Kensington, NH* 305
SAWYER ANTIQUES, *West Stockbridge, MA* 275
WYNN SAYMAN, *Richmond, MA* 248
SCALA'S ANTIQUES, *Georgetown, MA* 213
JOYCE SCARBOROUGH ANTIQUES, *New Canaan, CT* 78
SCARLET LETTER BOOKS & PRINTS, *Sherman, CT* 93
KARL SCHICK, *Montague, MA* 230
SUZANNE SCHLOSSBERG BOOKS, *Newton Centre, MA* 237
SCHOEN & SON BOOKSELLERS, *Northampton, MA* 241

GLADYS SCHOFIELD ANTIQUES, *South Egremont, MA* 260
SCHOMMER ANTIQUES, *Newfane, VT* 363
SCHOOLHOUSE ANTIQUES, *Saxtons River, VT* 369
SCHOOLHOUSE TEN ANTIQUES, *Brownsville, VT* 350
DAVID A SCHORSCH, *Greenwich, CT* 65
DORRIE SCHREINER GALLERY ANTIQUE, *Darien, CT* 56
SCHUELER ANTIQUES, *Camden, ME* 123
SCHUTZ & COMPANY, *Greenwich, CT* 65
THOMAS SCHWENKE, INC, *Wilton, CT* 107
W M SCHWIND, JR ANTIQUES, *Yarmouth, ME* 158
SCIENTIA BOOKS, *Arlington, MA* 164
STEPHEN SCORE, *Essex, MA* 209
CHERYL & PAUL SCOTT ANTIQUES, *Hillsboro, NH* 301
BARRY SCOTT, *Fairhaven, MA* 210
ALLEN SCOTT/BOOKS, *Portland, ME* 146
SCOTT'S ANTIQUES, *Warner, NH* 324
SCOTT'S BOOKS, *Brewer, ME* 121
LEWIS W SCRANTON ANTIQUES, *Killingworth, CT* 70
SCRANTON'S SHOPS, *South Woodstock, CT* 95
THE SCRAPBOOK, *Essex, MA* 209
JAMES E SCUDDER, *Carolina, RI* 330
SEABOARD AUCTION GALLERY, *Eliot, ME* 127
SEAGULL ANTIQUES, *Acton, MA* 162
SECOND LIFE BOOKS, *Lanesborough, MA* 222
SECOND TYME AROUND, *Arlington, MA* 164
SEDLER'S ANTIQUE VILLAGE, *Georgetown, MA* 213
SENTIMENTAL JOURNEY, *West Brewster, MA* 272
SERGEANT, *Redding, CT* 90
SEVEN SOUTH STREET ANTIQUES, *Harwichport, MA* 219
SEVERED TIES, *Darien, CT* 56
SEVERED TIES, INC, *New Canaan, CT* 78
SEWARDS' FOLLY, BOOKS, *Providence, RI* 341
JOHN LARKIN SGRO, *York, ME* 159
THE SHADOW SHOP, *Hillsboro, NH* 302
SHAFER AUCTION GALLERY, *Madison, CT* 73
SHANNON FINE ARTS INC, *New Haven, CT* 81
B SHAW ANTIQUES, *Cummington, MA* 201
SHAWME POND ANTIQUES, *Sandwich, MA* 251
MONIQUE SHAY ANTIQUES, *Woodbury, CT* 113
NAN SHEA ANTIQUES, *Francestown, NH* 294
CARL & BEVERLY SHELDRAKE, *Moultonboro, NH* 311
SHER-MORR ANTIQUES, *Boston, MA* 185
SHIPPAN POINT GALLERY, *Stamford, CT* 97
SHIRETOWN ANTIQUE CENTER, *Alfred, ME* 116
THE SHOP AT BLACK HILL, *Paxton, MA* 244
THE SHOP IN THE BARN, *Lancaster, NH* 306
SHOP ON THE HILL, *Boston, MA* 187
SHREVE, CRUMP & LOW, *Boston, MA* 187
SHUTE AUCTION GALLERY, *West Bridgewater, MA* 272
SIBLEYS VILLAGE WORKSHOP, *Newfane, VT* 363
THE SIDE DOOR, *Dennisport, MA* 204
MEL SIEGEL ANTIQUES, *Johnson, VT* 358
SIGN OF THE DIAL CLOCK SHOP, *St Johnsbury, VT* 372
SIGN OF THE OWL, *Lincolnville Beach, ME* 137
SIGN OF THE RAVEN, *Saxtons River, VT* 369

SIGN OF THE UNICORN BOOKSHOP, *Peace Dale, RI* 339
SIGOURNEYS' ANTIQUES, *Cavendish, VT* 351
THE SILK PURSE, *New Canaan, CT* 78
THE SILK PURSE, *Ridgefield, CT* 91
SUSAN SILVER ANTIQUES, *Sheffield, MA* 256
SILVER LADY ANTIQUES, *Foxboro, MA* 212
SIMMONS & SIMMONS, *Newport, RI* 337
SIMPLER PLEASURES, *Chatham, MA* 199
SIMPLY COUNTRY, *South Burlington, VT* 371
ALICE SIMPSON ANTIQUES, *Newport, RI* 337
ROBERT W SKINNER INC, *Bolton, MA* 167
ROBERT W SKINNER INC, *Boston, MA* 187
EARL J SLACK ANTIQUES, *Marble Dale, CT* 73
SLEIGH MILL ANTIQUES, *Snowville, NH* 320
SLENSKA'S ANTIQUES & INTERIORS, *Boston, MA* 187
SAM SLOAT COINS, INC, *Westport, CT* 106
JOSIAH SMITH ANTIQUES, *Hallowell, ME* 131
SMITH ANTIQUES, *South Brewster, MA* 259
NANCY A SMITH APPRAISAL ASSOC, *Brookline, MA* 194
R W SMITH-BOOKSELLER, *New Haven, CT* 81
BRAD SMITH, *Wyoming, RI* 345
NATHAN SMITH HOUSE, *Cornish, NH* 290
SMITH MARBLE LTD, *Newport, RI* 337
PATTI SMITH, *Harwich, MA* 219
ROBERT E SMITH, *Somerville, MA* 258
STEPHEN H SMITH, CABINETMAKER, *Clinton, CT* 51
CHRISTOPHER L SNOW ASSOCIATES, *Newburyport, MA* 236
EDWARD SNOW HOUSE ANTIQUES, *Brewster, MA* 191
SNOWBOUND BOOKS, *Norridgewock, ME* 141
SNUG HARBOR BOOKS, *Wells, ME* 155
ELLIOTT & GRACE SNYDER, *South Egremont, MA* 260
SNYDER'S STORE, *Great Barrington, MA* 216
SOMEWHERE IN TIME ANTIQUES, *Lyme, NH* 308
SOPHIA'S GREAT DAMES, *Greenwich, CT* 66
SOPHIE'S COLLECTIQUES, *Rutland, VT* 368
SOTHEBY'S, *Boston, MA* 187
THE SOULES-ANTIQUES, *Hopkinton, NH* 303
SOUTH ESSEX ANTIQUES, *Essex, MA* 210
SOUTHAMPTON ANTIQUES, *Southampton, MA* 261
SOUTHBURY ANTIQUES CTR, *Southbury, CT* 96
SOUTHFORD ANTIQUES, *Woodbury, CT* 113
SOUTHPAW BOOKS, *Roxbury, MA* 249
M SPENCER, *Bridgton, ME* 121
SPINNING WHEEL ANTIQUES, *Richmond, NH* 318
SPIVACK'S ANTIQUES, *Wellesley, MA* 269
SPLENDID PEASANT, *South Egremont, MA* 260
SPNEA CONSERVATION CENTER, *Waltham, MA* 268
SPRAGUE HOUSE ANTIQUES, *Danvers, MA* 201
SPRIG OF THYME ANTIQUES, *Wiscasset, ME* 157
SPRING HILL FARM ANTIQUES, *Springfield, NH* 321
LOIS W SPRING, *Sheffield, MA* 256
THE SPYGLASS, *Chatham, MA* 199
SQUAM LAKE GALLERY, *Holderness, NH* 302
STANLEY BOOKS, *Wilder, VT* 375
STARR BOOK CO INC, *Melrose, MA* 230
THE STARR BOOK SHOP, *Cambridge, MA* 197

STARTING OVER LTD, *Hyannis, MA* 222
STATEN HOOK BOOKS, *Harwich Center, MA* 219
STATIONHOUSE ANTIQUES CENTER, *North Adams, MA* 238
PATRICIA STAUBLE ANTIQUES, *Wiscasset, ME* 157
JOHN STEELE BOOK SHOP, *Litchfield, CT* 71
STEEPLE BOOKS, *Southbridge, MA* 262
JEF & TERRI STEINGRIBE, *Bradford, NH* 286
SUSAN STELLA ANTIQUES, *Essex, MA* 210
STEPHEN-DOUGLAS ANTIQUES, *Rockingham Village, VT* 367
STERLING AUCTIONS LTD, *Woodbury, CT* 113
STEVENSON GALLERY, *Manchester, VT* 359
STEWARTS OF NEEDHAM, *Needham, MA* 234
THE STITCHERY IN SANDWICH, *Sandwich, MA* 251
D B STOCK PERSIAN CARPETS, *Wellesley, MA* 269
STOCK EXCHANGE, *Barrington, RI* 330
THE STOCK MARKET, *Southport, CT* 97
STOCK TRANSFER, *Milford, CT* 76
EDGAR STOCKWELL DECORATING/ANTIQ, *Orange, MA* 242
EVE STONE & SON ANTIQUES, *Woodbury, CT* 113
STONE HOUSE ANTIQUES, *Seabrook, NH* 320
STONE LEDGE ART GALLERIES, *Noank, CT* 84
STONE OF SCONE ANTIQUES, *Canterbury, CT* 49
STONE SOUP BOOKS, *Camden, ME* 123
STONE VILLAGE ANTIQUARIAN BOOKS, *Chester Depot, VT* 352
STONE'S ANTIQUE SHOP, *Hyannis, MA* 222
STONE'S THROW ANTIQUES, *Lenox, MA* 224
C A STONEHILL INC, *New Haven, CT* 81
STONEWALL ANTIQUES, *Francestown, NH* 295
STONY CREEK VILLAGE STORE, *Stony Creek, CT* 99
THE STORE, INC, *Waitsfield, VT* 373
H RICHARD STRAND FINE ANTIQUES, *Sandwich, MA* 251
STRAWBERRY HILL ANTIQUES, *New Preston, CT* 83
THE STRAWBERRY PATCH, *Brookline, MA* 194
HARRY W STROUSE, *Litchfield, CT* 71
MARY STUART COLLECTION, *Lenox, MA* 224
ROBERT O STUART, *Limington, ME* 136
THE STUDIO, *New Canaan, CT* 78
THE STUFF SHOP, *Ossipee, NH* 315
STURBRIDGE ANTIQUE SHOPS, *Sturbridge, MA* 264
GEORGE SUBKOFF ANTIQUES, INC., *Wilton, CT* 107
SUGAR HOUSE ANTIQUES, *Rutland, VT* 368
GARY SULLIVAN ANTIQUES, *West Townsend, MA* 275
KATHLEEN SULLIVAN-CHILDREN'S BKS, *Coventry, CT* 53
SUMMER HILL SHOP, *Springfield, VT* 371
SUMNER & STILLMAN, *Yarmouth, ME* 158
SUN GALLERIES, *Southbridge, MA* 262
SUNDERLAND PERIOD HOMES INC, *South Windsor, CT* 95
SUNNY DAYS, *Providence, RI* 341
SUNSMITH HOUSE - ANTIQUES, *Brewster, MA* 191
SUZANNE'S BOOK SHOPPE, *Pawtucket, RI* 339
SWEET PEA ANTIQUES, *Old Saybrook, CT* 87

MARY S SWIFT ANTIQUES, *Glastonbury, CT* 62
SYKES & FLANDERS ANTIQUARIAN BKS, *Weare, NH* 324
FRANK F SYLVIA ANTIQUES, *Nantucket, MA* 232
T'OTHER HOUSE ANTIQUES, *Morris, CT* 76
TAILOR'S ANTIQUES, *Burlington, VT* 351
TAKE YOUR LIFE IN YOUR HANDS, *Hanover, NH* 300
TALIN BOOKBINDERY, *Brewster, MA* 191
FRANK J TAMMARO, *Townsend, MA* 267
TANSY FARM ANTIQUES, *Swanton, VT* 372
THE TATES ANTIQUES, *Londonderry, NH* 307
TATEWELL GALLERY, *Hillsboro, NH* 302
LEON TEBBETTS BOOK SHOP, *Hallowell, ME* 132
TEN EYCK BOOKS, *Southborough, MA* 261
TEN EYCK-EMERICH ANTIQUES, *Southport, CT* 97
TEN POUND ISLAND BOOK CO, *Gloucester, MA* 214
TERI ANTIQUES, *Boston, MA* 187
TERRAMEDIA BOOKS, *Wellesley, MA* 269
TEXTILE REPRODUCTIONS, *West Chesterfield, MA* 273
ROBERT THAYER AMERICAN ANTIQUES, *Ashley Falls, MA* 165
CHARLES & PATRICIA THILL ANTIQUE, *Essex (Centerbrook), CT* 60
THINGS OF YESTERYEAR, *Poultney, VT* 366
THINGS, *Westport, CT* 106
THISTLE'S, *Fairfield, ME* 128
ISAIAH THOMAS BOOKS & PRINTS, *Worcester, MA* 280
WM THOMPSON, ANTIQUARIAN BKSELLR, *Greenland, NH* 297
ROY & BETSY THOMPSON ANTIQUES, *Glastonbury, CT* 62
JANET L THOMPSON, *Wakefield, RI* 342
WESTON THORN ANTIQUES, *Bantam, CT* 45
THREE BAGS FULL, *Harvard, MA* 218
THREE RAVENS ANTIQUES, *Salisbury, CT* 92
THREE SEWALL STREET ANTIQUES, *Marblehead, MA* 228
TIGER LILY, *Boston, MA* 187
TIGER LILY, *Newport, RI* 337
C. TILEY ANTIQUES, *Middlebury, VT* 361
TILLER ANTIQUES, *Nantucket, MA* 233
PETER H TILLOU - FINE ARTS, *Litchfield, CT* 71
TIME AFTER TIME, *Danbury, CT* 54
TIME AND AGAIN ANTIQUES, *Round Pond, ME* 147
TIME PAST ANTIQUES, *South Windsor, CT* 95
TIMELESS BOOKS, *New Milford, CT* 82
THE TIN LANTERN, *Windham, CT* 108
TINTAGEL ANTIQUES, *Washington, NH* 324
MAGDA TISZA RARE BOOKS, *Chestnut Hill, MA* 200
TITCOMB'S BOOKSHOP, *East Sandwich, MA* 206
TOBEY HOUSE ANTIQUES, *Sandwich, MA* 252
TODBURN, *Westport, CT* 106
TODD FARM, *Rowley, MA* 249
TONKIN OF NANTUCKET, *Nantucket, MA* 233
TOOMEY'S HAVEN ANTIQUES, *Southborough, MA* 262
TOP KNOTCH ANTIQUES, *Scarborough, ME* 148
TOPSHAM FAIR MALL, *Topsham, ME* 152
TOUCH OF CLASS, *Old Saybrook, CT* 87
A TOUCH OF CLASS, *Cambridge, MA* 197
TOUCHMARK ANTIQUES, *Wolfeboro, NH* 327

TOWN CRIER ANTIQUES, *Yarmouth Port, MA* 282
TOWN PUMP ANTIQUES, *Northwood, NH* 314
TOWNE ANTIQUES, *Brookline Village, MA* 195
THE TOWNE HOUSE, *Jaffrey, NH* 304
THE TOY SHOP, *Southwick, MA* 262
TRADE WINDS GALLERY, *Mystic, CT* 77
TRADE WINDS, THE 1749 HOUSE, *Goshen, CT* 63
TRANQUIL CORNERS ANTIQUES, *Nantucket, MA* 233
TRANQUIL THINGS, *Derby Line, VT* 353
BARBARA B TRASK, APPRAISALS, *Manchester Center, VT* 360
TREASURES & TRIFLES, *Milford, CT* 76
TREBIZOND RARE BOOKS, *New Preston, CT* 83
TREFLER ANTIQUE RESTORING STUDIO, *Newton Highlands, MA* 237
TRI-COUNTY LIQUIDATORS, *New Milford, CT* 82
TRIFLES, *Bath, ME* 118
TRITON ANTIQUES, *Newport, RI* 337
RUTH TROIANI FINE ANTIQUES, *Avon, CT* 45
TROTTING HILL PARK BOOKS, *Springfield, MA* 263
TRUEMAN AUCTION CO, *Newcastle, ME* 140
TRULY UNIQUE ANTIQUES, *Rutland, VT* 368
TRUMPETER, *New Preston, CT* 83
TRUNKWORKS, *Portsmouth, NH* 318
THE TULIP TREE COLLECTION, *Washington Depot, CT* 102
TURKEY HILL BOOKS, *Westport, CT* 106
TURTLE CREEK ANTIQUES, *Essex, CT* 60
TUTTLE ANTIQUARIAN BOOKS INC, *Rutland, VT* 369
KENNETH AND PAULETTE TUTTLE, *Pittston, ME* 144
ESTHER TUVESON, *Needham, MA* 234
TWIN MAPLES ANTIQUES, *Ferrisburg, VT* 356
TWO AT WISCASSET, *Wiscasset, ME* 158
J. OGDEN TYLDSLEY, JR, *Brewster, MA* 191
THE TYPOGRAPHEUM BOOKSHOP, *Francestown, NH* 295
TYSON'S OLD & RARE BOOKS, *Providence, RI* 341
UNA GALLERIES, *St Johnsbury Ctr, VT* 372
UNDER THE DOGWOOD TREE, *Ridgefield, CT* 91
UNDERBRIDGE ANTIQUES, *Shelburne Village, VT* 370
UNICORN ANTIQUES, *Nashua, NH* 311
UNION STREET ANTIQUES, *Salem, MA* 250
UNIQUE ANTIQUES & COLLECTIBLES, *Yalesville, CT* 114
THE UNIQUE ANTIQUE, *Hartford, CT* 67
UNIQUE ANTIQUE, *Putney, VT* 366
UNIQUE ANTIQUES, *Newport, RI* 337
UNITED HOUSE WRECKING, *Stamford, CT* 98
UPLAND ACRES ANTIQUES, *Waterbury, VT* 375
UPTON HOUSE ANTIQUES, *Littleton, MA* 225
VALLEY BOOKS, *Amherst, MA* 163
VALLEY FARM ANTIQUES, *Essex, CT* 60
VALLIN GALLERIES, *Wilton, CT* 107
VALYOU AUCTIONS, *West Newbury, MA* 274
KENNETH W VAN BLARCOM, *Sherborne, MA* 257
VAN CARTER HALE FINE ART, *Clinton, CT* 51
VAN DALE GALLERY, *Providence, RI* 341
VANDERWEG ANTIQUES, *Natick, MA* 234

WILLIAM VAREIKA FINE ARTS, *Newport, RI* 338
VARNEY'S VOLUMES, *South Casco, ME* 150
TOM VEILLEUX GALLERY, *Farmington, ME* 129
MELINDA VENTRE, *Norwalk, CT* 85
VENTURE ANTIQUES, *Portland, ME* 146
VERDE ANTIQUES & BOOKS, *Winsted, CT* 108
VICTORIAN BARN ANTIQUES, *Manchester, NH* 308
VICTORIAN HOUSE BOOK BARN, *Stockton Springs, ME* 151
VICTORIAN LIGHT/WATERTOWER PINES, *Kennebunk, ME* 134
THE VICTORIAN ON MAIN STREET, *Haverhill, NH* 300
VICTORIA PLACE, *Milford, NH* 310
VICTORIA STATION, *Stonington, CT* 99
VILLA'S AUCTION GALLERY, *New Hartford, CT* 79
VILLAGE ANTIQUE GROUP SHOP, *Warren Village, ME* 153
VILLAGE ANTIQUES, *Holden, MA* 220
VILLAGE ANTIQUES, *North Scituate, RI* 338
VILLAGE ANTIQUES, *Rowley, MA* 249
VILLAGE ANTIQUES, *Coventry, CT* 53
THE VILLAGE ATTIC, *Middle Haddam, CT* 74
VILLAGE BARN ANTIQUE COOP, *West Falmouth, MA* 273
VILLAGE BOOKS, *Rumney, NH* 319
VILLAGE FRANCAIS, *New Haven, CT* 81
VILLAGE PEDLAR CLOCK SHOP, *Dennis, MA* 203
VILLAGE STORE OF MIDDLEBURY, *Middlebury, VT* 361
CHARLES VINCENT - BOOKS, *Brunswick, ME* 122
VISUALLY SPEAKING, *Gilford Village, NH* 296
THE VOLLMERS, *Ashley Falls, MA* 165
VOSE GALLERIES OF BOSTON, INC., *Boston, MA* 187
VOSE SMITH ANTIQUES, *Portland, ME* 146
W HARTFORD BK SHOP AT PARK PLACE, *West Hartford, CT* 103
WALDEN'S ANTIQUES & BOOKS, *Lanesborough, MA* 223
WALDRON & RHODES FINE JEWELERS, *Rutland, VT* 369
WALES & HAMBLEN ANTIQUE CENTER, *Bridgton, ME* 121
WALFIELD THISTLE, *Brunswick, ME* 122
ROBERT S WALIN ANTIQUES, *Woodbury, CT* 113
SHIRLEY WALKER ANTIQUES, *Chatham, MA* 199
ALFRED J WALKER FINE ART, *Boston, MA* 188
WALKER HOUSE ANTIQUES, *Hinesburg Village, VT* 358
C WALLENSTEIN AUCTIONWORLD INC, *Concord, NH* 289
WALLINGFORD ANTIQUE CENTER, *Wallingford, VT* 374
WALLINGFORD ANTIQUES COLLECTIVE, *Wallingford, CT* 102
WALNUT HILL ANTIQUES, *Chester, NH* 288
ANN & DAN WALSH, *Dublin, NH* 291
JOHN WALTON INC, *Jewett City, CT* 68
WALTS ANTIQUES, *Norwich, CT* 86
BARBARA WALZER, BOOKSELLER, *Providence, RI* 341
WARD'S BOOK BARN, *Steep Falls, ME* 151

MARIA & PETER WARREN ANTIQUES, *Wilton, CT* 108
WARREN ANTIQUES, *Warren, VT* 374
WASHINGTON STREET BOOK STORE, *South Norwalk, CT* 94
WATER STREET ANTIQUES, *Stonington, CT* 99
WATERBORO EMPORIUM, *Waterboro, ME* 153
WATERCRESS ANTIQUES, *Meriden, NH* 310
H B & DOROTHY WATSON, *Wellfleet, MA* 270
WAYLAND ANTIQUE EXCHANGE, *Wayland, MA* 269
WAYSIDE ANTIQUES, *Marlboro, MA* 229
WAYSIDE EXCHANGE, *Wilton, CT* 108
WEBB & PARSONS NORTH, *Burlington, VT* 351
H G WEBBER, *Hampton, NH* 298
WEE BARN ANTIQUES, *Thomaston, ME* 151
WEINER'S ANTIQUE SHOP, *Boston, MA* 188
I M WIESE, ANTIQUARIAN, *Southbury, CT* 96
SAMUEL WEISER BOOKS, *York Beach, ME* 159
DAVID M WEISS, *Sheffield, MA* 257
ED WEISSMAN, *Portsmouth, NH* 318
MARGARET & PAUL WELD, *Middletown, CT* 75
WELL SWEEP ANTIQUES, *Hillsboro, NH* 302
WELLS ANTIQUE MART, *Wells, ME* 155
WELLS UNION ANTIQUE CENTER, *Wells, ME* 155
WENHAM CROSS ANTIQUES, *Boston, MA* 188
MADELINE WEST ANTIQUES, *Woodbury, CT* 113
WEST COUNTRY ANTIQUES, *Woodbury, CT* 113
WEST GATE ANTIQUES, *New Haven, CT* 81
WESTERLY ENTERPRISES, *Westerly, RI* 344
WESTERN HEMISPHERE INC, *Stoughton, MA* 264
WESTFORD VALLEY ANTIQUES, *Westford, MA* 276
MICHAEL WESTMAN FINE ARTS, *Newport, RI* 338
WESTVILLE ANTIQUE CENTER, *New Haven, CT* 81
ELDRED WHEELER, *Osterville, MA* 243
THE WHIPPLETREE, *West Barnstable, MA* 271
RICHARD WHITE ANTIQUES, *Winchester, NH* 327
WHITE BARN ANTIQUES, *Augusta, ME* 117
WHITE DOVE ANTIQUES, *Georgetown-Wilton, CT* 62
THE WHITE ELEPHANT SHOP, *Essex, MA* 210
WHITE FARMS ANTIQUES, *Essex, CT* 60
GUSTAVES J.S. WHITE, *Newport, RI* 338
THE WHITE HOUSE ANTIQUES, *Northwood, NH* 315
WHITLEY GALLERY, *Old Lyme, CT* 86
WHITLOCK FARM, BOOKSELLERS, *Bethany, CT* 45
WHITLOCK'S INC, *New Haven, CT* 81
FRED P WHITTIER III, *Weare, NH* 324
THE WICKER LADY INC, *Needham, MA* 234
THE WICKER PORCH, *Nantucket, MA* 233
LILLIAN WIENER, *Bedford, NH* 286
WIKHEGAN BOOKS, *Mount Desert Island, ME* 138
WILD GOOSE CHASE, *Haddam, CT* 66
WILDER SHOP, *Holliston, MA* 220
WILDFLOWER, *Coventry, CT* 54
WILKERSON BOOKS, *Lincoln, MA* 225
WILLARD RESTORATIONS INC, *Old Wethersfield, CT* 87
LYNDA WILLAUER ANTIQUES, *Nantucket, MA* 233

WILLIAMS PORT ANTIQUES, *Rowayton, CT* 91
ROBERT B WILLIAMS, *Bethany, CT* 45
THOMAS D & CONSTANCE R WILLIAMS, *Litchfield, CT* 71
BETTY WILLIS ANTIQUES, INC, *Marlborough, NH* 308
PEG WILLIS ANTIQUES, *Westwood, MA* 277
WILLOW HOLLOW ANTIQUES, *Northwood, NH* 315
WILLOWBROOK, *West Bridgewater, MA* 272
WILMA'S ANTIQUES & ACCESSORIES, *Portland, ME* 146
WILMINGTON FLEA MARKET, *Wilmington, VT* 376
WIND-BORNE FRAME & RESTORATION, *Darien, CT* 56
WINDFALL ANTIQUES, *Kennebunkport, ME* 135
WINDHAM ANTIQUES, *West Lebanon, NH* 325
WINDSOR ANTIQUES MARKET, *Windsor, VT* 376
WINDSOR ANTIQUES LTD, *Darien, CT* 56
THE WINDSOR CHAIR, *Kittery, ME* 136
WINDY TOP ANTIQUES, *Rockport, ME* 147
WING CARRIAGE HOUSE, *Westport, MA* 277
WINGS OF A DOVE CONSIGNMENT, *Norwalk, CT* 85
WINSOR ANTIQUES, *Fairfield, CT* 61
WINTER ASSOCIATES INC, *Plainville, CT* 88
WINTER HILL FARM, *Kennebunkport, ME* 136
WISCASSET BAY GALLERY, *Wiscasset, ME* 158
ALEXANDRA WISE ANTIQUES, *Stamford, CT* 98
WISHING WELL ANTIQUES, *Milford, CT* 76
WISTERIA TREE, *Portsmouth, NH* 318
WISWALL HOUSE, *Durham, NH* 291
RICHARD W WITHINGTON AUCTIONEER, *Hillsboro, NH* 302
LAURENCE WITTEN RARE BOOKS, *Southport, CT* 97
MANFRED R WOERNER, *Westerly, RI* 344
WOMEN'S WORDS BOOKS, *Hopkinton, NH* 303
CHARLES B WOOD, III INC, *Boston, MA* 189
STEPHANIE ADAMS WOOD, *Saunderstown, RI* 342
WOOD*WORKS, *Litchfield, CT* 71
WOOD-SHED ANTIQUES, *Amherst, MA* 163
WAYNE & PEGGY WOODARD ANTIQUES, *Hopkinton, NH* 303
WOODBRIDGE BOOK STORE, *Woodbridge, CT* 108
WOODBURY BLACKSMITH & FORGE CO, *Woodbury, CT* 113
WOODBURY HOMESTEAD ANTIQUES, *Francestown, NH* 295
WOODBURY HOUSE, *Woodbury, CT* 114
WOODBURY PEWTERERS, *Woodbury, CT* 114
WOODS ANTIQUES, *Pawcatuck, CT* 88
JOHN A WOODS, APPRAISERS, *South Windsor, CT* 95
F P WOODS, BOOKS, *Saco, ME* 148
WOODSHED ANTIQUES, *Grafton, VT* 356
WOODWARDS ANTIQUES, *Marlborough, NH* 309
GARY W WOOLSON, BOOKSELLER, *Hamden, ME* 132
WRENTHAM ANTIQUE COMPANY, *Wrentham, MA* 280
WRIGHT TAVERN ANTIQUES, *Templeton, MA* 266
WYNDHURST FARM ANTIQUES, *Hillsboro, NH* 302

THE YANKEE BOOK & ART GALLERY, *Plymouth, MA* 246
YANKEE CRAFTSMAN, *Wayland, MA* 269
YANKEE GEM CORP, *Roxbury, ME* 147
YANKEE HERITAGE ANTIQUES, *West Boylston, MA* 272
YANKEE MAID ANTIQUES, *Wallingford, VT* 374
THE YANKEE MERCHANT GROUP, *Boston, MA* 189
YANKEE PEDLAR'S ANTIQUES, *Essex Junction, VT* 355
YANKEE TRADER, *Brewster, MA* 191
THE YARD SALE, *Keene, NH* 305
YARMOUTHPORT ANTIQUES, *Yarmouth Port, MA* 282

YE OLDE LANTERN ANTIQUES, *Rockport, MA* 248
YE OLDE SHAVEHORSE WORKSHOP, *Wilmot Flat, NH* 326
YE PRINTERS' ANTIQUES, *Rockland, MA* 248
YELLOW HOUSE ANTIQUES, *Reading, VT* 367
YESTERDAY'S THREADS, *Branford, CT* 47
YESTERDAYS ANTIQUE CENTER, *Sturbridge, MA* 264
YESTERYEAR SHOP, *Coventry, VT* 352
YORKSHIRE HOUSE, *Brewster, MA* 191
YOUNG FINE ARTS GALLERY, INC., *North Berwick, ME* 141
PRISCILLA H ZIESMER, *Pomfret Center, CT* 89
ZIMMERS HEIRLOOM CLOCKS, *Trumbull, CT* 101

PAGE NUMBERS FOR QUICKCODE™ INDEX

1 Americana 407
2 Andirons/Fenders 408
3 Antiquities 408
4 Appraisal 408
5 Architectural Antiques 409
6 Arms/Military 409
7 Art Deco/Art Nouveau 409
8 Auction 410
9 Autographs/Manuscripts 411
10 Barometers 411
11 Baseball Cards 411
12 Bookbinding/Restoration 411
13 Books/Antiquarian 411
14 Books 415
15 Bottles 415
16 Brass/Copper/Metalwork 415
17 Bronzes 416
18 Buttons/Badges 416
19 Cabinet Makers 416
20 Cameras/Daguerreotypes 416
21 Carpets/Rugs 416
22 Chair Caning 417
23 Clocks/Watches 417
24 Coins/Medals 418
25 Conservation 418
26 Consultation/Research 418
27 Country Antiques 419
28 Crocks/Stoneware 420
29 Decorative Accessories 421
30 Decoys 422
31 Display Stands/Glass 422
32 Dolls/Toys 422
33 Ephemera 423
34 Folk Art 423
35 French Antiques 424
36 Furniture 424
37 Furniture/American 427
38 Furniture/Continental 428
39 Furniture/English 429
40 Furniture/Oak 429
41 Furniture/Painted 430
42 Furniture/Pine 430
43 Furniture/Reproduction 431
44 Glass 431

45 Garden Statuary 433
46 Interior Decoration 433
47 Jewelry 433
48 Lace/Linen 434
49 Lead Soldiers 435
50 Lighting 435
51 Maps 436
52 Miniatures 436
53 Mirrors 436
54 Models 436
55 Music/Musical Instruments 437
56 Nautical/Marine Items 437
57 Needlework/Samplers 437
58 Objets d'Art 437
59 Oil Paintings 438
60 Oriental Art 439
61 Paperweights 440
62 Photographs 440
63 Porcelain/Pottery 440
64 Post Cards 442
65 Primitives 442
66 Prints/Drawings 443
67 Quilts/Patchwork 444
68 Repairs 445
69 Replication 445
70 Reproduction 445
71 Restoration 446
72 Scientific/Medical Instruments 447
73 Sculpture 447
74 Services to Period Homes 447
75 Shipping/Packing/Storage 448
76 Shop Signs 448
77 Silver 448
78 Sporting Art/Equipment 448
79 Stamps 449
80 Textiles 449
81 Tools 449
82 Tribal Art 449
83 Victorian Antiques 450
84 Vintage Cars/Carriages 450
85 Vintage Clothing/Costumes 450
86 Wicker 450
87 Weather Vanes 451

INDEX BY QUICKCODE™
CATEGORY

1 Americana

Connecticut

Ashford, *MERRYTHOUGHT* 44
Bolton, *AUTUMN POND ANTIQUES* 46
Canterbury, *STONE OF SCONE ANTIQUES* 49
Cornwall Bridge, *THE BRASS BUGLE* 52
Darien, *DORRIE SCHREINER GALLERY ANTIQUE* 56
Essex, *FRANCIS BEALEY AMERICAN ARTS* 59
Glastonbury, *ROY & BETSY THOMPSON ANTIQUES* 62
Greenwich, *DAVID A SCHORSCH* 65
Guilford, *CORNUCOPIA ANTIQUE CONSIGNMENTS* 66
Jewett City, *JOHN WALTON INC* 68
Middletown, *MARGARET & PAUL WELD* 75
Plainville, *WINTER ASSOCIATES INC* 88
Pomfret Center, *MEADOW ROCK FARM ANTIQUES* 89
Ridgefield, *THE RED PETTICOAT* 91
Salisbury, *THREE RAVENS ANTIQUES* 92
Stonington, *ANN LEHMANN ANTIQUES* 98
Stonington, *MARGUERITE RIORDAN* 99
Woodbury, *CARRIAGE HOUSE ANTIQUES* 109
Woodbury, *HAROLD E COLE ANTIQUES* 110
Woodbury, *DAVID DUNTON/ANTIQUES* 111
Woodbury, *ART & PEGGY PAPPAS ANTIQUES* 112
Woodbury, *WOODBURY HOUSE* 114

Maine

Bar Harbor, *ROSE W OLSTEAD* 117
Camden, *SCHUELER ANTIQUES* 123
Cape Elizabeth, *HANSON'S CARRIAGE HOUSE* 123
Deer Isle, *BELCHER'S ANTIQUES* 126
Hallowell, *JAMES H. LE FURGY BOOKS & ANT.* 131
Hope, *THE BLUEBERRY PATCH* 132
Limerick, *TOM JOSEPH & DAVID RAMSAY* 136
North Edgecomb, *THE DITTY BOX* 141
North Edgecomb, *JACK PARTRIDGE* 141
Northeast Harbor, *PINE BOUGH* 142
South China, *COUNTRY ANTIQUES* 150
Wiscasset, *MARSTON HOUSE AMERICAN ANTIQUES* 156
Wiscasset, *TWO AT WISCASSET* 158

Massachusetts

Arlington, *IRREVERENT RELICS* 164
Ashley Falls, *ROBERT THAYER AMERICAN ANTIQUES* 165
Boston, *H GROSSMAN* 178
Boston, *HALEY & STEELE INC* 178
Boston, *HERITAGE ART* 178
Boston, *SAMUEL L LOWE JR ANTIQUES INC* 181
Boston, *THE NOSTALGIA FACTORY* 182
Charlestown, *THE FISKE HOUSE* 198
Chesterfield, *CHESTERFIELD ANTIQUES* 199
Dedham, *DEDHAM ANTIQUE SHOP* 202
Dennis, *ELLIPSE ANTIQUES* 202
Groton, *BOSTON ROAD ANTIQUES* 216
Groton, *JOS KILBRIDGE CHINA TRADE ANTIQU* 216
Halifax, *WILLEM & INGER LEMMENS ANTIQUES* 218
Lee, *FERRELL'S ANTIQUES & WOODWORKING* 223
Nantucket, *FORAGER HOUSE COLLECTION* 231
Nantucket, *NINA HELLMAN* 231
Nantucket, *ISLAND ATTIC INDUSTRIES INC* 231
Orleans, *LILAC HEDGE ANTIQUES* 243
Plainville, *BRIAR PATCH ANTIQUES & COLLECTIB* 245
Provincetown, *JULIE HELLER GALLERY* 246
Sheffield, *DAVID M WEISS* 257
South Egremont, *BIRD CAGE ANTIQUES* 259
South Orleans, *PLEASANT BAY ANTIQUES* 261
Sudbury, *FARMHOUSE COLLECTIBLES* 265
Upton, *DAVID ROSE ANTIQUES* 267
Worthington, *COUNTRY CRICKET VILLAGE INN* 280

New Hampshire

Bedford, *DRUMMER BOY ANTIQUES* 286
Concord, *VERNA H MORRILL* 289
Fitzwilliam, *WILLIAM LEWAN ANTIQUES* 294
Hampton, *RONALD BOURGEAULT ANTIQUES* 297
Hampton, *HEYDAY ANTIQUES OF HAMPTON* 298
Manchester, *VICTORIAN BARN ANTIQUES* 308
Moultonboro, *ANTIQUES AT MOULTONBORO* 311
Rochester, *PETER CARSWELL ANTIQUES* 319
Stratham, *COMPASS ROSE ANTIQUES* 321
Stratham, *JOHN PIPER HOUSE* 321
Tuftonboro, *LOG CABIN ANTIQUES* 322
Wentworth, *RETOUCH THE PAST* 324
Winchester, *RICHARD WHITE ANTIQUES* 327

Rhode Island

Charlestown, *SALT BOX ANTIQUES* 331
Newport, *R KAZARIAN* 335

Newport, *OLD FASHION SHOP* 337
Providence, *CAROL LOMBARDI ANTIQUES* 340

Vermont

East Montpelier, *JEFFREY R CUETO ANTIQUES* 354
Grafton, *GABRIELS' BARN ANTIQUES* 356
Johnson, *MEL SIEGEL ANTIQUES* 358
Reading, *YELLOW HOUSE ANTIQUES* 367
Rockingham Village, *STEPHEN-DOUGLAS ANTIQUES* 367
Saxtons River, *SCHOOLHOUSE ANTIQUES* 369
Saxtons River, *SIGN OF THE RAVEN* 369
Shelburne, *HARRINGTON HOUSE 1800* 370
Townshend, *COLT BARN ANTIQUES* 373

2 Andirons/Fenders

Connecticut

Essex, *THE ESSEX FORGE* 59
Middletown, *MARGARET & PAUL WELD* 75
Westbrook, *HANES RUSKIN* 104
Woodbury, *KENNETH HAMMITT ANTIQUES* 111
Woodbury, *NEW ENGLAND FIREBACKS* 112
Woodbury, *WOODBURY BLACKSMITH & FORGE CO* 113

Maine

Wells, *R JORGENSEN ANTIQUES* 154

Massachusetts

Amherst, *R & R FRENCH ANTIQUES* 162
Boston, *HOWARD CHADWICK ANTIQUES* 173
Brewster, *THE PFLOCK'S-ANTIQUES* 190
Brimfield, *BRIMFIELD ANTIQUES* 192
Marblehead, *S & S GALLERIES* 228
Sandwich, *SHAWME POND ANTIQUES* 251

New Hampshire

Hudson, *COLONIAL SHOPPE* 304

Vermont

Shraftsbury, *NORMAN GRONNING ANTIQ/ARCH ITEMS* 370

3 Antiquities

Maine

Boothbay Harbor, *BAY STREET ANTIQUES* 120
Newcastle, *NEWCASTLE ANTIQUES* 140

Massachusetts

Cambridge, *BERNHEIMER'S ANTIQUE ARTS* 195
Cambridge, *HURST GALLERY* 196
South Natick, *COMING OF AGE ANTIQUES* 261

4 Appraisal

Connecticut

Cheshire, *J MUENNICH ASSOCIATES, INC* 50
Chester, *SAGE AUCTION GALLERIES* 51
Clinton, *VAN CARTER HALE FINE ART* 51
Colebrook, *RINHART GALLERIES* 52
Coventry, *ALLINSON GALLERY INC* 53
Essex, *ESSEX AUCTION & APPRAISAL* 59
Fairfield, *G G G ANTIQUES* 61
Greenwich, *BETTERIDGE JEWELERS INC* 64
Greenwich, *CHELSEA ANTIQUES OF GREENWICH* 64
Greenwich, *SCHUTZ & COMPANY* 65
Madison, *SHAFER AUCTION GALLERY* 73

Newtown, *MARIE LOUISE KANE* 84
Norwalk, *KEVIN B MCCLELLAN* 85
Ridgefield, *GERALD GRUNSELL & ASSOCIATES* 90
South Glastonbury, *RIBA AUCTIONS* 93
South Windsor, *JOHN A WOODS, APPRAISERS* 95
Southport, *HANSEN & CO* 96
Southport, *POMEROY ANDERSON* 96
Stamford, *FENDELMAN & SCHWARTZ* 97
Trumbull, *APPRAISAL ASSOCIATES* 101
Wallingford, *MAISON AUCTION COMPANY INC* 102
West Hartford, *SAMUEL S T CHEN* 103
West Hartford, *ALICE KUGELMAN* 103
Westport, *CONNECTICUT FINE ARTS, INC* 105
Wethersfield, *CLEARING HOUSE AUCTION GALLERIES* 106
Wilton, *AMABEL BARROWS ANTIQUES* 107
Winthrop, *JAS E ELLIOTT ANTIQUES* 108
Woodbury, *WOODBURY HOUSE* 114

Maine

Kennebunk, *JUDITH A KEATING, GG* 133
Portland, *F O BAILEY ANTIQUARIANS* 144

Massachusetts

Auburn, *KENNETH ANDERSON* 165
Beverly, *A R M ASSOCIATES* 166
Bolton, *ROBERT W SKINNER INC* 167
Boston, *BRATTLE BOOK SHOP* 171
Boston, *BROMER BOOKSELLERS INC* 171
Boston, *MAURY A BROMSEN ASSOCIATES, INC* 173
Boston, *GROGAN & COMPANY* 178
Boston, *HARPER & FAYE INC* 178
Boston, *LYNNE KORTENHAUS* 180
Boston, *LEON OHANIAN & SONS CO INC* 185
Boston, *ROSE & CLEAVES* 185
Brookline, *NANCY A SMITH APPRAISAL ASSOC* 194
Cambridge, *F B HUBLEY & CO* 196
Cambridge, *HURST GALLERY* 196
Chestnut Hill, *DALE POLLOCK APPRAISAL SERVICES* 199
Dedham, *CENTURY SHOP* 202
East Dennis, *ROBERT C ELDRED CO, INC* 205
Essex, *L A LANDRY ANTIQUES* 209
Foxboro, *SILVER LADY ANTIQUES* 212
Gloucester, *GLOUCESTER FINE ARTS & ANTIQUARI* 214
Gloucester, *TEN POUND ISLAND BOOK CO* 214
Halifax, *WILLEM & INGER LEMMENS ANTIQUES* 218
Hingham, *PIERCE GALLERIES INC* 220
Hyannis, *RICHARD A BOURNE CO INC* 221
Hyannis, *HYANNIS AUCTION* 221
Lee, *CAROPRESO GALLERY* 223
Lee, *HENRY B HOLT INC* 223
Lowell, *R P DURKIN & COMPANY INC* 226
Marshfield, *WILLIS HENRY AUCTIONS* 229
Nantucket, *RAFAEL OSONA AUCTIONEER* 232
Needham, *HORST KLOSS* 234
Newburyport, *CHRISTOPHER L SNOW ASSOCIATES* 236
Orleans, *FRANK H HOGAN FINE ARTS INC* 243
Salem, *AMERICAN MARINE MODEL GALLERY* 249
Salem, *JER-RHO ANTIQUES* 250
Salem, *MARINE ARTS GALLERY* 250
Seekonk, *LEONARD'S ANTIQUES, INC.* 252

South Deerfield, *DOUGLAS AUCTIONEERS* 259
West Bridgewater, *SHUTE AUCTION GALLERY* 272
Williamsburg, *GEORGE THOMAS LEWIS* 278

New Hampshire
Francestown, *BERT MC CLEARY AUCTIONEER* 294
Hampton, *RONALD BOURGEAULT ANTIQUES* 297
Hampton, *NORTHEAST AUCTIONS* 298
Henniker, *RONALD J ROSENBLEETH INC* 301
Hillsboro, *RICHARD W WITHINGTON AUCTIONEER* 302
Hollis, *COUGHLIN ANTIQUE/ESTATE APPRAISA* 303
Northwood, *HARTLEY'S ANTIQUES* 314
Plainfield, *PLAINFIELD AUCTION GALLERY* 316

Rhode Island
Newport, *BELLEVUE GOLD* 333
Newport, *ROGER KING GALLERY OF FINE ART* 335
Newport, *NEWPORT FINE ARTS INVESTMENT CO* 336
Providence, *ASSOCIATES APPRAISERS INC* 339
Providence, *CHAMBERLAIN ANTIQUES LTD* 340

Vermont
Brattleboro, *PAUL LAWTON & SON* 349
Manchester Center, *BARBARA B TRASK, APPRAISALS* 360
Reading, *YELLOW HOUSE ANTIQUES* 367
Rutland, *WALDRON & RHODES FINE JEWELERS* 369

5 Architectural Antiques

Connecticut
Ashford, *JERALD PAUL JORDON GALLERY* 44
Greenwich, *BANKSVILLE ANTIQUES* 64
Middletown, *MARGARET & PAUL WELD* 75
New Haven, *PETER G HILL & ASSOCIATES* 80
Redding, *SERGEANT* 90
South Willington, *SOUTH WILLINGTON ANTIQUES* 94
Southbury, *I M WIESE, ANTIQUARIAN* 96
Stamford, *UNITED HOUSE WRECKING* 98
Woodbury, *ART & PEGGY PAPPAS ANTIQUES* 112
Woodbury, *RAMASE* 113

Maine
Belfast, *APEX ANTIQUES* 118
Damariscotta, *PATRICIA ANNE REED ANTIQUES* 125
Kennebunkport, *ANTIQUES AT NINE* 134
Limerick, *TOM JOSEPH & DAVID RAMSAY* 136
Sanford, *JOHN LEEKE, PRESERVATION CONSULT* 148
Wells, *RIVERBANK ANTIQUES* 154

Massachusetts
Boston, *TIGER LILY* 187
Dorchester, *OLDE BOSTONIAN* 204
Hanover, *RESTORATION RESOURCES* 218
Marblehead, *EVIE'S CORNER* 227
Northampton, *RUMPLESTILTSKIN* 241
Pittsfield, *BERKSHIRE ANTIQUES* 245
Rowley, *NORTH FIELDS RESTORATIONS* 249
Somerville, *LONDONTOWNE GALLERIES* 258

Swansea, *FERGUSON & D'ARRUDA* 265
West Barnstable, *SALT & CHESTNUT WEATHERVANES* 271

New Hampshire
Deerfield, *DAVID OTTINGER* 290
Hampton, *GARGOYLES & GRIFFINS* 298
Lyme Center, *JOAN & GAGE ELLIS* 308
South Hampton, *R G BETTCHER RESTORATIONS* 320

Rhode Island
Ashaway, *STEPHEN P MACK* 330
Newport, *AARDVARK ANTIQUES* 333
Newport, *R KAZARIAN* 335

Vermont
Montpelier, *GREAT AMERICAN SALVAGE COMPANY* 362
Shraftsbury, *NORMAN GRONNING ANTIQ/ARCH ITEMS* 370

6 Arms/Military

Connecticut
Canterbury, *STONE OF SCONE ANTIQUES* 49
East Haddam, *CENTERPIECE ANTIQUES* 57
Essex, *VALLEY FARM ANTIQUES* 60
Greenwich, *HALLOWELL & CO* 65
Madison, *ORDNANCE CHEST* 72
Southport, *HANSEN & CO* 96

Maine
Brewer, *MCLEOD MILITARY ANTIQUES* 121
Gardiner, *FRED ROBBINS* 130
Roxbury, *YANKEE GEM CORP* 147

Massachusetts
Ashley Falls, *THE VOLLMERS* 165
Brewster, *THE HOMESTEAD ANTIQUES* 190
Malden, *EXCALIBUR HOBBIES* 226

New Hampshire
Bedford, *DRUMMER BOY ANTIQUES* 286
Bridgewater, *IDLE-A-WHILE COUNTRY ANTIQUES* 286
Stratham, *COMPASS ROSE ANTIQUES* 321

Vermont
Dorset, *AMERICAN SPORTING ANTIQUES* 353

7 Art Deco/Art Nouveau

Connecticut
Suffield, *NIKKI & TOM DEUPREE* 100
Westport, *FRIEDMAN GALLERY* 105

Maine
Auburn, *ORPHAN ANNIE'S* 116
Bernard, *ONCE UPON A TIME* 119
Portland, *NELSON RARITIES, INC* 145

Massachusetts
Acton, *SEAGULL ANTIQUES* 162
Boston, *DIVINE DECADENCE* 175
Boston, *FUSCO & FOUR ASSOCIATES* 176
Boston, *KNOLLWOOD ANTIQUES* 180
Brookline Village, *BECKERMAN NEAL ANTIQUES* 194
Brookline, *ANTIQUERS III* 192
Brookline, *APPLETON ANTIQUES* 192
Newburyport, *ELIZABETH'S 20TH CENTURY* 235
Norfolk, *ROBERT F. GRABOWSKY* 238

Northampton, *AMERICAN DECORATIVE ARTS* 240

Provincetown, *INTERIOR ARTS GALLERY* 246

Provincetown, *REMEMBRANCES OF THINGS PAST* 246

Rockport, *RECUERDO* 248

Sandwich, *THE BROWN JUG* 251

New Hampshire

Tuftonboro Corner, *DOW'S CORNER SHOP* 322

Rhode Island

Newport, *FULL SWING* 334

Vermont

Fairfax, *THE CAT'S MEOW ANTIQUES* 355

8 Auction

Connecticut

Canton, *CANTON BARN AUCTIONS* 50

Chester, *SAGE AUCTION GALLERIES* 51

Colchester, *NADEAU'S AUCTION GALLERY* 52

Essex, *ESSEX AUCTION & APPRAISAL* 59

Fairfield, *CONNECTICUT BOOK AUCTION* 60

Jewett City, *LEONE'S AUCTION GALLERY* 68

Litchfield, *LITCHFIELD AUCTION GALLERY* 71

Madison, *SHAFER AUCTION GALLERY* 73

New Hartford, *VILLA'S AUCTION GALLERY* 79

New Milford, *AUCTION BARN* 82

New Milford, *TRI-COUNTY LIQUIDATORS* 82

Norwalk, *KEVIN B MCCLELLAN* 85

Plainville, *GOLDEN SALES & AUCTIONS* 88

Plainville, *WINTER ASSOCIATES INC* 88

South Glastonbury, *RIBA AUCTIONS* 93

Southport, *JOSKO & SONS AUCTIONS* 96

Sterling, *ROBERT H GLASS AUCTIONEERS* 98

Torrington, *COUNTRY AUCTION SERVICE* 100

Wallingford, *MAISON AUCTION COMPANY INC* 102

Wethersfield, *CLEARING HOUSE AUCTION GALLERIES* 106

Willimantic, *ERNEST ELDRIDGE AUCTIONEER* 107

Woodbury, *STERLING AUCTIONS LTD* 113

Woodstock Valley, *NORMAN C HECKLER & CO* 114

Woodstock, *ARMAN ABSENTEE AUCTION* 114

Maine

Anson, *PHILL A MC INTYRE & DAUGHTERS* 116

Belfast, *ANDREWS & ANDREWS* 118

Denmark, *BRUCE D COLLINS FINE ART* 126

Denmark, *C E GUARINO* 126

Eliot, *SEABOARD AUCTION GALLERY* 127

Fairfield, *JAMES D JULIA AUCTIONEERS* 128

Kennebunk, *J J KEATING INC* 133

Kennebunk, *RICHARD W OLIVER AUCTIONEERS* 133

Mechanic Falls, *MCMORROW AUCTION COMPANY* 138

New Sharon, *FREDERICK BAUER* 139

Newcastle, *FOSTER'S AUCTION GALLERY* 140

Newcastle, *TRUEMAN AUCTION CO* 140

Portland, *F O BAILEY ANTIQUARIANS* 144

Yarmouth, *GERALD W BELL AUCTIONEER* 158

York, *MARITIME AUCTIONS* 159

Massachusetts

Abington, *ABINGTON AUCTION GALLERY* 162

Bolton, *ROBERT W SKINNER INC* 167

Boston, *GROGAN & COMPANY* 178

Boston, *ROSE & CLEAVES* 185

Boston, *ROBERT W SKINNER INC* 187

Boston, *SOTHEBY'S* 187

Cambridge, *JAMES R BAKKER ANTIQUES INC.* 195

Cambridge, *F B HUBLEY & CO* 196

Cambridge, *CARL R NORDBLOM* 197

Dedham, *CENTURY SHOP* 202

East Dennis, *ROBERT C ELDRED CO, INC* 205

Essex, *BLACKWOOD MARCH* 208

Essex, *L A LANDRY ANTIQUES* 209

Halifax, *JOAN F CADDIGAN* 217

Hyannis, *RICHARD A BOURNE CO INC* 221

Hyannis, *HYANNIS AUCTION* 221

Lee, *CAROPRESO GALLERY* 223

Lowell, *R P DURKIN & COMPANY INC* 226

Marshfield, *WILLIS HENRY AUCTIONS* 229

Nantucket, *RAFAEL OSONA AUCTIONEER* 232

Newburyport, *CHRISTOPHER L SNOW ASSOCIATES* 236

North Amherst, *PIONEER AUCTION OF AMHERST* 239

North Brookfield Ctr, *PAUL R LANGEVIN AUCTIONEER* 240

North Eastham, *EASTHAM AUCTION HOUSE* 240

Pittsfield, *FONTAINE'S AUCTION GALLERY* 245

Sandwich, *SANDWICH AUCTION HOUSE* 251

Sheffield, *BRADFORD GALLERIES, LTD* 254

Sherborne, *KENNETH W VAN BLARCOM* 257

South Bellingham, *COYLE'S AUCTION GALLERY* 258

South Deerfield, *DOUGLAS AUCTIONEERS* 259

South Deerfield, *INTERNATIONAL AUCTION SCHOOL* 259

Stoneham, *FRANK C KAMINSKI* 263

Waltham, *FIREMATIC SPECIALTIES* 268

West Bridgewater, *SHUTE AUCTION GALLERY* 272

West Newbury, *VALYOU AUCTIONS* 274

Williamsburg, *GEORGE THOMAS LEWIS* 278

New Hampshire

Concord, *C WALLENSTEIN AUCTIONWORLD INC* 289

Dover, *MICHAEL G BENNETT AUCTIONS* 290

Francestown, *BERT MC CLEARY AUCTIONEER* 294

Greenland, *DANIEL OLMSTEAD ANTIQUES/AUCTION* 297

Hampton Falls, *PAUL MC INNIS, INC.* 299

Hampton, *NORTHEAST AUCTIONS* 298

Henniker, *RONALD J ROSENBLEETH INC* 301

Hillsboro, *RICHARD W WITHINGTON AUCTIONEER* 302

North Weare, *NEW HAMPSHIRE BOOK AUCTIONS* 313

Plainfield, *PLAINFIELD AUCTION GALLERY* 316

Tamworth, *SANDERS & MOCK, ASSOCIATES* 322

Weare, *FRED P WHITTIER III* 324

Wolfeboro, *AUCTIONS BY BOWERS & MERENA, INC* 327

Rhode Island

Newport, *GUSTAVES J.S. WHITE* 338

Providence, *ASSOCIATES APPRAISERS INC* 339

Smithfield, *MARTY'S ANTIQUE AUCTION SERVICE* 342

West Greenwich, *MARTONE'S GALLERY* 343

Vermont
Brattleboro, *PAUL LAWTON & SON* 349
Hardwick, *WILLIAM F HILL* 357
Milton, *BARSALOW AUCTIONS* 362
Pittsford, *IRON HORSE ANTIQUES, INC* 365
Williston, *DUANE E MERRILL* 376

9 Autographs/Manuscripts

Connecticut
Branford, *BRANFORD RARE BOOK & ART GALLERY* 47
Cos Cob, *THE BOOK BLOCK* 52
New Haven, *C A STONEHILL INC* 81
New Preston, *TRUMPETER* 83
Southport, *LAURENCE WITTEN RARE BOOKS* 97
Wilton, *ARCHIVES HISTORICAL AUTOGRAPHS* 107

Maine
Dresden, *MATHOM BOOKSHOP & BINDERY* 126
Eliot, *BOOKS & AUTOGRAPHS* 127
Northport, *LORD SEAGRAVE'S* 142
Portland, *CARLSON AND TURNER BOOKS* 144
Portland, *F M O'BRIEN-ANTIQUARIAN BOOKS* 145
Wells, *THE BOOK BARN* 153
Wells, *EAST COAST BOOKS* 154
Wells, *SNUG HARBOR BOOKS* 155

Massachusetts
Blandford, *ROBERT F LUCAS* 166
Boston, *BOSTON BOOK ANNEX* 171
Boston, *BRATTLE BOOK SHOP* 171
Boston, *MAURY A BROMSEN ASSOCIATES, INC* 173
Boston, *PRISCILLA JUVELIS INC* 180
Fairhaven, *BARRY SCOTT* 210
Gardner, *PAUL C RICHARDS AUTOGRAPHS* 212
Great Barrington, *J & J LUBRANO ANTIQUARIAN BOOKS* 215
Great Barrington, *GEORGE R MINKOFF, INC* 215
Newton, *KENNETH W RENDELL, INC* 237
Onset, *JOSEPH A DERMONT, BOOKSELLER* 242
Randolph, *B & B AUTOGRAPHS* 247
Sharon, *PEPPER & STERN RARE BOOKS, INC* 253
Sheffield, *HOWARD S MOTT INC* 255
Waban, *DIANA J RENDELL, INC* 268
Weston, *M & S RARE BOOKS, INC* 277

New Hampshire
Hillsboro, *THE SHADOW SHOP* 302
Hollis, *GEORGE LABARRE GALLERIES, INC.* 303

Vermont
Norwich, *F J MANASEK* 364
Putney, *UNIQUE ANTIQUE* 366
Woodstock, *PLEASANT STREET BOOKS* 377

10 Barometers

Maine
Cushing, *NEVILLE ANTIQUES* 125

Massachusetts
Chatham, *THE SPYGLASS* 199

New Hampshire
Portsmouth, *SAUNDERS & COOKE INC* 318
Wolfeboro, *RALPH K REED ANTIQUES* 327

11 Baseball Cards

Connecticut
Avon, *EAGLES NEST* 44
Darien, *GILANN SUMMER BOOK SHOP* 55

Maine
Waterboro, *WATERBORO EMPORIUM* 153
Wells, *THE BOOK BARN* 153

Massachusetts
Chatham, *HOUSE ON THE HILL* 198
Southwick, *THE TOY SHOP* 262

12 Bookbinding/Restoration

Connecticut
Cos Cob, *THE BOOK BLOCK* 52

Maine
Bernard, *NANCY NEALE TYPECRAFT* 119
Brunswick, *MARILYN NULMAN, BOOK REPAIR* 122
Dresden, *MATHOM BOOKSHOP & BINDERY* 126

Massachusetts
Brewster, *TALIN BOOKBINDERY* 191

New Hampshire
Marlborough, *HOMESTEAD BOOKSHOP* 308

13 Books/Antiquarian

Connecticut
Avon, *NATURAL SELECTION BOOKS* 44
Barkhamstead, *BETTY MESSENGER* 45
Bethany, *THE ANTIQUARIUM* 45
Bethany, *WHITLOCK FARM, BOOKSELLERS* 45
Bethany, *ROBERT B WILLIAMS* 45
Bloomfield, *ARS ANTIQUA BOOKS* 46
Branford, *BRANFORD RARE BOOK & ART GALLERY* 47
Brookfield, *BERT & PHYLLIS BOYSON* 48
Canterbury, *STONE OF SCONE ANTIQUES* 49
Canton, *BOOK STORE* 50
Colebrook, *COLEBROOK BOOK BARN* 52
Colebrook, *RINHART GALLERIES* 52
Collinsville, *COUNTRY LANE BOOKS* 52
Collinsville, *LAWRENCE GOLDER, RARE BOOKS* 52
Cos Cob, *THE BOOK BLOCK* 52
Coventry, *COVENTRY BOOK SHOP* 53
Coventry, *KATHLEEN SULLIVAN-CHILDREN'S BKS* 53
Danbury, *ORPHEUS BOOKS* 54
Darien, *GILANN SUMMER BOOK SHOP* 55
Deep River, *W B GOTTLEIB - BOOKS* 56
Derby, *BOOKS BY THE FALLS* 56
East Haddam, *CONNECTICUT RIVER BOOKSHOP* 57
East Haddam, *MAGIC HORN LTD* 57
East Hampton, *BIBLIOLATREE* 57
Fairfield, *CONNECTICUT BOOK AUCTION* 60
Fairfield, *A. LUCAS, BOOKS* 61
Fairfield, *MUSEUM GALLERY BOOK SHOP* 61

Falls Village, *R & D EMERSON, BOOKSELLERS*
  61
Goshen, *ANGLER'S & SHOOTER'S*
  BOOKSHELF 63
Granby, *WILLIAM & LOIS M PINKNEY* 63
Guilford, *LAMB HOUSE FINE BOOKS* 66
Hamden, *AMERICAN WORLDS BOOKS* 66
Hamden, *ANTIQUE BOOKS* 66
Hamden, *BOOKCELL BOOKS* 67
Hamden, *MCBLAIN BOOKS* 67
Hartford, *THE JUMPING FROG* 67
Litchfield, *JOHN STEELE BOOK SHOP* 71
Manchester, *BOOKS & BIRDS* 73
Mansfield Center, *SHIELA B AMDUR - BOOKS*
  73
Meriden, *DUNN'S MYSTERIES OF CHOICE* 74
Middlebury, *MICHAEL C DOOLING* 74
New Haven, *BRYN MAWR BOOK SHOP* 79
New Haven, *WILLIAM REESE COMPANY* 81
New Haven, *R W SMITH-BOOKSELLER* 81
New Haven, *C A STONEHILL INC* 81
New Haven, *WHITLOCK'S INC* 81
New Milford, *TIMELESS BOOKS* 82
New Preston, *BRITANNIA BOOKSHOP* 82
New Preston, *TIMOTHY MAWSON BOOKS &*
  PRINTS 83
New Preston, *TREBIZOND RARE BOOKS* 83
Newtown, *BANCROFT BOOK MEWS* 84
Newtown, *THE PAGES OF YESTERYEAR* 84
Plainville, *THE BOOK EXCHANGE* 88
Pomfret Center, *POMFRET BOOK SHOP* 89
Pomfret, *BO & CO* 88
Ridgefield, *THE CHARLES DALY COLLECTION*
  90
Salisbury, *LION'S HEAD BOOKS* 92
Sandy Hook, *CHISWICK BOOK SHOP INC* 92
Sherman, *PAST TIME BOOKS* 93
Sherman, *SCARLET LETTER BOOKS & PRINTS*
  93
South Norwalk, *WASHINGTON STREET BOOK*
  STORE 94
South Willington, *KINGSMILL BOOK SHOP* 94
Southbury, *CHISWICK BOOK SHOP, INC.* 95
Southport, *OLD SOUTHPORT BOOKS* 96
Southport, *LAURENCE WITTEN RARE BOOKS*
  97
Stamford, *AVIS & ROCKWELL GARDINER* 97
Storrs, *RAINBOW BOOKS* 100
Torrington, *NUTMEG BOOKS* 101
Washington Depot, *HICKORY STICK*
  BOOKSHOP 102
West Cornwall, *DEBORAH BENSON*
  BOOKSELLER 102
West Cornwall, *BARBARA FARNSWORTH* 103
West Hartford, *W HARTFORD BK SHOP AT*
  PARK PLACE 103
Westport, *GUTHMAN AMERICANA* 105
Westport, *TURKEY HILL BOOKS* 106
Wilton, *ARCHIVES HISTORICAL*
  AUTOGRAPHS 107
Windsor, *CEDRIC L ROBINSON-BOOKSELLER*
  108
Winsted, *VERDE ANTIQUES & BOOKS* 108
Woodbridge, *WOODBRIDGE BOOK STORE* 108
Yalesville, *VICTOR A DENETTE*
  BOOKS/EPHEMERA 114

Maine
  Augusta, *READING TREASURES BOOKSHOP*
  117

Bangor, *LIPPINCOTT BOOKS* 117
Bar Harbor, *STEVE POWELL* 118
Belfast, *BOOKLOVER'S ATTIC* 118
Brewer, *SCOTT'S BOOKS* 121
Bridgton, *BRIDGTON BOOK HOUSE* 121
Brooklin, *GEORGE & PATRICIA FOWLER,*
  BOOKS 121
Brunswick, *CROSS HILL BOOKS* 122
Brunswick, *ROBERT E DYSINGER - BOOKS* 122
Brunswick, *GORDON'S BOOKSHOP* 122
Brunswick, *OLD BOOKS* 122
Brunswick, *CHARLES VINCENT - BOOKS* 122
Brunswick, *WALFIELD THISTLE* 122
Bryant Pond, *MOLL OCKETT* 122
Buckfield, *PATRICIA LEDLIE-BOOKSELLER*
  ABAA 122
Camden, *ABCDEF BOOKSTORE* 123
Camden, *STONE SOUP BOOKS* 123
Cape Elizabeth, *LOMBARD ANTIQUARIAN*
  MAP/PRINTS 123
Castine, *BARBARA FALK - BOOKSELLER* 124
Cundys Harbor, *BOOK PEDLARS* 125
Damariscotta, *COOPER'S RED BARN* 125
Damariscotta, *ELLIOTT HEALY*
  PHOTOGRAPHICA 125
Dresden, *MATHOM BOOKSHOP & BINDERY*
  126
East Lebanon, *MICKLESTREET RARE*
  BOOKS/MOD 1STS 126
East Livermore, *ALDEN PRATT, BOOKS* 127
Eliot, *BOOKS & AUTOGRAPHS* 127
Ellsworth, *BIG CHICKEN BARN - BOOKS* 127
Eustis, *MACDONALD'S MILITARY* 128
Fairfield, *THISTLE'S* 128
Farmington Falls, *FALLS BOOK BARN* 129
Freeport, *BOOK CELLAR* 129
Gardiner, *BUNKHOUSE BOOKS* 129
Garland, *FREDERICA DEBEURS - BOOKS* 130
Hallowell, *LEON TEBBETTS BOOK SHOP* 132
Hamden, *GARY W WOOLSON, BOOKSELLER*
  132
Jay, *RIVER OAKS BOOKS* 133
Lincolnville Beach, *GOOSE RIVER EXCHANGE*
  137
Madison, *BOOKS BOUGHT AND SOLD* 138
Manchester, *CHARLES ROBINSON RARE*
  BOOKS 138
Mount Desert Island, *WIKHEGAN BOOKS* 138
New Gloucester, *DONALD CHANDLER -*
  BOOKS 139
New Harbor, *RICHARDSON BOOKS LTD* 139
New Sharon, *ATTIC OWL BOOKS* 139
Newcastle, *BARN STAGES BOOKSHOP* 139
Newcastle, *SAIL LOFT* 140
Norridgewock, *SNOWBOUND BOOKS* 141
North Edgecomb, *EDGECOMB BOOK BARN* 141
North Monmouth, *JOYCE B KEELER - BOOKS*
  142
Northeast Harbor, *PINE BOUGH* 142
Northport, *LORD SEAGRAVE'S* 142
Paris, *HAUNTED BOOKSHOP* 143
Poland Spring, *CIDERPRESS BOOKSTORE* 144
Portland, *CARLSON AND TURNER BOOKS* 144
Portland, *CUNNINGHAM BOOKS* 144
Portland, *FLYNN BOOKS* 144
Portland, *F M O'BRIEN-ANTIQUARIAN BOOKS*
  145
Portland, *OUT-OF-PRINT SHOP* 145
Portland, *ALLEN SCOTT/BOOKS* 146

Round Pond, *CARRIAGE HOUSE* 147
Saco, *F P WOODS, BOOKS* 148
Sanford, *BOOK ADDICT* 148
Skowhegan, *MAIN(E)LY BOOKS* 150
South Casco, *VARNEY'S VOLUMES* 150
South China, *GRAY MATTER SERVICE* 150
South Portland, *J. GLATTER BOOKS* 150
Springvale, *HARLAND EASTMAN - BOOKS* 150
Springvale, *GEORGE E MILKEY BOOKS* 151
Steep Falls, *WARD'S BOOK BARN* 151
Stockton Springs, *VICTORIAN HOUSE BOOK BARN* 151
Waldoboro, *OLD LIBRARY BOOKSTORE* 153
Wells, *THE ARRINGTONS* 153
Wells, *THE BOOK BARN* 153
Wells, *EAST COAST BOOKS* 154
Wells, *HARDINGS BOOK SHOP* 154
Wells, *A DAVID PAULHUS BOOKS* 154
Wells, *SNUG HARBOR BOOKS* 155
Westbrook, *PEG GERAGHTY-BOOKS* 155
Yarmouth, *SUMNER & STILLMAN* 158
York Beach, *SAMUEL WEISER BOOKS* 159
York, *POST ROAD ANTIQUES & BOOKS* 159

Massachusetts

Amherst, *BOOK MARKS* 162
Amherst, *LEIF LAUDAMUS, RARE BOOKS* 163
Amherst, *VALLEY BOOKS* 163
Andover, *ANDOVER ANTIQUARIAN BOOKS* 163
Arlington, *SCIENTIA BOOKS* 164
Auburn, *KENNETH ANDERSON* 165
Belmont, *PAYSON HALL BOOKSHOP* 166
Bernardston, *BERNARDSTON BOOKS* 166
Beverly, *JEAN S MC KENNA BOOK SHOP* 166
Blandford, *ROBERT F LUCAS* 166
Boston, *ANTIQUARIAN BOOKSELLERS INC* 167
Boston, *ARS LIBRI* 168
Boston, *THOMAS G BOSS-FINE BOOKS* 171
Boston, *BOSTON BOOK ANNEX* 171
Boston, *BRATTLE BOOK SHOP* 171
Boston, *BROMER BOOKSELLERS INC* 171
Boston, *MAURY A BROMSEN ASSOCIATES, INC* 173
Boston, *BUDDENBROOKS* 173
Boston, *CHOREOGRAPHICA* 174
Boston, *GOODSPEED'S BOOK SHOP INC* 176
Boston, *PRISCILLA JUVELIS INC* 180
Boston, *RALPH KRISTIANSEN BOOKSELLER* 180
Boston, *THE NOSTALGIA FACTORY* 182
Boston, *JAMES F O'NEIL* 182
Boston, *THE PRINTERS' DEVIL* 185
Boston, *SHER-MORR ANTIQUES* 185
Boston, *CHARLES B WOOD, III INC* 189
Brewster, *BARBARA GRANT - ANTIQUES* 190
Brewster, *KINGS WAY BOOKS & ANTIQUES* 190
Brewster, *THE PUNKHORN BOOKSHOP* 190
Brookline Village, *BROOKLINE VILLAGE BOOKSHOP* 194
Brookline, *ROBERT H RUBIN, BOOKS* 193
Cambridge, *ROBIN BLEDSOE* 195
Cambridge, *H MENDELSOHN FINE EUROPEAN BOOKS* 197
Cambridge, *THE STARR BOOK SHOP* 197
Chatham, *PAPYRUS BOOKS* 199
Chestnut Hill, *MAGDA TISZA RARE BOOKS* 200
Concord, *THE BARROW BOOKSTORE* 200
Concord, *BOOKS WITH A PAST* 200
Concord, *JOSLIN HALL RARE BOOKS* 200
Conway, *ROBERT L MERRIAM* 201

Dennis Village, *ANOTHER TIME & PLACE* 203
Dracut, *THE ANTIQUARIAN SCIENTIST* 204
East Longmeadow, *W D HALL* 205
East Otis, *LYMAN BOOKS - THEATRE* 205
East Sandwich, *TITCOMB'S BOOKSHOP* 206
Fairhaven, *EDWARD J LEFKOWICZ INC* 210
Fairhaven, *BARRY SCOTT* 210
Fall River, *DORCAS BOOKS* 211
Gardner, *IRENE'S BOOK SHOP* 212
Gardner, *PAUL C RICHARDS AUTOGRAPHS* 212
Georgetown, *JANE FIELD BOOKS* 213
Gloucester, *TEN POUND ISLAND BOOK CO* 214
Great Barrington, *J & J LUBRANO ANTIQUARIAN BOOKS* 215
Great Barrington, *GEORGE R MINKOFF, INC* 215
Hadley, *KEN LOPEZ BOOKSELLER* 217
Hamilton, *ELMCRESS BOOKS* 218
Harwich Center, *STATEN HOOK BOOKS* 219
Harwichport, *HARWICH BOOKSTORE* 219
Haverhill, *CONSTANCE MORELLE BOOKS* 219
Haydenville, *THE MILLER'S DAUGHTER* 220
Lanesborough, *SAVOY BOOKS* 222
Lanesborough, *SECOND LIFE BOOKS* 222
Lanesborough, *WALDEN'S ANTIQUES & BOOKS* 223
Lexington, *EVA AROND* 224
Lexington, *PATRIOT ANTIQUARIAN BOOKS* 224
Lexington, *RAINY DAY BOOKS* 225
Lincoln, *WILKERSON BOOKS* 225
Marblehead, *LORRAINE ALLISON* 226
Marblehead, *MUCH ADO* 228
Marlboro, *DOWER HOUSE* 228
Marshfield, *LORD RANDALL BOOKSHOP* 229
Medway, *MARJORIE PARROTT ADAMS BOOKS* 229
Melrose, *ROBINSON MURRAY III, BOOKSELLER* 230
Melrose, *STARR BOOK CO INC* 230
Montague, *PETER L MASI BOOKS* 230
Montague, *KARL SCHICK* 230
Needham, *ESTHER TUVESON* 234
New Salem, *THE COMMON READER BOOKSHOP* 235
Newton Centre, *EDWARD MORRILL & SON* 237
Newton Centre, *SUZANNE SCHLOSSBERG BOOKS* 237
Newton, *THE BOOK COLLECTOR* 236
Newton, *HARD-TO-FIND NEEDLEWORK BOOKS* 237
Newton, *KENNETH W RENDELL, INC* 237
North Orange, *ARMCHAIR BOOKS* 240
Northampton, *BARBARA L FERET, BOOKSELLER* 241
Northampton, *GLOBE BOOKSHOP* 241
Northampton, *SCHOEN & SON BOOKSELLERS* 241
Onset, *JOSEPH A DERMONT, BOOKSELLER* 242
Orleans, *HAUNTED BOOK SHOP* 243
Pittsfield, *RUNNING FENCE BOOKS* 245
Plymouth, *THE YANKEE BOOK & ART GALLERY* 246
Roxbury, *SOUTHPAW BOOKS* 249
Salem, *ROBERT A MURPHY BOOKSELLER* 250
Sharon, *ANTIQUARIAN BOOKWORM* 253
Sharon, *BLAND'S BOOK BIN* 253

Sharon, *MICHAEL GINSBERG BOOKS INC* 253
Sharon, *PEPPER & STERN RARE BOOKS, INC* 253
Sheffield, *HOWARD S MOTT INC* 255
South Egremont, *BRUCE & SUSAN GVENTER, BOOKS* 260
South Harwich, *CAPE COLLECTOR* 261
Southborough, *TEN EYCK BOOKS* 261
Southbridge, *STEEPLE BOOKS* 262
Spencer, *QUABOAG USED BOOKS* 262
Springfield, *JOHNSON'S SECONDHAND BOOKSHOP* 262
Springfield, *TROTTING HILL PARK BOOKS* 263
Stockbridge, *OVERLEE FARM BOOKS* 263
Stockbridge, *JOHN R SANDERSON* 263
Stoughton, *WESTERN HEMISPHERE INC* 264
Sunderland, *RICHARD E OINONEN* 265
Waban, *DIANA J RENDELL, INC* 268
Waltham, *HAROLD M BURSTEIN & CO* 268
Wellesley, *TERRAMEDIA BOOKS* 269
West Brookfield, *BOOK BEAR* 272
West Newbury, *MOODY-RIDGEWAY HOUSE* 274
West Stockbridge, *DOROTHY ELSBERG BOOKS* 275
Weston, *JANE CHORAS, BOOKS* 276
Weston, *M & S RARE BOOKS, INC* 277
Wilbraham, *MURRAY BOOKS* 277
Williamstown, *CARRIAGE BARN BOOKS* 278
Williamstown, *SETH NEMEROFF, ANTIQUARIAN BOOKS* 278
Worcester, *JEFFREY D MANCEVICE INC* 280
Worcester, *ISAIAH THOMAS BOOKS & PRINTS* 280
Yarmouth Port, *PARNASSUS BOOK SERVICE* 281

New Hampshire
Andover, *THE CILLEYVILLE BOOKSTORE* 285
Bedford, *CLOAK & DAGGER BOOKS* 285
Bedford, *RICHARDSON BOOKS, LTD* 286
Bradford, *KALONBOOKS* 286
Canterbury, *CRABTREE'S COLLECTION* 287
Center Sandwich, *HILL COUNTRY BOOKS* 287
Concord, *BOOKSHELF SHOP* 289
Concord, *CARR BOOKS* 289
Concord, *THE OLD ALMANACK SHOP* 289
Contoocook, *THE ARNOLDS* 289
Contoocook, *CHURCHILLBOOKS* 289
Contoocook, *EMERY'S BOOKS* 289
Derry, *BERT BABCOCK BOOKSELLER* 290
Exeter, *A THOUSAND WORDS* 292
Exeter, *COLOPHON BOOK SHOP* 292
Exeter, *EXETER OLD BOOK BARN* 293
Exeter, *JANE ROBIE - LANDSCAPE BOOKS* 293
Farmington, *THE BOOKERY* 293
Francestown, *THE TYPOGRAPHEUM BOOKSHOP* 295
Franklin, *EVELYN CLEMENT* 295
Freedom, *FREEDOM BOOKSHOP* 296
Gilford Village, *VISUALLY SPEAKING* 296
Gilford, *LOUISE FRAZIER, BOOKS* 296
Goffstown, *SACRED & PROFANE* 297
Goshen, *NELSON CRAFTS & USED BOOKS* 297
Greenland, *WM THOMPSON, ANTIQUARIAN BKSELLR* 297
Guild, *PAUL & MARIE MAJOROS* 297
Hancock, *OLD BENNINGTON BOOKS* 300
Hanover, *G B MANASEK, INC* 300

Hanover, *TAKE YOUR LIFE IN YOUR HANDS* 300
Harrisville, *BEN'S OLD BOOKS* 300
Henniker, *OLD NUMBER SIX BOOK DEPOT* 301
Hillsboro, *THE SHADOW SHOP* 302
Hopkinton, *WOMEN'S WORDS BOOKS* 303
Laconia, *BARN LOFT BOOKSHOP* 305
Laconia, *COTTON HILL BOOKS* 305
Lancaster, *BRETTON HALL ANTIQUITIES* 306
Lancaster, *ELM STREET & STOLCRAFT BOOKS* 306
Lisbon, *EARTH BOOKS* 306
Manchester, *ANITA'S ANTIQUARIAN BOOKS* 308
Marlborough, *HOMESTEAD BOOKSHOP* 308
Meredith, *MARY ROBERTSON - BOOKS* 309
Nashua, *PAUL HENDERSON* 311
New London, *BURPEE HILL BOOKS* 312
Newport, *JUNIPER HILL BOOKS* 312
North Weare, *NEW HAMPSHIRE BOOK AUCTIONS* 313
Peterborough, *PETERBOROUGH USED BOOKS & PRINTS* 316
Portsmouth, *BOOK GUILD OF PORTSMOUTH* 316
Portsmouth, *PORTSMOUTH BOOKSHOP* 317
Portsmouth, *TRUNKWORKS* 318
Richmond, *NORTH COUNTRY BOOKSHOP* 318
Rumney, *JOHN F HENDSEY -BOOKSELLER* 319
Rumney, *ELIZABETH OLCOTT BOOKS* 319
Rumney, *VILLAGE BOOKS* 319
Twin Mountain, *BRETTON HALL ANTIQUITIES* 322
Warner, *HILLSIDE BOOKS* 323
Weare, *SYKES & FLANDERS ANTIQUARIAN BKS* 324
Westmoreland, *CELTIC CROSS BOOKS* 326
Westmoreland, *HURLEY BOOKS* 326

Rhode Island
Newport, *ANCHOR & DOLPHIN BOOKS* 333
Newport, *SIMMONS & SIMMONS* 337
Pawtucket, *SUZANNE'S BOOK SHOPPE* 339
Peace Dale, *SIGN OF THE UNICORN BOOKSHOP* 339
Providence, *CELLAR STORIES BOOKS* 340
Providence, *METACOMET BOOKS* 340
Providence, *SEWARDS' FOLLY, BOOKS* 341
Providence, *TYSON'S OLD & RARE BOOKS* 341
Providence, *BARBARA WALZER, BOOKSELLER* 341
Warwick, *FORTUNATE FINDS BOOKSTORE* 343
Watch Hill, *THE BOOK & TACKLE SHOP* 343

Vermont
Adamant, *ADAMANT BOOKS* 348
Bellows Falls, *ARCH BRIDGE BOOKSHOP* 348
Bennington, *AISLINN BOOK & RESEARCH* 348
Bennington, *BRADFORD BOOKS* 348
Bennington, *NEW ENGLANDIANA* 349
Bennington, *NOW AND THEN BOOKS* 349
Bethel, *OLD BOOKS & EPHEMERA* 349
Bristol, *TERRY HARPER, BOOKSELLER* 350
Burlington, *ASHLEY BOOK COMPANY* 350
Burlington, *BYGONE BOOKS* 350
Burlington, *CODEX BOOKS* 350
Burlington, *JAMES FRASER* 351
Chelsea, *BOOKS AT CHELSEA* 351
Chester Depot, *STONE VILLAGE ANTIQUARIAN BOOKS* 352

Craftsbury Common, *CRAFTSBURY COMMON ANTIQUARIAN* 352
Cuttingsville, *HAUNTED MANSION BOOKSHOP* 352
Derby Line, *TRANQUIL THINGS* 353
East Middlebury, *BREADLOAF BOOKS* 354
Fairfax, *THE BOOKSTORE* 355
Greensboro, *RECOVERY BOOKS* 357
Groton, *OLD BOOKS* 357
Lyndonville, *GREEN MOUNTAIN BOOKS & PRINTS* 359
Manchester Village, *JOHNNY APPLESEED BOOKSHOP* 361
Middlebury, *POOR RICHARDS USED BOOKS* 361
Morrisville, *BRICK HOUSE BOOKSHOP* 362
Newbury, *OXBOW BOOKS* 363
Newfane, *NU-TIQUE SHOP* 363
Newport, *MICHAEL DUNN - BOOKS* 363
North Bennington, *NATURAL HISTORY BOOKS* 363
North Pomfret, *RICHARD H ADELSON ANTIQUARIAN BK* 364
Norwich, *LILAC HEDGE BOOKSHOP* 364
Norwich, *F J MANASEK* 364
Plainfield, *THE COUNTRY BOOKSHOP* 366
Quechee, *QUECHEE BOOKS* 366
Rutland, *TUTTLE ANTIQUARIAN BOOKS INC* 369
Shelburne, *WILLIAM L PARKINSON BOOKS* 370
South Hero, *FRANCES L ROBINSON* 371
St George, *A J BELLIVEAU BOOKS* 372
St Johnsbury Ctr, *UNA GALLERIES* 372
Waitsfield, *RARE & WELL DONE BOOKS* 373
West Brattleboro, *THE BEAR BOOK SHOP* 375
Wilder, *STANLEY BOOKS* 375
Woodstock, *PLEASANT STREET BOOKS* 377

14 Books

Connecticut
Derby, *BOOKS BY THE FALLS* 56
Fairfield, *MUSEUM GALLERY BOOK SHOP* 61
South Windsor, *JOHN A WOODS, APPRAISERS* 95
Woodbury, *BOOKS ABOUT ANTIQUES* 109

Maine
Camden, *STONE SOUP BOOKS* 123
Sebago, *THE GALLERY SHOP* 149
Springvale, *HARLAND EASTMAN - BOOKS* 150

Massachusetts
Amherst, *VALLEY BOOKS* 163
Bernardston, *BERNARDSTON BOOKS* 166
Brookline Village, *BROOKLINE VILLAGE BOOKSHOP* 194
Concord, *JOSLIN HALL RARE BOOKS* 200
Harwichport, *HARWICH BOOKSTORE* 219
Huntington, *PAULSON'S ANTIQUARIAN PAPER/BOOK* 221
Newton, *THE BOOK COLLECTOR* 236

New Hampshire
Wolfeboro, *NEW ENGLAND GALLERY* 327

Rhode Island
Providence, *CELLAR STORIES BOOKS* 340
Wakefield, *JIGGER'S ANTIQUES* 342

15 Bottles

Connecticut
Norwalk, *BARTER SHOP* 85

Maine
South China, *COUNTRY ANTIQUES* 150

New Hampshire
Exeter, *HOLLIS & TRISHA BRODRICK* 292

16 Brass/Copper/Metalwork

Connecticut
Avon, *GARLAND AND FRANCES PASS* 44
Cromwell, *HORTON BRASSES* 54
Darien, *H P MC LANE ANTIQUES INC* 55
Essex, *VALLEY FARM ANTIQUES* 60
Fairfield, *JAMES BOK ANTIQUES* 60
Killingworth, *LEWIS W SCRANTON ANTIQUES* 70
Lisbon-Jewett City, *MR & MRS JEROME BLUM* 70
Litchfield, *COUNTRY HOUSE CONSIGNMENTS* 70
Litchfield, *THOMAS D & CONSTANCE R WILLIAMS* 71
Madison, *RIVER CROFT* 72
New Haven, *ARK ANTIQUES* 79
Simsbury, *C RUSSELL NOYES* 93
Southport, *PAT GUTHMAN ANTIQUES* 96
Stamford, *UNITED HOUSE WRECKING* 98
Stonington, *CHRISTOPHER & KATHLEEN COLE* 98
Westbrook, *HANES RUSKIN* 104
Woodbury, *ANTIQUES ON THE GREEN* 109
Woodbury, *CROSSWAYS ANTIQUES* 110
Woodbury, *EVE STONE & SON ANTIQUES* 113
Woodbury, *WOODBURY PEWTERERS* 114

Maine
Bernard, *NANCY NEALE TYPECRAFT* 119
Gardiner, *MCKAY'S ANTIQUES* 130
Newcastle, *MARY HODES* 140
Norway, *DIXON'S ANTIQUES* 142
Portland, *VOSE SMITH ANTIQUES* 146
Rockport, *WINDY TOP ANTIQUES* 147
Wells, *THE FARM* 154
Winter Harbor, *POND HOUSE ANTIQUES* 156
Wiscasset, *LILAC COTTAGE* 156

Massachusetts
Amherst, *WOOD-SHED ANTIQUES* 163
Ashley Falls, *DON ABARBANEL* 164
Brewster, *THE PFLOCK'S-ANTIQUES* 190
Brimfield, *BRIMFIELD ANTIQUES* 192
Conway, *CONWAY HOUSE* 201
Eastham, *QUAIL SONG ANTIQUES* 206
Great Barrington, *COMPASS ANTIQUES* 215
Hyannis, *STONE'S ANTIQUE SHOP* 222
Millis, *BIRCHKNOLL ANTIQUES* 230
Newton, *BRASS BUFF ANTIQUES* 236
Sandwich, *FAULCONNER HOUSE ANTIQUES* 251
Sheffield, *FALCON ANTIQUES* 255
Shelburne, *ORCHARD HILL ANTIQUES* 257
South Brewster, *SMITH ANTIQUES* 259
South Egremont, *ELLIOTT & GRACE SNYDER* 260
Templeton, *WRIGHT TAVERN ANTIQUES* 266
Westborough, *OLD SCHOOLHOUSE ANTIQUES* 276

Yarmouth Port, *NICKERSON'S ANTIQUES* 281

New Hampshire
Alexandria, *COLE HILL FARM ANTIQUES* 284
Chester, *OLDE CHESTER ANTIQUES* 288
Dublin, *ANN & DAN WALSH* 291
Franconia, *COLONIAL COTTAGE* 295
Hancock, *HARDINGS OF HANCOCK* 299
Hillsboro, *OLD DUNBAR HOUSE* 301
Hollis, *THE BLUE LANTERN ANTIQUES* 302
Hopkinton, *THE SOULES ANTIQUES* 303
Hopkinton, *WAYNE & PEGGY WOODARD ANTIQUES* 303
Laconia, *THE HOFFMANS* 305
Marlow, *PEACE BARN ANTIQUES* 309
New London, *MAD EAGLE INC FINE ANTIQUES* 312
Portsmouth, *MARGARET SCOTT CARTER, INC.* 317
Portsmouth, *ED WEISSMAN* 318
South Hampton, *R G BETTCHER RESTORATIONS* 320

Rhode Island
Ashaway, *ASHAWAY ANTIQUES STORE* 330

Vermont
Burlington, *CONANT CUSTOM BRASS* 350
Cavendish, *SIGOURNEYS' ANTIQUES* 351
Derby Line, *CARRIAGE HOUSE ANTIQUES* 353
Fairfax, *GLENORTON COUNTRY ANTIQUES* 355
Jeffersonville, *MARY'S GLASS & COLLECTIBLES* 358
Middlebury, *VILLAGE STORE OF MIDDLEBURY* 361
Springfield, *PASTIMES ANTIQUES* 371
St Albans, *PAULETTE'S ANTIQUES/COLLECTIBL* 371
Stowe, *ENGLISH COUNTRY ANTIQUES* 372
Waterbury, *CABELL ANTIQUES* 374
Waterbury, *UPLAND ACRES ANTIQUES* 375

17 Bronzes

Maine
Kennebunkport, *MARITIME MUSEUM SHOP* 135
Portland, *VOSE SMITH ANTIQUES* 146
Stockton Springs, *BRICK HOUSE ANTIQUES* 151

Massachusetts
Boston, *BEDELLE INC* 170
Boston, *KAY BEE FURNITURE COMPANY* 180
Brookline, *CYPRESS TRADING POST* 193
Charlestown, *BUNKER HILL RELICS* 198
Hyannis, *ALBERT ARTS & ANTIQUES* 221
Marblehead, *EVIE'S CORNER* 227

Vermont
Manchester, *PARAPHERNALIA ANTIQUES* 359

18 Buttons/Badges

Maine
Rockport, *WINDY TOP ANTIQUES* 147

Massachusetts
Marblehead, *ANTIQUEWEAR* 227

Rhode Island
Providence, *MY FAVORITE THINGS* 340

19 Cabinet Makers

Connecticut
Bethlehem, *WOODY MOSCH CABINETMAKERS* 46
Clinton, *STEPHEN H SMITH, CABINETMAKER* 51
New Milford, *PHOENIX ANTIQUE RESTORATION* 82
South Windsor, *EARLY NEW ENGLAND ROOMS* 95
Woodbury, *NININGER & COMPANY LTD* 112

Maine
Waldoboro, *WILLIAM EVANS, CABINETMAKER* 152

Massachusetts
Ashby, *COUNTRY BED SHOP* 164
Easthampton, *PETER FRANKLIN CABINETMAKERS* 207
Somerville, *ROBERT E SMITH* 258
South Ashfield, *RUSS LOOMIS JR* 258
Wayland, *GREAT MEADOWS JOINERY* 268
West Chesterfield, *TIMOTHY GORHAM, CABINET MAKER* 273

New Hampshire
Alexandria, *ALEXANDRIA WOOD JOINERY* 284
Enfield, *DANA ROBES WOOD CRAFTSMEN* 291
Milford, *THE RENAISSANCE MAN* 310

Rhode Island
West Kingstown, *G R CLIDENCE, 18TH C WOODWORKS* 344

20 Cameras/Daguerreotypes

Maine
Brewer, *MCLEOD MILITARY ANTIQUES* 121
Gardiner, *FRED ROBBINS* 130
Lincolnville Beach, *GOOSE RIVER EXCHANGE* 137

New Hampshire
Plymouth, *SUSAN B LARSEN ANTIQUES* 316

21 Carpets/Rugs

Connecticut
Bethel, *PICKWICK HOUSE ANTIQUES* 46
Clinton, *HEY-DAY ANTIQUES* 51
Essex, *A MATHEWS ANDERSON ANTIQUES* 59
Fairfield, *PATTY GAGARIN ANTIQUES* 61
Greenwich, *BANKSVILLE ANTIQUES* 64
Mystic, *ORIENTAL RUGS LTD* 77
Norwalk, *WINGS OF A DOVE CONSIGNMENT* 85
Old Greenwich, *NEW ENGLAND SHOP* 86
Southport, *J B RICHARDSON GALLERY* 97
Stonington, *OPUS I* 99
Stonington, *ORKNEY & YOST ANTIQUES* 99
Washington Depot, *THE TULIP TREE COLLECTION* 102
Wilton, *WAYSIDE EXCHANGE* 108
Woodbury, *CLAPP AND TUTTLE* 109
Woodbury, *COUNTRY LOFT ANTIQUES* 110
Woodbury, *EMILIE J RAHHAL* 112

Maine
Bangor, *T J BURKE ORIENTAL RUGS* 117
Falmouth, *HARD CIDER FARM ORIENTAL RUGS* 128

Gorham, *COUNTRY SQUIRE ANTIQUES* 130
Gorham, *LONGVIEW ANTIQUES* 130
Limington, *EDWARD & ELAINE CASAZZA* 136
Newcastle, *GORDON NICOLL* 140
Pittston, *KENNETH AND PAULETTE TUTTLE*
144
Searsport, *THE CAPTAIN'S HOUSE ANTIQUES*
149
Trenton, *MAYO ANTIQUES GALLERY* 152
Wiscasset, *MARGARET B OFSLAGER* 157
York, *LAWRENCE FORLANO* 159

Massachusetts
Boston, *ARABY RUG* 168
Boston, *ARKELYAN RUGS* 168
Boston, *BROOKS, GILL & CO INC.* 173
Boston, *COLLECTOR'S SHOP* 174
Boston, *KAY BEE FURNITURE COMPANY* 180
Brewster, *WILLIAM M BAXTER ANTIQUES* 190
Brewster, *J. OGDEN TYLDSLEY, JR* 191
Essex, *FRIENDSHIP ANTIQUES* 208
Essex, *RIDER & CLARKE ANTIQUES* 209
Gloucester, *CAPE ANN ANTIQUES &*
ORIENTALS 213
Hopkinton, *HERITAGE ANTIQUES* 220
Hyannis, *PRECIOUS PAST* 221
Millis, *BIRCHKNOLL ANTIQUES* 230
Nantucket, *ARKELYAN RUGS* 231
Newburyport, *JOHN J COLLINS, JR.* 235
Newton Lower Falls, *ARTHUR T GREGORIAN*
INC 238
Rockport, *ELIOT ANTIQUES* 248
Rockport, *MOUNT VERNON ANTIQUES* 248
Sandwich, *TOBEY HOUSE ANTIQUES* 252
Wellesley, *D B STOCK PERSIAN CARPETS* 269
Winchester, *KOKO BOODAKIAN & SONS* 279
Yarmouth Port, *CONSTANCE GOFF* 281

New Hampshire
Center Strafford, *HALF THE BARN* 287
Concord, *ART RUG* 288
Franconia, *ELEANOR M LYNN/ELIZABETH*
MONAHAN 295
Hampton, *H G WEBBER* 298
Hancock, *THE BARN OF HANCOCK VILLAGE*
299
Keene, *PETER PAP ORIENTAL RUGS INC* 305
New Ipswich, *ESTELLE M GLAVEY, INC.* 312
Peterborough, *THE COBBS ANTIQUES* 315
Peterborough, *OLD TOWN FARM ANTIQUES*
316
Raymond, *CALOUBAR COLLECTABLES* 318
Seabrook, *STONE HOUSE ANTIQUES* 320
Winchester, *RICHARD WHITE ANTIQUES* 327

Rhode Island
Little Compton, *THE GALLERY ON THE*
COMMONS 333
Newport, *ARAKEL H BOZYAN STORE* 334
Newport, *OLD FASHION SHOP* 337

Vermont
Castleton Corners, *OLD HOMESTEAD*
ANTIQUES 351
Manchester Center, *BELLWETHER GALLERY*
360
Manchester, *HOOKED RUG RESTORATION* 359
Richmond, *VINCENT J FERNANDEZ*
ORIENTAL RUG 367
Rutland, *CONWAY'S ANTIQUES & DECOR* 368
Shraftsbury, *NORMAN GRONNING*
ANTIQ/ARCH ITEMS 370

Williamstown, *CLELAND E SELBY* 376

22 Chair Caning

Connecticut
Avon, *IMPERIAL DECORATING &*
UPHOLSTERY 44
Manchester, *CONNECTICUT CANE & REED CO*
73

Maine
Warren, *ABLE TO CANE* 153

Massachusetts
Beverly, *PRICE HOUSE ANTIQUES* 166
Peabody, *HERITAGE CANING* 244
Rehoboth, *JIM NEARY ANTIQUES* 247

New Hampshire
Hampton Falls, *APPLE COUNTRY ANTIQUES*
299
Hudson, *COLONIAL SHOPPE* 304
Wentworth, *RETOUCH THE PAST* 324

23 Clocks/Watches

Connecticut
Bethel, *PICKWICK HOUSE ANTIQUES* 46
Brookfield Center, *ANTIQUE CLOCK SHOP* 49
Canton, *THE HOUSE OF CLOCKS* 50
Clinton, *MEURS RENEHAN* 51
East Norwalk, *THE CLOCKERY* 58
Greenwich, *RENE GROSJEAN ANTIQUES* 64
Kent, *HARRY HOLMES ANTIQUES* 69
Madison, *KIRT & ELIZABETH CRUMP* 72
New Haven, *WEST GATE ANTIQUES* 81
New Milford, *BRUCE W ANDERSON*
ANTIQUES 81
Norwich, *WALTS ANTIQUES* 86
Ridgefield, *GERALD GRUNSELL &*
ASSOCIATES 90
South Windsor, *TIME PAST ANTIQUES* 95
Trumbull, *ZIMMERS HEIRLOOM CLOCKS* 101
Woodbury, *DAVIS ANTIQUES* 111
Woodbury, *WOODBURY HOUSE* 114
Yalesville, *UNIQUE ANTIQUES &*
COLLECTIBLES 114

Maine
Augusta, *PINE TREE STABLES ANTIQUES* 117
Bernard, *1895 SHOP* 119
Boothbay Harbor, *COLLECTOR SHOP* 120
Caribou, *THE BARN DOOR* 124
Hallowell, *D & R ANTIQUES* 131
Hallowell, *GARY F ELWELL ANTIQUES* 131
Hanover, *LYONS' DEN ANTIQUES* 132
Newcastle, *KAJA VEILLUX ART & ANTIQUES*
140
Portland, *NELSON RARITIES, INC* 145

Massachusetts
Amherst, *POLISSACK ANTIQUE JEWELRY* 163
Boston, *FINE TIME VINTAGE TIMEPIECES* 176
Boston, *THE FINEST HOUR* 176
Boston, *KAY BEE FURNITURE COMPANY* 180
Chatham, *OLDE VILLAGE COUNTRY BARN* 199
Dennis, *VILLAGE PEDLAR CLOCK SHOP* 203
Salem, *UNION STREET ANTIQUES* 250
Scituate, *GREENHOUSE ANTIQUES* 252
Sheffield, *1750 HOUSE ANTIQUES* 253
Sheffield, *CENTURYHURST ANTIQUES* 254
Sheffield, *DOVETAIL ANTIQUES* 254

Stockbridge, *TOM CAREY'S PLACE* 263
West Barnstable, *THE CLOCK SHELF* 271
West Boylston, *OBADIAH PINE ANTIQUES* 271
West Townsend, *JOHN & BARBARA DELANEY CLOCKS* 275

New Hampshire
Brookline, *1786 HOUSE ANTIQUES* 286
Contoocook, *GOLD DRAGON ANTIQUES* 289
Enfield, *THE CLOCK SHOP* 291
Exeter, *HERSCHEL B BURT* 292
Fitzwilliam, *CLOCKS ON THE COMMON* 293
Francestown, *MILL VILLAGE ANTIQUES* 294
Hampton, *H G WEBBER* 298
Hillsboro, *BEAR TRACK FARM ANTIQUES* 301
Kensington, *PETER SAWYER ANTIQUES* 305
Loudon, *CHIMES & TIMES CLOCK SHOP* 307
Plymouth, *SUSAN B LARSEN ANTIQUES* 316
Raymond, *BURT DIAL COMPANY* 318
Salem, *SANDERS ANTIQUES* 319
Union, *CARSWELL'S ANTIQUES* 323
Walpole, *GOLDEN PAST OF WALPOLE* 323
Winchester, *RICHARD WHITE ANTIQUES* 327

Rhode Island
Newport, *THE CLASSIC TOUCH* 334
Newport, *A & A GAINES* 335
Newport, *LAMPLIGHTER ANTIQUES* 336
Westerly, *HERITAGE ANTIQUES* 344

Vermont
Clarendon Springs, *CLARENDON HOUSE ANTIQUES* 352
Manchester, *THE CLOCK EMPORIUM* 359
Middletown Springs, *CLOCK DOCTOR* 361
Middletown Springs, *OLD SPA SHOP ANTIQUES* 362
Randolph Center, *RED BRICK HOUSE* 367
St Johnsbury, *SIGN OF THE DIAL CLOCK SHOP* 372
Vergennes, *FITZ-GERALDS' ANTIQUES* 373
Westminster, *LARSON'S CLOCK SHOP* 375
Williston, *GREEN MOUNTAIN CLOCK SHOP* 376
Wilmington, *DEERFIELD VALLEY ANTIQUES* 376

24 Coins/Medals

Connecticut
Avon, *EAGLES NEST* 44
Greenwich, *CHELSEA ANTIQUES OF GREENWICH* 64
Madison, *ORDNANCE CHEST* 72
Norwich, *WALTS ANTIQUES* 86
Westport, *SAM SLOAT COINS, INC* 106

Maine
Lincolnville Beach, *BETTY'S TRADING POST* 137
Roxbury, *YANKEE GEM CORP* 147

Massachusetts
Franklin, *JOHNSTON ANTIQUES* 212
Worcester, *J & N FORTIER INC* 280

New Hampshire
Fitzwilliam, *EXPRESSIONS* 294
West Swanzey, *FREDERICK MAC PHAIL ANTIQUES* 325
Winchester, *FAT CHANCE ANTIQUES* 326
Wolfeboro, *AUCTIONS BY BOWERS & MERENA, INC* 327

Rhode Island
Newport, *BELLEVUE GOLD* 333
Westerly, *WESTERLY ENTERPRISES* 344

Vermont
Jamaica, *ANTIQUES ANONYMOUS* 358

25 Conservation

Connecticut
Darien, *WIND-BORNE FRAME & RESTORATION* 56
Ivoryton, *COMSTOCK HSE ANTIQUE RESTORATION* 68

Massachusetts
Amherst, *ROSENTHAL PAPER RESTORATION* 163
Brewster, *TALIN BOOKBINDERY* 191
Brookline, *ROSINE GREEN ASSOCIATES, INC.* 193
Cambridge, *THE MUSIC EMPORIUM* 197
Duxbury, *LOWY FRAME & RESTORING COMPANY* 204
Foxboro, *POND HOUSE WOODWORKING* 211
Lee, *HENRY B HOLT INC* 223
Newton Highlands, *TREFLER ANTIQUE RESTORING STUDIO* 237
Waltham, *RESTORATION SERVICES* 268
Waltham, *SPNEA CONSERVATION CENTER* 268

New Hampshire
Portsmouth, *W MORIN FURNITURE RESTORATION* 317
Warner, *LINDA L DONOVAN* 323

Rhode Island
Tiverton, *METAL RESTORATION SERVICES* 342

26 Consultation/Research

Connecticut
Clinton, *VAN CARTER HALE FINE ART* 51
Madison, *P HASTINGS FALK SOUND VIEW PRESS* 72
South Windsor, *JOHN A WOODS, APPRAISERS* 95
Southport, *POMEROY ANDERSON* 96

Maine
Sanford, *JOHN LEEKE, PRESERVATION CONSULT* 148

Massachusetts
Boston, *FUSCO & FOUR ASSOCIATES* 176
Boston, *HERITAGE ART* 178
Brookline, *NANCY A SMITH APPRAISAL ASSOC* 194
Lincoln, *BROWN-CORBIN FINE ART* 225
Waban, *ANTIQUE RESEARCHERS* 267
Waltham, *SPNEA CONSERVATION CENTER* 268
West Newbury, *HELIGE ANDE ARTS* 274
West Newton, *AUCTION INDEX INC* 274
West Townsend, *JOHN & BARBARA DELANEY CLOCKS* 275
Winchester, *ACQUIS LTD* 279
Winchester, *KOKO BOODAKIAN & SONS* 279

New Hampshire
Northwood, *HARTLEY'S ANTIQUES* 314

Rhode Island
Peace Dale, *SIGN OF THE UNICORN BOOKSHOP* 339

27 Country Antiques

Connecticut

Bolton, *HAILSTON HOUSE INC* 47
Bolton, *QUAKER LADY ANTIQUES* 47
Brookfield, *EUROPEAN COUNTRY ANTIQUES* 48
Canterbury, *CACKLEBERRY FARMS ANTIQUES* 49
Coventry, *WILDFLOWER* 54
Essex, *A MATHEWS ANDERSON ANTIQUES* 59
Harwinton, *RYAN'S ANTIQUES* 68
Kent, *THE FORRER'S* 68
Madison, *NOSEY GOOSE* 72
Marble Dale, *LIMEROCK FARMS ANTIQUES* 73
Monroe, *BARBARA'S BARN ANTIQUES* 76
Morris, *MARTINGALE FARM ANTIQUES* 76
New Milford, *BIT OF COUNTRY* 82
Norwich, *1840 HOUSE* 86
Pine Meadow, *1847 HOUSE ANTIQUES* 88
South Norwalk, *OLD WELL ANTIQUES* 94
South Windsor, *COUNTRY BARN* 94
Trumbull, *GWENDOLYN DONAHUE* 101
West Simsbury, *NANCY DAVIS* 104
Westport, *COUNTRY SWEDISH ANTIQUES* 105
Westport, *PARC MONCEAU* 106
Westport, *TODBURN* 106
Wilton, *THE PINE CHEST, INC.* 107
Woodbury, *WEST COUNTRY ANTIQUES* 113

Maine

Alfred, *ALFRED TRADING COMPANY* 116
Alfred, *PATRICIAN DESIGNS* 116
Cape Elizabeth, *HANSON'S CARRIAGE HOUSE* 123
Cape Porpoise, *PADDY'S COVE ANTIQUES* 124
Caribou, *JUDY'S ANTIQUES* 124
Damariscotta, *THE MAPLES* 125
Damariscotta, *PINE CHESTS & THINGS* 125
Farmington, *MAPLE AVENUE ANTIQUES* 129
Freeport, *OLD THYME SHOP* 129
Hallowell, *BERDAN'S ANTIQUES* 131
Holden, *DOUGLAS MARSHALL* 132
Jefferson, *BUNKER HILL ANTIQUES* 133
Kennebunkport, *CATTAILS ANTIQUES* 134
Moody, *KENNETH & IDA MANKO* 138
Newcastle, *MILLING AROUND* 140
Portland, *WILMA'S ANTIQUES & ACCESSORIES* 146
Round Pond, *THE HOLMES* 147
Round Pond, *ROUND POND ANTIQUES* 147
Searsport, *RED KETTLE ANTIQUES* 149
South China, *COUNTRY ANTIQUES* 150
Southwest Harbor, *MARIANNE CLARK FINE ANTIQUES* 150
Troy, *GREEN'S CORNER ANTIQUES* 152
Wells, *1774 HOUSE ANTIQUES* 153
West Brooklin, *LOUISA GOODYEAR ANTIQUES* 155
Wiscasset, *SHEILA & EDWIN RIDEOUT* 157

Massachusetts

Acton, *ENCORES* 162
Ashley Falls, *THE VOLLMERS* 165
Brewster, *BAYBERRY ANTIQUES* 190
Cambridge, *EASY CHAIRS* 196
Chatham, *BACKYARD ANTIQUES* 198
Chatham, *CHAPDELAINE ANTIQUES* 198
Chatham, *SIMPLER PLEASURES* 199
Chatham, *SHIRLEY WALKER ANTIQUES* 199
Concord, *CANTERBURY ANTIQUES* 200

Cummaquid, *THE OWL'S NEST ANTIQUES* 201
Dennis, *DOVETAIL ANTIQUES* 202
Dover, *INTERIOR MOTIVES, INC.* 204
Essex, *COUNTRY CORNER ANTIQUES* 208
Essex, *THE WHITE ELEPHANT SHOP* 210
Grafton, *PEGGY PLACE ANTIQUES* 214
Great Barrington, *BY SHAKER HANDS* 214
Great Barrington, *CORASHIRE ANTIQUES* 215
Great Barrington, *RED HORSE ANTIQUES* 216
Great Barrington, *SNYDER'S STORE* 216
Groton, *THE ANNEX* 216
Groton, *BOSTON ROAD ANTIQUES* 216
Hancock, *MOUNTAIN ROAD ANTIQUES* 218
Hingham, *ONE TEN NORTH* 220
Holden, *DAVIDIAN AMERICANA* 220
Lenox, *OCTOBER MOUNTAIN ANTIQUES* 224
Littleton, *HAMLET ANTIQUES* 225
Littleton, *UPTON HOUSE ANTIQUES* 225
Marblehead, *S & S GALLERIES* 228
Nantucket, *AMERICAN PIE* 231
Newton Highlands, *MARCIA & BEA ANTIQUES* 237
Norfolk, *NORFOLK ANTIQUES* 238
North Andover, *COUNTRY IN ANDOVER* 239
Salisbury, *FORT HILL ANTIQUES* 251
Sandwich, *FAULCONNER HOUSE ANTIQUES* 251
Sandwich, *THE STITCHERY IN SANDWICH* 251
Seekonk, *ANTIQUES AT HEARTHSTONE HOUSE* 252
Sheffield, *CENTURYHURST ANTIQUES* 254
Sheffield, *CORNER HOUSE ANTIQUES* 254
Sheffield, *OLE T J'S ANTIQUE BARN* 255
Sheffield, *LOIS W SPRING* 256
Shelburne Falls, *LUELLA MC CLOUD ANTIQUES* 257
Shelburne, *ORCHARD HILL ANTIQUES* 257
South Egremont, *HOWARD'S ANTIQUES* 260
South Egremont, *LITTLE HOUSE STUDIO* 260
South Egremont, *SPLENDID PEASANT* 260
Stockbridge, *TOM CAREY'S PLACE* 263
Sturbridge, *THE GREEN APPLE* 264
Sudbury, *ADAMS ANTIQUES USA* 264
Sudbury, *FARMHOUSE COLLECTIBLES* 265
Templeton, *1800 HOUSE ANTIQUES, LTD* 266
Templeton, *WRIGHT TAVERN ANTIQUES* 266
Wellfleet, *MORTAR & PESTLE ANTIQUES* 270
West Barnstable, *LUDWIG'S ANTIQUES* 271
West Barnstable, *THE WHIPPLETREE* 271
West Boylston, *OBADIAH PINE ANTIQUES* 271
Westborough, *MAYNARD HOUSE* 275
Westborough, *OLD SCHOOLHOUSE ANTIQUES* 276
Westborough, *SALT-BOX HOUSE ANTIQUES* 276
Yarmouth Port, *COLLECTOR'S CORNER* 281
Yarmouth Port, *NICKERSON'S ANTIQUES* 281

New Hampshire

Amherst, *CARRIAGE SHED ANTIQUES* 284
Barnstead (North), *COOPER SHOP ANTIQUES* 285
Bedford, *BEDFORD CENTER ANTIQUES* 285
Bedford, *LILLIAN WIENER* 286
Bradford, *JEF & TERRI STEINGRIBE* 286
Canaan, *ERNIE'S ANTIQUES* 287
Center Strafford, *BERT & GAIL SAVAGE* 288
Chester, *OLDE CHESTER ANTIQUES* 288
Chester, *WALNUT HILL ANTIQUES* 288
Contoocook, *PIATT'S COPPER COW* 289

Contoocook, *SHIRLEY D QUINN ANTIQUES* 290

Epping, *PLEASANT HILL ANTIQUES* 292

Exeter, *SANDY ELLIOTT, COUNTRY ANTIQUES* 293

Exeter, *OCTOBER STONE ANTIQUES* 293

Fitzwilliam, *BLOOMIN' ANTIQUES* 293

Fitzwilliam, *DAVIS HOMESTEAD* 293

Fitzwilliam, *WILLIAM LEWAN ANTIQUES* 294

Hampton Falls, *AMERICAN PRIDE* 298

Hampton, *HEYDAY ANTIQUES OF HAMPTON* 298

Hancock, *CROOKED ONION FARM ANTIQUE* 299

Hancock, *HARDINGS OF HANCOCK* 299

Hanover, *COUNTRY LOOK ANTIQUES* 300

Haverhill, *SUZANNE BRUCKNER 1812 HOUSE* 300

Hillsboro, *BARBARA'S ANTIQUES* 301

Hollis, *THE COOPERAGE* 302

Hudson, *COLONIAL SHOPPE* 304

Laconia, *THE HOFFMANS* 305

Londonderry, *THE TATES ANTIQUES* 307

Loudon, *COUNTRY ANTIQUES* 307

Marlborough, *WOODWARDS ANTIQUES* 309

Marlow, *PEACE BARN ANTIQUES* 309

Meriden, *WATERCRESS ANTIQUES* 310

Moultonboro, *BENCHMARK ANTIQUES* 311

Nashua, *RUSTIC ACCENTS, INC.* 311

New London, *LEE BURGESS ANTIQUES* 312

New London, *MOSES BURPEE FARM ANTIQUES* 312

Newton, *STEVEN J ROWE* 313

Peterborough, *OLD TOWN FARM ANTIQUES* 316

Plymouth, *PAULINE CHARON ANTIQUES* 316

Portsmouth, *MARGARET SCOTT CARTER, INC.* 317

Richmond, *SPINNING WHEEL ANTIQUES* 318

Stratham, *JOHN PIPER HOUSE* 321

Union, *CARSWELL'S ANTIQUES* 323

Warner, *SCOTT'S ANTIQUES* 324

Washington, *TINTAGEL ANTIQUES* 324

Wilmot Flat, *PLEASANT ACRES ANTIQUES ETC* 326

Wolfeboro, *AREA CODE 603 ANTIQUES* 327

Wolfeboro, *TOUCHMARK ANTIQUES* 327

Rhode Island

Charlestown, *BUTTERNUT SHOP* 331

Charlestown, *FOX RUN COUNTRY ANTIQUES* 331

Chepachet, *JADED LION* 331

Little Compton, *BLUE FLAG ANTIQUES* 333

Newport, *NEW ENGLAND ANTIQUES* 336

Newport, *TRITON ANTIQUES* 337

Wakefield, *JANET L THOMPSON* 342

Westerly, *LAUREL LEDGE ANTIQUES* 344

Vermont

Brandon, *NUTTING HOUSE ANTIQUES* 349

Chester, *1828 HOUSE* 351

East Barre, *FARR'S ANTIQUES* 354

Grafton, *GRAFTON GATHERING PLACE* 356

Grafton, *PICKLE STREET ANTIQUES* 356

Grafton, *WOODSHED ANTIQUES* 356

Groton, *STEPHEN JONES ANTIQUES* 357

Hinesburg Village, *WALKER HOUSE ANTIQUES* 358

Hinesburg, *HAWK'S NEST ANTIQUES & DECOYS* 358

Ludlow, *RED CLOVER ANTIQUES* 359

Middlebury, *BIX ANTIQUES* 361

Newfane, *SIBLEYS VILLAGE WORKSHOP* 363

North Hero, *DORWALDT'S ANTIQUES* 364

Randolph Center, *PAGE JACKSON ANTIQUE GALLERY* 366

Reading, *LIBERTY HILL ANTIQUES* 367

Rutland, *SUGAR HOUSE ANTIQUES* 368

Rutland, *TRULY UNIQUE ANTIQUES* 368

Saxtons River, *SCHOOLHOUSE ANTIQUES* 369

South Barre, *COUNTRY LOFT ANTIQUES* 371

South Burlington, *ETHAN ALLEN ANTIQUE SHOP INC* 371

Taftsville, *FRASER'S ANTIQUES* 373

Wallingford, *YANKEE MAID ANTIQUES* 374

Weston, *GAY MEADOW FARM ANTIQUES* 375

Woodstock, *LOFTY IDEAS* 377

28 Crocks/Stoneware

Connecticut

Bantam, *GOOSEBORO BROOK ANTIQUES* 45

Killingworth, *LEWIS W SCRANTON ANTIQUES* 70

North Kent, *GOODE HILL ANTIQUES* 84

Maine

Pittston, *PHIPPS OF PITTSTON* 143

Portland, *MILK STREET ANTIQUES* 145

Searsport, *ANTIQUES AT THE HILLMANS* 149

Searsport, *PRIMROSE FARM ANTIQUES* 149

Winter Harbor, *POND HOUSE ANTIQUES* 156

Massachusetts

Arlington, *IRREVERENT RELICS* 164

Concord, *CANTERBURY ANTIQUES* 200

Harwich, *PATTI SMITH* 219

Holden, *DAVIDIAN AMERICANA* 220

Northampton, *L & M FURNITURE* 241

Petersham, *GROUND FLOOR ATTIC ANTIQUES* 244

Plainville, *BRIAR PATCH ANTIQUES & COLLECTIB* 245

New Hampshire

Chesterfield, *HEMLOCK HILL ANTIQUES* 288

Chester, *OLDE CHESTER ANTIQUES* 288

Fitzwilliam, *RED BARN ANTIQUES* 294

Laconia, *THE HOFFMANS* 305

Snowville, *SLEIGH MILL ANTIQUES* 320

Walpole, *FARQUHAR ANTIQUES* 323

Rhode Island

Portsmouth, *COUNTRY CUPBOARD* 339

West Kingston, *PETER POTS AUTHENTIC AMERICANA* 344

Vermont

Clarendon Springs, *CLARENDON HOUSE ANTIQUES* 352

Grafton, *GABRIELS' BARN ANTIQUES* 356

Grafton, *PICKLE STREET ANTIQUES* 356

Jamaica, *ANTIQUES ANONYMOUS* 358

Ludlow, *RED CLOVER ANTIQUES* 359

Reading, *MILL BROOK ANTIQUES* 367

Rutland, *PARK ANTIQUES* 368

Springfield, *PASTIMES ANTIQUES* 371

Wallingford, *COUNTRY HOUSE ANTIQUES* 374

29 Decorative Accessories

Connecticut
Bridgeport, *MARC THE 1ST ANTIQUES* 48
Cromwell, *CUSTOM HOUSE* 54
Durham, *HODGE PODGE LODGE* 57
Fairfield, *JAMES BOK ANTIQUES* 60
Fairfield, *PATTY GAGARIN ANTIQUES* 61
Greenwich, *ANTAN ANTIQUES LTD* 63
Greenwich, *ANTIQUES & INTERIORS AT THE MILL* 63
Greenwich, *GUILD ANTIQUES* 64
Greenwich, *LIBERTY WAY ANTIQUES* 65
Kent, *OLDE STATION ANTIQUES* 69
Mystic, *5 CHURCH STREET ANTIQUES* 76
New Canaan, *SALLEA ANTIQUES* 78
New Canaan, *SEVERED TIES, INC* 78
New Haven, *JASMINE* 80
New Preston, *JONATHAN PETERS* 83
Newtown, *CODFISH ANTIQUES* 84
Old Lyme, *BRIGER FAIRHOLME JONES* 86
Old Lyme, *THE ELEPHANT TRUNK* 86
Pomfret Center, *PRISCILLA H ZIESMER* 89
South Willington, *SOUTH WILLINGTON ANTIQUES* 94
Stonington, *DOWNSTAIRS AT HARBOR VIEW* 98
Stonington, *NEIL B EUSTACE* 98
Stonington, *MARY MAHLER ANTIQUES* 99
Stonington, *RONALD NOE ANTIQUES* 99
Stonington, *ORKNEY & YOST ANTIQUES* 99
Thompson, *RUSSIAN BEAR ANTIQUES* 100
West Willington, *RONALD & PENNY DIONNE* 104
Wilton, *WAYSIDE EXCHANGE* 108
Woodbury, *THE BAY TREE ANTIQUES* 109
Woodbury, *GRASS ROOTS ANTIQUES* 111
Woodbury, *MILL HOUSE ANTIQUES* 111
Woodbury, *PETER A NELSON* 112
Woodbury, *MADELINE WEST ANTIQUES* 113

Maine
Bath, *TRIFLES* 118
Blue Hill, *EMERSON'S ANTIQUES* 120
Camden, *LEVETT'S ANTIQUES* 123
Ellsworth, *CALISTA STERLING ANTIQUES* 127
Kennebunkport, *MARIE PLUMMER GOETT* 134
Kennebunkport, *RANDS ANTIQUES ON RAND GREEN* 135
Kennebunkport, *WINTER HILL FARM* 136
Limington, *ROBERT O STUART* 136
Lincolnville Beach, *NORTH HOUSE FINE ANTIQUES* 137
Newcastle, *CONSTANCE H HURST* 140
Newfield, *JOHN BAUER SONIA SEFTON ANTI* 141
Richmond, *THE LOFT ANTIQUES* 146
Round Pond, *THE HOLMES* 147
Rumford Center, *GROVE FARM ANTIQUES* 148
Southwest Harbor, *MARIANNE CLARK FINE ANTIQUES* 150
West Bath, *F BARRIE FREEMAN ANTIQUES* 155
York, *POST ROAD ANTIQUES & BOOKS* 159
York, *JOHN LARKIN SGRO* 159

Massachusetts
Ashley Falls, *RUSSELL LYONS* 165
Boston, *BELGRAVIA ANTIQUES INC* 170
Boston, *JAMES BILLINGS* 170
Boston, *BRODNEY INC* 171
Boston, *HOWARD CHADWICK ANTIQUES* 173

Boston, *CHESTNUT & COMPANY* 174
Boston, *DIVINE DECADENCE* 175
Boston, *GEORGE I GRAVERT ANTIQUES* 178
Boston, *KNOLLWOOD ANTIQUES* 180
Boston, *THE MARCH HARE, LTD* 182
Boston, *MARCOZ ANTIQUES & JEWELRY* 182
Boston, *MARIKA'S ANTIQUE SHOP, INC* 182
Boston, *C A RUPPERT* 185
Boston, *SHOP ON THE HILL* 187
Boston, *SLENSKA'S ANTIQUES & INTERIORS* 187
Boston, *WEINER'S ANTIQUE SHOP* 188
Boston, *WENHAM CROSS ANTIQUES* 188
Brookline Village, *THE ANTIQUE COMPANY* 194
Brookline, *JERRY FREEMAN LTD* 193
Brookline, *TIM GALLAGHER ANTIQUES* 193
Cambridge, *SHARON BOCCELLI & CO ANTIQUES* 196
Cambridge, *DOWN UNDER* 196
Cambridge, *MARC J MATZ* 197
Cummaquid, *CUMMAQUID FINE ARTS* 201
East Sandwich, *THE GILDED SWAN* 206
Gloucester, *BEAUPORT ANTIQUES* 213
Great Barrington, *CORASHIRE ANTIQUES* 215
Great Barrington, *PAUL & SUSAN KLEINWALD INC* 215
Groton, *PAM BOYNTON* 216
Groton, *JAMES MATTOZZI & MARILYN BURKE* 217
Harvard, *THREE BAGS FULL* 218
Lee, *AARDENBURG ANTIQUES* 223
Marblehead, *MARBLEHEAD ANTIQUES* 227
Nantucket, *NANTUCKET HOUSE ANTIQUES* 232
Osterville, *FERRAN'S INTERIORS* 243
Salem, *MARCHAND'S LAFAYETTE ANTIQUES* 250
Sandwich, *H RICHARD STRAND FINE ANTIQUES* 251
Seekonk, *ANTIQUES AT HEARTHSTONE HOUSE* 252
Sheffield, *COVERED BRIDGE ANTIQUES* 254
Sheffield, *FREDERICK HATFIELD ANTIQUES* 255
Sheffield, *KUTTNER ANTIQUES* 255
Sheffield, *OLE T J'S ANTIQUE BARN* 255
Sheffield, *DAVID M WEISS* 257
Somerville, *EMBELLISHMENTS* 257
South Egremont, *RED BARN ANTIQUES* 260
South Natick, *COMING OF AGE ANTIQUES* 261
Southampton, *SOUTHAMPTON ANTIQUES* 261
Southborough, *MAPLEDALE ANTIQUES* 261
Sudbury, *THE ANTIQUE EXCHANGE OF SUDBURY* 265
Sudbury, *FARMHOUSE COLLECTIBLES* 265
Upton, *DAVID ROSE ANTIQUES* 267
Wellesley, *LINDA RICKLES INTERIORS INC* 269
Wellesley, *SPIVACK'S ANTIQUES* 269
Wenham, *HENDERSON'S* 271
Weston, *HOLLYDAY HOUSE* 276
Williamstown, *LIBRARY ANTIQUES* 278

New Hampshire
Epsom, *BOB & RITA BECKER* 292
Fitzwilliam, *DAVIS HOMESTEAD* 293
Hillsboro, *LOON POND ANTIQUES* 301
Hillsboro, *CHERYL & PAUL SCOTT ANTIQUES* 301
Holderness, *SQUAM LAKE GALLERY* 302

Hollis, *THE COOPERAGE* 302
Hopkinton, *MEADOW HEARTH* 303
Loudon, *GODIVA ANTIQUES* 307
Lyme, *SOMEWHERE IN TIME ANTIQUES* 308
Marlborough, *THOMAS R LONGACRE* 308
Marlborough, *BETTY WILLIS ANTIQUES, INC*
308
Moultonboro, *CARL & BEVERLY SHELDRAKE*
311
North Conway, *RICHARD M PLUSCH*
ANTIQUES 313
Portsmouth, *COBBLESTONES OF MARKET*
SQUARE 317
Portsmouth, *ED WEISSMAN* 318
Salem, *SANDERS ANTIQUES* 319
Washington, *HALF-MOON ANTIQUES* 324

Rhode Island
Bristol, *ALFRED'S* 330
Chepachet, *JADED LION* 331
Newport, *TRITON ANTIQUES* 337
Newport, *MICHAEL WESTMAN FINE ARTS*
338
Newport, *GUSTAVES J.S. WHITE* 338
Wakefield, *DOVE AND DISTAFF ANTIQUES* 342
Warren, *CHRISTIE & HADLEY ANTIQUES* 342
West Kingston, *PETER POTS AUTHENTIC*
AMERICANA 344
Wyoming, *BRAD SMITH* 345

Vermont
Chester, *1828 HOUSE* 351
Dorset, *VIRGINIA POPE, INC.* 354
Manchester Village, *EQUINOX ANTIQUES* 360
Middlebury, *BRADY GALLERIES, INC.* 361
Middletown Springs, *NIMMO & HART*
ANTIQUES 362
Shaftsbury, *THE CHOCOLATE BARN*
ANTIQUES 370
Waitsfield, *THE STORE, INC* 373

30 Decoys

Connecticut
Bethel, *DIERINGERS ARTS & ANTIQUES* 46
Coventry, *ANTIQUE DE-LIGHTS* 53
Glastonbury, *MARY S SWIFT ANTIQUES* 62
Salisbury, *THREE RAVENS ANTIQUES* 92

Maine
Damariscotta, *THE MAPLES* 125
Damariscotta, *PINE CHESTS & THINGS* 125
Fairfield, *JAMES D JULIA AUCTIONEERS* 128
Hanover, *LYONS' DEN ANTIQUES* 132
Kennebunkport, *BARBARA DOHERTY* 134
Kennebunkport, *OLD FORT INN & ANTIQUES*
135

Massachusetts
Nantucket, *FOUR WINDS CRAFT GUILD* 231
South Orleans, *PLEASANT BAY ANTIQUES* 261

New Hampshire
Chesterfield, *HEMLOCK HILL ANTIQUES* 288
Dublin, *WM LARY-THOMAS SEAVER*
ANTIQUES 290
Francestown, *MILL VILLAGE ANTIQUES* 294
Holderness, *WILLIAM F DEMBIEC ANTIQUES*
302
Jaffrey, *INDIAN SUMMER ANTIQUES* 304
Lyme Center, *JOAN & GAGE ELLIS* 308
New London, *THE BLOCK HOUSE* 312

Rhode Island
Wickford, *THE BALL & CLAW* 344

Vermont
Dorset, *AMERICAN SPORTING ANTIQUES* 353
Hinesburg, *HAWK'S NEST ANTIQUES &*
DECOYS 358
Middlebury, *VILLAGE STORE OF*
MIDDLEBURY 361
Shelburne Village, *UNDERBRIDGE ANTIQUES*
370

31 Display Stands/Glass

Connecticut
Bristol, *RICHARD BLASCHKE* 48

New Hampshire
Raymond, *BURT DIAL COMPANY* 318

Rhode Island
Hopkinton, *THE ELEGANT DRAGON* 332

32 Dolls/Toys

Connecticut
Bethlehem, *THE NEW ENGLAND SHOP* 46
Bridgewater, *THE DOLL ROOM* 48
Coventry, *WILDFLOWER* 54
Greenwich, *THE HOUSE THAT JACK BUILT* 65
Kent, *THE FORRER'S* 68
Milford, *JENNY LEES ANTIQUES* 75
North Kent, *GOODE HILL ANTIQUES* 84
North Kent, *MAVIS* 85
Old Saybrook, *THE HOUSE OF PRETTY*
THINGS 87
South Norwalk, *OLD WELL ANTIQUES* 94
Westport, *TODBURN* 106

Maine
Albion, *COCK HILL FARM* 116
Augusta, *WHITE BARN ANTIQUES* 117
Caribou, *CHARLOTTE'S DOLLS &*
COLLECTIBLES 124
Lincolnville Beach, *BETTY'S TRADING POST*
137
Presque Isle, *THE COUNTRY STORE* 146
Roxbury, *YANKEE GEM CORP* 147
Searsport, *GOLD COAST ANTIQUES* 149
Searsport, *RED KETTLE ANTIQUES* 149
Thomaston, *WEE BARN ANTIQUES* 151
West Southport, *CATHERINE HILL ANTIQUES*
155
Wiscasset, *MARSTON HOUSE AMERICAN*
ANTIQUES 156
Wiscasset, *AARON & HANNAH PARKER*
ANTIQUES 157

Massachusetts
Brewster, *BAYBERRY ANTIQUES* 190
Brewster, *BRETON HOUSE* 190
Brewster, *SUNSMITH HOUSE - ANTIQUES* 191
Cummaquid, *THE OWL'S NEST ANTIQUES* 201
East Sandwich, *HORSEFEATHERS ANTIQUES*
206
Holden, *DAVIDIAN AMERICANA* 220
Hudson, *THE NEW ENGLAND ANTIQUE TOY*
MALL 220
Ipswich, *HILDA KNOWLES ANTIQUES* 222
Marlboro, *WAYNE PRATT & CO* 228
Milford, *DUNBAR'S GALLERY* 230
Northampton, *L & M FURNITURE* 241

Seekonk, *RUTH FALKINBURG'S DOLL SHOP* 252
South Egremont, *DALZELL HOUSE ANTIQUES* 259
Southwick, *THE TOY SHOP* 262
Waltham, *MISTER BIG TOYLAND* 268
Westborough, *THE BAYBERRYSHOP ANTIQUES* 275
Yarmouth Port, *TOWN CRIER ANTIQUES* 282

New Hampshire
Antrim, *GRIST MILL ANTIQUES* 285
Keene, *THE YARD SALE* 305
Laconia, *1893 ANN-TEEKS* 305
Lancaster, *THE SHOP IN THE BARN* 306
Portsmouth, *THE DOLL CONNECTION* 317
Springfield, *LAZY FOX ANTIQUES ET GALLERIE* 321
Stratham, *COMPASS ROSE ANTIQUES* 321

Rhode Island
Newport, *THE DOLL MUSEUM* 334

Vermont
Cavendish, *SIGOURNEYS' ANTIQUES* 351
Manchester, *THE CLOCK EMPORIUM* 359
Middlebury, *REBA BLAIR SALES* 361
Middlebury, *C. TILEY ANTIQUES* 361
Rutland, *EAGLE'S NEST ANTIQUES* 368
Springfield, *SUMMER HILL SHOP* 371
Swanton, *RAY & AL'S ANTIQUES* 372
Taftsville, *FRASER'S ANTIQUES* 373
Warren, *WARREN ANTIQUES* 374

33 Ephemera

Connecticut
Barkhamstead, *BETTY MESSENGER* 45
Bethany, *THE ANTIQUARIUM* 45
Danbury, *CARNIVAL HOUSE ANTIQUES* 54
Darien, *GILANN SUMMER BOOK SHOP* 55
East Haddam, *MAGIC HORN LTD* 57
Lakeville, *BAD CORNER ANTIQUES & DECORATION* 70
Meriden, *FAIR WEATHER ANTIQUES* 74
Monroe, *BARBARA'S BARN ANTIQUES* 76
Norfolk, *NOBODY EATS PARSLEY* 84
Norwalk, *BARTER SHOP* 85
Torrington, *NUTMEG BOOKS* 101
Winsted, *VERDE ANTIQUES & BOOKS* 108

Maine
Bangor, *LIPPINCOTT BOOKS* 117
Bryant Pond, *MOLL OCKETT* 122
Camden, *STONE SOUP BOOKS* 123
Castine, *BARBARA FALK - BOOKSELLER* 124
Farmington Falls, *FALLS BOOK BARN* 129
Lincolnville Beach, *GOOSE RIVER EXCHANGE* 137
Mount Desert Island, *WIKHEGAN BOOKS* 138
Northport, *LORD SEAGRAVE'S* 142
Wells, *COUNTRY BARN* 154
West Brooklin, *LOUISA GOODYEAR ANTIQUES* 155
Westbrook, *PEG GERAGHTY-BOOKS* 155

Massachusetts
Amherst, *GRIST MILL ANTIQUES* 162
Boston, *THE NOSTALGIA FACTORY* 182
Brewster, *THE HOMESTEAD ANTIQUES* 190
Brewster, *ROCKING CHAIR ANTIQUES* 191
Chatham, *HOUSE ON THE HILL* 198
Dennisport, *THE SIDE DOOR* 204

East Longmeadow, *W D HALL* 205
Gardner, *PAUL C RICHARDS AUTOGRAPHS* 212
Hamilton, *ELMCRESS BOOKS* 218
Haverhill, *CONSTANCE MORELLE BOOKS* 219
Hudson, *THE NEW ENGLAND ANTIQUE TOY MALL* 220
Huntington, *PAULSON'S ANTIQUARIAN PAPER/BOOK* 221
Lanesborough, *AMBER SPRING ANTIQUES* 222
Lexington, *RAINY DAY BOOKS* 225
Medway, *MARJORIE PARROTT ADAMS BOOKS* 229
Orange, *ORANGE TRADING COMPANY* 242
Provincetown, *REMEMBRANCES OF THINGS PAST* 246
Sheffield, *HOWARD S MOTT INC* 255
South Egremont, *ANTIQUES & VARIETIES* 259
South Egremont, *DALZELL HOUSE ANTIQUES* 259
Spencer, *QUABOAG USED BOOKS* 262
Waltham, *HAROLD M BURSTEIN & CO* 268
Weston, *JANE CHORAS, BOOKS* 276
Wilbraham, *MURRAY BOOKS* 277

New Hampshire
Charlestown, *ANTIQUES CENTER* 288
Concord, *THE OLD ALMANACK SHOP* 289
Freedom, *FREEDOM BOOKSHOP* 296
Hillsboro, *THE SHADOW SHOP* 302
Richmond, *NORTH COUNTRY BOOKSHOP* 318
Rumney, *VILLAGE BOOKS* 319

Rhode Island
Newport, *SIMMONS & SIMMONS* 337

Vermont
Adamant, *ADAMANT BOOKS* 348
Bethel, *OLD BOOKS & EPHEMERA* 349
Groton, *STEPHEN JONES ANTIQUES* 357
Pittsford, *NOSTALGIA NOOK* 365
Putney, *UNIQUE ANTIQUE* 366
Shelburne, *WILLIAM L PARKINSON BOOKS* 370
Woodstock, *PLEASANT STREET BOOKS* 377

34 Folk Art

Connecticut
Bethel, *DIERINGERS ARTS & ANTIQUES* 46
Clinton, *MEURS RENEHAN* 51
Coventry, *HANDS OF TIME* 53
Coventry, *WILDFLOWER* 54
Darien, *ANTIQUES UNLIMITED* 55
East Lyme, *STEPHEN & CAROL HUBER INC* 58
Easton, *RED SLEIGH* 58
Glastonbury, *MARY S SWIFT ANTIQUES* 62
Greenwich, *THE HOUSE THAT JACK BUILT* 65
Lakeville, *AMERICANA* 70
Litchfield, *PETER H TILLOU - FINE ARTS* 71
New Haven, *GIAMPIETRO ANTIQUES* 80
Sharon, *RANDALL AND KOBLENZ* 93
South Windsor, *COUNTRY BARN* 94
Southport, *J B RICHARDSON GALLERY* 97
Stonington, *ANN LEHMANN ANTIQUES* 98
Suffield, *NIKKI & TOM DEUPREE* 100
West Cornwall, *INDIAN LANE FARM* 103
Westport, *THE FAMILY ALBUM* 105
Woodbury, *DARIA OF WOODBURY* 111
Woodbury, *ROBERT S WALIN ANTIQUES* 113

Maine
Albion, *COCK HILL FARM* 116

Damariscotta, *PATRICIA ANNE REED ANTIQUES* 125
Deer Isle, *BELCHER'S ANTIQUES* 126
Hallowell, *BERDAN'S ANTIQUES* 131
Hallowell, *GARY F ELWELL ANTIQUES* 131
Holden, *DOUGLAS MARSHALL* 132
Kennebunkport, *BARBARA DOHERTY* 134
Lille, *THE OLD HOMESTEAD* 136
Moody, *KENNETH & IDA MANKO* 138
Peaks Island, *ISLAND TO ISLAND ANTIQUES* 143
Portland, *MILK STREET ANTIQUES* 145
Wells, *COREY DANIELS* 154
Wiscasset, *SPRIG OF THYME ANTIQUES* 157
Wiscasset, *TWO AT WISCASSET* 158

Massachusetts
Chatham, *SHIRLEY WALKER ANTIQUES* 199
Essex, *STEPHEN SCORE* 209
Groton, *BOSTON ROAD ANTIQUES* 216
Hancock, *MOUNTAIN ROAD ANTIQUES* 218
Lee, *PEMBROKE ANTIQUES* 223
Lenox, *CHARLES L FLINT* 223
Lenox, *OCTOBER MOUNTAIN ANTIQUES* 224
Milford, *DUNBAR'S GALLERY* 230
Nantucket, *FORAGER HOUSE COLLECTION* 231
Nantucket, *NINA HELLMAN* 231
Nantucket, *NANTUCKET HOUSE ANTIQUES* 232
Provincetown, *JULIE HELLER GALLERY* 246
Sandwich, *PAUL MADDEN ANTIQUES* 251
Sheffield, *CUPBOARDS & ROSES* 254
Shelburne Falls, *LUELLA MC CLOUD ANTIQUES* 257
South Egremont, *ANTIQUES & VARIETIES* 259
South Egremont, *LITTLE HOUSE STUDIO* 260
South Egremont, *SPLENDID PEASANT* 260
Sturbridge, *THE GREEN APPLE* 264
Taunton, *JO-ANN E ROSS* 266
Vineyard Haven, *EARLY SPRING FARM ANTIQUES* 267
West Barnstable, *THE WHIPPLETREE* 271
Westborough, *PUSHCART PLACE* 276

New Hampshire
Canaan, *AMERICAN CLASSICS* 287
Center Strafford, *BERT & GAIL SAVAGE* 288
Dublin, *WM LARY-THOMAS SEAVER ANTIQUES* 290
Epsom, *BOB & RITA BECKER* 292
Francestown, *THE FRANCESTOWN GALLERY* 294
Hampton Falls, *AMERICAN PRIDE* 298
Hillsboro, *WELL SWEEP ANTIQUES* 302
Jaffrey, *INDIAN SUMMER ANTIQUES* 304
Loudon, *COUNTRY ANTIQUES* 307
Merrimack, *JEANNINE DOBBS COUNTRY FOLK* 310
Mont Vernon, *CANDLEWICK ANTIQUES* 310
Mt Sunapee, *RED SLEIGH* 311
Peterborough, *THE COBBS ANTIQUES* 315
Portsmouth, *MILL POND ANTIQUES* 317
Sunapee, *FRANK & BARBARA POLLACK* 321
Wolfeboro, *RICHARD G MARDEN* 327

Rhode Island
Charlestown, *SALT BOX ANTIQUES* 331
Newport, *FAIR DE YORE* 334
Newport, *R KAZARIAN* 335

Vermont
Brandon, *BRANDON ANTIQUES* 349
Brandon, *H GRAY GILDERSLEEVE ANTIQUES* 349
Brandon, *NUTTING HOUSE ANTIQUES* 349
Burlington, *WEBB & PARSONS NORTH* 351
Dorset, *VIRGINIA POPE, INC.* 354
Fair Haven, *FOUNDATION ANTIQUES* 355
Manchester Center, *BARBARA B TRASK, APPRAISALS* 360
Manchester, *STEVENSON GALLERY* 359
Shelburne Village, *UNDERBRIDGE ANTIQUES* 370
Taftsville, *FRASER'S ANTIQUES* 373
Townshend, *COLT BARN ANTIQUES* 373

35 French Antiques

Connecticut
Colchester, *LES TROIS PROVINCES* 51
Darien, *LA CALECHE* 55
Fairfield, *LEMANOIR COUNTRY FRENCH ANTIQUES* 61
Fairfield, *WINSOR ANTIQUES* 61
Greenwich, *ANTAN ANTIQUES LTD* 63
Greenwich, *ELAINE DILLOF* 64
Greenwich, *HENRI-BURTON FRENCH ANTIQUES* 65
Greenwich, *PROVINCES DE FRANCE* 65
Madison, *ANTIQUES AT MADISON* 72
New Canaan, *SALLEA ANTIQUES* 78
New Haven, *VILLAGE FRANCAIS* 81
Westport, *PARC MONCEAU* 106
Wilton, *MARIA & PETER WARREN ANTIQUES* 108
Woodbury, *BRITISH COUNTRY ANTIQUES* 109
Woodbury, *COUNTRY LOFT ANTIQUES* 110
Woodbury, *MILL HOUSE ANTIQUES* 111

Massachusetts
Boston, *ANTIQUE PORCELAINS LTD* 167
Boston, *AUTREFOIS* 168
Brookline Village, *A ROOM WITH A VIEUX* 194
Brookline, *AUTREFOIS II* 192
Great Barrington, *MULLIN-JONES ANTIQUITIES* 216
Longmeadow, *LE PERIGORD* 226
Nantucket, *PETTICOAT ROW* 232
North Andover, *COUNTRY IN ANDOVER* 239
Seekonk, *PENNY LANE ANTIQUES & GIFTS INC* 253

36 Furniture

Connecticut
Bantam, *GOOSEBORO BROOK ANTIQUES* 45
Bethel, *J THOMAS MELVIN* 46
Bolton, *HAILSTON HOUSE INC* 47
Bridgeport, *GRAYNOOK ANTIQUES & INTERIORS* 48
Brookfield, *MC CAFFREY BOOTH ANTIQUES* 48
Brooklyn, *HEIRLOOM ANTIQUES* 49
Chester, *ONE-OF-A-KIND INC* 50
Colchester, *LES TROIS PROVINCES* 51
Coventry, *ANTIQUE DE-LIGHTS* 53
Coventry, *OLD COUNTRY STORE ANTIQUES* 53
Darien, *ROSE D'OR* 56
Durham, *HODGE PODGE LODGE* 57

East Haddam, *CENTERPIECE ANTIQUES* 57
East Hampton, *BELLTOWN TRADING POST* 57
East Hampton, *OPERA HOUSE ANTIQUES* 58
Fairfield, *JAMES BOK ANTIQUES* 60
Fairfield, *ENSINGER ANTIQUES LTD* 61
Fairfield, *LEMANOIR COUNTRY FRENCH ANTIQUES* 61
Glastonbury, *MARY S SWIFT ANTIQUES* 62
Glastonbury, *ROY & BETSY THOMPSON ANTIQUES* 62
Greenwich, *ANTIQUES & INTERIORS AT THE MILL* 63
Greenwich, *BANKSVILLE ANTIQUES* 64
Greenwich, *CONSIGN IT* 64
Greenwich, *LIBERTY WAY ANTIQUES* 65
Guilford, *ARNE E AHLBERG* 66
Haddam, *WILD GOOSE CHASE* 66
Hartford, *BACON ANTIQUES* 67
Hebron, *DAVID & DALE BLAND ANTIQUES* 68
Kent, *HARRY HOLMES ANTIQUES* 69
Kent, *OLDE STATION ANTIQUES* 69
Lakeville, *AMERICANA* 70
Lakeville, *BAD CORNER ANTIQUES & DECORATION* 70
Litchfield, *COUNTRY HOUSE CONSIGNMENTS* 70
Meriden, *FAIR WEATHER ANTIQUES* 74
Middletown, *COUNTRY ANTIQUES AT MIDDLETOWN* 74
Milford, *KAYES CONSIGNMENTS* 75
Milford, *JENNY LEES ANTIQUES* 75
Milford, *STOCK TRANSFER* 76
Milford, *TREASURES & TRIFLES* 76
New Canaan, *SEVERED TIES, INC* 78
New Haven, *JASMINE* 80
New Haven, *WEST GATE ANTIQUES* 81
New Milford, *LEON-VANDERBILT* 82
North Kent, *GOODE HILL ANTIQUES* 84
Norwalk, *WINGS OF A DOVE CONSIGNMENT* 85
Old Lyme, *BRIGER FAIRHOLME JONES* 86
Pine Meadow, *PINE MEADOW ANTIQUES* 88
Ridgefield, *GREENWILLOW ANTIQUES* 90
Ridgefield, *THE SILK PURSE* 91
Rowayton, *WILLIAMS PORT ANTIQUES* 91
Somers, *OLD HICKORY ANTIQUES* 93
South Norwalk, *FAIENCE* 94
South Willington, *SOUTH WILLINGTON ANTIQUES* 94
Stonington, *MARY MAHLER ANTIQUES* 99
Stonington, *RONALD NOE ANTIQUES* 99
Stonington, *OPUS I* 99
Stonington, *VICTORIA STATION* 99
Tolland, *HUNT COUNTRY ANTIQUES* 100
Torrington, *NORMAN'S ANTIQUES* 101
West Haven, *JOSEPH LOUIS NACCA* 104
Weston, *MILLICENT RUDD BEST* 104
Westport, *THINGS* 106
Wilton, *WAYSIDE EXCHANGE* 108
Woodbury, *MONIQUE SHAY ANTIQUES* 113

Maine
Bangor, *GAMAGE ANTIQUES* 117
Belfast, *APEX ANTIQUES* 118
Boothbay Harbor, *COLLECTOR SHOP* 120
Camden, *LEVETT'S ANTIQUES* 123
Camden, *THE RICHARDS ANTIQUES* 123
Camden, *SCHUELER ANTIQUES* 123
Damariscotta, *BROOKMEAD FARM* 125
Ellsworth, *CALISTA STERLING ANTIQUES* 127

Fairfield, *THISTLE'S* 128
Hanover, *LYONS' DEN ANTIQUES* 132
Kennebunk, *DYNAN FINE ARTS* 133
Kennebunkport, *MARIE PLUMMER GOETT* 134
Kennebunkport, *SAML'S STAIRS ANTIQUES* 135
Lincolnville Beach, *BETTY'S TRADING POST* 137
Lincolnville Beach, *NORTH HOUSE FINE ANTIQUES* 137
Newcastle, *MARY HODES* 140
Pittsfield, *KENNISTON'S ANTIQUES* 143
Presque Isle, *THE COUNTRY STORE* 146
Round Pond, *ROUND POND ANTIQUES* 147
Round Pond, *TIME AND AGAIN ANTIQUES* 147
Thomaston, *WEE BARN ANTIQUES* 151
Trenton, *MAYO ANTIQUES GALLERY* 152
West Southport, *CATHERINE HILL ANTIQUES* 155
Wiscasset, *COACH HOUSE ANTIQUES* 156
Yarmouth, *THE RED SHED* 158
Yarmouth, *W M SCHWIND, JR ANTIQUES* 158
York, *JOHN LARKIN SGRO* 159

Massachusetts
Acton, *SEAGULL ANTIQUES* 162
Amherst, *R & R FRENCH ANTIQUES* 162
Amherst, *GRIST MILL ANTIQUES* 162
Beverly, *PRICE HOUSE ANTIQUES* 166
Boston, *BELGRAVIA ANTIQUES INC* 170
Boston, *HOWARD CHADWICK ANTIQUES* 173
Boston, *DIVINE DECADENCE* 175
Boston, *HIGHGATE GALLERIES* 180
Boston, *LESLIE'S ANTIQUES & COLLECTIBLES* 181
Boston, *RERUNS ANTIQUES* 185
Boston, *TIGER LILY* 187
Boston, *WEINER'S ANTIQUE SHOP* 188
Boston, *WENHAM CROSS ANTIQUES* 188
Brewster, *DONALD B HOWES - ANTIQUES* 190
Brewster, *THE PFLOCK'S-ANTIQUES* 190
Brighton, *DINING ROOM SHOWCASE* 192
Brookline, *TIM GALLAGHER ANTIQUES* 193
Cambridge, *KARIN J PHILLIPS ANTIQUES* 197
Cambridge, *A TOUCH OF CLASS* 197
Concord, *CONCORD PATRIOT ANTIQUES* 200
Cummington, *B SHAW ANTIQUES* 201
Dedham, *HENRY HORNBLOWER III* 202
Essex, *BRICK HOUSE ANTIQUES* 208
Essex, *FRIENDSHIP ANTIQUES* 208
Georgetown, *PHEASANT HILL ANTIQUES* 213
Gloucester, *BEAUPORT ANTIQUES* 213
Gloucester, *CAPE ANN ANTIQUES & ORIENTALS* 213
Great Barrington, *ANTHONY'S ANTIQUES* 214
Great Barrington, *JONESES ANTIQUES* 215
Great Barrington, *RED HORSE ANTIQUES* 216
Groton, *PAM BOYNTON* 216
Groton, *JAMES MATTOZZI & MARILYN BURKE* 217
Hopkinton, *HERITAGE ANTIQUES* 220
Huntington, *PAULSON'S ANTIQUARIAN PAPER/BOOK* 221
Hyannis, *STONE'S ANTIQUE SHOP* 222
Lenox, *STONE'S THROW ANTIQUES* 224
Marblehead, *HEELTAPPERS ANTIQUES* 227
Marblehead, *MARBLEHEAD ANTIQUES* 227
Marblehead, *S & S GALLERIES* 228
Marlboro, *WAYNE PRATT & CO* 228
Nantucket, *ISLAND ATTIC INDUSTRIES INC* 231

Nantucket, *TILLER ANTIQUES* 233
Newtonville, *AROUND THE CORNER ANTIQUES* 238
Norton, *DUBOIS' OLD HOUSE* 241
Orleans, *CONTINUUM* 242
Osterville, *FERRAN'S INTERIORS* 243
Peabody, *AMERICANA ANTIQUES* 244
Plainfield, *DICK HALE ANTIQUES* 245
Rockport, *ELIOT ANTIQUES* 248
Rockport, *YE OLDE LANTERN ANTIQUES* 248
Salem, *MARCHAND'S LAFAYETTE ANTIQUES* 250
Sandwich, *H RICHARD STRAND FINE ANTIQUES* 251
Seekonk, *ANTIQUES AT HEARTHSTONE HOUSE* 252
Seekonk, *LEONARD'S ANTIQUES, INC.* 252
Sheffield, *COVERED BRIDGE ANTIQUES* 254
Sheffield, *FALCON ANTIQUES* 255
Sheffield, *OLE T J'S ANTIQUE BARN* 255
South Egremont, *BIRD CAGE ANTIQUES* 259
South Egremont, *COUNTRY LOFT ANTIQUES* 259
South Egremont, *RED BARN ANTIQUES* 260
South Egremont, *GLADYS SCHOFIELD ANTIQUES* 260
Southborough, *GOLDEN PARROT* 261
Southborough, *GOLDEN PONY ANTIQUES* 261
Southborough, *MAPLEDALE ANTIQUES* 261
Southborough, *TOOMEY'S HAVEN ANTIQUES* 262
Swansea, *FERGUSON & D'ARRUDA* 265
Townsend, *THE COUNTRY GENTLEMAN* 267
Townsend, *FRANK J TAMMARO* 267
Upton, *DAVID ROSE ANTIQUES* 267
Vineyard Haven, *EARLY SPRING FARM ANTIQUES* 267
Wayland, *YANKEE CRAFTSMAN* 269
Wellesley Hills, *COUNTRY INTERIORS* 270
Wenham, *FIREHOUSE ANTIQUES* 270
West Boylston, *YANKEE HERITAGE ANTIQUES* 272
West Bridgewater, *WILLOWBROOK* 272
Westwood, *PEG WILLIS ANTIQUES* 277
Williamsburg, *COUNTRY FINE ANTIQUES* 278
Williamstown, *LIBRARY ANTIQUES* 278
Worthington, *COUNTRY CRICKET VILLAGE INN* 280
Yarmouth Port, *STEPHEN H GARNER* 281

New Hampshire
Bedford, *BEDFORD CENTER ANTIQUES* 285
Brookline, *1786 HOUSE ANTIQUES* 286
Center Harbor, *ACCENTS FROM THE PAST* 287
Center Harbor, *HOLIDAY HOUSE ANTIQUES* 287
Charlestown, *ANTIQUES CENTER* 288
Durham, *WISWALL HOUSE* 291
Epsom, *BOB & RITA BECKER* 292
Epsom, *THE BETTY HOUSE* 292
Exeter, *DECOR ANTIQUES* 292
Fitzwilliam, *DENNIS & DAD ANTIQUES* 294
Francestown, *STONEWALL ANTIQUES* 295
Hampton, *GARGOYLES & GRIFFINS* 298
Hampton, *THE RED BARN ANTIQUES* 298
Hancock, *THE BARN OF HANCOCK VILLAGE* 299
Hillsboro, *APPLEYARD ANTIQUES* 301
Hillsboro, *LOON POND ANTIQUES* 301

Hillsboro, *CHERYL & PAUL SCOTT ANTIQUES* 301
Hillsboro, *TATEWELL GALLERY* 302
Hillsboro, *WELL SWEEP ANTIQUES* 302
Hollis, *THE COOPERAGE* 302
Hopkinton, *WAYNE & PEGGY WOODARD ANTIQUES* 303
Keene, *BEECH HILL GALLERY* 304
Laconia, *1893 ANN-TEEKS* 305
Lancaster, *GRANARY ANTIQUES* 306
Lancaster, *THE SHOP IN THE BARN* 306
Lisbon, *HOUSTON'S FURNITURE BARN* 306
Lyme Center, *JOAN & GAGE ELLIS* 308
Lyme, *SOMEWHERE IN TIME ANTIQUES* 308
Moultonboro, *ANTIQUES AT MOULTONBORO* 311
Moultonboro, *CARL & BEVERLY SHELDRAKE* 311
New Ipswich, *ESTELLE M GLAVEY, INC.* 312
New London, *PRISCILLA DRAKE ANTIQUES* 312
Raymond, *CALOUBAR COLLECTABLES* 318
Rochester, *PETER CARSWELL ANTIQUES* 319
Salisbury Heights, *BARKER'S OF SALISBURY HEIGHTS* 319
Spofford, *FINE ANTIQUES* 320
Walpole, *FARQUHAR ANTIQUES* 323
Walpole, *RHODES OF WASHINGTON SQUARE* 323
Washington, *HALF-MOON ANTIQUES* 324
West Lebanon, *WINDHAM ANTIQUES* 325

Rhode Island
Bristol, *ALFRED'S* 330
Carolina, *JAMES E SCUDDER* 330
Charlestown, *LION'S MANE ANTIQUES* 331
Hope Valley, *DUKSTA'S ANTIQUES* 332
Newport, *GALLERY '76 ANTIQUES INC* 335
Newport, *JOHN GIDLEY HOUSE* 335
Newport, *HARRY GREW* 335
Newport, *SMITH MARBLE LTD* 337
Newport, *UNIQUE ANTIQUES* 337
Newport, *GUSTAVES J.S. WHITE* 338
Westerly, *HERITAGE ANTIQUES* 344
Woonsocket, *THE CORNER CURIOSITY SHOPPE* 344
Wyoming, *BRAD SMITH* 345

Vermont
Addison, *OLD STONE HOUSE ANTIQUES* 348
Colchester, *MATTESON GALLERY OF ARTS* 352
Derby Line, *CARRIAGE HOUSE ANTIQUES* 353
Essex Junction, *YANKEE PEDLAR'S ANTIQUES* 355
Grafton, *GABRIELS' BARN ANTIQUES* 356
Grafton, *GRAFTON GATHERING PLACE* 356
Manchester Village, *EQUINOX ANTIQUES* 360
Middletown Springs, *OLD SPA SHOP ANTIQUES* 362
Newfane, *SCHOMMER ANTIQUES* 363
Pawlet, *EAST WEST ANTIQUES* 365
Reading, *MILL BROOK ANTIQUES* 367
Rutland, *PARK ANTIQUES* 368
Shaftsbury, *THE CHOCOLATE BARN ANTIQUES* 370
Stowe, *GREEN MOUNTAIN ANTIQUES* 372
Vergennes, *FITZ-GERALDS' ANTIQUES* 373
Waltham, *C J HARRIS ANTIQUES* 374
Warren, *WARREN ANTIQUES* 374
Waterbury, *UPLAND ACRES ANTIQUES* 375
Woodstock, *CHURCH STREET GALLERY* 376

Woodstock, *COUNTRY WOODSHED* 377

37 Furniture/American

Connecticut

Bantam, *KENT & YVONNE GILYARD ANTIQUES* 45
Bolton, *AUTUMN POND ANTIQUES* 46
Bolton, *QUAKER LADY ANTIQUES* 47
Bridgeport, *MARC THE 1ST ANTIQUES* 48
Canton, *1784 HOUSE ANTIQUES* 49
Colchester, *NATHAN LIVERANT & SON* 51
Darien, *ANTIQUES UNLIMITED* 55
Darien, *WINDSOR ANTIQUES LTD* 56
Essex, *FRANCIS BEALEY AMERICAN ARTS* 59
Essex, *TURTLE CREEK ANTIQUES* 60
Essex, *WHITE FARMS ANTIQUES* 60
Farmington, *LILLIAN BLANKLEY COGAN ANTIQUARY* 61
Greenwich, *ELAINE DILLOF* 64
Greenwich, *GUILD ANTIQUES* 64
Harwinton, *JOHN M DAVIS INC* 67
Jewett City, *JOHN WALTON INC* 68
Kent, *GOLDEN THISTLE ANTIQUES* 69
Kent, *ELIZABETH S MANKIN ANTIQUES* 69
Lisbon-Jewett City, *MR & MRS JEROME BLUM* 70
Madison, *ANTIQUES AT MADISON* 72
Madison, *KIRT & ELIZABETH CRUMP* 72
Marble Dale, *EARL J SLACK ANTIQUES* 73
New Canaan, *THE MORRIS HOUSE* 78
New Haven, *EDWIN C AHLBERG* 79
New Preston, *THE R COGSWELL COLLECTION* 83
Newtown, *CODFISH ANTIQUES* 84
Norwalk, *EAGLES LAIR ANTIQUES* 85
Pomfret Center, *PRISCILLA H ZIESMER* 89
Redding, *MELLIN'S ANTIQUES* 89
Redding, *SERGEANT* 90
Salisbury, *BUCKLEY & BUCKLEY ANTIQUES* 92
Salisbury, *COLLECTORS* 92
Simsbury, *C RUSSELL NOYES* 93
South Windsor, *HORACE PORTER ANTIQUES* 95
Southport, *J B RICHARDSON GALLERY* 97
Southport, *THE STOCK MARKET* 97
Southport, *TEN EYCK-EMERICH ANTIQUES* 97
Stamford, *SHIPPAN POINT GALLERY* 97
Stonington, *CHRISTOPHER & KATHLEEN COLE* 98
Stonington, *NEIL B EUSTACE* 98
Stonington, *ORKNEY & YOST ANTIQUES* 99
Thompson, *RUSSIAN BEAR ANTIQUES* 100
Washington Depot, *STEPHEN CALCAGNI* 102
West Cornwall, *INDIAN LANE FARM* 103
West Redding, *LINCOLN & JEAN SANDER INC* 104
West Willington, *RONALD & PENNY DIONNE* 104
Westport, *DORVAN L MANUS* 106
Wilton, *THE PINE CHEST, INC.* 107
Wilton, *THOMAS SCHWENKE, INC* 107
Wilton, *GEORGE SUBKOFF ANTIQUES, INC.* 107
Wilton, *MARIA & PETER WARREN ANTIQUES* 108
Woodbury, *CARRIAGE HOUSE ANTIQUES* 109
Woodbury, *CLAPP AND TUTTLE* 109
Woodbury, *HAROLD E COLE ANTIQUES* 110

Woodbury, *DARIA OF WOODBURY* 111
Woodbury, *DAVID DUNTON/ANTIQUES* 111
Woodbury, *GILDAY'S ANTIQUES* 111
Woodbury, *KENNETH HAMMITT ANTIQUES* 111
Woodbury, *FRANK C JENSEN ANTIQUES* 111
Woodbury, *PETER A NELSON* 112
Woodbury, *SOUTHFORD ANTIQUES* 113
Woodbury, *EVE STONE & SON ANTIQUES* 113
Woodbury, *ROBERT S WALIN ANTIQUES* 113

Maine

Bar Harbor, *ROSE W OLSTEAD* 117
Belfast, *AVIS HOWELLS ANTIQUES* 119
Damariscotta, *PETER/JEAN RICHARDS FINE ANTIQUE* 126
Kennebunkport, *ANTIQUES AT NINE* 134
Kennebunkport, *WINTER HILL FARM* 136
Limington, *ROBERT O STUART* 136
Newfield, *JOHN BAUER SONIA SEFTON ANTI* 141
Norway, *DIXON'S ANTIQUES* 142
Pittston, *KENNETH AND PAULETTE TUTTLE* 144
Rockport, *KATRIN PHOCAS LTD* 147
Searsport, *THE CAPTAIN'S HOUSE ANTIQUES* 149
Southwest Harbor, *MARIANNE CLARK FINE ANTIQUES* 150
Stockton Springs, *BRICK HOUSE ANTIQUES* 151
Union, *EBENEZER ALDEN HOUSE* 152
Wells, *COREY DANIELS* 154
Winterport, *RICHARD & PATRICIA BEAN* 156
Wiscasset, *LILAC COTTAGE* 156
Wiscasset, *PORRINGER & BRUCE MARCUS ANTIQUE* 157

Massachusetts

Andover, *NEW ENGLAND GALLERY INC* 163
Ashley Falls, *ASHLEY FALLS ANTIQUES* 164
Ashley Falls, *ROBERT THAYER AMERICAN ANTIQUES* 165
Boston, *H GROSSMAN* 178
Boston, *DAVID LAWRENCE GALLERY* 181
Brewster, *WILLIAM M BAXTER ANTIQUES* 190
Brewster, *EDWARD SNOW HOUSE ANTIQUES* 191
Brighton, *DERBY DESK COMPANY* 192
Brookline Village, *TOWNE ANTIQUES* 195
Brookline, *BROOKLINE ANTIQUES* 193
Brookline, *JERRY FREEMAN LTD* 193
Cambridge, *MARC J MATZ* 197
Charlestown, *THE FISKE HOUSE* 198
Chesterfield, *CHESTERFIELD ANTIQUES* 199
Danvers, *SPRAGUE HOUSE ANTIQUES* 201
Dedham, *DEDHAM ANTIQUE SHOP* 202
East Sandwich, *JESSE CALDWELL LEATHERWOOD* 206
Easthampton, *GLASKOWSKY & COMPANY* 207
Essex, *NORTH HILL ANTIQUES* 209
Framingham, *AVERY'S ANTIQUES* 212
Gloucester, *GLOUCESTER FINE ARTS & ANTIQUARI* 214
Great Barrington, *BY SHAKER HANDS* 214
Great Barrington, *CORASHIRE ANTIQUES* 215
Great Barrington, *PAUL & SUSAN KLEINWALD INC* 215
Hadley, *MOUNTAIN CREST ANTIQUES* 217
Halifax, *WILLEM & INGER LEMMENS ANTIQUES* 218
Hamilton, *RO-DAN ANTIQUES* 218

Hancock, *MOUNTAIN ROAD ANTIQUES* 218
Lanesborough, *AMBER SPRING ANTIQUES* 222
Lee, *AARDENBURG ANTIQUES* 223
Lee, *PEMBROKE ANTIQUES* 223
Lenox, *CHARLES L FLINT* 223
Lenox, *OCTOBER MOUNTAIN ANTIQUES* 224
Marlboro, *WAYNE PRATT & CO* 228
Nantucket, *NANTUCKET HOUSE ANTIQUES* 232
Nantucket, *TRANQUIL CORNERS ANTIQUES* 233
Nantucket, *THE WICKER PORCH* 233
Nantucket, *LYNDA WILLAUER ANTIQUES* 233
Needham, *GOLDEN FLEECE ANTIQUES* 234
Newburyport, *PETER EATON* 235
North Andover, *ROLAND B HAMMOND INC* 239
Pittsfield, *BERKSHIRE ANTIQUES* 245
Plymouth, *ANTIQUES UNLIMITED INC* 246
Rehoboth, *MENDES ANTIQUES* 247
Sheffield, *DARR ANTIQUES AND INTERIORS* 254
Sheffield, *DOVETAIL ANTIQUES* 254
Sheffield, *KUTTNER ANTIQUES* 255
Sheffield, *LOIS W SPRING* 256
Sheffield, *DAVID M WEISS* 257
South Egremont, *HOWARD'S ANTIQUES* 260
South Egremont, *ELLIOTT & GRACE SNYDER* 260
Sterling, *PUDDLE DUCK ANTIQUES* 263
Wellesley, *SPIVACK'S ANTIQUES* 269
West Boylston, *PUDDLE DUCK ANTIQUES* 272
West Granville, *IVES HILL ANTIQUES* 273
West Stockbridge, *SAWYER ANTIQUES* 275
West Townsend, *JOHN & BARBARA DELANEY CLOCKS* 275
West Townsend, *GARY SULLIVAN ANTIQUES* 275

New Hampshire
Amherst, *AMHERST VILLAGE ANTIQUE SHOP* 284
Canaan, *AMERICAN CLASSICS* 287
Chichester, *DOUGLAS H HAMEL* 288
Cornish, *NATHAN SMITH HOUSE* 290
East Lempster, *PETER HILL INC* 291
Exeter, *HOLLIS & TRISHA BRODRICK* 292
Fitzwilliam, *BLOOMIN' ANTIQUES* 293
Franconia, *ELEANOR M LYNN/ELIZABETH MONAHAN* 295
Hampton, *GUS JOHNSON ANTIQUES* 298
Hillsboro, *OLD DUNBAR HOUSE* 301
Hopkinton, *ANDERSON'S ANTIQUES, INC.* 303
Hopkinton, *MEADOW HEARTH* 303
Jaffrey, *AT THE SIGN OF THE FOX* 304
Kensington, *PETER SAWYER ANTIQUES* 305
Londonderry, *THE TATES ANTIQUES* 307
Lyme, *FALCON'S ROOST ANTIQUES* 307
Manchester, *VICTORIAN BARN ANTIQUES* 308
Marlborough, *THOMAS R LONGACRE* 308
Marlborough, *BETTY WILLIS ANTIQUES, INC* 308
Nashua, *RALPH KYLLOE* 311
New London, *MAD EAGLE INC FINE ANTIQUES* 312
Portsmouth, *COBBLESTONES OF MARKET SQUARE* 317
Portsmouth, *ED WEISSMAN* 318
Rindge, *SCOTT BASSOFF/SANDY JACOBS* 319
Seabrook, *STONE HOUSE ANTIQUES* 320

Sunapee, *FRANK & BARBARA POLLACK* 321
Walpole, *GOLDEN PAST OF WALPOLE* 323
Warner, *SCOTT'S ANTIQUES* 324
Rhode Island
Ashaway, *ASHAWAY ANTIQUES STORE* 330
Charlestown, *SALT BOX ANTIQUES* 331
Newport, *THE DRAWING ROOM ANTIQUES* 334
Newport, *LAMP WORKS* 336
Newport, *LAMPLIGHTER ANTIQUES* 336
North Kingstown, *LAFAYETTE ANTIQUES* 338
North Scituate, *VILLAGE ANTIQUES* 338
Portsmouth, *COUNTRY CUPBOARD* 339
Portsmouth, *BENJAMIN FISH HOUSE ANTIQUES* 339
Providence, *MARTIN CONLON AMERICAN ANTIQUES* 340
Providence, *THE RATHBUN GALLERY-SHAKER* 340
Wakefield, *DOVE AND DISTAFF ANTIQUES* 342
Vermont
Bennington, *FOUR CORNERS EAST, INC* 348
Brandon, *BRANDON ANTIQUES* 349
East Montpelier, *JEFFREY R CUETO ANTIQUES* 354
Fairfax, *GLENORTON COUNTRY ANTIQUES* 355
Middlebury, *BRADY GALLERIES, INC.* 361
Middlebury, *HOBNOB ANTIQUES* 361
Rockingham Village, *STEPHEN-DOUGLAS ANTIQUES* 367
Rutland, *CONWAY'S ANTIQUES & DECOR* 368
Waitsfield, *THE STORE, INC* 373
Wallingford, *COUNTRY HOUSE ANTIQUES* 374

38 Furniture/Continental

Connecticut
Essex, *BONSAL-DOUGLAS ANTIQUES* 59
Greenwich, *STEFANO MAGNI ANTIQUES/FINE ART* 65
Kent, *GOLDEN THISTLE ANTIQUES* 69
Killingworth, *THE BERGERON'S ANTIQUES* 69
Southport, *THE STOCK MARKET* 97
Stonington, *WATER STREET ANTIQUES* 99
Westport, *L'OBJET D'ART LTD* 105
Maine
Kennebunkport, *ANTIQUES AT NINE* 134
Kennebunkport, *WINTER HILL FARM* 136
Wells, *RIVERBANK ANTIQUES* 154
Massachusetts
Ashley Falls, *CIRCA* 164
Ashley Falls, *RUSSELL LYONS* 165
Boston, *AUTREFOIS* 168
Boston, *JAMES BILLINGS* 170
Boston, *GEORGE I GRAVERT ANTIQUES* 178
Boston, *SLENSKA'S ANTIQUES & INTERIORS* 187
Boston, *TIGER LILY* 187
Brewster, *WILLIAM M BAXTER ANTIQUES* 190
Brookline Village, *BECKERMAN NEAL ANTIQUES* 194
Brookline Village, *BROOKLINE VILLAGE ANTIQUES* 194
Brookline Village, *TOWNE ANTIQUES* 195
Brookline, *AUTREFOIS II* 192
Brookline, *BROOKLINE ANTIQUES* 193
Dover, *INTERIOR MOTIVES, INC.* 204

Great Barrington, *MULLIN-JONES ANTIQUITIES* 216
Hamilton, *RO-DAN ANTIQUES* 218
Lenox, *CHARLES L FLINT* 223
Natick, *VANDERWEG ANTIQUES* 234
Plymouth, *ANTIQUES UNLIMITED INC* 246
Wellesley, *EUROPEAN MANOR* 269
Wellesley, *MARCUS & MARSHALL ANTIQUES* 269

New Hampshire
Amherst, *AMHERST VILLAGE ANTIQUE SHOP* 284
Springfield, *LAZY FOX ANTIQUES ET GALLERIE* 321

Rhode Island
Newport, *TIGER LILY* 337
Providence, *CAROL LOMBARDI ANTIQUES* 340

Vermont
Bennington, *FOUR CORNERS EAST, INC* 348
Manchester, *PARAPHERNALIA ANTIQUES* 359
Old Bennington, *ANTIQUARIAN* 364

39 Furniture/English

Connecticut
Avon, *RUTH TROIANI FINE ANTIQUES* 45
Bantam, *WESTON THORN ANTIQUES* 45
Cos Cob, *PIERCE-ARCHER ANTIQUES* 52
Fairfield, *WINSOR ANTIQUES* 61
Greenwich, *ELAINE DILLOF* 64
Greenwich, *GEORGIAN ANTIQUES* 64
Greenwich, *GUILD ANTIQUES* 64
Harwinton, *JOHN M DAVIS INC* 67
Litchfield, *D W LINSLEY INC* 70
Madison, *ANTIQUES AT MADISON* 72
Marble Dale, *EARL J SLACK ANTIQUES* 73
New Canaan, *ENGLISH HERITAGE ANTIQUES, INC* 77
New Canaan, *MANOR ANTIQUES* 77
New Canaan, *JOYCE SCARBOROUGH ANTIQUES* 78
New Haven, *THE ANTIQUES MARKET* 79
New Preston, *BLACK SWAN ANTIQUES* 82
New Preston, *STRAWBERRY HILL ANTIQUES* 83
Salisbury, *COLLECTORS* 92
Salisbury, *MICHAEL COX ANTIQUES* 92
Scotland, *OLD ENGLISH ANTIQUES & TEA ROOM* 93
Southport, *THE STOCK MARKET* 97
Stamford, *SHIPPAN POINT GALLERY* 97
Stonington, *WATER STREET ANTIQUES* 99
Tolland, *HUNT COUNTRY ANTIQUES* 100
Washington Depot, *STEPHEN CALCAGNI* 102
Westport, *L'OBJET D'ART LTD* 105
Westport, *DORVAN L MANUS* 106
Westport, *PRINCE OF WALES* 106
Wilton, *GEORGE SUBKOFF ANTIQUES, INC.* 107
Wilton, *MARIA & PETER WARREN ANTIQUES* 108
Winthrop, *JAS E ELLIOTT ANTIQUES* 108
Woodbury, *THE BAY TREE ANTIQUES* 109
Woodbury, *BRITISH COUNTRY ANTIQUES* 109
Woodbury, *CROSSWAYS ANTIQUES* 110
Woodbury, *MILL HOUSE ANTIQUES* 111
Woodbury, *GERALD MURPHY ANTIQUES LTD* 112

Maine
Damariscotta, *PETER/JEAN RICHARDS FINE ANTIQUE* 126
Newcastle, *CONSTANCE H HURST* 140
North Edgecomb, *JACK PARTRIDGE* 141
Rockport, *KATRIN PHOCAS LTD* 147
Wells, *THE FARM* 154
Wells, *R JORGENSEN ANTIQUES* 154
Wiscasset, *LILAC COTTAGE* 156

Massachusetts
Ashley Falls, *LEWIS & WILSON* 165
Boston, *BEACON HILL FINE ARTS/ANTIQUES* 168
Boston, *JAMES BILLINGS* 170
Boston, *ISABELLE COLLINS OF LONDON* 175
Boston, *MARCOZ ANTIQUES & JEWELRY* 182
Boston, *C A RUPPERT* 185
Boston, *SHREVE, CRUMP & LOW* 187
Brookline Village, *BROOKLINE VILLAGE ANTIQUES* 194
Brookline Village, *TOWNE ANTIQUES* 195
East Orleans, *COUNTRYSIDE ANTIQUES* 205
Essex, *RIDER & CLARKE ANTIQUES* 209
Groton, *JOS KILBRIDGE CHINA TRADE ANTIQU* 216
Marblehead, *SACKS ANTIQUES* 228
Nantucket, *VAL MAITINO ANTIQUES* 232
Nantucket, *TILLER ANTIQUES* 233
Natick, *VANDERWEG ANTIQUES* 234
Sheffield, *GOOD & HUTCHINSON ASSOCIATES* 255
Sheffield, *KUTTNER ANTIQUES* 255
Sheffield, *SUSAN SILVER ANTIQUES* 256
Wellesley, *SPIVACK'S ANTIQUES* 269

New Hampshire
Alexandria, *COLE HILL FARM ANTIQUES* 284
Hampton, *RONALD BOURGEAULT ANTIQUES* 297
Marlborough, *BETTY WILLIS ANTIQUES, INC* 308
Milford, *VICTORIA PLACE* 310
Portsmouth, *COBBLESTONES OF MARKET SQUARE* 317
Springfield, *THE COLONEL'S SWORD* 320
Wolfeboro, *RALPH K REED ANTIQUES* 327

Rhode Island
Newport, *COUNTRY PLEASURES LTD* 334
Newport, *LAMP WORKS* 336
North Kingstown, *MENTOR ANTIQUES* 338

Vermont
Chester, *1828 HOUSE* 351
Middletown Springs, *NIMMO & HART ANTIQUES* 362
Wallingford, *TOM KAYE ANTIQUES LTD* 374

40 Furniture/Oak

Connecticut
Bristol, *DICK'S ANTIQUES* 48
Darien, *EMY JANE JONES ANTIQUES* 55
Killingworth, *THE BERGERON'S ANTIQUES* 69
Litchfield, *D W LINSLEY INC* 70
Middletown, *COUNTRY ANTIQUES AT MIDDLETOWN* 74
Milford, *ANTIQUES OF TOMORROW* 75
Milford, *MILFORD EMPORIUM* 75
New Milford, *BRUCE W ANDERSON ANTIQUES* 81

New Milford, *BIT OF COUNTRY* 82
Pawcatuck, *WOODS ANTIQUES* 88
Torrington, *NORMAN'S ANTIQUES* 101

Maine
Alfred, *ALFRED TRADING COMPANY* 116
Alfred, *PATRICIAN DESIGNS* 116
Auburn, *MORIN'S ANTIQUES* 116
Belgrade, *BORSSEN ANTIQUES* 119
Bernard, *ONCE UPON A TIME* 119
Ellsworth, *CINDY'S ANTIQUES* 127
Fairfield, *JULIA & POULIN ANTIQUES* 128
Fairfield, *JOHN D JULIA ANTIQUES* 128
Lincolnville Beach, *SIGN OF THE OWL* 137
Orrington, *MERRIMAC'S ANTIQUES* 143
Scarborough, *TOP KNOTCH ANTIQUES* 148
Searsport, *BETTER DAY'S ANTIQUES* 149
Searsport, *RED KETTLE ANTIQUES* 149
Troy, *GREEN'S CORNER ANTIQUES* 152
Wells, *COUNTRY BARN* 154

Massachusetts
Brewster, *ANTIQUES ETC* 189
Brookline, *THE STRAWBERRY PATCH* 194
Cambridge, *EASY CHAIRS* 196
Essex, *AMERICANA ANTIQUES* 207
Lincoln, *BROWN-CORBIN FINE ART* 225
Marlboro, *WAYSIDE ANTIQUES* 229
Newton Highlands, *BENCHMARK ANTIQUES* 237
Newton Highlands, *MARCIA & BEA ANTIQUES* 237
Newton Upper Falls, *NORTH WIND FURNISHINGS INC* 238
Northampton, *AMERICAN DECORATIVE ARTS* 240
Northampton, *L & M FURNITURE* 241
Palmer, *FURNITURE BARN* 243
South Egremont, *DOUGLAS ANTIQUES* 260
Southampton, *SOUTHAMPTON ANTIQUES* 261
Sterling, *PUDDLE DUCK ANTIQUES* 263
West Boylston, *OBADIAH PINE ANTIQUES* 271
West Boylston, *PUDDLE DUCK ANTIQUES* 272

New Hampshire
Antrim, *COURT'S CUPBOARD ANTIQUES* 285
Brookline, *BROOKLINE VILLAGE ANTIQUES* 286
Canaan, *ERNIE'S ANTIQUES* 287
Londonderry, *LONDONDERRY ANTIQUES* 307
Portsmouth, *TRUNKWORKS* 318
Troy, *RED SHED* 322
West Swanzey, *FREDERICK MAC PHAIL ANTIQUES* 325

Rhode Island
Chepachet, *CHESTNUT HILL ANTIQUES* 331
Newport, *MAINLY OAK LTD* 336

Vermont
Chester, *WILLIAM AUSTIN'S ANTIQUES* 351
Essex Junction, *ALL THINGS CONSIDERED* 355
Johnson, *MEL SIEGEL ANTIQUES* 358
Poultney, *DEN OF ANTIQUITY* 366
Quechee, *PEDLER'S ATTIC* 366
Rutland, *SUGAR HOUSE ANTIQUES* 368
South Burlington, *SIMPLY COUNTRY* 371
St Albans, *PAULETTE'S ANTIQUES/COLLECTIBL* 371
Swanton, *TANSY FARM ANTIQUES* 372
Vergennes, *EIGHTH ELM FARM ANTIQUES* 373

41 Furniture/Painted
Connecticut
East Lyme, *STEPHEN & CAROL HUBER INC* 58
Fairfield, *PATTY GAGARIN ANTIQUES* 61
Killingworth, *LEWIS W SCRANTON ANTIQUES* 70
Madison, *NOSEY GOOSE* 72
Pomfret Center, *MEADOW ROCK FARM ANTIQUES* 89
Salisbury, *RUSSELL CARRELL* 92
South Norwalk, *OLD WELL ANTIQUES* 94
Suffield, *NIKKI & TOM DEUPREE* 100
Washington Depot, *THE TULIP TREE COLLECTION* 102
Woodbury, *PINE WOODS ANTIQUES* 112
Woodbury, *MONIQUE SHAY ANTIQUES* 113

Maine
Hallowell, *JAMES H. LE FURGY BOOKS & ANT.* 131
Wiscasset, *MARSTON HOUSE AMERICAN ANTIQUES* 156
Wiscasset, *SPRIG OF THYME ANTIQUES* 157

Massachusetts
Boston, *SHOP ON THE HILL* 187
Essex, *STEPHEN SCORE* 209
Great Barrington, *MULLIN-JONES ANTIQUITIES* 216
Harvard, *THREE BAGS FULL* 218
Lee, *FERRELL'S ANTIQUES & WOODWORKING* 223
Littleton, *HAMLET ANTIQUES* 225
Nantucket, *PETTICOAT ROW* 232
Sheffield, *EGH PETER AMERICAN ANTIQUES* 256
Townsend, *MARTHA BOYNTON ANTIQUES* 266
West Chatham, *1736 HOUSE ANTIQUES* 272
Westborough, *SALT-BOX HOUSE ANTIQUES* 276
Yarmouth Port, *DESIGN WORKS* 281

New Hampshire
Cornish, *NATHAN SMITH HOUSE* 290
Fitzwilliam, *WILLIAM LEWAN ANTIQUES* 294
Francestown, *STONEWALL ANTIQUES* 295
Merrimack, *JEANNINE DOBBS COUNTRY FOLK* 310
Peterborough, *THE COBBS ANTIQUES* 315

Rhode Island
Newport, *ANTIQUES AT FIFTY NINE BELLEVUE* 333
Newport, *THE CLASSIC TOUCH* 334
Newport, *TIGER LILY* 337

Vermont
Hinesburg, *HAWK'S NEST ANTIQUES & DECOYS* 358

42 Furniture/Pine
Connecticut
Darien, *EMY JANE JONES ANTIQUES* 55
Deep River, *RIVERWIND ANTIQUE SHOP* 56
Easton, *RED SLEIGH* 58
Killingworth, *THE BERGERON'S ANTIQUES* 69
Litchfield, *D W LINSLEY INC* 70
New Canaan, *LISSARD HOUSE* 77
New Canaan, *JOYCE SCARBOROUGH ANTIQUES* 78

Pomfret Center, *MEADOW ROCK FARM ANTIQUES* 89
Ridgefield, *ISLAND HOUSE ANTIQUES* 91
Tolland, *HUNT COUNTRY ANTIQUES* 100
Washington Depot, *THE TULIP TREE COLLECTION* 102
Westport, *PRINCE OF WALES* 106
Wilton, *CASTLE ANTIQUE IMPORTERS* 107
Woodbury, *BRITISH COUNTRY ANTIQUES* 109
Woodbury, *PINE WOODS ANTIQUES* 112
Woodbury, *WEST COUNTRY ANTIQUES* 113

Maine
Alfred, *ALFRED TRADING COMPANY* 116
Fairfield, *JOHN D JULIA ANTIQUES* 128
Kennebunkport, *RANDS ANTIQUES ON RAND GREEN* 135
Lille, *THE OLD HOMESTEAD* 136
Pittston, *PHIPPS OF PITTSTON* 143
Portland, *MARY ALICE REILLEY* 145
Waterboro, *WATERBORO EMPORIUM* 153
Wells, *COUNTRY BARN* 154

Massachusetts
Acton, *ENCORES* 162
Arlington, *IRREVERENT RELICS* 164
Boston, *ISABELLE COLLINS OF LONDON* 175
Brewster, *ANTIQUES ETC* 189
Chatham, *OLDE VILLAGE COUNTRY BARN* 199
East Sandwich, *HEATHER HOUSE* 206
Essex, *AMERICANA ANTIQUES* 207
Great Barrington, *BYGONE DAYS* 214
Groton, *THE ANNEX* 216
Marlboro, *WAYSIDE ANTIQUES* 229
Nantucket, *ISLAND ATTIC INDUSTRIES INC* 231
Plainfield, *DICK HALE ANTIQUES* 245
Somerville, *LONDONTOWNE GALLERIES* 258
Sterling, *PUDDLE DUCK ANTIQUES* 263
Sudbury, *ADAMS ANTIQUES USA* 264
Wellfleet, *MORTAR & PESTLE ANTIQUES* 270
West Chatham, *1736 HOUSE ANTIQUES* 272
Williamsburg, *COUNTRY FINE ANTIQUES* 278
Yarmouth Port, *DESIGN WORKS* 281

New Hampshire
Antrim, *COURT'S CUPBOARD ANTIQUES* 285
Brookline, *BROOKLINE VILLAGE ANTIQUES* 286
Chesterfield, *HEMLOCK HILL ANTIQUES* 288
Hopkinton, *THE SOULES-ANTIQUES* 303
Mt Sunapee, *RED SLEIGH* 311
Troy, *RED SHED* 322
Wolfeboro, *TOUCHMARK ANTIQUES* 327

Rhode Island
Newport, *COUNTRY PLEASURES LTD* 334

Vermont
Pawlet, *EAST WEST ANTIQUES* 365
Quechee, *PEDLER'S ATTIC* 366
Stowe, *ENGLISH COUNTRY ANTIQUES* 372
Swanton, *TANSY FARM ANTIQUES* 372
Vergennes, *EIGHTH ELM FARM ANTIQUES* 373

43 Furniture/Reproduction

Connecticut
Ashford, *CLASSICS IN WOOD* 44
Ashford, *MERRYTHOUGHT* 44
Brookfield, *MC CAFFREY BOOTH ANTIQUES* 48
Milford, *MILFORD EMPORIUM* 75
New Milford, *CRICKET HILL CONSIGNMENT* 82
Old Lyme, *GARY R PARTELOW REPRODUCTIONS* 86
Ridgefield, *THE RED PETTICOAT* 91
South Norwalk, *BEAUFURN INC* 94
Southbury, *GARY LUNDIN* 96
Torrington, *NORMAN'S ANTIQUES* 101
Woodbury, *ART & PEGGY PAPPAS ANTIQUES* 112

Maine
Kittery, *THE WINDSOR CHAIR* 136

Massachusetts
Ashby, *COUNTRY BED SHOP* 164
Easthampton, *PETER FRANKLIN CABINETMAKERS* 207
Harvard, *CORNUCOPIA, INC* 218
Osterville, *ELDRED WHEELER* 243
Seekonk, *LEONARD'S ANTIQUES, INC.* 252
Somerville, *ROBERT E SMITH* 258
South Ashfield, *RUSS LOOMIS JR* 258
Sudbury, *ADAMS ANTIQUES USA* 264
Wayland, *GREAT MEADOWS JOINERY* 268
Westborough, *MAYNARD HOUSE* 275

New Hampshire
Enfield, *DANA ROBES WOOD CRAFTSMEN* 291
Gilmanton Iron Works, *STEPHEN P BEDARD* 297

Rhode Island
Bristol, *ROBERT BARROW, CABINETMAKER* 330
East Greenwich, *CONSTANTINE'S FINE FURNITURE* 332
Newport, *RAMSON HOUSE ANTIQUES* 337
Providence, *VAN DALE GALLERY* 341

Vermont
Corinth, *ROBERT CHAMBERS* 352
Manchester Center, *BELLWETHER GALLERY* 360

44 Glass

Connecticut
Bethel, *PICKWICK HOUSE ANTIQUES* 46
Burlington, *HADSELL'S ANTIQUES* 49
Canton, *1784 HOUSE ANTIQUES* 49
Danbury, *CARNIVAL HOUSE ANTIQUES* 54
Darien, *ROSE D'OR* 54
Essex, *A MATHEWS ANDERSON ANTIQUES* 59
Greenwich, *LIBERTY WAY ANTIQUES* 65
Hamden, *GALLERY 4* 67
Hartford, *BACON ANTIQUES* 67
Litchfield, *THOMAS MC BRIDE ANTIQUES* 71
Milford, *R & J GLASSWARE* 75
Morris, *T'OTHER HOUSE ANTIQUES* 76
New Haven, *FROM HERE TO ANTIQUITY* 80
New Milford, *CRICKET HILL CONSIGNMENT* 82
Newtown, *POVERTY HOLLOW ANTIQUES* 84
North Kent, *MAVIS* 85
Norwich, *WALTS ANTIQUES* 86
Old Greenwich, *NEW ENGLAND SHOP* 86
Old Saybrook, *THE HOUSE OF PRETTY THINGS* 87
Old Saybrook, *LITTLE HOUSE OF GLASS* 87
Old Saybrook, *SWEET PEA ANTIQUES* 87
Portland, *CRANE'S ANTIQUES, ETC* 89
Ridgefield, *GREENWILLOW ANTIQUES* 90

Riverside, *ESTATE TREASURES* 91
Somers, *OLD HICKORY ANTIQUES* 93
Stony Creek, *STONY CREEK VILLAGE STORE* 99
Woodbury, *GRASS ROOTS ANTIQUES* 111

Maine
Augusta, *PINE TREE STABLES ANTIQUES* 117
Augusta, *WHITE BARN ANTIQUES* 117
Bernard, *1895 SHOP* 119
Bernard, *THE OLD RED STORE* 119
Biddeford, *ELI THE COBBLER ANTIQUES* 120
Boothbay Harbor, *BAY STREET ANTIQUES* 120
Boothbay Harbor, *COLLECTOR SHOP* 120
Boothbay Harbor, *JOSEPHINE HURD ANTIQUES* 121
Boothbay, *BLUE UNICORN* 120
Bryant Pond, *MOLL OCKETT* 122
Caribou, *AUNTIE BEA'S ANTIQUES* 124
Caribou, *JUDY'S ANTIQUES* 124
Damariscotta, *ROGER & BEE BENNETT* 125
Damariscotta, *BROOKMEAD FARM* 125
Damariscotta, *COOPER'S RED BARN* 125
Farmington, *ANTIQUES FROM POWDER HOUSE HILL* 129
Gardiner, *MORRELL'S ANTIQUES* 130
Gorham, *COUNTRY SQUIRE ANTIQUES* 130
Hallowell, *D & R ANTIQUES* 131
Hallowell, *MAINELY ANTIQUES* 131
Hallowell, *JOSIAH SMITH ANTIQUES* 131
Hope, *THE BLUEBERRY PATCH* 132
Kennebunkport, *OLD FORT INN & ANTIQUES* 135
Lincolnville, *DUCK TRAP ANTIQUES* 137
Ogunquit, *BEAUPORT INN ANTIQUES* 142
Orono, *THE GREEN DOOR ANTIQUE SHOP* 143
Orrington, *MERRIMAC'S ANTIQUES* 143
Portland, *MARY ALICE REILLEY* 145
Portland, *VENTURE ANTIQUES* 146
Portland, *WILMA'S ANTIQUES & ACCESSORIES* 146
Presque Isle, *THE COUNTRY STORE* 146
Rangeley, *BLUEBERRY HILL FARM* 146
Round Pond, *TIME AND AGAIN ANTIQUES* 147
Sebago, *THE GALLERY SHOP* 149
Topsham, *MERRYMEETING ANTIQUES* 152
Woolwich, *ANTIQUES ETC* 158
York, *GORGEANA ANTIQUES* 159

Massachusetts
Amherst, *GRIST MILL ANTIQUES* 162
Boston, *HIGHGATE GALLERIES* 180
Buzzards Bay, *THE OLD HOUSE* 195
Cambridge, *FLEUR DE LIS GALLERY* 196
Chatham, *CHAPDELAINE ANTIQUES* 198
Concord, *CONCORD PATRIOT ANTIQUES* 200
Cummaquid, *THE PICKET FENCE* 201
Dennis, *ELLIPSE ANTIQUES* 202
Dennisport, *THE SIDE DOOR* 204
Dorchester, *OLDE BOSTONIAN* 204
Essex, *CHRISTIAN MOLLY ANTIQUES* 208
Essex, *HOWARD'S FLYING DRAGON ANTIQUES* 209
Essex, *THE WHITE ELEPHANT SHOP* 210
Fairhaven, *HARE & TORTOISE ANTIQUES/COLLECT* 210
Falmouth, *AURORA BOREALIS ANTIQUES* 211
Holden, *VILLAGE ANTIQUES* 220
Hyannis, *PRECIOUS PAST* 221
Hyannis, *STONE'S ANTIQUE SHOP* 222

Ipswich, *HILDA KNOWLES ANTIQUES* 222
Marblehead, *THE ANTIQUE SHOP* 226
New Bedford, *BROOKSIDE ANTIQUES* 235
Newtonville, *AROUND THE CORNER ANTIQUES* 238
Northampton, *ELEANOR KOCOT ANTIQUES* 241
Rockport, *YE OLDE LANTERN ANTIQUES* 248
Salem, *JER-RHO ANTIQUES* 250
Sandwich, *THE BROWN JUG* 251
Sandwich, *SHAWME POND ANTIQUES* 251
Sandwich, *THE STITCHERY IN SANDWICH* 251
Sandwich, *H RICHARD STRAND FINE ANTIQUES* 251
Sheffield, *1750 HOUSE ANTIQUES* 253
South Brewster, *SMITH ANTIQUES* 259
South Egremont, *COUNTRY LOFT ANTIQUES* 259
South Egremont, *GLADYS SCHOFIELD ANTIQUES* 260
Southborough, *GOLDEN PARROT* 261
Sudbury, *THE ANTIQUE EXCHANGE OF SUDBURY* 265
Templeton, *1800 HOUSE ANTIQUES, LTD* 266
Townsend, *THE COUNTRY GENTLEMAN* 267
West Boylston, *YANKEE HERITAGE ANTIQUES* 272
West Brewster, *SENTIMENTAL JOURNEY* 272
West Dennis, *RUMFORD ANTIQUES* 273
Yarmouth Port, *CC CANCER CONSIGNMENT EXCHANGE* 281
Yarmouth Port, *CONSTANCE GOFF* 281
Yarmouth Port, *BETSY HEWLETT* 281
Yarmouth Port, *LIL-BUD ANTIQUES* 281
Yarmouth Port, *TOWN CRIER ANTIQUES* 282

New Hampshire
Alton, *FLEUR-DE-LIS ANTIQUES* 284
Bedford, *BEDFORD CENTER ANTIQUES* 285
Center Harbor, *THE ROYALE MESS* 287
Charlestown, *ANTIQUES CENTER* 288
Contoocook, *GOLD DRAGON ANTIQUES* 289
Fitzwilliam, *DENNIS & DAD ANTIQUES* 294
Fitzwilliam, *EXPRESSIONS* 294
Fitzwilliam, *RED BARN ANTIQUES* 294
Francestown, *STONEWALL ANTIQUES* 295
Hampton, *THE RED BARN ANTIQUES* 298
Hampton, *H G WEBBER* 298
Hillsboro, *BARBARA'S ANTIQUES* 301
Hillsboro, *WYNDHURST FARM ANTIQUES* 302
Hollis, *THE BLUE LANTERN ANTIQUES* 302
Keene, *THE YARD SALE* 305
Meredith, *GORDONS ANTIQUES* 309
New London, *PRISCILLA DRAKE ANTIQUES* 312
Ossipee, *FLAG GATE FARM ANTIQUES* 315
Salisbury Heights, *BARKER'S OF SALISBURY HEIGHTS* 319
Springfield, *THE COLONEL'S SWORD* 320
Springfield, *SPRING HILL FARM ANTIQUES* 321
Walpole, *FARQUHAR ANTIQUES* 323
Whitefield, *THE FAIRWEATHER SHOP* 326
Wolfeboro, *RICHARD G MARDEN* 327
Wolfeboro, *MONIQUE'S ANTIQUES* 327

Rhode Island
Ashaway, *BRIGGS HOUSE ANTIQUES* 330
Bristol, *ALFRED'S* 330
Carolina, *JAMES E SCUDDER* 330

Charlestown, *FOX RUN COUNTRY ANTIQUES* 331

Newport, *BLACK SHEEP ANTIQUES* 333

Newport, *SMITH MARBLE LTD* 337

North Kingstown, *LILLIAN'S ANTIQUES* 338

Watch Hill, *OCEAN HOUSE ANTIQUES/CURIOSITIES* 343

West Greenwich, *MARTONE'S GALLERY* 343

Woonsocket, *THE CORNER CURIOSITY SHOPPE* 344

Vermont

Addison, *OLD STONE HOUSE ANTIQUES* 348

Burlington, *COLIN & ELIZABETH DUCOLON* 351

Burlington, *TAILOR'S ANTIQUES* 351

Castleton Corners, *OLD HOMESTEAD ANTIQUES* 351

East Barre, *FARR'S ANTIQUES* 354

Essex Junction, *YANKEE PEDLAR'S ANTIQUES* 355

Fairlee, *EDITH M ACKERMAN* 356

Grafton, *WOODSHED ANTIQUES* 356

Jeffersonville, *MARY'S GLASS & COLLECTIBLES* 358

Manchester Center, *BREWSTER ANTIQUES* 360

Middlebury, *BIX ANTIQUES* 361

Middlebury, *HOBNOB ANTIQUES* 361

Newfane, *SCHOMMER ANTIQUES* 363

Ryegate Corner, *RYEGATE CORNER ANTIQUES* 369

Shelburne, *GADHUE'S ANTIQUES* 370

St Albans, *PAULETTE'S ANTIQUES/COLLECTIBL* 371

Waterbury, *UPLAND ACRES ANTIQUES* 375

Wilmington, *DEERFIELD VALLEY ANTIQUES* 376

45 Garden Statuary

Connecticut

Essex, *HASTINGS HOUSE* 60

Wilton, *VALLIN GALLERIES* 107

Maine

Kennebunkport, *BARBARA DOHERTY* 134

Limerick, *TOM JOSEPH & DAVID RAMSAY* 136

Wells, *COREY DANIELS* 154

Wells, *RIVERBANK ANTIQUES* 154

Massachusetts

Boston, *SHOP ON THE HILL* 187

East Sandwich, *JESSE CALDWELL LEATHERWOOD* 206

Essex, *HOWARD'S FLYING DRAGON ANTIQUES* 209

Great Barrington, *JONESES ANTIQUES* 215

Nantucket, *AMERICAN PIE* 231

Nantucket, *FORAGER HOUSE COLLECTION* 231

Somerville, *LONDONTOWNE GALLERIES* 258

Rhode Island

Newport, *AARDVARK ANTIQUES* 333

North Kingstown, *MENTOR ANTIQUES* 338

46 Interior Decoration

Connecticut

Darien, *LA CALECHE* 55

South Norwalk, *FAIENCE* 94

Wallingford, *IMAGES, HEIRLOOM LINENS/LACE* 101

Massachusetts

Boston, *HIGHGATE GALLERIES* 180

Boston, *LINDERMAN SCHENCK* 181

Boston, *NEWBURY STREET JEWELRY & ANTIQUE* 182

Essex, *NORTH HILL ANTIQUES* 209

Groton, *OLD FASHIONED MILK PAINT COMPANY* 217

West Chesterfield, *TEXTILE REPRODUCTIONS* 273

West Newbury, *HELIGE ANDE ARTS* 274

New Hampshire

Gilmanton Iron Works, *STEPHEN P BEDARD* 297

Peterborough, *PARTRIDGE REPLICATIONS* 316

Portsmouth, *PARTRIDGE REPLICATIONS* 317

West Lebanon, *PARTRIDGE REPLICATIONS* 325

Rhode Island

Newport, *THE DRAWING ROOM ANTIQUES* 334

Newport, *FULL SWING* 334

47 Jewelry

Connecticut

Branford, *YESTERDAY'S THREADS* 47

Chester, *ONE-OF-A-KIND INC* 50

Darien, *EMY JANE JONES ANTIQUES* 55

Fairfield, *G G G ANTIQUES* 61

Greenwich, *BETTERIDGE JEWELERS INC* 64

Greenwich, *CONSIGN IT* 64

Greenwich, *RENE GROSJEAN ANTIQUES* 64

Greenwich, *SOPHIA'S GREAT DAMES* 66

Guilford, *CORNUCOPIA ANTIQUE CONSIGNMENTS* 66

Hartford, *THE UNIQUE ANTIQUE* 67

Kent, *PAULINE'S PLACE* 69

Milford, *KAYES CONSIGNMENTS* 75

Milford, *STOCK TRANSFER* 76

Milford, *TREASURES & TRIFLES* 76

Monroe, *BARBARA'S BARN ANTIQUES* 76

New Haven, *ANN MARIE'S VINTAGE BOUTIQUE* 79

New Haven, *SALLY GOODMAN ANTIQUES* 80

North Kent, *MAVIS* 85

Old Saybrook, *SWEET PEA ANTIQUES* 87

Ridgefield, *HUNTER'S CONSIGNMENT* 90

Ridgefield, *UNDER THE DOGWOOD TREE* 91

Riverside, *ESTATE TREASURES* 91

Scotland, *OLD ENGLISH ANTIQUES & TEA ROOM* 93

Sharon, *RANDALL AND KOBLENZ* 93

Southbury, *THE HONEY POT* 95

Stamford, *ALEXANDRA WISE ANTIQUES* 98

Stonington, *DOWNSTAIRS AT HARBOR VIEW* 98

Stonington, *RAYMOND IZBICKI* 98

Westport, *THE FAMILY ALBUM* 105

Westport, *FRIEDMAN GALLERY* 105

Willimantic, *ANTIQUES & THINGS* 107

Woodbury, *DAVIS ANTIQUES* 111

Woodbury, *SOUTHFORD ANTIQUES* 113

Maine

Bernard, *ONCE UPON A TIME* 119

Biddeford, *ELI THE COBBLER ANTIQUES* 120

Damariscotta, *BROOKMEAD FARM* 125

Hallowell, *MOTHER GOOSE ANTIQUES* 131
Kennebunkport, *GIBRAN ANTIQUE GALLERY* 134
Kennebunkport, *PORT ANTIQUES* 135
Newcastle, *KAJA VEILLUX ART & ANTIQUES* 140
Ogunquit, *POTPOURRI ANTIQUES* 142
Portland, *NELSON RARITIES, INC* 145
Thomaston, *ANCHOR FARM ANTIQUES* 151
Thomaston, *WEE BARN ANTIQUES* 151

Massachusetts
Arlington, *SECOND TYME AROUND* 164
Ashley Falls, *ASHLEY FALLS ANTIQUES* 164
Boston, *BEDELLE INC* 170
Boston, *BRODNEY INC* 171
Boston, *COLLECTOR'S SHOP* 174
Boston, *FINE TIME VINTAGE TIMEPIECES* 176
Boston, *FIRESTONE AND PARSON* 176
Boston, *GRAND TROUSSEAU* 176
Boston, *HARPER & FAYE INC* 178
Boston, *HOMER'S JEWELRY & ANTIQUES* 180
Boston, *LESLIE'S ANTIQUES & COLLECTIBLES* 181
Boston, *LEON OHANIAN & SONS CO INC* 185
Boston, *THE YANKEE MERCHANT GROUP* 189
Brookline Village, *THE ANTIQUE COMPANY* 194
Cambridge, *BERNHEIMER'S ANTIQUE ARTS* 195
Cambridge, *DOWN UNDER* 196
Cambridge, *FLEUR DE LIS GALLERY* 196
Chestnut Hill, *SONIA PAINE* 199
Dennis, *KING'S GRANT ANTIQUES* 203
Dennis, *THE LEANING TREE* 203
East Sandwich, *THE GILDED SWAN* 206
Essex, *CHRISTIAN MOLLY ANTIQUES* 208
Gloucester, *BANANAS* 213
Great Barrington, *KAHNS ANTIQUE & ESTATE JEWELRY* 215
Harwichport, *MAGGIE'S ANTIQUES & COLLECTIBLES* 219
Harwichport, *SEVEN SOUTH STREET ANTIQUES* 219
Lee, *THE KINGSLEIGH 1840* 223
Marblehead, *THREE SEWALL STREET ANTIQUES* 228
Nantucket, *AVANTI ANTIQUE JEWELRY* 231
Nantucket, *PUSS-N-BOOTS* 232
Newburyport, *ELIZABETH'S 20TH CENTURY* 235
Newtonville, *AROUND THE CORNER ANTIQUES* 238
Orleans, *LILAC HEDGE ANTIQUES* 243
Osterville, *OAK & IVORY* 243
Pittsfield, *GREYSTONE GARDENS* 245
Rockport, *ELIOT ANTIQUES* 248
Rockport, *RECUERDO* 248
Salem, *JER-RHO ANTIQUES* 250
Salem, *UNION STREET ANTIQUES* 250
Sheffield, *FREDERICK HATFIELD ANTIQUES* 255
South Egremont, *ANTIQUES & VARIETIES* 259
South Egremont, *COUNTRY LOFT ANTIQUES* 259
Wellfleet, *H B & DOROTHY WATSON* 270
West Brewster, *SENTIMENTAL JOURNEY* 272
Yarmouth Port, *COLLECTOR'S CORNER* 281

New Hampshire
Center Harbor, *THE ROYALE MESS* 287

Francestown, *WOODBURY HOMESTEAD ANTIQUES* 295
Hampton, *THE RED BARN ANTIQUES* 298
Hancock, *CROOKED ONION FARM ANTIQUE* 299
Hanover, *MARIE-LOUISE ANTIQUES* 300
Milford, *MILFORD ANTIQUES* 310
Plymouth, *SUSAN B LARSEN ANTIQUES* 316
Portsmouth, *WISTERIA TREE* 318
Union, *CARSWELL'S ANTIQUES* 323

Rhode Island
East Greenwich, *HARBOUR GALLERIES* 332
Newport, *BELLEVUE GOLD* 333
Newport, *FAIR DE YORE* 334
Newport, *ALICE SIMPSON ANTIQUES* 337
North Kingstown, *LILLIAN'S ANTIQUES* 338
Providence, *CAROL LOMBARDI ANTIQUES* 340
Providence, *SUNNY DAYS* 341
Warren, *CHRISTIE & HADLEY ANTIQUES* 342
Warwick, *THE EMPORIUM* 343
Westerly, *WESTERLY ENTERPRISES* 344

Vermont
Barre, *ARNHOLM'S ANTIQUES* 348
Fairfax, *THE CAT'S MEOW ANTIQUES* 355
Manchester Center, *BREWSTER ANTIQUES* 360
Rutland, *SOPHIE'S COLLECTIQUES* 368
Rutland, *WALDRON & RHODES FINE JEWELERS* 369

48 Lace/Linen

Connecticut
Hamden, *GALLERY 4* 67
Lebanon, *THE ETCETERA SHOPPE* 70
New Preston, *JONATHAN PETERS* 83
Riverton, *ANTIQUES AND HERBS OF RIVERTON* 91
Scotland, *OLD ENGLISH ANTIQUES & TEA ROOM* 93
Wallingford, *IMAGES, HEIRLOOM LINENS/LACE* 101
Willimantic, *ANTIQUES & THINGS* 107

Maine
Bath, *RECENT PAST* 118
Portland, *REMEMBER WHEN* 145
Richmond, *THE LOFT ANTIQUES* 146
Rumford, *CONNIE'S ANTIQUES* 148
Wiscasset, *AARON & HANNAH PARKER ANTIQUES* 157
Woolwich, *ANTIQUES ETC* 158
Yarmouth, *THE RED SHED* 158

Massachusetts
Arlington, *SECOND TYME AROUND* 164
Boston, *COLLECTOR'S SHOP* 174
Boston, *LACE BROKER* 180
Boston, *LONDON LACE* 181
Boston, *RUE DE FRANCE* 185
East Sandwich, *HORSEFEATHERS ANTIQUES* 206
Harwichport, *MAGGIE'S ANTIQUES & COLLECTIBLES* 219
Holden, *VILLAGE ANTIQUES* 220
Hyannis, *PRECIOUS PAST* 221
Malden, *FLIGHTS OF FANCY ANTIQUES* 226
Marblehead, *THREE SEWALL STREET ANTIQUES* 228
Maynard, *MOLLY'S VINTAGE CLOTHING PROMO'N* 229

Nantucket, *PETTICOAT ROW* 232
Pittsfield, *GREYSTONE GARDENS* 245
Rockport, *MOUNT VERNON ANTIQUES* 248
Sandwich, *SHAWME POND ANTIQUES* 251
Wellesley Hills, *LACES UNLIMITED* 270

New Hampshire
Brookline, *BROOKLINE VILLAGE ANTIQUES* 286
Haverhill, *THE VICTORIAN ON MAIN STREET* 300
Keene, *ANDERSON GALLERY* 304
Keene, *THE YARD SALE* 305
Meredith, *GORDONS ANTIQUES* 309
Tuftonboro, *LOG CABIN ANTIQUES* 322

Rhode Island
Newport, *ANTIQUES AT FIFTY NINE BELLEVUE* 333
Newport, *BLACK SHEEP ANTIQUES* 333
Newport, *FAIR DE YORE* 334
Providence, *MY FAVORITE THINGS* 340
Watch Hill, *FINITNEY & COMPANY* 343

Vermont
Jeffersonville, *MARY'S GLASS & COLLECTIBLES* 358
Stowe, *ENGLISH COUNTRY ANTIQUES* 372
Swanton, *RAY & AL'S ANTIQUES* 372

49 Lead Soldiers

Maine
Gardiner, *FRED ROBBINS* 130

Massachusetts
Malden, *EXCALIBUR HOBBIES* 226

Vermont
Cavendish, *SIGOURNEYS' ANTIQUES* 351

50 Lighting

Connecticut
Avon, *AUTHENTIC REPRODUCTION LIGHTING* 44
Brooklyn, *HEIRLOOM ANTIQUES* 49
Chester, *PERIOD LIGHTING FIXTURES* 50
Coventry, *ANTIQUE DE-LIGHTS* 53
Cromwell, *CUSTOM HOUSE* 54
Essex, *THE ESSEX FORGE* 59
Gaylordsville, *MICHAEL HALL ANTIQUES* 62
Lisbon-Jewett City, *MR & MRS JEROME BLUM* 70
New Canaan, *THE STUDIO* 78
Newtown, *POVERTY HOLLOW ANTIQUES* 84
Salisbury, *BUCKLEY & BUCKLEY ANTIQUES* 92
Westport, *FRIEDMAN GALLERY* 105
Windham, *THE TIN LANTERN* 108
Woodbury, *GILDAY'S ANTIQUES* 111

Maine
Augusta, *PINE TREE STABLES ANTIQUES* 117
Bangor, *GAMAGE ANTIQUES* 117
Camden, *THE RICHARDS ANTIQUES* 123
Cape Neddick, *CRANBERRY HILL ANTIQUES/LIGHTING* 124
Damariscotta, *ROGER & BEE BENNETT* 125
Hallowell, *D & R ANTIQUES* 131
Kennebunkport, *MARIE PLUMMER GOETT* 134
Kennebunk, *VICTORIAN LIGHT/WATERTOWER PINES* 134

Newcastle, *DIFFERENT DRUMMER ANTIQUES* 139
Northeast Harbor, *PINE BOUGH* 142
Portland, *OCTAVIA'S ANTIQUES* 145
Searsport, *ANTIQUES AT THE HILLMANS* 149
Searsport, *GOLD COAST ANTIQUES* 149
Wiscasset, *TWO AT WISCASSET* 158

Massachusetts
Boston, *AUTREFOIS* 168
Boston, *DAVID LAWRENCE GALLERY* 181
Boston, *PERIOD FURNITURE HARDWARE CO* 185
Boston, *RERUNS ANTIQUES* 185
Boston, *TERI ANTIQUES* 187
Brookline Village, *A ROOM WITH A VIEUX* 194
Brookline, *APPLETON ANTIQUES* 192
Brookline, *AUTREFOIS II* 192
Brookline, *BEAZE OF BROOKLINE* 192
Brookline, *RENOVATORS SUPPLY* 193
Cambridge, *CITY LIGHTS* 196
Cambridge, *EASY CHAIRS* 196
Cambridge, *LAMP GLASS* 197
Conway, *CONWAY HOUSE* 201
Dennis Village, *BOSTON BRASS WORKS* 203
Dennis, *ELLIPSE ANTIQUES* 202
Essex, *AMERICANA ANTIQUES* 207
Fairhaven, *FANTASY HOUSE ANTIQUES* 210
Hadley, *HOME FARM ANTIQUES* 217
Holden, *VILLAGE ANTIQUES* 220
Holliston, *WILDER SHOP* 220
Hyannis, *ALBERT ARTS & ANTIQUES* 221
Littleton, *P & J ANTIQUES* 225
Marblehead, *BRASS & BOUNTY* 227
Nantucket, *VAL MAITINO ANTIQUES* 232
Newburyport, *ON CONSIGNMENT GALLERIES* 236
Northampton, *RUMPLESTILTSKIN* 241
Orange, *EDGAR STOCKWELL DECORATING/ANTIQ* 242
Orleans, *CONTINUUM* 242
Sandwich, *THE BROWN JUG* 251
Sandwich, *TOBEY HOUSE ANTIQUES* 252
Scituate, *GREENHOUSE ANTIQUES* 252
Sheffield, *COVERED BRIDGE ANTIQUES* 254
Sheffield, *DARR ANTIQUES AND INTERIORS* 254
South Egremont, *HOWARD'S ANTIQUES* 260
South Egremont, *RED BARN ANTIQUES* 260
South Egremont, *GLADYS SCHOFIELD ANTIQUES* 260
Stockbridge, *TOM CAREY'S PLACE* 263
Sturbridge, *THE COPPERSMITH* 264
Templeton, *WRIGHT TAVERN ANTIQUES* 266
Wayland, *YANKEE CRAFTSMAN* 269
Wellfleet Ctr, *FINDERS KEEPERS* 270
Wellfleet, *H B & DOROTHY WATSON* 270
West Dennis, *RUMFORD ANTIQUES* 273
Westborough, *PUSHCART PLACE* 276
Worcester, *HAMMERWORKS* 280
Worthington, *COUNTRY CRICKET VILLAGE INN* 280

New Hampshire
Center Harbor, *ACCENTS FROM THE PAST* 287
East Lempster, *PETER HILL INC* 291
Epsom, *COPPER HOUSE* 292
Francestown, *WOODBURY HOMESTEAD ANTIQUES* 295
Hampton, *HISTORIC HARDWARE LTD* 298
Hillsboro, *TATEWELL GALLERY* 302

Hillsboro, *WELL SWEEP ANTIQUES* 302
Jaffrey, *THE TOWNE HOUSE* 304
Lancaster, *THE SHOP IN THE BARN* 306
Meredith, *ALEXANDRIA LAMP SHOP* 309
Ossipee, *FLAG GATE FARM ANTIQUES* 315
Snowville, *SLEIGH MILL ANTIQUES* 320

Rhode Island
Coventry, *CANDLE SNUFFER* 332
Newport, *AARDVARK ANTIQUES* 333
Newport, *C & T LAMP SHOP/ANTIQUE DEALERS* 334
Newport, *CHRISTOPHER FOSTER GLASS WORKS* 334
Newport, *JOHN GIDLEY HOUSE* 335
Newport, *LAMP WORKS* 336
Newport, *LAMPLIGHTER ANTIQUES* 336
Newport, *RAMSON HOUSE ANTIQUES* 337

Vermont
Burlington, *CONANT CUSTOM BRASS* 350
Fairfax, *GLENORTON COUNTRY ANTIQUES* 355
Manchester Center, *BELLWETHER GALLERY* 360
Middletown Springs, *THE LAMPLIGHTER* 362

51 Maps

Connecticut
Bethany, *WHITLOCK FARM, BOOKSELLERS* 45
Fairfield, *CONNECTICUT BOOK AUCTION* 60
Mystic, *TRADE WINDS GALLERY* 77
Pomfret Center, *POMFRET BOOK SHOP* 89

Maine
Blue Hill, *LIROS GALLERY* 120
Cape Elizabeth, *LOMBARD ANTIQUARIAN MAP/PRINTS* 123
Damariscotta, *ELLIOTT HEALY PHOTOGRAPHICA* 125
Denmark, *C E GUARINO* 126
Hamden, *GARY W WOOLSON, BOOKSELLER* 132
Manchester, *CHARLES ROBINSON RARE BOOKS* 138
Wells, *HARDINGS BOOK SHOP* 154

Massachusetts
Amherst, *AMHERST ANTIQUARIAN MAPS* 162
Andover, *ANDOVER ANTIQUARIAN BOOKS* 163
Boston, *EUGENE GALLERIES* 176
Boston, *GOODSPEED'S BOOK SHOP INC* 176
Dennis Village, *ANOTHER TIME & PLACE* 203
Essex, *THE SCRAPBOOK* 209
Fairhaven, *EDWARD J LEFKOWICZ INC* 210
Franklin, *JOHNSTON ANTIQUES* 212
Gloucester, *WILLIAM N GREENBAUM* 214
Nantucket, *SABOL AND CROSS, LTD* 232
Sharon, *MICHAEL GINSBERG BOOKS INC* 253
West Newbury, *MOODY-RIDGEWAY HOUSE* 274

New Hampshire
Concord, *THE OLD ALMANACK SHOP* 289
Contoocook, *EMERY'S BOOKS* 289
Hanover, *G B MANASEK, INC* 300
Peterborough, *PETERBOROUGH USED BOOKS & PRINTS* 316
Weare, *SYKES & FLANDERS ANTIQUARIAN BKS* 324
Wolfeboro, *AREA CODE 603 ANTIQUES* 327

Vermont
Middlebury, *HOBNOB ANTIQUES* 361
Norwich, *F J MANASEK* 364
Putney, *UNIQUE ANTIQUE* 366
Rutland, *TUTTLE ANTIQUARIAN BOOKS INC* 369
Shelburne, *WILLIAM L PARKINSON BOOKS* 370
Shoreham, *LAPHAM & DIBBLE GALLERY, INC.* 370

52 Miniatures

Maine
Searsport, *GOLD COAST ANTIQUES* 149

Massachusetts
Brewster, *ROCKING CHAIR ANTIQUES* 191

Rhode Island
Newport, *THE DOLL MUSEUM* 334

Vermont
Dorset, *THE ANGLOPHILE ANTIQUES* 353
Middlebury, *REBA BLAIR SALES* 361
Rutland, *EAGLE'S NEST ANTIQUES* 368
Waitsfield, *ROSIE BOREL'S L'ESCALIER* 373

53 Mirrors

Connecticut
Woodbury, *CROSSWAYS ANTIQUES* 110
Woodbury, *KENNETH HAMMITT ANTIQUES* 111

Maine
Wells, *THE FARM* 154

Massachusetts
Boston, *RERUNS ANTIQUES* 185
Boston, *SLENSKA'S ANTIQUES & INTERIORS* 187
Brookline Village, *A ROOM WITH A VIEUX* 194
Brookline Village, *BROOKLINE VILLAGE ANTIQUES* 194
Brookline, *JERRY FREEMAN LTD* 193
Great Barrington, *PAUL & SUSAN KLEINWALD INC* 215
Lee, *THE KINGSLEIGH 1840* 223
Newburyport, *ON CONSIGNMENT GALLERIES* 236
Sheffield, *SUSAN SILVER ANTIQUES* 256

New Hampshire
Franconia, *COLONIAL COTTAGE* 295

Rhode Island
Charlestown, *LION'S MANE ANTIQUES* 331
Newport, *MAINLY OAK LTD* 336

Vermont
Middlebury, *C. TILEY ANTIQUES* 361
Poultney, *DEN OF ANTIQUITY* 366
South Burlington, *SIMPLY COUNTRY* 371
Woodstock, *CHURCH STREET GALLERY* 376

54 Models

Connecticut
Stonington, *QUESTER GALLERY* 99

Maine
Portland, *PORT 'N STARBOARD* 145
Wiscasset, *MARINE ANTIQUES* 156

Massachusetts
  Hudson, *THE NEW ENGLAND ANTIQUE TOY MALL* 220
  Hyannis, *RICHARD J O'MALLEY* 221
  Nantucket, *FOUR WINDS CRAFT GUILD* 231
  Salem, *AMERICAN MARINE MODEL GALLERY* 249

55 Music/Musical Instruments

Connecticut
  Danbury, *ORPHEUS BOOKS* 54
  Norwalk, *BARTER SHOP* 85
  South Norwalk, *MECHANICAL MUSIC CENTER INC* 94
  Yalesville, *UNIQUE ANTIQUES & COLLECTIBLES* 114

Maine
  Wiscasset, *MUSICAL WONDER HOUSE* 157

Massachusetts
  Brookline Village, *THE COLLECTOR* 194
  Cambridge, *THE MUSIC EMPORIUM* 197
  Georgetown, *THOMAS A EDISON COLLECTION* 212
  Orange, *ORANGE TRADING COMPANY* 242
  Provincetown, *REMEMBRANCES OF THINGS PAST* 246
  Sheffield, *1750 HOUSE ANTIQUES* 253
  West Stockbridge, *DOROTHY ELSBERG BOOKS* 275

Vermont
  Manchester, *THE CLOCK EMPORIUM* 359
  Pittsford, *NOSTALGIA NOOK* 365
  West Brattleboro, *THE BEAR BOOK SHOP* 375
  Williston, *GREEN MOUNTAIN CLOCK SHOP* 376

56 Nautical/Marine Items

Connecticut
  Essex, *BONSAL-DOUGLAS ANTIQUES* 59
  Rowayton, *WILLIAMS PORT ANTIQUES* 91
  Stonington, *QUESTER GALLERY* 99

Maine
  Cushing, *NEVILLE ANTIQUES* 125
  Kennebunkport, *MARITIME MUSEUM SHOP* 135
  Kennebunkport, *NAUTICAL ANTIQUES* 135
  Limerick, *RYAN M COOPER* 136
  Newcastle, *NEWCASTLE ANTIQUES* 140
  Portland, *PORT 'N STARBOARD* 145
  Wiscasset, *MARINE ANTIQUES* 156

Massachusetts
  Boston, *HALEY & STEELE INC* 178
  Boston, *SAMUEL L LOWE JR ANTIQUES INC* 181
  Brewster, *THE HOMESTEAD ANTIQUES* 190
  Chatham, *OLDE VILLAGE COUNTRY BARN* 199
  Chatham, *THE SPYGLASS* 199
  Dennis, *HYLAND GRANBY ANTIQUES* 203
  East Sandwich, *JESSE CALDWELL LEATHERWOOD* 206
  Fairhaven, *EDWARD J LEFKOWICZ INC* 210
  Marblehead, *BRASS & BOUNTY* 227
  Nantucket, *FOUR WINDS CRAFT GUILD* 231
  Nantucket, *NINA HELLMAN* 231
  Nantucket, *VAL MAITINO ANTIQUES* 232

  Nantucket, *FRANK F SYLVIA ANTIQUES* 232
  Nantucket, *TONKIN OF NANTUCKET* 233
  Nantucket, *TRANQUIL CORNERS ANTIQUES* 233
  Newtonville, *VIRGINIA S CLARK* 238
  Salem, *AMERICAN MARINE MODEL GALLERY* 249
  Salem, *MARINE ARTS GALLERY* 250
  Sandwich, *PAUL MADDEN ANTIQUES* 251
  Westwood, *PEG WILLIS ANTIQUES* 277

New Hampshire
  Hollis, *THE BLUE LANTERN ANTIQUES* 302
  Wolfeboro, *RALPH K REED ANTIQUES* 327

Rhode Island
  Newport, *A & A GAINES* 335
  Newport, *THE NEWPORT GALLERY LTD* 336
  Newport, *NEWPORT SCRIMSHAW COMPANY* 336

Vermont
  Wallingford, *TOM KAYE ANTIQUES LTD* 374

57 Needlework/Samplers

Connecticut
  Avon, *RUTH TROIANI FINE ANTIQUES* 45
  Colchester, *BARBARA WOOD BROWN* 51
  East Lyme, *STEPHEN & CAROL HUBER INC* 58
  Salisbury, *BUCKLEY & BUCKLEY ANTIQUES* 92
  Stonington, *ANN LEHMANN ANTIQUES* 98
  Stonington, *MARGUERITE RIORDAN* 99

Maine
  North Edgecomb, *THE DITTY BOX* 141
  Wiscasset, *SHEILA & EDWIN RIDEOUT* 157

Massachusetts
  Ashley Falls, *DON ABARBANEL* 164
  Nantucket, *NANTUCKET NEEDLEWORKS* 232
  Newton, *HARD-TO-FIND NEEDLEWORK BOOKS* 237
  West Chesterfield, *TEXTILE REPRODUCTIONS* 273

New Hampshire
  Hopkinton, *THE SOULES-ANTIQUES* 303
  Hopkinton, *WAYNE & PEGGY WOODARD ANTIQUES* 303
  Portsmouth, *MARGARET SCOTT CARTER, INC.* 317

58 Objets d'Art

Connecticut
  Greenwich, *STEFANO MAGNI ANTIQUES/FINE ART* 65
  Litchfield, *HARRY W STROUSE* 71
  New Canaan, *MANOR ANTIQUES* 77
  New Haven, *WEST GATE ANTIQUES* 81
  New Preston, *BRITANNIA BOOKSHOP* 82
  Wallingford, *LEE MOHN ANTIQUES AND ART* 102
  Weston, *SANDI OLIVER FINE ART* 105

Maine
  North Edgecomb, *JACK PARTRIDGE* 141

Massachusetts
  Essex, *L A LANDRY ANTIQUES* 209
  Hopkinton, *HERITAGE ANTIQUES* 220
  Newburyport, *ON CONSIGNMENT GALLERIES* 236

North Eastham, *EASTHAM AUCTION HOUSE* 240
South Natick, *COMING OF AGE ANTIQUES* 261
Wellesley, *LINDA RICKLES INTERIORS INC* 269

Rhode Island
Newport, *ARAKEL H BOZYAN STORE* 334
Newport, *JOHN GIDLEY HOUSE* 335
Newport, *JB ANTIQUES* 335
Newport, *NEWPORT SCRIMSHAW COMPANY* 336
Newport, *PETTERUTI ANTIQUES* 337
Providence, *CHAMBERLAIN ANTIQUES LTD* 340
Watch Hill, *FINITNEY & COMPANY* 343

59 Oil Paintings

Connecticut
Avon, *RUTH TROIANI FINE ANTIQUES* 45
Bantam, *WESTON THORN ANTIQUES* 45
Bethany, *ROBERT B WILLIAMS* 45
Bethel, *J THOMAS MELVIN* 46
Bolton, *AUTUMN POND ANTIQUES* 46
Bozrah, *CHARLES GALLERY* 47
Clinton, *VAN CARTER HALE FINE ART* 51
Colchester, *NATHAN LIVERANT & SON* 51
Coventry, *ALLINSON GALLERY INC* 53
Darien, *WIND-BORNE FRAME & RESTORATION* 56
East Hampton, *OPERA HOUSE ANTIQUES* 58
Essex, *FRANCIS BEALEY AMERICAN ARTS* 59
Essex, *BONSAL-DOUGLAS ANTIQUES* 59
Greenwich, *AMERICAN TRADITION GALLERY* 63
Greenwich, *ANTAN ANTIQUES LTD* 63
Greenwich, *GEORGIAN ANTIQUES* 64
Greenwich, *STEFANO MAGNI ANTIQUES/FINE ART* 65
Greenwich, *PROVINCES DE FRANCE* 65
Kent, *ELIZABETH S MANKIN ANTIQUES* 69
Litchfield, *THOMAS MC BRIDE ANTIQUES* 71
Litchfield, *PETER H TILLOU - FINE ARTS* 71
Madison, *P HASTINGS FALK SOUND VIEW PRESS* 72
Marble Dale, *EARL J SLACK ANTIQUES* 73
Marlborough, *THE CONNECTICUT GALLERY* 74
Milford, *ANTIQUES OF TOMORROW* 75
Milford, *STOCK TRANSFER* 76
New Canaan, *ACAMPORA ART GALLERY* 77
New Canaan, *ENGLISH HERITAGE ANTIQUES, INC* 77
New Canaan, *HASTINGS ART, LTD* 77
New Canaan, *MANOR ANTIQUES* 77
New Hartford, *GALLERY FORTY FOUR* 78
New Haven, *THOMAS COLVILLE FINE ART* 79
New Haven, *FROM HERE TO ANTIQUITY* 80
New Haven, *GIAMPIETRO ANTIQUES* 80
New Haven, *SHANNON FINE ARTS INC* 81
New Milford, *BRUCE W ANDERSON ANTIQUES* 81
Noank, *STONE LEDGE ART GALLERIES* 84
Norwalk, *EAGLES LAIR ANTIQUES* 85
Old Lyme, *THE COOLEY GALLERY* 86
Old Lyme, *WHITLEY GALLERY* 86
Pomfret Center, *PRISCILLA H ZIESMER* 89
Southport, *GWS GALLERIES* 96
Stamford, *AVIS & ROCKWELL GARDINER* 97
Stamford, *SHIPPAN POINT GALLERY* 97

Stonington, *MARGUERITE RIORDAN* 99
Stonington, *VICTORIA STATION* 99
Stonington, *WATER STREET ANTIQUES* 99
Stratford, *AMERICA'S PAST* 100
West Cornwall, *INDIAN LANE FARM* 103
West Hartford, *ROBIN FERN GALLERY* 103
West Haven, *ARTISTIC VENTURES GALLERY* 103
Westport, *CONNECTICUT FINE ARTS, INC* 105
Wilton, *GEORGE SUBKOFF ANTIQUES, INC.* 107
Woodbury, *DAVID DUNTON/ANTIQUES* 111

Maine
Bangor, *GAMAGE ANTIQUES* 117
Blue Hill, *LIROS GALLERY* 120
Boothbay Harbor, *GLEASON FINE ART AT MCKOWN ST* 120
Bridgton, *M SPENCER* 121
Camden, *SCHUELER ANTIQUES* 123
Damariscotta, *PATRICIA ANNE REED ANTIQUES* 125
Fairfield, *JAMES D JULIA AUCTIONEERS* 128
Farmington, *TOM VEILLEUX GALLERY* 129
Gorham, *COUNTRY SQUIRE ANTIQUES* 130
Hallowell, *JAMES H. LE FURGY BOOKS & ANT.* 131
Hulls Cove, *HULLS COVE TOOL BARN* 133
Kennebunk, *DYNAN FINE ARTS* 133
Kennebunkport, *CATTAILS ANTIQUES* 134
Kennebunkport, *NAUTICAL ANTIQUES* 135
Kennebunkport, *SAML'S STAIRS ANTIQUES* 135
Limington, *EDWARD & ELAINE CASAZZA* 136
Newcastle, *KAJA VEILLUX ART & ANTIQUES* 140
Newcastle, *NEWCASTLE ANTIQUES* 140
Newcastle, *GORDON NICOLL* 140
North Berwick, *YOUNG FINE ARTS GALLERY, INC.* 141
Portland, *BARRIDOFF GALLERIES* 144
Portland, *REMEMBER WHEN* 145
Rockport, *KATRIN PHOCAS LTD* 147
Round Pond, *THE HOLMES* 147
Round Pond, *ROUND POND ANTIQUES* 147
Topsham, *MERRYMEETING ANTIQUES* 152
Union, *EBENEZER ALDEN HOUSE* 152
Wells, *R JORGENSEN ANTIQUES* 154
Wells, *A DAVID PAULHUS BOOKS* 154
Wiscasset, *COACH HOUSE ANTIQUES* 156
Wiscasset, *WISCASSET BAY GALLERY* 158
Yarmouth, *W M SCHWIND, JR ANTIQUES* 158

Massachusetts
Ashley Falls, *LEWIS & WILSON* 165
Ashley Falls, *THE VOLLMERS* 165
Boston, *FRANCESCA ANDERSON GALLERY* 167
Boston, *BEACON HILL FINE ARTS/ANTIQUES* 168
Boston, *CHILDS GALLERY* 174
Boston, *COMENOS FINE ARTS* 175
Boston, *CRANE COLLECTION* 175
Boston, *EUGENE GALLERIES* 176
Boston, *GUIDO* 178
Boston, *HERITAGE ART* 178
Boston, *SAMUEL L LOWE JR ANTIQUES INC* 181
Boston, *MARIKA'S ANTIQUE SHOP, INC* 182
Boston, *VOSE GALLERIES OF BOSTON, INC.* 187
Boston, *ALFRED J WALKER FINE ART* 188

Brewster, *DONALD B HOWES - ANTIQUES* 190
Brewster, *EDWARD SNOW HOUSE ANTIQUES* 191
Brimfield, *BRIMFIELD ANTIQUES* 192
Brookline, *BEAZE OF BROOKLINE* 192
Brookline, *TIM GALLAGHER ANTIQUES* 193
Cambridge, *JAMES R BAKKER ANTIQUES INC.* 195
Cambridge, *MARC J MATZ* 197
Dedham, *HENRY HORNBLOWER III* 202
Dennis, *KING'S GRANT ANTIQUES* 203
Dennis, *THE LEANING TREE* 203
Dennis, *VILLAGE PEDLAR CLOCK SHOP* 203
Essex, *BRICK HOUSE ANTIQUES* 208
Essex, *NORTH HILL ANTIQUES* 209
Essex, *RIDER & CLARKE ANTIQUES* 209
Fitchburg, *JOHN CLEMENT FINE ART* 211
Gloucester, *BURKE'S BAZAAR-POET'S ANTIQUES* 213
Gloucester, *CAPE ANN ANTIQUES & ORIENTALS* 213
Gloucester, *GLOUCESTER FINE ARTS & ANTIQUARI* 214
Hingham, *PIERCE GALLERIES INC* 220
Lee, *HENRY B HOLT INC* 223
Lee, *PEMBROKE ANTIQUES* 223
Lexington, *GALLERY ON THE GREEN LTD* 224
Lincoln, *BROWN-CORBIN FINE ART* 225
Millis, *BIRCHKNOLL ANTIQUES* 230
Needham, *GEORGE A DOWNER FINE ARTS* 234
Newburyport, *LEPORE FINE ARTS* 235
Newton, *PETER D COWEN* 236
North Andover, *ROLAND B HAMMOND INC* 239
Orleans, *FRANK H HOGAN FINE ARTS INC* 243
Pepperell, *GODWIN GALLERY* 244
Pittsfield, *BERKSHIRE ANTIQUES* 245
Provincetown, *JULIE HELLER GALLERY* 246
Salem, *MARINE ARTS GALLERY* 250
Sandwich, *PAUL MADDEN ANTIQUES* 251
Sheffield, *FREDERICK HATFIELD ANTIQUES* 255
South Orleans, *PLEASANT BAY ANTIQUES* 261
Southbridge, *SUN GALLERIES* 262
Swansea, *AMERICAN ART & ANTIQUES, INC* 265
Taunton, *JO-ANN E ROSS* 266
Wellesley Hills, *ERNEST S KRAMER FINE ARTS* 270
West Harwich, *RALPH DIAMOND ANTIQUES* 274
Weston, *HOLLYDAY HOUSE* 276
Yarmouth Port, *STEPHEN H GARNER* 281

New Hampshire
Fitzwilliam, *RED BARN ANTIQUES* 294
Francestown, *THE FRANCESTOWN GALLERY* 294
Hampton, *HEYDAY ANTIQUES OF HAMPTON* 298
Hancock, *THE BARN OF HANCOCK VILLAGE* 299
Holderness, *SQUAM LAKE GALLERY* 302
Hopkinton, *ANDERSON'S ANTIQUES, INC.* 303
Loudon, *COUNTRY ANTIQUES* 307
Marlborough, *THOMAS R LONGACRE* 308
New Ipswich, *ESTELLE M GLAVEY, INC.* 312
North Conway, *GRALYN ANTIQUES, INC* 313

North Conway, *RICHARD M PLUSCH ANTIQUES* 313
Peterborough, *OLD TOWN FARM ANTIQUES* 316
Seabrook, *STONE HOUSE ANTIQUES* 320
Spofford, *FINE ANTIQUES* 320
Walpole, *GOLDEN PAST OF WALPOLE* 323
Walpole, *RHODES OF WASHINGTON SQUARE* 323
Warren, *WM MERRIFIELD MERTSCH ANTIQUES* 324
Wolfeboro, *NEW ENGLAND GALLERY* 327

Rhode Island
Ashaway, *BRIGGS HOUSE ANTIQUES* 330
Charlestown, *ARTIST'S GUILD & GALLERY* 331
East Greenwich, *CONSTANTINE'S FINE FURNITURE* 332
Little Compton, *BLUE FLAG ANTIQUES* 333
Newport, *HARRY GREW* 335
Newport, *JB ANTIQUES* 335
Newport, *ROGER KING GALLERY OF FINE ART* 335
Newport, *NEWPORT FINE ARTS INVESTMENT CO* 336
Newport, *THE NEWPORT GALLERY LTD* 336
Newport, *PETTERUTI ANTIQUES* 337
Newport, *WILLIAM VAREIKA FINE ARTS* 338
Newport, *MICHAEL WESTMAN FINE ARTS* 338
Providence, *BERT GALLERY* 339
Providence, *VAN DALE GALLERY* 341
Saunderstown, *STEPHANIE ADAMS WOOD* 342
Wickford, *THE BALL & CLAW* 344
Wyoming, *BRAD SMITH* 345

Vermont
Bennington, *FOUR CORNERS EAST, INC* 348
Colchester, *MATTESON GALLERY OF ARTS* 352
Dorset, *VIRGINIA POPE, INC.* 354
East Poultney, *RIVERS EDGE ANTIQUES* 355
Manchester Center, *BARBARA B TRASK, APPRAISALS* 360
Manchester, *STEVENSON GALLERY* 359
Middlebury, *BRADY GALLERIES, INC.* 361
Old Bennington, *ANTIQUARIAN* 364
Pittsford, *ART INTERIORS ANTIQUES-PITTSFORD* 365
Saxtons River, *SIGN OF THE RAVEN* 369
Shelburne Village, *UNDERBRIDGE ANTIQUES* 370
Shoreham, *LAPHAM & DIBBLE GALLERY, INC.* 370

60 Oriental Art

Connecticut
Bethel, *J THOMAS MELVIN* 46
Darien, *ROSE D'OR* 56
Darien, *DORRIE SCHREINER GALLERY ANTIQUE* 56
East Haddam, *OLD BANK HOUSE GALLERY* 57
Essex, *HASTINGS HOUSE* 60
Gaylordsville, *MICHAEL HALL ANTIQUES* 62
Goshen, *TRADE WINDS, THE 1749 HOUSE* 63
Harwinton, *JOHN M DAVIS INC* 67
Milford, *ANTIQUES OF TOMORROW* 75
Old Lyme, *WHITLEY GALLERY* 86
Ridgefield, *RUTH COATES ANTIQUES* 90
Washington Depot, *STEPHEN CALCAGNI* 102
Westport, *L'OBJET D'ART LTD* 105

Wilton, *VALLIN GALLERIES* 107
Woodbury, *MADELINE WEST ANTIQUES* 113

Maine
Hallowell, *JOSIAH SMITH ANTIQUES* 131
Kennebunkport, *WINDFALL ANTIQUES* 135
Lincolnville Beach, *SIGN OF THE OWL* 137
Newcastle, *GORDON NICOLL* 140
Searsport, *THE CAPTAIN'S HOUSE ANTIQUES* 149

Massachusetts
Ashley Falls, *LEWIS & WILSON* 165
Boston, *ALBERTS-LANGDON, INC.* 167
Boston, *ANTIQUE PORCELAINS LTD* 167
Boston, *BELGRAVIA ANTIQUES INC* 170
Boston, *O'REILLY/EINSTADTER, LTD* 182
Boston, *SHER-MORR ANTIQUES* 185
Brookline, *BEAZE OF BROOKLINE* 192
Brookline, *CYPRESS TRADING POST* 193
Cambridge, *BERNHEIMER'S ANTIQUE ARTS* 195
Cambridge, *KARIN J PHILLIPS ANTIQUES* 197
Charlestown, *BUNKER HILL RELICS* 198
Charlestown, *THE FISKE HOUSE* 198
Chestnut Hill, *SONIA PAINE* 199
Fitchburg, *JOHN CLEMENT FINE ART* 211
Groton, *JOS KILBRIDGE CHINA TRADE ANTIQU* 216
Marblehead, *THE ANTIQUE SHOP* 226
Nantucket, *LYNDA WILLAUER ANTIQUES* 233
Salem, *ASIA HOUSE* 250
Salem, *MARCHAND'S LAFAYETTE ANTIQUES* 250
Sheffield, *GOOD & HUTCHINSON ASSOCIATES* 255

New Hampshire
Portsmouth, *GARAKUTA COLLECTION* 317

Rhode Island
East Greenwich, *CONSTANTINE'S FINE FURNITURE* 332
Hopkinton, *THE ELEGANT DRAGON* 332
Newport, *A & A GAINES* 335
Portsmouth, *BENJAMIN FISH HOUSE ANTIQUES* 339

61 Paperweights

Massachusetts
Boston, *TERI ANTIQUES* 187

62 Photographs

Maine
Damariscotta, *ELLIOTT HEALY PHOTOGRAPHICA* 125
Eliot, *BOOKS & AUTOGRAPHS* 127
Eustis, *MACDONALD'S MILITARY* 128
Limerick, *RYAN M COOPER* 136

Massachusetts
Brookline Village, *THE COLLECTOR* 194

Rhode Island
Little Compton, *BLUE FLAG ANTIQUES* 333
Providence, *QUE ANTIQUES* 340

63 Porcelain/Pottery

Connecticut
Bantam, *KENT & YVONNE GILYARD ANTIQUES* 45
Bantam, *WESTON THORN ANTIQUES* 45
Bolton, *HAILSTON HOUSE INC* 47
Canton, *1784 HOUSE ANTIQUES* 49
Colchester, *LES TROIS PROVINCES* 51
Danbury, *CARNIVAL HOUSE ANTIQUES* 54
Darien, *ANTIQUES UNLIMITED* 55
Darien, *H P MC LANE ANTIQUES INC* 55
Darien, *WINDSOR ANTIQUES LTD* 56
Essex, *VALLEY FARM ANTIQUES* 60
Fairfield, *ENSINGER ANTIQUES LTD* 61
Fairfield, *LEMANOIR COUNTRY FRENCH ANTIQUES* 61
Goshen, *TRADE WINDS, THE 1749 HOUSE* 63
Greenwich, *CHELSEA ANTIQUES OF GREENWICH* 64
Greenwich, *GEORGIAN ANTIQUES* 64
Hartford, *BACON ANTIQUES* 67
Kent, *GOLDEN THISTLE ANTIQUES* 69
Kent, *ELIZABETH S MANKIN ANTIQUES* 69
Litchfield, *COUNTRY HOUSE CONSIGNMENTS* 70
Litchfield, *THOMAS D & CONSTANCE R WILLIAMS* 71
Morris, *T'OTHER HOUSE ANTIQUES* 76
New Canaan, *ENGLISH HERITAGE ANTIQUES, INC* 77
New Haven, *THE ANTIQUES MARKET* 79
New Haven, *FROM HERE TO ANTIQUITY* 80
New Haven, *HER MAJESTY'S ANTIQUES* 80
New Milford, *CRICKET HILL CONSIGNMENT* 82
New Preston, *STRAWBERRY HILL ANTIQUES* 83
Newtown, *CODFISH ANTIQUES* 84
Newtown, *POVERTY HOLLOW ANTIQUES* 84
Old Greenwich, *NEW ENGLAND SHOP* 86
Old Lyme, *WHITLEY GALLERY* 86
Old Saybrook, *THE HOUSE OF PRETTY THINGS* 87
Old Saybrook, *LITTLE HOUSE OF GLASS* 87
Old Saybrook, *PRESENCE OF THE PAST* 87
Old Saybrook, *SWEET PEA ANTIQUES* 87
Pine Meadow, *1847 HOUSE ANTIQUES* 88
Portland, *CRANE'S ANTIQUES, ETC* 89
Redding, *MELLIN'S ANTIQUES* 89
Ridgefield, *GREENWILLOW ANTIQUES* 90
Ridgefield, *HUNTER'S CONSIGNMENT* 90
Ridgefield, *THE SILK PURSE* 91
Salisbury, *RUSSELL CARRELL* 92
Salisbury, *COLLECTORS* 92
Somers, *OLD HICKORY ANTIQUES* 93
Southport, *TEN EYCK-EMERICH ANTIQUES* 97
Stonington, *OPUS I* 99
Stonington, *QUIMPER FAIENCE* 99
Stonington, *VICTORIA STATION* 99
Stony Creek, *STONY CREEK VILLAGE STORE* 99
Wallingford, *LEE MOHN ANTIQUES AND ART* 102
Westbrook, *HANES RUSKIN* 104
Weston, *MILLICENT RUDD BEST* 104
Winthrop, *JAS E ELLIOTT ANTIQUES* 108
Woodbury, *GERALD MURPHY ANTIQUES LTD* 112

Maine

Augusta, *WHITE BARN ANTIQUES* 117
Belmont, *BARBARA PATTERSON'S ANTIQUES* 119
Bernard, *THE OLD RED STORE* 119
Boothbay Harbor, *BAY STREET ANTIQUES* 120
Caribou, *JUDY'S ANTIQUES* 124
Farmington, *ANTIQUES FROM POWDER HOUSE HILL* 129
Gardiner, *MCKAY'S ANTIQUES* 130
Gardiner, *MORRELL'S ANTIQUES* 130
Hallowell, *MAINELY ANTIQUES* 131
Hallowell, *JOSIAH SMITH ANTIQUES* 131
Kennebunkport, *WINDFALL ANTIQUES* 135
Lincolnville Beach, *NORTH HOUSE FINE ANTIQUES* 137
Lincolnville Beach, *SIGN OF THE OWL* 137
Lincolnville, *DUCK TRAP ANTIQUES* 137
North Edgecomb, *THE DITTY BOX* 141
Ogunquit, *BEAUPORT INN ANTIQUES* 142
Orono, *THE GREEN DOOR ANTIQUE SHOP* 143
Pittsfield, *KENNISTON'S ANTIQUES* 143
Pittston, *PHIPPS OF PITTSTON* 143
Portland, *VENTURE ANTIQUES* 146
Portland, *WILMA'S ANTIQUES & ACCESSORIES* 146
Round Pond, *TIME AND AGAIN ANTIQUES* 147
Sebago, *THE GALLERY SHOP* 149
Spruce Head, *ELFAST'S ANTIQUES* 151
Thomaston, *ANCHOR FARM ANTIQUES* 151
Topsham, *MERRYMEETING ANTIQUES* 152
Union, *EBENEZER ALDEN HOUSE* 152
Winterport, *RICHARD & PATRICIA BEAN* 156
Wiscasset, *SHEILA & EDWIN RIDEOUT* 157
Woolwich, *ANTIQUES ETC* 158
York, *GORGEANA ANTIQUES* 159

Massachusetts

Ashley Falls, *DON ABARBANEL* 164
Ashley Falls, *CIRCA* 164
Boston, *ALBERTS-LANGDON, INC.* 167
Boston, *ANTIQUE PORCELAINS LTD* 167
Boston, *H GROSSMAN* 178
Boston, *LINDERMAN SCHENCK* 181
Boston, *NELSON-MONROE, ANTIQUES* 182
Boston, *NEWBURY STREET JEWELRY & ANTIQUE* 182
Boston, *O'REILLY/EINSTADTER, LTD* 182
Boston, *C A RUPPERT* 185
Boston, *SHREVE, CRUMP & LOW* 187
Boston, *WEINER'S ANTIQUE SHOP* 188
Boston, *WENHAM CROSS ANTIQUES* 188
Brookline, *CYPRESS TRADING POST* 193
Buzzards Bay, *THE OLD HOUSE* 195
Cambridge, *SHARON BOCCELLI & CO ANTIQUES* 196
Cambridge, *FLEUR DE LIS GALLERY* 196
Charlestown, *BUNKER HILL RELICS* 198
Cummaquid, *THE PICKET FENCE* 201
Dennis, *LESLIE CURTIS ANTIQUES* 202
East Sandwich, *THE GILDED SWAN* 206
Eastham, *QUAIL SONG ANTIQUES* 206
Essex, *BRICK HOUSE ANTIQUES* 208
Essex, *THE WHITE ELEPHANT SHOP* 210
Fairhaven, *FANTASY HOUSE ANTIQUES* 210
Fairhaven, *HARE & TORTOISE ANTIQUES/COLLECT* 210
Falmouth, *AURORA BOREALIS ANTIQUES* 211
Gloucester, *BEAUPORT ANTIQUES* 213

Great Barrington, *ANTHONY'S ANTIQUES* 214
Hamilton, *RO-DAN ANTIQUES* 218
Harwichport, *SEVEN SOUTH STREET ANTIQUES* 219
Hyannis, *ALBERT ARTS & ANTIQUES* 221
Ipswich, *HILDA KNOWLES ANTIQUES* 222
Lenox, *HAMLET ANTIQUES* 224
Lenox, *STONE'S THROW ANTIQUES* 224
Malden, *FLIGHTS OF FANCY ANTIQUES* 226
Marblehead, *THE ANTIQUE SHOP* 226
Marblehead, *HEELTAPPERS ANTIQUES* 227
Marblehead, *MARBLEHEAD ANTIQUES* 227
Marblehead, *SACKS ANTIQUES* 228
Marblehead, *THREE SEWALL STREET ANTIQUES* 228
Middleboro, *CHARLES & BARBARA ADAMS* 230
Nantucket, *FRANK F SYLVIA ANTIQUES* 232
Nantucket, *TILLER ANTIQUES* 233
Natick, *VANDERWEG ANTIQUES* 234
Needham, *GOLDEN FLEECE ANTIQUES* 234
Northampton, *ELEANOR KOCOT ANTIQUES* 241
Norton, *DUBOIS' OLD HOUSE* 241
Orleans, *LILAC HEDGE ANTIQUES* 243
Richmond, *WYNN SAYMAN* 248
Rockport, *YE OLDE LANTERN ANTIQUES* 248
Salem, *ASIA HOUSE* 250
Salem, *UNION STREET ANTIQUES* 250
Salisbury, *FORT HILL ANTIQUES* 251
Sandwich, *DEN OF ANTIQUITY SLAVID INC* 251
Sandwich, *FAULCONNER HOUSE ANTIQUES* 251
Sheffield, *CENTURYHURST ANTIQUES* 254
Sheffield, *DARR ANTIQUES AND INTERIORS* 254
Sheffield, *GOOD & HUTCHINSON ASSOCIATES* 255
Sheffield, *SUSAN SILVER ANTIQUES* 256
Sudbury, *THE ANTIQUE EXCHANGE OF SUDBURY* 265
Templeton, *1800 HOUSE ANTIQUES, LTD* 266
Townsend, *THE COUNTRY GENTLEMAN* 267
Wellesley Hills, *COUNTRY INTERIORS* 270
Wellfleet, *H B & DOROTHY WATSON* 270
Wenham, *HENDERSON'S* 271
Westborough, *PUSHCART PLACE* 276
Yarmouth Port, *CC CANCER CONSIGNMENT EXCHANGE* 281
Yarmouth Port, *DESIGN WORKS* 281
Yarmouth Port, *CONSTANCE GOFF* 281
Yarmouth Port, *NICKERSON'S ANTIQUES* 281
Yarmouth Port, *TOWN CRIER ANTIQUES* 282

New Hampshire

Alton, *FLEUR-DE-LIS ANTIQUES* 284
Center Harbor, *ACCENTS FROM THE PAST* 287
Center Harbor, *HOLIDAY HOUSE ANTIQUES* 287
Center Harbor, *THE ROYALE MESS* 287
Contoocook, *GOLD DRAGON ANTIQUES* 289
Dublin, *ANN & DAN WALSH* 291
Exeter, *HOLLIS & TRISHA BRODRICK* 292
Exeter, *DECOR ANTIQUES* 292
Fitzwilliam, *DENNIS & DAD ANTIQUES* 294
Francestown, *NAN SHEA ANTIQUES* 294
Franconia, *COLONIAL COTTAGE* 295
Franconia, *ELEANOR M LYNN/ELIZABETH MONAHAN* 295

Hancock, *CROOKED ONION FARM ANTIQUE* 299

Hanover, *MARIE-LOUISE ANTIQUES* 300

Hillsboro, *BARBARA'S ANTIQUES* 301

Hillsboro, *OLD DUNBAR HOUSE* 301

Hillsboro, *TATEWELL GALLERY* 302

Hopkinton, *ANDERSON'S ANTIQUES, INC.* 303

Lancaster, *GRANARY ANTIQUES* 306

Littleton, *NILA PARKER* 307

Loudon, *GODIVA ANTIQUES* 307

Meredith, *GORDONS ANTIQUES* 309

Mont Vernon, *CANDLEWICK ANTIQUES* 310

New London, *PRISCILLA DRAKE ANTIQUES* 312

New London, *MAD EAGLE INC FINE ANTIQUES* 312

North Conway, *RICHARD M PLUSCH ANTIQUES* 313

Northwood, *DRAKE'S HILL ANTIQUES* 314

Northwood, *PIONEER AMERICA* 314

Springfield, *THE COLONEL'S SWORD* 320

Springfield, *LAZY FOX ANTIQUES ET GALLERIE* 321

Springfield, *SPRING HILL FARM ANTIQUES* 321

Washington, *TINTAGEL ANTIQUES* 324

West Lebanon, *WINDHAM ANTIQUES* 325

Whitefield, *THE FAIRWEATHER SHOP* 326

Wolfeboro, *RICHARD G MARDEN* 327

Rhode Island

Ashaway, *BRIGGS HOUSE ANTIQUES* 330

Carolina, *JAMES E SCUDDER* 330

Newport, *ANTIQUES AT FIFTY NINE BELLEVUE* 333

Newport, *GALLERY '76 ANTIQUES INC* 335

Newport, *HARRY GREW* 335

Newport, *JB ANTIQUES* 335

Newport, *ETHEL M KALIF ANTIQUES* 335

Newport, *NEW ENGLAND ANTIQUES* 336

Newport, *OLD FASHION SHOP* 337

Newport, *RAMSON HOUSE ANTIQUES* 337

Newport, *SMITH MARBLE LTD* 337

Portsmouth, *BENJAMIN FISH HOUSE ANTIQUES* 339

Vermont

Addison, *OLD STONE HOUSE ANTIQUES* 348

Dorset, *THE ANGLOPHILE ANTIQUES* 353

Essex Junction, *YANKEE PEDLAR'S ANTIQUES* 355

Ferrisburg, *TWIN MAPLES ANTIQUES* 356

Johnson, *MEL SIEGEL ANTIQUES* 358

Middletown Springs, *NIMMO & HART ANTIQUES* 362

Poultney, *DEN OF ANTIQUITY* 366

Randolph Center, *PAGE JACKSON ANTIQUE GALLERY* 366

Rutland, *CONWAY'S ANTIQUES & DECOR* 368

Rutland, *SUGAR HOUSE ANTIQUES* 368

Ryegate Corner, *RYEGATE CORNER ANTIQUES* 369

South Burlington, *ETHAN ALLEN ANTIQUE SHOP INC* 371

Waterbury, *CABELL ANTIQUES* 374

Wilmington, *DEERFIELD VALLEY ANTIQUES* 376

Woodstock, *CHURCH STREET GALLERY* 376

64 Post Cards

Connecticut

Litchfield, *JOHN STEELE BOOK SHOP* 71

Meriden, *FAIR WEATHER ANTIQUES* 74

Norfolk, *NOBODY EATS PARSLEY* 84

Pomfret Center, *POMFRET BOOK SHOP* 89

Wallingford, *LEE MOHN ANTIQUES AND ART* 102

Maine

Bernard, *1895 SHOP* 119

Rumford, *CONNIE'S ANTIQUES* 148

Massachusetts

Chatham, *HOUSE ON THE HILL* 198

Dennisport, *THE SIDE DOOR* 204

Fairhaven, *HARE & TORTOISE ANTIQUES/COLLECT* 210

Hamilton, *ELMCRESS BOOKS* 218

New Hampshire

Bridgewater, *IDLE-A-WHILE COUNTRY ANTIQUES* 286

Tuftonboro, *LOG CABIN ANTIQUES* 322

Winchester, *FAT CHANCE ANTIQUES* 326

Wolfeboro, *AREA CODE 603 ANTIQUES* 327

Rhode Island

Chepachet, *CHESTNUT HILL ANTIQUES* 331

Warwick, *THE EMPORIUM* 343

Watch Hill, *THE BOOK & TACKLE SHOP* 343

Vermont

Groton, *STEPHEN JONES ANTIQUES* 357

Newbury, *OXBOW BOOKS* 363

Pittsford, *NOSTALGIA NOOK* 365

65 Primitives

Connecticut

Ashford, *MERRYTHOUGHT* 44

Bethel, *DIERINGERS ARTS & ANTIQUES* 46

Bolton, *QUAKER LADY ANTIQUES* 47

Clinton, *MEURS RENEHAN* 51

Cornwall Bridge, *THE BRASS BUGLE* 52

Coventry, *HANDS OF TIME* 53

Deep River, *RIVERWIND ANTIQUE SHOP* 56

Easton, *RED SLEIGH* 58

Lakeville, *BAD CORNER ANTIQUES & DECORATION* 70

Sharon, *RANDALL AND KOBLENZ* 93

South Windsor, *COUNTRY BARN* 94

Stonington, *CHRISTOPHER & KATHLEEN COLE* 98

Woodbury, *ANTIQUES ON THE GREEN* 109

Woodbury, *DARIA OF WOODBURY* 111

Maine

Albion, *COCK HILL FARM* 116

Brewer, *FRAN & DEAN'S ANTIQUES* 121

Cape Neddick, *CRANBERRY HILL ANTIQUES/LIGHTING* 124

Cape Porpoise, *PADDY'S COVE ANTIQUES* 124

Damariscotta, *PINE CHESTS & THINGS* 125

Farmington, *MAPLE AVENUE ANTIQUES* 129

Gardiner, *MCKAY'S ANTIQUES* 130

Gorham, *LONGVIEW ANTIQUES* 130

Hallowell, *BERDAN'S ANTIQUES* 131

Jefferson, *BUNKER HILL ANTIQUES* 133

Kennebunkport, *THE GOOSE HANGS HIGH* 135

Kennebunkport, *OLD FORT INN & ANTIQUES* 135

Lille, *THE OLD HOMESTEAD* 136

Limington, *EDWARD & ELAINE CASAZZA* 136
Peaks Island, *ISLAND TO ISLAND ANTIQUES* 143
Portland, *MARY ALICE REILLEY* 145
Trenton, *THE ACADIA MEWS ANTIQUE CENTER* 152
Wells, *1774 HOUSE ANTIQUES* 153
West Brooklin, *LOUISA GOODYEAR ANTIQUES* 155
West Southport, *CATHERINE HILL ANTIQUES* 155
Wiscasset, *COACH HOUSE ANTIQUES* 156
Wiscasset, *MARGARET B OFSLAGER* 157
Wiscasset, *SPRIG OF THYME ANTIQUES* 157

Massachusetts
Brewster, *SUNSMITH HOUSE - ANTIQUES* 191
Centerville, *FOR OLDE TIME'S SAKE* 198
Chatham, *BACKYARD ANTIQUES* 198
Conway, *CONWAY HOUSE* 201
Cummaquid, *THE OWL'S NEST ANTIQUES* 201
Eastham, *QUAIL SONG ANTIQUES* 206
Essex, *STEPHEN SCORE* 209
Framingham, *AVERY'S ANTIQUES* 212
Grafton, *PEGGY PLACE ANTIQUES* 214
Great Barrington, *SNYDER'S STORE* 216
Plainville, *BRIAR PATCH ANTIQUES & COLLECTIB* 245
Sunderland, *SALT BOX ANTIQUES* 265
Vineyard Haven, *EARLY SPRING FARM ANTIQUES* 267
West Brewster, *SENTIMENTAL JOURNEY* 272
Westborough, *THE BAYBERRY SHOP ANTIQUES* 275
Westborough, *OLD SCHOOLHOUSE ANTIQUES* 276
Williamsburg, *COUNTRY FINE ANTIQUES* 278
Yarmouth Port, *COLLECTOR'S CORNER* 281

New Hampshire
Barnstead (North), *COOPER SHOP ANTIQUES* 285
Bedford, *DRUMMER BOY ANTIQUES* 286
Bridgewater, *IDLE-A-WHILE COUNTRY ANTIQUES* 286
Canaan, *ERNIE'S ANTIQUES* 287
Cornish, *NATHAN SMITH HOUSE* 290
Francestown, *MILL VILLAGE ANTIQUES* 294
Hillsboro, *BEAR TRACK FARM ANTIQUES* 301
Jackson, *RED SHED ANTIQUES* 304
Marlow, *PEACE BARN ANTIQUES* 309
Meriden, *WATERCRESS ANTIQUES* 310
Mt Sunapee, *RED SLEIGH* 311
Nashua, *RUSTIC ACCENTS, INC.* 311
Northwood, *PIONEER AMERICA* 314
Peterborough, *BRENNANS ANTIQUES* 315
Plymouth, *PAULINE CHARON ANTIQUES* 316
Rochester, *PETER CARSWELL ANTIQUES* 319
Sandwich, *ANTIQUES & AUCTIONS, LTD* 320
Shelburne, *CROW MOUNTAIN FARM ANTIQUES* 320
Spofford, *FINE ANTIQUES* 320
Stratham, *JOHN PIPER HOUSE* 321
Sunapee, *FRANK & BARBARA POLLACK* 321
Warren, *WM MERRIFIELD MERTSCH ANTIQUES* 324
Wolfeboro, *TOUCHMARK ANTIQUES* 327

Rhode Island
Charlestown, *BUTTERNUT SHOP* 331
Charlestown, *FOX RUN COUNTRY ANTIQUES* 331
Chepachet, *JADED LION* 331
Newport, *ETHEL M KALIF ANTIQUES* 335
Newport, *NEW ENGLAND ANTIQUES* 336
Woonsocket, *THE CORNER CURIOSITY SHOPPE* 344

Vermont
Brandon, *H GRAY GILDERSLEEVE ANTIQUES* 349
Burlington, *TAILOR'S ANTIQUES* 351
Castleton Corners, *OLD HOMESTEAD ANTIQUES* 351
East Barre, *FARR'S ANTIQUES* 354
Fair Haven, *FOUNDATION ANTIQUES* 355
Hinesburg Village, *WALKER HOUSE ANTIQUES* 358
North Hero, *DORWALDT'S ANTIQUES* 364
Pittsford, *IRON HORSE ANTIQUES, INC* 365
Reading, *MILL BROOK ANTIQUES* 367
Rutland, *EAGLE'S NEST ANTIQUES* 368
Rutland, *PARK ANTIQUES* 368
Saxtons River, *SCHOOLHOUSE ANTIQUES* 369
Shelburne, *GADHUE'S ANTIQUES* 370
Townshend, *COLT BARN ANTIQUES* 373
Wallingford, *COUNTRY HOUSE ANTIQUES* 374
Wallingford, *YANKEE MAID ANTIQUES* 374
Waltham, *C J HARRIS ANTIQUES* 374
Woodstock, *COUNTRY WOODSHED* 377

66 Prints/Drawings

Connecticut
Bethany, *WHITLOCK FARM, BOOKSELLERS* 45
Bethany, *ROBERT B WILLIAMS* 45
Branford, *BRANFORD RARE BOOK & ART GALLERY* 47
Coventry, *ALLINSON GALLERY INC* 53
Darien, *CATHERINE SYLVIA REISS* 55
East Haddam, *OLD BANK HOUSE GALLERY* 57
Granby, *WILLIAM & LOIS M PINKNEY* 63
Madison, *P HASTINGS FALK SOUND VIEW PRESS* 72
Mystic, *TRADE WINDS GALLERY* 77
New Canaan, *LISSARD HOUSE* 77
New Haven, *CITY POINT ANTIQUES* 79
New Haven, *THOMAS COLVILLE FINE ART* 79
New Preston, *BRITANNIA BOOKSHOP* 82
New Preston, *TIMOTHY MAWSON BOOKS & PRINTS* 83
New Preston, *STRAWBERRY HILL ANTIQUES* 83
New Preston, *TRUMPETER* 83
Newtown, *JANE COTTINGHAM ANTIQUES* 84
Norwalk, *WINGS OF A DOVE CONSIGNMENT* 85
Plainville, *WINTER ASSOCIATES INC* 88
Redding, *MELLIN'S ANTIQUES* 89
Sherman, *SCARLET LETTER BOOKS & PRINTS* 93
Stamford, *AVIS & ROCKWELL GARDINER* 97
Westport, *CONNECTICUT FINE ARTS, INC* 105
Woodbury, *THE BAY TREE ANTIQUES* 109
Woodbury, *CLAPP AND TUTTLE* 109

Maine
Blue Hill, *LIROS GALLERY* 120
Boothbay Harbor, *GLEASON FINE ART AT MCKOWN ST* 120
Bridgton, *M SPENCER* 121

Cape Elizabeth, *LOMBARD ANTIQUARIAN MAP/PRINTS* 123
Denmark, *C E GUARINO* 126
Fairfield, *THISTLE'S* 128
Farmington, *TOM VEILLEUX GALLERY* 129
Hamden, *GARY W WOOLSON, BOOKSELLER* 132
Kennebunkport, *CATTAILS ANTIQUES* 134
Manchester, *CHARLES ROBINSON RARE BOOKS* 138
North Edgecomb, *M.A.H. ANTIQUES* 141
Norway, *DIXON'S ANTIQUES* 142
Portland, *CARLSON AND TURNER BOOKS* 144
Portland, *F M O'BRIEN-ANTIQUARIAN BOOKS* 145
Portland, *PORT 'N STARBOARD* 145
Rockport, *JOAN HARTMAN ELLIS ANTIQUE PRINT* 147
Round Pond, *CARRIAGE HOUSE* 147
Rumford Center, *GROVE FARM ANTIQUES* 148
Wells, *EAST COAST BOOKS* 154
Wells, *HARDINGS BOOK SHOP* 154
Wells, *A DAVID PAULHUS BOOKS* 154
Wells, *SNUG HARBOR BOOKS* 155
Winter Harbor, *POND HOUSE ANTIQUES* 156
Wiscasset, *WISCASSET BAY GALLERY* 158
Yarmouth, *W M SCHWIND, JR ANTIQUES* 158

Massachusetts
Amherst, *AMHERST ANTIQUARIAN MAPS* 162
Andover, *ANDOVER ANTIQUARIAN BOOKS* 163
Boston, *CHILDS GALLERY* 174
Boston, *COMENOS FINE ARTS* 175
Boston, *EUGENE GALLERIES* 176
Boston, *GOODSPEED'S BOOK SHOP INC* 176
Boston, *HALEY & STEELE INC* 178
Boston, *PRISCILLA JUVELIS INC* 180
Boston, *SHER-MORR ANTIQUES* 185
Boston, *SHREVE, CRUMP & LOW* 187
Brewster, *DONALD B HOWES - ANTIQUES* 190
Brewster, *THE PUNKHORN BOOKSHOP* 190
Cambridge, *JAMES R BAKKER ANTIQUES INC.* 195
Concord, *BERNICE JACKSON* 200
Dedham, *HENRY HORNBLOWER III* 202
Dennis, *KING'S GRANT ANTIQUES* 203
Essex, *THE SCRAPBOOK* 209
Fitchburg, *JOHN CLEMENT FINE ART* 211
Georgetown, *PHEASANT HILL ANTIQUES* 213
Gloucester, *WILLIAM N GREENBAUM* 214
Great Barrington, *J & J LUBRANO ANTIQUARIAN BOOKS* 215
Great Barrington, *GEORGE R MINKOFF, INC* 215
Lexington, *RAINY DAY BOOKS* 225
Medway, *MARJORIE PARROTT ADAMS BOOKS* 229
Nantucket, *JANICE ALDRIDGE INC* 231
Nantucket, *SABOL AND CROSS, LTD* 232
Onset, *JOSEPH A DERMONT, BOOKSELLER* 242
Sharon, *ANTIQUARIAN BOOKWORM* 253
South Egremont, *BRUCE & SUSAN GVENTER, BOOKS* 260
Stockbridge, *REUSS GALLERIES* 263
Swansea, *AMERICAN ART & ANTIQUES, INC* 265
Waban, *PRIPET HOUSE ANTIQUE PRINTS* 267
Waltham, *HAROLD M BURSTEIN & CO* 268

Wellesley Hills, *ERNEST S KRAMER FINE ARTS* 270
Wellesley, *MARCUS & MARSHALL ANTIQUES* 269
West Newbury, *MOODY-RIDGEWAY HOUSE* 274
Wilbraham, *MURRAY BOOKS* 277
Worcester, *ISAIAH THOMAS BOOKS & PRINTS* 280

New Hampshire
Exeter, *A THOUSAND WORDS* 292
Gilford Village, *VISUALLY SPEAKING* 296
Hanover, *G B MANASEK, INC* 300
Jaffrey, *AT THE SIGN OF THE FOX* 304
Meredith, *THE OLD PRINT BARN* 309
Northwood, *PIONEER AMERICA* 314
Peterborough, *PETERBOROUGH USED BOOKS & PRINTS* 316
Weare, *SYKES & FLANDERS ANTIQUARIAN BKS* 324

Rhode Island
Newport, *SIMMONS & SIMMONS* 337
Newport, *WILLIAM VAREIKA FINE ARTS* 338
Newport, *MICHAEL WESTMAN FINE ARTS* 338
Providence, *QUE ANTIQUES* 340
Watch Hill, *THE BOOK & TACKLE SHOP* 343

Vermont
Burlington, *BYGONE BOOKS* 350
East Poultney, *RIVERS EDGE ANTIQUES* 355
Lyndonville, *GREEN MOUNTAIN BOOKS & PRINTS* 359
Newfane, *SCHOMMER ANTIQUES* 363
Randolph Center, *PAGE JACKSON ANTIQUE GALLERY* 366
Shoreham, *LAPHAM & DIBBLE GALLERY, INC.* 370
South Burlington, *ETHAN ALLEN ANTIQUE SHOP INC* 371
Waitsfield, *THE STORE, INC* 373
Warren, *WARREN ANTIQUES* 374

67 Quilts/Patchwork

Connecticut
Bantam, *GOOSEBORO BROOK ANTIQUES* 45
Colchester, *BARBARA WOOD BROWN* 51
Greenwich, *THE HOUSE THAT JACK BUILT* 65
Lakeville, *AMERICANA* 70
New Preston, *THE R COGSWELL COLLECTION* 83
Norwalk, *MELINDA VENTRE* 85
Salisbury, *THREE RAVENS ANTIQUES* 92
Westport, *THE FAMILY ALBUM* 105
Woodbury, *ANTIQUES ON THE GREEN* 109

Maine
Belmont, *BARBARA PATTERSON'S ANTIQUES* 119
Caribou, *THE BARN DOOR* 124
Gorham, *LONGVIEW ANTIQUES* 130
Jefferson, *BUNKER HILL ANTIQUES* 133
Portland, *MILK STREET ANTIQUES* 145
Portland, *VENTURE ANTIQUES* 146
Rangeley, *BLUEBERRY HILL FARM* 146
Searsport, *ANTIQUES AT THE HILLMANS* 149
Spruce Head, *ELFAST'S ANTIQUES* 151
Wells, *1774 HOUSE ANTIQUES* 153
Wiscasset, *MARGARET B OFSLAGER* 157

Wiscasset, *AARON & HANNAH PARKER ANTIQUES* 157

Massachusetts
Brewster, *BAYBERRY ANTIQUES* 190
Centerville, *FOR OLDE TIME'S SAKE* 198
Chatham, *CHAPDELAINE ANTIQUES* 198
Concord, *CANTERBURY ANTIQUES* 200
Dennis, *THE LEANING TREE* 203
Dover, *INTERIOR MOTIVES, INC.* 204
Georgetown, *PHEASANT HILL ANTIQUES* 213
Great Barrington, *SNYDER'S STORE* 216
Maynard, *MOLLY'S VINTAGE CLOTHING PROMO'N* 229
Nantucket, *TRANQUIL CORNERS ANTIQUES* 233
Nantucket, *LYNDA WILLAUER ANTIQUES* 233
Newton Highlands, *MARCIA & BEA ANTIQUES* 237
Newton Upper Falls, *NORTH WIND FURNISHINGS INC* 238
Rockport, *FIVE CORNERS ANTIQUES* 248
Salisbury, *FORT HILL ANTIQUES* 251
Sandwich, *TOBEY HOUSE ANTIQUES* 252
South Egremont, *DOUGLAS ANTIQUES* 260
Wellesley Hills, *COUNTRY INTERIORS* 270
West Granville, *IVES HILL ANTIQUES* 273
Westwood, *PEG WILLIS ANTIQUES* 277

New Hampshire
Antrim, *GRIST MILL ANTIQUES* 285
Canaan, *AMERICAN CLASSICS* 287
Center Strafford, *HALF THE BARN* 287
Contoocook, *SHIRLEY D QUINN ANTIQUES* 290
Hopkinton, *MEADOW HEARTH* 303
Jaffrey, *AT THE SIGN OF THE FOX* 304
Keene, *BEECH HILL GALLERY* 304
Lancaster, *GRANARY ANTIQUES* 306
Merrimack, *JEANNINE DOBBS COUNTRY FOLK* 310
Sandwich, *ANTIQUES & AUCTIONS, LTD* 320

Rhode Island
Ashaway, *ASHAWAY ANTIQUES STORE* 330
Newport, *BLACK SHEEP ANTIQUES* 333
Portsmouth, *COUNTRY CUPBOARD* 339
Wickford, *THE BALL & CLAW* 344

Vermont
Colchester, *MATTESON GALLERY OF ARTS* 352
Grafton, *PICKLE STREET ANTIQUES* 356
Jamaica, *ANTIQUES ANONYMOUS* 358
Reading, *YELLOW HOUSE ANTIQUES* 367
Stowe, *GREEN MOUNTAIN ANTIQUES* 372
Swanton, *TANSY FARM ANTIQUES* 372
Waitsfield, *ROSIE BOREL'S L'ESCALIER* 373

68 Repairs

Connecticut
Avon, *IMPERIAL DECORATING & UPHOLSTERY* 44
Branford, *BARBARA CHAMBERS RESTORATIONS* 47
Brookfield Center, *ANTIQUE CLOCK SHOP* 49
East Norwalk, *THE CLOCKERY* 58
Ivoryton, *COMSTOCK HSE ANTIQUE RESTORATION* 68
Litchfield, *WOOD*WORKS* 71
Madison, *RIVER CROFT* 72
Meriden, *ORUM SILVER CO* 74

Woodbury, *CRAIG FARROW CABINETMAKER* 111

Maine
Brunswick, *MARILYN NULMAN, BOOK REPAIR* 122

Massachusetts
Boston, *BESCO PLUMBING* 170
Boston, *THE BOSTON HAMMERSMITH* 171
Boston, *CENTER FOR ANTIQUES CONSERVATION* 173
Boston, *THE FINEST HOUR* 176
Brookline, *EMANUAL GENOVESE* 193
Brookline, *ROSINE GREEN ASSOCIATES, INC.* 193
Duxbury, *LOWY FRAME & RESTORING COMPANY* 204
Essex, *JOHN CUSHING ANTIQUE RESTORATION* 208
Foxboro, *POND HOUSE WOODWORKING* 211
Needham, *THE WICKER LADY INC* 234
Newton Highlands, *TREFLER ANTIQUE RESTORING STUDIO* 237
Peabody, *HERITAGE CANING* 244
West Chesterfield, *SUSAN K RILEY, SEAT WEAVER* 273
Woburn, *PATRICK J GILL & SONS* 279

New Hampshire
Alexandria, *ALEXANDRIA WOOD JOINERY* 284
Hillsboro, *STEPHEN SANBORN CLOCK REPAIR* 301
Portsmouth, *W MORIN FURNITURE RESTORATION* 317

Rhode Island
Peace Dale, *ANTIQUITY RESTORATIONS & REPRO'S* 339
Providence, *BRASSWORKS* 340
Tiverton, *METAL RESTORATION SERVICES* 342

Vermont
West Rupert, *AUTHENTIC DESIGNS* 375

69 Replication

Massachusetts
Orleans, *CONTINUUM* 242

New Hampshire
Gilmanton Iron Works, *STEPHEN P BEDARD* 297
Peterborough, *PARTRIDGE REPLICATIONS* 316
Portsmouth, *PARTRIDGE REPLICATIONS* 317
West Lebanon, *PARTRIDGE REPLICATIONS* 325

Vermont
Corinth, *ROBERT CHAMBERS* 352
West Rupert, *AUTHENTIC DESIGNS* 375

70 Reproduction

Connecticut
Avon, *AUTHENTIC REPRODUCTION LIGHTING* 44
Cromwell, *HORTON BRASSES* 54
Essex, *THE ESSEX FORGE* 59
Glastonbury, *MAURER & SHEPHERD, JOYNERS* 62
Mansfield Center, *JACK COLLINS WOODWORKING* 73
Old Lyme, *GARY R PARTELOW REPRODUCTIONS* 86

South Windsor, *EARLY NEW ENGLAND ROOMS* 95
West Willington, *RANDALL NELSON* 104
Windham, *THE TIN LANTERN* 108
Woodbury, *CRAIG FARROW CABINETMAKER* 111
Woodbury, *NEW ENGLAND FIREBACKS* 112
Woodbury, *NININGER & COMPANY LTD* 112
Woodbury, *WOODBURY PEWTERERS* 114

Maine
Harrison, *JEFF KOOPUS* 132
Kennebunk, *J J KEATING INC* 133
Waldoboro, *WILLIAM EVANS, CABINETMAKER* 152

Massachusetts
Ashby, *COUNTRY BED SHOP* 164
Boston, *BOSTON ORNAMENT COMPANY* 171
Boston, *PERIOD FURNITURE HARDWARE CO* 185
Brookline, *EMANUAL GENOVESE* 193
Brookline, *RENOVATORS SUPPLY* 193
Cambridge, *LAMP GLASS* 197
Duxbury, *LOWY FRAME & RESTORING COMPANY* 204
Easthampton, *PETER FRANKLIN CABINETMAKERS* 207
Groton, *OLD FASHIONED MILK PAINT COMPANY* 217
Somerville, *FAUX-ARTS ASSOCIATES* 257
Somerville, *ROBERT E SMITH* 258
South Ashfield, *RUSS LOOMIS JR* 258
Sturbridge, *THE COPPERSMITH* 264
Wayland, *GREAT MEADOWS JOINERY* 268
West Barnstable, *PACKET LANDING IRON* 271
West Chesterfield, *SUSAN K RILEY, SEAT WEAVER* 273

New Hampshire
Alexandria, *ALEXANDRIA WOOD JOINERY* 284
Enfield, *DANA ROBES WOOD CRAFTSMEN* 291
Epsom, *COPPER HOUSE* 292
Hampton, *HISTORIC HARDWARE LTD* 298
Milford, *THE RENAISSANCE MAN* 310
Portsmouth, *SAUNDERS & COOKE INC* 318

Rhode Island
Newport, *CHRISTOPHER FOSTER GLASS WORKS* 334
Peace Dale, *ANTIQUITY RESTORATIONS & REPRO'S* 339
West Kingstown, *G R CLIDENCE, 18TH C WOODWORKS* 344

Vermont
Hartland, *18TH CENTURY DESIGN* 357
West Rupert, *AUTHENTIC DESIGNS* 375

71 Restoration

Connecticut
Avon, *IMPERIAL DECORATING & UPHOLSTERY* 44
Branford, *BARBARA CHAMBERS RESTORATIONS* 47
Brookfield Center, *ANTIQUE CLOCK SHOP* 49
Darien, *WIND-BORNE FRAME & RESTORATION* 56
East Norwalk, *THE CLOCKERY* 58
Ivoryton, *COMSTOCK HSE ANTIQUE RESTORATION* 68
Kent, *HOLMES RESTORATIONS* 69

Litchfield, *WOOD*WORKS* 71
Madison, *RIVER CROFT* 72
Mansfield Center, *JACK COLLINS WOODWORKING* 73
Meriden, *ORUM SILVER CO* 74
New Haven, *EDWIN C AHLBERG* 79
New Milford, *LEON-VANDERBILT* 82
New Milford, *PHOENIX ANTIQUE RESTORATION* 82
Old Lyme, *THE COOLEY GALLERY* 86
Old Wethersfield, *WILLARD RESTORATIONS INC* 87
Ridgefield, *GIORDANO GRAZZINI* 90
Ridgefield, *GERALD GRUNSELL & ASSOCIATES* 90
Ridgefield, *THE METAL MENDER* 91
Stamford, *RAPHAEL'S ANTIQUE RESTORATION* 97
Trumbull, *ZIMMERS HEIRLOOM CLOCKS* 101
West Willington, *RANDALL NELSON* 104
Woodbury, *ANTIQUE FURNITURE RESTORATION* 109
Woodbury, *HAROLD E COLE ANTIQUES* 110
Woodbury, *CRAIG FARROW CABINETMAKER* 111
Woodbury, *NININGER & COMPANY LTD* 112
Woodbury, *WOODBURY BLACKSMITH & FORGE CO* 113

Maine
Kennebunk, *VICTORIAN LIGHT/WATERTOWER PINES* 134
Waldoboro, *WILLIAM EVANS, CABINETMAKER* 152
Wiscasset, *WISCASSET BAY GALLERY* 158

Massachusetts
Amherst, *ROSENTHAL PAPER RESTORATION* 163
Boston, *J R BURROWS & COMPANY* 173
Boston, *CENTER FOR ANTIQUES CONSERVATION* 173
Boston, *THE FINEST HOUR* 176
Boston, *GUIDO* 178
Brewster, *TALIN BOOKBINDERY* 191
Brookline, *BROOKLINE ANTIQUES* 193
Brookline, *ROSINE GREEN ASSOCIATES, INC.* 193
Essex, *JOHN CUSHING ANTIQUE RESTORATION* 208
Hadley, *HOME FARM ANTIQUES* 217
Hyannis, *STARTING OVER LTD* 222
Lee, *FERRELL'S ANTIQUES & WOODWORKING* 223
Needham, *THE WICKER LADY INC* 234
Newton Highlands, *BENCHMARK ANTIQUES* 237
Newton Highlands, *TREFLER ANTIQUE RESTORING STUDIO* 237
Newton, *BRASS BUFF ANTIQUES* 236
Peabody, *HERITAGE CANING* 244
Seekonk, *PENNY LANE ANTIQUES & GIFTS INC* 253
Sheffield, *CARRIAGE HOUSE ANTIQUES* 254
Swansea, *AMERICAN ART & ANTIQUES, INC* 265
Waltham, *RESTORATION SERVICES* 268
Wayland, *YANKEE CRAFTSMAN* 269
West Chesterfield, *SUSAN K RILEY, SEAT WEAVER* 273

West Harwich, *HOOKED RUG RESTORATION* 274
West Newbury, *HELIGE ANDE ARTS* 274
Winchester, *KOKO BOODAKIAN & SONS* 279
Woburn, *PATRICK J GILL & SONS* 279

New Hampshire
Hillsboro, *STEPHEN SANBORN CLOCK REPAIR* 301
Keene, *HAYS SCULPTURE STUDIO* 304
Milford, *THE RENAISSANCE MAN* 310
Portsmouth, *W MORIN FURNITURE RESTORATION* 317
Raymond, *BURT DIAL COMPANY* 318
Wentworth, *THE RE-STORE ANTIQUES* 324
Wentworth, *RETOUCH THE PAST* 324

Rhode Island
Ashaway, *STEPHEN P MACK* 330
Bristol, *ROBERT BARROW, CABINETMAKER* 330
Coventry, *CANDLE SNUFFER* 332
Cranston, *JEFFREY HERMAN* 332
East Greenwich, *HARBOUR GALLERIES* 332
Newport, *CHRISTOPHER FOSTER GLASS WORKS* 334
Newport, *ROGER KING GALLERY OF FINE ART* 335
Newport, *NEWELL'S CLOCK/CHINA RESTORATION* 336
Newport, *NEWPORT FINE ARTS INVESTMENT CO* 336
Peace Dale, *ANTIQUITY RESTORATIONS & REPRO'S* 339
Providence, *BRASSWORKS* 340
Tiverton, *METAL RESTORATION SERVICES* 342
Westerly, *MANFRED R WOERNER* 344

Vermont
Burlington, *CONANT CUSTOM BRASS* 350
Manchester, *HOOKED RUG RESTORATION* 359
St Johnsbury, *SIGN OF THE DIAL CLOCK SHOP* 372
Williston, *GREEN MOUNTAIN CLOCK SHOP* 376

72 Scientific/Medical

Connecticut
Greenwich, *HALLOWELL & CO* 65

Maine
Wiscasset, *MARINE ANTIQUES* 156

Massachusetts
Boston, *THE PRINTERS' DEVIL* 185
Falmouth, *AURORA BOREALIS ANTIQUES* 211
Nantucket, *TONKIN OF NANTUCKET* 233
Newton, *BRASS BUFF ANTIQUES* 236
Wellfleet, *MORTAR & PESTLE ANTIQUES* 270

Vermont
Wallingford, *TOM KAYE ANTIQUES LTD* 374

73 Sculpture

Connecticut
Darien, *DORRIE SCHREINER GALLERY ANTIQUE* 56
Litchfield, *PETER H TILLOU - FINE ARTS* 71
Stamford, *STEVE NEWMAN FINE ARTS* 97

Massachusetts
Boston, *CHILDS GALLERY* 174

Boston, *COMENOS FINE ARTS* 175
Brookline Village, *BECKERMAN NEAL ANTIQUES* 194

Rhode Island
Saunderstown, *STEPHANIE ADAMS WOOD* 342

74 Services to Period Homes

Connecticut
Ashford, *JERALD PAUL JORDON GALLERY* 44
Bethlehem, *WOODY MOSCH CABINETMAKERS* 46
Bristol, *RICHARD BLASCHKE* 48
Chester, *PERIOD LIGHTING FIXTURES* 50
Glastonbury, *MAURER & SHEPHERD, JOYNERS* 62
Old Wethersfield, *WILLARD RESTORATIONS INC* 87
South Windsor, *EARLY NEW ENGLAND ROOMS* 95
South Windsor, *SUNDERLAND PERIOD HOMES INC* 95
Stamford, *UNITED HOUSE WRECKING* 98
West Willington, *RANDALL NELSON* 104
Wilton, *THE PINE CHEST, INC.* 107
Woodbury, *NEW ENGLAND FIREBACKS* 112
Woodbury, *RAMASE* 113
Woodbury, *WOODBURY BLACKSMITH & FORGE CO* 113

Maine
Sanford, *JOHN LEEKE, PRESERVATION CONSULT* 148

Massachusetts
Boston, *BESCO PLUMBING* 170
Boston, *BOSTON ORNAMENT COMPANY* 171
Boston, *J R BURROWS & COMPANY* 173
Boston, *CENTER FOR ANTIQUES CONSERVATION* 173
Brookline, *RENOVATORS SUPPLY* 193
Dorchester, *OLDE BOSTONIAN* 204
Groton, *OLD FASHIONED MILK PAINT COMPANY* 217
Hanover, *RESTORATION RESOURCES* 218
Marblehead, *EVIE'S CORNER* 227
North Randolph, *MIKE MIHAICH* 240
Northampton, *RUMPLESTILTSKIN* 241
Rowley, *NORTH FIELDS RESTORATIONS* 249
Somerville, *A-1 ANTIQUE PLUMBING FIXTURES* 257
Waltham, *SPNEA CONSERVATION CENTER* 268
West Barnstable, *BARNSTABLE STOVE SHOP* 271
West Barnstable, *SALT & CHESTNUT WEATHERVANES* 271
West Chesterfield, *TEXTILE REPRODUCTIONS* 273
Weston, *HOLLYDAY HOUSE* 276
Winchester, *ACQUIS LTD* 279

New Hampshire
Deerfield, *DAVID OTTINGER* 290
Portsmouth, *NANCY BORDEN* 317
South Hampton, *R G BETTCHER RESTORATIONS* 320

Rhode Island
Ashaway, *STEPHEN P MACK* 330

Vermont
Hartland, *18TH CENTURY DESIGN* 357

Montpelier, *GREAT AMERICAN SALVAGE
COMPANY* 362

75 Shipping/Packing/Storage

Massachusetts
Boston, *THE FORTRESS CORPORATION* 176
Marblehead, *E R BUTLER & SONS* 227

77 Silver

Connecticut
Bridgeport, *MARC THE 1ST ANTIQUES* 48
Darien, *H P MC LANE ANTIQUES INC* 55
Greenwich, *CONSIGN IT* 64
Hamden, *GALLERY 4* 67
Litchfield, *THOMAS MC BRIDE ANTIQUES* 71
Litchfield, *HARRY W STROUSE* 71
New Haven, *ARK ANTIQUES* 79
New Haven, *SALLY GOODMAN ANTIQUES* 80
Ridgefield, *HUNTER'S CONSIGNMENT* 90
Ridgefield, *THE SILK PURSE* 91
Riverside, *ESTATE TREASURES* 91
Riverton, *ANTIQUES AND HERBS OF
RIVERTON* 91
Stamford, *ALEXANDRA WISE ANTIQUES* 98
Stonington, *RAYMOND IZBICKI* 98
Weston, *MILLICENT RUDD BEST* 104
Westport, *THINGS* 106
Woodbury, *GRASS ROOTS ANTIQUES* 111

Maine
Auburn, *ORPHAN ANNIE'S* 116
Damariscotta, *PETER/JEAN RICHARDS FINE
ANTIQUE* 126
Ellsworth, *CINDY'S ANTIQUES* 127
Kennebunkport, *GIBRAN ANTIQUE GALLERY*
134
Kennebunkport, *PORT ANTIQUES* 135
Kennebunkport, *SAML'S STAIRS ANTIQUES* 135
Kennebunkport, *WINDFALL ANTIQUES* 135
Kittery, *WILLIAM CORE DUFFY* 136
Orono, *THE GREEN DOOR ANTIQUE SHOP*
143
Pittsfield, *KENNISTON'S ANTIQUES* 143
Thomaston, *ANCHOR FARM ANTIQUES* 151
Yarmouth, *NATHAN D CUSHMAN INC* 158
Yarmouth, *THE RED SHED* 158

Massachusetts
Acton, *SEAGULL ANTIQUES* 162
Arlington, *SECOND TYME AROUND* 164
Boston, *BEACON HILL FINE ARTS/ANTIQUES*
168
Boston, *BRODNEY INC* 171
Boston, *FIRESTONE AND PARSON* 176
Boston, *HOMER'S JEWELRY & ANTIQUES* 180
Boston, *MARIKA'S ANTIQUE SHOP, INC* 182
Boston, *NELSON-MONROE, ANTIQUES* 182
Boston, *NEWBURY STREET JEWELRY &
ANTIQUE* 182
Boston, *THE YANKEE MERCHANT GROUP* 189
Brookline Village, *THE ANTIQUE COMPANY*
194
Chestnut Hill, *SONIA PAINE* 199
Concord, *CONCORD PATRIOT ANTIQUES* 200
Essex, *CHRISTIAN MOLLY ANTIQUES* 208
Foxboro, *SILVER LADY ANTIQUES* 212
Great Barrington, *ANTHONY'S ANTIQUES* 214

Great Barrington, *KAHNS ANTIQUE & ESTATE
JEWELRY* 215
Harwichport, *SEVEN SOUTH STREET
ANTIQUES* 219
Lenox, *STONE'S THROW ANTIQUES* 224
Lenox, *MARY STUART COLLECTION* 224
Marblehead, *HEELTAPPERS ANTIQUES* 227
Marblehead, *SACKS ANTIQUES* 228
Nantucket, *PUSS-N-BOOTS* 232
Nantucket, *FRANK F SYLVIA ANTIQUES* 232
Needham, *GOLDEN FLEECE ANTIQUES* 234
North Andover, *ROLAND B HAMMOND INC*
239
Rockport, *RECUERDO* 248
Salem, *ASIA HOUSE* 250
Sandwich, *THE STITCHERY IN SANDWICH* 251
South Brewster, *SMITH ANTIQUES* 259
South Egremont, *BIRD CAGE ANTIQUES* 259
Wenham, *HENDERSON'S* 271

New Hampshire
Brookline, *1786 HOUSE ANTIQUES* 286
Center Harbor, *HOLIDAY HOUSE ANTIQUES*
287
Exeter, *DECOR ANTIQUES* 292
Hanover, *MARIE-LOUISE ANTIQUES* 300
Keene, *ANDERSON GALLERY* 304
Springfield, *SPRING HILL FARM ANTIQUES*
321
Wolfeboro, *MONIQUE'S ANTIQUES* 327

Rhode Island
Charlestown, *LION'S MANE ANTIQUES* 331
Cranston, *JEFFREY HERMAN* 332
Newport, *GALLERY '76 ANTIQUES INC* 335
Newport, *ALICE SIMPSON ANTIQUES* 337
Providence, *CHAMBERLAIN ANTIQUES LTD*
340
Providence, *MY FAVORITE THINGS* 340
Warwick, *THE EMPORIUM* 343

Vermont
Dorset, *THE ANGLOPHILE ANTIQUES* 353
East Arlington, *GEBELEIN SILVERSMITHS* 354
Manchester Center, *BREWSTER ANTIQUES* 360
Manchester, *PARAPHERNALIA ANTIQUES* 359
Stowe, *GREEN MOUNTAIN ANTIQUES* 372
Waterbury, *CABELL ANTIQUES* 374

78 Sporting Art/Equipment

Connecticut
Bozrah, *CHARLES GALLERY* 47
Danbury, *TIME AFTER TIME* 54
Darien, *WINDSOR ANTIQUES LTD* 56
East Haddam, *OLD BANK HOUSE GALLERY* 57
Goshen, *ANGLER'S & SHOOTER'S
BOOKSHELF* 63
Greenwich, *HALLOWELL & CO* 65
Madison, *ORDNANCE CHEST* 72
New Canaan, *LISSARD HOUSE* 77
Stonington, *QUESTER GALLERY* 99
Westport, *THINGS* 106

New Hampshire
New London, *THE BLOCK HOUSE* 312

Rhode Island
Providence, *THE REEL MAN* 341

Vermont
Dorset, *AMERICAN SPORTING ANTIQUES* 353
East Poultney, *RIVERS EDGE ANTIQUES* 355

Grand Isle, *BACK DOOR ANTIQUES* 356

79 Stamps
Connecticut
Avon, *EAGLES NEST* 44
Milford, *R & J GLASSWARE* 75
Westport, *SAM SLOAT COINS, INC* 106

Massachusetts
Franklin, *JOHNSTON ANTIQUES* 212
Worcester, *J & N FORTIER INC* 280

New Hampshire
Winchester, *FAT CHANCE ANTIQUES* 326

80 Textiles
Connecticut
Bantam, *KENT & YVONNE GILYARD ANTIQUES* 45
Branford, *YESTERDAY'S THREADS* 47
Cornwall Bridge, *THE BRASS BUGLE* 52
Coventry, *HANDS OF TIME* 53
Essex, *HASTINGS HOUSE* 60
Gaylordsville, *MICHAEL HALL ANTIQUES* 62
Greenwich, *SOPHIA'S GREAT DAMES* 66
Guilford, *CORNUCOPIA ANTIQUE CONSIGNMENTS* 66
New Haven, *CITY POINT ANTIQUES* 79
Norwalk, *MELINDA VENTRE* 85
Wallingford, *IMAGES, HEIRLOOM LINENS/LACE* 101

Maine
Cape Elizabeth, *HANSON'S CARRIAGE HOUSE* 123
Newcastle, *MILLING AROUND* 140
Portland, *REMEMBER WHEN* 145
Portland, *VOSE SMITH ANTIQUES* 146
Scarsport, *PRIMROSE FARM ANTIQUES* 149
Spruce Head, *ELFAST'S ANTIQUES* 151
Waterboro, *WATERBORO EMPORIUM* 153

Massachusetts
Boston, *LACE BROKER* 180
Boston, *LONDON LACE* 181
Brewster, *EDWARD SNOW HOUSE ANTIQUES* 191
Rockport, *MOUNT VERNON ANTIQUES* 248
South Egremont, *ELLIOTT & GRACE SNYDER* 260
Wellesley, *EUROPEAN MANOR* 269

New Hampshire
Concord, *VERNA H MORRILL* 289
Contoocook, *PIATT'S COPPER COW* 289
Contoocook, *SHIRLEY D QUINN ANTIQUES* 290
Keene, *PETER PAP ORIENTAL RUGS INC* 305
Mont Vernon, *CANDLEWICK ANTIQUES* 310
Peterborough, *PARTRIDGE REPLICATIONS* 316
Portsmouth, *NANCY BORDEN* 317
Portsmouth, *PARTRIDGE REPLICATIONS* 317
West Lebanon, *PARTRIDGE REPLICATIONS* 325

Rhode Island
Newport, *FULL SWING* 334
Newport, *ALICE SIMPSON ANTIQUES* 337
Saunderstown, *STEPHANIE ADAMS WOOD* 342

Vermont
Brandon, *BRANDON ANTIQUES* 349
Brandon, *NUTTING HOUSE ANTIQUES* 349
Burlington, *COLIN & ELIZABETH DUCOLON* 351
Middlebury, *VILLAGE STORE OF MIDDLEBURY* 361
Pittsford, *ART INTERIORS ANTIQUES-PITTSFORD* 365
Rutland, *SOPHIE'S COLLECTIQUES* 368
Shelburne, *GADHUE'S ANTIQUES* 370
Waitsfield, *ROSIE BOREL'S L'ESCALIER* 373
Wallingford, *YANKEE MAID ANTIQUES* 374

81 Tools
Connecticut
Harwinton, *RYAN'S ANTIQUES* 68
Kent, *THE FORRER'S* 68

Maine
Brewer, *FRAN & DEAN'S ANTIQUES* 121
Caribou, *THE BARN DOOR* 124
Damariscotta, *ROGER & BEE BENNETT* 125
Damariscotta, *COOPER'S RED BARN* 125
Farmington, *ANTIQUES FROM POWDER HOUSE HILL* 129
Hulls Cove, *HULLS COVE TOOL BARN* 133
Newcastle, *MARY HODES* 140
Searsport, *PRIMROSE FARM ANTIQUES* 149
Stockton Springs, *BRICK HOUSE ANTIQUES* 151

Massachusetts
Dennis, *DOVETAIL ANTIQUES* 202
Great Barrington, *JONESES ANTIQUES* 215
Lancaster, *ANTIQUES TOOLS & CATALOGS* 222
Lanesborough, *AMBER SPRING ANTIQUES* 222
Norton, *DUBOIS' OLD HOUSE* 241
Petersham, *GROUND FLOOR ATTIC ANTIQUES* 244
Scituate, *GREENHOUSE ANTIQUES* 252
Sheffield, *FALCON ANTIQUES* 255
Shelburne, *ORCHARD HILL ANTIQUES* 257
South Weymouth, *DANA R JOHNSEN* 261
West Barnstable, *THE WHIPPLETREE* 271

New Hampshire
Epsom, *THE BETTY HOUSE* 292
Jackson, *RED SHED ANTIQUES* 304
Peterborough, *BRENNANS ANTIQUES* 315
Portsmouth, *TRUNKWORKS* 318
Salisbury Heights, *BARKER'S OF SALISBURY HEIGHTS* 319
Shelburne, *CROW MOUNTAIN FARM ANTIQUES* 320
Troy, *RED SHED* 322
Washington, *TINTAGEL ANTIQUES* 324

Vermont
Derby Line, *CARRIAGE HOUSE ANTIQUES* 353
Grafton, *WOODSHED ANTIQUES* 356
Ludlow, *RED CLOVER ANTIQUES* 359
Middlebury, *BIX ANTIQUES* 361
Pittsford, *ART INTERIORS ANTIQUES-PITTSFORD* 365
Pittsford, *IRON HORSE ANTIQUES, INC* 365
Reading, *LIBERTY HILL ANTIQUES* 367
Springfield, *PASTIMES ANTIQUES* 371
Vergennes, *FITZ-GERALDS' ANTIQUES* 373

82 Tribal Art
Maine
Newfield, *JOHN BAUER SONIA SEFTON ANTI* 141

Massachusetts
Boston, *O'REILLY/EINSTADTER, LTD* 182
Brookline Village, *THE COLLECTOR* 194
Cambridge, *HURST GALLERY* 196

New Hampshire
Keene, *PETER PAP ORIENTAL RUGS INC* 305

83 Victorian Antiques

Connecticut
Bristol, *DICK'S ANTIQUES* 48
East Hampton, *OPERA HOUSE ANTIQUES* 58
Middletown, *COUNTRY ANTIQUES AT MIDDLETOWN* 74
New Haven, *HER MAJESTY'S ANTIQUES* 80
New Preston, *TRUMPETER* 83
Pawcatuck, *WOODS ANTIQUES* 88
Woodbury, *SOUTHFORD ANTIQUES* 113
Woodbury, *EVE STONE & SON ANTIQUES* 113
Yalesville, *UNIQUE ANTIQUES & COLLECTIBLES* 114

Maine
Bath, *RECENT PAST* 118
Damariscotta, *THE MAPLES* 125
Gardiner, *MORRELL'S ANTIQUES* 130
Kennebunkport, *GIBRAN ANTIQUE GALLERY* 134
Orrington, *MERRIMAC'S ANTIQUES* 143
Portland, *OCTAVIA'S ANTIQUES* 145
Searsport, *BETTER DAY'S ANTIQUES* 149
Troy, *GREEN'S CORNER ANTIQUES* 152

Massachusetts
Boston, *KNOLLWOOD ANTIQUES* 180
Brookline, *APPLETON ANTIQUES* 192
Cambridge, *SHARON BOCCELLI & CO ANTIQUES* 196
Cambridge, *A TOUCH OF CLASS* 197
East Sandwich, *HORSEFEATHERS ANTIQUES* 206
Lee, *THE KINGSLEIGH 1840* 223
Newton Highlands, *BENCHMARK ANTIQUES* 237
Palmer, *FURNITURE BARN* 243
Peabody, *AMERICANA ANTIQUES* 244
Petersham, *GROUND FLOOR ATTIC ANTIQUES* 244
Seekonk, *PENNY LANE ANTIQUES & GIFTS INC* 253
South Egremont, *DOUGLAS ANTIQUES* 260
Springfield, *ANTIQUARIA* 262
Wellfleet Ctr, *FINDERS KEEPERS* 270

New Hampshire
Amherst, *AMHERST VILLAGE ANTIQUE SHOP* 284
East Lempster, *PETER HILL INC* 291
Fitzwilliam, *EXPRESSIONS* 294
Hampton, *GARGOYLES & GRIFFINS* 298
Snowville, *SLEIGH MILL ANTIQUES* 320
West Swanzey, *FREDERICK MAC PHAIL ANTIQUES* 325

Rhode Island
North Kingstown, *LAFAYETTE ANTIQUES* 338
Westerly, *HERITAGE ANTIQUES* 344

Vermont
Middletown Springs, *OLD SPA SHOP ANTIQUES* 362

84 Vintage Cars/Carriages

Maine
Pittston, *KENNETH AND PAULETTE TUTTLE* 144

Massachusetts
Beverly, *A R M ASSOCIATES* 166

Vermont
Quechee, *PEDLER'S ATTIC* 366
Rutland, *TRULY UNIQUE ANTIQUES* 368

85 Vintage Clothing/Costumes

Connecticut
Branford, *YESTERDAY'S THREADS* 47
Greenwich, *SOPHIA'S GREAT DAMES* 66
Lakeville, *LISA C INC* 70
Lebanon, *THE ETCETERA SHOPPE* 70
New Haven, *ANN MARIE'S VINTAGE BOUTIQUE* 79
Newington, *DOLL FACTORY* 83
Willimantic, *ANTIQUES & THINGS* 107

Maine
Auburn, *ORPHAN ANNIE'S* 116
Richmond, *THE LOFT ANTIQUES* 146
Rumford Center, *GROVE FARM ANTIQUES* 148
Rumford, *CONNIE'S ANTIQUES* 148

Massachusetts
Boston, *GRAND TROUSSEAU* 176
Brewster, *SUNSMITH HOUSE - ANTIQUES* 191
Cambridge, *KEEZER'S HARVARD COMMUNITY EXCH* 196
Gloucester, *BANANAS* 213
Harwichport, *MAGGIE'S ANTIQUES & COLLECTIBLES* 219
Malden, *FLIGHTS OF FANCY ANTIQUES* 226
Maynard, *MOLLY'S VINTAGE CLOTHING PROMO'N* 229
Newburyport, *ELIZABETH'S 20TH CENTURY* 235
Pittsfield, *GREYSTONE GARDENS* 245
Sudbury, *MAGGIE FLOOD* 265

New Hampshire
Haverhill, *THE VICTORIAN ON MAIN STREET* 300
Wolfeboro, *MONIQUE'S ANTIQUES* 327

Rhode Island
Providence, *SUNNY DAYS* 341

Vermont
Clarendon Springs, *CLARENDON HOUSE ANTIQUES* 352
Fairfax, *THE CAT'S MEOW ANTIQUES* 355
Rutland, *SOPHIE'S COLLECTIQUES* 368

86 Wicker

Connecticut
Guilford, *A SUMMER PLACE* 66
Madison, *NOSEY GOOSE* 72
Newington, *CONNECTICUT ANTIQUE WICKER* 83
Old Saybrook, *TOUCH OF CLASS* 87
Pawcatuck, *WOODS ANTIQUES* 88
Westport, *TODBURN* 106

Maine
Bernard, *ANTIQUE WICKER* 119
Ellsworth, *CINDY'S ANTIQUES* 127

Fairfield, *JOHN D JULIA ANTIQUES* 128
Searsport, *BETTER DAY'S ANTIQUES* 149
Trenton, *THE ACADIA MEWS ANTIQUE CENTER* 152
Trenton, *MAYO ANTIQUES GALLERY* 152

Massachusetts
Beverly, *PRICE HOUSE ANTIQUES* 166
Dennis, *LESLIE CURTIS ANTIQUES* 202
Marlboro, *WAYSIDE ANTIQUES* 229
Nantucket, *THE WICKER PORCH* 233
Needham, *THE WICKER LADY INC* 234
Newton Upper Falls, *NORTH WIND FURNISHINGS INC* 238
Sheffield, *CORNER HOUSE ANTIQUES* 254

Rhode Island
Newport, *MAINLY OAK LTD* 336
Newport, *PETTERUTI ANTIQUES* 337

North Kingstown, *LILLIAN'S ANTIQUES* 338
Vermont
Vergennes, *EIGHTH ELM FARM ANTIQUES* 373

87 Weather Vanes

Connecticut
Greenwich, *DAVID A SCHORSCH* 65

Massachusetts
Holliston, *WILDER SHOP* 220
Southampton, *SOUTHAMPTON ANTIQUES* 261
West Barnstable, *SALT & CHESTNUT WEATHERVANES* 271

New Hampshire
Epsom, *COPPER HOUSE* 292

INDEX TO GROUPSHOPS AND MULTIPLE DEALER SHOPS

Group Shops

Connecticut
Canton, *BALCONY ANTIQUES* 50
Coventry, *COVENTRY ANTIQUE CENTER* 53
Coventry, *MEMORY LANE ANTIQUE CENTER* 53
Coventry, *VILLAGE ANTIQUES* 53
Darien, *1860 HOUSE OF ANTIQUES* 54
Darien, *PURPLE DOOR ANTIQUES* 55
East Hampton, *OLD BANK ANTIQUES* 58
Essex (Centerbrook), *BRUSH FACTORY ANTIQUES* 60
Essex, *ESSEX ANTIQUES CENTER* 59
Essex, *ESSEX COLONY ANTIQUES* 59
Gaylordsville, *BITTERSWEET SHOP* 62
Georgetown-Wilton, *WHITE DOVE ANTIQUES* 62
Granby, *GRANBY ANTIQUES EMPORIUM* 63
Jewett City, *JEWETT CITY EMPORIUM* 68
Kent, *KENT ANTIQUES CENTER* 69
Milford, *MILFORD ANTIQUE CENTER* 75
Milford, *MILFORD GREEN ANTIQUES GALLERY* 75
Mystic, *MYSTIC RIVER ANTIQUES MARKET* 76
New Haven, *ANTIQUE CORNER* 79
New Haven, *WESTVILLE ANTIQUE CENTER* 81
Norwich, *NORWICHTOWN ANTIQUE CENTER* 86
Old Saybrook, *ESSEX-SAYBROOK ANTIQUES VILLAGE* 87
Pomfret Center, *COUNTRY COTTAGE ANTIQUES* 89
Pomfret, *POMFRET ANTIQUE WORLD* 89
Putnam, *GRAMS & PENNYWEIGHTS* 89
Ridgefield, *COUNTRY VILLAGE ANTIQUES* 90
Ridgefield, *RIDGEFIELD ANTIQUE SHOPS* 91
Salisbury, *SALISBURY ANTIQUES CENTER* 92
South Woodstock, *SCRANTON'S SHOPS* 95
Southbury, *SOUTHBURY ANTIQUES CTR* 96
Southport, *CHELSEA ANTIQUES* 96

Wallingford, *ANTIQUE CENTER OF WALLINGFORD* 101
Wallingford, *WALLINGFORD ANTIQUES COLLECTIVE* 102
West Hartford, *PARK PLACE ANTIQUES* 103
Westbrook, *THE CAPTAIN STANNARD HOUSE* 104

Maine
Alfred, *SHIRETOWN ANTIQUE CENTER* 116
Arundel, *ARUNDEL ANTIQUES* 116
Belfast, *CHECKERED PAST ANTIQUES CENTER* 118
Biddeford, *BIDDEFORD ANTIQUE CENTER* 120
Bridgton, *WALES & HAMBLEN ANTIQUE CENTER* 121
Cape Neddick, *THE BARN AT CAPE NEDDICK* 123
East Winthrop, *LAKESIDE ANTIQUES* 127
Ellsworth, *DOWNEAST ANTIQUE CENTER* 128
Freeport, *FREEPORT ANTIQUE MALL* 129
Gardiner, *PORT OF GARDINER ANTIQUES* 130
Gray, *THE BARN ON 26 ANTIQUE CENTER* 131
Kennebunk, *RIVERGATE ANTIQUES MALL* 133
Lincolnville Beach, *MAINE ANTIQUE MERCHANTS LTD* 137
Lisbon, *OLD LISBON SCHOOLHOUSE ANTIQUES* 137
Moody, *THE GRAY'S ANTIQUES* 138
Oxford, *OXFORD COMMON ANTIQUE CENTER* 143
Searsport, *PUMPKIN PATCH ANTIQUE CENTER* 149
Topsham, *TOPSHAM FAIR MALL* 152
Warren Village, *VILLAGE ANTIQUE GROUP SHOP* 153
Wells, *BO-MAR HALL* 153
Wells, *WELLS ANTIQUE MART* 155
Wells, *WELLS UNION ANTIQUE CENTER* 155
Windham, *CIDER MILL ANTIQUE MALL* 156
Wiscasset, *NONESUCH HOUSE* 157
Wiscasset, *PATRICIA STAUBLE ANTIQUES* 157

Massachusetts
Barnstable Village, *BARNSTABLE VILLAGE ANTIQUES* 165

Barnstable Village, *CAPE COD SHOPPER 165*

Boston, *BOSTON ANTIQUE COOPERATIVE II 171*

Brewster, *YORKSHIRE HOUSE 191*

Buzzards Bay, *THE ANTIQUE MART 195*

Concord, *CONCORD ANTIQUES 200*

Deerfield, *ELLIE'S ANTIQUE CENTER 202*

Dennis Village, *RED LION ANTIQUES 203*

Dennis, *OLD TOWNE ANTIQUES 203*

Duxbury, *ANTIQUES AT MILLBROOK 204*

East Bridgewater, *ANTIQUES AT FORGE POND 205*

Edgartown, *AUNTIES ATTIC ANTIQUES 207*

Elmwood, *DOING ANTIQUES AT ELMWOOD 207*

Essex, *ANNEX ANTIQUES 207*

Essex, *CHEBACCO ANTIQUES 208*

Essex, *HOTEL ESSEX ANTIQUES 208*

Essex, *MAIN STREET ANTIQUES 209*

Essex, *SOUTH ESSEX ANTIQUES 210*

Essex, *SUSAN STELLA ANTIQUES 210*

Fall River, *COLLECTORS JUNCTION 211*

Framingham, *FRANKLIN STREET ANTIQUE MALL 212*

Georgetown, *SCALA'S ANTIQUES 213*

Georgetown, *SEDLER'S ANTIQUE VILLAGE 213*

Gloucester, *MAIN STREET ARTS & ANTIQUES 214*

Great Barrington, *THE EMPORIUM 215*

Hadley, *HADLEY ANTIQUES CENTER 217*

Hadley, *OLDE HADLEY FLEA MARKET 217*

Harwich Center, *ANTIQUES AT THE BARN AT WINDSONG 219*

Haydenville, *BRASSWORKS ANTIQUES CENTER 219*

Ipswich, *ESSEX ANTIQUE CO-OP 222*

Marblehead, *OLD TOWN ANTIQUE CO-OP 228*

Maynard, *CHIPPENDALES ANTIQUES 229*

New Bedford, *NEW BEDFORD ANTIQUES COMPANY 235*

Newton Upper Falls, *THE MALL @ ECHO BRIDGE 238*

North Adams, *STATIONHOUSE ANTIQUES CENTER 238*

North Attleboro, *RYAN'S ANTIQUES & REFINISHING 239*

Northampton, *ANTIQUE CENTER OF NORTHAMPTON 240*

Norwood, *COUNTRY TURTLE 241*

Old Deerfield, *ANTIQUE CENTER OF OLD DEERFIELD 242*

Orange, *BLDG 38 ANTIQUE CENTER 242*

Palmer, *QUABOAG VALLEY ANTIQUE CENTER 243*

Paxton, *THE SHOP AT BLACK HILL 244*

Pembroke, *ENDLESS ANTIQUES 244*

Plymouth, *ANTIQUE CENTER OF PLYMOUTH 245*

Rockland, *YE PRINTERS' ANTIQUES 248*

Rowley, *ROWLEY ANTIQUE CENTER 249*

Rowley, *SALT MARSH ANTIQUES 249*

Rowley, *TODD FARM 249*

Rowley, *VILLAGE ANTIQUES 249*

Salem, *ANTIQUES GALLERY 250*

Sandwich, *MAYPOP LANE 251*

Sheffield, *ANTIQUE CENTER OF SHEFFIELD 253*

Southfield, *ANTIQUES @ BUGGY WHIP FACTORY 262*

Sturbridge, *R "n" G ANTIQUES & COLLECTIBLES 264*

Sturbridge, *STURBRIDGE ANTIQUE SHOPS 264*

Sturbridge, *YESTERDAYS ANTIQUE CENTER 264*

Townsend Harbor, *HARBORSIDE ANTIQUES 267*

Wellfleet, *THE FARMHOUSE 270*

West Boylston, *A & G ANTIQUES 271*

West Boylston, *THE DEACONS BENCH 271*

West Boylston, *THE ROSE COTTAGE 272*

West Falmouth, *VILLAGE BARN ANTIQUE COOP 273*

Westfield, *ANTIQUE MARKETPLACE 276*

Westford, *ANTIQUES ORCHARD 276*

Westford, *WESTFORD VALLEY ANTIQUES 276*

Westport, *WING CARRIAGE HOUSE 277*

Williamstown, *COUNTRY PEDLAR ANTIQUES 278*

Wrentham, *WRENTHAM ANTIQUE COMPANY 280*

Yarmouth Port, *YARMOUTHPORT ANTIQUES 282*

New Hampshire

Alstead, *PAPERMILL VILLAGE ANTIQUES 284*

Antrim, *BACKWARD LOOK ANTIQUES 285*

Bedford, *BELL HILL ANTIQUES 285*

Derry, *FARMER'S MARKET ANTIQUES 290*

Derry, *HILLTOP ANTIQUES 290*

East Swanzey, *PINE GROVE ANTIQUES 291*

Fitzwilliam, *ANTIQUES PLUS & STRAWBERRY ACRES 293*

Fitzwilliam, *FITZWILLIAM ANTIQUE CENTER 294*

Hampton Falls, *ANTIQUES AT HAMPTON FALLS 299*

Hampton Falls, *ANTIQUES NEW HAMPSHIRE 299*

Hampton Falls, *ANTIQUES ONE 299*

Hampton Falls, *THE BARN AT HAMPTON FALLS 299*

Kingston, *RED BELL ANTIQUES 305*

Kingston, *THE PEDDLER'S CART 305*

Lancaster, *LANCASTER MALL & ANTIQUES MARKET 306*

Lincoln, *MILLSIDE ANTIQUES 306*

Littleton, *THE BEAL HOUSE INN &
ANTIQUES 306*
Meredith, *BURLWOOD ANTIQUE CENTER 309*
Milford, *NEW HAMPSHIRE ANTIQUE CO-OP,
INC 310*
Nashua, *UNICORN ANTIQUES 311*
North Conway, *ANTIQUES & COLLECTIBLES
BARN 313*
North Hampton, *NORTH HAMPTON ANTIQUE
CENTER 313*
Northwood, *COUNTRY TAVERN OF
NORTHWOOD 314*
Northwood, *HAYLOFT ANTIQUE CENTER 314*
Northwood, *JUNCTION ANTIQUE CENTER 314*
Northwood, *NORTHWOOD INN ANTIQUE
CENTER 314*
Northwood, *PARKER FRENCH ANTIQUE
CENTER 314*
Northwood, *THE WHITE HOUSE ANTIQUES
315*
Northwood, *TOWN PUMP ANTIQUES 314*
Northwood, *WILLOW HOLLOW ANTIQUES
315*
Ossipee, *GREEN MOUNTAIN ANTIQUE
CENTER 315*
Pelham, *CARTER'S BARN ANTIQUES 315*
Peterborough, *PETERBOROUGH ANTIQUE
ASSOCIATES 316*
Stratham, *THE COURTYARD EMPORIUM 321*
Swanzey, *O'BRIEN ENTERPRISES 321*
Tuftonboro Center, *GOLDEN PAST ANTIQUE
MARKET 322*
West Lebanon, *COLONIAL PLAZA ANTIQUES
325*
West Nottingham, *MERRY HILL FARM 325*
West Swanzey, *KNOTTY PINE ANTIQUE
MARKET 325*
Westmoreland, *THE ANTIQUES SHOPS 326*
Wilmot Flat, *YE OLDE SHAVEHORSE
WORKSHOP 326*
Winchester, *GOOD OLD DAYS ANTIQUES 326*
Rhode Island
Chepachet, *KIMBALL HOUSE
1753/REMINGTON ANT 331*
Rumford, *ANTIQUES BEAUTIFUL 341*
Vermont
Brattleboro, *BLACK MOUNTAIN ANTIQUE
CENTER 349*
Danby, *DANBY ANTIQUES CENTER 353*
Danby, *MAIN STREET ANTIQUES CENTER 353*
East Arlington, *EAST ARLINGTON ANTIQUE
CENTER 354*

East Middlebury, *MIDDLEBURY ANTIQUE
CENTER 354*
Hardwick, *OLD FIREHOUSE ANTIQUES 357*
Jeffersonville, *1829 HOUSE ANTIQUES 358*
Ludlow, *LUDLOW ANTIQUE & GIFT CENTER
359*
Manchester Center, *1812 HOUSE ANTIQUE
CENTER 359*
Manchester Center, *CARRIAGE TRADE
ANTIQUES CENTER 360*
Manchester Center, *CENTER HILL PAST &
PRESENT ANTIQ 360*
New Haven, *COLLECTOR'S EMPORIUM
ANTIQUE CTR 362*
Newfane, *NEWFANE ANTIQUES CENTER 363*
North Ferrisburg, *MARTIN HOUSE ANTIQUE
CENTER 364*
Old Bennington, *ANTIQUE CENTER AT OLD
BENNINGTON 364*
Orwell, *HISTORIC BROOKSIDE FARMS
ANTIQUE 365*
Pittsford, *COUNTRY BARN ANTIQUE CENTER
365*
Pittsford, *PITTSFORD GREEN ANTIQUES 365*
Quechee, *ANTIQUE MALL AT TIMBER RAIL
VIL. 366*
Rutland, *ANTIQUES CENTER & SPECIALTY
SHOP 368*
Rutland, *RUTLAND ANTIQUES 368*
Vergennes, *FACTORY MARKETPLACE
ANTIQUES 373*
Wallingford, *WALLINGFORD ANTIQUE
CENTER 374*
Waterbury, *EARLY VERMONT ANTIQUES 374*
Windsor, *WINDSOR ANTIQUES MARKET 376*

Antiques Dealers
Auction Houses
Period Restoration Specialists
Antiquitarian Booksellers
Appraisers . . . . .

WE WOULD LIKE to consider you for listing in "Sloan's Green Guide to Antiques Dealers - New England". Please attach your card to this sheet of paper and mail it to:

The Antique Press
105 Charles Street - 140
Boston, MA 02114

AFFIX YOUR BUSINESS CARD HERE

DID YOU BORROW THIS GUIDE?

There's nothing like having your own personal copy of "Sloan's Green Guide to Antiques Dealers - New England". This unique guide enables you to identify dealers throughout New England. Armed with this guide, you will plan really successful "antiquing" tours. You can make notes in the margins. Best of all, with an extra copy in the glove compartment, you can refer to it spontaneously anywhere in New England to identify the antiques resources locally. To order your personal copy, another copy for the car or several as gifts for friends, simply complete the form below.

_____ **YES**, I'd like _____ copies of "Sloan's Green Guide to Antiques Dealers - New England".

Name _____

Address _____

City _____ State _____ Zip _____

Sloan's Green Guide @ $14.95 x (___) copies = _____	
Postage: $2.00 first book, 50¢ each additional book = _____	
State tax (MA residents add 5%) = _____	
	TOTAL = _____

Please make your check payable to *The Antique Press*.
Mail to: *The Antique Press*, 105 Charles Street - 140, Boston, MA 02114